THE POPULAR HANDBOOK
OF BRITISH BIRDS

LIST OF ARTISTS

Coloured Plates:

ROLAND GREEN
H. GRÖNVOLD
C. TALBOT KELLY
M. A. KOEKKOEK
G. E. LODGE
DAVID REID-HENRY
R. A. RICHARDSON
PHILIP RICKMAN
SIR PETER SCOTT

Black-and-white Plates:

H. GRÖNVOLD
J. C. HARRISON
D. I. M. WALLACE

Text Drawings:

P. R. COLSTON
ROBERT GILLMOR
P. J. HAYMAN
R. A. RICHARDSON
D. I. M. WALLACE
DONALD WATSON

The Popular Handbook of British Birds

P. A. D. HOLLOM

Co-author of *The Field Guide to the Birds of Britain and Europe* and *The Birds of the Middle East and North Africa*

H. F. & G. WITHERBY LTD

14 Henrietta Street, London WC2E 8QJ

First published in Great Britain 1952
5th revised edition, 1988

© H. F. & G. Witherby Ltd 1988

British Library Cataloguing in Publication Data
Hollom, P. A. D. (Philip Arthur Dominic), *1912*–
The popular handbook of British birds.—
5th ed.
1. Great Britain. Birds—Field guides
I. Title
598.2941

ISBN 0-85493-169-4

Photoset in Great Britain by
Rowland Phototypesetting Ltd
Bury St Edmunds, Suffolk
Printed in the Netherlands by
Lochemdruk BV, Lochem

PUBLISHER'S NOTE TO 1988 EDITION

This book is the lineal descendant of *The Handbook of British Birds*, a twentieth century classic and landmark for ornithologists. It is to the editors of this five-volume work and the many friends of ornithology whose names are acknowledged in its pages that the great indebtedness of all concerned with the present volume has been expressed.

This shortened version has been designed to meet, within the compass of a single volume, the broad interests of the field ornithologist and the general bird-watcher.

We believe their requirements extend beyond the mere identification features on which many guides now concentrate. This book's sustained success is in part due to the liberal information it provides on birds' habits, activities and idiosyncrasies; these are tremendously varied, often diagnostic, and can be as intriguing to the housewife as to the behaviourist. The field descriptions are supported by coloured illustrations showing each species in its natural habitat, and there is also a series of egg plates.

The sections in this book dealing with status and distribution have in particular been regularly revised and up-dated. These are the aspects of bird-life which are most liable to variation. The fortunes of a species depend largely on habitat or climatic changes, weather, pollution, protection or persecution; disturbance to birds is on the increase due to pressures put on them by man's activities, making it doubly important now to support the protection and conservation of the wonderful heritage of British bird-life.

CONTENTS

Egg Plates are between pages 198 and 199

Bird Plates are between pages 294 and 295

SYSTEMATIC LIST OF SPECIES

GLOSSARY OF TERMS

AXILLARY.   Of or belonging to the axilla (armpit).

CARPUS.   The wrist. The carpel joint of the wing is that one forming the forward prominence when the wing is closed.

CERE.   The bare and sometimes swollen and distinctively coloured skin in which the nostrils are situated at the base of the bill—a prominent feature in the hawks.

CULMEN.   The central longitudinal ridge of the upper mandible.

DIMORPHISM.   A difference in form, and also used generally in ornithology for a difference in colour (strictly dichromatism), constantly exhibited by different individuals of the same species.

DISTAL.   Remote from the base or point of attachment to the body or belonging to such portion of limb, etc. Opposed to PROXIMAL.

DORSAL.   Forming or belonging to the upper surface in the natural position of the body.

EMARGINATED.   Cut out or cut away in a slanting direction.

GAPE.   The angle formed by the lower border of the upper jaw and the upper border of the lower jaw, when the bill is open.

IRIS.   The, often distinctively, coloured portion of the eye, in the form of a circular curtain, having a central circular aperture, which is called the "pupil".

JUVENILE BIRD.   As here used refers to a bird in its first covering of true feathers, which usually immediately succeeds the down of the nestling.

KNEE.   The forwardly directed joint in the upper part of the bird's leg, always hidden by feathers. The more evident, distal and backwardly-directed joint is often erroneously called the bird's knee, but is in reality the ankle.

MANDIBLE.   The jaw—generally used with the qualifying adjectives upper or lower, including the horny sheaths as well as the bone.

NAIL.   The term applied to the inverted shield-shaped horny plate at the tip of the upper mandible in the ducks, geese, and swans.

ORBITAL.　Of or belonging to the orbit, the bony cavity containing the eye and its external mechanism.

SPECULUM.　A name used for any patch of feathers on the wing differing markedly in colour from those near them—especially applied to the metallic patch on the wing-feathers of fresh-water ducks.

SUB-SONG.　Term applied to very subdued and inward warblings more or less distinct from the full song ("recording" of bird-fanciers), employed by males of various Passerine species, chiefly outside the period of full song (and without reference to territory), by young birds, and sometimes also by females. With some species the only song which the bird possesses is so subdued, simple and feeble that they may be said to have only a sub-song, but there is no hard and fast line between sub-song and true song.

SUBSPECIES.　A species is subdivided into subspecies (or races) if different geographical populations of that species are separable from each other by measurement and/or plumage variation. In some cases races are claimed on such fine shades of colour difference, etc., that it becomes a matter of personal opinion as to whether the distinction is valid.

SUPERCILIARY.　Referring to the part immediately above the eye.

TARSUS.　Term currently used in ornithology for the most conspicuous portion of the bird's leg, which, except in a few genera, is covered with flattened horny scales. The toes are attached to its lower extremity. To be anatomically correct this part should strictly be called the metatarsus. The tarsus proper consists merely of two rows of small bones which, except in the embryo, are indistinguishably fused with the adjacent bones, the proximal row with the tibia and the distal row with the metatarsus.

WING-BAR.　A bar across the wing—often formed by the tips of the feathers of one of the series of wing-coverts differing in colour from the rest of the feathers.

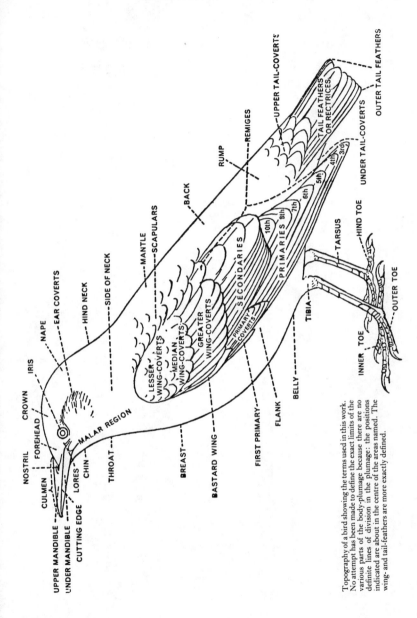

Topography of a bird showing the terms used in this work. No attempt has been made to define the exact limits of the various parts of the body-plumage because there are no definite lines of division in the plumage: the positions indicated are about in the centre of the areas named. The wing- and tail-feathers are more exactly defined.

RED-THROATED DIVER—*Gavia stellata*

BIRD PLATE I EGG PLATE XXIII (1)

A rather smaller bird than most Black-throated Divers, but for field purposes approximately the same size. In the breeding-season it is distinguished by *nearly uniform dark grey-brown upper-parts, grey head and sides of neck, dull red throat-patch and slender, distinctly uptilted appearance of the bill*, mainly due to distinct angulation of the lower mandible. The red colour of the throat is not at all noticeable in poor lights and may look black, but the absence of the bold black and white pattern of back, and the *retroussé* effect of the bill, recognizable at a considerable range, prevent any confusion with Black-throated Diver. In winter the bill is the character recognizable at longest range, but *fine white spots all over the upper parts* are distinctive at fairly close quarters; it is paler faced than other divers, with white cheeks and lores, and the dark of the crown barely reaches eye or ear-coverts. In adults the ground-colour of the upper-parts in winter is greyer, less brownish, than other divers, contrasting sharply with the very pure white of the under-parts, but immature birds are browner and darker, with less pronounced spotting and are sometimes confused with Black-throats. As with all divers the dates of assumption of summer and winter plumage vary greatly. Total length about 21–23 ins., body about 14–15 ins.

Habitat. Although also breeding on large lochs both on open moorland, swamp and in wooded country, it habitually does so on quite small tarns or mere pools, visiting larger ones or the sea to fish. Outside the breeding-season it is primarily marine, frequenting inshore waters, also occurring fairly often on open reservoirs and other waters inland.

General Habits. Flight is swift, direct and powerful, with regular rapid wing-beats and is frequently high up in the air. In descending, it planes down to water and lands with considerable impetus, striking the water breast first, as do grebes. Unlike Great Northern Diver it can rise without difficulty from quite small ponds and is the most active of the divers on the wing. When alarmed it can submerge the whole body and even head as well, so that it swims with only the bill protruding. When watching for fish the head is dipped under water to beyond the level of the eyes. In diving it usually sinks under almost instantaneously in a quiet and

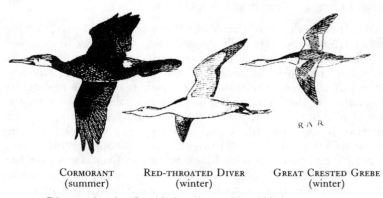

CORMORANT   RED-THROATED DIVER   GREAT CRESTED GREBE
(summer)   (winter)   (winter)

Divers and grebes fly with drooping necks and hindparts.

effortless manner, but sometimes with a considerable spring, and moves under water with remarkable speed. Small fish may be eaten under water, but larger ones, crabs, etc., are brought to the surface and may be beaten about or mutilated before being swallowed. It often sips water after feeding. It is more sociable than the other two divers, sometimes breeding in colonies, and even where this does not occur parties of 10–12 birds may be seen before the breeding-season is over. In winter it occurs often singly or in pairs and on fresh waters seldom otherwise, but sometimes, at migration-seasons and in winter, in considerable numbers together on the sea, though usually more or less scattered in small groups.

Ordinary note, often rapidly repeated in flight on the breeding-ground, is a rapid, deep, guttural, quacking note "kwuk-kwuk-kwuk . . .", much like Black-throated Diver's; also used as alarm.

Food is chiefly fish. Molluscs, crustacea, larger insects, and some vegetable matter have also been recorded.

Nests near the water's edge. The eggs, normally 2 but exceptionally 1 or 3, vary in ground-colour from yellowish-olive to dark brown. They are laid generally in late May or June in a nest which is sometimes merely a flattened patch in which grass has been pressed into a hollow on a hummock in the water or on the bank; at other times quite a substantial heap of wet moss and weeds is built up near the margin in shallow water. Incubation is by both sexes for about 24–29 days. The young are tended and fed by both sexes, probably for about 8 weeks. Single-brooded.

Status and Distribution. Present throughout the year, breeding from S. Argyll, Arran and Perthshire northwards, including a number of the western and northern Scottish islands; has also bred irregularly in S.W. Scotland, rarely with success. In Ireland it has bred for many years in Donegal, but the foothold here is precarious. Otherwise it is a regular winter-visitor to all our coasts and their estuaries and not rare inland, from mid-September to March or April, while in early May there is a well-marked passage off the east coast. Abroad the bird breeds in N. Asia, N. America, and in Europe from S. Sweden northwards, reaching the Mediterranean in winter. There are no subspecies.

BLACK-THROATED DIVER—*Gavia arctica*

BIRD PLATE I   EGG PLATE XXIII (6)

Divers, like grebes, are practically tail-less aquatic birds, with moderately long necks and pointed bills. They differ from grebes in larger size, bulkier bodies, and *stouter necks*, the last-named being the outstanding difference on the water; moreover, unlike grebes, in the breeding-season they have a bold pattern of white spots and bars on the back (except in Red-throated Diver) and lack any ornamental plumes on the head. They are essentially birds of open water, rarely if ever resorting to cover and, particularly on their breeding-ground, fly about more (the smaller species much more) than grebes, usually well up in the air. In flight the outline is very characteristic, the neck being extended in a markedly lower plane than the contour of the body, giving a peculiar, hunch-backed effect. The rather small pointed wings appear set far back; the feet are extended behind the tail.

The Black-throated Diver in breeding plumage has a *sharply defined area of broad white bands on scapulars and a smaller one on shoulders, contrasted with the black of the rest of back; these, together with grey head and back of neck* prevent any confusion with the black-headed and more uniformly spotted Great Northern Diver, while the bold pattern of the upper-parts separates it from Red-throated Diver even at long range. The throat and front of neck is black, with a beautifully regular pattern of black and white streaks at sides of the neck and breast. The under-parts and flanks are white; bill black. In winter plumage adults are distinguished by darker and uniform upper-parts from Great Northern Diver, which typically is larger and more thick-set, but young birds of the two species are often difficult to separate. Black-throats, however, have *more slender bills* and less heavy heads, and

R.A.R.

GREAT NORTHERN DIVER   BLACK-THROATED DIVER
                    RED-THROATED DIVER

Heads in Winter. Great Northern's is darker, more angular, than
Black-throat's; Red-throat has uptilt bill and white extending
above eye.

the light edgings to the back feathers tend to produce a spotted or
scaly effect, less barred than a Great Northern. The latter feature
can cause confusion with dark young Red-throated Divers, but the
latter have slightly uptilted bills and *more white on the cheeks*
and lores, while in Black-throated the dark of crown reaches
to base of lower mandible, and below eye. Total length about
22–27 ins.; body about 14–17 ins.

Habitat. In contrast to Red-throated Diver it normally breeds
on the deeper and larger lochs, often in hills, and both treeless and
forested country: rarely also on shallow and relatively small tarns.
It frequently resorts regularly to other lochs than those on which it
is nesting and to the sea or rivers for fishing purposes. Outside the
breeding-season it is found mainly on the sea near coasts and only
rarely inland.

General Habits. These and behaviour hardly differ from those
of Red-throated Diver except that, habitually breeding on larger
lochs, its visits to other lochs or to the sea, though often quite
frequent, are not as regular as in the case of Red-throated breeding
on small tarns. The mode of diving is identical.

Ordinary note is a guttural "kwuk-kwuk-kwuk . . ." often used
in flight and much like Red-throated Diver's.

Food includes fish, crustacea, molluscs and worms.

Nests usually on a small islet, but also occasionally on the shores
of lochs. The eggs, normally 2, but 1 and 3 recorded, varying in
ground-colour from greenish-olive to dark umber, are laid generally in May on little more than a flattened spot or scrape, quite close
to water and a foot or two above it. Incubation is apparently by
both sexes for about 29 days. The young are fed and tended by
both parents, and fly when about 60 days old. Single-brooded.

Status and Distribution. Present throughout the year, breeding in small numbers in Argyll, Perth and Outer Hebrides, rather more commonly in Inverness, Ross, Sutherland, Caithness; now seems established in S.W. Scotland. To Shetland it is a very rare visitor. Elsewhere a winter-visitor in small numbers and the rarest of the divers, being especially scarce on the W. coast of England and Wales and Ireland. On the Continent this race, *Gavia arctica arctica*, breeds from Scandinavia and N. Germany north to the Arctic Ocean and east into Siberia, wintering south to the Mediterranean. Other races occur in E. Asia and N. America.

GREAT NORTHERN DIVER—*Gavia immer*

BIRD PLATE I

Great Northern Diver is the largest species of diver and most obviously distinguished in breeding plumage by *black head and neck with an incomplete light collar and similar short throat-band*, both formed of parallel white streaks visible as such at close quarters, and by *white spots over the entire upper-parts*, the large bold ones of mantle and scapulars forming a regular pattern of oblique bars. The under-parts are white, with black streaks at sides of the breast. Head and neck have a purple and green gloss; the bill is blackish. In winter plumage it is very like Black-throated Diver, both having dark grey-brown upper-parts contrasted with white throat and underside of neck. Typically the Great Northern is a *good deal larger bird with thicker neck and noticeably stout, heavy bill*, but there is some overlap. In adults, Black-throat has a darker, almost blackish, and uniform back, while Great Northern is lighter, with pale edgings to the feathers, tending to produce an obscurely barred effect. But the immature Black-throat has similar plumage and most birds of both species seen in the British Isles in winter are immature, so that small and slender-billed immature Great Northerns are often almost impossible to identify with certainty. At close range the effect of transverse bars on the back tends to be bolder and more definite in the present species, and the head is darker, more sooty looking, usually looking darker than the back, while in Black-throat it is slightly paler and greyer-brown than back. Traces of summer plumage may suffice to settle identity, in particular Great Northern often shows a dark band almost encircling the base of the neck. Total length about 27–32 ins., body about 17–20 ins.

Habitat. In Britain it is primarily marine, frequenting inshore waters, but not very rare on open reservoirs, lakes and rivers inland. Non-breeding birds occur on sea-coast in summer.

General Habits. These and behaviour closely resemble those of Red-throated Diver but some differences are to be noted. It is much more reluctant to take wing and does so laboriously, flapping and splashing along the surface for some distance, though once under way flight is powerful, direct and rapid. From small pools, as from the ground, it appears to be unable to rise at all, and for pitching it also requires a fair stretch of water. At times, though commonly sleeping on water, it will come ashore to sleep or preen when undisturbed. It moves with amazing speed under water, abruptly appearing and re-appearing and churning up all the water around. The average duration of dive is probably about 40 seconds, and it rarely reaches 70 seconds. It is markedly inquisitive and can sometimes be attracted to close range. Sometimes it is aggressive towards other birds. In winter it usually occurs singly or in pairs, but at migration times may sometimes be seen on the sea in parties.

It is generally silent in winter.

Food is mainly fish, also crustacea, molluscs, worms and some algae.

Status and Distribution. Mainly a winter-visitor from mid-September to May, fairly generally distributed on all coasts, but most plentiful in the north. In N.W. Scotland and Shetland it is present at most times of the year, and has been thought several times to have bred in the latter; breeding was proved for the first time in 1970, on a loch in Wester Ross. It is occasional in summer in other parts, especially N. Scotland. More frequently seen inland than other divers in winter. The bird breeds in Iceland, Greenland, also in N. America. There are no subspecies.

LITTLE GREBE—*Tachybaptus ruficollis*

Bird Plate 2   Egg Plate XXIII (7)

The Little Grebe, often known as Dabchick, is the smallest and commonest of the grebes and is the only one entirely without head ornaments at all seasons. The neck is relatively short and thick compared with the large grebes and the characteristically rotund and stumpy form is often accentuated by fluffing out of feathers at the hind end of body, giving the effect of a very broad stern. *In summer the dark brown plumage, with chestnut cheeks, throat and foreneck* are distinctive. Flanks are dusky brown, not so dark as the upper-parts; the *base of the bill and gape are bright yellowish-green. In winter plumage the upper-parts are not so dark as in summer, the flanks are paler, the chestnut is lost, and the cheeks and sides of neck become buff shading to white on throat.* This plumage is always much browner than the dullest Black-necked Grebe and the *relatively stout straight bill* is quite different. Hardly any white shows in flight. Young in first winter are paler than adults, but juveniles are as dark and have dark streaks on sides of the head. Total length about 10½ ins., body about 6 ins.

Habitat. In the breeding-season it is more catholic in its choice of haunts than the other grebes, frequenting all sorts of still and slow-moving fresh waters providing some cover, from large lakes and reservoirs to relatively small ponds, moorland pools, etc., or even ornamental waters in towns; also quiet reaches of rivers. Most winter inland in mild seasons, though frequently resorting to waters where they do not breed, including reservoirs, etc., devoid of all cover; but others resort to salt water, though more to sheltered estuaries and inlets than the open coast.

General Habits. It is more inclined to fly than the other grebes, though in daytime usually only for short distances and low down over water. In diving it may submerge with hardly a ripple or with a distinct jump, sometimes kicking up a splash of water, and remains submerged for an average period of about ¼-minute, but recorded up to 25 seconds. When alarmed it may show only its head at the surface on rising and may remain thus in shelter of vegetation for some time, especially in the breeding-season. It is more skulking than the other grebes and where there are considerable reed-beds it would often be overlooked, but for its well-known rippling trill. Outside the breeding-season it is often seen singly or in twos and threes, but also quite often in flocks of one or two dozen or occasionally more, which sometimes dive and emerge in unison.

The most distinctive note is a shrill rippling whinny or trill which is occasionally heard from mid-January to mid-October or later, regularly from mid-March to mid-June.

Food includes small fish, molluscs, insects and crustacea, and some vegetable matter. Feathers are not often recorded.

Nests among beds of giant rush, flag, etc., or under shelter of overhanging branches. The eggs, usually 4–6, occasionally 2 and up to 10 recorded, are chalky-white or creamy at first, readily becoming stained to dark brown or red. They are laid generally in April, but at times a month or so earlier, in a nest, built by both sexes, consisting of a heap of water-weeds built up to above the surface of the water with a depression for eggs, which are covered before leaving by the incubating bird when disturbed. Incubation is by both sexes apparently for 19–20 days. The young when small are sometimes carried on their parents' back. They are fed by both parents, but if the hen nests again at 4–6 weeks the male takes charge. Double-brooded; possibly three occasionally.

Status and Distribution. Present throughout the year, breeding in all counties in England, Ireland and Wales except Pembroke, but less plentiful in northern Scotland, and absent from Shetland. Some British and Irish birds appear to be sedentary, but many, especially those breeding on smaller pieces of water, move to rivers and tidal waters for the winter. There is no evidence of migration beyond British waters. Migrants from the Continent arrive on the east coast from September to November, returning mid-March to early May. The race concerned, *Tachybaptus ruficollis ruficollis*, breeds in Europe north to the Baltic States, also in N.W. Africa and Mediterranean Asia. Other races occur in tropical Africa, much of central and S. Asia and Australasia.

GREAT CRESTED GREBE—*Podiceps cristatus*

BIRD PLATE 3   EGG PLATE XXIII (3)

Grebes are aquatic birds, adept at diving, flying but little except when migrating, and distinguished by having long or rather long necks, pointed bills, practically no tails and a tendency to develop ear-tufts or other head ornamentation, at least in the breeding plumage. The Great Crested Grebe is our *largest species* and unlikely to be confused with any other bird except the uncommon Red-necked Grebe. *Ear-tufts are present in all plumages except juvenile*, but are considerably smaller in winter. The bill is rather long, the neck slender. Back is dark grey-brown, the under-parts are silky white. Crown and ear-tufts are blackish, leaving a white line above the eye. In breeding plumage long *chestnut feathers, shading to blackish, on the sides of the face, form an expansible frill or "tippet"*, which is lost in autumn. First-winter birds have sides of the head pure white or merely tinged dusky. Nestling has the head boldly striped black and white, and body more obscurely so; *juvenile has striped head and neck*, but body much as adult. The wing in all post-nestling plumages has white secondaries, concealed when at rest, but conspicuous in flight. Bill of adult is mainly pinkish with white culmen; eye crimson. Total length about 19 ins., body about 12 ins.

Habitat. In the breeding-season typical haunts are lakes, reservoirs, large ponds (including flooded gravel-pits and the like), and more rarely quiet reaches of slow-flowing rivers, with more or less cover of reeds or other plants of similar growth which afford nesting-sites. Sometimes trees such as willows with branches in the water suffice for anchorage of nests, and it will occasionally breed on waters with little or no cover at all. It requires fairly shallow waters, generally not smaller than 5–7 acres. In winter northern birds and many in the south withdraw to the sea-coast and tidal estuaries, and fresh waters are largely or quite deserted, although locally birds remain inland in some numbers, and reservoirs, etc. wholly devoid of cover are regularly frequented, as they are also by non-breeders in summer. Exceptionally, non-breeding birds remain on sea in summer.

General Habits. It is in general disinclined to take wing, and when approached or startled it hardly ever does so, preferring to withdraw by diving, usually to open water rather than to cover. Flight, however, is strong and direct when undertaken, although the rapid wing-beats give a somewhat laboured effect. It flies with extended neck depressed below upper contour of the body, giving a rather hump-backed appearance, much like Goosander and Merganser, with feet extended behind. In rising it patters over the water for some distance before getting clear, and in pitching, unlike ducks, strikes the water breast first. It swims with body low in the water and slender neck erect, but when at rest the head is sunk on shoulders and bill often buried in feathers on one side of the neck. When preening it often rolls over on one side, displaying white under-parts. Dives up to 50 seconds duration have been recorded, but the average is about half this time. Though exceptionally it forms regular colonies in the breeding-season, it is

GREAT CRESTED GREBE   RED-NECKED GREBE

Heads in winter. Note white above eye, and whiter sides of head and neck of Great Crested Grebe.

usually seen singly, in pairs or in scattered parties, seldom in close flocks. Display is frequently seen from early spring onwards, and occasionally in winter. The commonest ceremony is head shaking when a pair face one another, with rigid necks, "ears" and ruff expanded. It very rarely comes to land voluntarily.

One of the principal notes is a loud, discordant bark "gorrr".

Food includes fish, insects, crustacea, molluscs, newts, tadpoles and vegetable matter; feathers are often swallowed.

Nests as a rule among reeds or other vegetation growing in water, but not far from the edge. The eggs, usually 3–4, sometimes 1–7, are chalky-white when fresh but rapidly becoming stained. They are laid generally from April or May onwards in a nest built by both sexes, of water-weeds, dead reeds and other aquatic vegetation or occasionally twigs or sticks, just above the surface of the water with a depression in the middle. Incubation is by both sexes for about 28 days. Weeds are pulled over the eggs when the incubating bird leaves. The young when small are habitually carried on the back of one parent while the other brings them food; these rôles are reversed periodically. The young are independent at 9–10 weeks. Generally one, sometimes two broods.

Status and Distribution. Present throughout the year, breeding regularly in England in most counties but not Devon or Cornwall, and in greatest strength on Norfolk Broads, Cheshire meres and London area gravel-pits and reservoirs. In Wales it is scarcer, not breeding in the west. In Scotland it breeds, or has bred, in nearly all counties from Perth and Angus southwards, being most numerous in the Tay area. Also breeds N. Aberdeen. In Ireland very local in the southern half of the country but abundant in some places in the north. Most breeding waters are abandoned mid-July to October and reoccupied between February and April, but there is no evidence of migration between this country and the Continent. Our birds belong to the race *Podiceps cristatus cristatus* which breeds in most parts in Europe north almost to the Arctic Circle in Finland, also N. Africa and parts of Asia east to China. Other races occur elsewhere in Africa, and in Australasia.

RED-NECKED GREBE—*Podiceps grisegena*

BIRD PLATE 4

In breeding plumage it is characterized by the rich *chestnut colour of front and sides of neck, pale grey cheeks and conspicuously yellow base of the otherwise black bill*; sometimes the bill appears all-yellow. Ear-tufts and crown of head to the level of the eye are black, sides of the head pale grey, back darker brown than in Great Crested Grebe, and flanks mottled brown. The pattern of the spread wing is much as in Great Crested Grebe. In winter it more resembles Great Crested Grebe, but is a *thicker-necked and stockier-looking bird*, as well as smaller, and *lacks the white superciliary streak*, the dark colour of the crown coming down to level of the eye. Below this level the sides of head are more or less dusky, shading to white on the throat, so that there is not the same sharp line of demarcation as in Great Crested Grebe. The sides of the neck are grey-brown, separating the white regions of throat and breast. The yellow of the bill is duller than in summer, but often quite noticeable. In complete winter plumage the top of the head is rounded, not flattened and angular-looking as in Great Crested Grebe. Immature birds are dingier and sometimes have neck and face mainly dark grey-brown. Total length about 17 ins., body about 10 ins.

Habitat. Outside the breeding-season it occurs chiefly on the sea close to shore or in tidal estuaries; occasionally on reservoirs and other fresh waters, but in the British Isles it is the rarest of the grebes inland.

General Habits. In the breeding-season it is more secretive and fonder of keeping near banks and cover than Great Crested Grebe, but not so skulking as Little Grebe or Black-necked. Otherwise habits and behaviour do not differ from those of Great Crested Grebe.

Ordinary note is "keck, keck", higher-pitched than Great Crested Grebe's.

Food includes small fish, frogs, molluscs, crustacea, insects, also feathers and some vegetable matter.

Status and Distribution. A winter-visitor from October to March, sometimes recorded in August, September and April. Summering, formerly rare everywhere, has occurred several times in Scotland since early 1970s with possibility of nesting. It occurs chiefly on the east side of Great Britain south of the Forth, is more occasional on the S. coast of England, rare on the west side of Great Britain and almost unknown in N.W. Scotland; it is a rare but annual vagrant in Ireland. It is usually seen on the coast in small numbers but at intervals considerable "weather-influxes" occur, when it is more widely dispersed and may appear on inland waters, where it is otherwise rare. The race concerned, *Podiceps grisegena grisegena*, breeds in Europe east from Denmark, south to Bulgaria and north almost to the Arctic Circle, and extends into Asia. An example of the race *Podiceps grisegena holboellii* which breeds in N.E. Asia and N. America, has occurred in Scotland, but is indistinguishable in the field, being similar to European birds in all but its slightly larger size.

SLAVONIAN GREBE—*Podiceps auritus*

BIRD PLATE 2   EGG PLATE XXIII (2)

In the breeding-season it is distinguished by *chestnut neck and breast, black head and tippet, with a tuft of yellow feathers projecting like horns from the eyes to beyond back of the head.* The back is dark brown, flanks chestnut. In winter plumages Slavonian and Black-necked Grebes are closely similar. Both are small grebes rather larger than Little Grebe and resembling it in shape, though not quite so squat-bodied, and appear black and white in the field instead of brown. At a distance they are indistinguishable, but at reasonable range can nearly always be identified by the difference in shape of the head and bill and the distribution of black and white on head. Slavonian has a low forehead, the angle of which follows more nearly the line of the bill (giving a rather snake-like appearance to the head) than the steep forehead and high crowned appearance of Black-necked. Slavonian also has normally a relatively stout, straight bill, in contrast to the slender, tip-tilted bill of the slightly smaller Black-neck, while the *dark colour of the crown does not extend below eye* and the white on sides of head tends almost to meet on the nape, so as to suggest a white ring round the neck, whereas Black-neck has usually a continuous broad dark line down the hind-neck. Occasional individuals are however barely separable. Slavonian also tends to keep its neck more erect than Black-neck, though the latter also swims with a straight neck at times. Flanks are marbled with dark grey. Young in autumn have the black and white pattern, especially of the head, less clear-cut, the white cheeks being more or less tinged dusky and the blacks are browner but are usually less dingy than young Black-necks. Total length about 13 ins., body about 8 ins.

Habitat. In the breeding-season it haunts northern lochs, and large or small ponds, with more or less (sometimes decidedly scanty) cover of reeds, rushes, or similar vegetation. On some breeding-waters birds may remain in winter if not frozen out, but outside the breeding-season it is mainly marine, frequenting inshore waters, especially in sheltered bays, estuaries, etc.; and occasionally occurs on open reservoirs, ponds, or rivers inland.

General Habits. It is the least shy of European grebes, but is more inclined to fly and less to dive than other species. Flight is strong and direct, with rapid wing-beats, once the bird is clear of the water. Ordinarily it swims rather high in the water, but when suspicious can sink the body till nearly or quite submerged. In diving it often makes a marked upward and forward leap in a manner recalling Shag, but can also submerge without such action. The average length of dive seems shorter than Great Crested Grebe's. Outside the breeding-season it is usually seen singly or in couples, or, on salt water, sometimes in small parties.

The chief breeding-note is a low, rippling trill.

Food is mainly insects, fish and crustacea, also some water-weeds and other vegetable matter and large quantities of feathers.

Nests in little bays where there is some growth of vegetation for cover: often singly, but where common several pairs may nest not far apart. The eggs, usually 3–5, but 6 recorded, are chalky white when first laid but rapidly become stained. They are laid generally from late May onwards in a nest which consists of a mass of water-weeds and decaying vegetation built up by both sexes in fairly shallow water till just above water-level, with a depression in the middle for eggs; the nest-material is pulled over the eggs by the incubating bird when leaving. Incubation is by both sexes for 20–25 days. The young are tended and fed for probably more than a month by both parents, being carried on their backs when small as in Great Crested Grebe. Occasionally double-brooded.

Status and Distribution. Present throughout the year, breeding on several lochs in Inverness, and in small numbers more or

SLAVONIAN GREBE   BLACK-NECKED GREBE

Heads in winter. Note flatter crown of Slavonian; dusky patch surrounding eye of Black-necked.

less regularly in other counties from Perth to Caithness. Otherwise it is a regular winter-visitor to parts of all coasts of Britain and Ireland including estuaries, and at times inland. It also occurs on passage in May and the first half of June and from early September to late November, and has been seen a good many times in summer. The race concerned, *Podiceps auritus auritus*, breeds in N. Asia, N. America, and in Europe in Iceland, N. Scandinavia, the Baltic and parts of Russia, wintering south occasionally to the Mediterranean. Another race occurs in N. America.

BLACK-NECKED GREBE—*Podiceps nigricollis*

BIRD PLATE 3   EGG PLATE XXIII (5)

It is only a trifle smaller than Slavonian Grebe but distinguished from it in breeding plumage by the *black neck and tuft of golden-brown feathers radiating fan-wise from behind the eye*, as well as by bill. The upper-parts are dull black, sides of breast and flanks are chestnut with an admixture of black; the belly white. The elongated feathers of the crown are often raised, giving an effect of steep forehead and peaked crown. In the black and white winter plumage it resembles Slavonian Grebe very closely. The most characteristic difference is the high crown and steep forehead below which the bill projects at a sharp angle, an effect which is often accentuated by the slender tip-tilted shape of the bill but in some birds, especially young ones, the up-tilt may be very slight. Furthermore, the *black usually extends below the eye and well down over the ear-coverts*, though in this there is some variation, and the broad dark line down the back of neck is not as a rule nearly interrupted at the nape as in most Slavonians. Young birds have cheeks more or less dusky and not sharply demarcated from dark crown. Total length about 12 ins., body about 7 ins.

Habitat. In the breeding-season it resorts to lakes, reservoirs, or large ponds with considerable reed-beds or rich growth of other aquatic vegetation affording good cover. Outside the breeding-season it often occurs on lakes, reservoirs or other waters with little or no cover, and on the sea close to shore.

General Habits. These and behaviour are much like Slavonian Grebe, but in the breeding-season it is normally a good deal shyer, readily taking cover and usually remaining near it by day, though more inclined to spread out on to open water towards dusk. In winter on open waters little difference in behaviour is observable. It often takes insects on the surface with quick right and left movements of the head. Sociable in the breeding-season but in winter it is often found singly, sometimes in twos and threes and small parties.

The ordinary call is a soft "pee-eep".

Food consists mainly of insects; also fish, molluscs and considerable quantities of feathers.

Nests usually in colonies in shallow water, generally sheltered by plant growth. The eggs, usually 3–4, occasionally 2–6, are chalky-white when first laid, but rapidly become stained. They are laid generally in the second half of May and June in a nest consisting of the usual heap of wet water-weeds and decaying vegetable matter, built up by both sexes and added to during incubation. Incubation is by both sexes for about 20–21 days. The young are fed by both parents and carried on their backs when small. They are expert divers at 17 days, but still in the charge of the old birds. Double-brooded at times.

Status and Distribution. Present throughout the year, breeding for the most part rather irregularly at a few widely scattered and varying localities in England, Wales and Scotland as far north as Perthshire. In most years the total number of pairs is very small, but in 1930 a colony in Co. Roscommon contained about 250 pairs; the bird no longer breeds in Ireland. Breeding localities are normally occupied in summer only, and the bird appears as a winter-visitor, and passage-migrant from mid-July to September and late March to mid-May, both inland and on the east and south coasts of England, also in Wales and in Scotland but is unknown in the N. and N.W.; it is very scarce in Ireland. It is fairly frequent inland from Cheshire and Yorkshire southwards including Somerset. The race concerned is *Podiceps nigricollis nigricollis* which breeds from S. Scandinavia south to N.W. Africa and eastwards far into Asia. Other races occur farther south in Africa and in N. America.

FULMAR—*Fulmarus glacialis*

Bird Plate 4   Egg Plate XXII (3)

Superficially rather like a gull, but the *thick neck and rigid-looking, rather narrow wings without black tips and only slightly curved instead of noticeably angled*, prevent confusion with any gull, while the flight is quite distinct from a gull's and is of the regular petrel type, with *long glides on stiffly extended wings varied by intervals of leisurely flapping*. It flaps, however, more than shearwaters and albatrosses and, like them, most in calm weather; it often tilts over like a shearwater so that one wing nearly touches the waves. The head, neck and under-parts are generally slightly yellowish-white, the back and tail pearl-grey, primaries dark grey, with a more or less pronounced pale patch near tip of the wing, but there is wide variation from this type to completely grey ones (the dark phase, or so-called "Blue Fulmar") which are, however, scarce in British waters. Length about 18½ ins.

Habitat. Pelagic in habitat, but it resorts for breeding purposes to cliffs, often largely turfy, and almost exclusively on the coast, but exceptionally as much as a mile or so inland; also to stacks and high islands and exceptionally to flat ground close to sea-level. It rarely flies inland except near breeding cliffs.

General Habits. At breeding places, when not actually in-cubating, it spends most of its time wheeling with rigid wings and fanned tail to and fro in front of cliff-faces and over the adjacent sea. It frequently seems to have difficulty in landing, sweeping in to a cliff, and even touching with its feet, time after time before settling. At breeding-places it settles chiefly on cliff ledges, though also where available on such other perches as walls or turf-banks, and even buildings. When alarmed and sometimes for no obvious reason, a spurt of oil with characteristic musky odour is ejected. The bird usually has difficulty in rising from flat ground. In rising from water it generally patters along the surface before getting

FULMAR

clear. Often a number are seen together and huge congregations occur where food is abundant, but it is not conspicuously gregarious except in so far as conditions of food-supply or nesting sites determine.

Note uttered at rest on water is a sort of chuckling sound somewhat resembling a low grunt. In display it employs a succession of guttural notes "urg-urg-urg . . ." repeated as a cackle, and there are other calls.

Food in temperate seas consists largely of molluscs, fish and fish-offal, crustacea, etc., also floating oil and occasionally dead birds.

Nests in colonies normally on steep slopes of coastal cliffs; exceptionally on buildings. The white egg, normally 1 only, but sometimes 2, is laid generally in late May, often on bare rock, but sometimes a hollow in soil or sand is formed by hen: small stones may be arranged round it. Incubation is by both sexes in turn in spells of about 4 days for about 8 weeks. The young one is brooded and fed by both parents, though the intervals are irregular. It flies when about 8 weeks old. Single-brooded.

Status and Distribution. Mainly a summer-visitor, arriving at nesting-places between early November and early February and leaving between mid-August and the end of September. Dispersal then takes place and the majority of occurrences elsewhere off British coasts are in October and November, but most birds appear not to remain in British waters. The bird has bred from time immemorial on St. Kilda, which was the sole breeding station in the British Isles until 1878. It remains the strongest colony but the bird now nests in large numbers in the Outer Hebrides, Shetland, Orkney and N. Scotland, and has spread down the east coast of Britain to the cliffs of Norfolk. On the west coast, principally on headlands, it nests south to Cornwall, in the Channel to Dorset, and more recently reached Sussex; in Ireland it breeds in all coastal counties except Louth, Meath and Leitrim which lack suitable cliffs. The habit of prospecting new sites before occupying them is frequent and may continue several years, the birds even resting on ledges as if incubating, so that records of breeding must be substantiated by sight of eggs or young. From the British Isles the race *Fulmarus glacialis glacialis* extends far into the north, breeding on European and Canadian islands in the N. Atlantic and Arctic; also on continental coasts in small numbers from Norway south to Brittany. Another race occurs in the N. Pacific.

CORY'S SHEARWATER—*Calonectris diomedea*

BIRD PLATE 4

It looks larger and paler than Great Shearwater, dark brown or grey-brown above, with quills darker, and pure white below, also it differs *in lacking the capped appearance, the throat and sides of neck being mottled with grey-brown, giving appearance of a cloudy downward extension of the dark colour of the upper-parts instead of the brown and white being sharply demarcated*. It also often lacks the white patch at the base of the tail. Other points are: the belly is pure white; the under-side of the wing is margined with pale ash-brown, which shades off into the white central coverts, giving the wing-linings an even, smooth appearance; the bill is yellow instead of dark. Young as adults. Length about 18–20 ins.

Habitat. An offshore bird, but it is also regular in the pelagic zone.

General Habits. Flight is like that of Great Shearwater in general character, but in calm weather, when the birds cannot glide so much as in wind, the wing-beats are rather slower than Great Shearwater's, interspersed with glides on markedly *angled wings*, with wing-tips held below body. General habits and behaviour are otherwise closely similar to those of Great Shearwater and like that species it will accompany schools of dolphins or other cetaceans.

No notes appear to be recorded away from the breeding places.

Food. Offal from fishing-boats, especially oily substances such as cod-liver is eagerly taken, also cuttle-fish.

Status and Distribution. Birds of this species are infrequently observed at sea in July, August and September, rarely October, off the south coast of Ireland and at the mouth of the English Channel. It probably occurs here regularly in autumn. It is also occasionally recorded off the east coast of England and Scotland, where it has occurred in winter. The races *Calonectris diomedea diomedea* (breeding in the Mediterranean) and *Calonectris diomedea borealis* (breeding on islands in the E. Atlantic north to the Azores and Berlengas) are inseparable in the field and it is not known to which subspecies most of the records apply. Other races occur in the Cape Verde Islands and the Indian Ocean. In autumn the bird ranges across the entire width of the Atlantic, but rarely north of Lat. 50°.

GREAT SHEARWATER—*Puffinus gravis*

BIRD PLATE 5

One of the large shearwaters, but smaller than Cory's Shear-water and easily distinguished by its *conspicuously capped appearance*, due to the sharp demarcation of the brown of head from the white of throat, sides and front of neck, the white almost meeting across the nape, this feature being visible at a great distance. Usually has a prominent white patch at the base of the tail, where Cory's too may show white. Further points are: the under-side of the wing is margined with dark brown, contrasted sharply with the white under-wing coverts and it has numerous brown spots and markings at the wing-roots and on the flanks; the belly is white, with a dark mid-ventral patch (lacking in Cory's), the lower tail-coverts appearing brownish. Moulting birds show a conspicuous irregular white band along the whole length of the wing. Bill is dark. Young resemble adults. Length about 17–18 ins.

Habitat. A pelagic bird in the northern hemisphere, but it is also regular in the offshore zone.

General Habits. It has a typical shearwater flight, following the contours of ocean waves for long intervals on rigid wings without apparent effort or wing movement; in calm weather it has to move the wings more and the wing-beats then appear more rapid than those of Cory's Shearwater, and it generally hugs the water more closely, though when prospecting for fish it will sometimes fly as high as 50 yards. When feeding, it alights every few yards or if necessary will dive in pursuit of prey. In rising it flaps along the surface, paddling feet for some distance before getting clear and in a perfect calm has difficulty in rising at all. It is often seen in flocks and the birds sit on the water in "rafts". Flocks often accompany whales or porpoises.

Harsh and raucous calls are uttered by feeding birds.

Food includes squid, entrails of fish, small fish, sand-eels, etc.

Status and Distribution. A summer- and autumn-visitor, recorded most frequently off the south and west coasts of Ireland (sometimes in considerable numbers), scarce in Hebridean seas, and off the coasts of Devon and Cornwall. It is regular but less frequent in Shetland, and there are a number of records off the Yorkshire coast but in all other parts it is rare and occasional. It is often in flocks and generally seen August to November, but on a fair number of occasions in the second half of June and July, and there are a few winter and spring records. It very seldom occurs close to land. The species breeds in the Tristan da Cunha islands in

GREAT SHEARWATER   CORY'S SHEARWATER

the S. Atlantic, and during our summer ranges north over the Atlantic, as far as Greenland and Iceland, numbers in the eastern N. Atlantic off Ireland reaching a maximum about the end of September. There are no subspecies.

SOOTY SHEARWATER—*Puffinus griseus*

BIRD PLATE 5

Its *large size and sooty-black colouring*, relieved only by somewhat paler bases of the quills and a paler tract which may grade to silvery along the middle of the under-side of the wing, but often not at all easily seen, distinguish it from all other species occurring in British waters except the darkest examples of the Balearic race of Manx Shearwater, which is a considerably smaller bird with a faster wing-beat. It is similar in size and flight to Great Shearwater, but the *body appears rather heavier and wings narrower*; the latter taper evenly to a point and are held very stiff and straight in gliding flight. Whitish feathers on the under-wing also separate it from all other dark-coloured petrels of similar size. Confusion is possible with distant young skuas which also "shear" waves sometimes and can appear black in poor light. Bill and legs are dark. Length about 16 ins.

Habitat. A pelagic species, but is also regular in the offshore zone, being proportionally more regular in the latter and less in the former than Great Shearwater.

SOOTY SHEARWATER

In calm air the wings would be held more rigid and less angled.

General Habits. Identical in every essential respect with those of Great Shearwater, with which it often associates in the Atlantic. It is chiefly seen in twos and threes or singly, but is very gregarious where common.

No notes appear to be recorded away from the breeding grounds although it is noisy if captured.

Food is chiefly squid. It is especially fond of oily food, such as cod-liver, and small fish are also taken.

Status and Distribution. An autumn-visitor, occurring mainly from August to October and less commonly from April to December. Movement is very marked along the west and south coasts of Ireland. Otherwise it is chiefly noticed, usually in small numbers, off the north Irish coast, in Hebridean seas, off Shetland, Firth of Forth, coast of Yorks., along Channel from Kent to Cornwall and off Pembroke coast. A few stragglers have been recorded elsewhere. It breeds in New Zealand and southern S. America, ranging on migration over much of the N. Atlantic and Pacific Oceans. There are no subspecies.

MANX SHEARWATER—*Puffinus puffinus*

BIRD PLATE 5   EGG PLATE XXII (4)

Shearwaters are larger and longer-bodied birds than the small petrels elsewhere described, with longer, narrower wings, and have also longer bills, hooked at the tip when seen at close range. Usually seen flying low over the waves with *rapid gliding flight on rigid wings, now tilting over to one side and now to the other, so that tip of the lower wing seems almost to cut the water, and occasionally varying this with a few rapid wing-beats.* They do not follow ships. Manx Shearwater is much the commonest species in British waters and is *black above and white below*, providing a sharp contrast in appearance as the flying bird tilts over almost at right angles, displaying now its upper- and now its under-side. Young resemble adults. Length about 14 ins.

Habitat. Like other shearwaters it is essentially maritime, but is an offshore bird rather than pelagic, being rare beyond the Continental shelf. For breeding it resorts to turfy, rock-girt islands and turfy slopes on cliffs, occasionally of mainland; sometimes also to screes and mainly rocky localities.

General Habits. Typical flight is as described above but sometimes is more purposeful and direct, as when flocks are travelling to and from feeding-grounds, which may be five or six hundred miles from the nesting site. It takes food chiefly at the surface but will also dive. It is active at sea by day, but at breeding-places is strictly nocturnal. Assembles offshore just before sunset in huge flocks, which rest on the water, washing, preening, drinking, and diving, or wheeling to and fro over the surface. Arrival at the breeding-ground is usually about 2 hours after sunset, but later on moonlight nights, when most birds do not come in at all. On land it has difficulty in taking off in absence of wind, and seeks some elevated point from which to launch out.

At breeding-stations at night it produces a babel of weird, gruff, cooing or crowing noises in rapid time, a typical version rendered as "kuk-kuk-kuk-koo", uttered in flight, as well as in burrows. Generally silent at sea.

Food is chiefly smaller fish, but also molluscs.

Nests in colonies in burrows, sometimes in enormous numbers. The dull white egg, one only, is laid generally between late April and mid-June in a burrow excavated by both sexes to a length of not less than 3 feet as a rule. The nesting-chamber usually contains only a little dry grass, roots, stalks, etc., and a few feathers. Incubation is for about 51–54 days by both sexes in turn for spells of up to 7–10 days without food. The young bird is deserted by its parents about the 60th day and is then fledged, but remains in the hole without food 11–15 days longer and leaves its nest for the sea when about 72–74 days old. Single-brooded. It may not breed until 5 years old.

Status and Distribution. A summer-visitor arriving between early February and third week of March, and leaving August to October. It breeds in the Scilly Isles, on islands off Pembroke and Caernarvon, Calf of Man, several of the Inner and Outer Hebrides including St. Kilda, in Orkney and Shetland, and in Ireland on a number of islands, particularly in the west, and a few promontories; also at least at times on Lundy and has bred in Durham. Summer occurrences elsewhere (e.g. regularly in the Firth of Forth) may be birds on feeding flights. In late August and September it becomes widely spread round the coasts and examples are sometimes picked up exhausted inland. Its winter quarters are not accurately known, but British waters are almost completely deserted, and ringed birds have been recovered in Brazilian waters. The race concerned, *Puffinus puffinus puffinus*, also breeds in the Faeroes and Iceland, off N.W. France, Madeiras and Azores. The race *Puffinus puffinus mauretanicus*, which breeds in the Balearic Islands, occurs regularly in the English Channel in autumn and especially between August and October off Portland Bill, Dorset; otherwise it is recorded chiefly off the east coast of England, most often Yorkshire, and a scattering in Scotland; also S.W. Ireland. In appearance it is quite distinct from our breeding bird, having the upper-parts noticeably paler (brown instead of black), flanks brownish, and although some have pale under-parts, others are much more uniform-looking, with no sharp demarcation between the colour of upper- and under-parts, most of the latter being more or less strongly tinged sooty-brown or greyish. In the case of the darkest examples care must be taken to avoid confusion with the considerably larger Sooty Shearwater. Another race of Manx Shearwater occurs in the E. Mediterranean.

WILSON'S PETREL—*Oceanites oceanicus*

BIRD PLATE 6

A small, sooty-black, white-rumped and square-tailed petrel resembling Storm Petrel, but distinguished by its long legs, the *yellow-webbed feet extending nearly half an inch beyond the tail in flight*. In its habit of following in wake of vessels it also resembles Storm Petrel (and differs from Leach's) though its wings are blunter and more rounded, and flight is direct and Swallow-like, with slow, steady wing beats. It often "walks" on the water in a characteristic attitude, with wings stretched level or slightly raised like a butterfly's and tail fanned, planing along in a series of hops with the feet dangling side by side. Length about 7 ins.

Habitat. It is purely an ocean-haunting bird in the northern hemisphere.

General Habits. These and behaviour resemble Storm Petrel's. It will often settle on the water, floating buoyantly like a phalarope. It can dive below the surface but does not do so commonly.

Food consists of remains of small fishes, floating oil, small molluscs, crustacea, etc.

Status and Distribution. A very rare vagrant which has occurred chiefly in the late autumn on the coasts of England, also once or twice in Scotland and Ireland. It is however more regular at sea west of Cornwall. The species breeds on Antarctic islands in the early part of the year, and outside the breeding-season, during our summer, migrates north into the N. Atlantic and does not reach the east side in numbers until autumn. There are no subspecies.

STORM PETREL—*Hydrobates pelagicus*

Bird Plate 6   Egg Plate XXII (2)

Petrels and shearwaters are birds of the ocean which come ashore only in connexion with breeding (though often long before eggs are laid) and never occur inland except as storm-driven waifs. The Storm Petrel is a *small sooty-coloured, white-rumped bird, suggesting a long-winged, square-tailed House Martin* in appearance, despite the dark under-parts. It shows a little white on under wing-coverts and flanks, but this is usually difficult to see. In fresh plumage the narrow whitish borders to the coverts form a narrow, but distinct wing-bar, but later this is lost through abrasion. Like Wilson's Petrel, and unlike Leach's, it *habitually follows vessels, fluttering* back and forth across the wake with *wavering bat-like flight* close to the water. Young resemble adults. Length about 6 ins.

Habitat. An essentially pelagic bird, resorting for breeding purposes to turfy or rocky and boulder-strewn islands. It occurs inland only when storm-driven.

General Habits. Wing-action is not rapid, but almost unceasing, gliding for only a few yards at a time before fluttering again. Occasionally it settles on the water and floats buoyantly. Though diurnal at sea, it is strictly nocturnal so far as its activities on land are concerned. Like other petrels, it has a characteristic musky smell by which occupied nests can generally be detected, and when irritated it ejects a similar smelling oil from mouth.

The usual note, used constantly in evening and at night from nesting-place until the chick hatches, is a not loud but penetrating sound consisting of a harsh uneven purring "urr-r-r-r-r" long sustained and ending abruptly with "chikka". It is very rarely uttered on the wing.

Food, in addition to fish, is probably derived from plankton or floating offal and oil.

Nests in colonies of varying size but not necessarily close together. The egg, one only, is dull white, sometimes unmarked but more often with a zone of fine red-brown speckles at the large end. It is laid generally in June, sometimes in a burrow made by the birds themselves in peaty soil, with a nest-chamber at the end: more often among loose stones or under boulders; also among ruined buildings. Nesting material is often entirely absent. Incubation is by both sexes for about 39–40 days, each adult commonly taking a 3-day shift. The young are fed by both parents, usually nightly, but intervals up to 2 or 3 days may occur. They normally fly when about 60–66 days old. Single-brooded.

Status and Distribution. Recorded throughout the year but it is mainly a summer-visitor arriving in late April and early May and leaving British waters during October and November. It has bred in S. Devon and does so regularly in the Scilly Isles (and probably N. Cornwall), Skokholm and Skomer (Pembroke) and a few birds elsewhere in Wales; on many of the western and northern islands of Scotland, and many islands off the west and southwest coasts of Ireland. It is sometimes driven inland in rough weather in autumn; also occasionally in winter when most are farther out in the Atlantic, and some penetrate deep into S. Atlantic. The species also breeds in the Mediterranean, Canaries, Spain, France, Channel Isles, Faeroes and Iceland. There are no subspecies.

LEACH'S PETREL—*Oceanodroma leucorhoa*

Bird Plate 6   Egg Plate XXII (6)

Somewhat like Storm and Wilson's Petrel but is, and looks, decidedly larger and browner than either, and has a distinct contrast between the blackish quills and the paler coverts, which Storm Petrel does not show. The fork in the tail can easily be missed except under the best conditions for observation, as can a smoky grey division down the centre of the white rump. Its wings are longer than those of Storm Petrel or Wilson's and it has *a distinctive flight, very buoyant and erratic, springing and bounding through the air with abrupt changes of direction*, now gliding like a miniature shearwater, now beating on buoyant wings like a nightjar, or turning with incredible swiftness. Length about 8 ins.

Habitat. In choice of habitat it resembles Storm Petrel.

General Habits. Apart from the points mentioned above, its general habits and behaviour are much like Storm Petrel's. In burrowing, the bill is used as a pick and loose earth is kicked out backwards by rapid movements of the legs, which are straddled out on either side of the body.

It calls freely on breeding-grounds, the principal call-notes being a crowing "her-kitti-werke" given on the wing, and a continuous crooning note given only from the burrow and frequently interrupted by the flight-call and variants.

STORM PETREL   LEACH'S PETREL

Food is derived from plankton and also from excreta of marine mammals, while small fish, crustacea and molluscs are occasionally taken.

Nests in colonies, forming burrows in peaty ground, or among heaps of stones or ruined buildings. The egg, one only, is dull white, usually with a zone of fine reddish spots at the big end. It is laid generally from mid-May onwards in a burrow excavated by male. The nest-chamber is sometimes lined with a pad of dry grass, thrift roots, moss, etc. Incubation is by both sexes for about 41–42 days. The chick is fed by both parents, at lengthening intervals towards fledging. It generally remains in the hole for 63–70 days. Single-brooded. It probably does not normally breed until 4–5 years old.

Status and Distribution. A summer-visitor arriving from April to June, and some linger on in British waters into December, but it is hardly ever recorded in the early months of the year. It breeds in numbers on some of the remotest Atlantic islands off N.W. Scotland (St. Kilda, N. Rona, Sula Sgeir, Flannans) perhaps a few pairs in Shetland, and there are some old scattered breeding records from islands off the west coast of Ireland. It is not often seen from shore, but is occasionally driven inland during autumn gales. The bird also breeds in the Faeroes, Iceland, N.E. American islands, and in the N. Pacific. There are no subspecies.

GANNET—*Sula bassana*

BIRD PLATE 7   EGG PLATE XXII (1)

It is generally seen in flight at sea, when adult appears as *a very large white bird with long, narrow, black-tipped wings, pointed tail, more distinct neck than a gull and stout pointed beak, which combine to give the body a characteristic "cigar-shape", pointed at both ends*. This form is unlike that of any other sea-bird and equally distinguishes the *blackish, white-speckled young* and the various pied plumages of intermediate ages, as also do its *spectacular headlong dives* from the air when fishing. Full adult plumage is apparently not attained until about the fifth year. Total length about 36 ins.; body about 23 ins.

Habitat. An essentially maritime species, typically frequenting offshore waters and breeding on rocky islands, generally with

D.W.

IMMATURE GANNETS

3rd autumn   2nd autumn   1st autumn

precipitous cliffs, at which some birds are present from February to October. It occurs only accidentally inland.

General Habits. Direct flight, which is commonly 30 ft. or so above the water, is accomplished by regular, rather rapid wing-beats with occasional glides, but it also often flies low over the surface, gliding and occasionally flapping, almost like a shear-water, or soars high in the air. It rests on the water, floating high and rising from it with some effort, flapping over the surface for some distance before it can rise clear. It does not come to land except to breeding-places or by accident. In fishing it dives from usually about 50–100 ft. In normal diving, flight is checked for a moment, or the bird may actually rise somewhat, and then shoots down in a headlong plunge with wings half open, but closes them just before entering the water with a terrific splash. Plunges may be practically vertical, but more often slanting, and the bird performs a half turn in its descent. Although a colonial nester, often travelling in strings to and from feeding-grounds and often seen in company at other seasons, it does not form close flocks and is frequently seen singly or in couples. Remains continuously at sea except in the breeding-season.

At breeding places the chief note is a loud hoarse "urrah". A similar call may be heard on take-off from the sea after a dive, and a repeated rasping croaking from parties on long-distance flights.

Food is almost entirely fish.

Nests in colonies, sometimes of enormous size, usually on cliff-ledges, but the nests may "overflow" on to cliff-tops where the birds are undisturbed and are often so close together as to touch. The egg, normally one only, is covered with a soft, chalky-white deposit, irregularly laid on and failing in places, disclosing bluish undershell. It is laid generally in April or May in a nest built often of seaweeds, though grasses and campion are also used. Incubation is by both sexes for about 43–45 days. The chick is fed by both parents for two months, and afterwards is left by its parents to starve for about 10 days, when it flies down to the sea and swims on the surface for 2 or 3 weeks before it begins to fish for itself. Single-brooded.

Status and Distribution. Present throughout the year, breeding in Scotland in large numbers on the Bass Rock, Noss and Hermaness (Shetland), Sule Stack (Orkney), Sula Sgeir (Outer Hebrides), St. Kilda and Ailsa Craig; fewer Scar Rocks (Wigtown), also Flannans, Fair Isle, Foula, Shiants. In Ireland about 10,000 pairs nest on Little Skellig (Kerry), and smaller colonies on Bull Rock (Cork) and on Great Saltee (Wexford). In Wales there is a large colony on Grassholm (Pembs) and in England a much smaller one at Bempton (Yorks). First year birds are mostly migratory, wintering mainly on the W. African coast south to Senegal. After their second year the great majority winter in British and W. European waters; a few enter the Mediterranean. The species also breeds in Brittany, the Channel Islands, Norway, Faeroes, Iceland and N.E. America. There are no subspecies.

CORMORANT—*Phalacrocorax carbo*

BIRD PLATE 7   EGG PLATE XXII (5)

A large, dark, fairly long-necked aquatic bird, with a moderately long bill distinctly hooked at the tip, and markedly upright carriage when settled. Only Shag amongst British birds resembles it at all closely, and adults of the two species are easily distinguished, Cormorant being characterized by a *white chin and sides of face, bronze-brown and black upper-parts, glossy bluish-black under-parts and neck, and in breeding dress by a conspicuous white thigh-patch, lack of crest, and hoary or white appearance of the head and neck*, due to long, greyish-white hair-like plumes. The bare skin of the lores and throat-pouch is yellow. Brown immature birds are less easy to distinguish, but Cormorant, in addition to being a considerably larger, more thick-set bird, with stouter neck and bill, has the *breast and abdomen dull white more or less mottled brown*, while young Shag has these parts entirely brown. It swims low in the water with neck erect and at a distance may sometimes be confused with divers, but the bill is inclined noticeably upwards, whereas a diver carries its bill horizontal or with only a slight upward inclination. Total length about 36 ins.; body about 22 ins.

Habitat. It haunts mainly marine localities, though not usually encountered out of sight of land, frequenting sea-coast, estuaries and tidal rivers, and is common about low-lying and sandy or muddy, as well as rocky shores; also often visiting adjacent fresh waters. In many districts of Scotland and Ireland it is of regular occurrence on the larger lochs and rivers far inland, even breeding on fresh waters in a few places, and elsewhere is a not infrequent visitor to inland reservoirs, rivers, etc.

General Habits. Flight is direct, fairly swift, with regular, rather rapid wing-beats, neck extended in front and feet under the tail, and it glides occasionally. Generally flies low down over water, but sometimes at a considerable elevation, and soars at times. It rises from water with some effort except in a strong wind. When not feeding it lands on shore, sandbanks, etc., where frequently long lines may be seen resting along the water's edge, or it perches on rocks, buoys, etc., in the water, often standing in a highly characteristic attitude with the wings held out and half spread to dry. When suspicious or alarmed it sinks body till only

CORMORANT

Breeding plumage.

the head and neck show above the surface. It dives either with a distinct jump, so that for a moment nearly the whole bird is out of the water, or by quiet submergence with scarcely a ripple. Dives of 20–30 secs. or less are frequent although up to 71 secs. recorded. It is often seen singly, but also often in numbers together.

It is usually silent away from nesting-sites and roosts, where the chief notes are various deep guttural noises, "karrk", "kworrk", etc.

Food consists almost entirely of fish, but crustacea and algae are also taken occasionally.

Nests close together in colonies, as a rule apart from Shags, on small rocky islands in lakes or sea, and on ledges of cliffs, generally on the coast, but occasionally inland and in some cases in trees, especially in Ireland. The eggs, usually 3–4 and rarely 6, have an unevenly deposited white chalky surface, which often almost conceals the pale blue undershell. They are laid generally in April and early May in the south, later in the north, in a nest built by both sexes, usually of seaweed, but at inland sites it may be composed of heather-stalks, sticks, etc., lined with grass, green rushes, straw, etc. Incubation is by both sexes for about 26–29 days. The young are fed by both parents and remain in the nest for over a month. Usually single-brooded.

Status and Distribution. Present throughout the year and generally distributed on all coasts at all seasons although there are considerable stretches where it does not breed or only does so sporadically, namely: between Isle of Wight and Flamborough (Yorks); between the Farne Islands and Easter Ross (except for an expanding colony in the Firth of Forth), between Cheshire and Cumberland, and very few on or near mainland between S. Ayr and N.W. Ross; in Ireland, none in Down and rather few breed on the east coast south of Antrim, apart from a big colony at Lambay. It also breeds in a few places on islands in inland waters and inland cliffs. Found virtually throughout year in lower Thames valley, occurring in flocks in winter, and has recently bred. British birds disperse rather than migrate, and some are to a large extent sedentary, but some reach N. Spain and Portugal. They belong to the race *Phalacrocorax carbo carbo* which breeds in Europe from Scandinavia to the White Sea, and in eastern N. America. Birds of the race *Phalacrocorax carbo sinensis* occur in this country mainly in winter between Suffolk and Dorset. It breeds from Denmark, Belgium, Holland and France, south to Tunisia and India and east to Japan. Other races occur elsewhere in Africa, Japan and Australia.

SHAG—*Phalacrocorax aristotelis*

BIRD PLATE 7   EGG PLATE XXII (7)

It is not unlike Cormorant, but is smaller and more slightly built, with a more slender bill, and easily distinguished when adult by the *dark oily-green plumage with no white*, and further, in the breeding-season, by its *recurved crest*. The yellow of the gape and gular region is deeper than in Cormorant. Immature birds differ from those of Cormorant in having *little or no white on brown breast*, as well as in smaller size, slimmer build and *markedly slender bill* (slenderer than adult's). They sometimes have a well-marked pure white spot on the chin. Total length about 30 ins.; body about 18 ins.

Habitat. In habitat it is more restricted than Cormorant, being exclusively marine and confined to rocky coasts, especially where there are caves and fissures. It is only a straggler to inland waters.

General Habits. Apart from difference in habitat, the Shag's habits and behaviour are very like Cormorant's, though it is more at home on rough seas and less inclined to perch on posts or buoys, preferring rocks and often assuming a rather less upright attitude than Cormorant; it spreads its wings in the same way. In diving it more habitually springs clear of the water, though it can also sink under without doing this. Sometimes plunge-dives from air.

Notes at breeding-places are harsh and croaking, recorded as "kroak-kraik-kroak".

Food is almost entirely fish; crustacea, molluscs and algae being taken occasionally.

Nests in colonies of varying size on ledges of sea-cliffs or in hollows under or among huge boulders, the nests often being placed close together. The eggs, normally 3, sometimes 2, and even 6, resemble those of Cormorant but are smaller. They are laid generally from April onwards in a nest built by both sexes, sometimes of sea-weed, often much decayed, but where available heather-stems and dry grass are also used, and green leaves, flowers, etc., may be added by way of lining or decoration. Incubation is by both sexes for about 33 days. Young are fed by both parents and fly when about 53 days old. Usually, if not always, single-brooded. Birds first breed when 3 or 4 years old.

Status and Distribution. Present throughout the year and fairly generally distributed on the Atlantic coasts of the British Isles, especially on the Scottish and Irish west coasts and western and northern isles. It breeds locally on the east coast of Scotland but not on the English east or south coasts between Flamborough

Head and the Isle of Wight, nor on the north-west coast of England. It breeds on the Isle of Man and locally in Wales, being numerous in Pembroke. In Ireland it does not breed on the east coast from Co. Antrim southwards, except in Co. Dublin. Our birds are relatively sedentary, although some wander up to 300 miles from home. They belong to the race *Phalacrocorax aristotelis aristotelis* which breeds in Europe from the Arctic Ocean to Portugal. Other races occur in the Mediterranean and Black Seas.

BITTERN—*Botaurus stellaris*

BIRD PLATE 10   EGG PLATE XXIII (4)

In the breeding-season male proclaims his presence by a booming note. When seen, the long pointed bill and *golden-brown plumage mottled and barred with black* distinguish it, whether it is flying with slow, rather owl-like action over the tops of the reeds, or standing with neck retracted, or extending it nearly vertically upwards in protective attitude. The crown and nape are black, the back richly mottled with black, sides of head and neck more uniform brown, under-side broadly streaked reddish-brown, and the wing-quills are barred rich brown and black. Young are much like adults. In a position of rest with neck retracted and bill pointing obliquely upwards, the contour of the neck is hidden by thick feathering, so that it appears short and thick and not clearly defined from the body. In flight the appearance is similar but the legs trail behind in typical heron fashion; wings broad and rounded. Total length about 30 ins.; body about 14 ins.

Habitat. It haunts more or less extensive reed-beds and rank vegetation of swamps or bordering meres, lagoons and sluggish rivers.

General Habits. Though essentially a skulking and secretive bird, keeping for the most part to the cover of reeds and swamp vegetation, Bittern may at times be seen standing in the open near the water's edge, especially in hard weather. Its habits are decidedly crepuscular, though it also feeds in the daytime. When feeding young, it may be seen regularly passing to and fro over reed-beds, but at other times is not often observed on the wing except when flushed. In cover it often progresses above ground or water-level by grasping reeds, several at a time, with the toes, moving in this manner with astonishing facility for so comparatively large a bird. It very rarely perches in trees, and is usually solitary.

Call of both sexes in a raucous "aark, aark"; alarm is "gok-gok-gok". The spring note of male is a deep resonant boom, not remarkably loud, but of extraordinary carrying power.

Food includes fish, frogs, newts, crustacea, insects, small mammals and birds, also some vegetable matter.

Nests in reed-beds among reed-stems of the previous year or among sedge, as a rule resting on matted roots and built up above the water-level. The eggs, usually 4–6, occasionally 3 or 7, olive-brown, sometimes with fine brown speckles, are laid generally in April or May in a nest rather carelessly built by female alone of bits of reeds, sedge, etc., and lined with finer materials. Incubation is by female alone for about 25 days. The young are fed by female only; they begin to leave the nest after 2 or 3 weeks, but are not fully fledged till nearly 8 weeks old. Single-brooded.

Status and Distribution. Present throughout the year. It breeds regularly in East Anglia, and in small numbers in Kent and N. Lancs.; it has done so irregularly elsewhere. Otherwise it is chiefly a winter-visitor, irregular in Scotland and Ireland. The race concerned, *Botaurus stellaris stellaris*, breeds from N.W. Africa north to the Baltic and east to E. Siberia. Other races occur in S. Africa and Australia.

AMERICAN BITTERN—*Botaurus lentiginosus*

BIRD PLATE 10

In general appearance it resembles European Bittern, but is rather smaller and differs in having the *upper-parts finely freckled instead of boldly mottled with black, the primaries uniform dark brownish-grey instead of barred, and the crown brown instead of black*. Total length about 26 ins.; body about 12 ins.

Habitat. It frequents country closely similar to the habitat of the European Bittern, but occurs more regularly in comparatively small areas of swamp and frequently visits more or less open meadows and pastures.

General Habits. Its habits closely resemble those of our bird, but is often seen feeding or flying in the open.

Flight-calls, not often given, are a nasal "haink" and a croaking "ok-ok-ok-ok".

Food is entirely animal matter, largely frogs or small fish.

Status and Distribution. A rare vagrant, most occurring in

October and November, some December to February. Most English records are from the south coast; there are a number of records from Ireland and a few from Scotland and Wales. The bird breeds in Canada and U.S.A. There are no subspecies.

LITTLE BITTERN—*Ixobrychus minutus*

BIRD PLATE 10

It is naturally secretive and skulking, and often difficult to flush, but if seen on the wing the *pattern of male, with whitish wing-coverts forming a sharply defined rounded area contrasted with the black of the rest of the wing and back*, is very distinctive and with legs trailing has appearance of a "black and buff Moorhen"; that of female, in which both light and dark parts are much browner, is a good deal less striking. At rest with neck retracted, it has a "Humpty Dumpty-like" outline with head and body all one, but when on the alert or clambering about in reeds or branches the neck is more extended, though still thick, and when assuming the protective, "stick-like" attitude it stretches it straight upwards to a startling length. At rest male appears a light buff-coloured bird with black back and crown. Female has a brown back, somewhat streaked, and under-parts are more streaked than in male. Young birds have a mottled and streaked appearance. Total length about 14 ins.; body about 6½ ins.

Habitat. It haunts reed-fringed meres, and rivers or canals, as well as more extensive reed-beds, especially where willows are mixed with reeds, and is not at all averse to comparatively frequented places.

General Habits. After rising with some effort it flies easily and lightly with fairly rapid wing-beats, usually low down, and with neck withdrawn and legs extended in usual heron manner. In general it keeps amongst reeds and willows, in which it climbs about rapidly and with the utmost facility. Though active to some extent by day, it is distinctly crepuscular, becoming more lively towards evening.

A call-note in flight is a low-toned "quer", short and sudden. There are several other notes.

Food is chiefly insects and fish.

Status and Distribution. A vagrant occurring chiefly from April to June and from August to October, occasionally in other

LITTLE EGRET   LITTLE BITTERN

male

months, and rarely in winter. It has been recorded in nearly every English and Welsh county, but most frequently on the south and east coast north to Yorkshire. It has probably bred in E. Anglia and one or two southern counties, and proved to do so recently in N. England. It is rare in Scotland and Ireland. The race concerned, *Ixobrychus minutus minutus*, breeds from N. Africa north to the Baltic States and eastwards to India. European birds winter in Africa. Other races occur in tropical and S. Africa, Madagascar and Australasia.

NIGHT HERON—*Nycticorax nycticorax*

BIRD PLATE 9

In flight a *short-bodied, compact-looking bird with closely re-tracted head appearing to merge directly into the rather stout body, so that the black of crown and mantle form a continuous area, contrasted with the grey of the broad, rounded wings and tail.* At rest it also appears compact and thick-set, with relatively short legs and with short stout neck appearing to merge directly into the body; under-parts greyish-white; three long filament-like white feathers on the nape. *Young birds are dull, dark brown above spotted and streaked with buffish-white, the under-parts dull greyish with dark streaks*; in flight the absence of long trailing legs helps separation from Bittern. Legs of adults are usually pale yellowish, though often appearing more or less greyish. Legs of young birds olive-green. Total length about 24 ins.; body about 12 ins.

NIGHT HERON
Adult

Habitat. It frequents wooded or bushy swamps and river-banks or the neighbourhood of other fresh waters or marshes where there are trees or other suitable cover, in which it remains inactive by day, but at dusk spreads out over almost any sort of open marsh or watersides that may be available.

General Habits. It is mainly crepuscular in habits, roosting in trees and other thick cover by day and flighting at dusk to feeding grounds; it is therefore liable to escape notice by day unless fortuitously flushed. It feeds in shallow water, swampy borders of reed-beds and along canals and ditches. It perches freely in trees and clambers about with much facility amongst both slender twigs and reeds, moving, however, with marked deliberation, as it does also on the ground. The beats of the short, much rounded wings appear rapid for a heron.

Call is a hoarse, not un-raven-like croak used freely when flighting at dusk.

Food is mainly small fish; also newts, frogs, molluscs, worms, leeches, aquatic insects, and crustacea.

Status and Distribution. A vagrant, many recorded on the south and east coasts of England from Cornwall to Yorkshire, and a good many inland, but rare in the west and north. Rare also in Wales, Ireland and Scotland (where there is a free-flying colony at Edinburgh Zoo). It has occurred in every month, but most in May and June and a good many in October and November. The race *Nycticorax nycticorax nycticorax* breeds in Europe north to Holland and Czechoslovakia, also over much of Africa and Asia. Northern birds migrate. Other races occur in N. and S. America.

SQUACCO HERON—*Ardeola ralloides*

BIRD PLATE 8

At rest it appears a *predominantly fawn-coloured bird* with long feathers of the head streaked pale buff and blackish, and can hardly be confused with any other species. This contrasts strikingly with its appearance in flight, when the *white wings* (largely concealed by mantle feathers when at rest) and the tail make it look predominantly white; at a distance it may even give the impression of being wholly white, though at reasonably close range the warm buff mantle and dingy-looking streaked head are usually fairly obvious. In winter the mantle is browner and the whole neck streaked blackish. Legs are generally yellowish-green, bill blackish, pale greenish at the base below, but in breeding birds bill becomes bright blue especially at base and legs reddish. Young are much like winter adults. When settled the neck looks thick, merging more or less gradually into the body and often giving a rather bittern-like appearance. Total length about 18 ins.; body about 9 ins.

Habitat. It frequents lush water-meadows and sedgy margins of marshes and flood-lands and banks of streams and lagoons.

General Habits. Wings are rather rounded and flight leisurely and heron-like with head drawn in. It is inclined to skulk in reeds or cover, being rather sluggish by day and becoming active towards evening. It perches quite freely in trees and bushes.

SQUACCO HERON

It is silent by day except at breeding colonies; at dusk often a harsh and shrill "karr".

Food is chiefly insects, also frogs, small fish, worms, molluscs, crustacea, and some vegetable matter.

Status and Distribution. A rare vagrant recorded chiefly from East Anglia, Sussex, Devon and Cornwall. There are records from a number of other English counties, and some from Wales, Ireland and Scotland. It has occurred mostly in May and June, several in July, and one or two in most other months. It breeds in many parts of S. and S.E. Europe, east into Asia, also in N.W., tropical and S. Africa. European birds are migratory. There are no subspecies.

LITTLE EGRET—*Egretta garzetta*

BIRD PLATE 9

An obvious heron with slender neck and *pure white plumage*. Amongst birds of about the same size it can only be confused with Cattle Egret (*Bubulcus ibis*), which looks equally white at a little distance, and (in flight only) with Squacco, which although head and body are fawn-coloured, looks mainly white on the wing. The *black bill and legs and yellowish feet* are characters to be looked for in flight and can be seen with glasses at a considerable distance.

LITTLE EGRET   CATTLE EGRET

Note long head-plumes of Little Egret (adult in summer); heavy protruding jowl of Cattle Egret.

When settled (except when at rest with neck withdrawn) the much slenderer, sinuous neck and slender bill are alone sufficient distinction from Cattle Egret. Total length about 22 ins.; body about 11 ins.

Habitat. It frequents open shallows in marshes and floodlands, and open shores or sandbanks of rivers, streams and lagoons.

General Habits. Flight and attitude of rest, with head retracted in both cases, also gait and manner of feeding are those of a typical heron; the wings are rather rounded and flight leisurely, sometimes gliding for a short distance.

It is generally silent except at breeding places.

Food includes small fish, frogs, crustacea, molluscs and insects.

Status and Distribution. Formerly a very rare vagrant but since 1952 has appeared annually, chiefly in spring or summer on the south and east coasts of England, not infrequent Ireland, but fewer elsewhere north to Shetland. The race concerned, *Egretta garzetta garzetta*, breeds in S. Europe north to northern France, Czechoslovakia, and Romania, also in N.W. and S. Africa and across Asia to Japan. Other races occur in Madagascar, Malaysia and Australasia. European birds winter from the Mediterranean southwards.

GREY HERON—*Ardea cinerea*

BIRD PLATE 8   EGG PLATE XXIII (8)

Grey Heron is the only bird of the stork kind occurring regularly and commonly in the British Isles, and is amongst the largest common British birds. *Its size, long bill and legs, and sober colouring of grey, white and black* are distinctive whether the bird has its long slender neck more or less extended, or is resting with head sunk between shoulders or flying with head drawn back, legs extended behind, and slow regular beats of broad, rounded wings. The upper-parts and tail are ash-grey; head and neck white with a black band running back from the eye to terminate in a long pendant crest, and blue-black streaks on the front of neck. The under-parts are greyish white with some black at the sides; wing-quills blackish. Bill usually yellow, legs brownish, but bill and legs are sometimes pinkish in the breeding-season. Immature birds are more uniform-looking than adults, with greyer neck, and no black on the head. Total length about 36 ins.; body about 16 ins.

GREY HERON   PURPLE HERON

Note deeper-pouched neck of Purple
Heron.

Habitat. It frequents almost any kind of country with waters
affording it a suitable food-supply and not too deep and shelving to
wade in. It ranges from coastal waters to mountain tarns and may
be met with equally on large or small rivers and lakes, reservoirs
and ponds, ditches, flood-waters, sea-shore, tidal estuaries and
brackish lagoons. At times foraging excursions may be extended
into fields far from water. Most actual breeding-sites are at low
elevation and birds may forage regularly up to 12 miles from the
nesting place.

General Habits. It spends much time on the ground where it
moves with a deliberate walk, and is frequently seen standing erect
and motionless, often on one leg by the water's edge, but it also
perches freely on trees, etc. When fishing it walks slowly along in
shallow water with neck curved ready to be shot out to seize prey;
at other times it stands motionless in shallows waiting for a fish to
pass within reach. Big fish may be taken ashore and the flesh picked
from the bones, and other prey is caught on the ground. It will
occasionally settle momentarily on the surface of deep water to
pick up food. It is especially active in the evening and near dawn.
Even outside the breeding-season it is rather gregarious.

Ordinary note is a loud, harsh "frarnk", but a wide variety of
weird and raucous noises are heard in a heronry.

Food is mainly fish, but water-voles and frogs are also frequently recorded; less frequently other mammals, birds, reptiles, molluscs, crustacea, insects, and some vegetable matter, also gralloch.

Nests generally in colonies normally in high trees, but in N.
Scotland, Orkney and Hebrides (and to slight extent elsewhere)
regularly on cliff-ledges, or in scrub, on ground, or in reeds. The
greenish-blue eggs, normally 3–5, but occasionally 2 or 6, are laid

generally in February or March in a nest which is small when first
built but may become very large as it is used year after year. It is
constructed of branches and sticks, lined with smaller twigs, and
sometimes roots, dead grass, etc., usually provided by the male
while the hen remains on the nest and builds. Incubation is by both
sexes apparently for about 25 days. The young are fed by both
sexes and fly when about 50–55 days old. Sometimes double-
brooded.

Status and Distribution. Present throughout the year and
generally distributed, nesting in all counties in Ireland and
throughout Britain except Shetland. After a series of mild winters
the breeding population of England and Wales ranges up to about
10,000 adults. In England breeding density is greatest in the
south-east. British birds are largely sedentary, but passage-
migrants and winter-visitors from the Continent arrive from mid-
July to early November and return from March to June. The race
concerned, *Ardea cinerea cinerea*, breeds from N. Scandinavia to
N. Africa, India and W. China. Other races occur in E. Asia and
Madagascar.

PURPLE HERON—*Ardea purpurea*

Bird Plate 8

In general appearance it resembles Grey Heron, but is slighter
and smaller and at a little distance *decidedly darker*, while at closer
quarters the *dark slate-grey back and wings and the strongly
striped, rufous neck* place identity beyond doubt. The crown is
entirely black, the breast chestnut with some black at sides. Head
and neck look slenderer and more "snaky" than Grey Heron. In
flight at some distance Grey Heron may appear dark in some
lights, but the quills are strongly contrasted with the rest of the
wing, whereas in the Purple Heron the contrast is much less
marked, and at times it may appear to have a nearly uniform wing;
moreover the outlines are different: the Purple looks slighter and
more "narrow-chested" with a more marked concavity where the
base of neck joins the breast, and as its toes are much longer than in
the common species its feet appear appreciably larger in flight.
Young birds are paler, with buffish under-parts, mainly chestnut
crown and without the prominent black stripes on head and neck.
Total length about 31 ins.; body about 15 ins.

Habitat. It resorts at all seasons and even on passage to marshes, lagoons, and inundated country where more or less extensive reed-beds, willow-thickets or other swamp vegetation afford good cover.

General Habits. In movement and carriage it resembles Grey Heron, but is a more secretive and less sociable bird, fond of skulking in reed-beds. It may quite frequently be seen in the open, but generally on sheltered pools or ditches close to reeds. It is also more terrestrial and at least as crepuscular as Grey Heron, often remaining active long after dusk.

Ordinary note resembles "frarnk" of Grey Heron, but not so loud and deep; it is a more silent bird.

Food is mainly fish, mammals, frogs, lizards and newts. Also small crustacea, worms, snails, etc.

Status and Distribution. A vagrant, now seen annually, which occurs mainly from April to October, and very rarely in winter, chiefly on the east coast of England, more rarely on the S. and S.W. coasts, and very rarely elsewhere, but it has been recorded in Wales, Scotland and Ireland. The race concerned, *Ardea purpurea purpurea*, breeds from Holland to N.W. Africa and east into Asia, also in many parts of tropical and S. Africa. Other races occur in tropical and E. Asia and Madagascar.

BLACK STORK—*Ciconia nigra*

BIRD PLATE 11

Form, flight and carriage are like White Stork, but the *whole plumage is black with a beautiful purple and green gloss, except for the white breast, belly and under tail-coverts; bill and legs red.* In flight overhead the all-black wings, neck and upper-breast contrast sharply with the white of the rest of the body, the white extending on to the axillaries to form white "armpits". Young are browner especially on the head and neck. Total length about 38 ins.; body about 20 ins.

Habitat. In the breeding-season it frequents chiefly wooded country interspersed with marsh or marshy meadows.

General Habits. In contrast to White Stork, it is shy and generally solitary in habits.

Note is "che lee, che lee", the "lee" being clear and drawn-out.

Food is chiefly fish.

BLACK STORK

Status and Distribution. A very rare vagrant, nearly all records occurring in English east and south coast counties from Durham to the Scillies. It has appeared in all months from March to November but chiefly May–June. It breeds in Spain, Portugal, the Baltic region and E. Europe, and from Asia Minor to China; also sometimes in S. Africa where it winters. There are no subspecies.

WHITE STORK—*Ciconia ciconia*

BIRD PLATE 9

The white (or dirty white) plumage with black wing-quills and scapulars, long neck and long red bill and legs make Stork easy to identify. It flies with rather slow, deliberate wing-beats and with legs and neck stretched out, but dropped a little below the plane of the body. It glides when about to pitch and also soars with rigid wings. Young birds have the black of the wings browner and the bill and legs brownish-red. Total length about 40 ins.; body about 21 ins.

Habitat. It frequents chiefly open grasslands and marsh country.

General Habits. Gait is a sedate walk. It perches on trees, buildings, etc., often resting on one leg, but away from nesting places it is often comparatively shy and wary.

Practically silent outside the breeding-season.

Food is principally frogs, also reptiles as well as insects, etc.

WHITE STORK

Soaring   Coming in to land.

Status and Distribution. A rare vagrant, most often recorded from March to June, but also in autumn, mainly in East Anglia and S. England; very rarely elsewhere. The race concerned, *Ciconia ciconia ciconia*, breeds in Europe from the Baltic to the Mediterranean; also in N.W. Africa and W. Asia; it winters mainly in central and E. Africa. Other races occur elsewhere in Asia.

GLOSSY IBIS—*Plegadis falcinellus*

BIRD PLATE 11

The curved bill gives appearance of a Curlew, and this combined with its *dark plumage*, which looks almost black at a little distance both in the air and on the ground, makes the bird readily recognizable. Unlike Curlew, however, the wings are broad and rounded and it flies with neck and legs extended, the legs drooping a little. The general colour in the breeding-season is rich deep purplish-brown, wings and tail darker, glossed green and purple. In winter it is duller, with the head and neck inconspicuously streaked whitish. Young birds are similar, but browner, with less white streaking. Total length about 22 ins.; body about 12 ins.

Habitat. It frequents chiefly reedy marshes, lagoons and inundated country, but also feeds on mud-flats and sea-shore, where most of those visiting Britain are observed.

General Habits. Wing-action is more rapid than in herons and egrets. It often flies high and sometimes glides for considerable distances. It is markedly sociable, often occurring in parties. When feeding, it probes mud and ooze with its long bill much like Curlew, but often wades in water and can swim on occasions.

Generally a silent bird, but it sometimes utters a harsh grating "gra-a-k".

Food includes leeches, insects, molluscs, amphibia, worms and some vegetable matter.

Status and Distribution. A vagrant occurring mainly from August to November, occasionally in winter and April/June. It has appeared chiefly on the S., S.W., or E. coasts of England, and there are a number of records from Irish south coast counties. Elsewhere in the British Isles it is very rare. The race concerned, *Plegadis falcinellus falcinellus*, breeds in S.E. Europe east to India, also in tropical Africa (where European birds mainly winter), and N. America. Another race occurs in S.E. Asia and Australia.

SPOONBILL—*Platalea leucorodia*

BIRD PLATE 11

The white colouring and remarkable spatulate bill at once distinguish Spoonbill. In size it is intermediate between Great White Heron and Little Egret, but *on the wing* it is at once separated from either by the *neck as well as legs being stretched out*. In side view on the wing the beak looks slender and slightly decurved at the tip. Build and carriage on the ground are heron-like, but the neck is shorter and less slender. At close quarters the orange-tawny patch on the throat of adult and in summer the buffish-yellow patch at base of the neck are visible. Legs black. Bill of adult is black with a yellow tip; of young, flesh coloured. Young birds have black tips to primaries. Total length about 34 ins.; body about 15 ins.

Habitat. Though mainly frequenting reedy meres and lagoons for breeding purposes, it is primarily a bird of open marshes and shallow waters which are at any rate not wholly reed-enclosed, and it feeds largely on mud-flats and estuaries.

General Habits. It flies rather slowly with regular Swan-like wing-beats, sometimes gliding, and will soar to considerable elevations. It feeds in the open in marshes and shallow water, in which it

SPOONBILL

Immature, as shown by black wing-tips.

wades with the end of bill immersed and swept from side to side. Sociable in disposition, and occurs commonly in small parties, but does not associate much with other species. Although feeding to some extent by day, it does so more regularly towards dusk.

A very silent bird.

Food includes small fish, molluscs, tadpoles, worms, insects, crustacea; also some vegetable matter.

Status and Distribution. A regular visitor to East Anglia, sometimes singly but often in parties, and almost regular on parts of the south coast of England and Ireland. It is only a vagrant elsewhere in the British Isles, rarely recorded in non-maritime counties. It has occurred in all months of the year, usually summer but it has recently wintered. The race *Platalea leucorodia leucorodia* is confined to Europe, breeding in S. Spain, Holland, sometimes Denmark, and south and east from Austria; it normally winters in tropical Africa. Other races occur in N.E. Africa and Asia.

FLAMINGO—*Phoenicopterus ruber*

BIRD PLATE 12

The enormously long legs and neck and peculiar downward deflected bill make Flamingo unmistakable. At rest it appears a rather "washed-out" pinkish-white colour, but the spreading of the wings brings into view the magnificent scarlet of the coverts set off by bold contrast with the black quills. The appearance *in flight* is just as unique as on the ground, the *neck and legs being fully extended*. Immature birds are smaller and have shorter legs and necks than adults and a more or less streaky brownish plumage with whiter under-parts, adult coloration being acquired gradually. Total length about 50 ins.; body about 21 ins.

Habitat. It frequents shallow, open freshwater, brackish or salt lagoons, and shallow coastal waters or estuaries.

General Habits. It flies with moderately rapid wing-beats at a fair speed (faster than Heron), often gliding a short distance before pitching and running several yards after doing so. It frequently takes a short run with flapping wings before getting under way. Purely terrestrial and never perching, it spends most of its time wading in shallow water, feeding with head partly or wholly immersed and with the normal position of the bill inverted, so that the dorsal surface is downwards. Though not ordinarily swimming, it will do so voluntarily on occasions.

Voice is remarkably goose-like.

Food includes both animal and vegetable matter.

Status and Distribution. A very rare vagrant in England and Wales and has occurred a very few times in Scotland and Ireland. Most reports probably refer to escapes from captivity. Abroad the race concerned, *Phoenicopterus ruber roseus*, breeds in Europe (S. France, sometimes S. Spain), W. and S.W. Asia, E. Africa, sometimes N. Africa and possibly elsewhere in Africa and Asia. Other races occur in America.

MUTE SWAN—*Cygnus olor*

Bird Plate 13 Egg Plate XX (2)

Swans are at once distinguished by their large size, pure white plumage and long slender necks. Mute Swan differs from Whooper and Bewick's Swans in having an *orange bill with the base, including prominent knob (smaller in female than in male), black*, while the other two species have the bill black at the end and yellow at the base. It also carries its neck in a more graceful S-shaped curve, and *tail slightly cocked*. Legs blackish. Downy young are grey. Juveniles are dingy brownish and have more or less grey bills without knob, and lead-grey legs; the succeeding plumage is *patchily* brown and white. Total length about 60 ins.; body about 30 ins.

Habitat. Birds of semi-wild stock occur on almost any sort of open, still or slow-moving waters providing a supply of vegetation at depths which they can reach, and they also frequent sheltered portions of the coast, even breeding on sheltered sea-lochs.

General Habits. The flight of all swans is similar, with neck fully extended and slow, regular and powerful wing-beats, the pinions producing in the present species *a musical, humming throb* which is audible for a considerable distance. It walks with a rather awkward waddle, and feeds by dipping the neck under water, also by "up-ending" in duck-like fashion. Outside the breeding-season it is sociable and often seen in parties, and in favoured localities flocks of non-breeding birds are found all the year round. It is usually aggressive and vicious towards other birds in the semi-artificial conditions in which it often lives. The well-known aggressive posture, with wings arched over the back, is not shared with the other two species. Young are sometimes carried on the back of the parents.

Compared with the other two species it is a silent bird. Note when irritated, or when nest or young are threatened, is an explosive, snorting sound subject to some variation. It also hisses.

Food is chiefly subaqueous vegetation. Some animal matter is also taken, including small frogs, worms, molluscs, occasionally small fish and insects.

Nests almost anywhere near water, sometimes in colonies. The eggs, normally 5–7, but 4–12 recorded, off-white with a greyish or bluish-green tinge, are laid generally in the second half of April or early May in a nest consisting of a large heap of reed-stems and roots of water-weeds, sticks, rushes and vegetable matter of any kind. Both sexes take part, male bringing the material, and female arranging it. Incubation is by both sexes, usually for about 35 days. The young remain in the nest for a day or so; both parents tend them and they are fully fledged in about 4½ months. Single-brooded.

Status and Distribution. A resident, generally distributed throughout the British Isles except Shetland, with a unique concentration of 200–500 pairs at Abbotsbury swannery (Dorset). The estimated population of Scotland is about 3,000–4,000 birds, and that of England and Wales about 10,000 or more birds. Abroad the bird breeds in a wild state in the Baltic region, Poland, parts of E. Europe and across Asia from the Black Sea to E. Siberia. It also occurs in a semi-domesticated state in many places. There are no subspecies.

BEWICK'S SWAN—*Cygnus columbianus*

BIRD PLATE 12

In many respects it resembles Whooper Swan, which see. Bewick's differs most notably in the *shorter bill, with the yellow area more or less abruptly truncated far behind nostril*, instead of tapering to a point below it. It is a smaller, rather shorter-necked bird than Whooper and in general stockier-looking and more "goosy". Young birds are greyish like young Whoopers, but at least by March show the specific bill-pattern quite plainly, though duller and less clear-cut than in adults, the black dingier and the future yellow area duller. Total length about 48 ins.; body about 24 ins.

Habitat. In the breeding-season it frequents arctic tundra; in winter prefers larger waters in more open country than Whooper.

General Habits. Flight and habits closely resemble those of Whooper. Young remain with parents till late autumn and often through the winter. It tends to occur in larger herds than Whooper.

Usual note a musical "hoo", becoming a conversational babble from feeding flocks.

Food is practically entirely vegetable matter, seeds, pond-grass, aquatic plants, also winter wheat, waste potatoes, etc.

Status and Distribution. A winter-visitor from October to April, sometimes May. Flocks occur regularly in various parts of England, notably Slimbridge (Glos.) and the Ouse Washes. In hard winter and on passage may occur anywhere in England and Wales, but is scarcer in Scotland. In Ireland now less numerous than Whooper Swan, but is a winter visitor to all provinces; occasionally summers. The race concerned, *Cygnus columbianus bewickii*, breeds in arctic Russia and Siberia. Other races occur in E. Siberia and N. America.

WHOOPER SWAN—*Cygnus cygnus*

BIRD PLATE 12   EGG PLATE XIX (3)

Whooper differs from Mute Swan in the *bill, which is yellow at the base and black at the tip and lacks a basal knob, and in lacking long, pointed tail*, as well as in strong development and constant

WHOOPER SWAN   BEWICK'S SWAN

Note difference in shape of (yellow) patch on bill.

use of vocal powers; it also frequently holds its neck more vertical and stiff. In these features it resembles Bewick's Swan, from which it differs in larger size (nearly as big as Mute), *longer, deeper bill* with a larger patch of yellow, *which extends in a wedge to below nostril or beyond, flatter forehead*, and in *note*. Young birds are *greyer and more uniform* than young Mutes, with bill a dirty flesh-colour, blackish at tip, but the basal part soon begins to show yellowish. The head is sometimes stained reddish. Total length about 60 ins.; body about 30 ins.

Habitat. In the breeding-season it haunts moorland lochs, hill tarns, and swamps. Outside the breeding-season it is found on the sea-coast, especially in sheltered bays and brackish lochs, also inland on lakes, larger rivers, flood-waters, etc., and indeed on any open waters that might be frequented by more or less wild Mute Swans. In some areas regularly feeds in fields well away from any water.

General Habits. Flight, mode of feeding and general characteristics are much like Mute Swan, but it does not arch its wings over back when angry, while in flight the wings produce merely the swishing sound common to many large birds and not the singing metallic throb of the Mute Swan. It walks much better than Mute Swan. The neck is *often bent rather sharply back for a considerable distance and then turned up stiffly*, but it can also be more gracefully curved; it usually looks longer and slenderer than Mute Swan's. Outside the breeding-season the bird occurs regularly in parties and flocks, sometimes of considerable numbers, but is never colonial when breeding. It feeds both by day and night, and flighting movements at dusk and dawn are influenced, as in ducks, by tide and moon.

Typical call on the wing is a loud bugle-like note rendered as "ahng", "whoop", etc., more goose-like than Bewick's.

Food is almost entirely vegetable matter, though worms, molluscs and aquatic insects are taken in small quantities.

Nests on islets in lakes or drier patches in swamps. The creamy-white eggs, normally 5–6, but 4–8 recorded, are laid generally in late May or early June in a nest consisting of a large heap of mosses and marsh plants, partly solidified with mud and with a depression in the middle lined with white down. Male assists in bringing material, but the female actually builds. Incubation is by female alone, for about 35–42 days. The young are tended by both parents and are fully fledged in about two months. Single-brooded.

Status and Distribution. Odd birds regularly summer in N. and W. Scotland and Ireland, and have occasionally bred in Scotland. Otherwise it is a winter-visitor from October or November to March or April, occasionally later; more numerous in Scotland (especially in the centre and north-east), N.E. England and N.W. Wales, than in the rest of England and Wales, and increasing in Ireland. Abroad the race concerned, *Cygnus cygnus cygnus*, breeds in Iceland, N. Scandinavia, N. Finland, Russia and N. Asia. It winters south to the Mediterranean. Another race occurs in N. America.

BEAN GOOSE—*Anser fabalis*

BIRD PLATE 15

Bean Goose is the brownest of the grey geese, and often conspicuously dark (but Greenland White-fronted can also be very dark). Typically it is much darker than Grey Lag, and even amongst the other species can often be picked out, when one is not close enough to see details, by its distinctly darker, more sooty appearance. The head and neck are not darker than the back, but usually distinctly contrasted with the paler chest, though less so than in the conspicuously dark-headed Pink-foot. The fore-wing is as dark as the rest. Light edges to feathers are often prominent. General appearance is rather long and slim, with a noticeably long neck. *Legs are orange or orange-yellow.* The *bill* is longer and stouter than in Pink-foot and coloured *orange-yellow and black* in varying proportions. Some birds have a narrow, but distinct, white band at the base of bill. There are no black markings on the under-parts. Total length about 28–35 ins.; body about 18–20 ins.

Habitat. In winter it frequents much the same habitat as Grey Lag, but in Scotland is fond of hill lochs and dry pastures, roosting on fresh water. It appears seldom, if ever, to feed on stubble in the British Isles.

General Habits. Do not differ from those of other grey geese, but it is more prone to roost inland, often remaining to sleep on marshes at night, even when associating with other species which retire to the coast to roost.

Note is usually very gruff, slightly reminiscent of baaing of sheep; it is the least vocal of British grey geese.

Food consists of grass, clover and leaves of young corn as well as many other plants.

Status and Distribution. A winter-visitor arriving usually from October to January and leaving in March, April or later. It is regular in small numbers in S.W. Scotland, rather more in E. Anglia. In S. and W. England and Wales and the Forth/Clyde valley it occurs as an irregular passage or winter-visitor, and in N. Scotland and most of the islands it is rare. In Ireland it is very scarce. The race concerned, *Anser fabalis fabalis*, breeds in Scandinavia, N. Finland, N. Russia and Siberia. Other races occur in E. Siberia.

PINK-FOOTED GOOSE—*Anser brachyrhynchus*

Bird Plate 16

Smaller than Grey Lag, it is characterized by the *contrast of dark head and neck with the rather pale body, by small short beak, which is black with a pink band, and pink legs.* In flight the fore-wing is noticeably pale greyish, though not so pale as in Grey Lag. Winter plumage is distinctly greyer than summer plumage, which is browner. There are no black markings on the under-parts. Young birds look darker and more uniform above, while the underside has a marbled appearance, not uniform grey as in adults; legs are a dirty greyish-pink or sometimes yellowish at first, then very pale pink quite different from adults. Total length about 24–30 ins.; body about 17–19 ins.

Habitat. Outside the breeding-season it frequents similar ground to the Grey Lag, though seldom actually the same, and is fond of stubble-, young corn- and potato-fields, resorting to fields on hills, such as the Wolds of Yorkshire, as well as to low ground.

General Habits. Habits are like those of other grey geese, and it often occurs in very large flocks. Chiefly roosts on sandbanks of coasts and estuaries, but will do so on marshes, inland lochs and moors where not disturbed.

General effect of notes is not so deep as Grey Lag's or so high-pitched as White-front's, lacking also the "laughing" quality of the latter.

Food includes grain from stubbles, potatoes, and young wheat and grass.

Status and Distribution. A winter-visitor, arriving usually in September and October and leaving in April and early May. It is found in some numbers in many places on the east side of Great Britain from Dornoch Firth to Norfolk, also Denbigh, N.W. England, Solway, and Clyde. Elsewhere it is scarce and irregular, rare in N. Scotland (except during active migration) and recorded annually in Ireland. It breeds in N.E. Greenland, Iceland and Spitzbergen. There are no subspecies.

WHITE-FRONTED GOOSE—*Anser albifrons*

BIRD PLATE 14

A darker bird than Grey Lag or Pink-foot and when adult it is the most readily recognizable of the grey geese owing to the *prominent white patch at the base of bill and the black barring on the breast*, which may be very extensive. Both these characters are lacking in young birds, but as they are generally with adults their recognition is simplified. Fore-wing is slightly paler than the rest. Differences from the very rare Lesser White-fronted Goose are given under that species. Bill of adult of the Siberian race is pink, shading to yellow on the culmen, with a white nail, but young birds sometimes have a dull yellowish bill; that of *flavirostris* is yellow or orange, with a white nail when adult; young birds of both races have the nail darker. Legs orange. Rim round eye brown or greyish. Total length about 26–30 ins.; body about 17–19 ins.

Habitat. Outside the breeding-season it frequents much the same type of country as Grey Lag, but resorts less to cultivated fields, preferring marshes and wet grasslands, saltings and the like.

General Habits. Much as Grey Lag, but it is more active in flight than other grey geese, and can rise almost perpendicularly from the ground. It often occurs in large flocks of hundreds, but is more apt than other grey geese to split up into family parties and small lots.

Note is higher-pitched and more "laughing" in quality than that of the other grey geese, most commonly of two syllables "kow-yow", etc.

Food in winter-quarters consists largely of grasses from marshes and pasture land.

Status and Distribution. A winter-visitor arriving from October to January and leaving from early March to April or May. The main haunts of the race breeding in W. Greenland, *Anser albifrons flavirostris*, are Ireland and W. and N. Scotland with small numbers in N.W. England and Wales. The race *Anser albifrons albifrons* occurs chiefly in southern and eastern England, especially on river Severn, but it is also regular in a number of other widely distributed coastal and low-lying inland areas, and is an irregular visitor to many more; it breeds in N.E. Russia, Siberia and arctic N. America; in Europe wintering south to France and the E. Mediterranean. In addition to the quite different bill colour described above, the Greenland race is darker plumaged than *Anser albifrons albifrons* and most individuals, but not all, may be separated in the field under good conditions. Another race occurs in arctic N. America.

LESSER WHITE-FRONTED GOOSE—*Anser erythropus*

BIRD PLATE 15

It is by no means merely a small edition of White-fronted Goose, adults being quite distinct-looking by reason of the *considerably greater extent of the white front, which reaches on to top of the head between the eyes, the shorter, smaller bill and the swollen lemon-yellow ring round the eye.* In White-fronted Goose the white rarely if ever extends beyond the level of the front of the eye and seldom reaches even so far, while the eyelids are brownish and not swollen. Lesser White-fronted is also distinctly darker and *the closed wings project beyond the tail*, which is not the case in the other species. It is also decidedly smaller than the average *albifrons*. The breast is barred black as in White-fronted Goose and equally variable, and the colour of the bill and legs is similar. Although the white front is absent in young birds, these already have the yellow eyelids. Total length about 21–26 ins.; body about 16–17 ins.

Habitat. Outside the breeding-season it is found in the same type of localities as White-fronted Goose.

General Habits. In habits it resembles other grey geese but tends to peck at a faster rate when feeding.

Call is very noticeably higher and more squeaky than that of White-fronted Goose, sounding like "ku-you".

Food is probably very similar to that of allied species.

Status and Distribution. Formerly regarded as a very rare vagrant, but in recent decades a bird or two have appeared most winters, mainly in Gloucester, sometimes Norfolk and Scotland; it has also occurred in Wales and Ireland. It breeds in central and N. Scandinavia, N. Finland, N. Russia and N. Siberia; and winters from E. central Europe eastward across Asia. There are no subspecies.

GREY LAG GOOSE—*Anser anser*

BIRD PLATE 14   EGG PLATE XVIII (3)

"Grey geese" are at once recognized as such by their obvious resemblance to the farm-yard bird, but the several species are much alike and cannot be distinguished when merely seen flying high overhead. With glasses at reasonable range on the ground or passing low enough on the wing, typical adults are distinguished by well-defined characteristics, but immaturity and individual variation, which is considerable, introduce complications. In general habits and behaviour they are all much like the present species, and the essential colouring is similar in all, grey-brown with lighter margins to the feathers of the body, white upper and under tail-coverts and appearing in flight to have a white tail, with a broad dark subterminal band. Grey Lag is the largest species and almost exactly like its domestic derivative, except that the wild bird is more lightly built and agile. It is characterized by a *large, stout bill and heavy head, noticeable in the air as well as on the ground, and by a pale grey fore-wing and rump*, the former conspicuous on the ground when stretching wing and also often very striking in flying birds; however, Pink-foot also has a distinctly pale fore-wing. The *bill is bright orange with no black* and with a white or sometimes brownish nail; there is sometimes a little white feathering at its base. Legs flesh coloured. Head and neck are not darker than the body. The breast is often spotted or blotched with black, sometimes heavily, but not barred as in White-front. Spotting is sparse or absent in immature birds, which also have more greyish legs. Total length about 30–35 ins.; body about 19–20 ins.

Habitat. In the breeding-season in the north it haunts hilly heather moors and "flow" country with scattered lochs, and also breeds on small islands well out to sea. Outside the breeding-season it frequents salt and fresh marshes and marshy grasslands, peat-mosses, etc., largely near estuaries and low-lying coasts, but also rivers and inundated country from the coast to long distances inland; it is also partial to fields of young grain, stubble and other cultivation, usually retiring at night to shoals and sandbanks or to secluded lakes.

General Habits. Flight is quite swift, flocks on migration flying in a V-formation but on short flights formation is often much more irregular. They rise easily from the ground, but not so easily from water. Flocks of this and other species of grey geese sometimes perform striking aerial evolutions with spiral nose-dives and side-slipping. All grey geese are essentially birds of open country and purely terrestrial, never perching even on low objects. In summer as the moult of adults approaches they resort, along with the young ones, to the most secluded localities, to pass the flightless period. Outside the breeding-season they are thoroughly gregarious, flocks being composed of family parties. All the species are essentially land-feeders, grazing on grasslands and marshes and resorting also to cultivation, but they will at times feed in shallow water. They are normally diurnal feeders flighting in the early morning, but when disturbed will feed at night. All grey geese are naturally wary and suspicious and may be very un-approachable.

Note is just like that of farm-yard bird, a loud, deep sonorous "aahng-ung-ung".

Food is chiefly grasses, but corn-fields are visited in autumn.

Nests on the ground among heather, preferably on islands. The creamy-white eggs, normally 4–6, occasionally 3–8, are laid generally in the second half of April in a nest built of heather twigs, grasses, mosses, etc., mixed with down and small feathers. Incubation is by female alone, for about 27–28 days. The young are tended by both parents and fly when about 8 weeks old. Single-brooded.

Status and Distribution. Present throughout the year in N. Scotland where a few breed in parts of Caithness, Sutherland, N.W. Ross, and especially Hebrides; feral groups exist in S.W. Scotland, N., central, E. and S.E. England. Otherwise it is a winter-visitor arriving between late September and mid-November and returning in March and April, sometimes May; it is found chiefly in parts of Tay and Forth areas, in S.W. Scotland, N.W. England, and a small scattering in N. and E. Ireland. Elsewhere it is a scarce or rare visitor. Abroad *Anser anser anser* breeds in Iceland, and from N. Scandinavia south to Denmark and Macedonia; it winters south to N. Africa. Another race extends from S.E. Europe to Siberia.

SNOW GOOSE—*Anser caerulescens*

Bird Plate 13

It has two colour-phases, white and "blue". The white phase is a *pure white goose* about the size of Pink-foot, with *black primaries, red bill with a white or whitish nail and black cutting edge, and pinkish-red legs.* The primary-coverts and bases of the primaries are grey, showing up in flight as a distinct pale area between the intense black of the primaries and pure white of the rest of the plumage. Bill is rather stout. Immature birds have the upper-parts dull brownish-grey with darker centres to the feathers of back and wing-coverts, the under-parts greyish-white, bill and legs leaden. The blue phase has head and neck white, upper- and under-parts dark bluish-grey, lower back paler; rump, upper and under tail-coverts white, tail grey. Innermost secondaries, dark with noticeable whitish edges, are long and drooping. Bill and feet as in white phase. Intermediate birds have belly and sometimes breast white. Immatures have dark greyish head and neck, body duller and

Snow Goose

SNOW GOOSE, Blue phase.

1st winter   Adult female   Adult male

browner, but wings paler and bluish. Total length about 25–28 ins.; body about 17–18 ins.

Habitat. Outside the breeding-season, like grey geese, it frequents both grasslands or marshes and fields of sprouting grain or stubble, but it also feeds on the open shore and mud-flats.

General Habits. Very like those of grey geese, and in winter-quarters it consorts freely with other species. It is not naturally shy, but becomes very wary where persecuted.

Note is a high-pitched "kaw" or rapidly repeated "ga-ga-ga".

Food on migration and in winter is almost entirely vegetable matter.

Status and Distribution. A vagrant which in recent years has occurred annually in very small numbers, mainly between October and April, recorded from several localities in Ireland, especially Wexford, Scotland and England. Some reports doubtless refer to escapes from captivity. Examples have occurred of both races, *Anser caerulescens atlanticus* (which does not have a blue phase), breeding in N.E. arctic America, and both white and blue phases of the slightly smaller *Anser caerulescens caerulescens* breeding elsewhere in arctic America and arctic E. Siberia.

CANADA GOOSE—*Branta canadensis*

BIRD PLATE 17   EGG PLATE XVIII (2)

A large grey-brown goose with black head and neck and a sharply defined white patch extending from chin up the sides of the head behind the eye. Wings and upper-parts are dark brown, flanks and sides paler brown, with light edgings to the feathers in both cases, the breast whitish, upper and under tail-coverts pure white, and a black tail. Bill and legs blackish. There should be no confusion with Barnacle Goose which is much smaller, is grey where Canada Goose is brown, has the whole face white, and has breast as well as neck black. Total length about 36–40 ins.; body about 21–24 ins.

Habitat. In the British Isles it frequents grasslands and marshes in the vicinity of lakes and fresh-water pools. Sometimes in parkland or well timbered localities.

General Habits. On short flights it does not adopt any definite formation, but on longer ones travels in the usual V-formation of geese or sometimes in oblique lines or single file. It is strongly gregarious outside the breeding-season, associating in this country in flocks of half-a-dozen or so to two or three hundred. It is normally a day-feeder, getting the bulk of its food by grazing on grasslands, but when feeding in water dips its neck and "up-ends" like other geese and ducks.

Note is a loud, resonant trumpet-like "ah-honk" or "aahonk".

Food chiefly consists of grass. Some insect and other animal food is also taken in summer.

Nests usually on the ground on islands in ponds, also on marshy spots sheltered by bushes and vegetation, sometimes in colonies. The white or creamy-white eggs, usually 5–6, but 2–11 recorded, are laid generally in April in a hollow lined with grasses, dead leaves, bits of reed, etc., down and feathers. Incubation is by goose only, with gander on watch, for about 28–29 days. The young are tended by goose with gander in attendance, and are fully grown at 6 weeks old. Single-brooded.

Status and Distribution. Introduced over 250 years ago and is now widespread in England although generally scarce in the S.W. and N.E., and in Wales. The population has increased ten-fold in the past 25 years, to reach 30,000–40,000 birds. A few hundred breed in Scotland north to Perth, and hundreds migrate from Yorkshire and the Midlands to Beauly Firth for summer moult. Movements otherwise are mainly rather local in Britain. In Ireland it nests in two areas in the north, and birds thought to be vagrants from America occur occasionally in winter. The species is a native of N. America. Our birds belong to the eastern race *Branta canadensis canadensis*, but individuals of one of the smaller races have been recorded in Scotland and Ireland.

BARNACLE GOOSE—*Branta leucopsis*

BIRD PLATE 17

The boldly contrasted black, white and grey of plumage is distinctive and permits identification at long range. The *crown, neck and breast* are *glossy black*, almost the *whole face and forehead creamy-white*, the *upper-parts lavender-grey with blackish bars narrowly bordered white*. The rump and under tail-coverts are white, and the rest of the under-parts pale greyish, flanks faintly barred. The quills and tail are black, as are the bill and legs. Bill is short, small and delicate. Young have the white of the face tinged dusky, rufous edgings to mantle-feathers, and the flanks more strongly barred. Total length about 23–27 ins.; body about 17–18 ins.

Habitat. Outside the breeding-season it resorts chiefly to pastures, marshes and grasslands close to shore, and will also feed at times on tidal flats and on bogs and cultivated land, especially if driven by frost. Occasionally straggles inland with grey geese.

General Habits. Flight, general habits and behaviour are much as other geese, but it is generally a good deal less wary and suspicious. It occasionally goes to sea to rest on very calm days, but is much more terrestrial than Brent. It feeds largely at night, but to some extent also by day. Flocks seldom associate with other geese, but odd birds or even small parties sometimes graze with grey geese.

Note is a series of rapidly repeated short barks, the chorus of flocks suggesting the shrill yelping of a pack of small terriers.

Food is mainly green grasses.

Status and Distribution. A winter-visitor arriving in October and early November, occasionally earlier, and leaving in April or May. Its main haunts are the Inner and Outer Hebrides, the Solway and islands off N. and W. coast of Ireland. It is scarce and irregular on most other parts of the coasts, but fairly regular on passage in Shetland, Orkney, Northumberland and Gloucester and odd birds are likely to occur in any large flock of Pink-feets. It breeds in N.E. Greenland, Spitzbergen and Novaya Zemlya. There are no subspecies.

BRENT GOOSE—*Branta bernicla*

BIRD PLATE 16

Brent is the smallest and much the darkest of the geese. *The whole head, neck and upper breast are black with a small whitish patch on the sides of neck. The upper-parts are dark grey-brown or slaty, with narrow lighter edgings to the feathers.* Upper and under tail-coverts and the region of the vent are pure white, in contrast to the rest. Quills and tail are black. There is no white mark on the neck of juvenile. In the dark-breasted race the lower breast and flanks are slaty and not strikingly paler than the upper-parts, though with paler bars on the flanks; the pale-breasted race has the lower breast and especially the flanks considerably paler, and shading to whitish. Both races are subject to a good deal of variation. It is rather stocky and duck-like in flight, *with the white stern conspicuous.* Bill and legs black. Total length about 22–24 ins.; body about 16–17 ins.

Habitat. Outside the breeding-season it was at one time exclusively maritime, frequenting tidal flats and estuaries, resting on the water at high tide and retiring to sea at night or if disturbed; however, in recent years it has increasingly taken to feeding also on farmland inside the sea-wall. It occurs exceptionally as a straggler well inland.

General Habits. Flight is swift, much like that of other geese, in irregular packs and usually at no great height. It is extremely gregarious, occurring in flocks up to many hundreds. Mainly a diurnal feeder, though the tide naturally affects movements.

Note is a guttural, croaking "krrowk", etc., using a single syllable.

Food is mainly marine vegetation.

Status and Distribution. A winter-visitor, from September and October but the bulk later, until the end of March, but some linger on to May. In England the main haunts are from Northumberland to Essex, and on the south coast west to Devon. Elsewhere on the west side of England and in Wales it is scarce and irregular. It very rarely occurs far inland. In Scotland it formerly occurred in large numbers in the E. coast estuaries but is now scarce and irregular. In Ireland it is found chiefly on the east and west coasts. The dark-breasted race *Branta bernicla bernicla* (breeding from the arctic Russian islands of Kolguev and Waigatz east to western arctic Siberia) predominates in England and is a rare vagrant in Ireland; the pale-breasted race *Branta bernicla hrota* (breeding in Spitzbergen, Greenland and E. arctic Canada) is the form which winters in Ireland, and occurs regularly in Northumberland also. One or two examples of the race *Branta bernicla nigricans* (breeding in E. Siberia, Alaska and N.W. Canada, and resembling *B. b. bernicla* but with a more extensive white collar) have been recorded in England. In Europe the species winters south to N. France.

RUDDY SHELDUCK—*Tadorna ferruginea*

BIRD PLATE 18

The *orange-brown coloration, with paler head, black wing-quills and tail and the white wing-coverts, which are nearly concealed when at rest but very conspicuous in flight*, are quite distinctive. Size is about that of Shelduck. Head of male is buffish, shading gradually to orange-brown on the neck; it has a narrow black collar and metallic-green speculum. Female is much the same, but has the head paler, almost whitish, and no collar. Juvenile is much as female, but duller, with a darker, browner back. Bill blackish, legs dark grey. Total length about 25 ins.; body about 16½ ins.

Habitat. Though at times seen on the sea, it is much less maritime than Shelduck, in the breeding-season frequenting open lakes, rivers, or streams. In winter-quarters it largely frequents sand-banks of larger rivers, but also lakes, lagoons, and other more or less extensive fresh or brackish waters, as well as fields and cultivation during the day.

General Habits. Flight is strong and fast, but rather heavy, with relatively slow wing-beats. Though swimming well enough, with neck erect, fore-parts low and stern high, it spends much of its time on land resting or walking about and grazing like a goose. It will perch on rocks, walls, and at times even trees. It is generally seen in pairs, but on migration these collect in loose flocks; it does not associate much with other species.

It has loud, nasal, honking notes, with a good deal of variation, the ordinary form rendered "ah-onk".

Food naturally consists chiefly of vegetable matter, grass, water-weeds, and growing crops, but also includes animal matter.

Status and Distribution. A rare vagrant which has occurred in a number of counties, mainly coastal, in England, Scotland, Ireland and Wales. An "invasion" occurred in the summer of 1892. The bird breeds in S.W. and S.E. Europe, N. Africa and across much of central Asia. There are no subspecies.

SHELDUCK—*Tadorna tadorna*

BIRD PLATES 18 and 124   EGG PLATE XXI (2)

A large duck with a goose-like pose and *boldly contrasted plumage pattern of black, white and chestnut*, while at close quarters the *bright red bill* and pink feet are also conspicuous. Head and neck are black with metallic-green lustre, the scapulars, primaries and tips of tail-feathers black, a broad chestnut band round the fore-part of the body, a dusky band down the centre of the belly, and speculum metallic-green bordered above (in closed wing) by chestnut; the rest of the plumage is white with under tail-coverts tinted chestnut. The chestnut band is conspicuous as such at fairly close range, but birds tend to appear black and white at longer distances. Female is merely a little duller, but lacks the knob at base of the bill which is conspicuous in drake. Both sexes have a rather duller plumage from July to October, corresponding to "eclipse" of other ducks, showing white about the face and throat and with the pectoral band much obscured. Juveniles have dark grey-brown upper-parts and head, with face and throat white, and lack the chestnut girdle; bill flesh-colour, legs livid grey. Downy young are marbled dark brown and white. Total length about 24 ins.; body about 16 ins.

Habitat. It chiefly frequents low-lying sandy and muddy coasts and estuaries, coastal sand-dunes, etc., but locally resorts for breeding purposes to rough, brambly ground above cliffs and locally also to lake borders, warrens, and even ordinary agricultural country some miles inland. Outside the breeding-season it is occasional on inland waters, but never in large numbers.

General Habits. Flight is slower than the typical ducks, with relatively slow wing-beats, and more like goose; and it rises easily. It swims buoyantly and often rests on the sea, but is less aquatic than most ducks and seldom goes far out. Thoroughly gregarious, it is seldom seen singly except in the case of stragglers inland, and hundreds are present on suitable bits of coast. It feeds chiefly on the ebb, wading in shallow water. Between tides birds generally rest on shore.

Usual note is a running "ak-ak-ak—" but in general it is a rather silent bird, though noisy at breeding-places where many nest.

Food is chiefly marine molluscs, small crustacea, occasionally insects, small fish and worms. Also vegetable matter.

Nests usually in a rabbit-hole or burrow, also under furze or bramble bushes, under rocks and occasionally almost in the open. The creamy-white eggs, normally about 8–15, but up to 20 recorded, are laid generally in May in a nest consisting almost entirely of pale grey down, also some marram grass, etc. Incubation is by female only, for about 28 days. The young are led from the nest to water by female alone or by both parents. At first they are tended by their parents, but where several pairs breed, broods unite to form packs with a couple of adults in attendance. The young fly when about 45 days old. Single-brooded.

Status and Distribution. Present throughout the year and generally distributed throughout the British Isles in suitable coastal localities. It occurs inland in very small numbers, breeding in several places. In some areas is a summer-resident only, arriving in mid-February or early March and leaving mid-July or August when a number of our birds migrate to moult on the E. side of the North Sea, some from the Irish Sea crossing the Pennines to do so; Bridgwater Bay is another important moulting area. Abroad it breeds from N. Scandinavia south to N. France and the Balkans and across much of Asia from Asia Minor to Manchuria. There are no subspecies.

WIGEON—*Anas penelope*

BIRD PLATES 20, 26 and 124   EGG PLATE XXI (8)

At a distance the colour-scheme of drake, with *chestnut head appearing markedly darker than the mainly grey body, and with a white mark along sides*, presents some superficial resemblance to that of the considerably smaller Teal, but the *yellow-buff forehead and crown are distinctive*. At closer quarters it is unmistakable, with vermiculated grey back and flanks, pinkish-brown breast and black under tail-coverts bordered by a pure white area in front. A *broad white patch on the wing-coverts* is the distinctive feature of adult drake in flight, no other duck (excepting the very rare American Wigeon) showing a *white patch on the front of the wing*; but most first year male Wigeon lack the white fore-wing although otherwise apparently in adult plumage. It usually keeps the neck more or less retracted, appearing a short-necked, compact bird. Female, intermediate in size between Mallard and Teal, differs from other surface-feeding ducks in small, short bill, more rufous plumage and pointed tail. The speculum, margined above (in closed wing) by white, is dark green broadly bordered black in male, dusky with little or no green and enclosed between white wing-bars in female. The pointed tail is an important field charac- ter in flight, when the white belly of both sexes is also noticeable. Complete or partial eclipse plumage may last from about June to October or November. Male in eclipse resembles female, but the crown and upper-parts are duskier, and flanks richer in colour, and it retains the characteristic wing-pattern with white shoulders. Juveniles are much like females. Bill blue-grey with black tip; legs greyish to brownish. Total length about 18 ins.; body about 12 ins.

Habitat. Typical haunts in the breeding-season are northern lochs, rivers and marshes, both on open moorlands and in cultiv- ated or wooded country, with a partiality for the last. Outside the breeding-season it is mainly maritime, frequenting chiefly muddy coasts and estuaries, but a good many winter on larger lakes, reservoirs, flood-waters, etc., inland and regularly visit fields and grasslands to feed.

General Habits. Flight is rapid, rising straight up off water. The rather long, narrow wings are more depressed below the body at the down-stroke than in Mallard. It comes to land freely, walks with ease and can run well. Thoroughly gregarious and is usually seen in parties or flocks, often resting off shore by day in compact flocks of many hundreds, which preserve a close formation in flight. Does not associate much with other ducks except Pintail, but often accompanies Brent Geese. Like Mallard it is not by preference a nocturnal feeder, but becomes so through persecution, flighting at dusk to feeding-grounds. It will feed by "up-ending" where necessary, but is less addicted to this practice than most surface-feeding ducks.

Call of male is a very distinctive loud, musical, whistling "*whee*-oo".

Food is almost entirely vegetable matter, mainly grasses and zostera.

Nests on the ground among heather, bracken or wiry grass. The cream or buff eggs, usually 7–8 but 6–10 recorded, are laid generally in May in a nest made by the duck and lined with grass, bracken or heather stems and down. Incubation is by duck alone, for about 24–25 days. The young are led to water by duck and tended by her, but drake usually rejoins the family; they fly when about 6 weeks old. Single-brooded.

Status and Distribution. Present throughout the year, widely distributed as a breeding bird on much of the mainland of Scotland south to Loch Leven, also Orkney, Outer Hebrides, Border hills and Yorkshire Pennines. It has also bred exceptionally in Shetland, S.E. England, Wales and Ireland. Otherwise it is a passage-migrant and winter-visitor, common on all coasts and many inland waters, arriving from the end of August to end of November and returning from early March to May. Abroad it breeds in Iceland, N. Europe south to Germany, and N. Asia; in winter it reaches tropical Africa. There are no subspecies.

AMERICAN WIGEON—*Anas americana*

BIRD PLATES 20 and 26

Drake is easily distinguished from Wigeon by its *grey head and white crown* and darker flanks contrasting more strongly with the white patch in front of the black under tail-coverts; a patch on the side of the head is glossy green, visible only in good light. At close quarters the sides of the head are finely speckled and streaked, and flanks brown instead of grey; otherwise characters are as Wigeon, including the white fore-wing. Duck is more difficult to distinguish, but head and neck look paler, more grey, instead of rufous, and under-parts show rather more white than our bird; the diagnostic point is white, instead of dusky, axillaries, but this can rarely be seen in the field. The eclipse plumages of the two species are very similar except for greyer head of the present species. Total length about 19 ins.; body about 13 ins.

Habitat. It occurs in much the same localities as Wigeon, but is generally less marine in habits, resorting outside the breeding-season largely to marshes and flooded lands, though also to tidal flats, estuaries, etc.

General Habits. Except for greater attachment to fresh waters, its habits, flight and general behaviour are very much like European Wigeon's.

Notes of both sexes are like those of Wigeon, but they are more silent birds.

Food is chiefly vegetable matter.

Status and Distribution. A vagrant; several are seen most years, mainly between October and May, occasionally June. The records are widely scattered from Shetland to Scilly, Wales and Ireland. It breeds in N. America, and winters south to Panama. There are no subspecies.

GADWALL—*Anas strepera*

BIRD PLATES 20, 26 and 124   EGG PLATE XXI (6)

Drake is rather smaller than Mallard, *at a distance looking fairly uniform grey-brown with black upper and under tail-coverts*; at closer quarters it shows fine "pepper and salt" speckling on the head and neck, *vermiculated pattern on back and flanks*, a bolder pattern of dark and light crescentic markings on the breast, and long secondaries mouse-grey. The *white speculum*, forming a prominent patch on the hind border of the spread wing, is diagnostic in flight, but on the water it is often concealed, as is a black band in front of it and (nearly always) the chestnut patch on the coverts, unless the bird preens or spreads its wings. Bill dark grey; legs orange-yellow. It tends to sit higher on the water than Mallard, with stern more elevated, but this is not always noticeable. Female is much like Mallard in plumage, but more slightly built. The white speculum at once identifies her when visible, but, as in male, it is often concealed when at rest; there is little or no chestnut on the coverts. *Orange at sides of the bill* is a good differentiating character, and orange-yellow, not orange-red, legs can be seen when she "up-ends"; in flight the white belly is a further distinction. Male in eclipse plumage, from about end of May to September or October, is like female but has darker upper-parts and retains chestnut on the wing-coverts. Immature birds resemble adult female, but have strongly spotted under-parts. Total length about 20 ins.; body about 13 ins.

Habitat. Especially in the breeding-season it prefers quiet lakes, marsh pools, and other still waters with good cover, or sluggish streams bordered by rank vegetation. It is occasionally seen on salt-water when migrating and will rest at sea by day.

General Habits. In flight the wings look more pointed than Mallard and the strokes are rather more rapid, the flight recalling Wigeon's. General habits are much as Mallard, though on the whole it is shyer and more retiring, and seldom seen in numbers together.

Note of female is a quack, less loud and coarse than Mallard duck's. Note of male is a deep nasal quack "nheck".

Food is chiefly vegetable matter, such as buds, leaves, seeds and roots of aquatic plants; animal matter in small quantity is also taken.

Nests usually on the ground in very thick vegetation and close to water. The warm creamy-buff eggs, normally 8–12, but 7 to 16 recorded, are laid generally in May or early June in a nest formed by duck of down, mixed with some grasses, sedges and vegetable matter. Incubation is by duck alone, for about 27–28 days. The young, after drying, are taken to water by the duck; they fly when about 7 weeks old. Single-brooded.

Status and Distribution. Present throughout year, breeding regularly in Norfolk, Suffolk and in Loch Leven neighbourhood, also Fenland, Gloucester/Somerset, S.E. and N.W. England, and few in Yorks., Outer Hebrides, and in Ireland. It also breeds sporadically in other parts, including Orkney. Elsewhere it is a winter-visitor, uncertain and scarce in most parts (but regular in Kerry), arriving between mid-August and late October and leaving in March or April. Abroad it breeds from Iceland and S. Scandinavia south to Algeria and eastwards across Europe and Asia; also in N. America. In winter it reaches tropical Africa. There are no subspecies.

TEAL—*Anas crecca*

BIRD PLATES 19, 26 and 124   EGG PLATE XXI (1)

Its small size distinguishes Teal from all European breeding ducks but Garganey. At long range *drake* appears *greyish with a dark head, a yellow-buff patch on either side of the black under tail-coverts and a whitish band along side above the wing.* At close quarters the vermiculated pattern of back and flanks, spotted breast, chestnut colouring of head and the broad metallic-green band narrowly outlined in buff which encloses eye and extends

GARGANEY   TEAL

female   female

Note Garganey's black fore-part of under-wing.

back to the nape, can be distinguished. Belly white. Female is mottled brown with cheeks paler than crown, and under-parts more or less strongly spotted in summer, whiter in winter. Both sexes have a *speculum half metallic-green and half black*, with two narrow, but distinct, white wing-bars in female, while drake has a very prominent (often buffish) anterior bar, but very faint posterior one. Complete or partial eclipse plumage lasts from about July to October. Eclipse and juvenile drakes are much like female, but with upper-parts rather darker and more uniform. Bill dark grey, legs greyish. Total length about 14 ins.; body about 10 ins.

Habitat. In the breeding-season it prefers rushy moorland and heath pools, bogs, and the like, often breeding far from water. In autumn and winter it occurs on lakes, ponds and reservoirs of all sorts, not only those with reeds or other cover but also with undisturbed mud-stretches or concrete banks, and also resorting largely to sewage-farms, flood-waters, etc., and to a less extent to sea-coast, estuaries, and mud-flats.

General Habits. Very agile on the wing, shooting straight upwards when flushed, and flying rapidly, wheeling and swerving in almost wader-like fashion, often in compact flocks. Outside the breeding-season it occurs in anything from pairs and small parties to flocks of a hundred or more, and males tend to gather into parties while the females are incubating. It is inclined to be sluggish and inactive by day, feeding mainly by night except when undisturbed.

Note of male is a low, far-sounding musical "krit, krit", that of female a short sharp "quack" seldom used except when alarmed, much higher and thinner than female Mallard's.

Food is largely vegetable matter such as duckweed, and seeds of many aquatic plants, also algae. Animal food includes insects, worms and molluscs.

Nests among heather, gorse, etc., on dry ground, in bracken-covered glades in woods, also in marshes. The eggs, normally 8–10, but 11–16 recorded, are pale stone-colour to light greenish-buff; they are laid generally in the latter part of April and early May in a nest made by duck and lined with dead leaves, dead bracken, etc., and down, which is very dark with light centres, but no white tips as with Garganey. Incubation is by duck only, for about 21–22 days. The drake often assists duck in tending the young, which fly when about 23 days old. Single-brooded.

Status and Distribution. Present throughout the year. It breeds in most eastern and northern English counties; in S. and S.W. England and S.E. Wales it is more scattered and often sporadic especially inland. In Scotland and Ireland it is more widely distributed. British birds are largely resident, although some may move S.W. or S. as far as central France. Passage-migrants and winter-visitors from N. and N.W. Europe arrive between early August and late November and return from late February to early May. The race concerned, *Anas crecca crecca*, breeds in Iceland, from N. Europe south to some of the Mediter-ranean countries, and across N. Asia. In N. America it is replaced by the Green-winged Teal, *Anas crecca carolinensis*, which occurs not infrequently in England, Ireland and Scotland; the male may be distinguished from our bird as it lacks the horizontal white stripe on the side and has instead a vertical white mark on the sides of the breast in front of the wing; it also lacks the cream line above the green band on the side of the head. The females are not distinguishable.

MALLARD—*Anas platyrhynchos*

BIRD PLATES 18, 26 and 124   EGG PLATE XXI (7)

Drake on the water shows a *dark green head, white collar, purplish-brown breast*, and *vermiculated pale grey back, shading to brownish above the flanks*, which are also pale grey; at a distance and in bright sunlight the greys may appear almost white. Centre of the back (showing in flight) is dark brown, the upper and under tail-covers black, tail whitish, but the four central feathers are black and curled upwards. *Wings* in both sexes are grey with a black-edged *violet-purple speculum bordered by white on both sides*, which, when visible, at once identifies the mottled brown and buff female. Male in eclipse plumage, from July to September, is much like female, but is darker and more uniform. Juveniles also resemble female. Bill of adult male is greenish-yellow, of adult female dark olive often with some orange at sides; legs orange-red. Total length about 23 ins.; body about 15 ins.

Habitat. It frequents not only large and small lakes, reservoirs, and quiet reaches of rivers, but breeds regularly on quite small woodland and other ponds seldom visited by other duck, marsh pools, hill tarns, islands, etc., and ponds in town parks where undisturbed. In winter large numbers also resort to sea-coast and estuaries, especially during frost, often resting in flocks off shore; floodlands are also much frequented. It will visit open fields and marshes some distance from any sheet of water to feed.

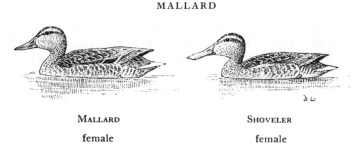

MALLARD
female

SHOVELER
female

General Habits. Flight is swift, with characteristic action in which the wings are not depressed much below the level of body; it rises straight off the water when flushed. Walks easily with less pronounced waddle than domestic duck and nearly horizontal carriage. Normally it only perches on low objects such as rocks, partly submerged stumps, etc. Gregarious in habits; flocks do not usually adopt any marked formation in flight. There is very seldom any marked disproportion in numbers of sexes in flocks, but drakes join up in little parties while the ducks are sitting or tending broods. Outside the breeding-season birds generally rest by day on open waters, and flight at dusk to marshes and other feeding places. Young birds dive for food fairly freely and adults will do so at times, especially in display.

The well-known loud, deep, coarse "quark" and its variants is peculiar to female. Male's note is a much more subdued but higher-pitched, rather grating "quek". Male also has a low whistling note in courtship.

Food is mainly vegetable matter. Animal food includes insects, molluscs, crustacea, worms and frogs.

Nests usually in fairly thick covert, under bushes, etc., on the ground within easy distance of water, but at times also in pollarded willows, holes of trees, old nests of Crows, etc. The eggs, 7 to 16, but normally about 10 or 12, are generally greyish-green or greenish-buff, occasionally clear pale blue. They are laid generally in March in a nest made by the duck and lined with dead leaves, grasses, etc., mixed with down and feathers. Incubation is by female alone, for about 28 days, sometimes less. The young when dried are led by duck to water and tended in many cases by her alone; they fly when about 7½ weeks old. Probably in a purely wild state single-brooded, but under protection may breed twice.

Status and Distribution. Present throughout the year and generally distributed. British birds are largely sedentary. Passage-migrants and winter-visitors from N. and N.W. Europe, Faeroes and Iceland arrive from mid-August to late November and return from mid-March to early May. The race concerned, *Anas platy-rhynchos platyrhynchos*, breeds throughout Europe, also in N.W. Africa, across Asia and N. America. Another race occurs in Greenland.

PINTAIL—*Anas acuta*

BIRD PLATES 19, 26 and 124   EGG PLATE XXI (5)

The drake is unmistakable. At long range a mainly grey bird with *chocolate head and neck and a white band extending down the side of the latter to join the white breast*, and it has a creamy patch in front of the black under tail-coverts. At closer quarters the *long pointed tail*, and vermiculated pattern of back and flanks add to its distinctive appearance. Belly white. General plumage of female is much like Mallard duck, but the combination of greyer colouring, more delicate form, slender neck, pointed tail (but not elongated like male's) and grey, not dark olive, bill readily separate her at reasonable range; the absence of white on the wing and orange on bill should prevent confusion with Gadwall duck. Bill is blue-grey in drake, legs grey. Speculum of male is bronzy-green, shading to black behind with a warm buff bar in front; that of female is obscure and brownish. In both sexes it is margined by white behind, and this forms a *light hinder border to the wing*, which is noticeable in flight and a good character of dull-winged duck, though the long slender neck, pointed tail, and narrow pointed wings are no less distinctive. Full or partial eclipse plumage lasts from about July to October, when both males and juveniles resemble the duck, but have upper-parts darker and more uniform. Total length about 22 ins.; body about 14 ins. (without the longer central tail-feathers).

Habitat. Typical haunts in the breeding-season are very much as Wigeon's, those with dry rather than marshy surroundings being generally preferred; also fresh-water and brackish lagoons in the south. Outside the breeding-season frequents sea-coasts and estuaries, also larger fresh waters inland.

General Habits. It is naturally shy and suspicious. Flight is very rapid, and it walks with ease and grace. Sometimes numerous on inland waters, and on the sea, as a rule in loose formation. It associates freely with other species. Feeding-habits are much like

Teal and Mallard and it is often a nocturnal feeder, even when undisturbed.

Notes are rarely heard, but male has a low double whistle like Teal's, but lower in pitch.

Food is apparently chiefly vegetable matter, but animal food includes insects, molluscs, worms, and frogs.

Nests socially on islands in lakes, but also in neighbourhood of lagoons, and on heather-covered shores, and among marram grass on dunes. The eggs, usually 7–9, but 6–12 on record, are generally yellowish-green or yellowish-cream, occasionally bluish. They are laid generally in May in a nest which is sometimes a mere hollow with some down and more exposed than most ducks' nests. Incubation is by duck alone, for about 23 days, the drake remaining in the neighbourhood. The young are tended by duck, but usually joined by drake; they fly when about 5–7 weeks old. Single-brooded.

Status and Distribution. Present throughout the year, with erratic breeding population of up to a few dozen pairs. In Scotland it is most nearly regular in Orkney and Caithness, in England around the Thames estuary and E. Anglian fens. Otherwise, nesting is recorded sporadically in widely scattered localities in England, Scotland and central or north Ireland. On passage and in winter (mid September–November until March–April) it is regular but local on coasts, but some estuaries and the fenland washes may hold hundreds, even thousands; otherwise inland numbers are generally very small. Our birds belong to the race *Anas acuta acuta* which breeds in Iceland, Faeroes, in Europe south to S. Spain, Hungary and Romania, across N. Asia, and in N. America. European birds winter south to E. Africa. Another race occurs in Kerguelen.

GARGANEY—*Anas querquedula*

Bird Plates 19, 26 and 124   Egg Plate XXI (3)

In size it is little larger than Teal. The outstanding features of drake Garganey are the *broad white band extending from eye to nape*, and in flight the *pale blue-grey fore wing* which remains even in eclipse. The *sharp demarcation of brown breast from vermiculated greyish flanks and white belly* is noticeable both at rest and on the wing. Long curved scapulars, blue-grey, black and white, overhang the wing which has a metallic-green speculum bordered white in front and behind. Duck closely resembles Teal, but has *only a very obscure speculum*, which distinguishes her on the wing from that species; longer neck in flight, slighter build and greyer wings are other finer points of difference. On the water the duck generally looks paler than duck Teal, but can only be definitely distinguished at close range by pure white instead of speckled brownish throat, whitish spot at base of the bill and a more distinct superciliary stripe. Drake assumes eclipse about the same time as Teal, and then is much like female except for the wings, and juveniles are similar except that the wing of juvenile male is duller than adult. Total length about 15 ins.; body about 10½ ins.

Habitat. In the breeding-season it prefers reedy meres, swampy pools and other shallow waters with rich vegetation, and water-meadows with creeks, ditches, or pools.

General Habits. These in many ways recall those of Shoveler. Flight is rapid, but generally without the sudden turns and downward plunges of Teal. It is commonly seen in pairs or small parties only.

Spring note of male is a peculiar low crackling sound. Note of female is a "quack" like female Teal's.

Food. Animal food includes young fish, frogs, crustacea, molluscs, worms, insects. Vegetable matter includes many waterplants.

Nests usually in long mowing grass in meadows near water. The warm creamy-buff eggs, normally 10 or 11, but from 7 to 14 recorded, are laid generally from late April and early May onwards in a nest lined with grasses and characteristic down with prominent pure white tips as well as centres. Incubation is by duck alone, for about 21–23 days. The young are tended by duck only. Single-brooded.

Status and Distribution. A scarce summer-visitor arriving in the second half of March and April, and leaving in August, sometimes October; it occurs exceptionally in winter. It breeds regularly in small numbers chiefly in coastal counties from the Wash to Kent, also Yorkshire and Somerset and sporadically in about a dozen other counties. Otherwise it is a scarce visitor, usually in spring, and fairly regular in Cornwall, Cheshire and Staffs. It is rare in Wales and Scotland but has bred in both countries. In Ireland it is now being recorded annually; it has bred twice and one or two may winter. Abroad it breeds from S. France north to Finland and Scandinavia and east across Asia. Our birds winter in tropical Africa. There are no subspecies.

SHOVELER—*Anas clypeata*

BIRD PLATES 21, 26 and 124   EGG PLATE XXI (4)

The outstanding character on water or in flight is the *enormous spatulate bill*. The plumage pattern of drake is also very striking, with *head dark green, breast and scapulars white, flanks and belly chestnut*, separated by a white patch from black under tail-coverts, and centre of the back dark brown. *Pale blue fore-wing* is also noticeable in flight, but in female it is a good deal duller, and often not noticeable. Female's plumage otherwise resembles Mallard duck, but on the water, in addition to the bill, her rather smaller size, shorter neck, heavier build and different carriage distinguish her. It swims with fore-parts deeply sunk and heavy bill inclined downwards. In flight the disproportionate size of bill make the wings appear set far back. Speculum is green with a white wing-bar in front and narrow white border behind. Legs orange, duller in female; bill blackish in male, brownish with some orange at the base in female. Drake remains long in eclipse, commencing about May or June and full plumage is often not completely recovered until December. In eclipse it is much like female except for brighter colouring of the wings, but back tends to be darker and more uniform. Juveniles are much the same, but wings duller. Length about 20 ins.; body about 12 ins.

Habitat. Owing to its feeding-habits it requires shallow and muddy waters. In the breeding-season, though regularly frequenting open lakes and reservoirs, usually with grassy borders, it is most addicted to reedy meres, pools and creeks of marshes and damp grasslands, bogs, sewage-farms and the like with ample cover. Outside the breeding-season it is more widely distributed on suitable shallow, fresh or brackish waters. Rests on the sea at times, but it visits salt-water less than other surface-feeders except Garganey.

General Habits. It is an active flier, rising almost as abruptly as Teal, and spends much time on the wing in spring. A poor walker. Usually it occurs singly or in pairs and parties up to 20 or so, though at times in large flocks and often with an excess of males. Typical mode of feeding is paddling rapidly about with head carried low all the time and bill continuously dabbling in the water. It is less fond of "up-ending" than most surface-feeders, and on rare occasions dives fairly freely for food.

Rather a silent bird. Flight-call and display-note of male is a low, guttural "took, took"; a creaking "quack" is female's note.

Food includes both animal and vegetable matter, but the latter apparently preponderating.

Nests usually on dry ground in an open site with some shelter from grass, heather, dead reeds, etc., on meadows near water, in open patches among reed-beds or on gorse-covered commons and heaths. The eggs, normally 8–12, but 7–14 recorded, nearly always have a tinge of green, though sometimes almost buff; they are laid generally in April or May in a nest lined with grass, down and feathers. Incubation is by duck alone, for about 23–25 days. The young are tended by duck with male occasionally in attendance; they fly when about 6 weeks old. Single-brooded.

Status and Distribution. Present throughout the year. It breeds in varying numbers in most English counties but very sparsely in the south (more in Kent and Somerset), and very sparsely in Wales; in Scotland in many counties principally in the south and east up to Loch Ness and E. Ross, also in Orkney and has bred in Shetland; in Ireland in every province. Most breeding places are forsaken in autumn and then, as in winter, it is more widely distributed. Passage-migrants and winter-visitors arrive from August to November and return from late February to late April. It breeds in Europe from the Baltic almost to the Mediterranean and eastwards across Asia to Mongolia; also N. America. European birds winter south to tropical Africa. There are no subspecies.

RED-CRESTED POCHARD—*Netta rufina*

BIRD PLATE 21

Male is very distinctive, with *crimson bill, rich chestnut head shading to more golden on top* and with *neck, breast, upper tail-coverts and whole under-parts glossy black*. The back is mouse-brown with a white mark across the shoulders, and flank-feathers white with a deeply serrated brownish pattern where they border the wing. A *broad white patch on flight-feathers* extends nearly the whole length of the expanded wing. Feathers of the crown are erectile, forming a sort of crest and making the head look large. Female is the only European duck except female Common Scoter which is more or less uniform brown with *pale cheek, but this is much more definite than in Scoter*, being *more greyish in colour and more sharply demarcated from the dark brown crown*;

moreover the upper-parts are soft, rather light, instead of dark, rather sooty, brown. The blackish bill shows more or less orange or reddish-brown towards the tip and there is a *white wing-patch* resembling, though duller than, male's. It usually sits noticeably higher on the water than most diving ducks. In May the drake begins to assume eclipse plumage which resembles female but is distinguished by the much more pronounced crest, greyer forewing, whiter wing-patch, and red bill. Legs of adult male orange, of female dull yellow. Total length about 22 ins.; body about 14 ins.

Habitat. It habitually frequents two rather distinct types of habitat, namely, extensive and moderately deep reed-fringed sheets of still or slow-moving water with abundant submerged vegetation; and open, shallow, saline or brackish lagoons often with little cover.

General Habits. It is more at home on land than other diving ducks, walking not only with greater ease, but with less of a roll and more horizontal carriage. Dives well and freely where water is deep enough, but often feeds in shallows by merely reaching down with neck or "up-ending" like surface-feeding ducks. The extreme duration of dive is estimated at 30 secs. Occasionally it even grazes on land. Except in the breeding-season it keeps mostly to open water and is not skulking, but is usually considered shy and wary.

Note of female, not often used, is a hoarse grating "kur-rr" similar to that of many diving ducks.

Food is mainly vegetable matter. Also occasionally some animal matter.

Status and Distribution. An annual autumn-visitor in small numbers from September to November, chiefly on waters in E. and S. England; a few also winter here. There are occasional records in Scotland and Ireland. Some occurrences doubtless do not refer to genuinely wild birds as a few pairs of feral origin breed in southern England. The increase here follows spread of breeding in Denmark, Holland and Germany; the breeding range extends in Europe to the Mediterranean, also Algeria, and in Asia from Syria to W. Siberia. There are no subspecies.

POCHARD—*Aythya ferina*

BIRD PLATES 21 and 124   EGG PLATE XIX (7)

The *chestnut-red head, vermiculated light grey back and flanks, and black breast and upper and under tail-coverts* separate male at once from other British diving ducks. *Female* is *dull brown with a hoary appearance about the base of the bill, cheeks and throat*; the back shows vermiculations at close quarters. In flight the absence of any white on the wing is characteristic of both sexes. The secondaries are paler and greyer than primaries. The male is in full plumage from the end of September, or later, to July; in eclipse plumage it resembles female or juvenile but has a much greyer back. Bill of adult is light blue with black base and tip, duller in female. Total length about 18 ins.; body about 12 ins.

Habitat. In the breeding-season it resorts to lakes, large ponds, and sluggish streams with beds of reeds, iris, etc. At other times it frequents a wide range of open fresh waters, including reservoirs entirely without cover, and tidal estuaries, but seldom resorts to the sea. It prefers waters of medium depth.

General Habits. Flight and general behaviour are typical of diving ducks; when disturbed it prefers shifting farther out on to open water to flying, and when it rises it does so in the usual laboured manner of the group, pattering over the surface for some distance before getting clear. When well started flight is straight and rapid, with quick beats of rather short wings; short flights are generally in compact formation. In spring it will fairly often rest on shore close to water, but is not otherwise much at home on land. Usually swims rather low with tail trailing. It is markedly gregarious; males form parties about the beginning of June, and outside the breeding-season it occurs in anything from small parties to flocks of many hundreds. It spends much of the day resting on open water, feeding principally in the morning and evening; it likes to dive in shallow waters, submerging generally for less than half a minute, and will occasionally "up-end" like a surface feeder.

It calls little outside the breeding-season when the note most frequently heard is the female's harsh growling "kur-r-r".

Food is mainly vegetable matter: roots, leaves, buds, seeds, etc., of aquatic plants. Animal matter includes crustacea, molluscs, insects, worms and frogs.

Nest, unlike that of most ducks, is built in or very close to water. The eggs, 6–11, but 13–15 recorded, are greenish-grey, sometimes with a tinge of buff. They are laid generally in late April or the first half of May, in a nest raised above water level on dead flags, broken reeds, etc., and lined with down generally much mixed with bits of dead reed. Incubation is by duck alone, for about 24–28 days. The young leave the nest the day after hatching, tended by duck, and fly when 7–8 weeks old. Single-brooded.

Status and Distribution. Present throughout the year. It breeds very locally but regularly in most counties in the eastern half of the country from Aberdeen to Hampshire, also Somerset, Anglesey and S.W. Scotland. It has also bred sporadically or for a series of years in many other counties in England, Scotland and Wales, also in Ireland. In winter it is widely distributed on inland waters and on coasts, our birds being augmented by visitors from the Continent between September and April. Abroad it breeds in N.W. Africa, in Europe north to the Baltic and east across Asia to Mongolia. There are no subspecies.

FERRUGINOUS DUCK—*Aythya nyroca*

Bird Plate 22

At close quarters the *general rich chestnut colouring with darker brown back and, in male, the white eye* are distinctive enough, but at longer range the colouring, especially in the case of the duller, brown-eyed female, often does not look very different from female Tufted Duck; the *conspicuous white under tail-coverts* are an important character on water at any distance, but this feature is also shown by a small proportion of Tufteds. The white wing-mark is often hidden in swimming bird, but when wings are flapped or in flight it is extremely conspicuous, forming a *broad roughly crescentic white band on the flight feathers*. Silky white under-parts shading into grey on the abdomen are also evident in flight, though duller in female. Male in eclipse and juveniles are much like females. The young birds, however, have not the pure white under tail-coverts and are not very unlike female Pochard, though the back is darker and rest more rufous; the white wing-bar is here the best distinction. Bill and legs of adult are blackish. Total length about 16 ins.; body about 10½ ins.

The possibility of confusion with hybrids, in particular Pochard × Ferruginous Duck (= Paget's Pochard type) cannot normally be eliminated except in the case of an adult male whose every field character has been critically examined under good viewing conditions. It is commonly kept in captivity.

Habitat. Though occurring on a wide variety of fresh waters its

FERRUGINOUS DUCK
Note high crown.

typical haunts are secluded pools and lagoons, often in swamps and marshes, with abundant cover of reeds, etc., and with growth of submerged and floating vegetation. Over much of its range it is a strictly fresh-water species, but in some areas occurs regularly on the sea in winter.

General Habits. It is generally retiring and somewhat secretive rather than shy, preferring the vicinity of cover and often skulking amongst reeds, etc., and is not easily alarmed. Flight and general behaviour are much as other diving ducks. An expert diver, but prefers shallow water, and will frequently rather dive than fly to escape danger. It will also "up-end" or merely reach down for food in shallows. It appears to be mainly a day-feeder and not as given to flighting as many diving ducks. It does not mix much with other species.

Note of female is a harsh sound much like Pochard's but less loud. That of male is a low, rather grating wheeze, not often heard.

Food is varied, vegetable matter preponderating.

Status and Distribution. A few appear every winter, recorded mainly in East Anglia, and it has also occurred in many other counties in England and Wales, especially in the south and east. There are also several records for Ireland and Scotland. The race concerned, *Aythya nyroca nyroca*, breeds in N.W. Africa and S. Europe north to E. France, Germany, Poland and Roumania, also in central Asia. Another race occurs in E. Siberia.

TUFTED DUCK—*Aythya fuligula*

BIRD PLATES 22 and 124   EGG PLATE XX (4)

The *bold contrast of pure white flanks with the black of the rest of the plumage* is distinctive of male, and the pendant *tuft at the back of its head* gives a characteristic appearance at close range, but is not always obvious at a distance unless blown clear. Female and juvenile are very dark brown, the former showing some whitish on the sides above the waterline in winter, but little or none in the breeding-season. A little whitish at base of the bill usually develops in autumn, and sometimes in adult females and juvenile males this is fairly extensive and conspicuous, giving rise to confusion with female Scaup, but there is almost never such a broad or sharply defined band as in adult female Scaup in full winter plumage. Distinction of some from immature Scaup may be difficult, but the Tufted's crest, though much shorter than in adult drake, is usually perceptible. Also in autumn adults, and to a lesser extent juveniles, may develop white under-tail coverts. *In flight* both sexes look black or nearly so with a white belly, except in breeding female, and show a *broad, white wing-bar*, which becomes dingier and less distinct on the primaries. Male in eclipse resembles female, but the dark parts are blacker and under-parts whiter; this plumage is usually complete in August and September, partial in July and October. Total length about 17 ins.; body about 11 ins.

Habitat. It frequents fresh waters of medium to large size, preferably with fringing reeds or other cover or secluded islands, though also regular in winter on reservoirs, etc., with no cover at all. In the breeding-season it prefers the more secluded waters. When undisturbed it will frequent lakes and ponds in town parks in some numbers in winter and even breeds regularly on some. It rarely occurs on sea, and hardly ever far from land.

General Habits. It readily becomes tame where protected. Flight, gait, diving and general habits are very much like Pochard. It is seen chiefly in small parties up to 25 or so, though large flocks occur in some localities. The favourite depth for diving appears to be slightly greater than in the case of Pochard, and duration of dive rather longer.

Note of female is the usual harsh, growling "kur-r-r, kur-r-r" common to females of most diving ducks. Male's note in the breeding-season is a low gentle whistle.

Food is chiefly animal matter including insects, molluscs, frogs, spawn and occasional small fish; vegetable matter includes grasses, duckweed and portions of many water-plants.

Nests generally within a few yards of water under shelter of bushes or amongst flags or other cover and also in tussocks of rushes or on grassy slopes in the open; sometimes considerable numbers may be found nesting together. The greenish-grey eggs, normally from 6 to 14, are laid generally in the second half of May or June in a nest lined with grasses or rushes and well supplied with down. Incubation is by duck alone, for about 23–26 days. The young are tended by duck, and learn to dive in a few hours; they are able to fly at about 6–7 weeks. Single-brooded.

Status and Distribution. Present throughout the year. It breeds in most counties where suitable waters exist, the main areas from which it is absent being most parts of Wales, S.W. England, the west side of the Scottish mainland from Argyll northwards and the eastern side of southern Ireland. It has recently colonized Shetland. British birds are to a large extent resident, with some southerly movement from mid-July onwards. In winter it is more widely distributed, numbers being augmented by visitors from Iceland, N.W. and N. Europe, which arrive from mid-September to mid-November and leave between late February and mid-May. Abroad it breeds in Iceland; on the continent south to Holland, Germany and Albania; and across Asia to Japan. There are no subspecies.

SCAUP—*Aythya marila*

Bird Plates 22 and 125   Egg Plate XX (1)

The *black head, shoulders, and breast*, the *vermiculated pale grey back, and white flanks* are distinctive of male; the head is glossed green, upper and under tail-coverts black. The wing of both sexes is very like Tufted Duck. At long range, and in broken water, Tufted, Pochard and even Mallard drakes can all be confused with it, all four having a dark head and breast and lighter body. However, except in the case of an isolated male Scaup, the white faces of accompanying females proclaim their identity. This *broad white band round the base of bill* is the outstanding feature of the dark brown duck in winter and is always *broader and more sharply defined in adults than in female or immature Tufted*. On the other hand, immature Scaup, also females in summer (which can then show a whitish crescent behind the ear-coverts), have less white on the face than adult female in winter, so that identification of isolated individuals may be very troublesome and indeed only possible with a very good and close view. The presence of more or less vermiculation on the back, which increases as the season advances, separates immature male Scaup from female Tufted at any age. The main difference between immature males in autumn is the stronger vermiculation of Scaup and, usually, traces of crest in Tufted, these differences becoming more pronounced as the season advances. Immature females are most difficult to separate although Scaup tend to be rather paler, slightly larger, with rather steeper forehead and broader bill, than Tufted. Some young female Scaup resemble juvenile male Tufted in having some vermiculation. Partial or eclipse plumage lasts from about July to early November, the male becoming duller but not resembling female. Bill and legs of adult blue-grey. Total length about 19 ins.; body about 12½ ins.

Isolated examples among Tufted or Pochard on inland waters in winter are generally suspect as hybrids and require meticulous examination of all features including bill pattern (only the narrow nail at the tip of the bill is dark in true Scaup).

Habitat. In the breeding-season it frequents lakes, lochs, and rivers of northern moorland. Outside the breeding-season it is thoroughly marine, frequenting chiefly bays and mouths of estuaries; in some districts freshwater lakes and lagoons close to shore are resorted to fairly freely, but it is rare on reservoirs and other fresh waters far inland.

General Habits. A hardy and robust species little affected by cold and stormy weather. It is thoroughly gregarious and flocks of many hundreds are of regular occurrence, but on the water the birds tend to disperse in small groups or *stretch out in long lines*. It can feed in deeper and rougher water than Tufted, and will also feed amongst pools and gutters on mudflats. Feeding hours are determined largely by tides, but it becomes mainly nocturnal where liable to disturbance.

It is very silent in winter, but female has a deep, harsh "karr-karr-karr".

Food is almost entirely animal matter, chiefly molluscs, crustacea and small insects.

Nests on the ground or in a tussock, at times in the open, but sometimes sheltered by heather or grass. The greenish or olive-grey eggs, normally 6–11, are laid generally in late May or June in a nest lined with the nearest material, down and feathers. Incubation is by duck alone, for about 27–28 days. The young are tended by duck and led almost when dry to water; they fly when about 5 or 6 weeks old. Single-brooded.

Status and Distribution. Chiefly a passage-migrant and winter-visitor to all coasts, only sporadically occurring on inland waters, arriving mid-September to mid-November and leaving from mid-March to early May. Odd birds sometimes summer and it has bred on several occasions in Orkney, W. Ross, the Outer Hebrides and elsewhere in N. Scotland. Abroad this race *Aythya marila marila*, breeds in Iceland, Faeroes, N. Europe and N. Siberia. Other races occur in the Bering Islands and N. America.

EIDER—*Somateria mollissima*

BIRD PLATES 23 and 125   EGG PLATE XX (3)

The bold contrast between the *black crown, flanks, belly and tail region and predominant white of the rest of the plumage* mark male at once. Breast is more or less strongly tinted pinkish, there are green patches on the sides of head and nape, and a white patch at sides of rump. The white inner secondaries are sickle-shaped and curve down over the closed wing. The black crown-patch is divided at the back by a median white band. It is a longer-bodied bird than the typical diving ducks, and has the tail often somewhat cocked up. *Female* is warm brown, streaked, barred and mottled with blackish, and is recognized by her heavy build and peculiar shape of head, the *rather flat profile of the fore-head being continued in an almost straight line by that of the broad-based bill*; there is sometimes a pale eye-stripe. In flight the bulky form and short, thick neck are very noticeable; in addition to the white areas already described, the whole fore-wing of male is white, contrasting with black quills in flight, while the brown female generally shows two rather obscure buffish wing-bars, but these may be almost absent or may develop into two broad white wing-bars, with a purple-blue speculum, much like a Mallard's. *In eclipse, the drake is dingy blackish except for white on the wing, which remains as in winter and shows as a white patch on sides*; a pale crescentic band curving up from base of the bill over the sides of the crown is developed to a varying extent and may be rather conspicuous. This plumage, complete or partial, lasts from about July to November or December; it is entirely different both from female and from male at other seasons, while transitions between it and full plumage and between the several plumages of immature birds produce a singular variety of patchy and mongrel-like patterns. Young birds mature very slowly, the plumage of males being approximately complete only in the third winter and not absolutely so until the fourth. Juvenile resembles female, but is darker and more uniform on the upper-parts, a light band curving over the eye region to the back of the crown. Total length about 23 ins.; body about 15 ins.

Habitat. A thoroughly maritime species. In the breeding-season it frequents chiefly low-lying coasts and islands with both rocky and sandy shores; also locally and rarely it resorts to islands in rivers and lakes some miles from the sea. Outside the breeding-season spends its time often well out to sea, though also frequently close inshore, off rocky, storm-swept and low-lying, sandy or muddy coasts, especially where mussel-banks and reefs afford

Male EIDER

Adult in eclipse.

1st winter moulting.

1st summer moulting.

good feeding, and is only of accidental occurrence on inland waters.

General Habits. Flight is usually within a few feet of the water, strong, steady and direct, parties generally flying in single file. It walks with a slow, rolling gait and erect attitude. In spring and autumn, but much less in winter, it comes to land very freely and spends much time resting and preening on rocks or sandbanks. It swims with head rather retracted, and feeds mainly by diving. The wings are often partly opened as the bird dives. It is often very tame and confiding at breeding-places, though shyer in winter.

Note of male is a low crooning or cooing sound rendered "ah-oo", etc., chiefly heard in spring. Female has hoarse, grating "kr-r-r-r" like other diving ducks, also a display note "coo-roo".

Food is very largely animal matter, especially molluscs and crustacea; some seaweed is also taken.

Nests in colonies, but isolated nests may also be found, sometimes in the open, at other times sheltered by rocks or inside a recess of building or rocks, and often concealed by growing vegetation. The eggs, normally 4–6, but 3 to 10 recorded, are usually pale olive or greenish-grey to buff, sometimes distinctly green and rarely deep blue. They are laid generally in the second half of May or June in a nest with a foundation of grass, seaweed, etc., plentifully lined with down and feathers. Incubation is by duck alone, for about 27–28 days. The young are taken by duck to the water as soon as dry; the chicks are independent, but attach themselves to and are tended by the nearest duck. Single-brooded.

Status and Distribution. A resident, increasing, breeding plentifully in Orkney, Shetland and Hebrides and extending down most of the east coast to Northumberland and the Farne Islands, and on the west coast to Wigtown; it has also bred in N. Lancs. since 1949. In Ireland it breeds in Sligo, Donegal, Antrim and Down. Summering records south of the breeding range have much increased recently and are now regular from most English east coast counties, also Sussex, Devon and Glamorgan. In winter it is found mainly within the breeding range but now also occurs, generally in small numbers, on all coasts from October to March. Abroad *Somateria mollissima mollissima* breeds in Iceland, Faeroes and in N.W. Europe from the Arctic Ocean south to Holland. Other races occur in N.E. Siberia, N. America, Greenland and Spitzbergen.

KING EIDER—*Somateria spectabilis*

Bird Plate 23

Male is at once distinguished from Eider by the *black back and striking shape and coloration of head and bill. The latter is orange with a broad shield at the base* expanding to form a huge and

King Eider

male

conspicuous knob in the breeding-season, rising up to the level of the top of the crown and bordered by black feathers. Crown and nape are pale blue-grey, sides of face white tinged pale green, and there is a black streak on either side of the throat meeting in a V in front. Fore-wing is not entirely white as in Eider, but bordered black in front. Female under favourable circumstances can be distinguished from Eider, having a decidedly rusty or buffy-brown rather than a sooty-brown appearance. The unstreaked throat is said to make this part appear lighter than the top of the head, giving a contrasted effect, which the Eider does not have; on the other hand, breeding birds in Spitzbergen appeared from a distance to have the whole head and back of neck uniform grey, while front of neck looked appreciably darker, giving an effect like Black-throated Diver. The feathers of the lesser wing-coverts and scapulars are buffy or rusty-brown with broad black centres, giving a contrasted effect, which is noticeable at a considerable distance. This is very different from the uniform sooty-brown wing of the Eider; moreover the shorter bill of female King Eider gives a more pointed and perky appearance to the face. Total length about 22 ins., body about 14 ins.

Habitat. Outside the breeding-season it is as much a sea-duck as Eider and its haunts do not differ from those of that species, though as a rule it appears to keep more out to sea.

General Habits. Flight and general habits outside the breeding-season scarcely differ from Eider's, though it has not the Eider's reluctance to fly over land and apparently tends to feed in deeper water and stay submerged longer.

Male has a cooing note resembling Eider's, and female has a hoarse "gak-gak-gak".

Food is chiefly molluscs and crustacea.

Status and Distribution. A vagrant or rare annual visitor appearing chiefly in autumn and winter, from October onwards, but there are several summer records. Apart from a few Irish birds, nearly all have occurred on the east coast from Shetland to Kent, and mainly in the north. It breeds on European and Asiatic islands in the Arctic Ocean, and in arctic N. America. There are no subspecies.

LONG-TAILED DUCK—*Clangula hyemalis*

BIRD PLATES 24 and 125

In winter the mainly white head, white flanks and belly of adults of both sexes are distinctive, as is the drake's bold pattern of dark brown and white and his long pointed tail, which is often trailed on the water but raised when excited; the *rather small delicate head, short bill and steep fore-head* are equally characteristic and aid recognition in other plumages. Male has head and neck, scapulars, belly and flanks white; with a patch on side of the neck, broad pectoral band and middle of the back dark brown. Female has the whole back mottled dark brown, white head with dusky crown and patch on upper neck, and white under-parts with an obscure brownish pectoral band. Both sexes have the wings uniform blackish without bars, and the white scapulars of drake in winter-plumage form two broad white streaks. Between February and June the drake assumes a distinct plumage (complete about May) with the *sides of the face white, but the rest of the head, neck, and breast dark brown, while the whole back, including scapulars, is warm brown with blackish centres to the feathers*. The eclipse, acquired in late July or August is duller, but much the same except for involving the loss of the long tail-feathers, and gives place to winter-plumage in early October or rather later. Female in summer has the head mainly dark with a whitish area surrounding the eye, the upper-parts darker and duller than in winter, breast brownish, and more or less an indication of a whitish collar. Juveniles have uniform dull grey backs, and heads somewhat like female, but much dingier, and greyish flanks. Bill of adult male is

LONG-TAILED DUCK

Male in summer.

pink or orange with black base and tip, of female blackish; legs slate-grey. Total length about 17 ins. exclusive of long central tail-feathers of male, which add about 5 ins. to length; body about 11½ ins.

Habitat. In the breeding-season it frequents fresh waters of the high north, including small fell pools and lochs, as well as larger lakes and rivers, but it also resorts to salt water. Out of the breeding-season it is thoroughly marine, usually resting and feeding well away from shore, and seldom resorting to coastal fresh waters, though doing so regularly in small numbers in some localities; rare on open lakes or reservoirs inland.

General Habits. A lively, restless, noisy bird delighting in the open sea, and usually not at all shy. Flight is distinctive, low down except when migrating, and swinging from side to side, so that now the white under- and now the dark upper-parts are turned to the observer. The wing-action is also peculiar; the wings are held more curved than in other ducks and are brought much less above the body on the upstroke and much lower on the downstroke. It has a habit of dropping abruptly breast first on to the water instead of gliding down like other ducks, and in winter is reluctant to fly over land when this can be avoided. It seldom comes on land. It is markedly gregarious, but seldom mixes with other species. Almost exclusively a day-feeder, with duration of dives often rather long, up to 60 or 90 seconds.

Call of male, used at all hours and on water or in air, is a loud resonant polysyllabic note, variously rendered "ow-ow-owdl-ow", "cah-cah-coralwee", etc., coming with quite musical effect from flocks at sea.

Food is mainly animal matter, especially molluscs.

Nests sometimes in the open among stunted heather, at other times sheltered by rocks. The olive-buff eggs, normally 6–8, are laid generally in late May or June. Incubation is by duck alone, for about 24 days. The young are tended by duck alone and fly when about 5 weeks old. Single-brooded.

Status and Distribution. It is mainly a winter-visitor, arriving between the end of September and end of October and leaving between March and May; numerous in Shetland, Orkney and Moray Basin, regular on much of east coast of Scotland and England, occasional on the S. and W. coasts of England and Wales, scarce in S.W. Scotland, but more in the Hebrides. In Ireland it is regular in small numbers, occurring chiefly on the N.W. coast. On inland waters it is a vagrant of infrequent occurrence. It occasionally stays the summer and breeding has been reported in the past in Orkney and Shetland. Abroad it breeds in Europe south

HARLEQUIN DUCK   LONG-TAILED DUCK

female   female

Note whiter belly of Long-tailed Duck.

to mid-Norway and west to Iceland, also in N. Asia and N. America. In Europe it winters south to N. France and the Black Sea. There are no subspecies.

COMMON SCOTER—*Melanitta nigra*

BIRD PLATES 25 and 125   EGG PLATE XIX (6)

Drake is entirely glossy black relieved only by a conspicuous patch of apricot-yellow on the otherwise black bill. The short pointed tail is elevated like Pintail's when the bird is swimming. The distinctive feature of the dark brown females and immatures is the *pale whitish-brown side of head*, which is conspicuous in the field and quite strongly contrasted with the dark crown; young birds especially in autumn have dirty whitish under-parts. The head-pattern of female Red-crested Pochard is rather similar, but different habits give little opportunity for confusion except in the case of solitary birds on fresh water. The wing in both sexes is uniform, without bars. Male only assumes an extremely imperfect eclipse, which is seldom seen, in which the head and neck are merely rather duller black, and flanks and under-parts browner than in full plumage. Bill of adult female is blackish, legs blackish in male, browner in female. Total length about 19 ins.; body about 12½ ins.

Habitat. In the breeding-season it usually frequents lochs of hilly moorland or sometimes in mountain country at considerable elevation, but main Irish haunt is a large lake with wooded islands. Outside the breeding-season it is exclusively marine, preferring open stretches of sea not far from the coast and generally avoiding broken water. Individuals on migration as well as storm-driven or "oiled" birds occur at times on inland lakes and reservoirs. Some non-breeding birds remain on the sea during summer.

General Habits. It is usually considered a shy species. Though capable of riding out heavy seas it avoids rough water when it can. It rises with some difficulty, and usually flies low over the waves or fairly low, but at times at a considerable height, and is not averse to short cuts over land where not shot at. Flies in long wavering lines or sometimes in wedge formation or denser irregular flocks. Except in the breeding-season, or when oiled, it is rarely seen on land, but it sometimes rests on sandbanks, etc. In spite of heavy build it is very buoyant, riding lightly on the water, but when alarmed swims with body deeply sunk, and head straight up. It occurs in suitable localities in large numbers. Seems to be mainly a day-feeder and to prefer moderate depths, dives not ordinarily exceeding about half-a-minute.

Notes of male are low, rather musical, plaintive piping call of several syllables "peu-peu-peu", and a double call "tuk-*tuk*". Female has horse "kr-r-r-r" much like other diving ducks.

Food for the greater part of the year is molluscs; also small crustacea, and on fresh water in summer insects, worms, and buds, etc., of water-plants.

Nests generally in heather within a few yards of water. The creamy to buff eggs, normally 5–7 but 8–10 recorded, are laid generally in early June in a hollow lined with grasses and down, mixed with mosses and lichens. Incubation is by duck alone, for

COMMON SCOTER   VELVET SCOTER

Bills of adult males.

about 27–28 days. The young are tended by duck only and fly when about 6–7 weeks old. Single-brooded.

Status and Distribution. Present throughout the year, breeding in small numbers on the Scottish mainland north from Loch Lomond, also Islay and Shetland; in Ireland regularly in Fermanagh and Mayo. It is mainly a common winter-visitor to most coasts of Great Britain where young birds often remain through the summer; in Orkney, Shetland, and on N. and N.W. Scottish coasts it is generally scarce. In Ireland it is a regular winter-visitor to most coasts except in the south, while Kerry also has a considerable summering population. Passage-migrants and winter-visitors arrive between early September and late October and leave from end of April to early June. Abroad the race *Melanitta nigra nigra* breeds in Iceland, N. Europe south to mid-S. Norway, and in N. Siberia, wintering south to the N.W. African coast. Another race occurs in N.E. Asia and N. America.

SURF SCOTER—*Melanitta perspicillata*

BIRD PLATE 25

At sufficiently close range the male may be identified by the *two patches of white on top of the head and brilliant red, yellow and white bill*. There is no white on the wing. Females and immatures usually have two whitish patches on the side of the head like Velvet Scoter, from which, as ordinarily seen on the sea, they are indistinguishable unless absence of white in the wing can be definitely established. The curious line of head and bill, more like an Eider, and quite different from other scoters, may however be noticeable. Some, but not all, adult females have a more or less distinct whitish patch on the nape in the same position as male's, and if this shows clearly no other clue is needed. Immature birds have much lighter under-parts than adult female, sometimes practically white. Bill of female is dark, leg colour much as Velvet Scoter. Total length about 21 ins.; body about 14½ ins.

Habitat. Outside the breeding-season it is maritime like Velvet Scoter.

General Habits. Much like Velvet Scoter's, but flight is described as not quite so heavy, resembling that of Common Scoter. It usually keeps well away from shore and like other scoters often partially opens wings in submerging.

A very silent bird.

Food is chiefly molluscs.

Status and Distribution. A vagrant, a few occurring most years both in Britain and Ireland, sometimes several together, and some individuals have remained for long periods. Widely scattered on most coasts (including E.), but mainly Scotland and Ireland, fewest on English south coast, and very rarely inland. They have generally been noted in winter from October onwards, but there are a number of spring and summer records. It breeds in N. America. There are no subspecies.

VELVET SCOTER—*Melanitta fusca*

BIRD PLATES 25 and 125

In form and habit it resembles Common Scoter, but is decidedly larger and distinguished by a *white wing-patch*, conspicuous on the hinder aspect of the wing in flight or when birds flap their wings on the water, and also sometimes visible at rest, but then often hidden by flank-feathers. At closer quarters other differences are: a small white patch just below the eye, bill with most of the side yellow or orange, with (black) knob only slightly developed, and reddish feet, which show when the bird dives. In case of immatures, and to a lesser extent females the *two whitish patches on the face, respectively in front of and behind eye*, afford a good guide to identity at a fair distance even if the wing-patch is not visible. The eclipse is very little developed, the drake merely becoming duller. Bill of adult female blackish, legs duller than male. Total length about 22 ins.; body about 14 ins.

Habitat. It is maritime outside the breeding-season like Common Scoter and often found in the same places, though on the one hand perhaps more indifferent to exposed and stormy waters, and on the other more inclined to frequent estuaries and vicinity of shore where muddy mussel-banks afford a good food-supply. It is rarer than Common Scoter on inland waters.

General Habits. It is generally much tamer than other scoters. It rises from the water with a good deal of labour and often flies low over the waves, when the heavy head and thick neck are noticeable. Seldom comes to land. It rarely occurs in large flocks and even where numerous is generally observed in scattered parties, and single birds are frequent. Feeds largely in rocky localities and well out to sea, but also on mussel-beds close inshore, where it may mingle with Eiders. It associates more regularly with Common Scoters. It often partially opens its wings as it dives and seldom remains submerged for more than a minute.

In contrast to Common Scoter it is very silent.

Food outside the breeding-season is almost exclusively marine: molluscs and some crustacea.

Status and Distribution. Mainly a passage-migrant and winter-visitor arriving between mid-September and November and leaving in late April or May, but some individuals stay the summer, and moulting flocks of unknown origins and uncertain regularity can occur off E. Scotland in August–September. It is decreasing and generally scarce, but locally common in Orkney and Moray Basin, and still regular at a number of places along the North Sea coast south to Rye Bay (Sussex); with few exceptions is very scarce in the south-west and west; it is a scarce visitor to Ireland. It is rare on inland waters, but has been suspected of breeding in Scotland on various occasions. The race concerned, *Melanitta fusca fusca*, breeds in N. Europe, southwards over most of Norway and the Baltic countries, and in the east to Transcaucasia; also in central Asia and W. Siberia. W. European birds winter south to Portugal. Other races occur in N.E. Asia and N. America.

GOLDENEYE—*Bucephala clangula*

BIRD PLATES 23 and 125

The *bold black and white pattern of drake with black head, showing a green and purple gloss at close quarters, and a circular white patch between eye and bill* are distinctive even at long range. The back and tail are black, the neck, under-parts and sides white, with black streaks on the scapulars and edge of flanks. The *wings* are black with a *conspicuous broad white patch on the basal half* extending nearly to the front edge of wing. The *short bill and peaked crown give a "triangular" outline to the head* which is characteristic, and this is a noticeable feature of the less conspicuous females and young, which are *chocolate-headed, mottled grey birds*, with the wing-patch showing as a white mark on the sides when the bird is not flying. Adult females have an obscure whitish collar which immature birds lack. Eclipse is complete in August and September when male is much like female, but retains some dark green feathers on the head. He comes out of eclipse between mid-October and late December but complete adult plumage is not attained until the second winter. Bill of adults blackish, yellowish at tip in female; legs orange in male, paler in female. Total length about 18 ins.; body about 12 ins.; female considerably smaller.

Habitat. In the breeding-season it frequents lakes and rivers in forested country. Outside the breeding-season it is mainly marine, frequenting sea-coast and tidal estuaries or river mouths. It is also quite frequent in small numbers on the larger fresh waters inland, while in Scotland parties often spend the whole winter on inland reaches of rivers.

General Habits. Like Scaup it is a hardy species little incommoded by severe weather. It rises more easily and directly from the water than other diving ducks, and the wing-beats are especially rapid. The *wings produce a characteristic loud "singing"* sound. It is restless in disposition and spends much time on the wing, but seldom comes to land. When excited the neck is stretched upwards and head-feathers puffed out, giving the head a peculiar "swollen" appearance. It is usually seen in quite small parties, which often dive simultaneously, and rarely associates with other waterfowl, but in some localities (e.g. Firth of Forth) flocks of over 1,000 regularly occur. Indefatigable divers, they will often dive in preference to swimming when making for a given spot. Dives average less than half-a-minute.

Generally a silent bird, but female has a loud, hoarse note like that of other diving ducks.

Food is almost entirely animal matter, chiefly molluscs, crustacea, and insects.

Nests normally in holes of trees and stumps, but has nested in rabbit-burrows. The bluish-green eggs, 6–15, are laid from mid-April onwards. Incubation is by duck alone, for about 26–30 days. The young scramble out of nest and drop to the ground; they are tended by duck only and fly when about 57–60 days old. Single-brooded.

Status and Distribution. Present throughout the year but mainly a winter-visitor, most arriving from mid-October to mid-November, and leaving from March to early May. It is widely distributed on estuaries and fresh waters in all parts of the British Isles, considerable flocks occurring in E. Scotland, Essex and N. Ireland. It is frequently seen in summer, especially in Scotland, and first proved to nest there in 1970 in Inverness, where a successful breeding population of over 50 pairs has since become established. The race concerned, *Bucephala clangula clangula*, breeds in Europe from the Arctic Ocean south to mid-Scandinavia, Germany, Jugoslavia and N. Bulgaria; also in N. Asia. European birds winter south to the Mediterranean. Another race occurs in N. America.

SMEW—*Mergus albellus*

BIRD PLATES 24 and 125

A much smaller and shorter-billed bird than other "saw-bills". Adult drake attracts attention by *mainly pure white plumage with a black patch on the face and band from behind the eye to the nape*. The drooping crest, black centre of back, band on side above the flanks and two curved bands at the sides of the breast are not conspicuous unless the bird is comparatively close, and the fine grey pencilling of the flanks shows only when closer still. In flight it shows much more black, presenting a pied effect, the wings being black with a prominent white patch on the coverts. Female and immature birds are quite as characteristic, with *pure white throat and cheeks contrasted with the chestnut red of the rest of the head*. Back, breast and flanks are grey, belly white; they also have a small, short bill, high forehead, and a small but distinct crest forming a peak at the back of the head. The white wing-patch is smaller and less sharply defined than in male, but still quite conspicuous. Full plumage of male is complete from about the end of November to June; in eclipse male resembles female except for larger size, blacker mantle and more white in the wing. Juveniles resemble female, but have the white wing-patch more or less obscured by brownish. Bill and legs grey. Total length (ad. male) about 16 ins.; body about 10 ins.; female smaller.

Habitat. Outside the breeding-season it resorts to rivers, lakes, reservoirs, and sometimes to floodlands, as well as to estuaries and inlets on the coast, but very seldom to the open sea. It is rather fond of quite small and shallow fresh-water pools which other "saw-bills" would avoid.

General Habits. It shows the usual Merganser outline on the wing, and flight is very rapid. In general it is decidedly shy, taking wing very readily, and if startled it leaps up from the water with almost the agility of Teal. It seldom comes ashore in winter, and ordinarily swims buoyantly, but like its allies sinks the body deeper when alarmed. It is most commonly seen in parties of half-a-dozen to twenty or so, and often associates with Goldeneye and other duck. An expert diver, submerging with almost startling rapidity, for a period sometimes of 40 seconds or more.

A very silent bird.

Food is mainly animal matter, chiefly fish; occasionally a little vegetable matter.

Status and Distribution. A winter-visitor, regular in small numbers in S.E. England but scarce elsewhere, irregular in Wales and N. England, Scotland, and Ireland. Numbers in the southeast, which have declined in recent decades, may be augmented during severe weather on the continent. It breeds in N. Scandinavia, N. Russia, N. Asia and perhaps N. Caspian region. European birds winter south to the Mediterranean. There are no subspecies.

RED-BREASTED MERGANSER—*Mergus serrator*

Bird Plates 27 and 125   Egg Plate XVIII (1)

The general form and habits resemble those of Goosander, though Merganser is a slimmer-necked bird, smaller than Mallard. *Male* is at once distinguished, however, by the *chestnut breast, noticeable as a dark band even when too far off to see colours*, by vermiculated grey flanks and by *noticeable crest*, standing out rather stiffly and distinctly divided into two. Head is bottle-green and bill red, as Goosander. Lower neck white forming a collar, and the belly is white. *Female* is less distinct, but at reasonable range is recognized by *brownish-grey, instead of clear blue-grey back and by dingy white throat-patch merging into the brown of the head, which itself shades off gradually at the neck*, whereas in Goosander the chestnut of the head is sharply demarcated at the neck, a difference often quite conspicuous in flight when fairly close, and the throat-patch is usually purer white and more sharply defined. The brown of the head is also usually paler and duller in female Merganser, and the *crest though smaller than in drake is similar and stands out quite prominently*, instead of hanging down the back of neck in a more mane-like fashion as in Goosander. Merganser often moves its neck backward and forward in swimming, like Moorhen. In flight male differs from Goosander in having a dark breast-band and less white in wing, the fore-wing

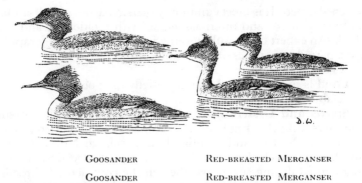

| GOOSANDER | RED-BREASTED MERGANSER |
| GOOSANDER | RED-BREASTED MERGANSER |

Females. Birds in foreground have crests blown by tail-wind.

being blackish and the broad white speculum is crossed by two black bands; a distinct black band also crosses white speculum of female, this being absent or much less distinct in the female Goosander; Goosander looks much longer bodied in flight. Moult into eclipse begins in April or May and full plumage is recovered about the end of November. Eclipse is complete in August and early September, when male closely resembles female except for more white in the wing and shorter crest. Juveniles are also very like females except for shorter crest and greyer back. Bill and legs of both sexes are red, less bright in female. Length about 23 ins.; body about 14 ins.

Habitat. In the breeding-season it frequents clear rivers and large or small lakes both in wooded districts and in treeless northern regions, commonly near the coast, but also far inland; also regularly about the coasts and islands of sea lochs and inlets. Outside the breeding-season it is a maritime species, generally keeping fairly near land in bays and estuaries; fresh and brackish waters are often visited if available close to the coast, and a few winter on lakes, etc., far inland in Ireland, but in England and Scotland it is then very uncommon on fresh waters inland.

General Habits. Actions and general behaviour are like Goosander. It feeds by day and often flights at dusk from shallows and inlets where it has been feeding to more open sea, returning at dawn. Full-grown birds are not often seen in large or close flocks.

Male rarely utters any sound except in display. Female has a loud harsh "kar-r-r" like Goosander.

Food is mainly fish, also small crustacea, worms and insects.

Nests on the ground generally under the protection of brambles, in a hollow among tree-roots, among boulders, sheltered by long heather or grass, or in a shallow burrow. The stone-drab to greenish-buff eggs, usually 7–12, but 13–17 recorded, are laid generally in late May or early June in a nest lined with grass, dead leaves, etc., and down. Incubation is by duck alone, for about 29 days. The young are tended by duck alone. Single-brooded.

Status and Distribution. Present throughout the year. It breeds commonly in all counties of Scotland south to Dumfries on the west side, and to Angus on the east side, and less commonly in several other counties. Since 1950 has spread into N.W. England, W. Yorks, Anglesey, N. and S. Wales. In Ireland it breeds commonly on many inland and several marine loughs and islands, but is scarce in the south-east. In winter it is widespread on coasts throughout the British Isles and more numerous in Scotland than elsewhere. Abroad it breeds in Iceland, Faeroes, N. Europe south to N. Germany, Poland and Armenia, and eastwards across N. Asia; also N. America. European birds winter south to the Mediterranean and N. African coast. There are no subspecies.

GOOSANDER—*Mergus merganser*

BIRD PLATES 24 and 125   EGG PLATE XVIII (4)

Goosander is the largest of the "saw-billed" ducks, and is bigger than Mallard. Drake has a *bottle-green head* which looks *black at a distance, white breast and sides, suffused with salmon-pink, and a black back*. The head lacks a distinct crest. Rump and tail are grey; bill blood-red. Female has *back and flanks ash-grey, a rich chestnut head, sharply defined white patch on the throat, and white breast and under-parts*; also a mane-like crest which comes to a kind of peak at the back of the lower neck, and a white wing-patch often concealed by the flank-feathers, but prominent on the hinder aspect of the wing when the wing is spread. In flight the black and white appearance of drake is striking, the under-parts, sides, and practically the whole basal half of the wing being white, while the back, primaries, and head appear black. The distinctions of both sexes from Red-breasted Merganser are given under that species. In eclipse the male resembles female, but retains the white fore-wing and has a darker and browner back; this plumage begins to appear in May and full plumage is not recovered until November or December. Juveniles resemble female, but have shorter crest, upper-parts browner, white on throat duller, and breast greyish, not white. Legs are red like bill, both less bright in female. Total length (ad. male) about 26 ins.; body about 18 ins.; female smaller.

Habitat. In the breeding-season it frequents clear lakes and rivers chiefly in forested districts, or at least where some trees are present; also sometimes on sheltered inlets of the sea. Outside the breeding-season it is much less marine than Red-breasted Merganser, frequenting lakes, lochs, and larger rivers, and is locally common on reservoirs, but also on estuaries and inlets of sea.

General Habits. Flight is of the usual Merganser type close to the water, and on rivers often following every bend of the stream, though at times it will rise high. Unless aided by wind it rises with some difficulty, splashing and flapping along the surface for some way before getting clear. The typical swimming position is low, and when alarmed it will sink body till the back is almost awash; it swims rapidly. In winter it does not seem to come ashore much, but in spring spends a good deal of time resting and preening on shore close to water. It also perches on branches overhanging water, and well up in trees when prospecting for nesting-holes. Markedly sociable, though seldom occurring in flocks of any considerable size. Males leave the females as soon as incubation begins and form small parties. It is essentially diurnal in feeding habits, often swimming with tip of bill and even the whole front of the head immersed as it watches for fish. The usual diving-period is less than half-a-minute. It can travel surprising distances under water, and often travels rapidly on the surface between dives. "Brown heads" generally arrive in their winter-haunts considerably before old drakes.

Male is very silent except in display, when a soft, low, croaking note is used. Female has a hoarse, guttural "kar-r-r" more often heard than male's note.

Food is apparently entirely animal matter, mainly fish.

Nests within easy reach of a river or loch, most commonly in a hollow tree, sometimes high up but also nests in cavities among boulders and in holes in banks sheltered by heather. The creamy-white eggs, usually 7–13, but 14–16 recorded, are laid from about mid-April onwards, in many cases no nest material being used beyond dead wood and plentiful down. Incubation is by duck alone, for about 34–35 days. The young remain in the nest 2–3 days; they scramble to the entrance and normally flutter to the ground or water when called by duck which alone tends them. Single-brooded.

Status and Distribution. Present throughout the year, breeding in many Scottish counties from Sutherland to the border but mainly in north; it has spread widely into N. England south to Yorkshire, and there are subsequent records from central Wales, Devon and N.W. Ireland. Elsewhere it is a winter-visitor to estuaries and inland waters, being especially numerous on reservoirs in the lower Thames valley, but scarce in Orkney, Shetland and Outer Hebrides, and somewhat irregular in S.W. England, Wales and Ireland, arriving mainly from late November to February and leaving between March and May. Abroad *Mergus merganser merganser* breeds in Iceland; in Europe south to Denmark, Switzerland and Jugoslavia; and across Asia to N.W. Mongolia. Other races occur in the Himalayas and N. America.

HONEY BUZZARD—*Pernis apivorus*

BIRD PLATE 28　EGG PLATE XII (3)

In flight it resembles a common Buzzard, but the *wings are rather longer and narrower and tail longer*, moreover in gliding flight the *wings are held slightly drooped* below horizontal; the *small head and neck are usually rather more extended* and the banding of tail is different. Seen from below, Buzzard shows the whole tail narrowly barred, with a broad subterminal band, whereas Honey Buzzard has several broad dark bands, of which the distal

P. J. H.

HONEY BUZZARD

Female overhead, soaring (has slightly heavier outline than Buzzard). Head-on, showing characteristic glide attitude with wings drooping slightly below level of back.

HONEY BUZZARD

Various flight attitudes.

In left-hand figure note the similarity of profile of leading and trailing edges. Male's wings are relatively narrower than Buzzard's.

one and the next are more widely separated than the rest; however, these details may be hard to see, particularly in darker examples. The flight feathers usually show a distinct pattern of transverse bars when viewed from below. The plumage is very variable; upper-parts dark brown, and under-parts usually more boldly variegated than in Buzzard, but sometimes upper- and under-parts are almost uniform chocolate. Length about 20–23 ins.

Habitat. In the breeding-season it is found in or near broad-leaved (often beech) or mixed woods and copses, as well as in pure conifers, preferring a rather open growth of trees or places where woodland is interspersed with glades or open places.

General Habits. Though soaring fairly freely, spends less time in the air than Buzzard. It perches on trees, etc., and settles freely on the ground, where it walks with ease. The characteristic mode of feeding is by digging out wasps', and more rarely humble-bees', nests with its feet.

Ordinary note on the wing is "piha", with variants, but it is a much more silent bird than Buzzard.

Food is mainly insects and especially wasp and other grubs. Small mammals, birds, frogs, etc., are also occasionally taken.

Nests in forest trees of good size, usually on a side branch at a considerable height. The eggs, normally 2, occasionally 1–3, have the white ground often almost entirely hidden by a wash or markings of reddish or chocolate. They are laid in the second half of May or first half of June in a nest usually built up on the foundation of an old nest of some kind, and variable in size, but small when built mainly or altogether by the birds themselves. Both sexes appear to bring decorative sprays to line the nest. Incubation is by both sexes for about 30–35 days. The young are fed by both parents and fly when about 40–45 days old.

Status and Distribution. Very scarce summer-visitor, and irregular passage-migrant chiefly in September–October and May–June appearing mainly on the east coast of Great Britain. It breeds regularly in very small numbers in southern and central England, and sporadic nesting has been attempted as far north as Fife. A rare vagrant in Ireland. The race concerned, *Pernis apivorus apivorus*, breeds in Europe from N. Sweden south in some parts to the Mediterranean; also in W. Siberia, and winters in tropical and S. Africa. Another race occurs in E. Siberia.

RED KITE—*Milvus milvus*

Bird Plate 28   Egg Plate XII (2)

In its great soaring powers the Red Kite exceeds Buzzard, but the *much longer, narrower and more angled wings and deeply forked tail* give it a quite different appearance. A *large whitish*

RED KITE   BLACK KITE

Black Kite (viewed here from above and below) has nearly square-cut tail and dingy pale wing patches compared with Red Kite.

patch on the underside of the wing is also distinctive. In gliding flight the wings are level, whereas harriers hold them in a shallow V. The upper-parts are dark brown with lighter borders to the feathers; the under-parts rusty-red with dark streaks, and head greyish with dark streaks, but nearly white in old birds. Primaries blackish, and tail rufous. Young are paler and duller, with browner head and shallower tail fork. Length about 24–25 ins.

Habitat. In Britain it is now confined to wild, hilly country with wooded valleys.

General Habits. Like Buzzard it will sail for hours in wide circles high in the air, and at such times the steering action of the tail is often very noticeable. Direct flight is also not unlike that of Buzzard, but perceptibly lighter and more buoyant, with generally longer glides and wing-beats appreciably slower. It will hover momentarily while prospecting for prey. It perches chiefly on trees. Practically all prey is taken on the ground.

Usual note is a shrill, mewing "weeoo-weeoo-weeoo", recalling Buzzard's, but higher pitched and more rapidly repeated, though much less frequently used.

Food includes mammals, birds, carrion, frogs and worms.

Nests usually close to the main stem in tall slender oaks, sometimes ivy-grown, in hanging woods on hillsides. The eggs, 2–3, rarely 4, are white, often feebly but sometimes strongly marked. They are laid usually from early April onwards, in a nest built by both sexes of sticks solidified by earth, noticeably flat on

P. J. H.

RED KITE

Adult overhead, gliding; and head-on to show horizontal set of wings in glide.

top and lined with lumps of wool, moss, sometimes hair and, whenever available, rags or paper. Incubation is undertaken mainly by female, for about 28–30 days. Young are fed by both parents and fly when about 50–54 days old. Single-brooded.

Status and Distribution. Adults are mainly resident but there is evidence of movement of some juveniles across southern England in autumn and return in spring. Once widespread, but fewer than a dozen pairs, confined to mid-Wales, remained during the early years of the present century. They have gradually increased to about 50 pairs by the mid-1980s. It is a very rare straggler to Scotland and Ireland. This race, *Milvus milvus milvus*, breeds from the Baltic to N.W. Africa and east to Iran. Another race occurs in the Cape Verde Islands.

WHITE-TAILED EAGLE—*Haliaeetus albicilla*

BIRD PLATE 30

In flight it is distinguished by its large size, *enormously wide wings which are usually held very straight, rectangular-shaped and blunt-ended, and a much shorter and more wedge-shaped tail than Golden Eagle*, which give it a quite vulturine appearance when soaring. The *light coloured, almost white head and*

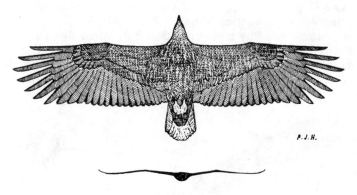

WHITE-TAILED EAGLE

Adult overhead, soaring (note whitish wedge-shaped tail); and head-on view, gliding, when wings held substantially horizontally but raised slightly at carpal joint.

transparent-looking white tail of adult make confusion with Golden or other eagles impossible, but *immature birds have tail dark brown.* At rest it is a heavy, lumpish-looking bird lacking the alertness of Golden Eagle, while at close range the huge deep bill and tarsi not feathered to the base of toes are further points of difference. Length about 27–36 ins.

Habitat. It frequents cliffed and rocky coasts and islands, inland lakes in wooded districts, and the vicinity of marshes, estuaries, etc. In winter it visits coasts and waters where it does not breed and the young especially are great wanderers.

General Habits. The flapping flight, with rather slow wing-beats, appears somewhat laboured and heavy, and has been compared to that of Grey Heron; wings are then more or less angled, but in soaring they are held perfectly straight with primaries widely separated. It perches both on rocks, trees, etc., and on the ground where it will stand motionless for hours in or near water. The usual mode of fishing is to fly low over water, often picking up fish from the surface, but sometimes plunging right in. Low flight is equally characteristic when hunting other prey, in the capture of which it relies mainly on surprise, sometimes poising in a kind of hover.

Usual cry is a querulous chatter "krikrikrikri . . .", insignificant for so large a bird.

Food includes fish, mammals and birds.

Nests usually on sea-cliffs or trees, rarely on flat islets in lochs. The white, unmarked eggs, normally 2, but occasionally 1–3, are laid generally in April in a nest built of sticks or heather stalks, driftwood, grass, moss, seaweed, etc., lined with luzula, grass, and at times wool. Incubation is mainly by female, for about 6 weeks. The young are fed by both parents and fly when about 10 weeks old. Single-brooded.

Status and Distribution. A former resident which bred until 1916. Thereafter stray immatures occurred irregularly, mainly in

P.J.H.

WHITE-TAILED EAGLE

On left, immature gliding (tail wedge-shaped but dark). On right, note lumpish appearance in steady flapping flight.

GOLDEN EAGLE   WHITE-TAILED EAGLE

White-tailed has an upright " dog-on-haunches " resting
attitude on shore, as well as a stance almost as horizontal
as that of Golden Eagle on ground.

winter near the east coasts, but a re-introduction project from
Norway to the Inner Hebrides, begun in 1968, led to successful breeding in the wild in 1985. The race *Haliaeetus albicilla
albicilla* breeds in Iceland and from N. Scandinavia south to N.
Germany and the Balkans, also in W. and N. Asia. Another race
occurs in Greenland.

MARSH HARRIER—*Circus aeruginosus*

BIRD PLATE 31   EGG PLATE XVII (2)

Harriers are large, long-winged, long-tailed, and long-legged
hawks frequenting open country. Their flight is characteristic,
often only a few feet from the ground or above the tops of reeds or
crops, several leisurely wing-beats being followed by a *glide on
half-raised wings*; and at times, especially in the breeding-season,
they will rise in wide circles to considerable heights. When hunting
they quarter the ground with much regularity and seize their prey
by a sudden pounce. The Marsh Harrier is the *largest European
species, with broader, more rounded wings held more horizontally
when gliding, slower flight and heavier build* than the others. The
plumage is predominantly dark rusty-brown, much the commonest phase (female and immature males) having *lighter, buffish
shoulders and head*, though the plumage varies much in detail.
The tail is not barred. Juveniles and first winter birds are uniform
very dark brown, usually with golden-yellow cap and throat. *Adult*

P. J. H.

MARSH HARRIER

Above: Female   Male

Below: Immature hunting, gliding on partly raised wings,
as do all harriers.

male has the tail, secondaries, and some coverts ash-grey, so that
in flight the wing shows a broad oblique band of grey contrasted
with black primaries, and there may be a little white at base of the
tail in old birds; this plumage looks very different in the field from
the others. Length about 19–22 ins.

Habitat. It frequents extensive reed-beds, marshes, and reedy
swamps at all seasons, hunting at times over neighbouring grasslands and open country; in recent years several successful nests in
England have been built in arable crops. Except as passage-
migrant or vagrant, it is seldom far from its typical haunts.

General Habits. It is usually seen hunting over marshes and
reed-beds, into which it drops occasionally in a rather clumsy
fashion. It settles on the ground or on posts, bushes, etc., but
never normally at any height in trees.

Spring note of male is a plaintive shrill "kweeoo", somewhat variable in sound, at times not unlike Lapwing. Generally 'silent outside the breeding-season.

Food includes many marsh animals, from frogs, birds and eggs to small mammals.

Nests usually among reeds and rank vegetation growing in water. The eggs, usually 4–5, occasionally 3–7, bluish-white and often stained, are laid generally from late April onwards in a nest, sometimes very bulky, built of dead reed-stems or roots, sedge and water plants, with sometimes thorns or branches of alder and sallow worked in, and lined with finer marsh grasses. It is built by hen, but male also makes a supplementary nest and at times carries material to the nest after incubation has begun. Incubation is largely by female for about 30–38 days. The young are fed mainly by female on food which is generally passed to her in the air by the male; they remain in or near the nest for about 35 to 40 days, but are not fully fledged till about 3 weeks later.

Status and Distribution. Mainly a summer-visitor, but a few individuals may winter. Breeding numbers are very low, fluctuating between about 2 and 30 pairs, located mainly in East Anglia and probably supported by a flourishing Dutch population. Nesting has also occurred in several other counties in England, also in Wales and apparently attempted in Scotland. Elsewhere in Great Britain and Ireland it is a rare vagrant. The race *Circus aeruginosus aeruginosus* breeds in Europe from the Baltic south to Portugal and the Balkans, also in W. Asia. Another race occurs in S. Spain and N.W. Africa.

HEN HARRIER—*Circus cyaneus*

Bird Plate 31   Egg Plate XVII (3)

It resembles Montagu's Harrier, but the blue-grey male has a *large and prominent pure white patch on the rump*, is rather paler, and *lacks the black mark on secondaries and streaks on flanks*. Female and young also tend to have a purer and more extensive white patch on the rump, but the difference is not absolute. For remarks on difference in build between the two species, see under Montagu's Harrier. Length about 17–20 ins.

Habitat. In the breeding-season it is now confined to wild moorlands and moorland valleys; in winter it also frequents open country, including fens, heaths, coastal sand-dunes, large open fields, downland, etc.

PALLID HARRIER   HEN HARRIER

Adult males in flight.

Hen Harrier has dusky band along hind border of under-
wing (and upper-wing), broader wings and more extensive
black on wing tips.

General Habits. It has a typical harrier flight and mode of
hunting, but will occasionally pursue and seize birds as well as
pounce on them. It settles on the ground or on rocks, stumps,
posts. Has a gregarious tendency in winter roosting.

Usual cry is a rapid quacking chatter "ke ke ke ke . . .", seldom
heard away from the nest.

Food is chiefly birds and mammals taken by surprise on the
ground.

Nests usually in a hollow on the ground. The eggs, usually 4–5,
sometimes 3–6, are bluish-white, rarely with reddish markings.
They are laid generally in the first half of May in a nest which is
chiefly the work of the female and is lined with a thick pad of dead
rushes or grasses, with often a number of heather stalks or twigs of
birch arranged round it. Incubation is by female alone, for about
29–30 days. During incubation and the first part of fledging the
male provides the food, calling the female off and "passing" the
prey in the air directly to her from foot to foot, or by a drop in the

HARRIERS IN FLIGHT

Male Marsh Harrier, female Hen Harrier, female Montagu's Harrier,
immature male Hen Harrier.

air. The young fly when 5–6 weeks old, but are attended by parents for 2 or 3 weeks longer. Single-brooded.

Status and Distribution. Present throughout the year. With breeding strength over 500 pairs it has increased outstandingly in the British Isles since 1945; during this time it has spread from Orkney and Outer Hebrides to nest, sometimes in groups, in widely scattered areas on the Scottish mainland, in Wales and in England mainly in the north. In Ireland too it has spread, with breeding taking place in eight counties by 1966. Otherwise it is only a winter-visitor and autumn- and spring-migrant. The race concerned, *Circus cyaneus cyaneus*, breeds from N. Scandinavia south to Portugal and the Balkans and across much of N. Asia. Another race occurs in N. America.

MONTAGU'S HARRIER—*Circus pygargus*

BIRD PLATE 31   EGG PLATE XVII (1)

European harriers other than Marsh Harrier are all distinctly smaller, more lightly built and narrower-winged than that species; they are birds of lighter and more buoyant flight, and adult males have more or less uniform grey upper-parts and black wing-tips. Male of Montagu's Harrier differs from Hen Harrier in having *dark bar across base of secondaries* (showing also on the underside of the wing), and a *grey or sometimes greyish-white rump* —but never a broad area of pure white as in Hen Harrier. At close quarters *rufous streaks on the flanks* can be seen. The female resembles that of Hen Harrier but the white at the base of tail is generally narrower and less pure, although this difference is not clear-cut enough to be really diagnostic. Montagu's Harrier is also more slightly built, with longer, narrower wings and longer tail, but this distinction must be used with care since males of both are noticeably more slender than females. Juvenile differs from adult female and from any plumage of Hen Harrier in having *rufous-buff under-parts without streaks*. Length about 15½–18 ins.

Habitat. In the breeding-season it equally frequents reedy and sedgy marshes and fens or dry moors, rough commons, sand-dunes, etc., often where such ground is interspersed with young conifer plantations.

General Habits. Flight is graceful and buoyant with typical harrier action, several wing-beats and then a glide with wings inclined upwards at a small angle to the horizontal. It settles on the ground or on a stump or post, occasionally on a bush or young conifer. General habits are as Hen Harrier.

Chattering note in the neighbourhood of nest is softer and much less penetrating, but higher-pitched than that of Hen Harrier, like "yick-yick-yick . . .".

Food is chiefly frogs, toads, snakes, birds' eggs, and small birds or mammals. Also earthworms and larger insects.

Nests in rank marsh vegetation, also on heaths with gorse bushes, heather, bramble thickets, etc., as covert. The eggs,

P.J.H.

MONTAGU'S HARRIER

Male in flight.

usually 4–5, sometimes 3–6, are pale bluish-white or white, exceptionally with rusty-brown marks. They are laid generally in late May or early June in a nest composed of rushes, sedge, or coarse grasses and lined with finer material. Sometimes both sexes take part in building, but the female in most cases does practically all the work. Incubation is normally by female alone, for about 30 days. The young fly when about 32–35 days old. Throughout incubation and most of the fledging period, all food is provided by male, the female remaining at the nest until called off to take it by a pass in the air from the male, either from foot to foot or dropped by male and caught by the female. Single-brooded.

Status and Distribution. A rare summer-visitor from about mid-April to mid-September, of unpredictably scattered, erratic occurrence in varying numbers; up to about 50 pairs in the 1950s, 20 in the mid-1960s, perhaps none in mid-1970s, about 3 to 10 in the mid-1980s. Nesting has been fairly regular in East Anglia, but was for a time concentrated in S.W. England; has also bred N. Wales and occasionally north to Scotland. In Ireland a pair or two have bred irregularly in two or three counties, but otherwise the bird is a rare vagrant. It breeds in Europe from S. Sweden south to most of the Mediterranean countries, also in Morocco and W. Asia, and winters mainly in tropical and S. Africa. There are no subspecies.

GOSHAWK—*Accipiter gentilis*

BIRD PLATE 28   EGG PLATE XII (4)

It *resembles a huge Sparrowhawk, having the same long tail and rounded wings*, though male, as in that species, is considerably smaller than female. Sexes do not differ except in size, and the *colouring recalls that of female Sparrowhawk*, the European race being dark ashy-brown (exceptionally, bluish) above, with a prominent whitish streak from eye over ear-coverts, whitish below closely barred with dark brown, and tail strongly barred. The *pure white under tail-coverts* are often conspicuous in flight. Juveniles and first-year birds have the upper-parts lighter, more rufous, and less uniform, and *under-parts warm buff streaked, not barred, with broad, drop-like markings* of dark brown. In ordinary flight the wing-tips are usually held pointed, so that it can sometimes be confused with Peregrine in brief views, but in soaring the spread wings and tail give it a very different appearance from that seen in ordinary flight. Length about 19–23 ins.

Habitat. It frequents forests and wooded districts in both plains and mountains, with a liking for places where woodland is bordered by or interspersed with fields or other open ground.

General Habits. Ordinary flight and habits are much like Sparrowhawk's. In its hunting flights it combines speed and a perfect control of movement, the short wings and long tail enabling it to thread its way swiftly amongst tree-trunks or other obstacles and to perform abrupt turns with the utmost facility. It will wait on the watch for prey on a suitable perch or fly low amongst trees or along borders of woods and fields, relying in either case on a lightning dash on its quarry.

A silent bird except in the vicinity of nest. The alarm note is a rapid, hoarse, strident "gek-gek-gek-gek . . ."

Food is mainly mammals and birds up to a considerable size.

Nests in both coniferous and deciduous trees. The eggs, usually 3–4, but 1–5 recorded, are bluish or sometimes dead white, generally unmarked but occasionally with light rusty-brown markings. They are laid generally in April or May in a substantial nest, built largely if not altogether by female, of sticks and boughs, with smaller twigs and green sprays round the cup; it is sometimes founded on an old nest. Incubation is almost entirely by female,

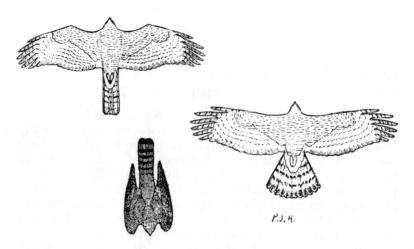

P.J.H.

GOSHAWK

Ordinary flight or glide.   Male display soaring.

Display plunge.

GOSHAWK

Immature going away; and tail-on view showing sailing attitude
of wings. Note white under tail-coverts.

for about 36–38 days. The young are fed by both parents, take to
the branches when about 41–43 days old, and can fly soon afterwards. Single-brooded.

Status and Distribution. Mainly resident. It was probably a
breeding species until some two centuries ago in England, more
recently in Scotland, and then became a rare vagrant until the
re-establishment of a pair or two in Sussex from the inter-war years
until 1951. It now breeds in several widely separated areas in
England, Wales and Scotland with a population estimated at 70
pairs in 1984. It is rarely reported in Ireland. The race concerned,
Accipiter gentilis gentilis, breeds in Europe from the Pyrenees to S.
Russia and north to N. Scandinavia. A few examples of the N.
American race *Accipiter gentilis atricapillus* have been found in
Ireland in winter, also recorded from the Scillies and Perth; this
race differs from the normal W. European bird in having the
upper-parts slate-grey, with crown almost black, and under-parts
with considerably less bold and definite barring. Other races occur
in S.W. and S.E. Europe, N.E. Russia and Asia.

SPARROWHAWK—*Accipiter nisus*

BIRD PLATE 29   EGG PLATE XI (5A & 5B)

The *long tail, broad rounded wings, barred not streaked under-
parts and characteristic mode of hunting*, distinguish Sparrowhawk
from our other smaller native birds-of-prey. Male has dark slate-

SPARROWHAWK

Adult female soaring.   Adult males in flight.

grey upper-parts, with barred under-parts more or less rufous. The conspicuously larger female has upper-parts considerably browner and the under-parts whitish, or only slightly rufous except on the flanks, and a whitish superciliary stripe. Both sexes have some whitish on the nape and there is much individual variation in plumage. Immature birds have the upper-parts brown. Length about 11–15 ins.

Habitat. It frequents mainly well-wooded country, but chiefly cultivated districts with scattered woods or at least those where woodland is varied by cultivation or other open ground. It is fond of conifer and mixed woods or copses.

General Habits. When hunting it flies fast and low along wood borders or rides, hedgerows, or watercourses. When working a hedge it slips over from one side to the other at intervals. Though preferring to secure its prey by surprise, it will not infrequently pursue and fairly out-fly in the open. It will also suddenly invade, or keep watch at, places where small birds congregate to feed, etc., suddenly stooping down and seizing one before they have time to take cover. Soars at times, the bird circling upwards generally with 3 or 4 wing-beats from time to time, to a high elevation. Often very unobtrusive.

Alarm note in the vicinity of the nest is a rapid, harsh "kek-kek-kek-kek . . ." or variants.

Food consists mainly of birds, insects and mammals.

Nests generally in a tree near the main stem, preferring a conifer if available. The eggs, normally 4–5, occasionally 3–7, have whitish, normally bluish-white, ground-colour, sometimes without markings. They are laid generally in the first half of May in a nest nearly always built by the birds themselves and frequently by the female alone, but at times on the foundation of an old nest of another species. Incubation is normally by female alone, for about 32–35 days. The young are fed by female on food brought by the male; they fly when about 24–30 days old. Single-brooded.

Status and Distribution. It was formerly a generally distributed resident where suitable woodland cover was available, although scarce in Orkney and extreme N. Scotland; but with the advent of toxic agricultural chemicals it decreased markedly during 1955–64 in most areas, almost disappearing from much of S.E. and central England. Following restrictions on chemicals, the population had recovered by the mid-1980s, to an estimated total of 20,000 pairs. In Ireland it breeds in every county. Our birds seem sedentary, but continental visitors appear on passage on the east coast from mid-September to mid-November and again in March and April. The race concerned, *Accipiter nisus nisus*, breeds in Europe from the Mediterranean northwards, also in W. Asia. Other races occur in N.W. Africa and central and E. Asia.

BUZZARD—*Buteo buteo*

BIRD PLATE 29   EGG PLATE XI (1A & 1B)

In the field the most characteristic feature of Buzzard is its majestic *soaring flight*, as it sweeps round in wide spirals with *broad rounded wings held straight and slightly above horizontal, and the broad, slightly rounded tail expanded.* The tips of the upward curved primaries are separated like fingers. The head does not extend far beyond the front border of the wings. At rest its size, robust build, dark brown upper-parts, and under-parts mottled

BUZZARD

Various flight attitudes.

and barred or streaked with brown and white are good characters. The amount of white on the under-parts varies considerably, as does the pattern of under-wing as seen in flight. In some a dark patch in the carpal region is fairly well-defined, but not as pronounced as is usual in Rough-legged Buzzard; only exceptional examples appear as pale below as that species, and lack of white in the tail is normally a reliable distinction. Length about 20–22 ins.

Habitat. Purely agricultural country with trees, or part moorland and part agricultural, supports denser population than moorland or forest. It is however widespread in uncultivated hilly and mountainous districts, and forests, and in the neighbourhood of rocky coasts in rather barren areas.

General Habits. In soaring it will often rise to great heights with scarcely a perceptible wing movement. In contrast to this, direct flight, especially when the bird is flushed, is slow and heavy with rather laboured flapping. Prey is seized on the ground by a sudden pounce as the bird hunts comparatively low down over open country. Sometimes it hovers for brief periods with considerable persistence while hunting, though it has not the lightness and grace of Kestrel. Where common it is not unusual to see half-a-dozen or more on the wing together.

Ordinary cry is a prolonged, plaintive, mewing "peeioo".

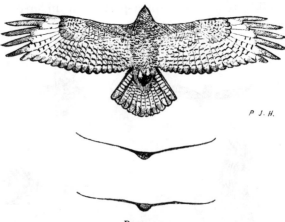

P J. H.

BUZZARD

Overhead, soaring. Head-on views: (*upper*) soaring when wings are held in shallow V; (*lower*) gliding when wing-tips although lower remain somewhat above body level.

Food is chiefly smaller mammals, especially rabbits, also carrion, occasionally birds and earthworms. Some reptiles, molluscs, insects and berries also recorded.

Nests chiefly in trees, or sometimes on a ledge of sea-cliff, but in hilly districts frequently on low bluffs or on the ground on broken hillsides, sheltered by bushes. The eggs, normally 2–3, rarely 1–5, white or bluish-white, sometimes almost unmarked, sometimes heavily marked with red and chocolate-brown. They are laid generally in April or early May in a bulky nest built of boughs or heather stalks, lined with bracken, moss, bark, grass, rushes, and on the coast seaweed; the interior decorated, apparently by female, with freshly plucked sprays of pine, ivy, birch, wood-rush, red and green seaweeds, fern, etc., regularly renewed. Incubation is by both sexes for up to 34–38 days. The young are fed by both parents and fly when 6 or 7 weeks old. Single-brooded.

Status and Distribution. A resident which has greatly increased and spread since 1900 and by 1954 had become the commonest bird of prey in much of its range with an estimated total of about 12,000 pairs. It then bred in most counties of England, Wales and Scotland except those lying east of a line from .London to Edinburgh; density was highest in S.W. England, Wales and W. Scotland from Kintyre to Skye, and numbers were still considerable east to the New Forest, Worcester, in N.W. England and most of Scotland north of the Tay including Outer Hebrides but not Shetland. Numbers fell after 1954, following decimation of rabbits through myxomatosis, but have since recovered. It may occur as a vagrant at any time of year outside breeding areas, and is an irregular autumn migrant on the east coast. In Ireland it was exterminated by the end of last century, but has been breeding again in the north since the 1950s. Our birds belong to the race *Buteo buteo buteo* which breeds from about the Arctic Circle in Norway south to the Mediterranean and into Asia Minor. One or two examples have occurred in England of the race *Buteo buteo vulpinus* which breeds from Sweden, Poland, Bulgaria east into Asia; it tends to be more rufous than our bird, especially in the tail. Other races occur in the Azores, Madeira, Canaries, Corsica, Sardinia and from W. Siberia to Japan.

ROUGH-LEGGED BUZZARD—*Buteo lagopus*

BIRD PLATE 29

A trifle larger than Buzzard, with noticeably *longer, narrower wings and tail*. The plumage is variable, but the commonest type is white or whitish on the head, underparts and underwings, with a blackish belly-patch and *well-defined black patches under the carpal joints*. Viewed from above the *tail is white with a broad blackish terminal band*. Immature birds are less well-marked, and occasional pale Buzzards can confuse the unwary, but experienced observers can separate these species by shape alone. When settled, the *feathered tarsi* can sometimes be discerned. It is much more addicted to hovering than Buzzard, suggesting a gigantic, ponderous Kestrel but with much slower wing action. Length about 20–24 ins.

Habitat. Outside the breeding-season it keeps chiefly to open country, haunting marshes, moors, downs and hill country, heaths, sand-dunes and the like.

General Habits. In winter it generally prefers a post or an eminence on the ground to trees as a perch.

Note resembles that of Buzzard, but is in general louder and lower-pitched.

Food in winter is chiefly rabbits; often also brown rats and occasionally voles.

Status and Distribution. A winter-visitor, usually scarce, and rarely arriving before October and leaving from March to May. It occurs most years on the northern isles and E. coast of Scotland

P.J.H.

ROUGH-LEGGED BUZZARD

Overhead, soaring.

Note large black carpal patches, blackish belly and tail-band.

and England as far south as Suffolk. It is also fairly frequent along the Pennine Chain, is rare in S.E. England, and only an occasional vagrant elsewhere including Ireland. The race *Buteo lagopus lagopus* breeds from Scandinavia east to the Urals. Other races occur in N. Asia and N. Canada.

SPOTTED EAGLE—*Aquila clanga*

BIRD PLATE 27

A dark purplish-brown eagle, rather smaller than Golden Eagle but with proportionately broader wings and a *short, slightly wedge-shaped tail*. It is unspotted when adult. In immature plumage it is strongly marked with *broad whitish or buff spots* which on the wing form two or three slightly broken but distinct lines giving a banded effect; a white patch at the base of the tail. Length about 26–29 ins.

Habitat. It frequents chiefly the neighbourhood of water or marshes.

General Habits. Head projects in flight in typical eagle manner, but flight is heavy and laboured; seldom soars. Wings characteristically *droop down* in gliding flight, and tips of primaries sometimes bend down, not up as in most birds of prey. It perches chiefly on trees, and is rather like White-tailed Eagle in habits.

Note resembles the barking of a high-voiced small dog.

Food is mainly frogs, but reptiles and at times fish, birds, small mammals and carrion are also included.

SPOTTED EAGLE

1st year immature overhead, gliding; and head-on view gliding, when wings droop noticeably (similar when soaring).

Status and Distribution. A very rare vagrant in England, and reported once or twice from Scotland and Ireland. It has nearly always occurred in winter or autumn. It breeds from Finland south to Jugoslavia and eastwards through Siberia. There are no subspecies.

GOLDEN EAGLE—*Aquila chrysaetos*

BIRD PLATE 30   EGG PLATE XII (1A & 1B)

The flight and outline in the air, with broad wings and widespread, upward-curving primaries, recall those of Buzzard. At a distance the much greater size is not always apparent, but *the head of Eagle projects farther beyond the front border of the wings, and both wings and tail are relatively rather longer*, while an occasional downward stroke of the wings interrupting for a moment the majestic soaring flight conveys, even at long range, an impression of immense power peculiar to this and other raptors of comparable size. At closer range size alone is a sufficient distinction and the much more powerful bill gives a different outline to the head. The plumage is dark, varying in adults from almost uniform tawny to chocolate-brown, with *a tinge of yellowish on the head. Young birds have the tail white, with a broad black band at the end and white bases to secondaries and inner primaries*, and are not infrequently

GOLDEN EAGLE

Adult overhead, gliding: and head-on view to show the substantially horizontal set of the wings when gliding (shallow V when soaring).

GOLDEN EAGLE

| Adult gliding. | Immature sailing. | Hunting. |

confused with White-tailed Eagle, from which, however, the longer squarer tail distinguishes Golden Eagle at all ages. Length about 30–35 ins.

Habitat. It haunts wild and barren mountainous tracts, more rarely forested country in mountains and occasionally sea-cliffs.

General Habits. The wing-beats are regular, leisurely, and powerful, but it may glide for long stretches with no perceptible movement of wings, and frequently soars to great heights. When soaring, wings are raised in a slight V, like Buzzard's. It perches on crags or trees, and often has favourite places where it will sit immobile for hours. When hunting it beats over the hillsides low down or comparatively so, flying down its quarry in a swift rush or swooping to seize it from the ground. It is usually seen singly, but pairs will hunt in company in winter. The young remain with their parents until winter.

Usually a silent bird, but it has a thin, shrill yelp, rarely heard near the nest, and a whistling, Buzzard-like alarm note "twee-o"; also barking cries.

Food consists largely of blue hares, Red Grouse and Ptarmigan. Other birds and mammals, including young lambs, also carrion, are taken at times.

Nests frequently on a ledge of cliff, exceptionally on the ground among boulders, and sometimes in trees, generally Scots pine.

The same nest may be used for many years, but alternately used sites, when available, are more frequent. The eggs normally number 2, occasionally 1 or 3, and one of them is often white or nearly so, others so heavily marked with various shades of red-brown and ash-grey that little white is visible. They are laid generally in early April in a bulky nest built by both sexes and added to throughout the breeding-season. The foundation is of branches, heather stems or bracken and the lining includes dead grass, decorated with wood-rush, fern or green pine branches. Incubation is almost entirely by hen, for about 6 weeks. The young are fed by both parents and do not fly until at least 11 weeks old. Single-brooded.

Status and Distribution. Resident (with rather more than 400 pairs in 1982, about half of which bred successfully) in Scotland in the Highlands, Inner and Outer Hebrides and in very small numbers in the south-west; a very scarce visitor elsewhere. In Ireland it became exterminated about 1910, but bred again in Antrim from 1953 to 1960. A pair has frequented the Lake District for several years recently, but otherwise in England and Wales it is a very rare vagrant, hardly ever found south of Yorkshire. Abroad the race concerned, *Aquila chrysaetos chrysaetos*, breeds from N. Norway south to the Pyrenees and west into Asia. Other races occur in the Iberian peninsula, N.W. Africa, parts of Asia and in N. America.

P.J.H.

GOLDEN EAGLE

Immature soaring.

Note great amount of white in wings and tail.

OSPREY—*Pandion haliaetus*

BIRD PLATE 27

Constant association with water and the *contrast of dark brown upper-parts with white under-parts and the whitish head with a broad dark band on the side* are characteristic of Osprey. Wings are long and narrow, *distinctly angled in ordinary flight*. Much of the underwing is whitish, with most flight-feathers narrowly barred dark brown and white, a black mark in the carpal region and blackish wing-tips. Tail is of medium length, rather narrow. It has a light brown pectoral band and the feathers of the back of crown somewhat elongated as a kind of crest. Immature birds have light tips to the feathers of the upper-parts. Length about 20–23 ins.

Habitat. It always frequents the neighbourhood of water. In the breeding-season it is confined inland to lakes or rivers in the neighbourhood of woods, and on the coast mainly to districts with suitable cliffs for nesting.

General Habits. In fishing it usually flies 30–100 ft. above water with alternate flapping and gliding, and on sighting a fish hovers for a moment before plunging. It sometimes snatches fish from the surface without preliminary hover and plunge. As a perch it likes a dead or bare bough of a tree or a post in the water; also

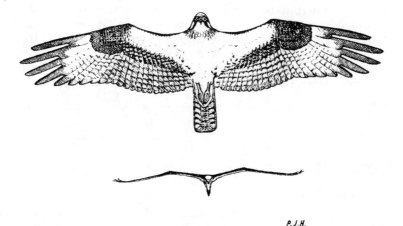

P.J.H.

OSPREY

Adult overhead; and carrying fish. In head-on view note the pronounced kink at carpal joint.

rocks. In soaring, the wings are less flexed than in ordinary flight, but more so than in Buzzard, which also differs by raising its wings in a shallow V.

Ordinary note is short, shrill musical whistle repeated a number of times "tchip-tchip-tchip . . .".

Food is almost entirely fish.

Nests mainly on rocky islets, and sometimes in pines. The eggs, 2–3, exceptionally 4, are boldly blotched and spotted with deep chocolate or red-brown and ashy shell-marks on a white ground. They are laid generally in late April or early May in a nest which is often of considerable size, being added to year after year; it is built by both sexes, of sticks, heather-stems, seaweed, bones, moss or almost any material available, and lined with grasses and finer materials, with a feather or two. Incubation is chiefly by hen for about 36 days. The young are mainly fed by the hen on food provided by male, and fly when about 7½–10 weeks old. Single-brooded.

Status and Distribution. A rare but regular passage-migrant in England occurring every year on some part of the coast or on inland waters, but most regularly in Norfolk, in September or October and April or May, and sometimes in summer, rarely winter. In Scotland after an interval of nearly half a century the bird nested again in Inverness in 1954, and regularly from 1959; by 1984 the population exceeded 30 pairs. A very few occur fairly regularly on passage in S. and central Scotland, and Orkney and Shetland but the bird is very rare on the west coast or west Highland lochs. It occurs rarely in Wales and Ireland. The race concerned, *Pandion haliaetus haliaetus*, breeds from N. Scandinavia to the N. African coast and in Asia. N. European birds winter south to tropical Africa. Other races occur in N. America, Malaysia and Australia.

LESSER KESTREL—*Falco naumanni*

BIRD PLATE 34

It closely resembles common Kestrel. Male is rather smaller and more delicately built than Kestrel and more brightly coloured, with a *richer red and unspotted mantle* and the head and tail often looking almost blue in sunlight; it also has a large, bluish area on the secondaries. The black tail-band is appreciably wider than

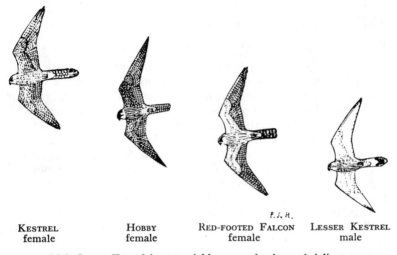

P. J. H.

| KESTREL | HOBBY | RED-FOOTED FALCON | LESSER KESTREL |
| female | female | female | male |

Male Lesser Kestrel is appreciably more slender and delicate
than Kestrel and its wings flash white even from a distance.

Kestrel's. Female closely resembles Kestrel in plumage, but is
noticeably slimmer, with rapid wing-beats and a longer, more
tapering and very thin tail. A further character common to both
sexes is the usually whitish colour of the claws, but this requires
closer observation than is generally possible. Length about 12 ins.

Habitat. In the breeding-season it frequents especially the
vicinity of old buildings and ruins, often in towns and villages, as
well as sometimes that of cliffs, hunting over any sort of open
country.

General Habits. Apart from its gregariousness which is not of
significance in this country, its habits hardly differ from those of
Kestrel except that it hovers much less and is more addicted to
almost Swallow-like hawking after insects in the air.

The commonest note is a chattering "kik-kik-kik-kik", higher
pitched and much more frequently uttered than Kestrel's.

Food is largely insects.

Status and Distribution. A very rare vagrant in England, also
recorded from Scotland and Ireland. It has occurred a few times
in October and November but mainly in spring from February
to May. The breeding range of this race, *Falco naumanni
naumanni*, is in N.W. Africa, Mediterranean Europe north to
central Spain, S. France, Hungary and Romania, and in Asia east
to Iran. It winters in tropical and S. Africa. Another race extends
from S.E. Russia to China.

KESTREL—*Falco tinnunculus*

BIRD PLATE 33   EGG PLATE XI (2A & 2B)

Habitual *hovering* is Kestrel's most distinctive feature. Also characteristic is the coloration of the male with *black-spotted chestnut upper-parts, and bluish-grey head, rump and tail, the last with a black subterminal band.* Under-parts are buff with dark streaks and markings; the quills mainly blackish. The head is more or less tinged brown in young birds. Colours of the female are less striking, being *rufous-brown with blackish barrings above, paler below with dark streaks; tail barred.* In addition, the pointed wings distinguish it from Sparrowhawk, which it resembles in having a rather long tail. Length about 13–14 ins.

Habitat. It inhabits a wide variety of country ranging from well-timbered cultivated districts and open woodlands to bare moors, marshes, hill country and rocky coasts; also the vicinity of old buildings, ruins, etc., and even large towns.

General Habits. It perches on trees, overhead wires, build-ings, rocks, etc. Flight is more leisurely than Hobby or Merlin, with rapid wing-beats and an occasional short glide usually about 20–30 ft. up, and well out in the open, not skulking along hedgerows, etc., within a few feet of the ground like Sparrow-hawk. Its course is constantly checked while the bird hovers, scanning the ground below for some quarry on which to drop. It will sometimes use a post as look-out, from which it flies down on insects, etc., and will also capture insects on the wing.

Usual cry is a loud, shrill "kee-kee-kee", with some variation in form and pitch, but it is rather silent away from breeding places.

Food. Mice and voles and other small mammals; insects, small birds, worms, etc., are also taken.

Nests on a ledge of cliff, often sheltered by ivy; in wooded districts in old nests of Crow or Magpie or other species; occasionally in a hollow tree, or recess in ruins, or buildings. The eggs, usually 4–5, rarely 7, have the white ground colour often quite hidden by dark red-brown markings; sometimes with mark-ings quite pale yellowish brown. They are laid generally from mid-April onwards, in a scrape, etc., to which no nesting material is added. Incubation is mainly by female for about 27–29 days. The young are fed by both sexes and fly when about 27–30 days old. Single-brooded.

Status and Distribution. Present throughout the year and generally distributed; it suffered only slightly from pesticides, and in 1984 the population was regarded as stable at about 70,000 pairs. Is only a passage migrant in Shetland, and is much scarcer in winter than summer in N. Scotland and N. and E. Ireland. Few British birds appear to leave the country in winter, but Continental migrants arrive from August to November and return from mid-March to May. The race concerned, *Falco tinnunculus tinnunculus*, breeds from N. Scandinavia south to N. Africa and in Asia east to Mongolia. Other races occur elsewhere in Africa and Asia.

RED-FOOTED FALCON—*Falco vespertinus*

BIRD PLATE 33

In size, shape, and flight it is very like Hobby, but is rather more finely built. *Male is dark slate-grey*, slightly paler below with *vent and under tail-coverts chestnut*; the legs, cere, and round the eye are orange-red. The less distinctive female shows *crown, nape, and under-parts rufous-buff* with forehead, throat, and sides of the face paler, blackish round the eye, and upper-parts slate-grey barred darker. Young birds are something like female, but with more rufous upper-parts, and under-parts paler with broad brown streaks; nape sometimes whitish; legs yellow. The wings reach nearly to the tip of the tail and young are much like young Hobbies, but differ in having less boldly marked under-parts, with brown, not black, markings, pale forehead, and paler upper-parts with more definite light bars especially on the tail. Length about 11–12 ins.

Habitat. In the breeding-season it chiefly frequents plains and steppe country with scattered groves and clumps of trees,

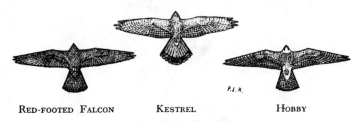

RED-FOOTED FALCON   KESTREL   HOBBY

Males soaring.

Kestrel's wings are held further forward, Hobby's (and to lesser extent Red-footed's) are more angled.

meadows with scattered bushes, and borders of forest within reach of open ground. It often occurs near farms and habitations.

General Habits. It hovers like Kestrel, but not so persistently, and usually hunts in fairly open ground. In addition it will dart down to seize prey on the ground from some look-out, such as a tree-top, telegraph wires, fence or bushes, on which it often perches, as it does freely on the ground. When hawking insects in the air both shape and flight suggest Hobby but the wings of Red-footed are a little broader at base. It is rather markedly crepuscular, frequently hunting late in the evening.

Note is much like Kestrel, but slightly sharper.

Food is mainly insects; frogs, lizards, and small mammals also recorded.

Status and Distribution. Occurs annually in England chiefly in the east and south; rarer in Scotland and very rare in Ireland. Most occurrences have been in May, several in June and April, and occasionally in autumn. Abroad the race concerned, *Falco vespertinus vespertinus*, breeds in E. Europe north to S. Austria and Estonia and in W. Asia, wintering in tropical and S. Africa. Another race occurs in E. Asia.

MERLIN—*Falco columbarius*

Bird Plate 33   Egg Plate XI (4)

The small size of male, which is not much larger than Mistle Thrush, alone precludes confusion with other falcons. *Upperparts are slate-blue, the nape and under-parts warm, often rufous,*

P.J.H.

MERLIN

Stooping

buff, the latter with dark streaks; the tail has a broad black band, and the bird lacks a moustachial stripe. The larger female might be confused with hen Kestrel, but is more compact-looking, with *shorter tail, upper-parts dark brown, not reddish-brown, and the brown-streaked under-parts whitish*, instead of pinkish-buff. The flight is also quite different, being buoyant, impetuous and dashing, with quick, winnowing wing-beats and occasional intervals of gliding, often with noticeable dips and swerves, and commonly close to the ground. Apart from colour differences, the less narrow and pointed wings distinguish it from Hobby. Young resemble female. Length about 10½–13 ins.

Habitat. In the breeding-season it frequents moors and hill country, bogs, heathy brows above sea-cliffs, and coastal sand-dunes. At other times it resorts also to marshes, low-lying coasts, and open country generally.

General Habits. It perches on boulders, walls, fences, etc., and on bare patches on the ground, and such sites near the nest are used as plucking-places. It will also perch on trees. In hunting it flies low, capturing birds by swift pursuit and rising above them in order to strike. Prey is also occasionally taken from the ground, and moths or other insects occasionally hawked. It sometimes hovers.

Usual cry when nesting-ground is invaded is a rapid, shrill, grating chatter "quik-ik-ik-ik . . .".

Food consists of small birds, occasionally insects and small mammals.

Nests on the ground among heather; but in cliffs and when breeding in trees the old nests of Carrion or Hooded Crow are usually annexed. The eggs, usually 4, sometimes 3–6, are normally thickly stippled with purplish-brown, exceptionally showing much light ground, with only pale markings or rich red. They are laid generally in May in a scrape or with an apology for a nest in the shape of a few heather stalks, bits of moss, and lining of bents. Incubation is by both sexes for about 28–32 days. The young are mainly fed by the female with prey caught by the male; they fly when about 25–27 days old. Single-brooded.

Status and Distribution. Present throughout the year. It breeds in many parts of Wales, the Pennine Range and other moors in N. England and in Scotland and Ireland in suitable localities; also very thinly on Exmoor and Dartmoor. There has been widespread, continuing decrease since 1950. To breeding areas on higher ground Merlins are summer-visitors, dispersing in autumn and becoming much more widely distributed. Numbers are augmented by continental migrants and birds from Iceland of the race *Falco columbarius subaesalon*, which arrive from mid-August to mid-November and return in April and May. Our birds belong to the race *Falco columbarius aesalon* which breeds in most of Europe from the Baltic northwards. An example of the N. American race *Falco columbarius columbarius* has occurred in Outer Hebrides. Other races occur in N.E. Russia and N. Asia.

HOBBY—*Falco subbuteo*

BIRD PLATE 32   EGG PLATE XI (6)

Hobby is the most graceful and agile of British falcons; in size approximately as Kestrel, but with *long, scythe-like wings, a comparatively short tail and Peregrine-like flight*, consisting of a rapid winnowing alternating with glides on extended wings. At medium range the *dark slaty upper-parts, white on side of neck, broad black moustachial stripe, white under-parts with conspicuous black streaks, and rusty-red thighs and under tail-coverts* are characteristic. Young are browner above, but very dark, with under-parts more buff and more heavily streaked, and without red on the thighs and under the tail. See also Red-footed Falcon. Length about 12–14 ins.

Habitat. In the breeding-season it frequents downlands, heaths, and undulating country with scattered clumps and belts of trees, especially pines, the outskirts or open parts of woodland, and agricultural country well supplied with hedgerow timber.

General Habits. It displays marvellous mastery and speed of

P.J.H.

HOBBY

Catching flying insects.

HOBBY

Pursuing House Martins.

flight, and is well capable of capturing even such rapid fliers as Swifts on the wing. In hunting birds it employs on occasions all the tactics of Peregrine, viz., the stoop, pursuit and capture without stoop, or seizure from below, but it will also dash straight through a flock of hirundines, seizing one in passing without any abatement of speed. Unlike Peregrine it feeds very largely on flying insects which are seized with claws and held to the beak while eaten. It hunts chiefly over open country, frequently where there are scattered trees and copses, but keeping clear of closed woodland, and it sometimes hovers for a few seconds. It often remains active till well after twilight. Pairs indulge in long soaring flights, also perform spectacular and wild aerobatics, and during the breeding-season the male not uncommonly passes food to the female on the wing. It ordinarily perches in trees.

The usual note is a clear repeated "kew-kew-kew-kew-kew" very variable both in form and timbre.

Food consists almost entirely of small birds and insects.

Nests mostly in pines in the southern counties, but in the Midlands commonly in deciduous trees, taking possession of an unoccupied nest usually of Carrion Crow, but occasionally of Rook, Sparrowhawk or other bird, or squirrel; it does not build its own. The eggs, normally 3, sometimes 2–4, are on average much paler than Merlin's or Kestrel's. They are laid generally about mid-June. Incubation is chiefly by female for about 28 days. The young are fed by both parents and fly when about 28–32 days old. Single-brooded.

Status and Distribution. A summer-visitor from the second half of April until September, very rarely winter. Numbers in England appear to remain rather stable, in the region of 200 pairs. The main concentration is from Sussex to Dorset and north to Oxfordshire; some pairs are also regular in most counties fringing this area, and breeding occurs at least at times west to Cornwall and Wales, north to Yorks, and very rarely in Norfolk. Little more than a vagrant in Scotland, and has occurred several times in Ireland. In Europe this race, *Falco subbuteo subbuteo*, breeds from the Mediterranean northwards, reaching the Arctic Circle in Sweden, and it extends to central Asia. Other races occur in E. Asia, Africa, S. America and Australia. Our birds winter in Africa.

GYR FALCON—*Falco rusticolus*

BIRD PLATE 32

The Gyr Falcon, Iceland Falcon and Greenland Falcon are geographical races of one species *Falco rusticolus*, although they are generally sufficiently distinct from each other to have earned separate English names. Gyr Falcons are *larger, more uniform-looking and generally paler birds than Peregrine, with the moustachial stripe obscure or lacking*. In the air it appears more angular than Peregrine, with *longer, less tapering, tail*, broader wings with the carpal joint relatively further from the body, and slower wing-beats. At rest wings fall well short of tail (see sketch p. 139). The Gyr Falcon is the darkest of the three races of this species recorded in the British Isles, and has on the upper-parts a broadly blotched and barred pattern of dark and light grey, under-parts whitish with blackish streaks, flanks barred. Iceland Falcon typically is larger than Gyr Falcon and paler especially on the head which is whitish and has no moustachial stripe; a typical Greenland Falcon, being pure white with black markings, can hardly be confused with any other bird. However, between the darkest and palest forms of these falcons, all intermediates occur. Young birds are browner and particularly difficult to separate. Length about 20–24 ins.

Habitat. It frequents open wild country in the vicinity of cliffs and rocky fells, sometimes inland but in this country chiefly coastal.

GYR FALCON

In flight overhead. Male in plumage most like immature Peregrine but note palish area on primaries.

General Habits. General habits are like Peregrine, but it usually hunts low over the ground in the manner of a Merlin.

It is a decidedly silent bird outside the breeding-season.

Food consists of birds of many species, especially Ptarmigan, and mammals to the size of rabbit and hare.

Status and Distribution. The Greenland Falcon, *Falco rusticolus candicans*, which breeds in Greenland and arctic Canada, is the race that has occurred least rarely here, being an irregular winter- and spring-visitor chiefly in the Scottish islands, also the mainland of Scotland, occasionally Ireland and N. England, and very rarely elsewhere; the Iceland Falcon, *Falco rusticolus islandus*, breeding in Iceland, is a rare vagrant which has been recorded generally in winter, in a number of localities from Shetland to the Scilly Islands, also in N. and W. Ireland; the Gyr Falcon, *Falco rusticolus rusticolus*, breeding in Scandinavia and arctic Europe, is a very rare vagrant which has not been identified here for about a century. Other races occur in N. Asia and N. America.

PEREGRINE—*Falco peregrinus*

Bird Plate 32   Egg Plate XI (3A & 3B)

Falcons are characterized by quick dashing flight and pointed wings. The Peregrine, the largest British breeding falcon, is a compact, robust-looking bird on the wing with *long sharply pointed wings, and a medium-length, rather tapering tail*. It has a very characteristic flight, swift and direct, with a *few rapid, winnowing beats alternating with a long glide on extended wings*;

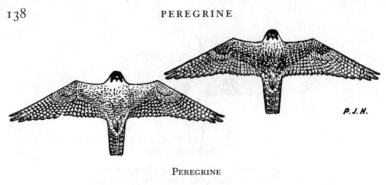

PEREGRINE

Adult   Immature

In flight overhead. Note different wing proportions between
Peregrine and Gyr Falcon, and shorter tail of Peregrine.

the action often not unlike that of a pigeon. At rest the dark
blue-grey upper-parts, with crown and sides of head and well-
marked moustachial stripe almost black, and buffy-white under-
parts barred black, are distinctive. The female is larger and usually
darker. Young birds are browner above, with under-parts
streaked, not barred. Length about 15–19 ins.

Habitat. It occurs chiefly in open, more or less treeless country.
In the breeding-season it frequents the vicinity of coastal or inland
cliffs, moors and mountain-sides; also locally more cultivated or
wooded country inland where suitable nesting-sites are available.
Outside breeding-season it ranges more widely, occurring in
almost any part of the country about estuaries, marshes, and open
country generally, and at times even in tolerably well-wooded
localities or built-up areas.

General Habits. Perches chiefly on rocks, commonly on some
ledge or pinnacle of a cliff, in an upright attitude with head sunk
between the shoulders. Peregrine typically strikes down its prey by
a magnificent headlong stoop at almost incredible speed, with
wings folded. Occasionally it will hover for a few seconds. It has
usually special plucking places to which the prey is carried. When
nesting, and especially when the young are small, the tiercel does
most of the hunting and passes food to the hen in the air, having
called her off the nest. She may take the prey from his feet or catch
it in mid-air after male has dropped it.

Usually silent outside the breeding-season, but often very noisy
when the breeding-place is invaded. Main cries are a shrill,
chattering "kek-kek-kek-kek . . ." and a hoarse, almost quacking
"kwaahk-kwaahk-kwaahk . . ." of more intense excitement.

PEREGRINE

Various flight attitudes.

Food is chiefly birds taken on the wing, especially pigeons and sea birds. Some mammals up to the size of rabbit are also taken.

Nests normally on a ledge or hole in a cliff, but at times annexes an old nest of Raven or other bird. The eggs, usually 3–4, sometimes 2–5, varying in ground-colour from orange-tawny to deep red, are laid generally in April in a bare scrape, no nesting material being used. Incubation is by both sexes for about 28–29 days. The young are tended by both parents and fly when 5 or 6 weeks old. Single-brooded.

Status and Distribution. Present throughout the year. In 1956 the population of Britain and Ireland was estimated at 650–750 breeding pairs, chiefly coastal in S. and S.W. England, but more widespread in Wales, N. England, Scotland and Ireland. During the next few years a drastic decline occurred, for which poisonous agricultural chemicals were responsible and by 1963 there remained only about one-tenth of the former breeding population in

GYR FALCON

female intermediate phase

GYR FALCON

male white phase

Peregrine

male

Note Gyr's (especially female) wing tips fall short of tail-end, and its leg feathering is baggier than Peregrine's.

Great Britain and one-third in Ireland; the Scottish Highlands were least affected. Recovery followed restrictions on chemicals, and by 1984 numbers were thought to be up to about 800 pairs, and still increasing. In autumn Scandinavian birds pass through on migration, while in winter our residents may wander inland. The race concerned, *Falco peregrinus peregrinus*, breeds over most of Europe from the Arctic Ocean southwards; other races occur in the Mediterranean region and in Asia, Africa, America and Australia. Two examples have been recorded in England of N. American race *Falco peregrinus anatum*, which is inseparable in the field except perhaps in its very dark immature plumage.

RED GROUSE—*Lagopus lagopus*

Bird Plate 35   Egg Plate X (7)

The characteristic game-bird of open moorlands, recognized by its *dark red-brown coloration*, which may look almost black at a distance, and when visible, by its whitish feathered legs, which together with smaller size, redder plumage and unforked tail distinguish it from Greyhen. Wing-quills and tail are blackish; red wattle above the eye is larger than in other grouse. The winter plumage of the male is red-brown with fine black barrings; summer plumage is paler, less red. Female in winter is much like male in summer, while the summer plumage is yellower. Juvenile is

RED GROUSE
female

BLACK GROUSE
female

Note Greyhen's forked tail and slight wing bars.

much like female in summer. Length: male about 14–15½ ins., female about 13–14 ins.

Habitat. Principal haunts are upland moors and lower-lying peat-bogs or mosses where heather and other heaths dominate the vegetation, but it also flourishes on grassy and rushy tracts, especially those where crowberry grows. In autumn numbers may occasionally visit stubble-fields on lower ground.

General Habits. Generally seen as it rises from heather with a whirr and travels with strong and swift, but deliberate flight close to the ground, rapid wing-beats alternating with long glides on bowed wings. In severe weather it will pitch on trees and bushes to feed on berries and will burrow into snow for food. In autumn and winter it forms into flocks or "packs", generally with a large predominance of one sex.

The usual note when flushed is a cackling "kowk, kok-ok-ok-ok . . .", with variations. Crowing, normally associated with display flights, ends after alighting with "go-bak, go-bak-bak-bak-bak".

Food is mainly vegetable, predominantly shoots, flowers and seed-heads of heather or ling. It also eats other shoots, buds and berries and in autumn takes cereals. Young chicks feed predominantly on insects.

Nests on the ground usually sheltered by heather, rushes or a tussock. The eggs, usually 6–11, occasionally 4–17, are laid generally in the second half of April or early May, in a hollow scraped by female, sometimes scantily lined. Incubation is by female only, for about 21–26 days. The young are led away by female shortly after hatching, the male usually accompanying and guarding them. They can fly about the 12th or 13th day. Single-brooded.

Status and Distribution. A resident, which has declined considerably during the past 50 years. It breeds in, and west and north of, Carmarthen, Brecon, Monmouth, Hereford, Salop, Staffs, Derby, Yorks (except E. Riding), also by introduction on Dartmoor and Exmoor. It is generally distributed throughout Scotland, and widely but sparsely distributed in Ireland. In some districts many habitually shift from the most elevated moorlands to lower ones in winter; otherwise distribution is the same as in summer. The birds in Ireland and the Outer Hebrides belong to the race *Lagopus lagopus hibernicus*, and in the rest of Great Britain to the race *Lagopus lagopus scoticus*. Other races (Willow Grouse) occur across the northern parts of Europe, Asia and America.

PTARMIGAN—*Lagopus mutus*

Bird Plate 35   Egg Plate X (13)

A grouse-like bird of high mountains, unmistakable *in winter* on account of its *pure white plumage*, excepting the black tail tipped white and, in the male only, black lores; and *at other seasons* on account of its *white wings and under-parts*. It has distinct summer and autumn plumages. In autumn plumage the upper-parts, breast and flanks are grey finely barred and vermiculated with black; female is browner than male. In summer plumage the male has these same parts darker, browner and more coarsely marked, while the female is considerably yellower. Red wattle over the eye is much larger in cock than hen; legs feathered. Juveniles are not unlike summer adults, but have primaries blackish. Length about 13–14 ins.

Habitat. In summer it is found on barren ground of the alpine zone of higher mountains, with broken rocks and rock detritus and more or less scanty vegetation, generally from about 2,500 ft., but locally at about 2,000 ft. In winter it ordinarily remains at considerable elevations, but may be temporarily driven down to more sheltered corries by blizzards.

Ptarmigan

Summer plumage; the white wings are barely visible at rest.

General Habits. Flight is usually much like Grouse, but it will shoot up or down a precipice of several hundred feet without apparent effort. It crouches when uneasy, harmonizing beautifully with its surroundings, and is often reluctant to fly. Often extremely tame and approachable, at other times shy. It is fond of basking in sun and of dusting. In winter it will if necessary burrow into loose snow to get at food. Unmated males may flock together in the breeding-season and there is a tendency to gather into packs at other times, especially in winter.

Call of male (rarely female) on flushing is a belching "aar-aa-ka-ka", which may be followed by prolonged cackling. In display-flight the first syllable is omitted. Flight intention note "kuk-kuk-kuk". Female's contact note a sharp "kee-ah".

Food is almost entirely vegetable, shoots and leaves, also berries and seeds. Insects are occasionally taken.

Nests on stony ground or among plants of crowberry, short grass or heather, often sheltered by a rock. The eggs, normally 5–9, sometimes 3–12, are laid generally from the last week of May onwards, in a mere hollow scraped by female, sometimes scantily lined with grass, etc., added during the laying period. Incubation is by female only, for about 22–24 days, the male remaining nearby. The young, at first brooded by female and guarded by male, can fly about the 10th day. Single-brooded.

Status and Distribution. A resident on the high mountains of the Scottish mainland from Perth (perhaps Stirling) northwards, also a few in Mull, Skye, Arran and perhaps Jura. The race *Lagopus mutus millaisi* is confined to Scotland. Other races occur in the Arctic (including some islands) of Europe, Asia and America, in Europe extending south to the Alps and Pyrenees.

BLACK GROUSE—*Tetrao tetrix*

Bird Plate 34   Egg Plate X (12)

Male or Blackcock is unmistakable, *glossy black with a lyre-shaped tail and white wing-bar*. Under tail-coverts and a patch at the carpal joint of wing are white; it has a red wattle over the eye. Female or Greyhen is warm brown, freckled and barred black, larger and less ruddy than Red Grouse, smaller and *less richly and boldly barred* than Capercaillie, and unlike either it has a slight double white wing-bar and distinctly forked tail. In late summer

BLACK GROUSE, female.

RED GROUSE, female.

male develops for a short time a partial "eclipse" plumage with some dark mottling on the head, neck and mantle and some whitish on the throat. Juvenile is much like female, but smaller. Length: male about 20–22 ins.; female about 16–17 ins.

Habitat. It haunts fringes of moorland rather than open moors, resorting to rough, heather-grown or bushy land, sparsely wooded places and marshy ground; also lowland heaths, frequently, though not always, with scattered birches or other trees.

General Habits. Flight is of the regular game-bird type, strong and rapid, though usually maintained for a comparatively short distance, low in cover but on open moors often appreciably higher than Red Grouse, and the bird has a tendency to circle round on rising and before landing. On the ground its movements are usually slow and sedate. It perches freely on trees and usually roosts on the ground. Packs in autumn normally number about 10–25. The bird is polygamous, both sexes assembling at special display grounds or "leks" in the spring, and males visit them again in October.

The crowing note of male at the lek is a loud "to-wha" or "whushee", and the "song" is a musical bubbling dove-like sound often uttered in long continuous phrases. Away from the lek the male is usually silent. The note of the hen is a loud "tchuk-tchuk".

Food is mainly vegetable, in winter chiefly buds of birch and other trees. In summer it also eats leaves and shoots of ground vegetation, and seeds, berries and fruit; also some insects. Stubble fields are regularly frequented in autumn.

Nests usually on the ground in the shelter of grasses or heather, exceptionally in an old nest in a tree up to 20 ft. The eggs, usually 6–10, occasionally 5–13, are laid generally from mid-May onwards in a hollow scraped by female. Incubation is by female only, for about 24–29 days. The young are tended by female only, and fledge in 2 to 3 weeks. Single-brooded.

Status and Distribution. A resident which decreased markedly in late 19th and early 20th centuries in many parts. In S.W. England it is now confined to Devon and Somerset, is more numerous in Wales breeding in the north and centre south to Brecon. It also breeds from N. Staffs northwards in England. Widely distributed on the mainland of Scotland and some Inner Hebrides, but not Outer Hebrides, Orkney or Shetland. The race *Tetrao tetrix britannicus* is confined to Great Britain. Other races are found in Europe from the Arctic south to the Pyrenees, Alps, Balkans and Russia, also over large areas of north and central Asia.

CAPERCAILLIE—*Tetrao urogallus*

BIRD PLATE 34   EGG PLATE X (1)

Great size and dark colouring suffice to distinguish the male from other game-birds. The general colouring is dark slaty-grey with fine vermiculations at close range. The wing-coverts are warm dark brown, there is a white patch at the carpal joint, throat and sides of head are black, breast dark glossy blue-green, tail black with some white markings, upper tail-coverts with white tips, and the belly and under tail-coverts are marked with white. It has bright red skin over the eye; the bill is whitish, legs feathered. Female has plumage barred and mottled with buff, black and greyish-white, and is distinguished from Greyhen by *decidedly larger size, rufous patch on the breast, rounded, not forked tail*, bolder black barring of the upper-parts and lack of white wing-bar. Juvenile is much like adult female. Length: male about 33–35 ins.; female about 23–25 ins.

Habitat. It frequents mature coniferous woodland of medium density with a fair amount of undergrowth. In autumn, spring and winter numbers make local movements to low-lying woods of oak, birch and larch; in autumn it is sometimes found amongst heather at some distance from woods and also visits stubble-fields.

General Habits. Flight is of the regular game-bird type, a succession of quick wing-beats alternating with more or less prolonged glides with down-curved primaries; neck extended. It is noisy and flapping as it breaks out of cover, but silent, rapid and easy when under way; amongst trees it displays striking dexterity. It perches freely in trees especially in winter, when it also tends to be gregarious, but in summer and autumn female and young are found mainly on the ground. It is fond of dust-baths.

"Song" of male, feeble for the size of the bird and occurring in April and May, begins with notes sounding like the knocking together of two small sticks at intervals of 10–15 secs. at first, but getting quicker at the end, followed without break by a sound like the drawing of a cork and ending with one like grinding a knife. Apart from display calls the male is otherwise silent, but the female has a loud harsh note "kock-kock".

Food from October to April consists almost entirely of shoots and buds of conifers. During summer other vegetable food is taken including grass, clover-leaves, bracken-shoots, seeds, berries and fruits; also insect larvae.

Nests usually among ground-vegetation in forests, also in juniper scrub, etc., and sometimes in deep heather on open moor. The eggs, normally 5–8, sometimes 4–15, are laid generally from mid- or late April onwards, in a hollow scraped in the ground by female, usually at the foot of a tree; lining material is added during the egg-laying period. Incubation is by female only, for about 27–29 days. The young are tended by female only, and can flutter after 2 or 3 weeks. Single-brooded.

Status and Distribution. A resident which became extinct about the middle of the 18th century, and was reintroduced in the first half of the 19th century. It now breeds in the Tay, Dee and Moray areas as far north as Golspie, also in the Forth area, Stirling and Dunbarton. It has occurred in a number of other Scottish counties. The race *Tetrao urogallus urogallus* inhabits coniferous forests of north and central Europe from Norway to the Alps and Bulgaria, and N.W. Asia. Other races occur in N. Spain, Pyrenees, central Russia and Asia.

RED-LEGGED PARTRIDGE—*Alectoris rufa*

BIRD PLATE 36   EGG PLATE X (10)

It is rather larger than Grey Partridge and at some distance is easily confused with it, especially as it shows a similar rufous tail in flight. At close quarters, however, Red-legged is at once distinguished by *white cheeks and throat bordered by a black band, by flanks beautifully barred with black, white and chestnut, and by red bill and legs*. Other less striking differences are: the upperparts are uniform hair-brown shading to grey on front of crown, the breast and ground-colour of the barred flanks are lavender grey and the belly is warm buff; it has a white superciliary stripe, bordered by black below. The black border to white of throat starts at the base of the bill, passes through eye and, curving downwards, merges at the sides and below into a kind of gorget of black streaks and spots. The sexes are similar. Juvenile has none of the bright colours of the adults and is not unlike young Grey Partridge, but is spotted rather than streaked. Length about 13½ ins.

Habitat. Its choice of habitat is not sharply distinguished from that of Grey Partridge, but it frequents especially chalky and sandy heaths, down and open fields. Is also found on coastal shingle and occurs locally on heavy soils and even on moist rushy ground.

General Habits. These and behaviour are much like Grey Partridge, but this bird is more restless and nervous. Its movements on the ground are generally quicker than those of Partridge and it is even more addicted to running in preference to flight. Coveys are more inclined to scatter when disturbed instead of keeping together. It perches fairly frequently on fences, barns, etc., and in low trees, even amongst foliage.

Display-note is a remarkable sound, a deliberate, harsh "chucka chucka", with variations in detail. When running or taking flight a sharp "kuk-kuk".

Food is mainly vegetable, very similar to that of Grey Partridge.

Nests usually among herbage or sheltered by a bush. The eggs, usually 10–16, sometimes 7–20, are laid generally at the end of April or in May in a hollow scraped in the ground, scantily lined with dead leaves, grass, etc. Incubation is for about 23–24 days, but sometimes does not begin until several weeks after the eggs have been laid. Sometimes, perhaps often, two separate nests are made and two clutches laid which are then incubated simultaneously, one by the male and the other by the female, and hatch within a few days of each other. Each parent then usually tends its own brood independently. Single-brooded apart from double clutch laying.

Status and Distribution. A resident, which following introduction in Suffolk about 1770, and subsequently in many other places, is widespread in S. and E. England, north to N. Yorkshire and Shropshire, and scarcer in N. Wales, and west to Somerset; also Isle of Man. Many releases, and some breeding in the wild, have occurred in Scotland in recent years, from the border to Caithness. The race concerned, *Alectoris rufa rufa*, is a native of mid- and S. France, parts of Switzerland, N. and central Italy and Corsica. Other races occur in the Iberian peninsula and the Canaries.

Note. The recently introduced Chukar *Alectoris chukar* (which resembles Red-legged, but lacks streaks on breast below the black collar and has no black on lores) readily breeds with Red-legged, producing hybrids which are easily confused with Red-legged.

GREY PARTRIDGE—*Perdix perdix*

BIRD PLATE 36   EGG PLATE X (8)

It is easily recognized by its *rotund form, orange-brown head, vermiculated grey neck and under-parts, and chestnut-barred flanks*; and in flight by its *rufous tail* coupled with regular game-bird form and flight, comprising successions of quick wing-beats alternating with glides on bowed wings. For distinctions from Red-legged Partridge, with which alone it is likely to be confused, see that species. The back is brown streaked buff, the flanks have narrow whitish streaks in addition to the chestnut bars, the crown is duller brown than rest of the head and bordered greyish. There is a broad and prominent *horseshoe-shaped patch of dark chestnut* on the lower breast of male, usually little developed or almost absent in older females, but more prevalent in first-year birds. Juvenile lacks the orange-brown and chestnut, having streaked brown under-parts and neck, and is not unlike a young Pheasant, but is smaller, more streaked and with a shorter tail. Length about 12 ins.

Habitat. It is found principally in agricultural country, especially in corn-growing districts and on light soils, but avoids too intensive cultivation, requiring a certain amount of rough cover. It also occurs regularly on moorlands and heaths bordering on cultivation and to a less extent on hillsides (up to 2,000 ft.), heaths, marshes, and sand-dunes, etc., in almost uncultivated areas. It will also feed regularly on coastal shingle.

General Habits. Rises with a whirr of wings and flies swiftly and strongly but seldom far, usually low down, skimming over the hedges and trees. Gait is a walk or run. It ordinarily walks with rounded back and neck withdrawn, but assumes a more erect carriage with neck stretched up when suspicious or when running for cover. If alarmed it may crouch, when it is difficult to detect on bare ground. Does not normally perch. It is fond of dusting. Family parties keep together in coveys through the winter.

The chief note is a loud, hoarse "kar-wit, kar-wit" or "kirr-ic, kirr-ic", aptly compared to the sound of a rusty key turning in a lock.

Food is mainly vegetable, including green food, fruits, seeds and grain and in summer buds and flowers; animal matter consists largely of ants and other insects; also worms and slugs.

Nests in bottoms of hedgerows or under bushes, also in crops and grass. The eggs, usually 9–20, occasionally 8–23, are, exceptionally, whitish or bluish. They are laid generally at the end of April or early May in a hollow scraped in ground by female, sheltered by growing vegetation and lined with dry grasses and dead leaves. Incubation is by female for about 23–25 days. The young leave the nest soon after hatching. They are tended by both parents, begin to flutter when 10–11 days old and can fly at about 16 days. Single-brooded.

Status and Distribution. A resident, declining. Widespread in England, but absent from many parts of W. and S.W. Wales. Widespread too in Scotland north to Argyll in the west and to Dornoch Firth in the east, but local in parts of Sutherland and Caithness, and virtually absent from the islands. Few left in Ireland, mainly in the east. It does not migrate. Our birds belonged to the race *Perdix perdix perdix* which breeds in Europe from southern Scandinavia and Finland south to N.E. France, Switzerland and Balkans, but they are now hybrid through the introduction of other races which occur in S.W., central and E. Europe and in W. Asia.

QUAIL—*Coturnix coturnix*

Bird Plate 36   Egg Plate X (9)

In general appearance it is *much like a very small, delicately-built Partridge*, which it also resembles in flight if flushed, but its presence is more often detected by the *characteristic note of male* than by the bird being seen. The general effect is more sandy than in Grey Partridge. The upper-parts and flanks are strongly streaked pale buff, with some black barring, the breast is sandy with narrow pale streaks, spotted blackish in female but not in male. There is a buff streak down the centre of dark crown, and a buff superciliary stripe prolonged to the base of the neck. The throat of male is buffish-white with a blackish central stripe and two dark bands (sometimes only obscurely developed) curving up from the base of the throat to the ear-coverts; the throat of female lacks the central band and the others are only indicated. Juvenile is much like adult female. Length about 7 ins.

Habitat. It frequents chiefly rough tussocky grasslands, and fields of cereals and green crops, also stubble and weedy fallows, and in autumn root-fields.

General Habits. These and actions are Partridge-like. If flushed it flies low and for a short distance only, but it is reluctant to fly and in its regular haunts, with ample cover of grass or plants, is seldom put up except by dogs. Found in family parties or bevies in autumn and on migration, but is not otherwise notably gregarious.

Call of male is a liquid "quic, qui-ic" usually repeated several times. It is heard by night as well as day and usually from the latter half of May through June and July.

Food is probably similar to that of Grey Partridge.

Nests in crops or grass. The eggs, usually 7–12, sometimes 6–18, may be boldly blotched or sometimes thickly sprinkled with spots. They are laid in the latter half of May or in June, or later, in a hollow in the ground scraped by female, scantily lined with a few bits of grass or other herbage. Incubation is by female only, for about 16–21 days. Young leave the nest within a few hours of hatching, tended by female only, flutter when 11 days old and fly well at about 19 days. Normally single-brooded.

Status and Distribution. Normally a scarce summer-visitor, arriving between the last week of April and mid-June and leaving probably in September or October, occasionally recorded in winter. Numbers fluctuate greatly and in most areas breeding is irregular or sporadic, and hard to prove. It seems regular in southern and south-central England but may occur in almost any county. In Scotland it is similarly erratic, mainly in the south and east, rarely reaching Shetland; it is scarcer in Wales. In Ireland it used to breed in one or two areas in the east, but has not been regularly reported recently. This race *Coturnix coturnix coturnix* breeds in N. Africa, the Mediterranean, in Europe north almost to the Arctic Circle, and east to central Asia. Other races occur in E. Asia and Africa south of the Sahara. Our birds winter mainly in the Mediterranean area and N. tropical Africa.

PHEASANT—*Phasianus colchicus*

BIRD PLATE 37   EGG PLATE X (3)

The *long tail* is the outstanding feature in all circumstances, both of the burnished copper-coloured male, with his metallic dark green head and neck, red wattles surrounding the eye, and ear-like tufts at the back of crown, and of the more soberly plumaged brown female. Male has bold purple-black crescentic markings on breast and flanks, and black bars on the tail. Details of plumage vary but a white neck ring generally shows. Juvenile is not unlike adult female in plumage. Total length: adult male about 30–35 ins. (tail varying considerably, about 20 ins. in biggest birds); female about 21–25 ins. (tail about 8–10 ins.).

Habitat. It flourishes chiefly in partly cultivated and well-watered districts, especially on light soils, with thick plantations affording ample cover of long grass and other undergrowth, varied by open parkland or cultivation. Fond of feeding in damp, rushy fields.

General Habits. In spite of its largely artificial status in game-preserving districts the Pheasant is often a shy and wary bird. When disturbed it prefers to run for shelter rather than take flight, or may crouch in cover, but it flies fairly readily, with neck moderately extended and tail somewhat spread. Flight is rapid, direct and strong while it lasts, but is usually not long sustained, beginning with rapid wing-beats which give place to a glide. Essentially a terrestrial bird, getting its food on the ground, but it takes to trees to escape danger and, generally, for roosting purposes. Young, however, roost amongst cover on the ground until about October.

The usual call of male is a far-sounding, resonant "korrk-korrk" or "karrk-karrk", with variants. The female uses a peevish whistle when frightened or flushed.

Food is very varied. Vegetable matter includes roots, stems, leaves, fruits and seeds; animal matter includes insects, earthworms, slugs, snails. Lizards and field-voles are also recorded.

Nests on the ground, usually under cover of brambles, coarse grass or other herbage; exceptionally in such sites as a haystack or old Woodpigeon's nest. The eggs, usually 8–15, occasionally only 7, are normally uniform olive-brown but, exceptionally, pale blue. They are laid generally from early May onwards in a hollow scraped by female, carelessly lined with a few stems of grass, dead leaves, etc. Incubation is normally by female only, but exceptionally by male, for about 22–27 days. The young are fed

and tended by female only, and can fly after 12–14 days.
Single-brooded.

Status and Distribution. An introduced resident, probably
from Roman times, and generally distributed although local in
N.W. Scotland and Cornwall. It is scarce in Ireland in places
where it is not preserved but breeds in every county. Our birds are
of mixed stock and cannot be assigned to any one race. The species
breeds in a wild state in S.E. Russia and Asia and has been
introduced to most European countries, also N. America and New
Zealand.

WATER RAIL—*Rallus aquaticus*

Bird Plate 37   Egg Plate X (4)

More often heard than seen, the Water Rail most frequently
reveals its presence amongst cover of reed-beds and swampy places
by its very distinctive, discordant notes. If seen, the *long bill* alone
is sufficient to distinguish it from other rails and crakes, while the
*olive-brown upper-parts streaked black, the slate-grey breast,
throat and sides of head, and the flanks barred blackish and white*
confirm its identity. Under tail-coverts are whitish. Bill is red,
blackish towards the end and along culmen, duller in winter; legs
are brownish flesh-colour or inclining to olive. Often only seen as it
bolts into shelter with lowered head, but like all crakes and rails it
occasionally allows itself to be observed quite easily. Juvenile has
under-parts brownish with darker mottlings and barrings. Length
about 11 ins.

Habitat. It frequents reed-beds and swamps with ample cover
of coarse marsh plants, with or without trees and bushes of alder,
etc., and the swampy borders of rivers and ponds with similar
vegetation. Outside the breeding-season it also occurs on
overgrown or reedy banks of ditches or water-cress beds,
sewage-farms, etc., where it does not nest.

General Habits. Flight as usually seen is of a weak fluttering
character low down, with legs dangling, and lasting for a few
seconds only. It walks with a deliberate, rather high-stepping gait,
with head somewhat raised when undisturbed and the tail either
carried horizontally or somewhat depressed, or else cocked and
frequently jerked spasmodically upwards like Moorhen, especially
when nervously excited. Its slender body enables it to move with

ease amongst marsh vegetation, and it has a habit of standing motionless when suspicious. It will occasionally perch on low bushes, especially during frost. Swims readily for short distances near cover, with Moorhen-like action.

Its most distinctive note, by which an unseen bird frequently announces its presence, is a singular discordant noise generally beginning as a kind of grunting and ending as a squeal, rather reminiscent of the squealing of pigs, and sometimes rising to a regular scream. It has also a sharp "kik-kik-kik", often followed by a trill, which may be repeated with great persistence in spring at dusk and through much of the night.

Food is varied, including insects, spiders, crustacea, molluscs, worms and small fish. Vegetable food includes roots, grass, grain, seeds and berries.

Nests among broken-down dead reeds or sedge, sometimes at some height above water-level, or among growing reeds, often concealed from above. The eggs, usually 6–11, occasionally 5–16, are laid generally from early April onward to July in a nest usually built of dead leaves of reeds. Incubation is by both sexes for about 19–20 days. The young are tended by both parents at least at first. They leave the nest soon after hatching and are fledged when 7–8 weeks old. Double-brooded.

Status and Distribution. Present throughout the year, breeding locally in marshy districts especially in East Anglia, and in Ireland where it apparently breeds in every county. It may often be overlooked, but it is not regarded as a regular breeder in more than half the counties in England and Wales; also Scotland where it is absent from Argyll northwards on the west side of the mainland, and most of the islands. Arrivals from the Continent and Iceland make it commoner and more widespread in winter, passage occurring mainly from second week of September to the third week of November and from early March to mid-May. British breeding birds probably migrate to some extent. They belong to the race *Rallus aquaticus aquaticus* which breeds in Europe from the Mediterranean to southern Scandinavia and central Russia, also in N. Africa and W. Asia, and winters south to Arabia. Other races occur in central and E. Asia and perhaps Iceland.

SPOTTED CRAKE—*Porzana porzana*

BIRD PLATE 38   EGG PLATE X (6)

This and the following two species are skulking marsh birds much like Water Rail in their general habits and behaviour, and are generally seen, if seen at all, only for a moment as they dart into cover or, if taken by surprise, spring up and fly with dangling legs and weak, fluttering action of broad, rather short wings for a few yards only before dropping into cover again, in either case probably disappearing for good. Seen thus in flight Spotted Crake looks rather like a *miniature olive-brown Moorhen or still more like a small dark Corncrake*, and even in such a hurried view as described, *white speckling on the upper-parts* may be noticed. The white outer web of the outer primary may also be seen. At a little distance it may look very dark. On the ground the comparison to a small Corncrake holds equally good, though the colouring, if seen clearly, is quite distinct; crown and upper-parts are olive-brown with blackish centres to feathers; throat, breast and stripe over the eye more or less grey, freely speckled with white on the neck and breast; white streaks and spots on back; the flanks barred brown and whitish, and the uniform buff *under tail-coverts* are conspicuous with frequent cocking of the tail. The bill is greenish-yellow, reddish at base; legs olive-green. Winter plumage is somewhat duller and female duller than male, with less grey on breast, etc. Juvenile is much as female, but breast buffish with few spots. Length about 9 ins.

Habitat. In the breeding-season it frequents waterlogged margins of swamps, fens, and bogs and water margins with ample cover of sedges and similar plants. Outside the breeding-season it also occurs in swamps, fens, etc., but at any rate during migration period may be met with in quite small areas of marshy ground and even along ditches.

General Habits. Like all crakes, it is skulking rather than particularly shy and is an adept at making its way unseen even amongst comparatively short plants, but on occasions will show itself quite freely in the open. Its habits are largely crepuscular. In ordinary gait the body is carried rather low, with legs flexed and tarsus at acute angle with ground. If suspicious the tail is cocked and flirted up at each step like a Moorhen's. If frightened the body and head are sunk still lower, with neck somewhat extended, and plumage compressed so that it looks very slim. This is the carriage of the bird bolting into cover. Swims readily with carriage and action like Moorhen. Not at all gregarious.

Note of male is typically "hwhip" like a short whiplash, usually repeated at brief regular intervals for long periods, uttered as a rule only in the evening, at night, or early morning.

Food is chiefly small molluscs, aquatic insects and their larvae, and seeds of various marsh plants.

Nests usually in a clump or tussock of sedge or marsh-grass, but sometimes on the ground. The eggs, usually 8–12, sometimes 6–15, are laid generally in the second half of May or early June in a nest built of coarse vegetable matter with lining of grasses. Incubation is apparently shared by sexes for about 18–21 days. Male takes some share in care of the young. Double-brooded.

Status and Distribution. A rare summer-visitor and scarce passage-migrant from mid-March to May and August to November, but most in September and October, occasionally wintering but normally migrating south to Africa. This elusive bird may perhaps breed annually but definite records are sporadic. Over a period of years suggestions of breeding have come from S. England from Kent to Somerset, East Anglia, N. England, S. Scotland, Highlands and one or two other areas including Wales. In Ireland it is a vagrant. It breeds in Europe from the Mediterranean north almost to the Arctic Circle; also in W. Asia and perhaps N.W. Africa, wintering south to N.W. Africa, E. Africa and N. India. There are no subspecies.

LITTLE CRAKE—*Porzana parva*

BIRD PLATE 38

Little and Baillon's Crakes are *so much smaller* than the more stockily built and rounder-bodied Spotted Crake that they can be distinguished from it even in a hurried view. To distinguish them from one another a good view is needed, but is not always obtainable. Male of present species and both sexes of Baillon's Crake have the *upper parts brown with dark streaks* (but see under Baillon's Crake), *the under-parts including sides of face and neck are slate-grey* and the under tail-coverts barred blackish and white. But the male Little Crake differs from Baillon's Crake in having *no white streaks on the wing-coverts* (and only some indistinct pale flecks on mantle) and *flanks uniform grey like the breast, not barred*. Female is quite different from Baillon's Crake, having some grey on the sides of the head, but *throat is white and the rest of the under-parts buff.* Hence any very small adult crake with buff under-parts must be a female Little, even if no details are seen. Bill is green with reddish base; legs green. Juvenile has no grey, its breast is obscurely barred whitish and brown and the flanks more strongly so, and it has some whitish spots on wing-coverts. This plumage is retained well into winter. When other characters cannot be seen it is often possible to note that the wing-tip is much longer and more pointed than Baillon's. Length about 7½ ins.

Habitat. Frequents flooded swamps, fens, and swampy borders of sluggish rivers with ample cover, sometimes with scattered willow bushes and often with much floating vegetation such as water-lilies, also reed-beds. On migration it may occur, like the Spotted Crake, in much smaller marshy areas.

General Habits. Behaviour and habits hardly differ from Spotted Crake's. It swims and dives readily and sometimes wades in shallows or walks about over floating vegetation close to cover.

The song is a series of notes which starts slowly and then grows faster, falling rapidly in tone. It also has a Moorhen-like call "kirrook".

Food includes insects, spiders and molluscs; also worms and seeds.

Status and Distribution. A vagrant, recorded in all months, chiefly March–April, and November, but rarely winter, mainly from eastern and southern counties of England; also a few in Wales, Scotland and Ireland. The species breeds locally in central and eastern Europe from N. Italy and the Balkans north to the Baltic States, and probably at times in France, Spain and N.W. Africa. Also in S.W. Asia. It winters in the Mediterranean region, N.E. Africa and S.W. Asia. There are no subspecies.

BAILLON'S CRAKE—*Porzana pusilla*

BIRD PLATE 38

A tiny crake even smaller than Little Crake (though size is hardly to be relied on in the field), with *sexes similar* and much like male of Little Crake, but distinguished by having the *flanks boldly barred blackish and white* like under tail-coverts. Seen well in a good light the upper-parts of Baillon's are a reddish or chestnut tinge, fairly markedly distinct from the paler olive-brown of Little

Crake; moreover Baillon's upper-parts are clearly marked with sharp-cut, even partly black-bordered, irregular white scratches, and the white outer web of its first primary may show as a narrow white leading edge to the wing. Bill is green without red at the base; legs brownish or greyish flesh-colour, not green. Juvenile resembles juvenile Little Crake, but has much more distinct pale markings on upper-parts, and belly is often more strongly barred. Length about 7 ins.

Habitat. It frequents swamps, fens, unreclaimed borders of rivers, lakes and ponds with abundant cover, and shallow lagoons or inundated overgrown areas, apparently preferring finer, lower and denser vegetation than Little Crake. It is said to prefer small marshes and pools, especially where there is a fringe of tamarisk or other bushes, rather than the meres and more open waters frequented by the Little Crake, but both species are decidedly more aquatic than Spotted Crake.

General Habits. These and behaviour scarcely differ from Little Crake's. Sometimes it is seen in the open, wading about deliberately, close to heavy cover, and walks about on floating vegetation.

Usually silent by day. The song is said to consist of a few separate notes followed by a short but distinct trill, like a hurried version of Little Crake's.

Food includes insects, molluscs, green plants and seeds.

Nests in thick growth of swamp vegetation, sometimes low down in thick sedge, occasionally a foot or two above water level in a bush but always cleverly concealed from above. The eggs, usually 6–8, but sometimes 4–9, have ochreous ground-colour, finely stippled and spotted with yellowish-umber. They are laid from end of April onwards in a nest built of dead leaves of reed or aquatic grasses, with a neatly rounded cup. Incubation is by both sexes for about 20–21 days.

Status and Distribution. A rare vagrant, very seldom recorded in recent decades; formerly bred a few times but last recorded in 1889 in Norfolk. It used to occur chiefly in spring or autumn, and exceptionally in summer and winter, most frequently in Norfolk, but also in many other counties in England and several in Wales, Scotland and Ireland. The race occurring in Britain *Porzana pusilla intermedia*, breeds in most Mediterranean and European countries north to Germany and probably winters in N. Africa. There are other races in Russia, Asia, Africa and Australasia.

CORNCRAKE—*Crex crex*

BIRD PLATE 37   EGG PLATE X (5)

In the breeding-season its presence is chiefly proclaimed by the unmistakable note of male. If it can be flushed, the general yellowish-buff colouring of the body and conspicuously *chestnut-coloured wings* at once identify it as it flies sluggishly for a few yards with dangling legs and drops into cover again. When seen in the open its *appearance is rather that of a small, slender game-bird with tapering body, yellowish-buff above with broad dark centres to the feathers*, and paler below with broad reddish-brown bars on flanks and under tail-coverts. It has a grey streak above the eye and, especially in summer, more or less grey on the throat, breast and cheeks. Juvenile shows no grey and has flanks less barred than adult. Length about 10½ ins.

Habitat. In the breeding-season its chief haunts are grasslands of fairly varied type, from low-lying meadows to rough pastures on the sides of mountains; also other localities with rank vegetation, but not as a rule in really wet places. Although it sometimes breeds in crops, cornfields are not a common habitat.

General Habits. It spends most of its time concealed in long grass, through which it runs away if disturbed and will crane its head above the grass to reconnoitre. When walking about undisturbed the head is moved to and fro with each step, and the tail may be moved up and down rather like Moorhen, but it is rarely seen in the open in England although in some parts, notably in Ireland, it shows itself decidedly more freely. Distinctly crepuscular in habits, most active about sunset and may continue so, particularly in fine weather, till dawn.

Characteristic note of male is a loud rasping disyllabic sound repeated with great persistence by day and night, often for long stretches without a break, represented crudely by syllables "arp-arp".

Food is varied, consisting mainly of insects, also slugs, snails, earthworms, millipedes and spiders, and some vegetable matter such as seeds and green weed.

Nests on the ground among long grass and rank vegetation. The eggs, usually 8–12, sometimes 6–14, vary in ground-colour from pale greenish-grey to reddish-brown. They are laid generally in the second half of May and early June on a pad of dead grasses apparently constructed by female. Incubation is normally by female only, for about 14–21 days. The young leave the nest soon after hatching and soon learn to feed themselves. They begin to flutter after 30 days and can fly about 4 days later, but are not fully feathered till 7–8 weeks old. Probably normally single-brooded.

Status and Distribution. A summer visitor, greatly decreased but still not uncommon in western Ireland and parts of the Hebrides. The bird has now almost ceased to nest anywhere in England, Wales and eastern Scotland. On the west Scottish mainland, Sutherland was the only area in 1979 with more than a few pairs left. Serious decline has continued since then, and in Ireland breeding is increasingly intermittent except in the west and north. Irregular nesting still occurs even in S. England. On migration from mid-April to the end of May and late July to early October, it is met with particularly in S. and S.W. England. It winters occasionally, particularly in the west and in Ireland. The species breeds in Europe from the Pyrenees, Alps and Bulgaria north to the Arctic Circle, also in W. Asia, and winters mainly in Africa south to Cape Province. There are no subspecies.

MOORHEN—*Gallinula chloropus*

Bird Plate 39   Egg Plate X (2)

A familiar water-bird easily recognizable by its *brownish-black plumage with oblique white stripes on the flanks, blending to a more or less continuous band, and a red frontal shield and base of bill*. It is perky and lively in action with a characteristic flirting movement of the cocked tail when nervous or excited, in which the *white under tail-coverts, divided by black down the centre, are conspicuous*. Flanks and under-parts are greyer, more slate-coloured, than back; the legs green with a red "garter" at base, and the tip of the bill is yellow. Juvenile and first winter birds are much browner than adults, with bill and frontal shield greenish-brown at first, but assuming adult colouring during the winter. Length about 13 ins.

Habitat. It frequents a wide range of still and slow-flowing fresh waters with banks affording some vegetable cover, preferring quite small or medium-sized ponds, dykes, quiet river reaches and ornamental urban waters rather than the larger, more open, lakes and reservoirs. Also occurs, but much less commonly, on moorland or mountainous areas. It feeds freely on meadows and grassland adjacent to or sometimes at some distance from water. Outside the breeding season it tends to congregate on sheltered lakes and ponds and especially on sewage farms.

General Habits. Though it will run for cover when disturbed on land, it is far less secretive than its relatives the rails and crakes, swimming about freely and buoyantly on open water, though generally keeping within reach of cover. Flight appears laboured as a rule, the bird rising with an effort, legs dangling at first and then gathered up so that they project behind the tail, as it flies low down for a short distance only. In rising it half flies and half runs over the surface for several yards before getting clear. It has a jaunty gait with head somewhat raised. It perches, also roosts, fairly often on branches of low trees and bushes. Birds which have dived when startled frequently remain almost submerged, preferably under cover, exposing beak only at first.

Chief notes are a loud, croaking "currc" or "curruc", apparently mainly a warning note, and "*kitt*ick", with variants.

Food is varied, but predominantly vegetable, comprising seeds and fruits of weeds and bushes, grass, leaves, moss, etc. Animal food includes insects, earthworms, slugs, snails, tadpoles and fish.

Nest is built, by both sexes, of dead reeds, sedge, etc., generally among aquatic plants or near water's edge, but also in bushes or trees not far from water. The eggs, 2–20 or more (? laid by two females), but usually 5–11, vary in ground-colour from whitish-grey to buff or greenish. They are laid generally from April onwards, but occasionally breeding has been recorded in winter. Incubation is by both sexes for about 19–22 days. The young remain in nest for 2 or 3 days if not disturbed; they are fed by both parents and sometimes by the young of previous broods for about 5 weeks, and are able to fly in 6–7 weeks. Generally double-brooded and frequently three broods are reared in a season.

Status and Distribution. Generally a common resident, but is scarce in Shetland, much of N. and N.W. Scotland, and parts of W. Ireland. Most of our birds are sedentary, but a few appear to migrate, and in winter visitors in small numbers arrive on eastern coasts from October to December. It is an almost cosmopolitan species of which only the race *Gallinula chloropus chloropus* occurs in this country, and through Europe from mid-Scandinavia southwards, N. Africa and much of Asia.

COOT—*Fulica atra*

<small>BIRD PLATE 39   EGG PLATE X (1)</small>

A larger, more thick-set bird than Moorhen, with *black plumage only relieved by the white frontal shield and bill.* Head and neck are glossy black, the rest slaty-black. A narrow whitish border shows along the inner part of the trailing edge of the wing in flight. Juvenile is brownish-grey with throat and breast whitish. Length about 15 ins.

Habitat. It does not frequent such small waters as Moorhen, but breeds on lakes, reservoirs, larger ponds, etc., with at least some marginal cover of reeds or similar vegetation, and to a less extent on quiet, reed-fringed reaches of rivers. Outside the breeding-season it also occurs on reservoirs, flood-waters, etc., entirely devoid of cover, and locally in Ireland regularly on land-locked arms of the sea, on which it even nests. In winter and especially in hard weather also sometimes on the sea close to shore, and on tidal estuaries.

General Habits. More gregarious than Moorhen and seen more habitually on open water far from cover, often associated with ducks, amongst which it stands out even at long range by reason of the rounded contour of the back. It rises from water with difficulty, pattering with feet along the surface for some distance. It flies, like Moorhen, with neck extended and heavy-looking feet stretched out behind, often looking like a rather long tail. Flight appears laboured and birds rarely fly far by day. It constantly dives to bring up water-weeds, etc., and may remain below surface for nearly ½-minute, but usually less than half this period. In diving the bird takes a distinct jump. A rather quarrelsome, aggressive bird. Outside the breeding-season it congregates on suitable large waters in great numbers.

Common note is a quite loud monosyllable varying a good deal in pitch, from "kowk" to a higher-pitched, quite pleasant-sounding "kewk", etc.

Food is chiefly vegetable matter, especially soft green stalks of reed and aquatic plants obtained by diving; also grass. Animal food includes molluscs, worms, insects, fish and fish ova.

Nests, often in company with other birds of the same species, usually amongst reed or other aquatic vegetation. Eggs, usually 6–9, sometimes up to 15, are laid from about the second week of March onwards, but often not till much later, in a large nest, built by both sexes of dead leaves of reed and flag. It is raised above water-level sometimes to a height of a foot, often with a runway made of nesting material leading up to it. Incubation is by both sexes for about 21–24 days. The young leave the nest within 3–4 days, but return to it to be brooded at night. On the water each parent feeds part of the brood. The young begin to dive and seek their own food after 30 days, and are independent at about 8 weeks. Sometimes double-brooded and three broods reared occasionally.

Status and Distribution. Present throughout the year, being fairly generally distributed and locally very numerous; few in Caithness and Orkney, but is scarce or absent from most of the Highlands and islands. Probably more or less sedentary in southern English and Irish counties, but many higher-lying and more northerly nesting haunts are unoccupied through the winter, movement occurring from July to November and end of February to April. At the same time some winter-visitors or passage-migrants arrive from the Continent. In addition to migration, hard-weather movements may occur of birds driven by frost from inland waters to the open sea. Our birds belong to the race *Fulica atra atra* which breeds throughout Europe north to Finland, in temperate Asia and N. Africa. Another race occurs in Australia.

CRANE—*Grus grus*

BIRD PLATE 39

A tall, graceful, long-necked and long-legged bird recalling the stork and heron type, with body uniform lead-grey and recognizable at a considerable distance by the *apparently large and loosely feathered tail* formed by elongated secondaries. At close quarters the *red patch on the back of the crown and the black and white of the head and neck* are characteristic. The primaries are black. Juvenile has head and neck brownish and body rather darker than adult. Legs black. In flight at a distance the *loud clanging notes* distinguish it from Stork and herons. Total length about 44 ins.; body about 23 ins.

Habitat. Outside the breeding-season it occurs only in open country, including not only marshes and lagoons, or sand-banks of rivers, but dry grasslands, steppe country, and cultivation.

General Habits. A markedly shy and wary bird. It flies with measured wing-beats with a peculiar jerky upstroke, neck and legs are extended horizontally, not slightly drooped like Stork. On migration it often soars high in the air, but otherwise does not glide

CRANE

Note straight extended neck
and legs.

much except preparatory to pitching. Normal gait is a sedate walk
with long strides, and all movements are more graceful than Stork
and herons. When standing still the carriage of the body is more or
less markedly slanting, with the neck only slightly curved or, if
alert or suspicious, stretched straight up. It is normally gregarious
outside the breeding-season.

It has a loud, clanging, trumpeting note in flight and on the
ground, by night as well as day, which may be rendered "krooh".

Food comprises vegetable matter including grain and seeds of
all kinds; also insects, molluscs, sometimes small mammals and
other animal food.

Status and Distribution. A rare vagrant in the first half of the
present century although it was probably a regular winter-visitor
100 years or more ago. Recently, however, it has been reported
annually, chiefly on passage, has summered in one or two localities, also wintered. It has occurred in most English counties,
more rarely in Wales and Scotland, and very rarely in Ireland. A
remarkable influx of some hundreds occurred in late October 1963
on the south coast of England. The race concerned, *Grus grus
grus*, breeds from Scandinavia and Germany east to the Volga,
with isolated colonies in south-east Europe and in Asia Minor. It
winters in the Mediterranean area and E. Africa. Another race
occurs in S.E. Russia and parts of Asia.

LITTLE BUSTARD—*Tetrax tetrax*

BIRD PLATE 40

It is quite a *small bird as compared with Great Bustard*, and like it has a mottled sandy-brown mantle and white under-parts. In flight its shape is surprisingly duck-like, but it *shows much white on the wing* and at some height appears almost entirely white in the distance. The male's *black neck with white bands* is very characteristic; the sides of head and throat are bluish-slate. The primaries are black, but their bases, with the secondaries and most of the coverts, are white. Female is rather more coarsely marked above than male, with the front of the neck and breast buffish, streaked and barred black. Male in winter and young birds are much like female. Legs dull yellowish. Length about 17 ins.

Habitat. It frequents chiefly undulating grasslands interpersed with corn- and clover-fields.

General Habits. As a rule a very shy and wary bird, difficult to see until it flies. Unlike Great Bustard it will crouch with neck extended in order to escape observation and is more disposed to run at times. It rises with a considerable rattle of wings and in full flight the wings make a peculiar hissing sound. The wing-action has been compared to that of a Partridge, with beats much faster than those of Great Bustard. When flushed it will rise high and go long distances, but may fly only a relatively short distance and quite low if suitable cover such as a cornfield is at hand.

Note on flushing is a short, not very loud "dahg".

Food is largely vegetable matter, including turnip-tops, clover,

LITTLE BUSTARD
female and male.

grass, and leaves of various plants; also some insects, snails and worms.

Status and Distribution. A vagrant which has appeared usually between October and January, and occasionally in other months. Occurrences have been fairly numerous in Yorkshire, East Anglia and some south coast counties, but very occasional elsewhere. There are several records for Scotland and Ireland. Nearly all refer to the race *Tetrax tetrax orientalis* which breeds in E. Europe from the Danube valley north to central Russia and south to Sardinia and the Balkans, also in W. Asia; a few British records refer to the race *Tetrax tetrax tetrax* which breeds in France, Spain, Portugal and N.W. Africa, and has the ground-colour of the upper-parts a warmer shade of buff. The two races are inseparable in the field. The bird is migratory in the northern part of its range.

GREAT BUSTARD—*Otis tarda*

BIRD PLATE 40

On the ground in the open the *great size, especially of male, and sandy upper-parts barred with black* are quite distinctive. *In flight the great bulk of the body, as compared with the wings, and very prominent breast* produce an appearance unlike any other European bird and the *great amount of white in the wing*, mostly concealed when at rest, is striking. The neck extends in front and the feet under tail. The head and neck are lavender grey, the breast and base of neck chestnut with black markings; under-parts white; the wings are mainly white with black primaries. In winter plumage there is less chestnut on the breast. Females are much smaller and slimmer than adult males and lack their moustachial feathers and the chestnut on breast. Young males are much like females. Length: adult male about 40 ins., female about 30–33 ins.

Habitat. It formerly frequented open downs and chalk uplands, and the grassy heaths and "brecks" of East Anglia.

General Habits. A shy and wary species, adept at taking cover when alarmed, but also readily taking wing. Flight is rapid, being much faster than it appears, with regular beats of broad wings, and not as a rule high. Ordinary gait is a stately walk.

A comparatively silent bird. Main note is a low gruff bark or hoarse grunt.

Food of adults mainly vegetable matter, including every kind of cereal, also other crops, grass, leaves and seeds. Animal matter such as field-voles, frogs, slugs, worms and grasshoppers also occasionally taken. Young birds feed largely on insects.

Status and Distribution. It died out as a breeding bird before the middle of the 19th century and is now a very rare vagrant which has occurred during the present century a very few times in England, Scotland, Ireland and Wales, chiefly in winter. The bird is mainly sedentary and breeds in Portugal, S. Spain and N. Morocco; also in E. Europe from Germany to the Balkans and in Asia. There are no subspecies.

OYSTERCATCHER—*Haematopus ostralegus*

BIRD PLATES 41 and 121   EGG PLATE IX (2A & 2B)

The boldly pied plumage, long orange-red bill and pink legs make Oystercatcher unmistakable. The head, breast, back, and wings are glossy black, with a broad white wing-band; underparts and rump are white, tail white with a broad black terminal band. In winter plumage there is a white half collar on the throat. Juvenile has upper parts more or less mottled brown. Length about 17 ins.

Habitat. Both in and out of the breeding-season it is chiefly characteristic of the sea-shore, resorting alike to rock-bound coasts, pebble-ridges, sandy shores and estuarine mud-flats, as well as to turfy islands and coastal links or warrens. In Scotland it also breeds freely on shingle banks of rivers and the shores of lochs, and less commonly in fields, many miles inland, feeding regularly on the neighbouring pastures and arable fields, and even on moorlands. It is irregular as a migrant on inland waters away from breeding areas.

General Habits. A noisy, excitable, wary bird. It generally flies rather low over shore or sea with rather shallow wing-beats. The ordinary gait is a sedate walk, but it can run rapidly. It can swim well when so disposed and flocks have occasionally been observed settling on the sea far from land. Autumn and winter flocks run into hundreds on favourable coasts, and large non-breeding flocks are also regular in some districts in summer. It is often active and noisy at night.

Ordinary note is a loud, clear, shrill "klee-eep, klee-eep"; also a short, sharp "pic-pic" or "kic-kic". The "piping performance" is a development of the ordinary call into a trill; it is regular from late February to late July, less so till late August and exceptional in autumn.

Food is chiefly molluscs, crustacea, worms and insects.

Nests on the ground. The eggs, normally 3 but sometimes 2–4, are yellowish-stone or clay-buff in ground-colour, sometimes greenish or brownish. They are laid generally in May, some earlier, in a nest which, when on shingle, consists of a shallow depression lined with small stones or shells; when on rocks, sand and turf, sometimes no nesting material, but bits of dead vegetation, rabbit-droppings, etc., may be used. Incubation is by both sexes, for about 25–28 days. The young usually leave the nest within 12 hours; they are tended by both parents, and fly when about 34–37 days old. Single-brooded.

Status and Distribution. Present throughout the year. It breeds on almost all coasts, plentifully in Scotland and Ireland, less so in Wales and England, but several localities in S. and E. England have been recolonized during recent decades, and numbers in parts of East Anglia are now considerable. It is extending inland into central England. At the same time it has become widespread inland along river valleys in N. England and S. Scotland and increased inland in N. Scotland. Inland breeding also occurs in Ireland. Breeding territories are taken up between mid-February and mid-April, and most birds move south again in July or August. Passage of these birds and immigrants lasts until November, and the return movement continues until mid-May. As a passage-migrant and winter-visitor it is widely distributed on all coasts and non-breeding birds are frequent in summer; inland it is an irregular and very scarce visitor except in breeding localities in Scotland and N. England. The race concerned, *Haematopus ostralegus ostralegus*, also breeds in Iceland, Faeroes, North Europe south to parts of the Mediterranean, and Asia Minor. Other races occur in Canary Islands, S. Africa, Asia, America and Australasia.

BLACK-WINGED STILT—*Himantopus himantopus*

BIRD PLATE 40

Its *enormously long pink legs, straight black bill and boldly contrasted black and white plumage* make Stilt quite unmistakable. It is equally striking on the ground or in flight, when the legs extending far beyond the tail and the uniform black (dark brown in female or immature) of the mantle and of both surfaces of the pointed wings give an appearance quite unlike any other bird. In adult plumage, attained after 2 years, the head and neck of female are white but often with some dusky fleckings in winter; the male is the same in winter, but in summer has more or less black on the head and neck. Immature birds have the crown and neck brown or greyish. Length about 15 ins.; legs project about 6½–7 ins. beyond the tail in flight; bill about 2½ ins.

Habitat. It frequents the vicinity of shallow pools and lagoons or flooded marshes and grasslands. It delights especially in open, more or less weedy, shallows with floating vegetation and often tussocks of rush, etc., but never closely overgrown with reeds or similar tall vegetation. Outside the breeding-season it is also sometimes found on shallow reaches of quiet streams and rivers, but hardly ever on the sea-shore.

General Habits. In direct flight the neck is only slightly extended and the legs, held close together, extend rigidly out behind. It sometimes glides for some distance on still wings when well up in the air, as well as prior to pitching. The gait on land is a graceful, deliberate walk with long strides, quickened occasionally to almost a run. At rest the head may be sunk on shoulders or the bill tucked behind a wing, and like most waders the bird will rest on one leg with the other drawn up. To pick up food from the ground the legs have to be flexed considerably, but it feeds mainly when wading, picking insects from the water's surface and from floating vegetation. When suspicious it moves its head backwards and forwards much like Redshank.

Ordinary notes on the breeding-ground are a repeated, sharp "kik-kik-kik . . .", and a disyllabic note with minor variations, "kiwik".

Food is chiefly insects, molluscs, worms, tadpoles and frog-spawn.

Nests in large or small colonies, usually close to, or actually in, shallow water with a muddy bottom, at times also on dry mud. The eggs, normally 3–4, sometimes 5, usually have clay-coloured ground-colour with black spots and irregular blotches, exceptionally almost unmarked. They are laid generally in May in a nest which varies considerably, some built up of stalks and mud, and quite substantial; others merely an apology for a nest, consisting of a few bits of dead reed, etc., arranged round a hollow. Incubation is by both sexes for about 25–26 days. The young leave the nest soon after hatching, and fly after about a month. Single-brooded.

Status and Distribution. A rare vagrant which has occurred

BLACK-WINGED STILT

chiefly in April, May and September, but even as late as December, most on the south and east coasts of England, especially Norfolk. Elsewhere, including several inland counties, it is a very rare vagrant, but 2 pairs bred in Notts in 1945, a pair in Cambridge in 1983, and Norfolk in 1987. There are a few records for Scotland including the northern isles, and for Ireland. The race concerned, *Himantopus himantopus himantopus*, is a summer-visitor to Europe, breeding especially in the S.E. and S.W., north to central France and Hungary, and in some recent years in Holland and Belgium. It also breeds in many parts of Africa south to the Cape, and Asia east to China. Other races occur in S.E. Asia, Australasia and N. and S. America.

AVOCET—*Recurvirostra avosetta*

Bird Plates 41 and 121   Egg Plate VIII (6)

The beautiful *snow-white plumage boldly patterned with black and the conspicuously up-curved, slender, black bill* make Avocet unmistakable. The nape and top of the head to below the eye and two broad somewhat convergent bands on the back are black, as are about the distal third of the wing (both sides) and (on dorsal side) a broad oblique band near the front of the more basal part, producing a very striking pattern. *Legs blue-grey.* Immature birds have blacks browner and the white parts more or less suffused with brownish. Length about 17 ins.; bill about 3¼ ins.

Habitat. In the breeding-season it resorts to localities on or near flat coasts or in river deltas which provide a combination of suitable feeding-grounds in the form of extensive muddy flats or brackish lagoons on salt-marshes, saline pastures, or reclaimed land, with open sandy flats or expanses of dried mud, on which it can nest. It is found more rarely on the borders of inland lakes, especially saline, affording the requisite conditions. Outside the breeding-season it frequents muddy coasts, shoals and sand banks at the mouths of estuaries, and flats bordering large inland lakes and rivers.

General Habits. It flies with the neck only slightly extended, so that it looks comparatively short and thick, with fairly rapid, regular wing-beats, gliding when about to pitch, but seldom otherwise. The legs extend considerably beyond the tail, but at times it may fly a short distance with legs drawn up. Normal gait is a fairly brisk walk with body horizontal and neck carried in a gentle curve, although when suspicious the body is slanted more and the neck is stretched up straighter. It feeds on mud or in shallow water with a side to side swing of the upcurved bill, skimming food from the surface and swallowing it with a short backward jerk of the head. In deeper water it will dip its head below the surface and when out of its depth swims readily and buoyantly, and will "up-end" like a duck. Single birds or parties will sometimes pitch on the water and swim gracefully. Resting birds often stand on one leg with the bill tucked into the scapulars. When excited or suspicious the head is bobbed up and down by an alternate extension and retraction of the neck, but without much movement of the body. It is markedly gregarious.

Ordinary call and alarm-note is a melodious, clear, liquid "kluut".

Food includes insects, molluscs, crustacea, worms, and fish spawn.

Nests on the ground, usually in colonies of varying size within easy reach of water, on sandy flats or islands covered with salt-scrub. The eggs, usually 4, sometimes 3–5, have clay-buff ground-colour, rarely pale or darker. They are laid generally in May in a nest which on bare sand may be merely a slight hollow, quite unlined; at other times any kind of dead vegetation or flood refuse may be collected and arranged round the eggs. Incubation is by both sexes for about 22 to 24 days. The young are tended by both parents; they are able to feed themselves from the time of hatching and fly when about 5 weeks old. Single-brooded.

Status and Distribution. Having been extinct as a breeding species for nearly a century, 2 pairs bred in Ireland in 1938, one pair in Norfolk in 1941, and in Suffolk a substantial colony has become established on Havergate Island since 1947 and another at Minsmere since 1963; nesting in Norfolk now seems regular, and it has bred occasionally south to Kent. Otherwise it is mainly a scarce migrant, occurring with some regularity .in Norfolk, Suffolk, Kent, Sussex and Hants, from the end of March to June and less often July and September; it has also occurred in all other months. In recent years a few birds have wintered, especially in Devon or Cornwall, often Cork. It is very rare elsewhere in the British Isles at all seasons. In Europe it breeds locally on the coasts of the North Sea and Baltic, inland in central Europe, and on the Mediterranean and Black Seas. It also breeds southwards to S. Africa and in Asia east to China. Northern birds are migratory. There are no subspecies.

STONE CURLEW—*Burhinus oedicnemus*

Bird Plates 41 and 121   Egg Plate IX (4A & 4B)

Although its protective colouring renders it inconspicuous till it flies, Stone Curlew is unmistakable when seen. On the ground it appears as *a rather large, bullet-headed, plover-like bird with streaked sandy-brown plumage and large, yellow eyes*, usually seen withdrawing in a rapid but stealthy manner, with short pattering steps, head lowered and neck retracted. On taking flight it reveals a rather conspicuous wing-pattern, *the secondaries and the whole wing beyond the wrist being black with white marks on the primaries and two conspicuous whitish bars on the basal part*. An oblique pale band with irregular borders shows to a varying degree on the closed wing. Breast and flanks are streaked, belly white. The tail is brown showing white at the sides and black tips. Legs pale yellow. Juvenile is much as adult. Length about 16 ins.

Habitat. In the breeding-season it frequents sandy heaths, open stony fallows and waste land, and barren, flint-strewn tracts of chalk uplands, with scanty ground vegetation; rarely also on sand-dunes. It is breeding increasingly on arable land, notably in E. Anglia. It is not averse to the presence of trees, generally pines, in fair quantity, provided fairly extensive bare areas are left free. It may visit cultivation or marshes for feeding purposes and sometimes the sea-shore or estuaries in winter or on passage.

General Habits. Flight is usually rather low down, with regular, rather slow wing-beats, sometimes with a long glide. In the evening flights are sometimes higher up and more erratic, and flocks will sometimes perform co-ordinated evolutions. When standing still the carriage is usually markedly upright with the back sloping rather steeply. When suspicious it often makes a sudden downward bob of the head with a corresponding elevation of the hind part of the body. It never perches, but rests on its belly or sitting with the whole length of tarsus on the ground. The freezing attitude, flattened out on the ground with head and neck extending, which is assumed by young birds and also by adults if taken by surprise, is characteristic. It is sociably inclined at all times; even in the breeding-season it is sometimes seen in parties, and is more markedly gregarious in autumn. It feeds to some extent by day, but principally by night.

Ordinary flight-note is a plaintive, wailing "coor-lee" or "coo-eee", rather like Curlew's note, but shriller.

Food is mainly snails and slugs, worms and insects. Field-mice and voles, and occasionally frogs and chicks of game-birds, are also taken.

Nests on the ground. The eggs, normally 2, but 3 occasionally recorded, vary in ground-colour from light yellowish-stone to pale brown. They are laid generally in late April and early May, on the bare ground without nesting materials apart from rabbit-droppings or small stones, which are often present. Incubation is by both sexes for about 25–27 days. The young leave the nest within a day, tended by both parents, and fly when about 6 weeks old. Occasionally double-brooded.

Status and Distribution. Although bird has sometimes wintered in S.W. England, and occasionally elsewhere, it is mainly a summer-visitor from March or April to October or November. It breeds in small numbers in E. and S. England, east of a line from Hertford to the Wash, and in the triangle Oxford-Dorset-Sussex. Elsewhere it is a vagrant, very rare in Wales, N. England, Scotland and Ireland. Our birds belong to the race *Burhinus oedicnemus oedicnemus* which breeds in Europe from the Baltic to the Mediterranean and in S.W. Asia, and winters from W. France south to E. Africa. Other races occur in N. Africa, Asia Minor, and S. Africa.

CREAM-COLOURED COURSER—*Cursorius cursor*

BIRD PLATE 56

A sandy-buff, plover-like bird with the terminal half and the whole under-side of the wing black, very conspicuous when it flies. The nape is pale grey, and a broad white band extends from eye to nape, with a black band below, and at the back of the head it is also bordered black above. The secondaries have blackish inner webs and white tips. The tail has a blackish subterminal band and white tips, conspicuous at the sides. Legs creamy. Bill is tapering and curved, not like a plover's. The bird looks small on the ground, not much larger than a Starling, but its size is exaggerated in flight. Young have dark, wavy markings on the upper-parts, and eye-stripe is buff. Length about 9 ins.

Habitat. It inhabits sandy desert and semi-desert or steppe country.

General Habits. Actions in general are suggestive of Golden Plover. It runs rapidly, usually in short spurts with pauses between, and if flushed does not as a rule fly far, though it can fly swiftly and high on occasions. It has a concealing attitude with head flat on the ground, something like Stone Curlew's.

Call, not often heard, is a harsh "hark, hark".

Food is chiefly insects, also small lizards and snails.

Status and Distribution. A rare vagrant which has been mainly recorded from the east and south coast counties of

CREAM-COLOURED COURSER

In flight the black under-wing and black outer part of upper-wing
is arresting.

England, between October and December. It has also occurred in Wales, Scotland and Ireland. These birds have belonged to the race *Cursorius cursor cursor* which breeds in N. Africa and S.W. Asia. Other races occur elsewhere in Africa and Asia.

COLLARED PRATINCOLE—*Glareola pratincola*

BIRD PLATE 56

In flight the shape and action are strongly suggestive of a huge brown swallow having a deeply forked tail, white at the base and the rest black. At other times the buoyant flight, forked tail, and especially the note equally recall terns. On the ground it is more plover-like, though the long wings give an elongated effect which is not really like any other bird. Chin and throat are light buff, with a narrow black border in summer and in winter more or less streaked and spotted. The bird has been regarded as having two colour phases, the typical form which is more or less dominant in the western part of range having the axillaries and under wing-coverts chestnut. The Black-winged form (*"nordmanni"*) has this under-wing area black, but the colouring is surprisingly hard to determine even when the bird is overhead; it is more visible on take-off. The appearance of the upper-parts is a better guide: the Collared Pratincole shows considerable contrast between the blackish primaries and the paler inner wing and mantle, accentuated by the white trailing edge of the secondaries; the Black-winged bird has secondaries black like the primaries and rather dark wing-coverts and mantle, giving an almost uniform effect. (See plate 17 in the *Popular Handbook of Rarer British Birds*.) Juveniles are mottled on the upper-parts, sides of head and breast. Legs black. Length about 10 ins. (to base of fork of tail about 7½ ins.).

Habitat. It frequents open and barren localities, such as stretches of sun-baked mud in marshy districts, on borders of lakes or lagoons, or on islands, and plains, pastures and fallows, etc. It is often, but not necessarily, found near water.

General Habits. Flight is swift and buoyant, often dashing and erratic, and it frequently hawks insects on the wing, especially over water. Does not perch, and walks or runs rapidly on the ground with a quick, tripping action like a plover, with horizontal carriage of the body. It sometimes wades in shallow water. It is to some extent crepuscular.

Note is a sharp, rippling "kikki-kirr*ik*, kikki-kirr*ik*" and variants.

Food consists almost exclusively of insects.

Status and Distribution. A vagrant which has been recorded almost annually in recent years occurring in many English counties, especially in the east and south. It has also been recorded in Scotland several times (including Shetland) and in Wales and Ireland. It has appeared in most months of the year except December and January, chiefly in May. The race concerned, *Glareola pratincola pratincola*, breeds in the Mediterranean area, also Hungary, Roumania, S. Russia, and W. Asia south to Sind. Northern birds winter in N. Africa. Other races occur elsewhere in Africa and in Arabia.

Note. The Black-winged Pratincole is now regarded by tax-onomists as a distinct species, *Glareola nordmanni*. Although it scarcely breeds farther west than the Black Sea, it has provided about half the pratincole records in recent years referred to above, mainly in autumn.

LITTLE RINGED PLOVER—*Charadrius dubius*

BIRD PLATES 43 and 123   EGG PLATE VIII (9)

Much like Ringed Plover, but smaller and slighter, this being a noticeable difference if the birds are seen together, but not always so at other times. The best characters are the *absence of any white wing-bar and the distinct note*, which suffice for certain identification even if the bird merely flies by. Subsidiary characters are: legs flesh-coloured or inclining to pale yellowish-green, never bright yellow or orange; yellow ring round the eye noticeable at close range. Young differ from adults in the same respects as in Ringed Plover. Length about 6 ins.

Habitat. Markedly more a fresh-water bird than Ringed Plover, in this country mainly frequenting disused gravel pits, otherwise sand and gravel banks on rivers or borders of lakes, and when found breeding on the coast usually at the mouth of a river or stream; it also breeds by pools with gravelly, sandy or rubbly waste ground adjacent.

General Habits. Apart from differences in habitat and the usually more excitable, noisy and demonstrative behaviour when breeding, its general habits and behaviour hardly differ from Ringed Plover's.

Ordinary note, also alarm note on the breeding-ground, is "*pee*-u"; in song flight a repeated "gree-a".

Food is chiefly insects; also spiders, small molluscs, and occasionally worms.

Nests on shingle or sand, also on dry mud and among grass. The eggs, normally 4, sometimes 3–5, are laid generally in May in a hollow, in some cases lined with stalks of plants, bits of shell or small stones or often without any added material. Incubation is by both sexes for about 24–26 days. The young leave the nest when dry, tended by both parents, and fly when about 24 days old. Mainly single-brooded.

Status and Distribution. Before 1938 a very rare vagrant, but now a regular summer-visitor which after establishment in the S.E., has spread to breed in small numbers in most English eastern counties and west to Gloucester and Lancashire. Population was nearly 200 pairs in 1964, and 450–500 pairs in 1973, then levelling off. A vagrant in S. Scotland (has bred), and Ireland. It arrives from late March to May and leaves from July to September. Our birds belong to the race *Charadrius dubius curonicus* which breeds from Finland and S. Norway south to Morocco and east to Japan. European birds winter in the Mediterranean area and farther south. Other races occur in India, and parts of S.E. Asia.

RINGED PLOVER—*Charadrius hiaticula*

BIRD PLATES 43 and 123   EGG PLATE VIII (10)

A small, robustly built plover whose outstanding characteristics are a *prominent black collar*, broad in front and narrow behind, and *bold black and white markings on the side and front of the head*. Back and crown are hair-brown. The under-parts white, the white of the throat being continued round the neck as a narrow collar bordering the black. The tail is brown in the centre, white at sides with white tips to feathers and a blackish subterminal band. A *well-marked, narrow white wing-bar* at once distinguishes it in flight from Little Ringed Plover. *Legs are orange-yellow or yellow*, more flesh-coloured in young; bill orange at base and black at the tip. Juveniles show a somewhat scale-like pattern at close range, have blackish bills and are altogether duller, with no black band on

LITTLE RINGED PLOVER   RINGED PLOVER

Little Ringed Plover often has a rather furtive appearance.

the crown, the other markings being dusky-brown instead of black, and the collar interrupted (or almost so) in front. They are sometimes confused with Kentish Plover, but yellowish, instead of blackish, legs at once separate them, apart from other differences. Length about 7½ ins.

Habitat. In the breeding-season it is mainly a bird of sandy and pebbly seashores, but in some districts breeds regularly on fallow land, mud of drained marshes, etc., near coast, as well as locally on sandy heaths and on rivers or lakes with pebbly margins or islands many miles inland. Outside the breeding-season inland breeding-haunts are abandoned and birds are generally distributed on sandy and muddy shores, especially the latter. It is also frequent in passage-seasons and to a less extent in winter on sewage-farms and muddy margins of rivers, reservoirs, etc., inland.

General Habits. Actions are energetic and lively. Like all the small plovers, and unlike Dunlin and other small shore-haunting waders, when feeding it runs rapidly here and there with head up, pausing for a moment every few yards, and when taking food seizes it with a quick tilt-over of the whole body, as though hinged on its legs. When suspicious it bobs its head up and down in a nervous way, and when leaving nest at the approach of an intruder a crouching carriage is usually adopted. Feeding parties scatter, and as a rule maintain only a loose contact, though flocks on the wing are often more compact, manoeuvring with the same precision as Dunlin, but in smaller parties. Flight is rapid, generally low down. It associates freely with Dunlin, Redshank, etc.

Ordinary note when disturbed is a melodious, liquid "tooi". Another is a liquid, piping "kluup". The song is a sort of trill, based on the ordinary note and is heard regularly from early March until early July, exceptionally from January to mid-September. It is given in nuptial flights when the bird sweeps about at low elevation with soft, rather slow beats of fully expanded wings.

Food includes molluscs, insects, also worms and some vegetable matter.

Nests mainly on sand, turf or shingle. The eggs, usually 4, sometimes 3–5, range in ground-colour from bluish-grey to warm reddish-yellow. They are laid generally in May and June in a hollow, in some cases quite open, in others sheltered by growing plants, and sometimes lined with small stones and bits of shell; sometimes quite substantial nests may be built of bents and other plants where material is available. Incubation is by both sexes, for 24–25 days as a rule. Young are tended by both sexes. They leave the nest soon after hatching, and fly when about 25 days old. Double-brooded and probably three at times.

Status and Distribution. Present throughout the year. Where undisturbed it is generally distributed as a breeding bird on low-lying coasts and islands, but none now remains in Cornwall, few in Devon and many sites have been deserted in other areas. Some also breed inland in many parts of Scotland and Ireland, also in N. England, East Anglia and the lower Thames valley. The nesting grounds are mainly deserted from mid-July until February or later, some of our birds wintering across the channel. On passage and in winter it is common on the coasts and frequent inland, movement in autumn lasting until late October and in spring until late June. Continental visitors include some of the race *Charadrius hiaticula tundrae* breeding in arctic Europe and Asia; otherwise residents and immigrants belong to the race *Charadrius hiaticula hiaticula* which breeds from Italy north to the Baltic and west to Greenland and E. Baffin Island. The bird winters south to S. Africa.

KILLDEER—*Charadrius vociferus*

Bird Plate 44

Apart from its larger size it is separable from other "ringed" plovers by the *double black band across breast, the rufous rump, longish tail and distinctive loud notes*. The crown and back are dark brown, the fore-head is white bordered black above. The white of the throat continues as a collar round the neck, and the tail is rufous with a subterminal black bar and white tips. It has a conspicuous white wing-bar. Legs vary from flesh colour to pale greyish-yellow. Young have less black, and buff edgings to the feathers of the upper-parts. Length about 9½ ins.

Habitat. It frequents meadows and dry uplands, sometimes near ponds but often far from water; also arable and cultivated land. In winter it also frequents the sea-shore, but seldom alights on coastal marshes.

General Habits. An excitable, noisy bird. Flight is rapid, but it usually flies about singly in a wavering and erratic manner. General behaviour is much like Ringed Plover's; it runs and stops in the same way with head up, picks up food with the same quick tilt over of the body, and bobs in a similar manner when suspicious. Where not interfered with, it becomes very tame.

Calls include upturning "kildee", plaintive "dee-ee" and many variants.

Food is mainly insects; also centipedes, spiders, worms, snails, crustacea and a little vegetable matter.

Status and Distribution. A very rare vagrant recorded from England, Ireland and Scotland mainly in winter or spring. The race which has occurred here, *Charadrius vociferus vociferus*, breeds in N. America from Canada to Mexico and winters south to Peru. Other races occur elsewhere in America.

KENTISH PLOVER—*Charadrius alexandrinus*

Bird Plates 43 and 123   Egg Plate VIII (8)

A decidedly smaller and slighter bird than Ringed Plover. The general plumage pattern is not unlike that species, but *upper-parts are noticeably paler, the legs and bill are blackish and the black markings are less extensive and fainter*, the pectoral band being represented merely by an *obscure blackish or dusky patch on sides of the breast*. Male has a white fore-head with a black mark above it, and a relatively narrow blackish mark through the eye with a white band above it; in summer the crown is more rufous than the back. Female has no dark mark on the fore-head, and the breast patches and band through eye are dusky brown. The bird has a narrow white wing-bar. Young are much like female, but with the same scaly pattern of the upper-parts as in Ringed Plover, which they resemble superficially. Ringed Plover, however, at all ages has yellowish legs (unless mud-coated) and a more robust build, while Kentish Plover has blackish legs and *very different note*. Length about 6¼ ins.

Habitat. In the breeding-season it frequents shingly and sandy beaches or flats, with a liking for an admixture of sand and mud.

General Habits. These and behaviour are very like Ringed Plover's, but it is much more active in its movements, darting over flats with surprising speed, but with the same frequent pauses.

Two main notes are a monosyllabic "wit", and "chirr".

Food is largely insects, also molluscs, worms, crustacea and spiders.

Nests in this country have nearly all been on shingle beds with a little wiry grass. The eggs, normally 3, but sometimes 2–4, have very variable ground-colour from stone-buff to dark greenish-olive or deep umber-brown. They are laid generally from early May onwards among pebbles, or on dead seaweed or in a hollow in sand. Bits of dead vegetation are sometimes used as a lining but are often absent. Incubation is by both sexes for about 24 days. The young are tended by both parents. Probably double-brooded in some cases.

Status and Distribution. Mainly a very rare passage-migrant in April–May, and August–September, along the S. coast to Devon and Cornwall and up the E. coast to Yorks; exceptional in winter. Formerly a summer-visitor, breeding in Kent and Sussex until 1956; nested Lincs in 1979, Norfolk 1983. A very rare vagrant in Ireland and has occurred in Scotland. The race concerned, *Charadrius alexandrinus alexandrinus*, breeds in Europe from S. Scandinavia to the Mediterranean, also in N. Africa, W. and central Asia. It winters throughout Africa and in S. Asia. Other races occur in E. Asia, Ceylon and America.

DOTTEREL—*Charadrius morinellus*

BIRD PLATES 44 and 123   EGG PLATE VIII (7)

It is *not unlike a small, dark-backed Golden Plover with prominent, broad white eye-stripes meeting on the nape*. Notwithstanding the rather striking colour-scheme, it is actually very inconspicuous in its natural haunts. The crown and upper-parts are blackish-brown, cheeks and throat whitish, the *brown breast is separated by a white band from chestnut lower breast and flanks*, belly is black, tail bordered white. Females usually much brighter than males. In autumn and winter and in young birds the eye-stripe is duller, and the striking pattern of the under-parts is lacking, breast and flanks being brown with an obscure pale pectoral band more or less indicated. Legs dull yellow. Length about 8½ ins.

Habitat. In the breeding-season it frequents mossy or tussocky ground or stony ridges and plateaux on barren mountain tops and high level fells above 2,500 ft. or more. On passage it prefers to halt on moors and hill pastures, but also does so in lowlands on rough pastures, heaths, and fallows, sea-shore, coastal marshes, etc., and has often fairly regular stopping-places. It is rarely, if ever, seen on low ground in the nesting-area.

General Habits. The Dotterel has a reputation for extra-ordinary tameness, which many birds fully merit, but others are quite wild and rise long before one is near them. Its flight has been compared to Golden Plover's, but is sometimes rather heavy. It has a typical plover gait, with a quick run and then a pause, often to pick up food, and in general behaviour is like other plovers. It usually occurs on migration in small "trips" of 4 or 5 to a dozen or more. On the breeding-ground females form into small bands while the males are sitting. It is fond of bathing and dusting.

Usual note of both sexes when disturbed is a sweet, twittering whistle "wit-e-wee, wit-e-wee". Autumn migrants give a Dunlin-like "dzeee" or "prrrit", and a clear fluty "rip, rip".

Food is mainly insects, also spiders. During migration small molluscs are occasionally recorded, and some vegetable matter.

Nests on the ground. The eggs, normally 3, occasionally 2, vary in ground-colour from clay-colour to light olivaceous, rarely deep tawny-buff. They are laid generally at the end of May and early in June in a depression hollowed by the birds and unlined or sparing-ly lined with mosses, lichens or grasses. Incubation is by male, almost or entirely alone, usually for 25 to 27½ days. The young may remain in the nest for 24 hours, tended mainly by male, though female occasionally takes some part; they are fully fledged in about a month. Single-brooded.

Status and Distribution. A summer-visitor in small numbers, breeding in the Cairngorms and Grampian ranges and perhaps W. Ross and Kirkcudbright; also, perhaps irregularly, in the Lake District. As a passage-migrant it has occurred in many localities in England and S. Scotland and occasionally Wales, but only rarely elsewhere in Scotland and a few times in Ireland. It arrives between mid-April and the end of May, and leaves from early

August to October and is much less frequently observed on autumn passage than spring. Abroad it breeds in arctic Europe and on high ground in S. Scandinavia and parts of central Europe; also in N. Asia. Our birds winter in N. Africa. There are no subspecies.

LESSER GOLDEN PLOVER—*Pluvialis dominica*

BIRD PLATE 42

Closely similar to Golden Plover but with longer legs, and wings which at rest extend well beyond the tail. This arctic-breeding species has subspecies in Asia and North America which can often be distinguished in the field. Asiatic form is *distinctly smaller than Golden Plover*, but American form is almost as large. The diagnostic feature in all plumages is the *greyish, instead of whitish axillaries*, but this is hard to see in the field and the underwing usually looks only slightly darker than Golden Plover's. In breeding plumage it resembles a brightly-patterned Golden Plover, with less white on flanks and *under-tail-coverts mainly black*. Breeding plumage is often retained until autumn passage in September, and is then sometimes very worn, the back appearing largely black. At all seasons most birds have less yellow on upper-parts than Golden Plover, and *American birds often have much less, some appearing as grey as Grey Plovers*. Some Asiatic birds, however, especially juveniles, are closely spangled with yellow. In winter and juvenile plumage it always shows a prominent eyestripe, and American birds are often very grey below, with little or no streaking on breast. *Some call-notes are diagnostic*. Length 9½–11 ins.

Habitat. Outside the breeding-season its favourite haunts are much like those of European Golden Plovers, chiefly on grasslands, sometimes on shore and in cultivation.

General Habits. General behaviour does not differ from Golden Plover's.

Usual flight-note of American race is a distinctive "quee-d-l-eee", with a double "catch" in the middle; other notes resemble Golden Plover's but are less musical. Asiatic race in full flight has a musical, clear disyllabic "klee-yee" or "tu-ee", recalling Spotted Redshank, but when moving only a few yards a single call like Golden Plover's.

Food is mainly insects; also small molluscs, crustacea and a little vegetable matter.

Status and Distribution. A very rare vagrant, which has occurred mainly in the autumn between August and November in England, Scotland and Ireland. The race *Pluvialis dominica dominica* which breeds in arctic N. America, has appeared a few times; but several records refer to the race *Pluvialis dominica fulva* breeding in N. Siberia and Alaska, which is rather the smaller and more brightly coloured of the two, and when juvenile has a much yellower appearance on head, neck and back. The species winters in S. Asia, Australia, New Zealand and S. America.

Note. The forms described above as races of Lesser Golden Plover have been re-classified as two separate species. The name Lesser Golden Plover has been dropped, the American form now being called American Golden Plover *Pluvialis dominica*, and the Asiatic form becomes Pacific Golden Plover *Pluvialis fulva*.

GOLDEN PLOVER—*Pluvialis apricaria*

Bird Plates 42 and 123   Egg Plate IX (3A & 3B)

A typical plover with rounded head and slender, straight bill of medium length. At all seasons the *spangled black and gold pattern of the upper-parts is distinctive* of Golden Plover, though young Grey Plover comes fairly near. In summer the northern race *altifrons* typically has the face, cheeks, and under-parts black and a broad white band from fore-head over the eye and down the sides of neck and breast to the flanks; this plumage is sometimes seen on migrants in late spring. Our breeding birds, which belong to the southern race, typically have this *pattern much less clear cut*, with face and throat dusky and mottled, the white band obscure or nearly absent, and the black of the breast and belly more or less mixed with white or yellowish. There is however a good deal of variation especially in Scottish Highlands where some breeding birds show the characteristics of the northern race. In winter plumage the black is lost and the under-parts are whitish with golden and dusky mottlings. *The axillaries are pure white, the under-wing whitish, and the rump and tail appear dark in flight.* It

LESSER GOLDEN PLOVER   GOLDEN PLOVER

Note the drabber underwing of Lesser Golden Plover.

has a whitish wing-bar. Legs greenish-grey. Young are rather paler above than adults and more dusky below. Length about 11 ins.

Habitat. In the breeding-season it haunts chiefly upland moors and peat-mosses with stunted heather and sometimes with a good deal of short moor grass; sometimes on similar ground not far from sea-level. Outside the breeding-season it occurs on wet or dry grass-fields, arable land, stubble, etc., both on hills and in lowlands, and sometimes on shore and mud-flats, especially in hard weather, but it is much less of a shore-bird than Grey Plover.

General Habits. Flight is rapid. On the ground it runs in the usual plover manner, stopping every now and again and tilting the whole body to pick up food. When stationary it stands rather upright, especially if at all suspicious. In the breeding-season it is fond of standing on some small eminence such as a peaty hummock, and breeding birds commonly meet and follow intruders a long way from the nest, with anxious pipings. Feeding flocks scatter over the ground, but on taking wing they gather into more compact bodies, which move with the astonishing precision common to many wader flocks. It is eminently gregarious and usually met with in flocks. It often associates with Lapwings, but the species tend to separate in the air. It is conservative with regard to feeding and roosting grounds, often resorting year after year to the same restricted areas.

Ordinary note is a musical liquid whistle "tlui". The song is a rippling "too-roo, too-roo" uttered in the air and on the ground. It is heard from March to early June, exceptionally in February or to the end of June and in autumn.

Food includes insects, molluscs, worms, crustacea, spiders and vegetable matter, such as seeds, berries, grasses and moss.

Nests on the ground, in burnt or short heather, also peat hags. The eggs, normally 4, but 3 not unusual, range in ground-colour from cartridge-buff to rich reddish-brown. They are laid generally in late April or early May in a mere depression in peat, with a scanty lining of heather-twigs, lichens, etc., prepared by both sexes. Incubation is by both sexes, usually for 27–28 days. The young usually leave the nest within a few hours of hatching, tended by both sexes, and fly when about 4 weeks old. Single-brooded.

Status and Distribution. Present throughout the year, breeding in reduced numbers in the Pennines, also N.E. Yorks and northwards; in Scotland it breeds in all counties except Fife, more commonly north of the Forth, also in the islands, but is scarce in the Outer Hebrides. It is also fairly plentiful in N. Wales, breeds sparingly in Brecon and Cardigan; on Dartmoor a few pairs are breeding again regularly. In Ireland numbers are now small and confined to about six counties in the north and north-west. Birds arrive in the breeding areas mainly between mid-February and the end of March, and flocking begins again as soon as the young can fly, generally early in July. In autumn and winter they are well distributed on the coasts and inland, being augmented by passage-migrants and winter-visitors which arrive September to November and return from February to May. Irregular movements occur during winter. Our birds belong to the race *Pluvialis apricaria apricaria* which also breeds in Holland, Denmark, N. Germany and S. Scandinavia. Immigrants include birds of the race *Pluvialis apricaria altifrons*, which in winter plumage is indistinguishable from our native race but in summer may be separated as indicated above; its normal breeding range is Iceland, Faeroes, N. Europe and N. Siberia, but some birds resembling this type have been found breeding in Britain. The species winters south to the Mediterranean region and S.W. Asia.

GREY PLOVER—*Pluvialis squatarola*

BIRD PLATES 42 and 123

The plumage pattern in both winter and summer resembles Golden Plover's, but it is a rather larger and stouter bird, with a stouter bill and in summer has *silver-grey spangling instead of gold* on the upper-parts. Adults in winter have the *upper-parts brownish-grey and much more uniform than any plumage of*

GREY PLOVER
Note the black axillaries.

Golden Plover, with only obscure mottlings. Young birds, on the other hand, have upper-parts spangled and tinged with yellowish and can be easily confused with Golden Plover, but in flight the conspicuous *black axillaries, whitish rump and tail* are diagnostic at all ages, as is the note. In Golden Plover the rump and tail look wholly dark. Both species have a whitish wing-bar. Legs grey. Length about 11 ins.

Habitat. From autumn to spring it frequents the sea-shore, mud-flats and estuaries, and is uncommon inland at reservoirs, sewage-farms, etc.

General Habits. Flight, carriage and general behaviour are very much like Golden Plover's. In Britain it is usually met with in twos and threes or small parties, often associating with other shore-birds. If larger numbers are met with, they are more usually scattered over the flats in small groups than in compact gatherings of any size. Generally it is a shy, wary bird. It occasionally wades in water.

Ordinary flight-note is longer than Golden Plover's, also higher-pitched and typically trisyllabic, "tlee-oo-ee".

Food includes molluscs, worms, crustacea, insects, and some vegetable matter.

Status and Distribution. Mainly a winter-visitor and passage-migrant, arriving from mid-July to mid-November and leaving from mid-March to early June; a few stay the summer. It is generally distributed on the east and south coasts of England, and in small numbers on the west coast and in Scotland where it is scarce north of Solway on the west, and north of Inverness on the

east. In Ireland it visits all coasts. It is a vagrant inland in all parts
of Britain. The bird breeds in arctic Russia, Siberia and America,
and in winter occurs on the coasts of Europe, Africa, S. Asia, N.
and S. America and Australia. There are no subspecies.

LAPWING—*Vanellus vanellus*

BIRD PLATES 42 and 121   EGG PLATE IX (1A, 1B & 1C)

From its prevalence in ordinary agricultural country, and its
striking appearance and call, Lapwing is the most familiar of
waders. On the ground the *long crest and apparently black and
white plumage, the upper-parts showing metallic green at closer
range*, are unmistakable, and in the air the *boldly black and white
effect, broad, rounded wings and relatively slow, flapping action*
are equally distinctive. The crown and broad pectoral band (also
throat in summer) are black, sides and back of head and neck
white, the tail white with a broad, black terminal band, and under
tail-coverts are rufous-buff. Legs reddish-flesh. Young are duller
than adults with buff edgings to feathers of upper-parts and a very
short crest. Length about 12 ins.

Habitat. It likes large or medium-sized open spaces, wherever
the soil is easily accessible, either naked or under some fairly light
vegetation cover. It is predominantly a farm bird, and favours
arable land, especially when newly ploughed or fallow, also
pastures and hayfields. Moist rushy fields and moorlands are
considerably more favoured for breeding than at other periods.
High ground is commonly deserted during winter, but some birds
do not move far and regularly visit their breeding grounds at dusk.
Margins of fresh waters, including temporary floods, and sewage
farms are frequented, especially where there is mud or sand, and
on the coast flocks occur regularly on muddy, sandy and stony
shores, often attaining huge dimensions on mud-flats and estuaries
when birds are driven from inland haunts by hard weather.

General Habits. The flight with slow wing-beats for a wader,
and characteristic "wobbly" action makes identification easy, even
at long range. Flocks do not manoeuvre with the agility of many
waders, but perform more leisurely and less co-ordinated evolutions, and tend to trail out into elongated formations. Ordinary
gait is a not very quick run with a pause every few yards, but it can
also run quite fast. It picks up food like other plovers, by tilting the

body without flexing the legs. It is very gregarious, and outside the breeding-season is nearly always in flocks, sometimes of great size. It can swim well on occasion, though adults do not often do so.

The typical spring song "peerrweet-weet-weet . . . peer-weet" is given in a conspicuous display flight by the male. The bird rises slowly from the ground then quickens pace, rising at an abrupt angle, and suddenly plunges down, turning and twisting, with wings thrown about as though out of control, often appearing to turn a somersault, and then sweeps off with erratic flight. It is heard regularly from early March to late May, sometimes extending a few weeks longer, and exceptionally from late January. Ordinary note uttered sometimes on the ground, but chiefly on wing, is a shrill, rather wheezy *"pee-wit"*.

Food is mainly insects; also molluscs, worms, spiders, crustacea and vegetable matter.

Nests on the ground generally on a slightly raised site, several pairs usually breeding in company. The eggs, normally 4, occasionally 3–5, range in ground-colour usually from clay to olive or umber-brown, but at times from bluish-white to deep green, reddish-brown or light pink. They are laid generally from the first half of April onwards in a muddied hollow, lined with grass stalks, etc., and sometimes quite substantially built. Incubation is by both sexes, usually for 24–27 days, sometimes longer. The young are tended mainly by female, and are fully fledged and flying at 33–42 days. Single-brooded.

Status and Distribution. It is present throughout the year, generally distributed, and breeding in all parts, including most islands, although long-term decrease has made it a scarce bird in some areas as far apart as central Wales and Suffolk; in winter very few remain in parts of N. Scotland. In autumn large numbers arrive from the continent and some of our home-bred birds, especially from northern districts, migrate to Ireland and south to S. Spain. Movement lasts from June to November or later in autumn, and in spring from mid-February till the second half of May. Abroad it breeds in the Faeroes and from N. Scandinavia south to the Mediterranean, also in parts of central Asia and Siberia. It reaches N. Africa and India in winter. There are no subspecies.

KNOT—*Calidris canutus*

BIRD PLATES 51 and 122

It is recognizable, in numbers, by its habit of *feeding in densely packed masses*, and individually by *its considerably larger size than Dunlin, stocky build, grey and white plumage in autumn and winter* (but not so grey and white as Sanderling). The bill is straight, relatively shorter than Dunlin's, legs rather short. In flight in winter plumage it is a grey bird with an inconspicuous white wing-bar, rump and tail paler than back, and tail of uniform appearance, not dark in the centre and white at sides like Dunlin, Sanderling, etc. Under-parts are white with grey markings on the flanks, breast and sides of neck; primaries blackish. Juveniles have a scaly pattern on the upper-parts, and under-parts are generally somewhat suffused with buff. In breeding plumage the back is boldly mottled with black and chestnut, and the *head and under-parts are chestnut*. Length about 10 ins.

Habitat. Outside the breeding-season it frequents coastal and estuarine sand- and mud-flats, especially the more extensive. It is uncommon inland, generally appearing singly or in small parties on sewage-farms, muddy borders of reservoirs, rivers, etc. Non-breeding birds occur on shore in summer.

General Habits. General carriage, flight and method of feeding are much like Dunlin's. On less favoured shores, small parties and even single birds occur at times but typically Knot is very gregarious, and on extensive flats flocks of two or three thousand are not unusual even in mid-winter.

Two main notes are a slightly hoarse monosyllable, the lowest-pitched of the common wader notes, usually rendered as "knut", and a more mellow, whistling, "quick-ick".

Food in winter-quarters includes crustacea, earthworms, insects and molluscs.

Status and Distribution. Mainly a passage-migrant and winter-visitor arriving from mid-July to November and leaving from mid-March to mid-June, but small parties of non-breeders may occur in summer. It is abundant on parts of the E. coast of Great Britain from Dornoch Firth southwards; on the W. coast from the Solway to the Severn Estuary: and on the east coast of Ireland. It is less abundant on the S. coast of England, and elsewhere scarcer. The race concerned, *Calidris canutus canutus*, breeds mainly in Siberia, wintering south to the Mediterranean and W. African coast, also Australia. Another race occurs in N. America.

SANDERLING—*Calidris alba*

BIRD PLATES 51 and 122

A plump little bird slightly larger than Dunlin, with shorter straight bill, and *characterized almost as much by its extreme activity as by the very pale appearance in autumn and winter, with whole under-parts and most of the head white*. The upper-parts are then pale grey with faint dark markings, but the dark front of the closed wing is often noticeable. In flight it shows a *prominent white wing-bar* with quills and front of wing blackish, thus having a more contrasted pattern than Dunlin. The tail has a dark centre showing white at the sides. Young in autumn have the upper-parts chequered black and pale grey, sometimes with a tinge of buff on back and breast. In summer plumage the upper-parts are light chestnut, mottled with black, paler than but not unlike Dunlin. But in Sanderling the *whole head, neck and upper breast are light chestnut rather sharply defined from the pure white belly* and with fine dark markings producing a speckled rather than streaked effect at close range, and its appearance is thus quite different from Dunlin. Length about 8 ins.

Habitat. Outside the breeding-season it is a strictly coastal species preferring sandy shores and flats, though regular in small numbers on mud in some places, and only occurs infrequently on passage on sewage-farms, borders of reservoirs, etc., inland.

General Habits. Although general habits are much like Dunlin's they differ in some ways. Sanderling seems always in a hurry, darting over the sand at an astonishing speed, like a clockwork toy. More than all other small waders it delights to feed along the tide edge, darting after the backwash to snatch sandhoppers, etc., and adroitly avoiding the oncoming breakers. The smaller parties in which it so frequently occurs are often very tame, running along the water's edge in front of the observer. Scattered birds and little groups frequently mix with Dunlin, Ringed Plovers, Knots, etc., but it is very often seen in unmixed flocks.

Note in flight or when flushed is a shrill, but liquid and pleasant sounding "twick, twick".

Food consists especially of small crustacea, molluscs and marine worms. Remains of fish and some vegetable matter are also taken.

Status and Distribution. A passage-migrant and winter-visitor passing south from mid-July to mid-November and returning from March to mid-June. It is widely distributed but occurs chiefly on sandy coasts and is only occasional in the N.W. and

extreme N. Scottish mainland, where it seldom winters. In most
other parts it usually winters in smaller numbers than occur on
passage. Some non-breeding birds may be found in summer. It is
infrequent inland, most often in May. It breeds in arctic Europe,
Asia and America, mainly in remote northern islands, and winters
south to S. Africa, S. Asia, Australia and S. America. There are no
subspecies.

LITTLE STINT—*Calidris minuta*

BIRD PLATES 51 and 122

Stints are the smallest waders. Little Stint is easily distinguishable from Dunlin, to which it has some superficial resemblance, by
its *diminutive size, shorter, straight bill, and white appearance of
breast*; in summer plumage also by the absence of black on the
under-parts. Except in winter, the *upper-parts are predominantly
rufous or buff, mottled black*, while the rarer Temminck's Stint
(which see for fuller details) is a much greyer bird. Most Little
Stints seen in the British Isles are young in autumn plumage, when
the white breast is suffused with buff; the fore-head, cheeks and
superciliary stripe are more or less whitish and the upper-parts
buff and creamy, mottled blackish, the light markings forming a
backwardly directed V on the back. In summer plumage the
upper-parts are richer, more rufous, and the breast is washed with
rufous, with some dark spots at the sides. Wing is much as Dunlin,
with a narrow white wing-bar, not very conspicuous. Adults in
winter plumage are much greyer above with only rather obscure
darker markings, and the whole of the under-parts white with only
faint dusky streakings on sides of breast. Rump and centre of tail
are dark in all plumages, with lateral tail-coverts showing white at
the sides. Legs black. Length about 5¾ ins.
    Habitat. Outside the breeding-season it occurs in the same type
of habitat as Curlew Sandpiper.
    General Habits. More lively in action and even quicker on the
wing than Dunlin, with which it often consorts, and seems to feed
more by picking on the surface than by probing, but otherwise its
habits outside the breeding-season are closely similar. It is seen on
the coast chiefly in small parties or associating with Dunlin,
Curlew Sandpipers, etc., but at times in autumn in flocks of fair
size. Inland it occurs often singly or in small parties. Generally
very tame.

Common note when flushed is a monosyllabic "chit" or "tit" repeated about three times.

Food is mainly insects, small crustacea, molluscs and worms.

Status and Distribution. A passage-migrant in fluctuating numbers in autumn, scarce in spring, appearing from August to October and from mid-April to early June. There are also winter records. It occurs chiefly on the E. and W. coasts, south of Aberdeen and the Solway, less commonly inland and on the south coast. It is also regular in Ireland on E. coast and W. Kerry. Elsewhere it is scarce and irregular. Breeding range is from north-east Norway eastwards across arctic Europe and Asia, and the bird winters south to S. Africa. There are no subspecies.

TEMMINCK'S STINT—*Calidris temminckii*

BIRD PLATES 52 and 122

At all times it is *much greyer than Little Stint, more uniform in colouring and with more or less grey, instead of more or less white, breast*; it may be likened to a miniature Common Sandpiper. Temminck's Stint also differs in its *note*, in the type of ground preferred, and in its behaviour. While Little Stint is essentially a bird of open flats, Temminck's Stint not infrequently resorts to cover amongst low plants and tends to "tower" when flushed. The white instead of grey outer tail-feathers are conspicuous at times (as in rising and alighting); but must not be confused with the white lateral tail-coverts of Little Stint. Adult in breeding-plumage is mouse-grey above, marked with blackish-brown, and with rufous edgings to some of the feathers. In winter the dark and rufous markings are lacking. Young in autumn are quite different from Little Stints, looking uniform grey above and at close quarters showing a delicately pencilled scaly pattern. Legs vary in colour from brown to greenish or yellow, never black as in Little Stint. Length about 5½ ins.

Habitat. In the breeding-season typical haunts are flats covered with short grass or sedge, often with scanty scrub, or of more heathy character near fresh-water pools or streams. Outside the breeding-season in contrast to Little Stint, which is primarily a shore-bird, Temminck's Stint is primarily a fresh-water bird, chiefly resorting to muddy places on marshes, sewage-farms, etc., or by lakes and pools, especially where vegetation affords some cover, and on the coast it prefers creeks and gutters to the open shore.

General Habits. Flight is erratic and twisting. Carriage on the ground is like Dunlin, with quick and lively movements. On the breeding-ground it perches freely on rocks, fences and low bushes, and is usually tame. In general it shows less inclination than most waders to consort with other species and generally occurs singly or in small parties.

Note when flushed is a high-pitched, trilling titter, almost cricket-like, never at all like the monosyllabic "tit, tit, tit" which is the common note of Little Stint.

Food is chiefly insects; also worms.

Nests in a hollow in the ground, lined with grass. The eggs, usually 4, have a greenish ground-colour, usually thickly and fairly evenly spotted with small liver-brown markings. They are laid generally in June. Incubation is by both sexes. The young fly when about 3 weeks old. Single-brooded.

Status and Distribution. Mainly a scarce and irregular passage-migrant occurring from late July to mid-Sept., and in

TEMMINCK'S STINT

May and early June, chiefly south of a line from the Wash to the Scillies. Elsewhere, including Ireland, a rare vagrant, but it has nested in E. Ross and has attempted to do so several times in Inverness, also Yorks. It breeds in N. Europe south to central Norway, and in Siberia, and winters south to central Africa; also in S. Asia. There are no subspecies.

WHITE-RUMPED SANDPIPER—*Calidris fuscicollis*

BIRD PLATE 52

It is the size of a small Dunlin with a shorter, slender bill, straight or with slight decurvature at tip. At favourable angles the diagnostic *white patch crossing above the rather dark tail* is conspicuous, and there is a pale shade on the wing, much less marked than the white wing-stripe of Dunlin. In breeding-plumage the upper-parts are much like those of Little Stint in summer, but the breast is prominently streaked and spotted. Juvenile has a variagated back pattern of warm brown, black and grey. Winter plumage is greyer, not unlike a rather small,

WHITE-RUMPED SANDPIPER

The wings may appear
sickle-shaped.

short-billed Dunlin but the *wings extend well beyond the tail* at rest. The very much shorter, straight bill precludes confusion with Curlew Sandpiper in winter plumage. Legs are dusky greenish or greenish-black. Length about 6¾ ins.

Habitat. On passage it occurs on coastal flats or rocky beaches, especially the latter, and creeks or pools of salt-marshes; also borders of lakes and ponds.

General Habits. These and behaviour seem to be almost exactly like Dunlin's. It is generally tame and confiding and sometimes takes advantage of concealing coloration by crouching.

In general it is rather silent, but has a peculiar and diagnostic flight-note like the squeak of a mouse—"jeet".

Food includes worms, molluscs, crustacea, insects and seeds.

Status and Distribution. A vagrant which has been recorded several times in most recent years chiefly August to October, but also in spring and winter, often on the S.W. or S. coasts of England, also farther north and east, and in Scotland and especially Ireland. It breeds in arctic N. America and winters in S. America. There are no subspecies.

PECTORAL SANDPIPER—*Calidris melanotos*

BIRD PLATE 52

Varying in size between Dunlin and Reeve, it resembles the latter in shape, with a more slender bill, just perceptibly decurved. The crown, neck and back are dark-streaked, the light buff feather-edgings on back usually *aligned into Snipe-like stripes*. Neck and breast are grey-buff, closely streaked blackish, the *streaked region ending abruptly, so as to define a kind of gorget*, contrasted with the white belly, this being its most distinctive feature. In flight the pale grey tail with dark central feathers is sometimes conspicuous as it rises, and the wing has a pale lengthwise shade. It frequently stretches the neck up, when it may look rather slender. Upper-parts are more rufous in summer than in winter plumage. Juveniles are much as adults in summer, but feather-edgings of the upper-parts are brighter, and the breast is more buff or yellowish. *Legs are usually dull yellowish or greenish-yellow.* Length about 7–8 ins. Male larger than female.

Habitat. On passage it is rare on sandy flats or beaches, but frequents wet fresh and salt meadows, preferably where the grass

PECTORAL SANDPIPER

has been cut, and which after a rain are covered with shallow pools of water; also margins of marshy creeks; in winter-quarters is usually found in marshy land with long water weeds abounding.

General Habits. It habitually calls on rising and is inclined to zig-zag as it leaves, erratic at first, but swift and direct when well under way. It has a Snipe-like habit of often standing motionless in grass, and moves slowly when feeding, probing with rapid strokes or picking on surface.

Flight-note is a loud, reedy "kerr" or "trrip-trrip".

Food consists chiefly of insects, also crustacea, worms and some vegetable matter.

Status and Distribution. The most regular American wader, appearing annually in England, Ireland and Scotland, mainly from late August to mid-October, occasionally November, even December; also a few earlier in autumn, and in spring from April onwards. In England and Ireland many records are from S.W., also E. coasts; in Scotland from the northern isles. It breeds in arctic N. America and N.E. Siberia, and winters in S. America. There are no subspecies.

CURLEW SANDPIPER—*Calidris ferruginea*

BIRD PLATES 54 and 122

In autumn and winter it is sufficiently like Dunlin to be fairly easily overlooked amongst flocks of that species. *Though typically the bill is longer, finer and more decurved than Dunlin's*, this is not, taken alone, a safe character, as there is some overlap, and the diagnostic distinction is the *white rump*. The wing is as Dunlin's. Most birds seen in autumn are young, with breast and flanks a delicate buff shading to white on belly, *without spots or streaks*, and the plumage, especially of under-parts, looks much cleaner than that of the dusky-breasted Dunlins, while the general effect of the upper-parts is more spotted or mottled and less streaky than in Dunlin. Other good characters are distinctly longer legs, more definite eye-stripe, slender form, graceful pose, and often more upright carriage. The winter-plumage of adults, not much seen in Britain, is grey above and white below and very like Dunlin's except for the rump. Breeding plumage is unmistakable, *rich chestnut, like Knot, boldly mottled black on the back*. In this plumage the upper tail-coverts are barred blackish and look less white in flight, and females are less richly coloured than males. Length about 7½ ins.

Habitat. Outside the breeding-season like Dunlin it frequents sand and mud-flats, creeks and gullies of salt-marshes; also sewage-farms and muddy patches in marshes and round inland waters.

General Habits. These and behaviour are almost exactly like those of Dunlin, with which it very commonly associates.

Ordinary note is a soft and rather pleasing "chirrip".

Food includes small crustacea, small molluscs, worms, also occasionally vegetable matter.

Status and Distribution. A passage-migrant in fluctuating numbers appearing from mid-July to mid-October, rarely later or in winter, and again from mid-April to early June, but it is much more scarce and irregular in spring. It occurs chiefly on the E. coast of Great Britain and in Midlands, is scarcer on the S. and W. coasts and unknown in the extreme N.W. of Scotland; scarce Shetland and Orkney; in Ireland chiefly on the E. and N. coasts, but is extremely rare in spring. The bird breeds in E. arctic Asia and winters south to S. Africa and New Zealand. There are no subspecies.

PURPLE SANDPIPER—*Calidris maritima*

BIRD PLATES 53 and 122

Distinctly larger than Dunlin, it is a robust and portly little bird, which is *chiefly met with on rocks, is darker in colour than other sandpipers* and has rather short, dull *yellow legs*. In winter the back is dark, almost blackish, the brown showing a purplish gloss at close quarters. Head, neck and breast are sooty-brown, throat whitish and flanks white with prominent dark markings. In breeding plumage rufous edgings to the feathers of the back give a more variegated effect, and the sides of the face are paler. It has then a certain resemblance to a large, dark stocky Dunlin without black belly. The wing has a *white bar on the secondaries* which is noticeable in flight. Length about 8¼ ins.

Habitat. Outside the breeding-season it is strictly a coastal species, chiefly frequenting rocky or boulder-strewn shores and weedy reefs or islets; locally and in small numbers also on muddy shores with stony patches, but on many such it is hardly ever seen, and on sand or mud without stones or rocks it is exceptional and rarely stays long. It is frequently found about piers, groynes, and similar masonry constructions.

General Habits. In winter-quarters it is tamest of waders. Flight is swift and on the whole more direct than most sandpipers, but it seldom flies far and usually keeps low over the water. It is chiefly seen in small parties on rocks newly uncovered by the tide where it forages with tireless activity, turning over sea-weed or debris, and dodging the waves with the utmost agility. It is quite at home swimming in the water if swept off its feet and sometimes even alights on the water voluntarily. It commonly associates with Turnstones.

Rather a silent species as a rule in winter, but it may utter a low "weet-wit" on rising.

Food includes small fish, insects, crustacea, molluscs, also vegetable matter.

Status and Distribution. Mainly a passage-migrant and winter-visitor appearing from mid-July to November and leaving from mid-March to early June. It is widely spread on all coasts, especially rocky ones; on flat coasts it occurs chiefly on passage. A few regularly summer in Orkney and Shetland, and rarely elsewhere. In most years since 1978 a pair or two have bred in the Scottish Highlands. Otherwise it is exceptional inland. The race concerned, *Calidris maritima maritima*, breeds mainly in the Arctic from Canada to N. Scandinavia and Siberia. Other races occur in Alaska and N. Pacific islands. In Europe the bird winters south to the Atlantic coast.

1a, 1b, 1c, 1d. Red-backed Shrike. 2a, 2b. Tree Sparrow. 3a, 3b. House Sparrow. 4a, 4b. Snow   Plate
Bunting. 5a, 5b. Reed Bunting. 6a, 6b. Cirl Bunting. 7a, 7b, 7c. Yellowhammer. 8a, 8b. Corn   I
Bunting. 9a, 9b, 9c. Chaffinch. 10. Crossbill. 11. Starling. 12a, 12b. Bullfinch.
13a, 13b. Linnet. 14. Lesser Redpoll. 15. Goldfinch. 16. Siskin. 17a, 17b. Greenfinch.

PLATE 1a, 1b, 1c, 1d, 1e, 1f. TREE PIPIT. 2. TWITE. 3a, 3b. HAWFINCH. 4a. ROCK PIPIT. 4b, 5. MEADOW
II PIPIT. 6a, 6b. YELLOW WAGTAIL. 7a, 7b. PIED WAGTAIL. 8a, 8b. GREY WAGTAIL. 9a, 9b. SPOTTED
FLYCATCHER. 10. PIED FLYCATCHER. 11. GOLDCREST. 12a, 12b. WOOD WARBLER. 13. CHIFF-
CHAFF. 14a, 14b. WILLOW WARBLER. 15a, 15b. GRASSHOPPER WARBLER. 16. REED WARBLER.
17a, 17b. MARSH WARBLER. 18a, 18b. SEDGE WARBLER. 19a, 19b. GARDEN WARBLER.

1a, 1b. Mistle Thrush.   2a, 2b. Song Thrush.   3. Redwing.   4a, 4b. Ring Ouzel.   Plate
5a, 5b, 5c. Blackbird.   6a, 6b. Blackcap.   7a, 7b. Whitethroat.   8. Lesser Whitethroat.   III
9. Dartford Warbler.   10. Wheatear.   11. Whinchat.   12. Stonechat.   13. Redstart.
14a, 14b. Nightingale.   15a, 15b. Robin.   16. Dunnock.   17a, 17b. Wren.
18. Nuthatch.

PLATE
IV

1a, 1b. RAVEN. 2a, 2b. HOODED CROW. 3a, 3b. CARRION CROW.
4a, 4b. ROOK. 5. CHOUGH. 6. MAGPIE. 7. JAY. 8a, 8b. JACKDAW.

1a, 1b. Treecreeper. 2a, 2b. Great Tit. 3. Blue Tit. 4. Coal Tit. 5. Crested Tit.
6. Marsh Tit. 7. Willow Tit. 8a, 8b. Long-tailed Tit. 9. Bearded Tit. 10a, 10b. Swallow.
11. Hoopoe. 12. Skylark. 13. Woodlark. 14. Golden Oriole. 15. Arctic Skua. 16a, 16b.
Nightjar. 17a, 17b, 17c. Black-headed Gull.

Plate
V

PLATE
VI

1a, 1b, 1c. SANDWICH TERN. 2a, 2b. COMMON TERN. 3. BLACK TERN.
4a, 4b. LITTLE TERN. 5a, 5b. ROSEATE TERN. 6a, 6b. ARCTIC TERN.

1a, 1b. CURLEW. 2a, 2b. COMMON SANDPIPER. 3. BLACK-TAILED
GODWIT. 4a, 4b. DUNLIN. 5a, 5b. REDSHANK. 6. WHIMBREL.

PLATE
VII

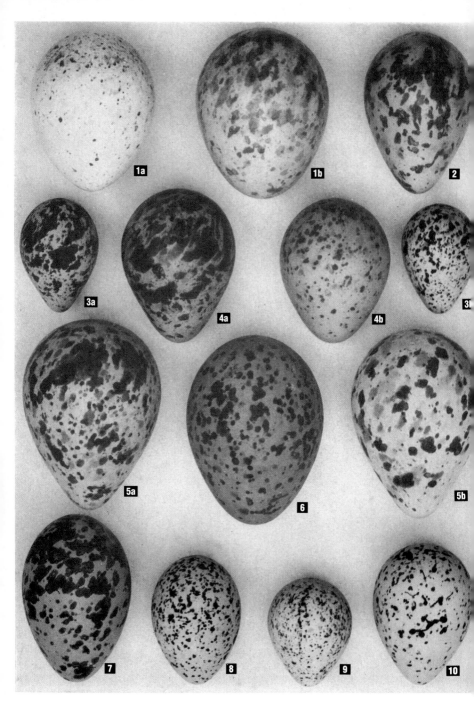

PLATE 1a, 1b. Woodcock. 2. Ruff. 3a, 3b. Red-necked Phalarope. 4a, 4b. Snipe. 5a, 5b. Greenshank.
VIII 6. Avocet. 7. Dotterel. 8. Kentish Plover. 9. Little Ringed Plover. 10. Ringed Plover.

1a, 1b, 1c. Lapwing. 2a, 2b. Oystercatcher.
3a, 3b. Golden Plover. 4a, 4b. Stone Curlew.

Plate
IX

PLATE   1. Coot.   2. Moorhen.   3. Pheasant.   4. Water Rail.   5. Corncrake.   6. Spotted Crake.
X   7. Red Grouse.   8. Grey Partridge   9. Quail.   10. Red-legged Partridge.
11. Capercaillie.   12. Black Grouse.   13. Ptarmigan.

1a, 1b. Buzzard. 2a, 2b. Kestrel. 3a, 3b. Peregrine.
4. Merlin. 5a, 5b. Sparrowhawk. 6. Hobby.

Plate
XI

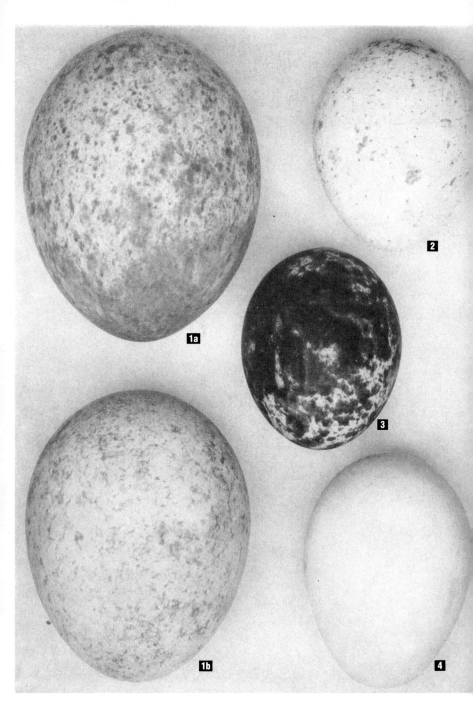

Plate
XII

1a, 1b. Golden Eagle.   2. Red Kite.   3. Honey Buzzard.   4. Goshawk.

Types of Eggs of Common Cuckoo (*Cuculus canorus canorus*) 1. Cuckoo with 1a Meadow Pipit. 2. Cuckoo with 2a Meadow Pipit. 3. Cuckoo with 3a Pied Wagtail. 4. Cuckoo with 4a Pied Wagtail. 5. Cuckoo with 5a Reed Warbler. 6. Cuckoo with 6a Reed Warbler. 7. Cuckoo with 7a Robin. 8. Cuckoo with 8a Robin. 9. Cuckoo with 9a Dunnock. 10. Cuckoo with 10a Dunnock.

Plate XIII

PLATE 1. GREAT BLACK-BACKED GULL. 2. HERRING GULL. 3. COMMON GULL. 4. LESSER BLACK-BACKED
XIV   GULL. 5. KITTIWAKE.

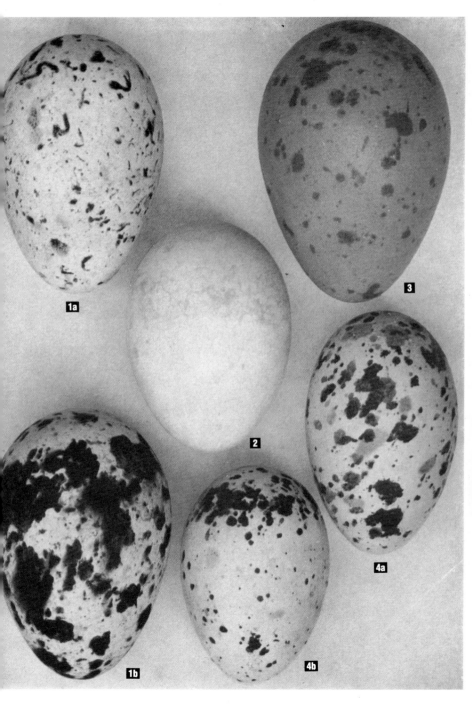

1a, 1b. RAZORBILL. 2. PUFFIN. 3. GREAT SKUA. 4a, 4b. BLACK GUILLEMOT. PLATE
XV

PLATE
XVI

1a, 1b, 1c, 1d. GUILLEMOT.

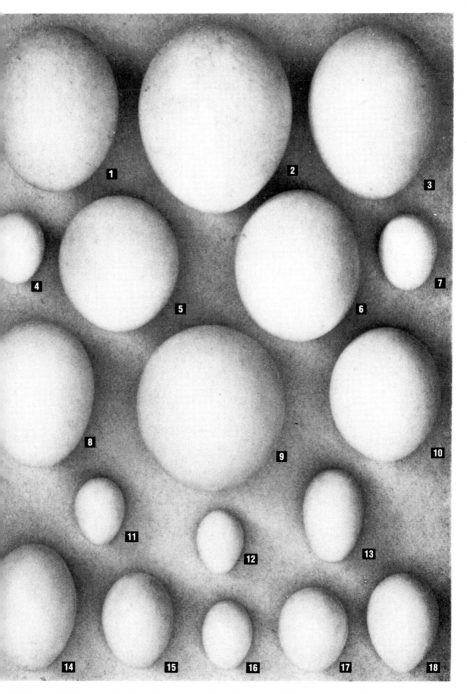

1. Montagu's Harrier.   2. Marsh Harrier.   3. Hen Harrier.   4. Black Redstart.   5. Short-   Plate
eared Owl.   6. Long-eared Owl.   7. Wryneck.   8. Barn Owl.   9. Tawny Owl.   10. Little   XVII
Owl.   11. House Martin.   12. Sand Martin.   13. Swift.   14. Green Woodpecker.   15. Great
Spotted Woodpecker.   16. Lesser Spotted Woodpecker.   17. Kingfisher.   18. Dipper.

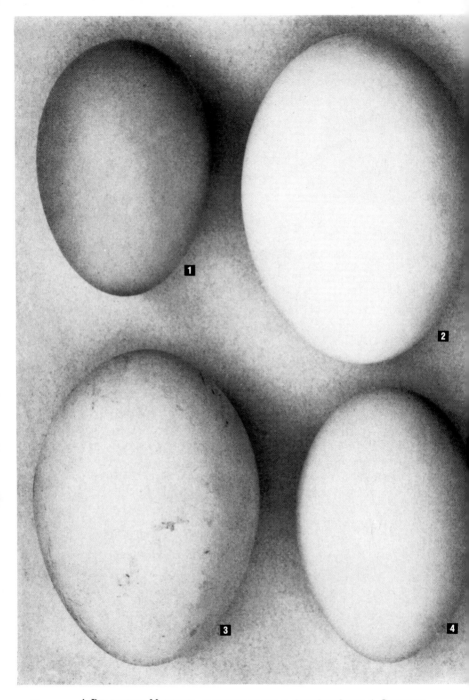

PLATE
XVIII

1. Red-breasted Merganser   2. Canada Goose.   3. Grey Lag Goose.   4. Goosander.

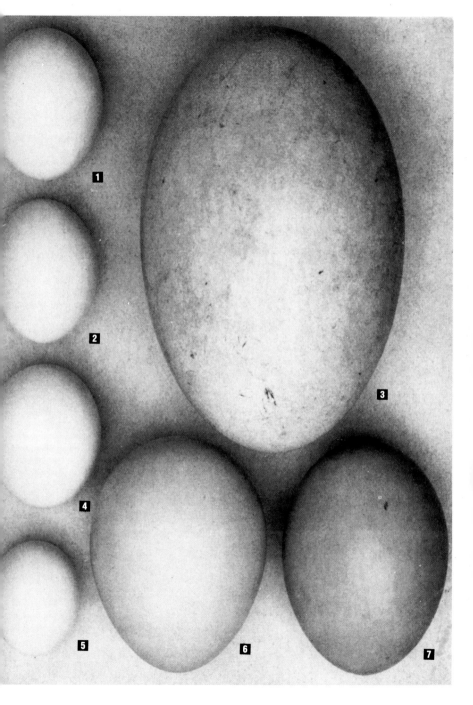

1. Woodpigeon. 2. Stock Dove. 3. Whooper Swan. 4. Rock Dove. 5. Turtle Dove.
6. Common Scoter. 7. Pochard.

Plate
XIX

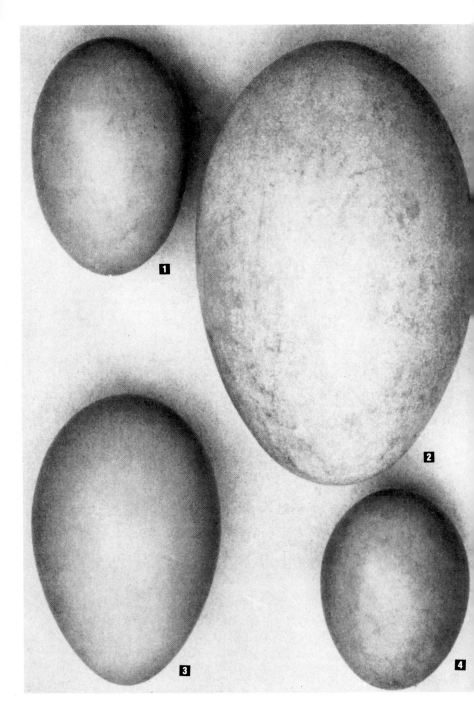

PLATE
XX

1. SCAUP. 2. MUTE SWAN. 3. EIDER. 4. TUFTED DUCK.

1. TEAL. 2. SHELDUCK. 3. GARGANEY. 4. SHOVELER. 5. PINTAIL.
6. GADWALL. 7. MALLARD. 8. WIGEON.

PLATE
XXI

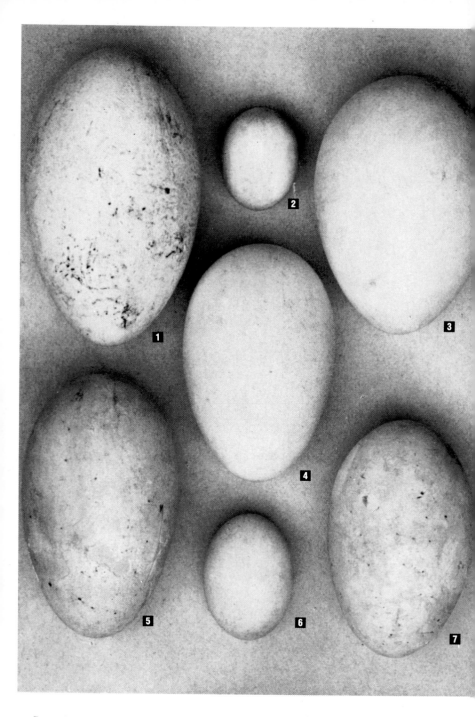

PLATE 1. GANNET. 2. STORM PETREL. 3. FULMAR. 4. MANX SHEARWATER. 5. CORMORANT. 6. LEACH'S
XXII   PETREL. 7. SHAG.

1. RED-THROATED DIVER.   2. SLAVONIAN GREBE.   3. GREAT CRESTED GREBE.   4. BITTERN.   Plate
5. BLACK-NECKED GREBE.   6. BLACK-THROATED DIVER.   7. LITTLE GREBE.   8. GREY HERON.   XXIII

DUNLIN—*Calidris alpina*

Bird Plates 53 and 122   Egg Plate VII (4A & 4B)

Dunlin is the commonest and most ubiquitous of shore-birds. A small wader with a *fairly long, practically straight or slightly decurved bill* and characteristic round-shouldered pose, distinguished in winter plumage by *brownish-grey upper-parts and greyish breast* (not clear, clean grey and pure white like Sanderling), and more strikingly in summer by chestnut and black back and a *black patch on the lower breast*. A fairly noticeable whitish wing-bar—but a good deal less conspicuous than in Sanderling—shows in flight, but the narrow white sides of the dark central area of rump and tail are much the same. Sides of the head, neck and upper breast are greyish with dark streaks; wing-quills blackish, coverts mostly grey. As in many waders the dates of moult vary greatly and birds in nearly complete winter and summer plumage may be seen together. Young in autumn have upper-parts much as adults, but the feather edgings are more buff than chestnut, and throat and breast are rather dingy buff with dark streaks. Bill is noticeably variable, in some markedly longer and more distinctly curved than in others. Length about 6¾ ins. to 7½ ins.

Habitat. In the breeding-season it frequents elevated moorlands, typically hummocky grass moors with peaty pools and boggy tracts; also a few lowland peat-mosses, and grassy salt- or fresh-water marshes with pools. Outside the breeding-season it frequents muddy, sandy or shingly, coastal or estuarine shores of almost every type, but chiefly wide mud-flats and the creeks and gutters of adjoining salt-marshes, and is a frequent visitor to sewage-farms, muddy borders of lakes, reservoirs or rivers, and marshes inland. Non-breeding parties occur on shore in summer.

General Habits. In general behaviour and habits outside the breeding-season, Dunlin may be taken as typical of all the small shore-birds of the stint type. It is extremely gregarious and generally met with in company, from small groups to flocks of hundreds on the more extensive flats. It associates freely with Ringed Plover and other small waders, and flocks frequently feed on the same ground as Redshank and larger species. Often it feeds along the tide-line and where water is quiet it will wade in shallows and can swim if obliged to; but much food is obtained away from immediate contact with water on recently uncovered flats. On the shore the smaller parties, especially of young birds, are often very tame, but the big flocks are difficult to approach. On taking wing, a compact flock is formed which sweeps along over the sea or flats with an astonishing unison of movement, changing shape as it goes, the birds wheeling and swerving, and tilting as they do so, so that a flock now appears dark and now flashes white, as first the upper- and then the under-side of every bird is turned towards the observer. As the tide rises the Dunlin, with other waders, gather on raised banks or higher parts of the beach or salt-marsh to await the ebb. Times of feeding and resting or sleeping are naturally mainly conditioned by tides, and birds feed both by day and night.

Ordinary note when flushed is a shrill, rather nasal "dzeep". Song is a rich purring trill of varying length which is uttered in ordinary flight, in a more definite display-flight, and on the ground. It is heard regularly in May, June and July, and to a lesser extent from late March to early October, occasionally on the shore.

Food consists almost entirely of insects, molluscs, crustacea and worms.

Nests on the ground, almost always close to water. The eggs, normally 4, but 2–6 recorded, have ground-colour ranging from pale bluish-green to brown. They are laid generally from mid-May onwards in a neat little cup hollowed out in a tussock of grass, lined with bents and sometimes a few dead leaves, but on moorlands among heather in a hollow lined with leaves. Incubation is by both sexes for about 21–22 days. The young are usually attended by both parents. Single-brooded.

Status and Distribution. Present throughout the year, breeding in Scotland widely in Orkney, Shetland, Outer Hebrides and N. mainland, rarer elsewhere, and mainly absent from central and eastern areas. In England it breeds thinly on the Pennines south to N. Derby, and on low ground in the north-west, and a pair or two on Dartmoor; in central and N. Wales sparingly on moorland, and in Ireland in small numbers in the centre, north-west and north. Breeding grounds are occupied about the end of April and abandoned as soon as the young can fly. Some birds, probably non-breeders, remain on the coast through the summer, and it is frequent on all coasts and often inland in winter, and especially on passage. Passage-migrants and winter-visitors arrive from August to November and leave from late February to late May. Our breeding birds belong to the race *Calidris alpina schinzii* whose range extends from Iceland to the Baltic, but winter-visitors belong almost exclusively to the race *Calidris alpina alpina* which is seldom separable in the field although on average larger and longer-billed, and which breeds in arctic Europe and W. Siberia, wintering south to the Cape of Good Hope. Another race occurs in N.E. Siberia and N. America.

BROAD-BILLED SANDPIPER—*Limicola falcinellus*

BIRD PLATE 54

The general form is not unlike a small Dunlin, though the shorter legs give a *squat appearance*, but in summer plumage the *very dark Snipe-like pattern of the back* is unlike any other sandpiper. The feathers are black, edged with light buffish, the light edgings giving an effect of stripes. In addition to a broad light eye-stripe, there is a light line at the side of the blackish crown giving the *head a more or less striped effect*, but the markings are not always equally distinct. The throat, breast, and sides of neck are strongly streaked, the rest of the under-parts white. In winter upper-parts are grey, Dunlin-like, usually with black patch at carpal joint but which many Dunlin show too, and the *very white throat and double eye-stripe* are good distinctions; the latter is less prominent than in summer but visible at 50 yards in side view, the superciliary stripe being whiter than that which forks off it up to the side of the crown. Juvenile is much as adult in winter, but under-parts are more buff. On the wing the rump shows a blackish centre and pale sides, but the wing-bar is poorly marked and sometimes not visible. The bill is longer than Dunlin's, rather heavy looking and slightly decurved, sometimes appearing to be angled (rather than curved) downwards towards the tip. Length about 6½ ins.

Habitat. On passage in Europe it seldom appears far inland, but chiefly on salt-marshes, muddy creeks and inlets or muddy patches on marshy ground or bordering lagoons and pools near the coast, rather than on the open shore.

BROAD-BILLED SANDPIPER

Note stripes above eye.

General Habits. It usually flies low over water, often not going far, and is inclined to be rather quiet and inactive. It is not much inclined to associate with other species, though found with Dunlins, etc., at times.

Ordinary note when flushed is a dry, deep trill, "chrreep" or "trreerrk".

Food includes worms, molluscs, insects and vegetable matter.

Status and Distribution. A rare vagrant which has occurred chiefly from August to October, and a few times in spring. Most records are from Norfolk and Sussex; it has also occurred in Scotland and Ireland. The race concerned, *Limicola falcinellus falcinellus*, breeds in Scandinavia and probably N. Russia, and winters in the Mediterranean and S.W. Asia. Another race occurs in E. Siberia.

BUFF-BREASTED SANDPIPER—*Tryngites subruficollis*

BIRD PLATE 53

It usually frequents inland and upland fields and is the only small wader (about size of Common Sandpiper) which has the *whole of the under-parts, including throat and sides of face, coloured buff*. On some birds the buff fades to whitish on the belly and under tail-coverts. The back has a clear-cut pattern of blackish feathers with sharply defined buff borders much like juvenile Ruff. The bill is short for a sandpiper, and the head noticeably small and rounded. *Lacks conspicuous markings on wings and tail*, but in flight overhead the under-side of the wing is seen to be crossed by peculiar black and white scale-like marks. Summer adult and winter plumage scarcely differ. Young are much as adults, but the colours are less contrasted above, the feathers edged whitish. Length about 7¼–8 ins.

Habitat. On passage it is sometimes found on the borders of lakes, etc., but prefers grasslands, and in winter-quarters chiefly on dry open ground.

General Habits. It flies with neck drawn in, generally low down, with many turns and zig-zags. Its carriage and pose are very much like a plover and it is noticeably alert, the long neck always being stretched up when it is approached, though the bird is excessively tame. It feeds with legs bent, giving a crouching attitude, and has a high-stepping gait as if stepping over grass. It easily escapes notice on the ground owing to its habit of "freezing" when approached.

Not a noisy bird. The spring (or adult) note recalls two stones chipped together, but quiet and very short. Note of young in autumn is extremely like Pectoral Sandpiper's.

Food is chiefly insects and a few seeds.

Status and Distribution. Formerly a very rare vagrant, but with the increased flow of records during the past 30 years several are reported annually, many in Ireland and S.W. England, especially Scilly, and almost annually in Scotland including a sprinkling on E. Coast. It has occurred in most months from May to November, but mainly in September. The bird breeds in arctic N. America and winters in S. America. There are no subspecies.

RUFF—*Philomachus pugnax*

BIRD PLATES 55 and 123   EGG PLATE VIII (2)

The extraordinary *ruff and ear-tufts* render male in breeding-plumage unmistakable, but birds on spring passage in the British Isles seldom show them, although males in full plumage do occur. In its other plumages the species lacks outstanding features and is apt to puzzle the inexperienced. It is a medium-sized wader with shorter bill and rather shorter legs than Redshank, showing a very slight pale wing-bar when it flies, and an *oval white patch on each side of the dark central area of the tail* is a good character at all ages; occasionally the white oval patches are extended to form a white horseshoe across the base of the tail. The feet project a little beyond tail in flight. Size varies markedly; mostly birds seen in Britain are young on autumn passage, which are smaller than adults and show a *neat bold pattern on the back as the black-brown feathers have sharply defined buff borders*, with fore-neck and sides of breast pinkish-buff. Female (or Reeve) in breeding-plumage is much the same but often greyer. Winter plumage is much greyer and more uniform and the sexes are generally similar except for size, but some males have white on head or neck. Ruff and ear-tufts of breeding male are extraordinarily variable in colour and pattern, barred or unbarred, and showing white, black, purple, chestnut, and buff in different combinations; the back also may be patchily marked; usually the breast and flanks are largely black. The bill is straight or just perceptibly decurved. Colour of

legs is variable, showing different shades of orange, yellow, greenish, brownish, and grey. Length of adult male about 11–12 ins.,
female about 8½–10 ins.

Habitat. In the breeding-season it resorts to grassy marshes,
fens, and moist meadows, in widely differing surroundings. On
passage it frequents chiefly swamps, marshes, wet meadows,
marshy and muddy borders of inland waters, sewage-farms, etc.;
it also occurs, but much less regularly, on muddy shores, estuaries,
etc., where it prefers creeks and tidal gutters to open flats. In
winter it often moves on to meadows or plough, consorting with
Lapwings.

General Habits. Flight is much like Redshank but more
deliberate. When standing still the carriage is generally more erect
than Redshank and sandpipers, but when moving the body is held
more horizontal. Breeding birds resort to special display grounds.

In general a very silent bird but when flushed it occasionally
calls a low "tu-whit".

Food is chiefly insects; also worms, molluscs and seeds.

Nests mainly among grass which, if thick, completely hides the
nest from above. The eggs, normally 4, but rarely 3, are laid
generally in May in a hollow neatly lined with fine grasses.
Incubation is by female alone, for about 21 days. The young are
tended by hen, but become independent after a few days. Single-
brooded.

Status and Distribution. Mainly a passage-migrant from late
June to October, and March to May, and is occasional in summer,
but a number have wintered recently in various areas as far north as
S.E. Scotland. It had only rarely bred in this country during the
present century until nesting began in 1963, perhaps earlier, on the
Ouse Washes (Cambs/Norfolk); it has since been proved in several
other counties including Lancs and Sutherland, and may occur
annually. It is more numerous in autumn than spring, appearing
mostly on the east side of Great Britain from the Forth southwards, and in the Midlands, but it also occurs regularly in most
English counties. In Ireland it is now regularly reported in a
number of localities including the S.W., mainly in autumn, but
some also winter. It breeds from N. Scandinavia south to
W. France and Hungary, extending eastwards into Siberia,
and it winters south to Cape Province and Sri Lanka. There are no
subspecies.

JACK SNIPE—*Lymnocryptes minimus*

BIRD PLATES 50 and 123

It is *smaller than Snipe, with a relatively shorter bill*, and *rises silently* with a slower flight, not zig-zagging so abruptly and generally pitching again after a short distance; usually it is reluctant to fly at all. The crown pattern differs from Snipe's, lacking the pale central stripe and having one on either side separated by a narrow black border from a less prominent pale stripe above the eye; the plumage has more metallic green and purple gloss and the flanks show dark mottlings instead of distinct bars. The effect of two light buff stripes on either side of the back produced by light edgings of the mantle feathers is often very marked. Legs greenish. Length about 7½ ins.; bill about 1⅝ ins.

Habitat. Outside the breeding-season it occurs in much the same types of country as Snipe.

General Habits. In contrast to the frequently gregarious Snipe, it is nearly always flushed singly, though some numbers may be present on the same ground, and they rarely join together in the air. Otherwise general habits and behaviour do not differ much from Snipe's.

It is normally silent when flushed, but does occasionally utter a feeble Snipe-like "skaap".

Food is mainly earthworms, molluscs and insects; also some vegetable matter such as seeds.

Status and Distribution. A winter-visitor and passage-migrant, arriving September to November and returning from early March to late April, while hard weather movements occur through the winter. It is widely distributed but decidedly local, and numbers are variable though usually small. It has occasionally been recorded in summer. The bird breeds in N. Europe south to Poland, occasionally N. Germany also Siberia, wintering south to central Africa. There are no subspecies.

SNIPE—*Gallinago gallinago*

BIRD PLATES 50 and 123 EGG PLATE VIII (4A & 4B)

Characterized by *very long, straight bill and longitudinal striped effect of dark, richly patterned upper-parts*, Snipe is most often seen as it *rises from marsh or pool with a hoarse note and zig-zags rapidly for a few yards* before going clear away. For differences from Great and Jack Snipe, see those species. The crown is black with a central buffish streak, the sides of head are brown with buff streaks above and below eye, the neck and breast are buff with dark brown markings, the flanks paler and barred. There are narrow white tips to the secondaries; the tail is irregularly barred black and tawny, showing a little white at the sides. Legs pale greenish. Juvenile has the longitudinal light stripes on the upper-parts considerably narrower than in adult. A well-defined melanistic variety is the so-called "Sabine's Snipe". Length about 10½ ins.; bill about 2½ ins.

Habitat. It frequents open grassy and sedgy marshes, lowland and hill bogs, peat-moors, ill-drained rushy fields, sewage-farms, marshy borders of lakes or streams; also occurring sometimes on coastal salt-marshes and exceptionally even on shore. In parts of Scotland it occurs regularly amongst heather, etc., on quite dry hillsides. It is met with in winter on small areas of marsh, etc., where it does not breed.

General Habits. Snipe are much less seen in the open than most waders, being largely crepuscular and spending most of the day resting in cover of coarse vegetation, but they also feed to a varying extent by day, in the open. When taken unawares the bird often crouches and does not fly till obliged. In pitching it is fond of dropping from a height, rather than descending gradually. In spring and summer it perches on posts, fences, etc., and not very uncommonly on the top branches of dead or bare trees. For feeding it delights in semi-liquid ooze of bogs, sewage-farms, etc., and the wet mud on the edge of standing waters. It is not markedly gregarious, frequently rising singly even where many are present on the same ground, but "wisps" of half-a-dozen or more are often seen flying together with the same co-ordination as other waders and occasionally regular flocks of much larger size may be met with, flying and feeding together. Where good cover is not available on the feeding ground, regular flighting movements occur towards dusk. The well-known drumming or bleating flight may occur at almost any time of year but is regular from about late March to mid-June, and less frequent earlier in March and until the end of July. In performing it, the bird dives down at an angle of about 45° with tail spread, the descent being accompanied by a resonant, tremulous sound lasting about two seconds and caused by the vibration of the outer pair of tail feathers. The bird frequently climbs again to repeat the display over and over again.

Note usually, but not always, uttered when flushed and often continued when well on the wing, is a hoarse, grating "scaap".

Spring note, and alarm, is a persistent, quick, rhythmical, throbbing "chip-per, chip-per, chip-per . . .".

Food consists very largely of worms; also insects, molluscs and woodlice. Vegetable matter includes grass and seeds.

Nests on the ground in a grass tussock, clump of rushes, or occasionally among heather, but not far from water or bog. The eggs, normally 4, 3–6 also recorded, have ground-colour varying as a rule from olive-grey to olive-brown, also pale blue to deep umber. They are laid generally from early April onwards in a hollow lined with grasses. Incubation is by female only, for about 19½–20 days. The young leave the nest when dry, tended by both parents and can fly soon after 14 days old, although not fully grown until about 7 weeks old. Double-brooded in some cases. There are several records of young chicks being carried by their parents, in a similar manner to Woodcock.

Status and Distribution. Present throughout the year, breeding widely but locally. It is declining, particularly on lowland farmland, and now scarce or irregular in many parts of south and central England; Norfolk holds about a quarter of the population of England and Wales. Some northern and Scottish birds winter in Ireland but there is little evidence of British birds migrating abroad. On passage and in winter the species is abundant and widely spread, sometimes in large congregations; visitors from N.W. Europe, Faeroes and Iceland arrive from September to November and return in March, April and early May. The birds breeding in Orkney and Shetland belong to the race *Gallinago gallinago faeroeensis* which also breeds in Iceland and the Faeroes. It is indistinguishable in the field from the race *Gallinago gallinago gallinago* which occupies the rest of the British Isles, also most of Europe south to North Portugal and Bulgaria, and Asia to the Himalayas. A single example has occurred in the Outer Hebrides of the N. American race *Gallinago gallinago delicata* which is inseparable in the field from our bird. Other races occur in N.E. Asia and Africa.

GREAT SNIPE—*Gallinago media*

Bird Plates 49 and 123

It tends to haunt drier situations than the Snipe, compared with which it is a *larger, heavier and darker bird on the wing*, with a conspicuous amount of white on the sides of the tail, visible if bird flies directly away, but otherwise can be inconspicuous. On being flushed it goes off usually to no great distance with *slower and more direct flight, without the twistings of common Snipe*. It generally rises reluctantly and without calling. The flight silhouette recalls Woodcock. The markings closely resemble those of Snipe, but the *flanks are more boldly barred* and the wing-coverts have prominent white tips, giving a more barred effect. These points, however, are generally of little use in the field, as it is seldom that one gets a good view on the ground, and juveniles, since they lack the conspicuous white on the tail, are practically not identifiable with certainty at all except in the hand. Length about 11 ins.; bill about 2½ ins.

Habitat. Outside the breeding-season it frequently occurs on more or less dry ground, such as rough pastures, fields, moorlands, sand-dunes, wood-borders, etc., and amongst such cover as bracken, crops or stubble, although also regularly in marshy localities.

General Habits. It is mainly nocturnal, and in fine weather sits very close. General habits seem to be much like Snipe but in flight wings are more bowed and bill held more horizontally.

It occasionally utters a monosyllabic guttural croak on rising.

Food is chiefly earthworms; also molluscs and insects.

Status and Distribution. A vagrant, perhaps occurring annually (formerly more frequent) August to mid-November but chiefly September, more rarely spring, sometimes in winter. Most have been recorded in N. Scotland (mainly on Fair Isle), in S.E. England, and Scilly Isles; very rarely in Ireland. It breeds from about the Arctic Circle in Scandinavia south to N. Germany and east through Asia to E. Siberia. It winters south to Cape Province. There are no subspecies.

SHORT-BILLED DOWITCHER—*Limnodromus griseus*

BIRD PLATE 49

‑ A rather stocky, short-legged bird of open mud-flats, about the size of a Knot but with a *very long snipe-like bill*. In flight it shows a *narrow white patch in the centre of the dark back*, much like Spotted Redshank; the upper tail-coverts and tail are barred but look brownish at a distance. In breeding plumage *the whole under-parts are dull rufous*. In autumn and winter the upper-parts are ashy- or brownish-grey, the under-parts greyish- or buffish-white with the flanks barred and spotted; there is a distinct pale eyestripe. Often impossible to separate from Long-billed Dowitcher, which see for distinctions. Length about 10 ins.

Habitat. Outside the breeding-season it frequents mud- and sand-flats of sheltered bays and estuaries, less commonly borders of lakes, and salt-marsh pools. In addition to open flats, it regularly visits reed-fringed bays of lakes, which most other waders avoid.

General Habits. On the wing it appears stout and compact, flight being swift and steady with head drawn in and bill pointed somewhat downward. Its gait is leisurely and graceful. Normally, it carries the head well tucked into the shoulders and bill pointing down at an angle of about 45 degrees, noticeably less horizontal than a Godwit. In feeding it probes in mud and sand or shallow water with quick deep perpendicular strokes. It associates quite freely with other waders, such as Grey Plover and Lesser Yellow-legs, and is generally tame and unsuspicious.

Flight-note is a quick, rather nasal "chu-chu-chu", with a somewhat Turnstone-like quality; monosyllabic calls are rare.

Food includes insects, leeches, molluscs and some vegetable matter.

Status and Distribution. A vagrant, previously generally confused with Long-billed Dowitcher. Out of over 40 past dow-itcher records up to 1960 most are now indeterminate, but several of them, and more recent records, are referred to this species. They are mainly from E. and S. England in September–November (exceptionally winter or spring); also recorded in Ireland. They include one definite example of the race *Limno-dromus griseus hendersoni* which breeds from Hudson Bay to N. Alberta and north to Great Slave Lake, and an almost certain example of *Limnodromus griseus griseus* which breeds from Ungava east of Hudson Bay; these races winter from southern U.S.A. south to Brazil. A third race breeds in Alaska.

LONG-BILLED DOWITCHER—*Limnodromus scolopaceus*

Bird Plate 49

Extremely similar to Short-billed Dowitcher, which see for general description. The best field indications appear to be the voice (see below), and bill length. The bill averages longer in this

LONG-BILLED DOWITCHER

Note barring on flanks
near tail.

species, but there is so much overlap that this character is seldom diagnostic; birds with bill more than twice length of head are likely to be Long-billed, and those with bill not exceeding 1½ times length of head are probably Short-billed. Generally the undertail coverts of Long-billed are barred and those of Short-billed are spotted, but the difference is marginal and even if established it cannot always be relied upon, as some Short-billed have barred coverts, and some Long-billed spotted; moreover individuals which have spent some months here have appeared spotted in winter plumage and barred in summer. In summer plumage the breast of Long-billed is deep salmon or brick-red heavily barred transversely, while that of Short-billed is paler, more orange, and may be spotted or unmarked.

Habitat. More arctic in the breeding-season than Short-billed Dowitcher, it nests on open tundra. On passage it is *largely a fresh-water species*, frequenting lake-shores and quite small marsh pools.

General Habits. Exactly as Short-billed, though perhaps less gregarious.

A shrill "keeek", usually uttered singly, though occasionally doubled or trebled, is considered diagnostic, but other calls can resemble those regarded as more typical of Short-billed.

Food is not known to differ materially from that of Short-billed.

Status and Distribution. A vagrant, seen annually. The species has only recently been separated from the Short-billed Dowitcher, and it remains difficult to know with certainty to which species to assign most past, and some present, British records. The majority however evidently refer to Long-billed which has been identified at points on the S., E. and W. coasts of England, in Scotland, Wales and Ireland. It has occurred from September to November but chiefly in October; exceptionally in winter. It breeds in N. and W. Alaska and N.W. Canada and winters south at least to Mexico. There are no subspecies.

WOODCOCK—*Scolopax rusticola*

BIRD PLATES 50 and 123   EGG PLATE VIII (1A & 1B)

It is generally seen as a *medium-sized, round-winged, russet-coloured bird, with long straight bill, which rises from cover in open woodland and flies off with a twisting flight amongst trees*. If seen on the ground the long bill, much larger size and stouter build than Snipe, upper-parts beautifully marbled with rich browns, buff and black, and light brown under-parts finely barred with dark brown make it unmistakable. There are black transverse bars on the back of the crown and neck. When incubating or at rest the colour-pattern harmonizes amazingly with dead leaves and earth, and bird is very difficult to see. Juvenile is much like adult. Length about 13½ ins.; bill about 3 ins.

Habitat. It chiefly frequents moist woods of oak, birch or conifers, with open glades or rides and good cover of bracken, brambles and bushes, especially evergreens; also rough ground with more scattered trees, scrub and ground cover of the type indicated. Woods with swampy hollows and overgrown ditches are often frequented, but the bird requires dry ground to rest in by day, and flights at dusk to feed on marshes, boggy ground and spongy places about springs and rills. In the breeding-season seclusion and freedom from disturbance appear important. In autumn before the onset of cold weather, it is found largely on moorlands and hill country, sheltering in tall heather and bracken, and in Ireland it also breeds on bracken- and furze-clad hillsides and even treeless marine islands.

General Habits. The mode of flight varies, strong and rapid on occasions, but when undisturbed often rather slow and wavering; bill inclined downwards. When flushed it often rises with consider-able noise of wings and, dodging swiftly amongst tree-trunks, frequently drops into cover again at no great distance. Crepuscular in habits, Woodcock rest by day amongst ground vegetation, and flight at dusk with great regularity to feeding-grounds. When dark nights have curtailed the hours of feeding and still more when open ground is frozen, it will feed by day along ditches or in boggy hollows in woods. In display flight, known as "roding", the male at dusk repeatedly traverses a regular circuit flying quite fast, but with a slow, owl-like wing-action, a little above the tree-tops. This occurs mainly between early March and early July, sometimes 2 or 3 birds together. Otherwise it is among the least sociable of waders and is practically always seen singly.

In "roding" it gives a thrice-repeated low croaking sound followed immediately by a thin "tsiwick". The "tsiwick" is also used in non-roding flights.

Food is largely earthworms, but also insects and their larvae, and some other animal matter; also seeds and grass.

Nests often at the foot of a tree, sometimes quite open, sometimes sheltered by undergrowth. The eggs, normally 4, occasionally 3, and 6 recorded, have ground-colour ranging from greyish-white to warm brown. They are laid generally from mid-March or April onwards in a mere hollow in mossy ground lined only with dead leaves which lie in profusion around. Incubation is by female only, for about 20–21 days. Transporting the young by air, usually carried between the parent's thighs and often pressed against the breast, is well-established as a regular, if infrequent, habit. Double-brooded.

Status and Distribution. Present throughout the year. It breeds in every county in Ireland; in Scotland it breeds commonly north to E. Ross and E. Sutherland, and locally further north, but is absent from Outer Hebrides, Orkney and Shetland. Widespread in much of England and E. Wales, but scarcer in the triangle Thames–Severn–Humber, and rare in S.W. England and W. Wales. Most British birds are sedentary, but in winter some from the north go to Ireland and others as far as Portugal. Continental immigrants arrive in this country from mid-September but mainly in the second half of October and November, returning from mid-March to early May. They are quite widely distributed in winter, but in hard weather some seek the vicinity of the coasts, especially in the west. The race concerned, *Scolopax rusticola rusticola*, breeds in Europe from N. Scandinavia south to the Pyrenees and Bulgaria, also in Azores, Madeira, Canaries, and in Asia east to Japan. Another race occurs in the Riu Kiu islands.

BLACK-TAILED GODWIT—*Limosa limosa*

BIRD PLATES 45 and 121   EGG PLATE VII (3)

In flight it is easily distinguished from Bar-tailed Godwit by a *broad white wing-bar and long legs projecting conspicuously beyond the tail*; also, as the bird flies away, by its *dark, not white, rump and pure white tail with broad terminal band of black*. On the ground its appearance is also distinct, as its *longer legs give it a noticeably taller, more upstanding, appearance*, in contrast to Bar-tailed whose legs look rather short for the bird's size; and its *bill is longer and quite straight or only very faintly up-curved*. In winter plumage the back is brownish-grey, darker than Bar-tailed Godwit's. In summer the head, neck and breast become chestnut but this is duller than in the Bar-tailed and does not extend to the under tail-coverts, while blackish markings are more conspicuous on both under- and upper-parts. Female is usually duller than male. The bill is pink shading to blackish towards the tip; legs greenish-black. Juveniles are much like adult winter, but have neck and breast more or less tinged rufous. Length about 15–17 ins.; bill about 3¾–4¾ ins.

Habitat. In the breeding-season it frequents reclaimed grass-lands or rough pasture in marshy or well-watered districts, tussocky swamps, and bogs; more sparingly on heaths, and scrub-grown tracts. Outside the breeding-season, though occurring regularly on mud-flats and shore, it is fonder of the mixed mud and salt-marsh on the borders of estuaries, etc., than the open shore and is much more of an inland bird than Bar-tailed Godwit, visiting fresh-water marshes, sewage-farms, and muddy borders of inland lakes and reservoirs.

General Habits. Apart from the above differences, its general habits and behaviour are much like Bar-tailed Godwit's. It is in general a taller and more graceful-looking bird, the neck often looking longer and more slender. In feeding it seems inclined to wade relatively more deeply, often up to the belly. On the breeding-ground it perches freely on fences and stumps, and on bushes or trees where present. It is generally seen in small parties or flocks, sometimes running into hundreds.

Flight-call, heard chiefly from flocks on the move, is a loud clear "wicka-wicka-wicka". Song is a repeated "wotta-we-do" with emphasis on last syllable.

Food on the breeding-grounds is chiefly insects and their larvae; elsewhere also small crustacea, worms, and molluscs.

Nests on the ground. The eggs, normally 4, occasionally 3–5, have ground-colour varying from pale blue-green to darkish brown, sometimes almost unmarked. They are laid generally in May in a nest which is usually a substantial pad of dead grasses and bents in a hollow made in luxuriant grass; if sheltered by scrub it is much slighter and lined with leaves and down. Incubation is by both sexes for about 24 days. The young leave the nest when dry, accompanied by both parents. Single-brooded.

Status and Distribution. Present throughout the year. Since 1952 it has become established (65 pairs in 1972) on the Ouse Washes in E. Anglia; it also nests in several near-coastal localities from Norfolk to Kent, and is scarce or irregular in Somerset, Lancs, Solway and Shetland, occasionally elsewhere. Otherwise it is a regular visitor, occurring as a passage-migrant from the beginning of July to September, and in March–May, but many stay the winter especially in the west and south. It is most frequent in England in the south coast counties, and E. Anglia, and Lincs.; also regular in the north-east and in parts on the W. side, especially Lancs and Carmarthen. Elsewhere it occurs not so regularly on all coasts and often by inland waters. In Scotland it is a passage-migrant and occasional visitor, some wintering, generally rare on the west side. In Ireland it is a numerous passage-migrant and winter-visitor, mainly in the southern half including some inland counties; some birds summer. Irish birds belong chiefly to Icelandic race *Limosa limosa islandica*. Elsewhere the race concerned is *Limosa limosa limosa*, which breeds in mid-Europe in S. Sweden, Öland and Gotland, otherwise only south of the Baltic west to France and east to Romania and Russia, also in W. Asia. Another race occurs in N.E. Asia. European birds winter mainly in Africa.

BAR-TAILED GODWIT—*Limosa lapponica*

Bird Plates 45 and 121

Markedly larger than Redshank and much smaller than Curlew, godwits are easily recognized among shore-birds by their *long, straight or upward curved bills*. From the present species, Black-tailed Godwit is at once distinguished by a broad white wing-bar, broad black subterminal band on the otherwise pure white tail, and long legs projecting beyond the tail in flight, apart from other differences. In contrast to this, the present species has relatively short legs, so that the *feet project only slightly beyond the tail, and wings lack conspicuous pattern*. In winter plumage the whole pattern of the upper-parts is much like Curlew, with *dull white rump* and tail rather darker, but with whiter under-parts. Young, however, have the breast buff, more or less markedly mottled and streaked. In summer plumage male has the *whole head, neck and under-parts chestnut-red* and the light portions of the feathers of the back are also rufous, but female is much duller and browner. In contrast to Black-tailed Godwit, the bill is often noticeably up-curved, though both length and degree of curvature vary quite considerably. Bill has basal part pink, rest blackish; legs grey. Length about 14–15 ins.; bill about 3–4 ins.

Habitat. Outside the breeding-season it is found on both muddy and sandy shores of sea-coast and estuaries. It is rare inland on marshes, sewage-farms and muddy borders of lakes or reservoirs. Flocks of non-breeding birds remain on our shores in summer.

General Habits. Flight is tolerably rapid with neck withdrawn, so that the shape looks compact and stocky, gliding before pitching and sometimes while well up in the air. Flocks usually fly in rather loose, straggling formations. At times they perform intricate gambols in the air, plunging down from a height, shooting upwards, dashing and twisting. Flocks feed in the shallows as the tide recedes, often wading deeply and they both snap up small organisms on the surface and probe for worms, etc., often driving the bill deep into the mud with a vigorous side-to-side movement of the head. Often in unmixed flocks, but it associates quite freely with Oystercatcher, Redshank, and other species. Small parties and even single birds occur on the less favoured shores.

The usual flight-note of flocks (also sometimes used by single birds and small groups) is a rather low "kirruc, kirruc", also a louder "kurruc" and other variants.

Food includes crustacea, worms, small molluscs, small fish-fry and insects.

Status and Distribution. A passage-migrant and winter-visitor arriving from mid-July to mid-November, but mainly in August and September, and leaving or passing through again from March to June. It occurs on most coasts, especially those with estuaries, but is rather scarce in Shetland, and only occasional in the N.W. and extreme N. Scottish mainland; seldom inland. Largest numbers are present at times of passage, but many stay the winter especially on parts of the E. coast between Moray and Norfolk, parts of the W. coast, Outer Hebrides, and E. and W. coasts of Ireland. A good many non-breeders stay through the summer in some parts. The race concerned, *Limosa lapponica lapponica*, breeds from N. Scandinavia to N. Siberia and winters south to W. Africa and the Indian Ocean. Another race occurs in N.E. Siberia and Alaska.

WHIMBREL—*Numenius phaeopus*

BIRD PLATES 46 and 121   EGG PLATE VII (6)

It resembles Curlew, but *has a quite different note, and is smaller, with a relatively shorter bill and distinctive pattern on the crown consisting of two broad dark bands, divided by a narrow pale streak*. As it is usually much more approachable than Curlew this pattern can generally be made out. Upper-parts are somewhat darker than Curlew and in the juvenile darker still, with light markings more contrasted. Legs greenish-grey. Length about 15–16 ins., bill about 3½ ins.

Habitat. In the breeding-season it resorts to northern moorlands and heaths. In Shetland typical haunts are stretches covered with cotton-grass, dwarf heather and moss, broken up with peaty channels. Outside the breeding-season it is found in much the same country as Curlew, but is especially fond of fields and grassland near the coast and is perhaps more frequent than Curlew on rocky shores. In England it is rarer inland than Curlew, but frequent on inland bogs and lake borders in Ireland. Small numbers of non-breeders remain locally on the coast in summer.

General Habits. Much tamer than Curlew, but otherwise its habits differ little. Wing-beats and gait are, however, often quicker. In Britain it is chiefly known as a passage-bird occurring singly or in parties and small flocks, but at times flocks reach a considerable size on the coast.

Ordinary note of passage-birds is a rapid tittering "titti-titti-titti-titti-titti-tit" with even emphasis throughout. The song is a bubbling trill, very like Curlew's.

Food includes crustacea, molluscs, worms, and when inland insects and berries.

Nests on the ground among grass or heath, but not in wet parts of marshes. The eggs, normally 4, 3 and 5 also recorded, vary in ground-colour from pale green to brown, more boldly marked as a rule than eggs of Curlew. They are laid generally in the latter part of May and first half of June, in a hollow usually quite open, and sparingly lined with grasses, fragments of moss, heather, twigs, etc. Incubation is by both sexes for about 24 days. Young leave the nest when dry, led away by both parents, and fly when about 4 weeks old. Single-brooded.

Status and Distribution. Mainly a passage-migrant occurring on all coasts and often inland between mid-April and mid-June, and from July to October. It breeds regularly in Shetland, sporadically or in very small numbers in the Outer Hebrides, and a few pairs on the N. Scottish mainland. A few non-breeders stay the summer on the coast and it has exceptionally been recorded in winter. Our birds belong to the race *Numenius phaeopus phaeopus* which breeds in Iceland, Faeroes, N. Europe, and N.W. Asia and winters south to S. Africa. The Hudsonian Whimbrel, *Numenius phaeopus hudsonicus*, which breeds in N. America, has occurred on Fair Isle and in Ireland; it lacks the white rump. Another race breeds in N.E. Asia.

CURLEW—*Numenius arquata*

BIRD PLATES 46 and 121   EGG PLATE VII (1A & 1B)

The largest and amongst the most familiar of the waders, with *long, strongly curved bill and streaky brown plumage*, Curlew can only be confused with Whimbrel. Compared with that species Curlew is *larger and coarser, with longer bill, and lacks the distinctive stripes on the crown*. It is also much shyer and its usual *note* is quite different. The head, neck, breast and mantle are light brown with dark brown streaks and markings; the rump is white, but not very sharply defined from the rather darker tail. Summer and winter plumages differ little, but the latter is rather paler. Juveniles are much as adult in summer, but upper-parts are warmer brown, under-parts more buff, and bill shorter. Legs greenish-grey. Length 19–25 ins., generally about 22–23 ins.; bill generally about 5 ins., the longest-billed birds being females.

Habitat. In the breeding-season it haunts chiefly boggy grass-moors of hill country, or hill pastures and rushy upland fields. It is less plentiful in lowlands, on sand-dunes, marshy fields, bogs and heaths with scattered trees and patches of swamp, and has spread onto pasture and even arable land. Outside the breeding-season it occurs in greatest numbers on mud-flats and saltings of estuaries, but also on sandy and to a less extent on rocky shores often resorting regularly to neighbouring grass- and arable-land, especially during the period of high water, when parties may travel several miles inland. As a migrant inland it is not much attracted by sewage-farms, resorting more to grassy marshes, and sometimes rough pastures and fallows. Non-breeding flocks occur on shore in summer.

General Habits. It is amongst the shyest and most wary of waders and is difficult to approach on the shore. Flight is swift, but with slower wing-beats than most waders, not unlike a gull, often well up in air and when coming down to feeding-grounds it often planes for some distance. Flocks travelling for any distance tend to do so in irregular lines and angled formations. On the breeding-ground it will perch on trees and bushes where these are present. Feeding birds often scatter rather widely on flats, where it probes deeply in the mud, wading in the water; it can swim well on occasion, and has, rarely, been observed actually to settle on the sea. It is markedly gregarious and commonly occurs in flocks, sometimes of great size, though single birds and small parties are frequent enough. Flocks of any size are uncommon well inland except in Ireland. On shore it associates freely with other larger waders, such as Oystercatcher, godwits, etc., and its habits are like those of other gregarious shore-birds.

The commonest notes are a loud, musical "quoi, quoi", and "croo*ee*, croo*ee*, croo*ee* . . ." with the second syllable higher-pitched and more emphatic than the first and often uttered in long sequences. Song begins as a succession of low, drawn-out liquid notes, then gains speed and passes into a louder and higher-pitched bubbling trill impossible to render in words, finally sinking again. It is to be heard throughout the year, regularly from late February to mid-June, but only exceptionally during most of July and the first half of August. It is uttered by the male in display-flight on the breeding-ground and by both sexes in ordinary flight, also on shore at all seasons.

Food on the coast includes molluscs, crustacea, fishes, worms, and some vegetable matter; when inland, insects and larvae, worms, small frogs, molluscs; also berries, seeds of grasses, etc., and occasionally grain.

Nests on the ground. The eggs, normally 4, occasionally 3–6 recorded, vary in ground-colour from light greenish to dark umber-brown. They are laid generally in the second half of April or early May in a hollow about 5–5½ ins. across, lined with grasses and sheltered by vegetation in low-lying meadows, but in heather much slighter, with a scanty lining of heather twigs or a few grasses. Incubation is by both sexes for about 28–30 days. The young leave the nest when dry, tended by both parents, and can fly in about 5–6 weeks. Single-brooded.

Status and Distribution. Present throughout the year. In Ireland it breeds in every county. In Scotland it breeds generally and commonly, except in the Outer Hebrides, where nesting has rarely been proved, and several Inner Hebridean islands. In Wales it nests commonly. In England it nests in all counties from Staffs and Derby northwards, and on the Welsh border and in S.W. England, also more sparingly into the middle of England; but is absent from most of the country east of Humber – Isle of Wight, apart from a pair or two in Surrey and Sussex, and a more flourishing population in Breckland (E. Anglia). Outside the breeding-season it is common on all coasts and frequent inland. The breeding-grounds are occupied from March or late February to June–August when most but not all our birds move west or south, succeeded by winter-visitors or passage-migrants from N.W. Europe. In addition, hard weather movements may occur through the winter. The race concerned, *Numenius arquata arquata*, breeds in Europe from N. Scandinavia, south to France and east to Romania and Russia, extending into W. Asia. In winter it reaches S. Africa. Another race occurs in Siberia.

UPLAND SANDPIPER—*Bartramia longicauda*

BIRD PLATE 44

A bird with the appearance of a sandpiper and behaviour of a plover, in *size about that of Reeve, with a general brown coloration, proportionately short bill, fairly short legs, slender neck, and noticeably long tail*. There are no wing-bars or other striking field-marks, but the *axillaries and under-wing are* strongly barred, displayed by the bird's habit of holding its wings elevated on alighting. When flushed, the tail with dark centre and pale margins and the white on sides of the rump appear sandpiper-like, and the wings look excessively long, but its carriage and habit of running quickly for a short distance, stopping suddenly to peck on the ground and then running again, are those of a plover. The upper-parts are dark brown with buff markings, the breast is streaked dark and the flanks barred. Legs are dull yellowish. Length about 10–11 ins.

Habitat. It is a bird of large open fields, rough grasslands and prairies, in some regions with a preference for moister tracts, but often on quite dry ground.

General Habits. Ordinary flight is swift with strong, steady wing-beats. It seldom associates with other species.

Usual call on migration a rich, mellow, trilling whistle.

Food consists mainly of insects. Some other animal matter and seeds are also taken.

Status and Distribution. A rare vagrant, which has occurred mainly in September–October, also November, December and April, in some inland as well as coastal localities. Many records are from Ireland or Scilly/Cornwall, but it has reached N.E. England and Scotland. It breeds in Canada and U.S.A., and winters in S. America. There are no subspecies.

SPOTTED REDSHANK—*Tringa erythropus*

BIRD PLATES 47 and 122

In summer the *black plumage spotted with white on the back* is quite unlike any other wader. In winter plumage it is not so outstandingly distinct from Redshank, but it is still readily ident-ified, being an appreciably larger, *more ashy-grey bird with rel-atively longer bill and legs, the wing-coverts and scapulars being noticeably barred and spotted with white instead of uniform, and lacking the conspicuous white on the secondaries in flight*. The *note* also is quite distinct. Both species have white backs, the white running far up the back between the wings. Juvenile is darker and

P.J.H.

SPOTTED REDSHANK

browner than adult in winter with light edges and marginal spots to feathers of the upper-parts. Bill is blackish, dull red at the base of lower mandible. Legs reddish. Length about 12 ins.

Habitat. Outside the breeding-season it occurs both on coastal mud-flats and salt-marshes, and on marshes, sewage-farms and borders of lakes, reservoirs, etc., inland.

General Habits. Actions and general behaviour hardly differ from Redshank's, and on the whole it is rather shy. In the British Isles it is chiefly seen singly or in small parties. It associates freely with other species such as Redshank and Greenshank.

Flight note is a characteristic, disyllabic "tchueet".

Food is mainly insects; also molluscs, worms, crustacea, small fishes and frogs.

Status and Distribution. Passage-migrant from the 3rd week of June to mid-October, uncommon in most areas, scarcer in spring but wintering regularly and a few are seen in summer. It has increased in recent years occurring chiefly on the coast from S. Lincs to Hants. It is also regular on passage in many other counties in England, Wales, Scotland (confined mainly to Solway, Forth and Moray areas) and Ireland. Small numbers winter locally on the same coasts. The bird breeds in N. Europe and Siberia, and winters mainly in the Mediterranean area and S. Africa. There are no subspecies.

REDSHANK—*Tringa totanus*

Bird Plates 47 and 122   Egg Plate VII (5A & 5B)

A medium-sized, grey-brown wader with *orange-red legs* (*yellower in young*), orange base of bill, a *conspicuous flight-pattern showing the white rump and tail-coverts and broad white patch on the hind border of the wing*, and a musical whistling note. Back in winter is ash-brown, the head, neck and breast greyish with dark streaks. In summer the ground-colour is warmer brown, the back strongly marked with black, head and neck strongly streaked black, and so appears much darker than in winter. Juvenile has upper-parts much as adult in summer, but more heavily marked. Length about 11 ins.

Habitat. In the breeding-season it frequents grassy marshes and lowland moors on coast and inland, water-side meadows, sewage-farms and coastal saltings; locally also hill moors and damp ground on heaths, etc. On passage it resorts freely to marshes, sewage-farms and borders of lakes, reservoirs, etc., where it does not breed, and some linger inland in winter, but most resort to tidal estuaries, mud-flats and to a lesser extent sandy and rocky shores. Birds breeding on the coast will visit the shore to feed and non-breeding birds occur on shore throughout the summer.

General Habits. A shy, restless and noisy bird. Flight is strong, swift and rather erratic. The bobbing action when suspicious, common to most sandpipers, is perhaps more conspicuous in Redshank than in any; another common action, especially noticeable in Redshank, is the graceful holding of the wings raised above the back for a moment after alighting. In the breeding-season it perches freely on fences, etc., and sometimes on branches of trees and buildings. When feeding it often wades in water up to the belly and swims readily. Inland it generally does not occur in large parties, but on the coast in any number from singly to large flocks. It associates freely with other waders.

Typical notes have a musical, whistling quality. The commonest are a single "tuuu" and triple "tu-hu-hu", the second two notes rather lower than the first. Song, consisting of a yodelling repeated "tu-udle . . ." may accompany display-flight, or be given on the ground.

Food includes insects, molluscs, crustacea, worms, spiders, occasionally small fish; also vegetable matter such as leaves, grasses, buds, seeds, berries.

Nests on the ground, generally well concealed in the middle of a long grass tuft, which hides the eggs from above. The eggs, normally 4, occasionally 3–5, with ground-colour varying from bluish-white to yellowish-brown, are laid generally from mid-April onwards in a hollow lined by the female with dry grasses. Incubation is by both sexes for about 22–24 days. The young leave the nest soon after hatching, tended by both parents, and fly when about a month old. Single-brooded.

Status and Distribution. Present throughout the year, but decreasing. It nests in good numbers in most of Scotland and northern England, the coastal fringe from the Wash to Dorset, and fairly widely in parts of central and northern Ireland. It becomes scarcer in the Scottish lowlands, central and southern England and Wales, particularly in agricultural lowlands subject to drainage; it is almost absent from southern Wales except coastal, from S.W. England and the southern third of Ireland. Most inland breeding areas are occupied in February or March and are vacated as soon as the young can fly. Some birds reach Ireland or France, while visitors from Iceland and the Continent arrive June–September and return March–May. During autumn and winter the species is present on all coasts and frequent inland. Our breeding birds belong to the race *Tringa totanus britannica* and passage- or winter-visitors include examples of the race *Tringa totanus robusta* breeding in Iceland and probably Faeroes, and of the race *Tringa totanus totanus* breeding from N. Scandinavia, south to S. Spain and S. Russia, and extending into Asia. British birds in summer are paler than the other two races but they cannot be certainly identified in the field, and in winter the three races are inseparable even in the hand. They winter south to Africa and S. Asia. Other races occur in central and E. Asia.

GREENSHANK—*Tringa nebularia*

BIRD PLATES 47 and 122   EGG PLATE VIII (5A & 5B)

A larger, taller, and greyer bird than Redshank, with relatively longer, greenish legs, slightly upturned bill, no white in the wing and distinctive call; the lower back, rump, and tail are conspicuously white. In winter plumage the upper-parts appear grey; the *head, neck*, and sides of breast *pale grey* with darker streaks, the rest of the under-parts white. In summer plumage the back is largely black, but often with much grey, giving a rather patchy appearance; the breast is boldly spotted black, and with dark bars and markings also on the flanks. Juveniles are also dark, but have a more regular pattern of dark feathers with light borders. Legs rarely yellow. Length about 12 ins.

Habitat. In the breeding-season in Scotland it frequents extensive, treeless moorlands interspersed with lochs and "flows", which often serve as feeding-places for adults and young; also heathy tracts in forested country. Outside the breeding-season it is found on the borders of lakes, reservoirs, and rivers, and on marshes, sewage-farms, etc.; on the coast on estuaries, salt marshes, etc., and less frequently on open shores and flats.

General Habits. Flight is rapid and often rather twisting and erratic. When uneasy it bobs like Redshank, and other habits are much the same. It will feed in shallows with a side-to-side motion of the bill as well as by picking and probing; also by a succession of rapid dashes through water with neck extended and bill submerged. On the breeding-ground it perches freely on trees as well

GREENSHANK

as on fences, rocks, etc. Outside the breeding-season it is commonly seen singly or in small parties inland, but sometimes in larger
flocks on the coast.

Usual note when flushed is a loud, clear "tew, tew, tew",
lower-pitched than Redshank's note. The song is a rich "ru-tu,
ru-tu, ru-tu . . ." uttered in display-flight or while soaring and
often in ordinary flight, also while perched.

Food includes insects, crustacea, worms, molluscs, amphibia
and fish. Vegetable matter rarely occurs.

Nests on the ground, usually close to a mark of some sort such as
a bleached log, granite boulder or a pine. The eggs, usually 4,
occasionally 3–5, vary in ground-colour from cartridge-buff and
faint greenish to, exceptionally, reddish-ochreous. They are laid
generally from early May onwards in a hollow made by hen, lined
with leaves of heath plants, pine-needles, dead wood, etc. Incubation is by both sexes for about 24–25 days. The young leave the
nest within 24 hours, tended by both parents and fly when about
one month old. Single-brooded.

Status and Distribution. A summer-visitor and passage-
migrant; winters in small but increasing numbers in England and
Scotland (but few on E. coasts), Wales, and particularly Ireland.
It breeds in Scotland, very sparingly in Argyll, Aberdeen, Banff
and Hebrides, and more commonly from N. Perth and Inverness
northwards on the mainland. As a passage-migrant it is widespread
on all coasts and frequently inland, chiefly in autumn from the
second half of June, when nesting areas begin to be abandoned,
until late October, and more rarely appearing in spring from
mid-April to early June. Abroad it breeds in north and central
Scandinavia, the Baltic States, N. Russia and across N. Asia,
and winters south to S. Africa and Australasia. There are no
subspecies.

LESSER YELLOWLEGS—*Tringa flavipes*

BIRD PLATE 46

It is rather smaller than Redshank, but markedly slenderer and less stocky, with *longer, slender, bright yellow legs; the back is dark black-brown in summer, freely mottled and spotted with light markings*, producing a pattern much like Wood Sandpiper, but in winter plumage is lighter, more grey-brown and less spotted. *In flight the wings are uniform dark grey above, unrelieved by any paler mark or shade, the upper tail-coverts are white and the tail* (actually barred) *usually looks greyish-white*; the white is cut off more or less square above the tail-coverts and is not prolonged as a wedge up the back between the wings as in Greenshank. Head, neck, and breast are greyish with blackish streaks, the rest of the under-parts pure white. Bill is rather slenderer than Redshank's, about the same length and straight or just perceptibly up-curved, whereas the bill of the even rarer Greater Yellowlegs is relatively longer and stouter, and usually more distinctly up-curved. Length about 10 ins.

Habitat. Outside the breeding-season it frequents grassy marshes, margins of ponds, lakes or lagoons, and coastal mud-flats; sometimes also dry meadows.

General Habits. Flight is much as Redshank's, and like that bird it bobs when suspicious, but is usually much more approachable. Lively and graceful, it moves at an active walk or run with legs strongly flexed.

The usual note is a double (or triple) "hew hew", weaker than Greenshank's.

Food is mainly insects and crustacea, also some spiders, molluscs and fish-fry.

Status and Distribution. A vagrant now of annual occurrence

LESSER YELLOWLEGS

which has been recorded mainly in August and September at many localities, chiefly coastal, from the Scilly Isles in the south to Fair Isle in the north, also Ireland. There are a few spring records in April and May, and one or two in winter. It breeds in Canada and winters in S. America. There are no subspecies.

GREEN SANDPIPER—*Tringa ochropus*

BIRD PLATES 48 and 122

It is *larger, stouter and considerably darker above than Common Sandpiper.* Confusion is sometimes possible, but any doubt is dispelled when it rises, the *upper-parts in flight appearing black and in sharp contrast to pure white rump, tail, and belly*, like a kind of limicoline House Martin. The back in winter has a uniform appearance but in breeding plumage is quite freely spotted with buff or whitish, which can lead to confusion with Wood Sandpiper, though the spotting is finer, less of a mottling or chequering than in that species, from which in any case the black and white appearance in flight, and especially the *blackish under-side of the wing*, at once distinguishes it. As a rule a shy bird and more often first seen as it gets up, with distinctive notes, than on the ground; nevertheless, it is much attached to certain feeding-grounds and may be put up day after day from the same spot. Head, neck, and breast are streaky, greyish-brown, with a distinct whitish eye-stripe. There is no wing-bar. Juvenile has feathers of the back margined buff. Legs greenish. Length about 9 ins.

Habitat. In the breeding-season it frequents marshy, wooded districts. Outside the breeding-season it may be found on borders

MARSH SANDPIPER   GREEN SANDPIPER   WOOD SANDPIPER

of lakes and reservoirs, sewage-farms, marsh drains, and frequently on streams where other waders except Common Sandpiper
rarely occur; sometimes on quite small ponds. It likes the vicinity
of cover or the shelter of banks and as a rule avoids completely
exposed places. On the coast it frequents gutters and channels of
salt-marshes, but very rarely the open shore.

General Habits. As a rule when flushed it rises high, often
zig-zagging close to ground for a few yards before towering, and
goes off out of sight with a wheeling erratic flight and rather jerky
wing-beats. It bobs head and moves tail up and down in the same
way as Common Sandpiper, but much less persistently. It is
usually seen singly or in couples, and very seldom associates with
other species.

Usual note when flushed and in flight overhead is a full, clear
musical "tweet, weet-weet".

Food is chiefly insects; worms, crustacea, molluscs and some
vegetable matter also taken.

Nests in trees usually in old nests of other species, especially
thrushes. The eggs, usually 4, have ground-colour usually greenish to warm buff, rather sparingly spotted purplish brown and
with ashy shell-marks. They are laid generally between mid-April
and June. Incubation is chiefly by hen. The young at first are
tended by both sexes; their stay in the nest is brief. Probably
normally single-brooded.

Status and Distribution. As a passage-migrant it is widely
distributed, generally in small numbers, in England and Wales;
fairly frequent in autumn in E. Scotland, and rarer elsewhere,
being practically unknown in N.W. or N. mainland. To Ireland it
is an autumn- and winter-visitor in small numbers. Passage occurs
between early June and November and from mid-March to May. A
few winter, chiefly in S. England. A pair nested in Westmorland
in 1917, and Inverness in 1959; breeding has been suspected in
various other counties on many occcasions. The bird breeds in
Europe from about the Arctic Circle south to Denmark and S.
Russia, also in Asia. It winters in Africa and S. Asia. There are no
subspecies.

WOOD SANDPIPER—*Tringa glareola*

BIRD PLATES 48 and 122

It is rather smaller and more lightly built than Green Sandpiper, with rather longer legs so that the feet project well beyond the tail in flight. *In summer plumage the back is conspicuously mottled and chequered with whitish markings*, but in winter these are much reduced and the back may look almost as uniform as a Green Sandpiper's when the bird is on the ground. At all seasons, however, it *lacks the boldly black and white appearance of Green Sandpiper in flight*. The upper-parts appear greyish or brownish, the *under-side of the wing is light greyish*, not blackish, and the white rump, though conspicuous, is less prominent than the big splash of white in Green Sandpiper, where coverts and most of tail (barred in present species) are white too. The *note* also is distinct. Head, neck and breast are streaked greyish-brown, with a distinct whitish eye-stripe, much more conspicuous than in Green Sandpiper. There is no wing bar. Juvenile has the light markings more buff than in adults. Legs greenish or yellow. Length about 8 ins.

Habitat. Outside the breeding-season it frequents muddy patches on marshes, muddy and marshy borders of lakes, reservoirs, etc., sewage-farms, and boggy pools on moorlands; also occasionally gutters of salt-marshes, but very seldom on the open shore.

General Habits. It is often less shy than Green Sandpiper, but excitable and noisy, migrating parties when disturbed dashing round the marsh with a clamour of shrill cries. It does not have the towering habit to the same extent as Green Sandpiper and rarely wheels or zig-zags so much and may settle not far away. Otherwise movements and general behaviour are very much the same as Green Sandpiper's, though it is rather more gregarious.

Ordinary flight and flushing note is an excited, peevish "chip-yip-yip".

Food includes insects, worms, small molluscs, occasionally small fish and some vegetable matter.

Nests usually on open ground or in open patches in forest, but has been known to lay in old nests of other birds, such as Fieldfare. The eggs, usually 4, are very variable with ground-colour ranging from pale sea-green to brownish-olive or warm buff, and boldly blotched and spotted with dark or purplish brown and ashy smears, often forming a zone; they are laid generally in late May or June in a hollow lined with a few leaves and grasses. Incubation is by both sexes. The young leave nest soon after hatching and are first tended by both parents, but female soon leaves family. Single-brooded.

Status and Distribution. A passage-migrant appearing from early July to mid-September with stragglers later, and more uncommonly in spring from late April to early June. It occurs regularly in E. and S.E. coastal counties and the Midlands, but is scarcer in most other parts of the British Isles; it is annual in Ireland. A very few pairs have bred in N. Scotland since 1959, the records extending from Caithness to Inverness and probably Perth and Argyll; there is a century-old breeding record for Northumberland. It breeds in Europe from N. Norway south to Holland and central Russia, and extends eastwards into Siberia. It winters throughout Africa and in S. Asia and Australia. There are no subspecies.

COMMON SANDPIPER—*Actitis hypoleucos*

BIRD PLATES 48 and 122   EGG PLATE VII (2A & 2B)

In the breeding-season it is a characteristic bird of hill-streams and lakes, and on passage frequently occurs on streams where other waders are rarely seen. It is readily recognized as a *small sandpiper with brownish-grey upper-parts, ashy streaked breast, pure white belly and a well-defined white wing-bar; when disturbed it flies off low over the water with a shrill note and peculiarly spasmodic wing-action*, and usually pitches again a little farther on. On the ground its slender, graceful form and *constant up-and-down motion of the hinder part of the body*, like a short-tailed wagtail, are equally characteristic. The centre of the rump and tail are like back, but the sides are white. Juvenile has feathers of the upper-parts margined buff, and rather darker than adults. Legs greenish. Length about 7¾ ins.

Habitat. In the breeding-season it chiefly frequents the vicinity of clear, gravelly or rocky streams and borders of lochs, tarns and reservoirs in or close to hilly country and in both open and wooded localities, nesting more sporadically on streams or lakes of lowland districts. On passage it is regular on lowland streams, lakes and reservoirs, as well as on sewage-farms, etc., though less attracted than most waders by swampy ground, and in autumn occurs regularly on drains of salt-marshes and banks of estuaries and often amongst rocks on coasts, but very seldom on open shore or flats.

General Habits. Ordinary flight is distinct from any other European wader, very low over the water with a regular alternation of peculiar, flickering wing-beat and momentary glide with wings set in a characteristically bowed position at the bottom of down-stroke. In addition to the up-and-down movement of the tail it has also, like other sandpipers, a bobbing, up-and-down motion of the head, which occurs independently. In the breeding-season it perches fairly freely on posts, railings, etc., and branches over-hanging water, as well as on rocks and walls. Outside the breeding-season it is generally seen singly or sometimes 2–3 together. In late summer family parties occur and sometimes, even in spring, larger flocks are formed, but it is not in general gregarious. It will at least occasionally take to water and dive when suddenly startled, or to escape a hawk. Nestlings when startled also dive and swim well, using wing-stumps as well as legs.

Flight note is a shrill "twee-wee-wee". The song, uttered in flight, or on the ground, "kitti-weeit, kitti-weeit, kitti-weeit . . ." has much the same quality as the ordinary note. It is heard regularly from late April to early June.

Food includes insects, molluscs, crustacea, worms; also some vegetable matter.

Nests on the ground, often sloping and close to water, on river shingle beds, etc., sheltered by grass or burdock; locally on seashore, also occasionally in cornfields at some distance from water or in an elevated site such as pollard willow or old Ring Ousel nest. The eggs, normally 4, but occasionally 3–5, with ground-colour usually buffish but at times ranging from greyish-white to yellowish-brown, are laid generally from about mid-May to early June in a hollow lined with a few grasses, and bits of flood-wrack. Incubation is shared by both sexes for about 21–22 days. The young are tended by both sexes. Single-brooded.

Status and Distribution. A summer-visitor, breeding in Scotland, N. England south to a line from Scarborough to the Severn, and in most parts of Wales except the extreme south. In southern England it appears no longer to breed on Dartmoor, but does so sporadically elsewhere. In Ireland it is generally distri-buted except in the south-east. As a passage-migrant it is widely spread on all coasts and inland, arriving between the end of March and June, the return movement lasting from July to October, but a few winter in England, Wales and irregularly in Ireland. Our bird belongs to the race *Actitis hypoleucos hypoleucos* which breeds in Europe from N. Scandinavia south to central Spain and the Balkans, and in Asia east to Japan. It winters throughout Africa, in S. Asia and reaches Australia.

In addition a few examples of the Spotted Sandpiper, *Actitis macularia*, have been recorded as vagrants in E. and S. England, Scotland and Ireland. This is the N. American counterpart of the Common Sandpiper, once regarded as race but now generally as a separate species. It very closely resembles Common Sandpiper, from which young birds and adults in winter are hardly separable in the field but are greyer, with yellower legs. Adults in summer, however, are distinguished by round black spots on under-parts, and by bill mainly yellow but with dark tip. The ordinary note is a sharp "peet-weet"; it also sometimes gives a note identical to Common Sandpiper's. It breeds in N. America south to southern United States and winters south to Peru and S. Brazil.

TURNSTONE—*Arenaria interpres*

BIRD PLATES 49 and 123

The *mottled, "tortoise-shell" upper-parts, broad black or dark pectoral band and rather short orange legs* are distinctive; but it is often hard to see against a broken background although larger than Dunlin or Ringed Plover. Bill is pointed, rather short and stout. In winter the head is dusky brown with white throat and at a distance the whole back looks dark, but in the breeding-season the back becomes much more richly coloured with orange-brown and black, and in male the head and neck become boldly patterned with black and white, while female shows more or less of this pattern, but is much dingier. The *boldly pied pattern is distinctive in flight*, when it shows a lozenge-shaped white patch on the rump enclosed by black, tail with a broad black subterminal band and the rest white, a white wing-bar, more or less distinct whitish patch on shoulders, and the rest of the upper-parts look blackish. Young are much like winter adults, but duller. Length about 9 ins.

Habitat. Outside the breeding-season it is found chiefly on rocky and pebbly shores and weedy reefs and along tide-lines, but also on mainly sandy or muddy flats where mussel-scaups or stony patches or banks occur here and there, and at times on flat shores without stones or weed, but seldom for long or in any numbers. Sometimes inland on borders of reservoirs or rivers, sewage-farms and the like.

General Habits. It is chiefly met with in relatively small and often scattered parties, which when disturbed rise, often a few at a time, and fly a short distance, with somewhat slow, wavering flight, though when necessary they are swift and strong fliers. They run about actively on rocks or shore, jerking aside tangles of weed, and rooting about amongst stones. They also sometimes pick up food on the open shore and along tide-edge like other waders. The bird often associates with Purple Sandpipers, Dunlin and other small waders, but is rather pugnacious and quarrelsome.

Ordinary note of birds flushed on shore is a twittering, metallic "kitititit".

Food in winter-quarters is mainly molluscs, insects and crustacea.

Status and Distribution. Present most of the year. It is widely distributed on all coasts, chiefly in autumn and spring but many stay the winter; non-breeding birds are frequently observed through the summer, and nesting has been suspected in Orkney and Sutherland. It is fairly frequent inland on passage. Migration in autumn extends from mid-July to mid-November and in spring from mid-March to the beginning of June. The race concerned, *Arenaria interpres interpres*, breeds from Greenland east to Siberia, in Europe extending south to Rügen and other S. Baltic Islands. It winters south to S. Africa and Australia. Another race occurs in arctic N. America.

RED-NECKED PHALAROPE—*Phalaropus lobatus*

Bird Plates 55 and 123   Egg Plate VIII (3A & 3B)

It is distinguished from Grey Phalarope in summer by *black bill, slate-grey head and upper-parts, white throat and underparts, and an orange patch on sides of the neck*. There are some buff streaks on the back and a small, but often conspicuous white spot over the eye. Male is considerably duller than female, with more buff streaking on the upper-parts. In winter plumage the bird resembles Grey Phalarope but is distinguishable at close range by *longer and noticeably slender bill and less uniform, darker grey back with whitish streakings*; it is also rather smaller. The wings are also rather darker, so that the white wing-bar stands out more. Young in autumn have the back blackish, striped with rich buff, and fore-head and sides of head whiter than in Grey Phalarope and breast more or less tinged vinous; also a dark mark on sides of the head as adult in winter. Bill blackish and legs dark blue-grey. Length about 6½ ins.

Habitat. In the breeding-season its typical haunts are wet grassy flats and bogs with scattered pools and lagoons. Outside the breeding-season it occupies much the same habitat as Grey Phalarope, but in the British Isles away from breeding-grounds it is rarer than that species.

General Habits. These and behaviour hardly differ at all from Grey Phalarope's.

A common note, on wing or settled, is "twit" or "whit", lower-pitched than Grey Phalarope's.

Food is chiefly insects and larvae; also small molluscs and small worms.

Nests in small or large colonies on marshy ground within easy reach of open water. Sometimes polygamous. The eggs, normally 4, rarely more, and occasionally 3 only, are usually buffish in ground-colour, but exceptionally ranging from pale greenish to dark brown. They are laid generally from the end of May and early June onward, in a hollow in a tussock of grass, lined with grasses, occasionally with a few leaves. Incubation is by male alone for about 20 days. The young are tended by male alone for about 18–20 days. One brood.

Status and Distribution. A summer-visitor from mid-May to August, breeding in very limited numbers in Shetland, Outer Hebrides, and irregularly or doubtfully elsewhere in Hebrides, Orkney and N. Scotland, also W. Ireland. Elsewhere it is a scarce visitor, chiefly as a passage-migrant in May and August–Sept. and occurring most often on the S. and E. coasts of England (especially Norfolk), less frequent inland; most autumn records are of young birds with very dark brownish upper-parts. It breeds in continental Europe northwards from mid-Norway and Finland, also in the Faeroes, Iceland, N. America and Siberia, and winters off W. Africa and in the Indian and Pacific Oceans. There are no subspecies.

GREY PHALAROPE—*Phalaropus fulicarius*

BIRD PLATES 54 and 123

Their extreme confidence allows observation of phalaropes at close quarters. They are the *only small waders which habitually swim about on water*, where, owing to their buoyancy, they look not unlike miniature gulls. In breeding plumage the *mainly yellow bill, chestnut under-parts, white or whitish sides of face, and dark brown back striated with buff and chestnut* make the present species unmistakable. In contrast to most birds the male is markedly duller than female, especially on the head, and the female takes the initiative in courtship. The wings are dark grey with a white bar on the basal half of wing and white tips to the secondaries. In winter plumage Grey and Red-necked Phalaropes are more alike, having a grey and white plumage in which they can hardly be confused with anything but Sanderling, from which they are distinguished by a *dark patch extending from in front of the eye over the cheeks and a peculiarly long-bodied appearance.* Grey Phalarope is distinguishable from Red-necked at close range by having a shorter, broader bill and *more uniform, blue-grey back*, considerably paler than the wings; also it is rather larger, being larger than the largest Dunlin, while Red-necked is smaller than smallest Dunlin. Head and under-parts are pure white with a dark patch on back of crown and down the centre of the nape. Migrants in autumn often retain more or less of summer plumage on the upper-parts. Juvenile is much like adult in transition. Adult's legs are yellowish in summer, more horn-coloured in winter or often (in immatures?) blackish or dark blue-grey like Red-necked's. Bill is black in winter, sometimes showing some yellow at base. Length about 8 ins.

Habitat. In winter it is mainly pelagic, frequenting chiefly offshore waters, but on passage some occur on the coast and inland reservoirs, ponds, sewage-farm pools and other shallow fresh waters.

General Habits. Conspicuously tame, it is often reluctant to take wing. Action is much like Dunlin in sustained flight, but often flitting and erratic for short distances over pools. It floats buoyantly on water with neck held straight up; sometimes with tail well up,

GREY PHALAROPE   RED-NECKED PHALAROPE
immature   immature

Note much darker back of Red-necked.

or sometimes noticeably high at shoulders, with slanting back and tail rather depressed. It swims in an erratic course with a Moorhen-like bobbing of the head and quick dabs from side to side to pick up insects, etc., on the surface. It will also rise from water to seize insects in the air. In shallow water it will "up-end" like a duck, and has a trick of spinning round and round on the surface as if on a pivot. Will also feed on land close to water, running about with something of the restless activity of Sanderling. In the British Isles it is generally seen singly or in couples, but exceptionally hundreds together in S.W.

Ordinary note is a short, low monosyllable of whistling quality, "twit".

Food includes crustacea, molluscs, worms and insects, also some vegetable matter.

Status and Distribution. A passage-migrant, mainly from early September to early November, but extending from August to December or even further into the winter; very scarce in spring. It is seen, usually in small numbers, on the S.W., S., and E. coasts of England, less often in Wales and Ireland, and a very few in Scotland; occasional inland. In Europe it breeds in Iceland (a few pairs only) and some arctic islands, also in arctic Siberia and N. America, and winters in the S. Atlantic and Pacific. There are no subspecies.

POMARINE SKUA—*Stercorarius pomarinus*

BIRD PLATES 57 and 126

A larger, more robustly built bird than Arctic Skua, character-ized when adult by having the *elongated central tail-feathers broad, blunt and peculiarly twisted*, so that in side view the full breadth of the long feathers is shown, giving the tail a heavy awkward appearance in flight. But birds not fully mature have feathers not twisted, and not rarely they are short-grown. The colour scheme is much like that of the other smaller skuas, with a dark and light phase, the latter showing the top of the head and face blackish, yellowish ear-coverts and collar, rest of the upper-parts dark greyish brown; throat and belly white, under tail-coverts and under-side of wing grey-brown; flanks usually barred dusky and it usually has a dusky pectoral band. The dark form with nearly uniform dark brown plumage is scarce. In both forms the shafts and bases of the primaries are whitish, forming a more or less distinct pale area on both sides of the expanded wing (more definite than in Arctic Skua, but not a prominent white patch as in Great Skua). In autumn and winter colour and markings are very like Arctic Skua at the same season. Young birds with short central tail-feathers can be separated (by observers fully familiar with both) from Arctic Skua by heavier build, broader, more rounded wings, and heavier, more owl-like flight. Length of adult about 20 ins., of which about 2–3 ins. is due to projection of central feathers beyond rest of tail.

Habitat. Main winter-quarters appear to be in offshore waters, but it is a regular pelagic migrant. To a less extent it occurs as a coastal migrant, and occasionally appears in inshore waters in considerable numbers during stormy periods at the time of migration. Rare inland.

General Habits. It is a heavier bird in ordinary flight, but otherwise behaviour and habits are much like Arctic Skua.

Call a sharp "which-yew", and others.

Food is often obtained at sea by pursuing terns and gulls and forcing them to disgorge, but it also captures fish and takes ships' refuse, and devours stranded fish and carrion.

Status and Distribution. A tolerably regular autumn-visitor (August to November), sometimes present in winter; also recently shown to be regular in May when hundreds pass north off the Outer Hebrides, and hundreds off Irish coasts. In autumn it is seen mainly on east and to lesser extent on south coasts of England, less common east coast Scotland; regular Ireland. Usually keeps well out to sea. The species breeds in arctic America and Asia, but in Europe apparently only on Kanin Peninsula and in Novaya Zemlya. It is an oceanic migrant and winters off the west coast of Africa, east coast of Australia and in the Pacific. There are no subspecies.

ARCTIC SKUA—*Stercorarius parasiticus*

Bird Plates 57 and 126   Egg Plate V (15)

The smaller skuas are characterized by the *nearly uniform dark brown colour of either the whole plumage or, at least, of upper-parts, elongated central tail-feathers, rather hawk-like flight, and piratical habits*. Arctic Skua, the commonest species in the British Isles, is recognized when adult by the two *long straight feathers projecting from wedge-shaped tail*, distinct from either the broad, twisted feathers of the rather larger and heavier Pomarine Skua or the very long, slender streamers of the lighter and more graceful Long-tailed Skua. It has dark and light phases. Typically the former is nearly uniform dark brown, with neck and sides of the face similarly dark, while the light phase has more or less white ear-coverts, neck and under-parts (ear-coverts and neck tinged yellowish), so that the blackish top of the head appears as a well-defined cap, separated from the back by a light collar, with dusky under tail-coverts, and the brown of the back extending down the sides of the breast and often continued to form a dusky pectoral band. Many intermediates occur between the extremes; the dark phase is in a minority in Britain. There is often a quite noticeable pale area on the wing at the base of the primaries, more marked in young birds than in adults. Legs black. Young birds have the central tail-feathers only a trifle longer than the rest and are difficult to separate in life from young Pomarine and Long-tailed Skuas. They vary greatly in plumage, from nearly uniform dark brown to a boldly marked pattern with the back mottled and barred rusty buff and dark brown, the head and neck yellowish-brown with dark streaks. Length of adult about 17–18½ ins., of which about 2–3½ ins. is due to projection of the long central feathers beyond the rest of the tail.

Habitat. Resorts for breeding to moorlands or swampy ground and hill tracts of northern coastal districts and to heathy ground above cliffs or on marine islands. It spends the rest of its life at sea, apparently wintering mainly in the offshore zone, but is also regular on migration both in pelagic waters at a great distance from land and, to a less extent, as a coastal, and locally even overland, migrant, sometimes appearing inshore in considerable numbers during stormy periods at the height of migration.

General Habits. Flight is buoyant and graceful, with regular wing-beats, often varied by long glide, and the general effect is noticeably hawk-like. Very swift and agile in pursuit of sea-birds which it robs of their prey. Chief victims are terns, Kittiwakes, and the smaller gulls. The Skua follows every twist and swerve of its quarry in its endeavour to escape, till the latter drops the fish it is carrying or disgorges its last meal. It also forages for itself on both land and sea. At breeding-places it settles on the ground quite freely and is occasionally seen on shore at times of migration. It swims buoyantly like a gull, but does not settle on the water very freely and rarely does so on its oceanic migrations, in contrast to Great Skua. Bold in defence of nesting territory, swooping at intruders, but is also extremely prone to "injury-feigning".

Common note on breeding-ground is a wailing, miaowing cry, "ka-*aa*ow", and variations.

Food is very varied. On breeding-grounds it takes small mammals, eggs and birds, also carrion and insects; on the coast, fish, fish-spawn, molluscs and crustacea.

Nests usually in colonies of considerable size, but isolated pairs may also be met with. The eggs, 1–4, but usually 2, vary in ground-colour from greenish to umber-brown, exceptionally light blue. They are laid generally at the end of May and in early June in a nest that is little more than a neatly rounded depression in moss, grass or heather, sometimes slightly lined. Incubation is by both sexes for about 24–28 days. The young are fed by both parents, leave nest very soon and fly in 4–5 weeks. Single-brooded. Birds first breed when 4, sometimes 3 or 5, years old.

Status and Distribution. Summer-visitor and passage-migrant from end of April to end of May, and August or earlier to end of October. It breeds in many places in Shetland, Fair Isle and Orkney, also less commonly in the Hebrides, Sutherland and Caithness. Elsewhere it is a passage-migrant, chiefly in autumn in varying numbers; rare in winter. It is regular on the east and south coasts of Great Britain and in smaller numbers on W. coast and Ireland. Very rare inland except in Ireland where it is fairly regular in autumn. Birds have summered in an Irish locality for several years. The species is at the southern limit of its range in Britain, and breeds north to the high Arctic islands and northern coasts of Europe, Asia and America, wintering mainly in the southern hemisphere. There are no subspecies.

LONG-TAILED SKUA—*Stercorarius longicaudus*

BIRD PLATES 57 and 126

Adult resembles a rather small, lightly built Arctic Skua of the pale type with *extremely elongated, slender and flexible middle tail feathers*, but the following confirmatory characters should be looked for: no pectoral band or downward extension of dark colouring on the sides of the breast, little or no whitish on the under-side of the wing, back somewhat paler and greyer especially in front, forming a sharper contrast with the nearly black crown than in Arctic Skua, and legs grey or blue-grey (instead of black) with black feet and webs. A dark phase occurs but is excessively rare. Immature birds in the barred plumage are difficult to identify in the field, but are generally greyer, less rufous or yellowish than Arctic Skua and show little or no white in the wing; their wings are more slender and their flight is graceful and tern-like. Length about 20–22 ins., of which about 5–8 ins. is due to projection of long central feathers beyond the rest of the tail.

Habitat. It spends its life at sea outside the breeding-season and is more markedly pelagic in its migration than the Arctic Skua.

General Habits. It is the most graceful and easy flier of the three smaller skuas, with action more floating and tern-like than Arctic Skua. Frequently hovers like Kestrel or tern; it is also fond of sailing and soaring high in the air, and will chase in aerobatic play birds of its own or other species. Otherwise behaviour and habits differ little from Arctic Skua. It swims buoyantly with long tail pointed upward.

Apparently no calls recorded away from breeding-grounds.

Food is varied, especially on breeding-grounds. At sea it pursues terns and gulls, but perhaps less frequently than other skuas. Fish and offal also recorded.

Status and Distribution. Mainly a scarce passage-migrant; in autumn from mid-August to the end of October annually in Shetland, very small numbers on the east coast of England, with stragglers in the Outer Hebrides and west coast of Ireland, but very irregular elsewhere. In spring the main passage, sometimes of hundreds, is concentrated in May off the Outer Hebrides. Exceptional inland. Single birds have been recorded in summer in breeding colonies of Arctic Skuas. It is a mainly arctic breeding species, our birds belonging to the race *Stercorarius longicaudus longicaudus* which nests in arctic Europe (extending further south in Norway) and N.W. Asia. An example of the race *Stercorarius longicaudus pallescens* which breeds in N.E. Asia, N. America and Greenland, has occurred in Outer Hebrides. European birds migrate chiefly offshore to winter apparently in the S. Atlantic.

GREAT SKUA—*Stercorarius skua*

BIRD PLATES 56 and 126   EGG PLATE XV (3)

In flight it resembles a large, heavy, rather short-tailed gull of a *nearly uniform dark brown colour, when seen at any distance, and with a prominent white patch at the base of the primaries*. At close quarters the upper-parts show more or less streaking of tawny brown. When settled the stout build, shorter tail and shorter, thicker bill than those of a gull of the same size give it a rather heavy, lumpish appearance. Juvenile has nearly uniform plumage and the white on the wing is less extensive than in adults, and apparently this is not much changed until after the second winter. Bill and legs blackish. Length about 23 ins.

Habitat. A maritime species ranging over the offshore and pelagic zones without regard to depth or distance from shore; resorting in the breeding-season to more or less elevated moorlands, rough pastures and fells near the sea. Exceptional inland.

General Habits. Ordinary action on the wing is much like one of the large gulls, appearing rather heavy and laboured, but when in pursuit of other birds or defending nest it is much accelerated and becomes impressively swift and powerful. On nesting grounds it fiercely attacks human and animal intruders. Gait and carriage are like those of a gull and at sea it settles on the water more freely than the other skuas. Commonly seen singly at sea, or occasionally in twos and threes. Like other skuas it obtains much of its food at sea by piracy, harrying gulls and terns with unexpected dash and agility and with relentless persistence till they either drop fish which they are carrying or disgorge what they have already swallowed. It also fishes for itself and sometimes accompanies vessels. In the breeding-season it is fond of bathing in freshwater pools.

Records of calls are apparently confined to breeding-grounds and include a loud note "hah-hah-hah" used in display, and a deep "tuk-tuk" in attack.

Food consists mainly of fish, often obtained by forcing gulls, terns and Gannets to disgorge. Also takes birds and will feed on stranded fish and offal.

Nests in heather, moss or rough pasture, by preference in colonies, but not very close together, and sometimes one or two pairs may be met with far from any others. The eggs, usually 2, but sometimes 1–3, have ground-colour normally olive-grey to reddish-brown, sometimes very pale without markings. They are laid generally in the latter half of May and early June in little more than a scantily lined depression. Incubation is by both sexes for about 28–30 days. The young are tended by both parents and fly when 6–7 weeks old. Single-brooded. Recorded first breeding when 4–6 years old.

Status and Distribution. Mainly a summer-visitor, from early April to mid-September, breeding on many Shetland islands (large colonies on Foula, Unst, Noss, Yell and Fetlar) and in smaller numbers on Fair Isle; in Orkney particularly numerous on Hoy; has spread to Outer Hebrides (including St. Kilda), to Caithness (1949 onwards), and Sutherland (1964). Scarce on passage on all coasts Great Britain; more numerous S.W. Ireland. Our birds belong to the race *Stercorarius skua skua* which breeds also in Iceland, Faeroes and possibly Greenland, wintering in E. Atlantic from 60° N., south to Madeira and Sargasso Sea. Other races are found in S. Chile, S. New Zealand and the Antarctic.

MEDITERRANEAN GULL—*Larus melanocephalus*

BIRD PLATE 61

A trifle larger than Black-headed Gull, longer legged and slightly stouter, with a *heavy decurved bill*. Adults are very pale grey on mantle and wings, paling to *frosty grey on primaries*, both above and below, and which sometimes look almost white in the field; the trailing edge of the wing is pure white. In breeding plumage they have *jet-black hoods*. First-year birds have outer primaries blackish and at rest somewhat resemble immature Black-headed Gull, although in flight look much like young Common Gull but sometimes more black and white, having inner primaries

MEDITERRANEAN GULL
1st winter

The dark hind border of the wing is broken by the whitish inner primaries. Bill appears to droop slightly.

R.A.R.

MEDITERRANEAN GULL
2nd year

LITTLE GULL
2nd year

When adult, both species lose the black spots on
wing tips.

and secondaries whitish with a dark sub-terminal line across the
secondaries (in Common Gull dark on primaries and secondaries is
less clear-cut, less contrasting); a *dark patch extends from eye to
ear-coverts* and then turns as if to run up over the back of the
whitish crown but fades out; underwing white (whiter than Common Gull) but 'transparent' enough to show dark primaries and
bar on secondaries. Moreover, in this as in subsequent plumages,
the *mantle is pale pearly grey*, whereas in all equivalent plumages
the Common Gull has slightly darker, blue-grey mantle. In its first
winter the Mediterranean's pale mantle (whiter even than that of
Black-headed Gull) contrasts with the grey-brown wing-coverts,
but by the summer these have become as pale as the mantle while
in Common Gull the darker mantle may give a 'saddle' effect; the
legs and bill appear to be blackish generally, but bill may have
greyish or orange base. Second winter birds resemble adults but
have small black tips to outer primaries. Legs of adult dark red, bill
reddish black. Length about 15¼ ins.

Habitat. It chiefly frequents the coast, and nests around lagoons and marshes, often among Black-headed Gulls. In winter a
few penetrate far inland.

General Habits. Behaviour and habits are very much like
Black-headed Gull's. Walks with high-stepping gait.

Often silent in autumn, but can give a sharp tern-like "kee-er";
assertive note in spring is a deep-toned, far-carrying "kyow", quite
unlike any Black-headed's call.

Food is evidently varied and includes small fish, molluscs and insects.

Status and Distribution. Present throughout the year but mainly in winter; gradually increasing, with perhaps 100–200 wintering in the mid-1980s. Most arrive July–November and leave March–early April, principally in southern England, more thinly on other coasts of England and Wales, E. and S. Ireland, and rare but now annual in Scotland chiefly on E. coast. Breeding began in 1968 in Hampshire, expanding rather sporadically to a few pairs in several counties in S. and S.E. England. The main breeding area is around the N. Black Sea, but nesting, often sparse or irregular, extends to most W. European countries. In winter it ranges throughout the Mediterranean and to coasts of the Bay of Biscay and Morocco. There are no subspecies.

LITTLE GULL—*Larus minutus*

BIRD PLATES 61 and 127

The smallest gull, distinctly smaller than Black-headed Gull, from which adults differ in breeding plumage in having a *black (not dark brown) hood* and at all seasons in *absence of black on the wings, but having dark slaty under-side of wing* with white trailing edge, which is noticeable in flight. Wings are rather paddle-shaped, distinctively blunt-ended. In winter, when the head is like Black-headed Gull's at the same season, size and wing characters must be relied on. Juvenile has dark crown and the back sooty-blackish more or less barred with whitish, and white tail with black subterminal bar. In flight it shows a *black diagonal bar across the wing from base to the carpal joint, continued along the front edge of wing to outer primaries which are also black*; at rest the black on the wing appears as a broad horizontal stripe above the flanks. Juvenile wing- and tail-pattern is retained through the first winter and summer and the under-side of the wing is white until autumn moult of the second year, though the back and rest of the plumage become as adult. Bill of adult is reddish in summer, blackish in winter and young; legs red in adult, duller in winter and young. In some immature individuals the central tail feathers moult white while the outer feathers retain black near the tip, thus creating the illusion of the tail being graduated; moult can also make the tail appear forked. Length about 11 ins.

KITTIWAKE
1st winter

LITTLE GULL
1st winter

Note dark hind-collar on Kittiwake.

Habitat. In the breeding-season it frequents marshes and marshy lakes. During the rest of the year much as Black-headed Gull, frequenting both sea-coast and inshore waters, estuaries and the vicinity of lakes or lagoons at some distance inland.

General Habits. Flight light and buoyant, recalling a tern's. General habits are much like Black-headed Gull. It secures much of its food in flight from the surface of water or just beneath it, dipping down like a marsh tern; also takes much insect food on the wing.

Common note is "kek-kek-kek", lower pitched than Black-headed Gull's note. Also a higher, harder "ka-ka-ka".

Food includes small fish, crustacea, worms, molluscs, insects and a little vegetable matter.

Status and Distribution. Mainly an autumn- and winter-visitor (August to March), also fairly often April to May, rarer June to July. In England it occurs chiefly on the east coast, sometimes in small parties, and is also regular on south coast but less frequent west coast and Wales. In Scotland since the 1950s it has been a regular autumn-visitor in some numbers to S. Fife, and in even larger numbers at mouth of Tay; elsewhere recorded as an occasional visitor including Orkney, Shetland and Hebrides. In

Ireland too it has become regular in the south-east, sometimes reaching west coast. In England nesting has been attempted a few times in recent years. The bird breeds from Holland and Denmark, but mainly through the Baltic and Russia to N. Asia, and winters south to the Mediterranean. There are no subspecies.

SABINE'S GULL—*Larus sabini*

BIRD PLATE 62

A most beautiful and graceful little gull, about the size of a Common Tern. It is characterized at all seasons by a forked tail (often looking squarish) and *striking triple-triangle wing-pattern, with nearly the whole primary region up to the carpal joint black (also a conspicuous black border to rest of the fore-wing in adult), a broad white triangle in the region of the secondaries*, and the inner wing and mantle are grey. In breeding plumage the *dark grey hood*, narrowly bordered black where it meets white of neck, renders it still more distinctive, and at rest the broad white tips of the primaries produce a very regular effect of black and white bars on the ends of the wings. Bill is black with a yellow tip, legs greyish. In winter plumage the head is white and more or less dusky on sides and nape. Juvenile has crown and upper-parts grey-brown, with pale greyish borders to the feathers of the

SABINE'S GULL

Adult, winter.   Immature.

mantle; the rump and tail are white with a black terminal band. Wing-pattern is much as adult, but with white tips of the primaries much less developed, and the coverts, which are grey in adult, like mantle. First winter birds are much as winter adults with wings and tail as juvenile; in subsequent summer the grey feathers of head are mixed with white. Young Sabine's must be distinguished from second-winter Kittiwake which has pale hind wing, no dark diagonal wing bar, no dark collar on nape, but is considerably larger. Length about 13 ins.

Habitat. Outside the breeding-season it apparently chiefly frequents offshore waters, but a few occur inshore.

General Habits. In flight it is rather like a tern, being extremely light and agile on the wing. It feeds by picking food off the surface of water in flight, also feeds on mud-flats, running about like a wader. Except at breeding-places it is not very social, usually flying singly or two or three together.

It has a single, harsh, grating, but not very loud note, very similar to grating cry of Arctic Tern, but somewhat harsher and shorter.

Food includes insects and their larvae, crustacea, worms, molluscs, also small fishes.

Status and Distribution. A scarce autumn- and winter-visitor, rarely occurring in spring and summer. Most frequent in Cornwall, Yorks and Norfolk, but many have been recorded at intervals elsewhere in England and Wales, even in inland counties; and widely on Irish coasts. It is rarer in Scotland, although recorded from both E. and W. coasts and Shetland. Adults are very rare. It is an arctic species, breeding in Spitzbergen, Greenland, Siberia, and arctic Canada, and wintering in S. Atlantic and S. Pacific. There are no subspecies.

BLACK-HEADED GULL—*Larus ridibundus*

BIRD PLATES 60, 61 and 127   EGG PLATE V (17A, 17B & 17C)

Smaller and slighter in build than Common Gull or Kittiwake, with more slender bill; immediately recognized in breeding plumage by *chocolate brown hood* and in flight at all ages by a *broad white margin to the front of the narrow black-tipped wings*, without terminal white spots or mirrors, as well as by *red bill and legs*, very dark in breeding birds (yellowish-red in immature). In winter

BLACK-HEADED GULL
1st winter

BONAPARTE'S GULL
1st winter

Bonaparte's tends to have a firmer band across wing, and
a darker, clearer-cut hind-border.

plumage the head is white with a dark patch on ear coverts and a
smaller one in front of eye. Juvenile has the back and wing-coverts
soft, mottled brown, but under-parts white and head much as
adult in winter, and crown more or less mottled brownish; tail
white with a subterminal black-brown band. First winter birds
have tail and wings as juvenile, but the back more or less grey like
adult. In the following summer much as adult, but with some
brown on the wings and the brown hood has some admixture of
white feathers. Length about 14–15 ins.

Habitat. An inland as well as a coastal bird, breeding not only
on sandhills and saltings close to sea or on low islands off shore, but
on bogs, moorland pools, and on islands and rushy borders of
larger sheets of fresh water far from the sea, including northern
lochs in treeless country and lakes with well-wooded borders in
agricultural districts. It feeds freely on grass- and arable fields
inland, and outside the breeding-season occurs far up rivers and
commonly on meres, reservoirs, marshes, sewage-farms and the
like where it does not breed, including waters of great cities like
London. On coast it chiefly frequents low-lying shores, estuaries,
harbours, etc., not so much rocky shores or cliffs, and at sea
seldom extends much beyond inshore waters.

General Habits. The most abundant of British gulls inland.
Flight is more buoyant than in the larger species and more
approaching tern type. It is much addicted to hawking in the air for

flying ants and other insects; plunging under water from the air after food has been recorded occasionally, and trampling wet mud or sand or in shallow water to disturb prey is a regular habit. In fields it frequently snatches food from Lapwings and on lakes and reservoirs from diving ducks, grebes and Coots. Otherwise general behaviour and habits are much as other gulls.

It has various more or less harsh notes, of which "kwarr" and "kwup" are commonly used.

Food is very varied, consisting mainly of animal matter including fish, fish ova, crustacea, molluscs, insects and earthworms; sometimes also mice and small birds. Vegetable food includes seeds of cereals and weeds, berries, grass, seaweed, potatoes and turnips. Also takes bread, meat, garbage, etc.

Nests in colonies in very varied sites: on low vegetation, on the ground, in shallow water and occasionally on sheds or other buildings or in bushes or trees. The eggs, 2–6 but usually 3, vary in ground-colour from light buffish-stone to deep brown, sometimes blue. They are laid generally from mid-April onwards in a nest carelessly built of any available vegetable matter. Incubation is by both sexes usually for 22–24 days. The young are fed by both parents and fly when 5–6 weeks old. Single-brooded.

Status and Distribution. Present throughout the year. In England and Wales it nests in nearly all coastal counties, and many inland ones, but is mainly absent from S.W. England as a breeder. Nearly 40 per cent. of sites are 20 miles or more inland. Density is greatest and colonies are most numerous in the north. In Scotland it is generally distributed throughout the mainland (few in the N.W.) and islands, including Outer Hebrides and Shetland. In Ireland there are colonies, some vast, in most areas except in the south and parts of the east. Although the actual nesting colonies are abandoned by end of August and considerable dispersal takes place, the majority of British breeding birds are relatively sedentary, but some reach the Atlantic coasts of France, Spain and Portugal and occasionally go further. Between August and April there is an influx from the Baltic countries and W. Europe south to Holland and Switzerland, these birds wintering mainly in E. and S.E. England. Passage along the east coast of birds breeding further north than Britain lasts until the end of May in the northern isles. Both breeding birds and visitors belong to the race *Larus ridibundus ridibundus* which breeds from Iceland and N. Russia, south to France and Bulgaria, and extends far into Asia, wintering south to the tropics. Another race occurs in E. Asia.

COMMON GULL—*Larus canus*

BIRD PLATES 58 and 127   EGG PLATE XIV (3)

Adults of Herring Gull and the present species are the two common grey-backed gulls which have black ends of primaries tipped with white. Common Gull is *decidedly the smaller, with a relatively slender bill, giving the head a more refined appearance* which is often the best distinction from the rather coarse, heavy-billed Herring Gull in flight, when size may be difficult to judge. Other differences are *greenish-yellow legs and bill*, the latter lacking Herring Gull's red spot on lower mandible, and the mantle is slightly darker, a difference noticeable on the ground. When at rest the wings project further beyond the tail than in Herring Gull, giving the body a more tapering appearance. Head is strongly streaked dusky in winter. When not badly worn, the white tips of primaries (conspicuous in flight and more apparent from below than above) afford a distinction from similar sized Kittiwake which has ends of wings mainly black, as well as other differences. Distinctly larger and more robust than Black-headed Gull, whose red bill and legs, white fore-wing and black wing-tips in any case at once distinguish it. Juvenile is not unlike those of Herring and Black-backed Gulls, but with a bolder tail-pattern, the whitish basal part contrasting with the blackish subterminal band. Juvenile wing- and tail-pattern are retained during the first year; the rest of the plumage is like adult, with more or less admixture of brown feathers. Length about 16 ins.

Habitat. On the coast it frequents the same localities as Herring Gull, but does not range much beyond inshore waters, and is more

COMMON GULL
1st autumn

Note whitish tail with
broad dark band at tip.

of an inland bird than that species, breeding habitually on fresh-water lochs, moorlands and hillsides, and less commonly on grassy cliffs or low marine islands. Outside the breeding-season also often far inland, resorting to arable and grass-fields in both lowland and hilly regions. It also visits lakes, reservoirs and other inland waters.

General Habits. These and behaviour are like other gulls. Drops mollusc shells in the same way as Herring Gull.

Notes are higher pitched than the larger gulls, the commonest being a shrill almost whistling "*keee*-ya".

Food is very varied: inland chiefly insects, earthworms and seeds; on coast all sorts of marine invertebrates, dead fish and refuse. Also takes small mammals, small birds and eggs.

Nests on the ground, rocks, etc., usually in small or medium-sized colonies, but not rarely single pairs. The eggs, 2–5, but usually 3, vary in ground-colour from dark to light olive, occasionally pale greenish-blue. They are laid generally in the latter half of May and early June in a nest built of heather, grass or seaweed, as obtainable. Incubation is by both sexes for about 24–27 days. The young are fed by both parents, begin to use their wings when about 4 weeks old and can fly after 5 weeks. Single-brooded.

Status and Distribution. Present throughout the year. As a breeding bird it is only really common and well distributed in Scotland, north of the central lowlands; in Wales it started breeding in Anglesey in 1963; in England there is an old-established colony at Dungeness (Kent/Sussex) and the odd pair or two nest in East Anglia and Nottingham, and more in the Pennines. In Ireland it breeds mainly in Donegal, Mayo, Galway, with smaller numbers in several other counties including Kerry. It is also a winter-visitor (August/April) to all coasts as well as inland, and a passage-migrant, while immature birds are frequent in summer. Migration is mainly in a S.W. direction, our winter-visitors coming from the area Holland–Finland–Norway and occurring in greatest numbers in S.E. England. The race concerned is *Larus canus canus* which breeds in Europe south to Holland and east to the White Sea, and winters south to the Mediterranean. Other races are found in Northern Asia and N.W. North America.

LESSER BLACK-BACKED GULL—*Larus fuscus*

BIRD PLATES 59 and 127   EGG PLATE XIV (4)

Adult resembles Great Black-backed Gull, and individuals in some circumstances may be hard to separate, but typically the Lesser is much smaller, has *yellow legs in summer* (in winter not infrequently fading to pinkish or whitish grey) *and the upper-parts are slate-grey* rather than black, although in *L. f. fuscus* the tint is as deep as in the larger bird. Build is also appreciably slenderer and the *bill less stout*. Head is often streaked dusky in winter. Juvenile is like that of Herring Gull, but slightly darker, some individuals fairly easily recognizable, but others inseparable in the field. Discrimination becomes easier at each successive moult, the actual changes being very much as in Herring Gull. Legs of young are brownish or flesh-coloured, becoming yellow gradually. Length about 21 ins.

Habitat. On coast and at sea it occupies the same habitat as Herring Gull, but frequents offshore waters to an even greater extent and often breeds on fresh water and in inland localities, such as islands in lochs, upland moors and flows, and lowland bogs or peaty mosses. It also migrates overland more than Herring Gull.

General Habits. Behaviour and habits are very much as Herring Gull, but on the whole it is a bolder and more aggressive bird.

The various calls are in general deeper and louder than Herring Gull's, approaching those of Great Black-back.

Food is very varied and includes fish, crustacea, worms, molluscs, insects, mice and voles, birds and eggs, dead animals and garbage. Vegetable food includes grain and seaweed.

Nests on the ground, exceptionally on roofs, usually in colonies. The eggs, usually 3, but sometimes 1–4, are indistinguishable from those of Herring Gull, having ground-colour varying from pale greenish-blue to dark umber-brown, occasionally unmarked light blue. They are laid generally from early May onwards to June in a nest composed of any available material such as heather, grass, seaweed or lichen. Incubation is by both sexes for about 26–28 days. The young are fed by both parents and fly when about 5 weeks old. Single-brooded.

Status and Distribution. Mainly a summer-visitor, but substantial numbers are now also present in winter. In England it is a scarce or irregular breeder in Norfolk, Suffolk and the south-east, regular on most south-west and west coasts, and numerous in Scilly, Bristol Channel, S.W. Wales and Walney (Lancs); Farne

Islands on the east side; inland some sites are occupied on northern moors or reservoirs, in southern Wales, and occasional pairs nest in central England. In Scotland it breeds in many places on the coasts and isles, also inland; widely in Ireland, chiefly on marine islands, also some freshwater lakes. On autumn and spring migration (July–November, and end February–May) it is more widely distributed on coasts, and also appears inland, in some parts in considerable numbers. Non-breeding birds are frequent in summer on all coasts. British birds are mainly migratory, wintering in the west Mediterranean and on Atlantic coasts of Europe and Africa south to Nigeria. They belong to the race *Larus fuscus graellsii* whose breeding range is confined to the British Isles, Faeroes, Iceland, Channel Is., Brittany. Adults in particular are wintering increasingly, especially in England in the lower Thames valley, upper Bristol Channel area, W. Midlands and Pennines/ Lancashire where inland reservoirs and refuse tips provide roosting-sites and food, chiefly in the vicinity of large towns. A minority of the Lesser Black-backed Gulls seen in winter belong to the Scandinavian race *Larus fuscus fuscus* which breeds in North Russia, in Scandinavia and the Baltic. This latter race can usually be distinguished in the field by the much darker slate-black (not slate-grey) mantle which, as in Great Black-backed Gull, appears almost as dark as the wing-tips, but intermediate birds also occur.

HERRING GULL—*Larus argentatus*

BIRD PLATES 58, 59 and 127   EGG PLATE XIV (2)

Adults may be confused with Common Gull, but are *considerably larger, with markedly heavier and coarser bill and flesh-coloured, not greenish, legs and feet*. The terminal parts of the wings are black with white tips or "mirrors". Bill is yellow, with a red spot towards the tip of the lower mandible. Head and hindneck are streaked brown in winter. It takes three years to reach fully matured plumage. Juvenile and first winter birds are dusky, mottled brown, without much contrast in plumage except for dark brown primaries, though the mantle is darker than the rest; the whole tail is brown with terminal band darker, but not strongly contrasted with the rest as in Common Gull. They are very like juveniles of Lesser Black-backed Gull. First summer is paler, especially on the head and under-parts. Second summer resembles adult, but with more or less brown mottling on the back; the streaking on the head during winter is more pronounced and it has more whitish in the tail than first year, so that the dark subterminal band is more definite, and the under-parts have some brownish marks. Third year is as adult, but with some brown flecks and mottlings on wings and tail. Length about 22 ins.

Habitat. It chiefly frequents coasts, tidal estuaries and inshore waters, also offshore fishing grounds. It resorts for breeding to coastal cliffs, especially those with grassy slopes, also islands, sand-dunes, etc., and exceptionally it breeds on freshwater lakes, bogs or cliffs at some distance from the sea. In a number of areas it also occurs commonly on inland waters. Feeding grounds regularly include grass-fields and arable land.

General Habits. These and behaviour are typical of the larger gulls. Feeding habits include trampling wet sand to disturb prey, dropping shells on shore from the air to break them, plunging under water, hawking for insects, quartering open ground like a harrier, and some birds develop considerable skill in hunting small rodents. A gregarious tendency is in evidence at all seasons, and outside the breeding-season it roosts in large assemblages on sheltered waters, sandbanks, etc.

It has a variety of loud wailing and other cries, one of the commonest being a loud "kyow-kyow-kyow".

Food is very varied, principally marine organisms, carrion and garbage.

Nests usually in colonies, on cliff ledges, more locally on roofs, and sometimes on fairly flat ground. Eggs, 2–6, but usually 3, have umber-brown to olive ground-colour but are sometimes unmarked pale blue; they are indistinguishable from those of Lesser Black-backed Gull. They are laid generally in May in a large nest built of grass, seaweed, etc., by both sexes. Incubation is by both sexes for about 25–27 days. The young are fed by both parents, and fly when about 6 weeks old. Single-brooded.

Status and Distribution. A common resident, breeding on all coasts, but only locally in E. and S.E. England; also some inland areas mainly in Scotland and Ireland, a few in England and Wales. Nesting on buildings is now a regular habit, mainly in coastal towns, especially in S.W., S.E., N.E. England, S. and N. Wales, E. Scotland. The population is augmented in winter on east coast by visitors from N.W. Europe. British breeding birds are rather sedentary, movement being almost entirely one of dispersal in any direction, and the majority do not travel more than 200–300 miles. They are currently regarded as belonging to the race *Larus argentatus argenteus*, breeding from Iceland to southern North

Sea coasts. Winter visitors include many larger and darker *Larus argentatus argentatus* from Denmark, Scandinavia and N.W. Russia; also of regular occurrence but in very small numbers in autumn or winter, mainly in S.E. England, are examples of *Larus argentatus michahellis* from S.W. Europe, which has *yellow legs*, vermillion eye-ring, more extensive black on the primaries, and tends to be larger and darker than our bird. Other races occur elsewhere in Europe, Asia, N. America, also Madeira and Canaries.

ICELAND GULL—*Larus glaucoides*

BIRD PLATES 60 and 127

In plumage it resembles Glaucous Gull. It is typically considerably smaller, but the largest Iceland may be almost as big as the smallest Glaucous, and more reliable characters are the *shorter, less heavy bill* (the head and bill being markedly smaller than Herring Gull), and in adults in the breeding-season, the *brick-red, not yellow, eye-ring*. Build is more stream-lined than that of Glaucous Gull, on the water appearing even slimmer and smaller than Herring Gull, with *tips of the wings when fully grown projecting beyond the tail to a very conspicuous extent*, and giving a markedly tapering effect to the body. However, except in the case of first winter birds (which do not moult their juvenile flight feathers) fully grown wings are rarely seen in this country as the primaries are moulted in autumn and do not grow to full length again before early spring. Plumage of young birds is generally like immature Glaucous Gull, with the eye very dark brown in the first winter; but Icelands at this age have the *bill dark from the tip backwards for at least half its length*. Some first winter Icelands, however, are almost pure white, but apparently always have the bare parts as described above, besides having attenuated tips to the primaries. In second winter birds the eye is pale, and the dark area of the bill is somewhat smaller, with bill-tip pale. Legs are dusky pink in immaturity. Adult plumage is attained about the fifth year. Length about 21 ins.

Habitat. It is found in much the same type of habitat as Glaucous Gull.

General Habits. Flight is less heavy than Glaucous Gull, with quicker wing-action reminiscent of Black-headed Gull or

Kittiwake, and the longer, slenderer wings may be noticed by those with a good eye for such points. General behaviour and habits are much like Herring Gull.

Voice resembles Herring Gull's but is considerably shriller.

Food is largely small fish, dead birds, and offal and garbage of all kinds. It also takes crustacea, molluscs and seeds.

Status and Distribution. A scarce winter-visitor from mid-October or occasionally earlier, until mid-March with stragglers into May or later. Distribution is much the same as Glaucous Gull, but it is decidedly scarcer and more irregular and very rarely occurs in numbers. It is only known to breed in Greenland, wintering south to Scandinavia and New York. There are no subspecies.

GLAUCOUS GULL—*Larus hyperboreus*

BIRD PLATE 60

Adult Glaucous and Iceland Gulls differ from all other species in having *very pale grey mantle and white primaries*; in all stages of immature plumage they have the wing-tips noticeably paler than rest of wing. Although ranging in size from about that of Herring Gull to Great Black-backed Gull, Glaucous is typically a *considerably larger* and heavier bird than Iceland Gull, and has a *relatively longer and stouter bill*; this is the most definite and trustworthy single character for smaller examples of Glaucous Gull which approach Iceland in size. In the breeding-season it has a *lemon-yellow, not brick-red, eye-ring*, but in winter this is practically colourless. Legs flesh-coloured. The *wings are relatively shorter* than in Iceland Gull, but when they are fully grown may project quite considerably beyond the tail; this applies to adults and immatures in summer, and to juveniles in their first winter, but older birds moult the wing-feathers in autumn and these are slow in re-growing, so that in winter they may not, or scarcely, reach beyond the tip of the tail. Juvenile and first winter birds are *much paler* than those of other large gulls, with buffish, wavy barrings and mottlings and without a broad subterminal tail-band. They become progressively whiter and are not fully adult till the fourth or even fifth year. First winter birds have the *bill creamy flesh colour for three-quarters of its length*, with the tip dark brown, but in first winter Icelands the dark portion extends over at least the

GLAUCOUS GULL
1st winter

ICELAND GULL
1st winter

Note the greater proportion of black on Iceland Gull's bill.

distal half of the bill. In both species the dark portion is reduced with age. Length about 27 ins.

Habitat. Outside the breeding-season it is found chiefly on sea-coast, sometimes frequenting harbours with Herring Gulls or other species, but also sometimes visits inland lakes and rivers. At sea it frequents both inshore and offshore waters.

General Habits. These and behaviour are much like Great Black-backed Gull. It is similarly destructive to other sea-fowl, but is stated to be less fierce and rapacious, more sluggish and cowardly than Black-back. It has similar rather heavy but powerful flight, with comparatively slow wing action, and is similarly rather inclined to solitary habits, though also occurring in considerable flocks. It is also a pirate, robbing Eiders, etc., of food.

Commonest note is equivalent to "kyow-kyow-kyow" of Herring Gull although much shriller, but it is rather silent as a rule.

Food includes carrion, birds, either found dead or killed, fish, crustacea, molluscs, worms and seaweed.

Status and Distribution. A winter-visitor, generally from October to March or April, and usually in small numbers, but in severe winters sometimes much more numerous. Occasional in summer. It is most frequent in Shetland, Orkney, Outer Hebrides, and fewer down the east coast to Suffolk; also Cornwall and most Irish coasts. Elsewhere it is occasional and rarely occurs inland in the south except in the London area. Adults are very rare in the south and west. The race concerned, *Larus hyperboreus hyperboreus*, breeds in the Arctic from Iceland and the N. Russian coast northwards, also in N.W. Asia and N.E. America. Another race occurs in N.E. Asia and N.W. America.

GREAT BLACK-BACKED GULL—*Larus marinus*

BIRD PLATES 59 and 127   EGG PLATE XIV (1)

Adult is distinguished in summer from British Lesser Black-backed Gull by its great size, *flesh-coloured or whitish legs and black rather than dark grey mantle* and from Scandinavian race of the Lesser Black-back, which has mantle similar, by the first two characters; in winter, however, the legs of Lesser Black-backs quite often lose their yellow colour and may resemble those of the present species, and then the massive bill of the larger bird is distinctive; nevertheless care is necessary to avoid confusion. Primaries are tipped white, and the whole wing shows white hind border. The head is only sparsely streaked dusky in winter. Bill is yellow with a red patch towards tip of the lower mandible. Young birds in first year differ from young Herring Gulls, apart from larger size, in whiter head and under-parts, giving a less uniform appearance; the mantle too is cleaner giving a more chequered effect. In second year the contrast of light head and dark mantle is intensified, while third year birds are almost as adults, but with the mantle browner and wavy dark bars more or less developed on the white tail. Length about 25–27 ins.

Habitat. In the breeding-season it frequents principally the more rocky coasts and islands, but also sometimes breeds on freshwater lochs and mosses at some distance from sea. Outside breeding-season it is at least as common on low-lying, sandy or muddy shores and estuaries as on rocky coasts, and visits fresh-water lakes near the coast, and reservoirs. It is the least numerous of the commoner species of gulls at any considerable distance inland, but in recent years has been coming inland in increasing numbers. At sea it frequents both inshore and offshore waters and occurs in great numbers on fishing grounds but does not in general range so far from land as Herring and Lesser Black-backed Gulls.

General Habits. These are much as other large gulls, but it is the most rapacious and destructive to other sea-birds. Sometimes it robs food from other species but will also join in hawking for such "small game" as flying ants; it dives occasionally but rarely submerges completely. It is frequently seen singly or in couples, alone or in flocks of other gulls, but considerable gatherings are also of regular occurrence.

Notes are much like those of Herring and Lesser Black-backed Gull, but stronger and deeper than those even of the latter. The deep, hoarse, barking "aouk" and deep guttural "uk-uk-uk" heard especially from birds disturbed on breeding-ground, are characteristic.

Food is very varied, mainly animal matter including fish, crustacea, worms, molluscs, starfishes, insects, rats, voles and mice, garbage and all kinds of carrion. It also kills adults and young of many species of birds up to the size of Puffins and Shearwaters; also rabbits, and other mammals, and occasionally weakly ewes and lambs.

Nests in colonies where numerous, but some pairs nest singly, on islands, cliff ledges, etc.; rarely on salt-marsh or shingle. The eggs, 2–5, but usually 3, have ground-colour normally stone-buff to olive-brown, sometimes blue. They are laid generally from beginning of May to early June in a large nest composed of heather, sticks, seaweed, grass and a few feathers, built by both sexes. Incubation is by both sexes for about 26–28 days. The young are fed by both parents and fly when 7–8 weeks old. Single-brooded.

Status and Distribution. Present throughout the year. In England it breeds in Isle of Wight and Dorset (few), Devon, Cornwall, Scilly Isles, Lundy, Steep Holm (Somerset), most coastal counties in Wales, Isle of Man, sparingly from Lancashire to Cumberland, but nowhere regularly on the east coast although pairs have occasionally attempted nesting in Norfolk or Suffolk. In Scotland it breeds on most parts of the west coast and island groups north to Shetland, also Moray Firth; further south on the east side pairs are scarce, scattered but spreading nearly to the border. In Ireland it breeds on all coasts, also a few fresh-water lakes. The breeding population of the British Isles in 1970 was about 20–25,000 pairs, of which 70% were in Scotland. In winter it is widely dispersed on all British coasts (as are non-breeding birds in summer); it is also widely distributed inland in increasing numbers in both England and Scotland, especially up river valleys and over lowland moors. Also frequent far inland in Ireland. Some British birds migrate and east coast gatherings include a proportion of winter visitors from the Continent between August–October and March–April. The species breeds in N. America and in Europe east to Russia and south to Brittany, wintering south to the Mediterranean. There are no subspecies.

KITTIWAKE—*Rissa tridactyla*

BIRD PLATES 62 and 127   EGG PLATE XIV (5)

Adult most nearly resembles Common Gull, but is rather smaller and more lightly built, without conspicuous white tips to the black ends of the wings and *with black legs*. At long range can readily be recognized by its buoyant, bounding flight, more rapid shallow wing-beat and its *pale primaries, contrasting with darker grey coverts and mantle*; in addition the underwing is white so that bird's general appearance is appreciably paler than Common Gull. The crown and nape are greyish in winter, with a dark patch extending upwards from the ear-coverts. Bill is waxy yellow. The dark eye gives a gentler, less fierce expression than other gulls. Juvenile and first winter birds are quite different from Common Gull, with white head and under-parts, blue-grey mantle spotted with blackish, *a broad black band across the back of neck and a diagonal black band across wing*, giving a distinctive pattern in flight; the back of the head is more or less grey, there is a blackish patch on ear-coverts, and the tail has a terminal black band. Some sub-adults have mainly greenish-yellow legs. Tail is practically square in adult and very slightly forked in young. Length about 16 ins.

Habitat. More strictly marine than other gulls and largely oceanic, frequenting offshore and pelagic waters outside the

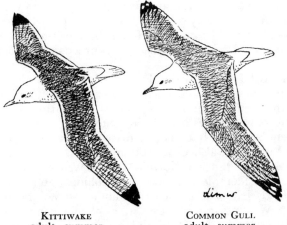

KITTIWAKE
adult, summer.

COMMON GULL
adult, summer.

Note that Kittiwake's outer wing is paler
than inner wing and back.

breeding-season, though also met with in the inshore zone and even inland at times. In the breeding-season it frequents chiefly the vicinity of rocky coasts where cliffs afford nesting sites. During this period even the immature, non-breeding birds move in towards the shallower waters and flocks, including both adults and young, not uncommonly rest on flat shores. Breeding birds will regularly visit freshwater lochs near shore to bathe, and it is showing a tendency to feed in fresh water.

General Habits. Flight is graceful, swift and buoyant with a quicker wing-action than the larger gulls. It habitually follows ships. Food is taken by deftly picking it up from the surface in flight, by settling and then diving, or by plunging in tern-like fashion from the air, often with complete immersion and at least sometimes using wings under water. It sometimes scavenges on beaches.

Chief note at breeding places is the well-known, pleasant-sounding "kitti-wa-a-k", but it is usually rather silent away from nesting-places.

Food is varied, comprising fish, crustacea, worms, molluscs, insects, aquatic plants, grass, moss, seeds (including cereals) and potato.

Nests in colonies on ledges of precipitous sea-cliffs or of sea-caves, sometimes on ledges of buildings. The eggs, usually 2, but sometimes 1–3, vary in ground-colour from pale bluish-grey to brown. They are laid at the end of May or in June in a neatly constructed nest with a well-defined cup, built by both sexes of moss, grass, sea-weed, etc., and fixed to some (often very slight) projection or irregularity of rock. Incubation is by both sexes for about 26–28 days. The young are fed by both parents and fly when about 6 weeks old. Single-brooded. First breeds when about 3 or 4 years old.

Status and Distribution. Present throughout the year. In Great Britain the greatest concentration is on the E. and N. coasts of Scotland and northern isles, but with southward spread a number of new colonies have been established elsewhere during the present century. It breeds at many places on the east coast south to Yorkshire, also Lowestoft and Kent, and has nested on sandy beaches or dunes in Norfolk. On the west coast of Scotland there are considerable gaps between colonies and it breeds in Cumberland, Isle of Man, several colonies in W. and S. Wales, Lundy, S.W. England and east in English Channel to Isle of Wight. In Ireland it breeds abundantly in most counties having precipitous coasts and islands. Non-breeding birds often occur in summer on S. and E. coasts of England. In winter it is widely distributed off all coasts of Great Britain, numbers being increased by immigrants, but in Ireland is scarcer in winter. Seldom inland. A general dispersal, with a tendency towards south and west, appears to be the chief movement in autumn reaching mid-Atlantic, and a few ringed birds have been recovered in N.E. American waters. The species breeds in arctic America, Asia and Europe south to Brittany, the race to which British birds belong, *Rissa tridactyla tridactyla*, extending from eastern N. America in the west to Chaun Bay (Siberia) in the east, and wintering south to the Tropic of Cancer.

IVORY GULL—*Pagophila eburnea*

BIRD PLATE 58

About size of Common Gull. Adult *pure white with dark eyes, short black legs, and stout yellowish bill with greyer base* and *reddish tip*. Juvenile and first year birds are also white, but with fore-head, throat and sides of head greyish, upper-parts more or less spotted with black, most of wing quills tipped black, and tail with subterminal black band. On the wing, with its long wings and snowy plumage, it is a bird of conspicuous beauty and grace, but it is not so graceful when settled, the rather short legs and puffed out, pigeon-like shape, with tail depressed and head raised, giving a slightly awkward appearance. Length about 17½ ins.

Habitat. Outside the breeding-season it frequents chiefly the fringe of the pack-ice.

General Habits. Flight is strong, buoyant and tern-like. In addition to walking, it can also run with some speed with action comparable to a plover's. It settles freely on ice, ground or rocks, but often shows great reluctance to settle on water, though at least immatures may do so at times and even bathe. Will attend on hunters to feed on carcasses. Fierce and aggressive in temperament, it is more than a match for the much larger Glaucous Gull.

Call is a fairly shrill disyllabic "kree-ar", rather tern-like, given singly or repeated a few times.

Food includes flesh of dead animals, also fish, crustacea, molluscs and insects.

Status and Distribution. A vagrant, most frequent in Shetland and Orkney, but which has occurred in many counties of

Great Britain and very rarely in Ireland, from autumn to spring and as late as June but chiefly in winter. It has a circumpolar range, breeding in N. Greenland, Spitzbergen and other islands in the far north, and normally does not extend south of the Arctic Circle even in winter. There are no subspecies.

GULL-BILLED TERN—*Gelochelidon nilotica*

BIRD PLATE 63

It is the same size as Sandwich Tern, but noticeably heavier in head and body, with broader wings and a *shorter tail with only shallow fork*. The diagnostic feature is the *short, very thick black bill without yellow tip*, which looks curiously "swollen" in the field (but beware of young Sandwich Terns with short black bills). The upper wing is greyer than a Sandwich Tern's, and the *tail is grey* like the back, not white. Winter adults and juveniles have the *head largely white*, with a more or less distinct dark patch round the eye; juvenile has buffish crown and underparts and brown mottling on the back. Its habitat and feeding habits often give the first clue to its identity, *the coarse notes are diagnostic* and the heavy, shallow wing-beats are much like a Black-headed Gull's. Length about 14–15 ins.

Habitat. In summer it frequents especially the vicinity of saline

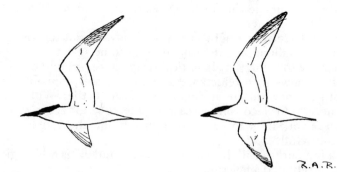

SANDWICH TERN
adult, summer.

GULL-BILLED TERN
adult, summer.

Note rather heavier body, broader wings and shorter tail
of Gull-billed Tern.

lagoons and salt-marshes; sometimes also on sandy coasts and freshwater lakes. In winter-quarters more on inland waters than coast.

General Habits. Flight tends to be rather heavier, steadier, and more leisurely than Sandwich Tern's, though very swift at times. Unlike that species it feeds to a considerable extent over land, being largely insectivorous and securing its prey by swift stoops to the ground or surface of water, as well as capturing them in flight. It also picks up food while walking on ground or in very shallow water. Otherwise its habits and behaviour are much like those of the sea-terns, although it rarely plunges right into the water.

Common notes are "ka-*huk*, ka-*huk*" "tirr*uck*-tirr*uck*" and a harsh "kaahk".

Food is varied, including small mammals, eggs and young of birds, lizards, frogs, tadpoles, small fish, crabs, worms and insects.

Nests on the shores of shallow lakes, etc. The eggs, normally 2–3, sometimes 5, are slightly smaller than Sandwich Tern's and spotted rather sparingly with browns, the ground-colour varying from creamy-whitish to brownish. They are laid in May or June in a hollow in sand or earth, scantily lined with grass, seaweed, etc. Incubation is by both sexes for about 22–23 days. The young can fly when about 4 weeks old. Single-brooded.

Status and Distribution. A vagrant or passage-migrant in very small numbers, appearing chiefly in May, less frequently other months from April to September; bred Essex 1950 and probably 1949. It occurs mainly on the south coast and in East Anglia; rare or very rare in northern England, Scotland and Ireland. The race concerned, *Gelochelidon nilotica nilotica*, breeds locally in Southern Europe north to Denmark, Austria, Romania, and S. Russia, also N.W. Africa and in Asia east to Burma, wintering on tropical Africa coasts, Red Sea and Persian Gulf. Other races occur in China, Malaysia, Australia and North and South America.

CASPIAN TERN—*Sterna caspia*

BIRD PLATE 64

A very large tern, as big as a Common Gull, with crown and sides of the head to below eye black, and a very stout, heavy coral-red bill. Primaries are dusky towards tip above and *appear mainly blackish from below.* Tail only slightly forked. Legs are black, rather long for a tern. In winter the crown is white closely streaked dark, becoming denser and blackish from eye over ear-coverts; lighter streaking extends on to the fore-head which in most other terns is plain white at this time of year. Juvenile has crown blackish-brown, back lightly mottled with brownish, bill paler and more orange. Length about 19–22 ins.

Habitat. Outside the breeding-season it is mainly maritime, but also occurs on larger inland rivers and lakes.

General Habits. Flight is powerful but graceful, and rather gull-like, not infrequently at a considerable height. Sometimes it soars high in the air. It plunges after fish in the usual manner of the sea-terns, but also settles on water to feed like a gull. Not as sociable as most terns and often seen singly.

Ordinary notes are a striking, deep, loud and raucous "kaah kaah" and a repeated monosyllable like "kuk-kuk-kuk".

Food is mainly fish, especially herring; occasionally young and eggs of birds.

Status and Distribution. A rare vagrant, chiefly in May and June but it has occurred in April and from July to October and has been recorded in November. It has appeared mainly on the east coast from Kent to Northumberland (mainly Norfolk and Suffolk), some on south coast, also Wales, Ireland, Scotland. The species breeds very locally in the Baltic and in the Gulf of Bothnia, a few places in the Mediterranean, also Black and Caspian Seas, and Asia, Africa, America and Australia. It winters mainly in the tropics. There are no subspecies.

SANDWICH TERN—*Sterna sandvicensis*

Bird Plate 64   Egg Plate VI (1a, 1b & 1c)

A distinctly *larger, heavier bird than the other common British terns, with tail less deeply forked and black bill with a yellow tip*; the yellow tip, however, is not always distinguishable on young birds in autumn (cf. Gull-billed Tern). It is a whiter looking bird than the other British breeding terns, except Roseate, and has relatively longer and narrower wings. The black feathers at back of the crown are elongated, and under-parts tinged salmon-pink. Legs are black, and comparatively long for a tern. In winter plumage the forehead and front of crown are white and what remains of the black cap is duller and less sharply defined owing to admixture of white. This plumage is assumed very early, in some adults before leaving the breeding-grounds. Young birds up to and including the summer after they were hatched are also like adult in winter. Juvenile has crown closely freckled, giving a brownish effect at a little distance, and back tinged buff and boldy marked with blackish bars. Length about 15–17 ins.

Habitat. In general a thoroughly maritime species, frequenting the vicinity of low-lying, sandy and shingly or pebbly, or occasionally rocky, coasts or islands in the breeding-season; but also breeding locally on lakes at a considerable distance inland. In some localities flocks will rest on meadows at high tide. It occasionally visits inland waters on passage.

General Habits. Flight is not quite so light and buoyant as the smaller terns, and the body does not rise and fall with the wing-beats although they are deep. It usually plunges from a greater height than the other terns, and remains under water perceptibly longer. In hovering preparatory to the plunge the tail is not generally depressed as in the other species. It is not so aggressive as Common and Arctic Tern. Otherwise habits hardly differ from Common Tern.

A noisy bird, calling very freely a distinctive loud grating "kirrick". The second syllable is generally higher pitched than the first.

Food is mainly fish; also worms and molluscs.

Nests in closely-packed colonies on shores of sea or, sometimes, of fresh water. The eggs, usually 1–2, sometimes 3, vary in ground colour from creamy-white to warm brownish, sometimes unmarked. They are laid generally from early May onwards in a mere hollow scratched in sand, sometimes lined with marram-grass. Incubation is by both sexes for about 21–24 days. The young are fed by both parents, and when about 7–15 days old they are brought to the shore where they assemble in troops. They can fly when 5 weeks old but some are still fed by parents after moving many miles from the nesting colony. Single-brooded.

Status and Distribution. A summer-visitor arriving from end of March to May and leaving between mid-July and mid-October; occasional birds winter, even in Scotland. Throughout the British Isles numbers at breeding colonies fluctuate and sites are often changed. These in recent years have included the following: in England, Ravenglass (Cumb.), Walney (Lancs), Farne Islands, Norfolk, Suffolk, Rye Bay, Hampshire; in Scotland, Firth of Forth, Aberdeen, Moray Firth, Caithness and Orkney. Breeding has occurred sporadically elsewhere. In Ireland there are generally

breeding-colonies on islands (both marine and freshwater) in
Donegal, Down, Sligo, Galway, Mayo, Wexford and Kerry. On
passage it occurs on many parts of the coast, but fewer in the
southern part of W. coast of England and Wales and rare on N.W.
Scottish mainland. British birds winter on W. and S. African
coasts extending into the Indian Ocean as far north as Natal. They
belong to the race *Sterna sandvicensis sandvicensis* which breeds
in S. Baltic, North Sea coast from Denmark to France, and
Mediterranean, Black and Caspian Seas. Another race occurs in
America.

ROSEATE TERN—*Sterna dougallii*

BIRD PLATE 65   EGG PLATE VI (5A & 5B)

Both in flight and on the ground it is a *much whiter looking bird
than Common or Arctic Tern, with conspicuously longer tail
streamers*, more slender form, and a *highly distinctive guttural
alarm note* by which even an odd pair can be picked out amongst
large numbers of other species. At close quarters the combination
of red legs and *black bill*, often with a little red at its base and round
the gape late in the breeding-season, is diagnostic. In full breeding
plumage the breast has beautiful rosy flush, but in sitting birds this
often disappears and breast looks "satiny" white. Forehead and
crown in winter plumage are much as in Common Tern, but the
whiter appearance and longer tail streamers are retained; bill is
then entirely black. Juvenile has upper-parts more boldly marked
than young Common Tern. Chicks in down have a more matted
appearance than the dry, fluffy look of Common or Arctic Tern
chicks, while Sandwich chicks look spiny, as if wet. Length about
14–15 ins.

Habitat. The Roseate Tern never breeds inland, but its
maritime haunts do not differ from those of Common and Arctic
Tern.

General Habits. Most habits hardly differ from those of
Common and Arctic Terns, but wing-beats are noticeably faster
and shallower, resembling flight of Little Tern. In buoyant display
flight wings are neither raised nor depressed to same extent as
Common and Arctic Terns.

Most distinctive note is the alarm-note, a guttural, rasping
"aach, aach".

Food is mainly small fish caught at sea.

Nests usually among coastal colonies of other terns, frequently on rocky islets, but at times also on sand, pebbles, or shinglebanks on shore. The eggs, normally 1–2, very rarely 3, have creamy or buff ground-colour. They are laid from early June onwards in a natural hollow, with practically no nest. Incubation is by both sexes for about 21–26 days. Single-brooded.

Status and Distribution. A summer-visitor from late April or May until mid-July to mid-September, very local, with erratic occupation of breeding sites, and fluctuating numbers. In England it breeds on the Farne Islands and Scillies. In Wales the main breeding strength is in Anglesey, with a colony sometimes in one or two other localities. In Scotland there are colonies on several islands in the Firth of Forth, but the sites in west Scotland (mainly in the Clyde) seem unoccupied at the present time. In Ireland there are colonies in Wexford, Dublin and Down. Almost anywhere in the British Isles a pair or two may occasionally nest in colonies of other terns. Away from breeding places it is a rare visitor. Our birds winter along the W. coast of Africa. They belong to the race *Sterna dougallii dougallii* which also breeds in eastern N. America, and N. and S. Africa. Other races occur in the Indian Ocean, W. Pacific and Australia.

COMMON TERN—*Sterna hirundo*

BIRD PLATE 64   EGG PLATE VI (2A & 2B)

All the sea-terns resemble one another rather closely in general appearance and behaviour. They are slenderly-built, graceful birds of medium size, with tapering bills and forked tails, the points of the fork generally prolonged into "Swallow-like" streamers. All the species of regular occurrence in Europe have pale grey backs, tails and under-parts white or nearly white, and black crowns in summer plumage. In winter plumage much of the black on the crown is lost. The flight is distinctive, very light and buoyant, with rather deliberate wing-beats, the body rising and sinking perceptibly at each down- and up-stroke respectively, but not so noticeable when hurried. When fishing they fly slowly or hover over the water, and plunge neatly in. Common Tern closely resembles Arctic Tern, but in flight Common has outer half-dozen primaries darker than remainder of upperwing, the innermost of

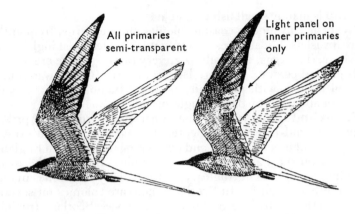

All primaries
semi-transparent

Light panel on
inner primaries
only

ARCTIC TERN   COMMON TERN

these outer primaries often being particularly dusky forming a
dark wedge tapering in from rear edge of wing and visible from a
considerable distance; in Arctic all primaries appear uniform,
clear grey. For underwing differences see the drawing above. At
close range Common Tern's sharply defined *black tip to orange-
red bill* is visible; Arctic Tern also sometimes has a black-tipped
bill. Occasionally a Common Tern has hardly any black tip, but
such birds can still be told by the shade of red of the bill, which is
distinct from the blood-red of Arctic Tern. Cheeks and underparts
are white, breast and belly tinged pale grey, sometimes with a
pinkish flush. Legs red. In winter plumage adults and first year
birds have the forehead and front of crown white, the latter part
more or less streaked blackish, under-parts pure white, a blackish
mark on the front of the wing in shoulder region, and bill more
black than in summer. In the case of juveniles, the spread primaries of Common are opaque and those of Arctic are translucent as in
adults: in addition the Common has a broad, rather poorly defined, dark band along the trailing edge of the outer wing, but in
the Arctic the corresponding feature is black, narrow and clear-
cut; from above the Common has grey secondaries (darker than
the secondary coverts) while the Arctic has white secondaries
(paler than the coverts); the forehead and mantle of young Common is more often tinged with gingery brown, while Arctic soon
acquires a white forehead; the bill of Common has a pale, flesh-
coloured base, which in migrant Arctic looks all black. Supplementary points in autumn and winter are: (1) The shoulder
mark in both adults and young is much more evident in the

Common, especially when perched, being blacker and more extensive than in the Arctic. (2) Bill of adult Common Tern apparently always retains some red in winter, while that of Arctic becomes completely black or blackish, but intermediate conditions may be expected to occur in Arctic. (3) Legs of Arctic Tern generally become blackish. See Arctic Tern for details of *"portlandica"* phase. Length (adult) about 13–14 ins., according to length of tail "streamers".

Habitat. In the breeding-season it frequents inshore waters in the vicinity of low-lying coasts and islands. Also breeds on rivers and lakes inland. On migration it is frequent on rivers, lakes, etc., inland, as well as on sea-coasts and inshore waters.

General Habits. Thoroughly gregarious. In addition to diving, food is sometimes picked up in flight from the surface of water, occasionally from the surface of sand, mud or even fields.

The best-known note is a high-pitched, grating *"keee-*yaah", heard when a colony is disturbed, and also from birds on passage. "Kik-kik-kik" is also freely used.

Food includes fish, crustacea, worms, molluscs and insects.

Nests in colonies on shingle-banks, sand-dunes, salt-marshes, rocky islets, etc. The eggs, usually 3, but sometimes 2–4, vary in ground-colour from stone-colour to brown, or sometimes blue and unmarked. They are laid generally in late May and early June in a hollow scratched out by female, sometimes quite unlined. Incubation is by both sexes for about 21–28 days. The young remain in nest about 3 days and are fed by both parents. They begin to fly when about 4 weeks old. Normally single-brooded. Does not usually breed until 3 or 4 years old.

Status and Distribution. A summer-visitor, breeding in many places on all coasts (but not S. Wales, and very local in S.W. England), also on many marine islands, and sporadically or in small numbers on some inland lakes and rivers. Reaches Shetland and Outer Hebrides but is less numerous in the north than Arctic Tern although apparently increasing. On migration from mid-April to mid-June and August to mid-October or later, it often appears inland. Our birds belong to the race *Sterna hirundo hirundo* which breeds from N. Africa to the Arctic Ocean, wintering mainly in African waters. It also breeds in W. Asia and America. Another race occurs in central and E. Asia.

ARCTIC TERN—*Sterna paradisaea*

Bird Plate 65   Egg Plate VI (6a & 6b)

For separation from Common Tern in flight, see that species; otherwise it is only distinguishable at close quarters, when the best character so long as breeding-season colours are retained is the *deep blood-red bill usually without black tip*, in contrast to the more scarlet-red and black-tipped bill of Common Tern. Arctic Tern, however, whose bill is mainly black in winter, does not always lose the black tip but the colour-transition is gradual, not sharply defined as in Common Tern. The bill also is usually rather shorter than Common Tern's. If settled where clearly visible, the *extremely short legs* afford a reliable distinction at all seasons for observers sufficiently familiar with the longer-legged Common Tern, but Common Tern may adopt a squatting stance producing a short-legged effect. Leg-colour is the same shade of red in both species. The more definite grey colour of the under-parts, and usually longer tail streamers and shorter wings, are not to be relied on. See Common Tern for distinguishing points in juvenile plumage. In winter and immature plumages it is only distinguishable from Common Tern under the most favourable conditions. In both species occasional examples may occur round breeding colonies in uncompleted moult, known as the "*portlandica*" phase, with features of winter plumage such as white forehead and collar, dark carpal bar, white underparts, dark bill and legs; in this plumage Arctic can be separated from Common Tern by white (not pale grey) rump and the translucency of the primaries. Length about 14–15 ins.

Habitat. This, in the main, is like Common Tern but more thoroughly maritime. Restriction to maritime breeding-grounds is not complete as it breeds regularly on some inland waters in Ireland and N. Scotland. Outside the breeding-season it occurs in both in- and offshore waters and is regular on migration in pelagic waters across the whole width of the Atlantic. Not rare on inland lakes, reservoirs, rivers, etc., on passage.

General Habits. These and behaviour scarcely differ from Common Tern's but it is inclined to be more aggressive on breeding-ground.

Notes are much like Common Tern's, but in the disyllabic anxiety-note the two syllables tend to be about equally stressed, while in Common the first syllable is usually more stressed and considerably more prolonged than the second. Very characteristic is a high whistling note "kee, kee", rising in pitch.

Food. Fish, crustacea, molluscs and insects.

Nests in colonies, sometimes associated with Common Terns, on rocky islets, grassy banks, sand-dunes, etc. The eggs, usually 2, but frequently 1–3, are normally more boldly marked than the Common Tern's, ground-colour varying from stone-colour to pale blue or brown, also sometimes blue almost unmarked. They are laid from end of May or early June onwards, in a hollow scratched out in sand by the female, or a depression in moss or on rock, frequently quite unlined, sometimes lined with marram-grass, shells, etc. Incubation is by both sexes for about 21–22 days. The young are fed by both parents and fly when about three weeks old but are fed by parents for more than a week longer. Not known to breed under 3 years old.

Status and Distribution. Summer-visitor and passage-migrant. It breeds in England and Wales on Farne Islands (Northumbs.), islets off Anglesey, Walney and odd pairs elsewhere in Lancs, Cumbria, Isle of Man, and erratically further south, notably N. Norfolk, Kent and Dorset. In Scotland on all coasts and groups of islands, sparingly in the south but outnumbers the Common Tern in north; in Ireland on all coasts. On passage (April to early June and August to October) it also occurs on many other parts of the coast and often inland. The species is near the southern limit of its range in Britain, extending north far into the Arctic in Europe, Asia and N. America. It winters in the Southern Ocean and on coasts of the Antarctic continent. There are no subspecies.

LITTLE TERN—*Sterna albifrons*

BIRD PLATE 65   EGG PLATE VI (4A & 4B)

Differs from the last three species in *smaller size, yellow bill with black tip, yellow legs and white forehead in breeding plumage.* Winter and juvenile plumage are much like those of Common Tern, but the bird is always distinguishable by its size and narrower-looking wing, in addition to the colour of the bill and feet in adult. Juvenile has bill and feet much duller. Length about 9–10 ins.

Habitat. It is almost entirely confined in the breeding-season to the vicinity of sea-shores and islands with sandy or shingly beaches, but occurs on inland waters on passage.

General Habits. Flies with quicker wing-beats than the larger terns and is less gregarious. Otherwise habits and behaviour are essentially similar.

Chief notes heard at nesting places are "kik-kik", a harsher rasping "kyik" and a quick "kirri-kikki, kirri-kikki".

Food includes crustacea, fish and molluscs; also insects caught on the wing.

Nests in colonies, usually small and often much scattered, on sand or fine shingle. The eggs, usually 2–3, rarely 4, vary in ground-colour from stone-colour to bluish or brownish. They are laid generally in the last half of May and early June in a mere hollow formed by female, very rarely lined with vegetable matter or small stones. Incubation is by both sexes for about 18–22 days. The young leave the nest within 24 hours of hatching and are fed by both parents. They begin to fly after 4 weeks.

Status and Distribution. A summer-visitor breeding in England and Wales in small colonies here and there on all coasts, numbers responding to protection but none now in south-west from Devon to Cardigan. In Scotland it breeds in most eastern counties, also in the south-west and Hebrides, but not on the N.W. mainland; on Irish coasts chiefly in the east and west, sometimes sporadically. On migration, from mid-April to mid-May, it occurs on many parts of the coast and sometimes inland. Our birds belong to the race *Sterna albifrons albifrons* which breeds in Europe from S. Baltic to the Mediterranean, wintering on tropical coasts. It also breeds in N.W. Africa and S.W. Asia, while other races occur elsewhere in Asia and Africa, also in America and Australia.

WHISKERED TERN—*Chlidonias hybridus*

BIRD PLATES 63 and 128

In breeding plumage the *combination of black cap, white sides of head and neck, and dark grey under-parts* is distinctive. The grey of under-side is darkest on flanks and belly, contrasting sharply with white under tail-coverts. Bill and feet are dark dull red. Tail grey, outer edge white and only slightly forked as in other marsh terns; under wing-coverts white. The white on sides of head and neck is not sharply defined from grey of throat and except at very close range the whole side of the face appears white. In winter the forehead and whole under-parts are white, crown streaked black and white, blackest at rear; bill blackish or partly so. Juvenile much as adult in winter, with some brownish markings on upper-parts; differences from White-winged Black Tern are given under that species. Whiskered juvenile has also to be separated from the "*portlandica*" phase of Common Tern, both having grey rumps, but Whiskered has blackish markings on mantle as well as upper-wing, and incomplete white collar. Slightly larger than other marsh-terns. Length about 11 ins.

Habitat. In choice of habitat it is much like Black Tern.

General Habits. These are much like Black Tern, but while Black Tern swoops to the water's surface to feed, Whiskered nearly always catches its food by plunge diving, although it subsequently sometimes washes its prey by dipping bill in water in flight. It bathes quite often and vigorously, sometimes immersing completely.

Ordinary note is a rasping sound tending more to a disyllable than Black Tern's usual "kik"—something like "kyo" or "kyick".

Food consists mainly of aquatic and water-haunting insects. Also freshwater shrimps, small fish, newts, tadpoles and small frogs and occasionally worms.

Status and Distribution. A rare vagrant which has been recorded usually May/June and August/September, mainly in southern England, a few in Wales and Ireland and extremely rare in Scotland. The race concerned, *Chlidonias hybridus hybridus*, breeds in the Mediterranean region and locally in southern Europe north to central France, S. Hungary, Romania, and S. Russia, also in S.W. Asia, wintering in northern tropical Africa. Other races occur elsewhere in Africa and Asia, and in Australia.

BLACK TERN—*Chlidonias niger*

BIRD PLATES 63 and 128   EGG PLATE VI (3)

Members of the genus *Chlidonias* are often known collectively as marsh-terns in contrast to the other terns, which are mostly marine in habits. In breeding plumage Black Tern is unmistakable, having *back, tail and wings slate-grey, shading to black on the head and under-parts, except for under tail-coverts, which are white*. Under-side of the wing is light grey. In winter and juvenile plumage the under-parts, fore-head and neck are white with a blackish area covering crown, nape and ear-coverts, and *the brownish-grey of the upper-parts extends downwards as a dark patch in front of the base of the wing.* Differences from the equivalent plumage of White-winged Black Tern are given under that species. The tail is only slightly forked. Bill is black or blackish, with some yellowish at the base in young birds; legs dark red-brown, yellower in young. Length about 9½ ins.

Habitat. In the breeding-season it frequents wet marshes, fens and the vicinity of reedy meres and lagoons, visiting rivers, lakes, ponds and reservoirs on migration. On autumn passage it is regular on sea-coast and inshore waters, even some way out from the coast, as well as on inland waters.

General Habits. Flight is of the regular buoyant tern type. When feeding it repeatedly dips to water to pick up food as it flies, and often hovers for a few seconds a foot or two from the surface, but only quite exceptionally submerges. It also catches insects on the wing. Sometimes it settles on shore but more often on posts, stones, etc., in the water, also occasionally on water. It frequently occurs in flocks up to 25–50, but maintaining only rather loose contact and also often singly.

A monosyllabic "kik, kik" is sometimes heard on migration and this is the common note at breeding-places.

Food consists mainly of aquatic and water-haunting insects (especially dragon-flies) and their larvae; also spiders, leeches, small fish, tadpoles and small frogs.

Nests generally in shallow water, and in colonies, but some-times in scattered pairs; also nests regularly amongst rough herb-age on quite firm ground in marshy localities. The eggs, usually 3, sometimes 2–4, have ground colour ochreous or brownish to greenish. They are laid generally from the second half of May onwards in a nest which is usually a floating heap of water-weeds, reeds, etc., lined with finer material, but on firm ground the nest is a scrape lined with a few bits of dead reed or grass. Incubation is chiefly by female for about 14–17 days. Both sexes feed and brood the young, which remain in nest about 2 weeks and are fully fledged after 4 weeks. Single-brooded.

Status and Distribution. A passage-migrant, from mid-April to early June, and July to early October, occurring regularly in England north to Yorks and Lancs. In Scotland it occurs annually, most regularly on the east coast. In Wales it is somewhat irregu-lar. In Ireland it is an annual passage-migrant in small numbers, recorded from all provinces. Formerly it bred in east England, ceasing to do so regularly about the middle of the nineteenth century. However, several pairs have intermittently bred there again since 1966; it has also bred more than once in Ireland in recent years. Our birds belong to the race *Chlidonias niger niger* which breeds from Denmark, S. Finland, Russia and W. Asia south to Spain, N. Italy and Black and Caspian Seas, and winters in tropical Africa. Another subspecies occurs in America.

WHITE-WINGED BLACK TERN—*Chlidonias leucopterus*

BIRD PLATES 62 and 128

In breeding plumage it is easily distinguished from Black Tern by *white shoulders, white tail and upper tail-coverts and red bill and legs*. The back as well as head and under-parts, including axillaries and under-wing, are dense black; under tail-coverts white. In winter and juvenile plumages—illustrated on plate 128—it is very like Black Tern and Whiskered Tern but the three can often be separated with careful observation, feature by feature, under good conditions. The White-winged and most Whiskered lack dark patches at *sides of breast* in front of wings, while these patches are generally but not always conspicuous on Black Tern and on young juvenile Whiskered.

The *bill* of White-winged is small and relatively stubby, that of Black is usually longer and thinner and slightly decurved, while adult male Whiskered has the longest and stoutest bill, angled on lower mandible (at gonys) like a *Sterna* sea-tern but juvenile female Whiskered's bill is only a little larger than White-winged Black.

The *head* of White-winged has crown white-flecked to a considerable extent, contrasting sharply with the nearly isolated black ear coverts; the pattern of Whiskered is rather similar although the black ear coverts are joined to black hind-crown; the Black Tern differs in having the blackish crown unflecked and united with similarly-coloured ear coverts, to form a complete hood (see text drawing on next page).

The *hind-necks* of young Black and White-winged Black are white, producing a fairly broad and complete white collar, but Whiskered's nape is often greyish and the collar therefore incomplete.

The *rump* is always brownish-grey in Black Tern in autumn, and pale grey in Whiskered, but is clear white in juvenile and moulting adult White-winged although becoming pale grey in late autumn when moult completed.

Head-patterns of marsh terns in non-breeding plumages (from skins): top left, White-winged Black Tern; top right, Whiskered Tern; bottom, Black Tern. In each case the upper head is a juvenile (from a late August or early September specimen) and the lower a winter adult (from an October specimen). Compare the amounts of flecking on the crowns and the extents to which the dark ear-coverts are or are not joined to the crown-caps, the presence or absence of shoulder-marks, the sizes and shapes of the bills, and the sizes of the triangular patches in front of the eyes.

The *tail* of Black is grey and often looks square cut at end, that of juvenile White-winged is similar and so contrasts with rump, while in Whiskered it is almost as pale grey as rump but always looks forked.

The mantle is diagnostic of juveniles: drab in case of Black and same colour as wing-coverts and only slightly darker than rump and tail; by contrast the dark brown back of the White-winged is as clear-cut as a saddle between the white collar and white rump and is darker than the greyish inner wings; Whiskered has mantle variegated with prominent buff markings, and wings pale grey. In full winter plumage the back of White-winged is ash grey, which may appear darker than rump, but the silvery-grey back of Whiskered may appear uniform with rump.

The White-winged has broader based wings and a tendency to a slower and shallower wing-beat than Black Tern, while the flight of the larger Whiskered is less flexible and resembles that of a sea-tern. Bill black in winter. Length about 9¼ ins.

Habitat. It occupies much the same habitat as Black Tern, but appears to be more restricted to fresh water outside breeding-season.

General Habits. In behaviour and habits it is much like Black Tern, with which it often associates.

A rather loud rattling or churring note is recorded.

Food consists mainly of aquatic and water-haunting insects.

Status and Distribution. A vagrant appearing annually in very small numbers in recent years in spring (chiefly May–June) and autumn (chiefly August–September). Records are widely scattered, with emphasis on east and south coastal counties, also Severn, sometimes well inland, and reaching Yorks/Lancs but rarely Scotland or Ireland. The species breeds in E. and S.E. Europe, perhaps west to France, and in Asia, wintering in the tropics and the southern hemisphere. There are no subspecies.

GUILLEMOT—*Uria aalge*

BIRD PLATE 67   EGG PLATE XVI (1A, 1B, 1C & 1D)

Differs from Razorbill in having a *slender pointed bill* and in the southern part of its range, when seen close enough, in *brown, not black upper-parts, especially the head*, but northern birds may have the body as dark as Razorbill. A more lightly built bird than Razorbill, with a more slender neck, which is stretched out more in flight, and a shorter, rounded tail. In winter plumage the throat, ear-coverts and front of neck are white like the rest of the under-parts, with a *black streak extending back over the ear-coverts from eye*. Juveniles have a somewhat scaly appearance at close quarters. The so-called "Ringed" or "Bridled Guillemot" is a variety having a white ring round the eye and a white line running back from it over the sides of the head. This variety constitutes 1 per cent. or less of the population in S. and S.W. England, increasing northwards to about 25 per cent. in Shetland. Legs and feet are pale brownish to yellowish, blackish at joints and at back of tarsus. Length about 16½ ins.

Habitat. It is confined in the breeding-season to cliffs with ledges, or flat-topped stacks; otherwise it occupies the same habitat as Razorbill.

General Habits. It breeds on suitable stretches of cliff in enormous numbers, and every available ledge is packed with birds. Apart from the difference in breeding sites, general behaviour is much like Razorbill's. Dives of a duration of 68 seconds and to a depth of 28 feet have been recorded.

Ordinary note is a prolonged, growling caw, "arrrr", with considerable modulations and variations of pitch, which rises from the breeding ledges in a remarkable volume of sound.

Food consists almost entirely of animal matter: fish, crustacea, worms and molluscs. Also some algae.

Nests in colonies, often on the same cliff with Razorbill, Kittiwake, Puffin, etc. The egg, only 1, is extremely variable in colour and markings, from deep blue-green or reddish to creamy or white, sometimes quite unmarked. It is laid generally from the second half of May onwards, on bare rock without any attempt at a nest, or occasionally in a crevice. Incubation is by both sexes for about 28–36 days, sometimes longer. The young are fed by both parents, and there is some communal feeding in large groups. About a fortnight to three weeks after hatching, when only half grown but well feathered, the young descend to sea in the same manner as young Razorbills. One or sometimes both parents attend the young on the sea. Single-brooded.

Status and Distribution. Present throughout the year, the northern race *Uria aalge aalge* breeding on suitable cliffs in Scotland northwards from Berwick on the east side and Islay (Argyll) on the west, and the southern race *Uria aalge albionis* in the rest of Great Britain and Ireland, but none breed between Yorks and the Isle of Wight. Visits to the nesting cliffs begin in late October–early February and sites are abandoned during August. In autumn and winter, augmented by continental visitors, they are fairly generally distributed at sea and occasionally storm-driven inland. Some of our birds reach Faeroes, Scandinavia, France and N. Spain. Outside the British Isles *Uria aalge albionis* breeds in Brittany, N.W. Spain and Portugal; and *Uria aalge aalge* in the Baltic, N. Europe, Greenland and eastern N. America. Other races occur in Bering Sea and N. Pacific.

BRÜNNICH'S GUILLEMOT—*Uria lomvia*

BIRD PLATE 66

At fairly close range it is separable from Guillemot by *decidedly shorter and thicker bill with a pale line along edge of the basal part of the upper mandible*. Flanks lack the dark striations of Guillemot, but this is not generally a character of much value in the field; mantle darker and crown and neck blacker than the chocolate-brown of northern Guillemot. In winter an additional distinction is that the present species *lacks the dark stripe on the white ear-coverts*, as the black of head extends down over ear-coverts. Care must be taken to avoid confusion with immature Razorbill which however is white behind the eye, has black legs, and tail tapering (not square). Moreover, in Brünnich's the length of the bill is about the same as distance from gape to eye, whereas in young Razorbill the bill length is only half the distance from gape to eye. Legs and feet are yellow with blackish bands at the joints. Length about 16½ ins.

Habitat. In choice of habitat it seems to have stronger pelagic tendencies than the Guillemot.

General Habits. Behaviour and habits outside the breeding-season scarcely differ from those of Guillemot.

Ordinary notes are similar to those of Guillemot.

Food includes small fish, crustacea and molluscs.

Status and Distribution. Almost annual in Scotland in recent years, but remaining a rare vagrant in England and Ireland. Most have been found dead, during winter. The race which occurs here, *Uria lomvia lomvia*, breeds on the N. Russian coast and arctic islands of Europe south to Iceland, also in Siberia and eastern N. America. Another race occurs in the Bering Sea and adjacent parts of the Arctic Ocean. European birds winter south to Norway.

RAZORBILL—*Alca torda*

BIRD PLATE 66   EGG PLATE XV (1A & 1B)

Auks are essentially marine birds, expert swimmers and divers, flying with rapid, whirring beats of small, narrow wings. Coming ashore only in the breeding-season, they have a more or less upright carriage on land, with clear-cut plumage patterns of black (or dark brown) and white. The Razorbill differs from Guillemot in having a *deep compressed bill crossed by a white line, and black, not brown upper-parts* (but Guillemots in the north of their range may be almost as dark) and in the breeding-season with a white line from base of the bill to the eye. On the water it is a more compact, plump-looking bird than Guillemot, with thicker neck and generally sitting higher on the water. Tail is longer, pointed, and commonly more or less elevated when swimming. Secondaries are tipped white, forming a white border to hind edge of the basal part of the wing in flight and appearing as a kind of wing-bar when at rest. In breeding plumage the whole head and neck are black; in winter the throat and sides of neck are white and the white mark from bill to eye is obscured. Juvenile has upper-parts and whole head and neck dark brown, but may have more or less white on the throat. First winter birds are like adults, but the bill is much shallower and less arched and without the white mark, so that confusion with northern Guillemot is possible, though the absence of a black streak behind eye should prevent this. Legs black. Length about 16 ins.

Habitat. It frequents in- and off-shore waters, resorting in the breeding-season to cliffs of mainland or islands and boulder-strewn shores. Outside the breeding-season it is usually found well out from coasts, though odd birds may sometimes be met with some way up estuaries. It returns early to inshore waters but occurs inland only when storm-driven.

General Habits. Although frequently associated with Guillemots on the cliffs, Razorbills are equally at home in the breeding-season on boulder-strewn shores with no cliffs at all, in localities where Guillemots are absent. In diving, it submerges with rather a flurry, with a distinct kick of legs and flick of partly opened wings as it goes under, but once under water it progresses with considerably more speed than in swimming on surface. Dives have been recorded of 52 seconds duration, and to a depth of 24 feet. Flight, although quite high at times, is for the most part low over the water, parties often travelling in lines. Markedly gregarious, commonly seen at all seasons in small groups and scattered parties, though also singly.

Chief notes are a tremulous, whirring sound and a prolonged, grating, growling "caarrrr".

Food consists almost entirely of animal matter: fish, crustacea, worms and molluscs.

Nests in colonies, frequently associated with Guillemot, but is especially partial to irregular, broken-faced cliffs and also nests among rocks and boulders on shore. The eggs, normally one, very rarely 2, may vary in ground-colour from light chocolate to white, occasionally greenish. They are laid generally from the second week of May onwards, in a crevice or hole, or beneath a boulder. No nest is made. Incubation is by both sexes for about 33–36 days. The young are fed by both parents and flutter down to the sea when 6 to 18 days old, long before they can fly properly. On the water they are first tended by both parents but later usually only by one. Single-brooded.

Status and Distribution. Present throughout the year, breeding on suitable cliffs on all coasts except between Yorkshire and

Isle of Wight. Birds are present in the neighbourhood of nesting sites from early spring to July–August. In autumn and winter they are fairly generally distributed at sea and occasionally storm-driven inland. The movement is mainly one of dispersal, but some birds reach Norway and E. Denmark, and the species winters regularly in the Mediterranean east to North Italy. Our birds belong to the race *Alca torda britannica* which also breeds in the Faeroes, Channel Isles and Brittany. The race *Alca torda torda* of which one example has been found in Kent in March, and one in Scotland, occupies the rest of the range of the species, breeding from Heligoland and the Baltic northwards to the White Sea, and west to the Canadian coast.

BLACK GUILLEMOT—*Cepphus grylle*

Bird Plate 67   Egg Plate XV (4a & 4b)

Smaller than the other long-billed auks, it is quite unlike any other sea-bird in plumage, being *uniformly black in summer except for a conspicuous broad white patch on wing*, covering most of the coverts, and *in winter with head and under-parts mainly white, the back barred blackish and white, and wings as in summer*; some dark mottlings on sides of head. At close quarters the *red feet* are noticeable. Birds in transition between summer and winter plumages show an odd and patchy appearance. Juveniles are much more dusky than winter adults, with the back nearly uniform blackish and the parts which are white in the adult, including the wing patches, are strongly mottled with sooty brown. Interior of gape is vermilion, orange in young, conspicuous when the bird utters its cry. Length about 13½ ins.

Habitat. In the breeding-season it frequents chiefly the vicinity of rocky and boulder-strewn coasts and islands. Outside the breeding-season it seems to be more confined to the vicinity of the shore than Guillemot and Razorbill. Inland only by accident and very rarely.

General Habits. Ashore it moves with more facility than Guillemot or Razorbill. It is much less abundant than Guillemot and is usually seen singly or in quite small parties. Dives recorded up to 75 seconds. Other habits and behaviour are much as Guillemot.

Note at breeding places is a shrill and feeble little whistling or

BLACK GUILLEMOT
winter

whining sound, "peeeeee", which may be repeated so as to become almost a twitter.

Food includes small fish, crustacea, molluscs, worms and seaweed.

Nesting. In this it is less social than other auks, but several pairs often nest not far apart in crevices of a cliff usually near its base, in hollows among or under boulders, or even in holes in masonry, also sometimes in holes in turf or earth-faced cliffs. The eggs, usually 2, sometimes 1–3, have ground-colour white, often with a tinge of bluish-green or buff. They are laid generally in May or early June. There is no nest. Incubation is by both sexes for 3–4 weeks. The young, fed by both parents, do not leave nest till fully fledged and able to take care of themselves at about 34–36 days old. Single-brooded.

Status and Distribution. A resident, breeding from Shetland south to Caithness, and on the west side of Scotland breeding in all the main island groups and on the mainland west coast south to Kirkcudbright; on the east side a few pairs in Banff; also Isle of Man and in small numbers in Cumberland (St. Bee's Head) and Anglesey. In Ireland it breeds locally in small numbers on rocky coasts and islands, especially in the west. Outside its breeding area it is only a scarce visitor, wintering south to Northumberland. Our birds belong to the race *Cepphus grylle grylle* which breeds in N. Europe east to the White Sea and south to the Baltic; also in N. America. Another race occurs in the high arctic of Europe, Asia and America.

LITTLE AUK—*Alle alle*

BIRD PLATE 66

Small size, black and white plumage and very short, stout bill distinguish this species and should preclude confusion with other auks. Young Puffin is liable to be mistaken for it, as that is also a rather small auk and the great difference of bill from adult Puffin's is not always realized, but it is also quite differently shaped from Little Auk's and much longer; moreover, unlike the Puffin, the black on the head of the Little Auk in all plumages extends well below the eye. Young Guillemots and Razorbills, also sometimes confused with it, are really considerably larger and less stumpy-billed birds. When flying over the sea it often looks at least as much like some odd kind of passerine bird as an auk. It has upper-parts black with scapulars streaked white, and white tips to secondaries. In winter the throat, breast and ear-coverts become white, more or less tinged dusky (black in summer), and the remainder of the under-parts is always white. The short thick-based bill is not very clearly defined from head and gives the latter a curious, rather frog-like appearance. Length about 8 ins.

Habitat. Outside the breeding-season it normally remains at sea, but during prolonged gales is liable to extensive "wrecks", when exhausted and starving birds are driven ashore and sometimes far inland.

General Habits. It flies like other auks, usually low over water with very rapid whirring wing-beats, but the appearance of flying very fast is to some extent illusory. Rises easily and directly from water. It is strongly gregarious and usually seen in flocks. It dives and "flies" under water in much the same way as other auks, for a maximum timed duration of 68 secs., but more frequently for less than half a minute.

Voice a quiet "wow", rarely heard in winter quarters.

Food is chiefly pelagic crustacea and other plankton organisms.

Status and Distribution. A winter-visitor of annual occurrence in variable but usually small numbers, from early October to mid-March, but mainly November to mid-February; a few summer records. It is regular in N. and E. Scotland and E. England but may occur on all coasts. The race concerned, *Alle alle alle*, breeds on arctic islands from W. Greenland to Novaya Zemlya. Another race occurs in Franz Josef Land. Normally most birds of this species winter further north than Britain.

PUFFIN—*Fratercula arctica*

BIRD PLATE 67   EGG PLATE XV (2)

Smaller than Guillemot and Razorbill, with the usual black and white plumage of auks, but adult is at once distinguished from any other species by its *remarkable, triangular, brightly-coloured bill and orange feet*. Crown and upper-parts are black, sides of the face dusky greyish, more blackish between eye and bill in winter, the black of the upper-parts being continued round the neck as a black collar. The beak in summer has the basal part blue-grey separated by a yellowish ridge from the bright red distal part. After the breeding-season the basal part of the bill-covering is shed, leaving the lower mandible more angular, and the bill becomes mainly yellow. Juvenile and first winter birds have plumage much like adults but duller, but the bill is quite different, much more slender and more "normal" in shape. Length about 12 ins.

Habitat. For breeding purposes it resorts to turfy islands and turfy slopes of cliffs and neighbouring waters. During the rest of the year it frequents chiefly offshore waters at no great distance from breeding places, but is also seen in deep water, several hundred miles from land. Inland only when storm-driven.

General Habits. Flight is with very quick strokes through a short arc. It stands with tarsus nearly vertical and not with tarsus resting on the ground like many auks, and with moderately upright carriage of body, but it often rests with body prone on ground or rock. Markedly gregarious and chiefly seen in parties or flocks, often of large size. At breeding places it is usually tame. The feeding range from a colony may be 50 miles or more.

Has only one note, uttered at or in burrows or on the sea, a low growling "arr", sometimes uttered singly, but generally thrice in slow succession, the first note higher than the second, and the third lowest of all.

Food consists mainly of fish, molluscs and other marine organisms, also a small proportion of algae.

Nests in colonies sometimes of great extent. The eggs, normally only 1, very rarely 2, are often white, but traces of markings are usually discernible. They are laid generally in early May in a slight hollow a few feet from the entrance of a shallow burrow either excavated by the birds or appropriated from a rabbit or shearwater, or in a natural crevice or hole under a boulder, rarely lined. Incubation is apparently sometimes by both sexes, for about 40–43 days. The young are tended by both parents, but about the 40th day are deserted by their parents and remain fasting in the hole for several days, finally emerging at night and fluttering or falling down to sea unattended by old birds; period in nest about 47–51 days. Single-brooded.

Status and Distribution. Present through the year in British waters. It breeds locally and in greatly reduced numbers on the south coast from the Isle of Wight westwards to the Scillies, and Lundy; it is rather more numerous in Wales. Farther north on the west side there are many colonies, and it is especially abundant in the Hebrides and Shetland. There are a few colonies on the east side of Scotland, and it breeds in Northumberland and Flamborough but not elsewhere on the east coast of England. Abundant in various parts of Ireland. It is seldom seen near the shore in winter, returning to the vicinity of breeding sites in March or April and leaving end July to late August. Our birds belong to the race *Fratercula arctica grabae* which also breeds in the Faeroes, S. Norway, W. Sweden, Channel Isles and Brittany. Some reach the Mediterranean in winter and ringed birds have been recovered in Newfoundland. Other races occur in arctic Europe and eastern N. America.

PALLAS'S SANDGROUSE—*Syrrhaptes paradoxus*

BIRD PLATE 69

Pallas's, like other sandgrouse, are hard to see on the barren ground they frequent and are generally difficult to approach. They have been compared to *light-coloured partridges with pigeon heads, and have long pointed wings and tail*; the very rapid flight is similar to Golden Plover's. *The wings are curved in flight and appear to be set very far forward* owing to the small head and short neck. The general colouring is sandy and the rather complex markings are inconspicuous except at close range, but the *black patch on the belly* is very noticeable in flight. Male has the back sandy-buff with black bars, the crown and nape greyer (unbarred), rest of the head and neck orange-buff with a grey mark from eye down the side of the neck; breast pale grey, more buff posteriorly, with a band of narrow black crescents; a black patch on belly; wing-quills largely pale grey; tail feathers barred, the central pair prolonged into long fine points, the lateral ones tipped white. Female is duller and more spotted, including crown, neck and wing-coverts; the orange-buff of her head and neck is paler, and the throat patch has a crescentic black border below; wings and tail do not taper to such long points. Legs are short, feathered to the toes; bill very short. Length about 13–16 ins., of which about 2½–3½ ins. represents the extension of long central tail-feathers beyond the rest of the tail.

Habitat. In its incursions into western Europe its principal haunts have been sand-dunes and sandy flats, .warrens, root and stubble-fields; also sandy shores at low tide and sometimes marshes and grasslands.

General Habits. It rises from the ground with rather an effort and with a clatter of wings like a pigeon, but once up flight is extremely rapid, the wings moving with regular, short, quick beats and producing a humming or whistling sound; sometimes in long, gentle undulations. It never settles except on the ground, where the carriage of the body is low and nearly horizontal and where it walks with very short steps and a waddling action. It delights to scratch holes in sandy or slaty ground and to dust itself in them. Markedly gregarious, members of a flock flying close together as a rule, usually low down.

Flight-call is "chack, chack" or something similar.

Food consists mainly of grain and other seeds.

Nests on the ground in little colonies. The eggs, usually 3, sometimes 2–4, have ground-colour varying from stone-buff to yellow-brown, spotted and blotched with purplish-brown and numerous ashy shell-marks. They have been laid from late May or June in this country. The nest is a mere scrape, often with no lining, but occasionally with a few grasses or shoots. Incubation is apparently by both sexes for about 23–27 days. Apparently two (or possibly three) broods.

Status and Distribution. An irregular visitor. The greatest invasions have been in 1863 and 1888 when the bird spread over much of the British Isles reaching even N.W. Ireland and the Outer Hebrides, and bred in Yorkshire and Moray. It has occurred in a number of other years but not between 1909 and 1963; four have been recorded since then. The species breeds in S.E. Russia and west central Asia, and has migrated in great numbers at irregular intervals westward through Europe. There are no subspecies.

ROCK DOVE—*Columba livia*

BIRD PLATE 69   EGG PLATE XIX (4)

It is distinguished from Stock Dove, which also frequents rocky coasts, by *much paler back, two distinct black wing-bars and white or whitish rump*; also, if seen from below, by white instead of grey axillaries and under wing-coverts. Head, breast, and belly are darker blue-grey than the back, and there is an iridescent green and purple patch on the sides of neck. Young are duller. So-called "Rock Doves" of inland cliffs in the British Isles are either Stock Doves or feral dovecote pigeons, and the latter not infrequently consort and breed with wild Rock Doves on coast-cliffs, sometimes even in remote districts. Length about 13 ins.

Habitat. In the British Isles it is now confined to the neighbourhood of rocky coasts, where caves and fissures afford breeding-sites. For foraging purposes it ranges from heathy brows and rough pastures above cliffs to fields and cultivation sometimes a considerable distance inland.

General Habits. Flight is conspicuously swift and dashing, often low down over water or land, often gliding freely, especially about cliff-faces; it rises with a similar clatter of wings to Wood-pigeon's, but settles only on rocks, ground, or sometimes buildings, and only very exceptionally, if ever, on trees. Otherwise general behaviour is as Woodpigeon's and, like it, it occasionally alights on water. Commonly seen singly or in pairs or small parties.

Voice appears not to differ at all from that of tame pigeon, whose main notes are: "oor-roo-cooo, oor-oor-roo-cooo", etc.

Food is chiefly grain, peas, beans, potatoes, seeds of many kinds, and seaweeds; also molluscs.

Nests in sea-caves or among rocks. This applies to only pure-bred birds. The white eggs, normally 2, occasionally 1 only, are laid especially in April, but to some extent throughout the year, in a nest consisting of merely a few bents, roots, heather-stems or even seaweed, carelessly arranged in a hole or on a ledge. Incubation is by both sexes for about 17–19 days. The young are fed by the parents at first with "pigeon's milk", and fly when about 35–37 days old. Evidently 2 or 3 broods annually.

Status and Distribution. A resident, decreasing in numbers. It is widely distributed in Scotland and Ireland, especially on the N. and W. coasts and isles (including Fair Isle where it is mainly a summer-visitor), but has ceased to breed south of the Firth of Forth on the E. side of Scotland, and has also disappeared from England and Wales in its pure wild state although in a number of places wild birds are mixed with feral domestic ones. Even in the north of Scotland few colonies are now 100 per cent pure. Birds of the same race, *Columba livia livia*, breed north to the Faeroes, and to the Arctic circle in Russia, south to the Mediterranean and N. Africa and east into W. Asia. Other races occur in W. Africa, Sahara, E. Mediterranean, S.W. and S. Asia.

STOCK DOVE—*Columba oenas*

BIRD PLATE 70   EGG PLATE XIX (2)

A rather smaller and more compact-looking bird than Wood-pigeon and at once distinguished not only by the *absence of white on wings and neck*, but by its *darker and bluer grey colouring*. Wing-quills and fringe of the tail are black. Sides of the neck show a patch of iridescent green at close quarters; throat and breast are vinous. Juvenile is duller. Length about 13 ins.

Habitat. It frequents not only woods, plantations and parkland with old timber, but the vicinity of maritime or inland cliffs and rocky places, sand-dunes, warrens, etc.; also sometimes old buildings and ruins. It feeds largely on fields and other open ground like Woodpigeon.

General Habits. Apart from habitat differences and its frequently faster, more dashing flight, in general habits and behaviour it hardly differs from Woodpigeon. Being less abundant it does not occur in such vast flocks as are often formed by Wood-pigeons, but in many districts flocks of 200–300 were not rare, although recently a considerable diminution has occurred. Small parties are regular and it frequently mingles with Woodpigeons.

The note is a rather deep, gruff "ooo-*woo*", the second syllable short, clipped and emphatic; it is regular from late February to early July, less frequent from January to early November, with a break during August.

Food is similar to that of Woodpigeon.

Nests. At times several pairs nest close together, in holes in old timber, also in rabbit-burrows, and in holes among outcrops of rock. The faintly creamy-white eggs, normally 2, exceptionally 1–4, are laid generally from the end of March to September on the floor of a hole without any material added; occasionally a few twigs, roots, straws or, in burrows, grass. Incubation is by both sexes for about 16–18 days. The young are fed by both sexes with

"pigeon's milk" and fly usually when they are 27–28 days, sometimes 20 days, old. At least two broods, sometimes three and even
five recorded in one year.

Status and Distribution. Present throughout the year, widely
distributed as a breeding bird in England and Wales but thinning
out somewhat towards the north and west. In Scotland was first
recorded nesting about 1877, and now breeds to S. Argyll on the
west side and to E. Ross on the east side. Further north it is only an
uncommon visitor. In Ireland it now breeds in most counties.
Adults seem to be sedentary in Britain, but there is some evidence
of emigration of young birds, and of autumn immigration from the
Continent. The species breeds in Europe north to mid-
Scandinavia, also in N.W. Africa and east to central Asia. There
are no subspecies.

WOODPIGEON—*Columba palumbus*

BIRD PLATE 69   EGG PLATE XIX (1)

A large, rather heavily built, blue-grey pigeon, characterized by
a *broad white band across the wing* and (except in young) a *white
patch on sides of neck*. Head and rump are bluer grey than the rest;
flanks and belly paler; breast vinous; sides of neck glossed purple
and green; wing-quills and tail mainly blackish. Young are duller,
with no white on the neck. Length about 16 ins.

Habitat. Normally frequents more or less wooded or well-
timbered country, haunting woods, plantations and copses, but
feeding largely on fields, cultivation or other open land, including
saltings. It is regular in town parks and some residential areas with
sufficient trees and gardens. It also frequents thickets on downs,
sea-coasts, etc., some way from woods and occurs sparingly in
some districts on islands with very few trees.

General Habits. When flushed from trees, and to a less extent
from ground, it dashes off with a loud clatter of wings. The breast
is prominent in flight which is strong and rapid. In the steeply
undulating display flight it commonly makes one to three vigorous
claps with its wings near the top of the rise. It feeds mostly on the
ground, where it walks with body carried horizontal and head
moving to and fro, but in spring also feeds often in trees on young
leaves, buds and flowers. In towns and suburban districts it
perches also on buildings. In drinking, this and other pigeons

take a continuous draught, instead of raising the head at each mouthful like most birds. It has been observed a good many times to alight on water and rise again without difficulty. From autumn to spring it commonly assembles in large flocks, though single birds and small groups may also be observed, and flocks in summer are also quite frequent. Shy and wary in the country, but in town parks it becomes singularly tame.

The coo, corresponding to song, has a well-marked rhythm, consisting of a repeated phrase usually of five notes "*Cooo*-coo, coo-coo, coo", the final note being abrupt. It may be heard throughout the year but is regular from mid-February to the end of September.

Food is nearly all vegetable, including cereals, seeds, leaves, roots, many fruits, berries and nuts. Animal food includes earthworms, snails and insects.

Nests in a wide variety of sites, mainly tall hedgerows or trees of any kind, also in ivy on forest trees, on old nests, rock ledges and on town buildings; exceptionally on ground. The white eggs, normally 2, occasionally 1–3, are laid mainly from mid-July to late September but have been recorded in every month of the year. The nest is very slight, being a mere lattice of small twigs, through which the shape of the eggs can often be seen from below; male provides the material but the female alone builds. Incubation is by both sexes for about 17–19 days. The young are fed with "pigeon's milk" produced in the crop of both sexes. Nestling period varies from 16–35 days. Two broods usually reared annually.

Status and Distribution. Present throughout the year, generally distributed. Rather local in N. Scotland owing to scarcity of suitable habitats, but breeds even in Orkney, Shetland irregularly, Outer Hebrides, and some treeless areas in W. Ireland. The race concerned, *Columba palumbus palumbus*, breeds in Europe from the Mediterranean almost to the Arctic circle and in W. Asia. Other races occur in N.W. Africa, Azores, Madeira and central Asia.

COLLARED DOVE—*Streptopelia decaocto*

BIRD PLATE 68

A dull-coloured bird, larger and looking heavier-bodied in flight than a Turtle Dove. It is drab, almost uniform pale grey-brown above, head paler and greyer with perhaps a slight tinge of pink;

below soft grey with a faint pinkish flush especially on breast. The main feature of the body plumage is a *narrow black half-collar* at the back of the neck, edged with white and not very prominent. The tail viewed from above is the same colour as the back, but with whitish showing in the outer feathers if spread; seen from below, at rest or in flight, it has a distinctive pattern with the *distal half white and basal half blackish. The primaries too are blackish* (although they can bleach paler during summer); the primary coverts are blue-grey, not conspicuous unless seen from above in flight. The blackish primaries are the best distinguishing feature from the rather similar domesticated and widespread Barbary Dove (*Streptopelia risoria*) which has grey-brown primaries and is a little smaller; however, the body plumage of Barbary Dove is generally cleaner and paler so that in the creamier examples the contrast between primaries and body plumage is as great as in Collared Dove. (The back and wing-coverts of Barbary are warm buff, sometimes almost buff-brown when new, but quickly bleach to pale cream if bird much exposed to sun and rain. Head and neck creamy-buff with very faint pink tinge on new feathers, which is quickly lost. But Barbary always looks buff, warm buff, creamy-buff or pale cream, while *decaocto* is pale greyish-fawn, dusty-fawn or vinous fawn; it almost always looks a much darker bird and completely lacks the *creamy* tint of Barbary.) Juvenile Collared Doves have upper-parts colder grey than adults, the feathers having paler edges which give a faintly patterned effect; under-parts drabber; the half collar is indicated, but poorly developed and often hard to see. The bill is dusty grey-black, legs livid pink (lead-grey in juveniles) and eye dark red. Length about 12½ ins.

Habitat. It has a marked preference for the vicinity of human habitation, frequenting villages, town parks, gardens and margins of cultivated land, and it habitually visits chicken-runs for feeding; where it is well established abroad it can become a bird of dusty streets where its plumage blends well.

General Habits. Largely a ground feeder, with waddling walk. Flight is direct and swift. It perches freely on prominent vantage points such as bare branches, wires, roofs, where it will spend long periods quiescent or preening. It is naturally wary but can become very tame. Outside the breeding-season it often forms flocks, usually not large.

The song of male is a distinctive three-syllabled "coo-cooo-cuk", mainly on one note (that of Barbary Dove is "koo-krr-oo" variable but always with a rolling "r" sound in the middle that is lacking in Collared): excitement call is "kwurr" (Barbary's equivalent is a jeering laugh "hek-hek-hek"). The female calls very little.

Food consists largely of grain and seeds, also a little fruit such as elderberries and cherries.

Nests generally in trees, particularly conifers such as cypresses, pines, cedars, also frequently in fruit and other deciduous trees, and ivy; exceptionally on buildings. The two white eggs, smooth and rather glossy, are laid from March or April onwards till September. The nest is a rough stick platform, and is sometimes lined with roots, grass or hair; it is generally 12 ft. or more above the ground, with limits about 5–50 ft. Incubation is by both sexes, mainly the male by day and the female by night, for about 14 days. The young are fed by both parents. They are fledged at about 18 days but do not finally leave the nest until a few days later. Usually 2 broods, and up to 5 may be attempted.

Status and Distribution. Resident. Following the initial colonization of north Norfolk (where birds bred at one site and were present at another in 1955, and bred at 3 sites in 1956 and 1957), there was explosive spread in 1957 with breeding in Moray, Lincoln and Kent. By 1960 breeding had occurred in 9 counties mainly on the eastern side of Britain, but also in S.W. Scotland, and individual birds seen at such outlying points as Scilly Isles, Bardsey (Caernarvon), Stornoway (Outer Hebrides), Fair Isle. Another great expansion in 1961 brought breeding pairs to 12 additional new counties including Cornwall and Pembroke. It is now widespread throughout England, most of Wales and Scotland (including Shetland), and in Ireland (where first recorded in 1959) is breeding in almost all coastal and many inland counties.

The arrival in Norfolk formed part of a remarkable expansion of range characterized by leaps of sometimes several hundred miles, mainly in N.W. direction. Thus this originally Asiatic species has spread since 1900 from the Balkans across Europe and is now resident in most continental countries bordering the North Sea. In Asia the race concerned, *Streptopelia decaocto decaocto*, breeds across the continent from Turkey to Japan and south to Sri Lanka. Other races occur in central and S.E. Asia.

TURTLE DOVE—*Streptopelia turtur*

BIRD PLATE 68   EGG PLATE XIX (5)

It can hardly be confused with other British pigeons. It is distinguished not only by its markedly smaller size and slighter build, but by the *rufous wing-coverts and scapulars with black centres to feathers, and the long graduated tail* which is black with broad white tips to all but the central feathers and is conspicuous in flight. The mantle, back and rump are brown, the head, neck and outer wing-coverts ash-grey, the throat and under-parts pale vinous, shading to white on belly and under tail-coverts. There is a patch of black and white feathers on the sides of the neck. Young are duller and browner, with no black and white patch on the neck. Length about 10¾ ins.

Habitat. Less addicted to thick woods than Woodpigeon, preferring open woodlands, copses, parkland, shrubberies, and large gardens, as well as open country where there are bushes and untrimmed hedgerows, etc. It feeds largely on open fields and cultivation, and is chiefly a bird of lowlands and valleys.

General Habits. The flight is rather rapid, with more flicking wing-beats than other pigeons. It perches more on low or medium-sized trees than on tall timber, also on bushes and telegraph-wires.

TURTLE DOVE   COLLARED DOVE

Note the expanse of white in Collared Dove's tail.

Apart from the preference for more open country, its general habits and behaviour differ little from Woodpigeon's. It often occurs singly or in pairs, and frequently in parties or small flocks in late summer.

"Song" is a deep crooning or purring note "rroorrrrr, rroorrrrr, rroorrrrr". It may be heard from the end of April until mid-August and is regular from mid-May to the end of July.

Food is almost entirely vegetable, mainly seeds and leaves. Small molluscs are occasionally taken.

Nests in tall bushes, high hedges, etc., especially blackthorn and whitethorn as well as spruces in plantations, and often shows a tendency to social breeding. The white eggs, usually 2, occasionally 1–3 recorded, are laid generally from mid-May onwards in a nest which is usually a very slight and flat structure of fine twigs, sometimes with roots or other material in the lining. Incubation is by both sexes for about 13–14 days. The young are fed by both parents; they leave the nest after about 18 days and fly 2–3 days later. Double-brooded as a rule.

Status and Distribution. A summer-visitor and to a small extent a passage-migrant, mainly arriving towards the end of April and in May, and leaving from early August to early October. It breeds chiefly in the south, east and Midlands, becoming rare in Devon and Cornwall, and parts of W. Wales. Although increasing in the northern part of its range, it does not breed in the Pennines or the Lake District. In Scotland it first bred in 1946 in Berwick and has done so once or twice since, also sporadically in other parts of S. Scotland; it occurs annually on passage, mainly in the northern half. In Ireland it breeds irregularly, mainly in Dublin; it is a regular but scarce visitor to the south coast and a vagrant elsewhere, occurring chiefly in May and June, less frequently in autumn. Our birds belong to the race *Streptopelia turtur turtur* which breeds in Europe north to the Baltic and Baltic States and in W. Asia, and winters in tropical Africa. Other races occur in N. Africa and mid-S.W. Asia.

PLATE
1

p. 5

Ad. m. summer   *Ad. f. winter*
GREAT NORTHERN DIVER (*ca.* ⅑)

p. 1

Ad. m. moulting   *Ad. f. summer*
RED-THROATED DIVER (*ca.* ⅑)

p. 3

Juv. m.   *Ad. f. moulting.*   *Ad. m. summer.*
BLACK-THROATED DIVER (*ca.* ⅑)

PLATE
2

p. 6

Ad. f. summer   *Ad. m. summer*
LITTLE GREBE (*ca.* ⅛)

p. 6

Juv. moulting from down   *Ad. m. winter*
LITTLE GREBE (*ca.* ⅕)

p. 12

Ad. m. summer   *Ad. f. moulting*   *Ad. m. winter*
SLAVONIAN GREBE (*ca.* ⅛)

PLATE
3

p. 14

Ad. m. winter   Juv. m.   Ad. m. summer
BLACK-NECKED GREBE (*ca.* ⅙)

p. 8

1st winter f.   Ad. m. winter   Juv. moulting from down
GREAT CRESTED GREBE (*ca.* ⅙)

p. 8

Ad. f. summer   Ad. m. summer
GREAT CRESTED GREBE (*ca.* ⅙)

PLATE
4

p. 11

Ad. m. winter   *Ad. f. winter* (*moulting*)
RED-NECKED GREBE (*ca.* ⅕)

p. 15

Ad.
FULMAR (*ca.* ⅐

p. 18

CORY'S SHEARWATER (*ca* ⅕)

PLATE
5

p. 19

GREAT SHEARWATER (*ca.* ⅕)

p. 20

SOOTY SHEARWATER (*ca.* ⅕)

p. 22

Ad. m.
MANX SHEARWATER (*ca.* ¼)

PLATE
6

p. 23

Ad. f.
WILSON'S PETREL *(ca. ¼)*

Ad. f.
FRIGATE PETREL

p. 24

Ad. f.
STORM PETREL *(ca. ⅓)*

p. 26

Ad. m.   *Ad. f.*
LEACH'S PETREL *(ca. ⅓)*

PLATE
7

p. 27

Nestling in down   *Ad. f.*   *Ad. m.*
GANNET (*ca.* ¹⁄₁₀)

p. 29

1st summer f.   *Ad. m. winter.*   *Juv. m.*
CORMORANT (*ca.* ¹⁄₁₀)

p. 32

Ad. m. summer   *Juv. f.*
SHAG (*ca.* ¹⁄₁₀)

PLATE
8

p. 38

p. 42

p. 40

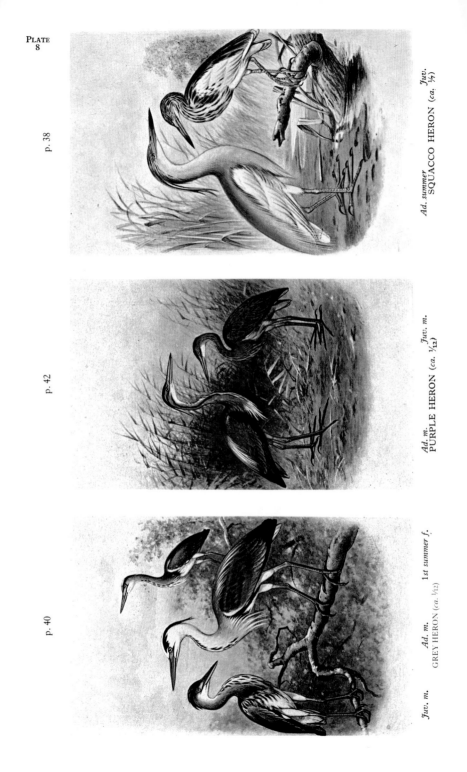

Ad. summer
SQUACCO HERON (*ca.* ¼)
Juv.

Ad. m.
PURPLE HERON (*ca.* ¹⁄₁₂)
Juv. m.

Juv. m.   *Ad. m.*   *1st summer f.*
GREY HERON (*ca.* ¹⁄₁₂)

Ad. m. NIGHT HERON (*ca.* ⅑) *Juv. m.*

Ad. winter *Ad. m. summer*
LITTLE EGRET (*ca.* ¼)

Ad. m. WHITE STORK (*ca.* ½₀) *Juv.*

p. 44

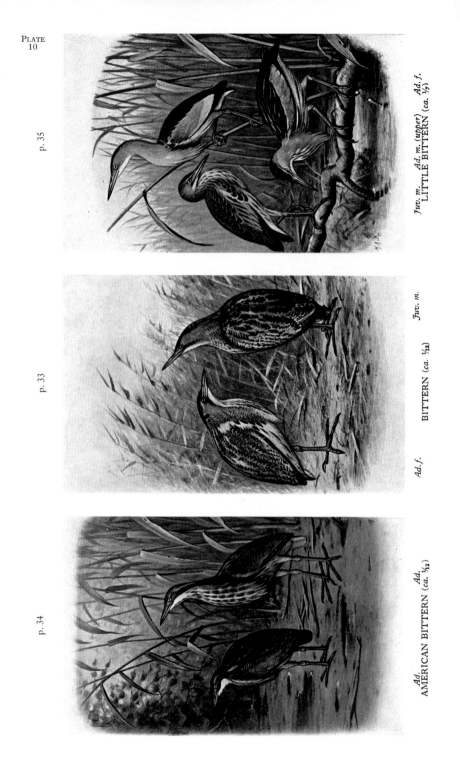

PLATE
10

p. 35

p. 33

p. 34

Juv. m. Ad. m. (upper) Ad. f.
LITTLE BITTERN (*ca.* ½)

Ad. f. BITTERN (*ca.* ⅟₁₁) *Juv. m.*

Ad.
AMERICAN BITTERN (*ca.* ⅟₁₂) *Ad.*

PLATE
11

p. 43

Ad. m.   BLACK STORK *(ca. ¹⁄₂₀)*   *Juv.*

p. 46

Juv.   *Ad. m. summer*
SPOONBILL *(ca. ¹⁄₁₂)*

p. 45

Ad. m. winter   *Ad. m. summer*
GLOSSY IBIS *(ca. ¹⁄₉)*

PLATE
12

p. 47

Ad. m.
FLAMINGO (*ca* ¹⁄₂₀)

p. 50

Ad. f.   *Juv. f.*
BEWICK'S SWAN (*ca.* ¹⁄₂₀)

p. 50

Ad. m.   *Juv. m*
WHOOPER SWAN (*ca.* ¹⁄₂₀)

PLATE 13

Juv. m. MUTE SWAN (*ca.* ⅟₂₀) *Ad. m.*

p. 48

Ad. *Ad.* SNOW GOOSE (*ca.* ⅟₁₃) *Juv.*

p. 58

PLATE 14

p. 56   *Ad.*   *Ad.*   *Juv.*   *Ad.*
GREY LAG GOOSE (*ca.* 1/10)

p. 54   *Adults.*   *Juv. (behind).*   *Juv.*
WHITE-FRONTED GOOSE (*ca.* 1/10)

PLATE 15

Ad.   *Ad.*   *Juv.*   p. 55
LESSER WHITE-FRONTED GOOSE (*ca.* ⅟₁₀)

Juv.   *Ad.*   *Ad.*   p. 52
BEAN GOOSE (*ca.* ⅟₁₀)

PLATE 16

Juv.　　*Ad.*　　*Juv.*　　　　　　　*Ad.*
PINK-FOOTED GOOSE (*ca.* ¹⁄₁₀)

Ad.　　*Ad.*　　　　　　*Ad.*　　*Juv.*
DARK-BREASTED BRENT GOOSE (*ca.* ¹⁄₁₀)　PALE-BREASTED BRENT GOOSE

PLATE 17

Ad.   Juv.   Ad.
BARNACLE GOOSE (*ca.* 1/10)

p. 61

p. 60

CANADA GOOSE (*ca.* 1/13)

PLATE
18

p. 63

Ad. f.   *Ad. m.*
RUDDY SHELDUCK (*ca.* ¹⁄₁₀)

p. 64

1st summer f.   *Ad. m.*
SHELDUCK (*ca.* ¹⁄₈)

p. 72

Ad. f.   MALLARD (*ca.* ¹⁄₈)   *Ad. m.*

PLATE
19

p. 70

Ad. m. eclipse   *Ad. f.*   *Ad. m.*
TEAL (*ca.* ⅛)

p. 75

Ad. m. eclipse   *Ad. m.*   *Ad. f.*
GARGANEY (*ca.* ⅛)

p. 74

Ad. f.   PINTAIL (*ca.* ⅛)   *Ad. m.*

Plate
20

p. 66

Ad. f.   *Ad. m.*   *1st winter m.*
WIGEON (*ca.* ⅛)

p. 68

Juv. m. (upper)   *Ad. m.*   *Ad. f.*
AMERICAN WIGEON (*ca.* ⅛)

p. 69

Ad. m.   *Ad. f.*
GADWALL (*ca.* ⅛)

PLATE
21

p. 77

Ad. f.   *Ad. m.*
SHOVELER (*ca.* ⅛)

p. 78

Ad. f.   *Ad. m.*
RED-CRESTED POCHARD (*ca.* ⅑)

p. 80

Ad. m.   *Ad. f.*
POCHARD (*ca.* ⅛)

PLATE
22

p. 82

Ad. m.   *Ad. f.*
TUFTED DUCK (*ca.* ⅛)

p. 84

Ad. f.   *Ad. m.*
SCAUP (*ca.* ⅛)

p. 81

Ad. f.   *Ad. m.*
FERRUGINOUS DUCK (*ca* ⅛)

PLATE
23

p. 96

Juv. m. (lower)   Ad. f. (upper)   Ad. m.
GOLDENEYE (*ca.* ⅛)

p. 86

*Ad. f.   EIDER (*ca.* ⅛)   Ad. m.*

p. 88

Ad. f.   Ad. m.   1st summer m.
KING EIDER (*ca.* ⅛)

PLATE
24

p. 90

Ad. m. *Ad. f.*
LONG-TAILED DUCK (*ca.* ⅛)

p. 98

Ad. f. *Ad. m.*
SMEW (*ca.* ⅛)

p. 101

Ad. m. *Ad. f.*
GOOSANDER (*ca.* ⅛)

PLATE
25

p. 92

Ad. f.   Ad. m.   *1st winter m.*
COMMON SCOTER (*ca.* ⅛)

p. 95

Juv. m.   *Ad. m.*   *Ad. f.*
VELVET SCOTER (*ca.* ⅛)

p. 94

Ad. f.   *Ad. m.*
SURF SCOTER (*ca.* ⅛)

PLATE 26

(1-3RD NATURAL SIZE)
Wing coverts and Specula of: 1. Mallard. 2. Teal. 3. Blue-winged
Teal. 4. Wigeon. 5. Shoveler. 6. Garganey. 7. Gadwall.
8. American Wigeon. 9. Pintail.

PLATE
27

p. 99

Ad. f.   *Ad. m.*
RED-BREASTED MERGANSER (*ca.* ⅛)

p. 127

Juv. f.   OSPREY (*ca.* ⅒)   *Ad. m.*

p. 123

Juv. m.   *2nd summer f.*   *Ad. m.*
SPOTTED EAGLE (*ca.* ⅒)

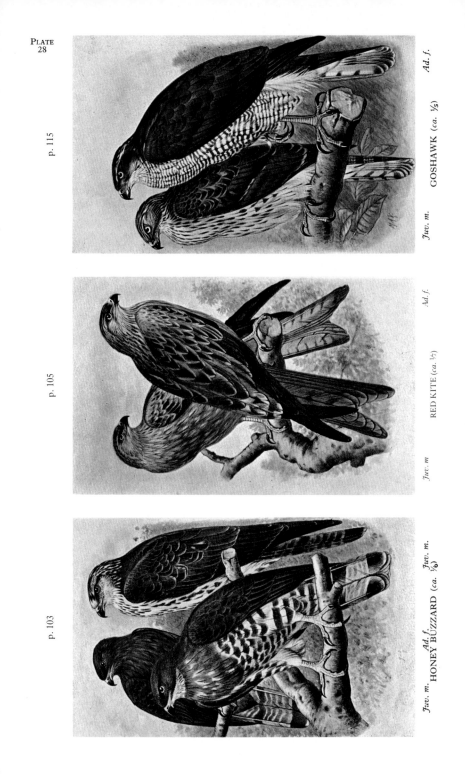

PLATE
28

p. 115

p. 105

p. 103

Ad. f. GOSHAWK (*ca.* ⅓) *Juv. m.*

Ad. f. RED KITE (*ca.* ⅐) *Juv. m.*

Juv. m. HONEY BUZZARD (*ca.* ⅙) *Ad. f.* *Juv. m.*

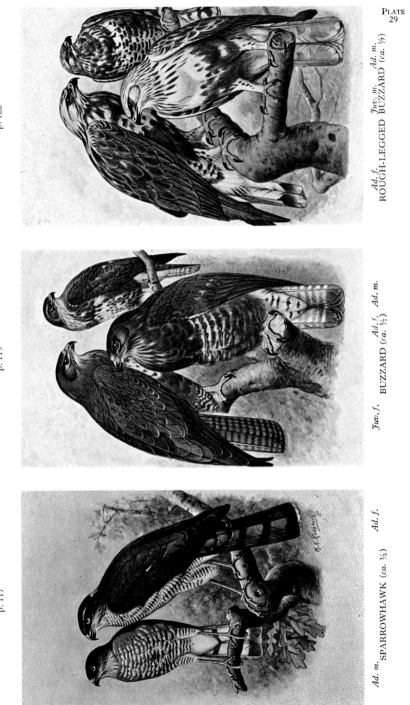

PLATE
29

p. 122

Ad. f.
ROUGH-LEGGED BUZZARD (*ca.* ¼) *Ad. m.* *Juv. m.*

p. 119

Juv. f. BUZZARD (*ca.* ¼) *Ad. f.* *Ad. m.*

p. 117

Ad. m. SPARROWHAWK (*ca.* ⅓) *Ad. f.*

PLATE
30

p. 124

Ad. f.   GOLDEN EAGLE (*ca.* ¹⁄₁₀)   *Ad. f.*

p. 107

Ad. f.   *Ad. m.*
WHITE-TAILED EAGLE (*ca.* $\frac{1}{10}$)

p. 107

Juv. f.   *2nd summer m.*
WHITE TAILED EAGLE (*ca.* $\frac{1}{10}$)

PLATE
31

p. 113

Ad. f.   *Ad. m.*   *Juv. f.*
MONTAGU'S HARRIER (*ca.* ⅙)

p. 111

Ad. m.   *Ad. f.*
HEN HARRIER (*ca.* ⅙)

p. 109

Ad. m.   *Ad. f.*
MARSH HARRIER (*ca.* ⅙)

PLATE
32

p. 134

Ad. m. *Juv.* *Ad. f.*
HOBBY *(ca. ⅓)*

. p. 137

Ad. f. PEREGRINE *(ca. ⅓)* *Ad. m.*

p. 136

Iceland *Ad. f.* Greenland *Ad. f. (upper) Juv. m. (lower)*
GYR FALCON *(ca. ⅙)*

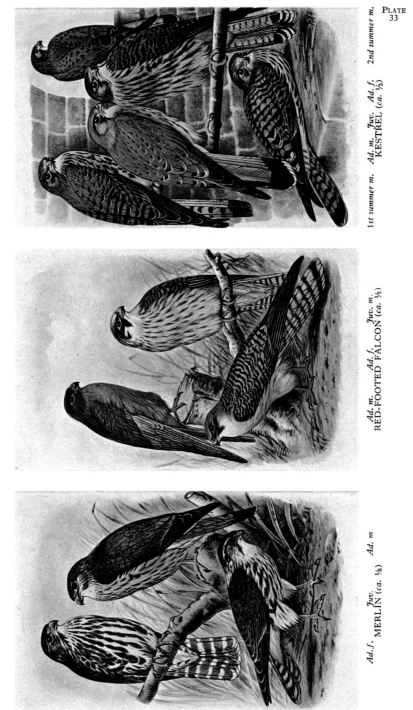

p. 130

PLATE
33

1st summer m.　Ad. m.　Juv.　Ad. f.　2nd summer m.
KESTREL (ca. ⅓)

p. 131

Ad. m.　Ad. f.　Juv. m.
RED-FOOTED FALCON (ca. ⅓)

p. 132

Ad. f.　Juv.　Ad. m.
MERLIN (ca. ⅖)

PLATE
34

p. 128

Ad. f.   **LESSER KESTREL** *(ca. ⅕)*   *Ad. m*

p. 145

Juv. m.   *Ad. m. winter*   *Ad. ƒ*
CAPERCAILLIE *(ca. 1/12)*

p. 143

Ad. f.   *Ad. m. winter*   *Juv. m. (in moult)*
BLACK GROUSE *(ca. ⅑)*

PLATE
35

p. 140

Juv. f.   Ad. m. (red variety)   Ad. f. summer   Ad. m. summer
RED GROUSE (*ca.* ½)

p. 142

Ad. m. summer   Ad. f. summer   Juv. m.
PTARMIGAN (*ca.* ½)

p. 147

Ad. m. autumn (upper)   Ad. f. autumn   Ad. f. winter   Ad. m. winter
PTARMIGAN (*ca.* ½)

PLATE
36

p. 147

Juv. (moulting)   Ad. m.   Ad. f.
RED-LEGGED PARTRIDGE (*ca.* ½)

p. 148

Ad. f. winter   Ad. m. winter   Variety "montana"
Ad. f. summer   Ad. m. summer
GREY PARTRIDGE (*ca.* ½)

p. 149

Ad. m.   Juv.   Ad   Ad. males (at back)
QUAIL (*ca.* ⅙)

PLATE
37

p. 151

Ad. m. (mutant)   *Ad. f. (mutant)*
Ad. m. (Ph. c. colchicus)   *Ad. m. (Ph. c. torquatus)*   *Ad. f.*   *Chick (normal) Chick (mutant)*
PHEASANT   *(ca.* ¹⁄₁₀)

p. 158

Ad. m. summer   *Juv. m.*
CORNCRAKE   *(ca.* ¼)

p. 152

1st winter m.   *Ad. f. summer*
WATER RAIL   *(ca.* ¼)

PLATE
38

p. 155

Ad. f. winter   *Ad. m. summer*   *Juv. m.*
LITTLE CRAKE (*ca.* ¼)

p. 156

Juv.   BAILLON'S CRAKE (*ca.* ¼)   *Ad. f. summer*

p. 154

Ad. m. summer   *Juv. m.*
SPOTTED CRAKE (*ca.* ¼)

PLATE
39

p. 159

Ad. m. summer   MOORHEN (*ca.* ⅟₇)   *Juv. f.*

p. 161

Juv. f.   COOT (*ca.* ⅟₇)   *Ad. m. summer*

p. 162

Juv. m.   *Ad. f.*   *Ad. m.*
CRANE (*ca.* ⅟₂₀)

PLATE
40

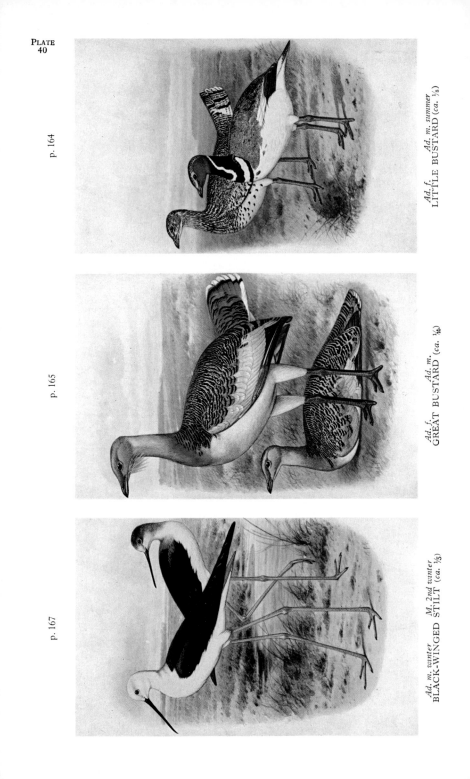

p. 164

Ad. f. *Ad. m. summer*
LITTLE BUSTARD (*ca.* ⅛)

p. 165

Ad. f. *Ad. m.*
GREAT BUSTARD (*ca.* ⅙)

p. 167

Ad. m. winter *M. 2nd winter*
BLACK-WINGED STILT (*ca.* ⅓)

PLATE
41

p. 171

Ad. m.   *Juv. m.*
STONE CURLEW (*ca.* ⅛)

p. 166

Juv. m.   *Ad. f. summer*   *Ad. m. winter*
OYSTERCATCHER (*ca.* ⅙)

p. 169

Ad. f. summer   *Juv. m.*
AVOCET (*ca.* ⅙)

PLATE
42

p. 187

Ad. m. summer   *Ad. f. summer*
LAPWING (*ca.* ½)

p. 185

Juv. m.   *Ad. m. summer*   *Ad. f. winter*
GREY PLOVER (*ca.* ¼)

p. 183

p. 182

Lesser, *juv. m.* Golden (Southern), *ad. m. summer.* Lesser, *ad. m. winter*
GOLDEN and LESSER GOLDEN PLOVERS (*ca.* ¼)

PLATE
43

p. 175

Ad. m. summer   *Juv.*
LITTLE RINGED PLOVER (*ca.* ¼)

p. 176

Ad. m. summer   *Ad. f. winter*   *Juv. f.*
RINGED PLOVER (*ca.* ¼)

p. 179

Ad. m. winter   *Juv. m.*   *Ad. m. summer*
KENTISH PLOVER (*ca.* ¼)

PLATE
44

p. 180

Ad. m. moulting   *Ad. m. winter*   *Ad. m. summer*
DOTTEREL (*ca.* ¼)

p. 178

Juv. m.   KILLDEER (*ca.* ¼)   *Ad. m. summer*

p. 219

Juv.   *Ad. f.*
UPLAND SANDPIPER (*ca.* ⅕)

PLATE
45

Ad. m. summer   *Ad. f. summer*
BAR-TAILED GODWIT (*ca.* ⅛)

p. 214

Juv. m.   *Ad. f. winter*
BAR-TAILED GODWIT (*ca.* ⅛)

p. 214

Juv.   *Juv. m.*   *Ad. f. winter*
BLACK-TAILED GODWIT (*ca.* ⅛)

p. 213

PLATE
46

p. 217

Juv. f.   *Ad. f.*

CURLEW (*ca.* ⅛)

p. 216

Ad. f.   *Juv. f.*

WHIMBREL (*ca.* ⅛)

p. 225

Ad. m. winter   *Ad. m. summer*   *Juv. f.*

LESSER YELLOWLEGS (*ca.* ⅕)

PLATE
47

p. 221

Juv. (lower)   Ad. m. winter (upper)   Ad. f. summer   Summer (on post)
REDSHANK *(ca. ⅕)*

p. 220

Ad. m. summer   Ad. f. winter   Juv. f.
SPOTTED REDSHANK *(ca. ⅕)*

p. 223

Juv. m.   Ad. m. winter
GREENSHANK *(ca. ⅕)*

PLATE
48

p. 229

Juv. f.   *Ad. f. winter*   *Ad. m. summer*
COMMON SANDPIPER (*ca.* ⅓)

p. 226

Ad. f summer   *Ad. m. winter*
GREEN SANDPIPER (*ca.* ⅕)

p. 228

Ad. m. summer   *Ad. f. winter*   *Juv. m.*
WOOD SANDPIPER (*ca.* ⅓)

PLATE
49

p. 231

Ad. m. winter   *Juv. f. (behind)*   *Ad. m. summer*
TURNSTONE (*ca.* ¼)

p. 208

p. 209

Long-billed, *Ad. m. winter* Short-billed, *Ad. f. summer;* and *Juv. m.*
LONG-BILLED and SHORT-BILLED DOWITCHERS

p. 207

Juv. f.   *Ad. m.*
GREAT SNIPE (*ca.* ¼)

PLATE
50

p. 205

Juv. f.   SNIPE (*ca.* ¼)   *Ad. m.*

p. 205

Ad. m.   JACK SNIPE (*ca.* ¼)   *Ad. f.*

p. 211

Ad. m.   *Juv.*   *Ad. f.*
WOODCOCK (*ca.* ¼)

PLATE
51

p. 190

Ad. m. summer   *Ad. m. winter*   *Juv. m.*
SANDERLING (*ca.* ¼)

p. 189

Ad. m. summer   *Juv. m.*   *Ad. f. winter*
KNOT (*ca.* ¼)

p. 191

Juv. f.   *Ad. winter*   *Ad. summer*
LITTLE STINT (*ca.* ¼)

PLATE
52

Ad. summer   *Ad. winter*   *Juv. m.*
TEMMINCK'S STINT (*ca.* ¼)

Ad. f. summer   *Ad. f. winter*   *Juv. m.*
WHITE-RUMPED SANDPIPER (*ca.* ¼)

Juv.   *Ad. summer*   *Ad. winter*
PECTORAL SANDPIPER (*ca.* ¼)

PLATE
53

p. 197

Ad. m. summer   *Ad. m. winter*   *Juv. f.*
PURPLE SANDPIPER (*ca.* ¼)

p. 202

Juv. f.   *Ad. m. summer*
BUFF-BREASTED SANDPIPER (*ca.* ¼)

p. 199

Ad. m. winter   *Ad. m. summer*   *Juv. f.*
DUNLIN (*ca.* ¼)

Plate
54

p. 196

Juv. m.   *Ad. f. winter*   *Ad. m. summer*
CURLEW SANDPIPER (*ca.* ¼)

p. 201

Juv. m.   *Ad. f. summer*
BROAD-BILLED SANDPIPER (*ca.* ¼)

p. 233

Ad. f. summer   *Ad. f. winter*   *Juv. m. moulting*
GREY PHALAROPE (*ca.* ¼)

PLATE
55

p. 232

Ad. m. winter   Juv. f.   Ad. f. summer
RED-NECKED PHALAROPE (*ca.* ¼)

p. 203

Adult males summer
RUFF (*ca.* ⅛)

p. 203

*Ad. m. winter   Ad. f. winter   Ad. m. moulting
Juv. m.   Juv. f.   Ad. m. winter*
RUFF (*ca.* ⅓)

PLATE
56

p. 173

Ad. m. summer   *First winter*
CREAM-COLOURED COURSER (*ca.* ¼)

p. 174

Ad. m. summer   *Juv.*
COLLARED PRATINCOLE (*ca.* ¼)

p. 239

Juv. f.   *Ad. m. summer*
GREAT SKUA (*ca.* ¹⁄₁₀)

PLATE
57

p. 235

Ad. summer (pale)   *Ad. summer (pale)*   *2nd summer (pale)*
POMARINE SKUA *(ca. ⅟₁₀)*

p. 236

Ad. (pale)   *Ad. (dark)*   *Ads. (pale)*
ARCTIC SKUA *(ca. ⅟₁₀)*

p. 238

Juv. m.   *1st summer m.*   *Ad. m. summer*
LONG-TAILED SKUA *(ca. ⅟₁₂)*

PLATE
58

p. 261

1st winter f.   *Ad. f.*
IVORY GULL *(ca.* ¹⁄₁₀)

p. 249

Ad. f. summer   *Ad. m. summer*   *Ad. f. winter*
COMMON GULL *(ca.* ¹⁄₁₀)

p. 252

Ad. m. winter   *Ad. m. and f. summer*
HERRING GULL *(ca.* ¹⁄₁₀)

PLATE
59

p. 252

2nd winter f.   *Juv. f.*   *2nd summer m.*

HERRING GULL (*ca.* ¹⁄₁₀)

p. 251

2nd summer   *Ad. f. summer*   *Juv. f.*

LESSER BLACK-BACKED GULL (*ca* ¹⁄₁₀)

p. 257

3rd winter f.   *Juv. m.*   *2nd winter m.*

GREAT BLACK-BACKED GULL (*ca.* ¹⁄₁₀)

PLATE
60

p. 255

Juv.   *2nd summer*
GLAUCOUS GULL *(ca.* ¹⁄₁₀*)*

p. 254

Ad. m. summer   *Ad. f. winter (behind) 2nd winter m.*   *3rd winter f.*
ICELAND GULL *(ca.* ¹⁄₁₀*)*

p. 246

Ad. f. winter 1st summer m. Ad. males moulting (at back) 1st winter m.
BLACK-HEADED GULL *(ca.* ¹⁄₁₀*)*

PLATE
61

p. 246

Ad. f. summer   *Ad. m. summer*   *Juv.*   *Juv. f.*
BLACK-HEADED GULL (*ca.* ¹⁄₁₀)

p. 241

Ad. m. winter   *Ad. m. summer*   *1st winter m.*
MEDITERRANEAN GULL (*ca.* ¹⁄₁₀)

p. 243

Juv. *1st winter m.* (*behind*) *Ad. m.* (*winter*) *1st summer f.* *Ad. males* (*summer*)
LITTLE GULL (*ca.* ¹⁄₁₀)

PLATE
62

p. 259

Ad. f. winter   Juv. f.   Ad. f. summer
KITTIWAKE *(ca.* ⅟₁₀*)*

p. 245

Juv. m.   Ad. m. winter   Ad. m. summer
SABINE'S GULL *(ca.* ⅟₁₀*)*

p. 275

Ad. f. winter   Ad. m. summer   Juv.   Ad. summer (flying)
WHITE-WINGED BLACK TERN *(ca.* ⅛*)*

PLATE
63

p. 273

Ad. m. summer   *Ad. f. summer*   *Juv. f.*
BLACK TERN (*ca.* ⅛)

p. 272

Juv. m.   *Ad. f. summer*   *Ad. f. winter* (*at back*)
WHISKERED TERN (*ca.* ⅛)

p. 262

Ad. m. winter   *Juv. m.*   *Ad. m. summer*
GULL-BILLED TERN (*ca.* ⅛)

PLATE
64

p. 264

Ad. m. summer　　*Juv. m.*　　　　*Juv. m*
SANDWICH TERN (*ca.* ⅛)

p. 263

Juv.　*Ad. winter*　*Ad. summer*
CASPIAN TERN (*ca.* ⅛)

p. 267

Ad. f. summer　　*Ad. m. summer*　　　*Juv.*
COMMON TERN (*ca.* ⅛)

PLATE
65

p. 270

Ad. f. summer   *Ad. m. summer*   *Juv.*
ARCTIC TERN (*ca.* ⅛)

p. 266

Ad. f. winter   *Ad. m. summer*   *Juv. m.*
ROSEATE TERN (*ca.* ⅛)

p. 271

Juv. m.   *1st winter f.*   *Ad. f. summer*   *Ad. m. winter*
LITTLE TERN (*ca.* ⅛)

PLATE
66

p. 283

Ad. f. (in moult)   *Ad. f. winter*   *Ad. f. summer*
LITTLE AUK *(ca. ⅛)*

p. 279

Juv. m.   *Ad. m. winter*   *Ad. f. summer*
RAZORBILL *(ca. ⅛)*

p. 278

Ad. f. winter   *Ad. f. summer*
BRÜNNICH'S GUILLEMOT *(ca. ⅛)*

PLATE
67

p. 277

Ad. m. winter (bridled)   1st *winter m.*   *Ad. females summer* (bridled, normal)
GUILLEMOT (*ca.* ⅙)

p. 281

Ad. m. summer.   *Juv. f.*   *Ad. f.* (moulting)   *Ad. f. winter*
BLACK GUILLEMOT (*ca.* ⅙)

p. 284

Ad. m. summer   *Ad. f. winter*   *Juv. f.*
PUFFIN (*ca.* ⅙)

PLATE
68

p. 290

Ad.   *Juv.*
COLLARED DOVE *(ca.* ⅓)

p. 293

Ad. m.   *Juv. f.*   *Ad. f.*
TURTLE DOVE *(ca.* ⅙)

PLATE
69

p. 285

Ad. m.   *Ad. f.*   *Ad. m.*
PALLAS'S SANDGROUSE (*ca.* ⅛)

p. 289

Ad. m.   *Juv. f. moulting from down*   *Juv. f.*
WOODPIGEON (*ca.* ⅛)

p. 287

Juv. m.   *Ad. m.*
ROCK DOVE (*ca.* ⅛)

PLATE
70

p. 288

Ad. f.   *Juv. f.*   *Ad. m.*
STOCK DOVE (*ca.* ⅛)

p. 296

Ad. m.   *Ad. f.*
BLACK-BILLED CUCKOO   YELLOW-BILLED CUCKOO (*ca.* ⅛)

p. 295

Ad. f.   1*st summer f.*   *Ad. m.*
CUCKOO (*ca* ¼)

PLATE
71

p. 297

White-breasted, *ad. m.*   *Juv.*   Dark-breasted, *ad. m.*   White-breasted, *ad. f.*
BARN OWL (*ca.* 1/6)

p. 300   p. 299

Ad. m.   *Ad. f.*
SNOWY OWL (*ca* 1/8)

Ad. m.
EAGLE OWL (*ca* 1/8)

PLATE
72

p. 306

American, *ad. m.*   *Ad. f.*
HAWK OWL.   TENGMALM'S OWL (*ca.* ⅙)

p. 298

Ad. f.   *Ad. m.*   *Ad. m.*
SCOPS OWL (*ca.* ⅙)

p. 301

Ad f.   *nestling.*   *Juv.*   *Ad. m.*
LITTLE OWL (*ca* ⅛)

PLATE
73

p. 305

Ad. m.   *Nestling.*   *Ad. f.*
SHORT-EARED OWL (*ca.* ⅙)

p. 303

Ad. m.   *Juv. f.*   *Ad. f.*
LONG-EARED OWL (*ca.* ⅙)

p. 302

Ad. f.   *Juv.*   *Ad. m.*
TAWNY OWL (*ca.* ⅙)

PLATE
74

p. 307

Juv.   *Ad. f.*   *Ad. m. (upper)*
NIGHTJAR *(ca. ⅓)*

p. 311

Ad. m.   *Ad. f.*
NEEDLE-TAILED SWIFT *(ca. ⅛)*   ALPINE SWIFT

p. 309

Ad. m.   *Juv. m.*   *Ad. f.*
SWIFT *(⅓)*

PLATE
75

p. 314

Ad. m. summer   *Juv.*
ROLLER (*ca.* ¼)

p. 311

Juv.   *Ad. f. (upper)*   *Ad. m.*
KINGFISHER (*ca.* ¼)

p. 312

Ad. m.   *Ad. f.*
BEE-EATER (*ca.* ⅓)

PLATE
76

p. 315

Ad. f.   *Juv. (not full grown)*   *Ad. m.*
HOOPOE (*ca.* ⅓)

p. 316

Ad. f.   *Ad. m.*   *Juv.*
WRYNECK (¼)

p. 321

Ad. m. (lower) Juv. f. (upper) Ad. f.
LESSER SPOTTED WOODPECKER (⅔)

p. 319

Ad. f. Juv. Ad. m.
GREAT SPOTTED WOODPECKER (ca. ¼)

p. 318

Ad. m. Juv. m. Ad. f.
GREEN WOODPECKER (ca. ⅛)

PLATE 77

PLATE
78

p. 327

Eastern, *ad.* (*upper*).   *Juv.*   *Ad. m. summer*   *Ad. f. winter* (*upper*)
SKYLARK (⅓)

p. 325

Ad. m.   *Juv.*   CRESTED LARK (¼)   *Ad. f.*

p. 326

Juv.   *Ad. f.*   *Ad. m.*
WOODLARK (⅓)

PLATE
79

p. 329

Ad. f. spring   Ad. m. spring   M. winter
SHORE LARK (⅓)

p. 323

EASTERN SHORT-TOED LARK (*ca* ⅕) SHORT-TOED LARK (⅓)
Juv. CALANDRA LARK (⅓) *Ad. m.*

p. 323

Ad. m. winter Ad. m. summer (ca ⅕) BLACK LARK *Ad. f. winter* (⅓)
Ad. m. WHITE-WINGED LARK (⅓) *Ad. f.*

PLATE
80

p. 330

Ad. m.   *Ad. f.*   *Juv. m.*
SAND MARTIN (⅓)

p. 333

Ad. m.   *Juv. m.*   *Ad. f.*
HOUSE MARTIN (⅓)

p. 331

Ad. m.   *Ad. m.*   *Juv.*   *Juv.*   *Ad. f.*
SWALLOW (⅓)

PLATE
81

p. 420

Ad. f.   *Juv. m.*   *Ad. m.*
GOLDEN ORIOLE (⅓)

p. 428

British, *Ad. f. and Juv.*   Continental, *Ad. m.*   Irish, *Ad. f. (lower).*
JAY (*ca.* ⅙)

p. 431

Ad. m.   *Juv.*
CHOUGH (*ca.* ⅕)

PLATE
82

p. 432

Ad. (upper).   *Juv.*   *Ad. m.*   *Ad. f.*
JACKDAW (*ca.* ⅙)

p. 430

Thick-billed, *F.*   Slender-billed, *M.*
NUTCRACKER (*ca.* ⅕)

p. 429

Juv. m.   MAGPIE (*ca.* ⅕)   *Ad. m.*

PLATE
83

p. 437

Ad. f.   *Ad. m.*
CARRION CROW (*ca.* ⅛)

p. 438

Juv. f.   *Ad. m.*
RAVEN (*ca.* ⅛)

p. 434

Juv. f.   *Ad. m.*
ROOK (*ca.* ⅛)

PLATE
84

p. 435

Ad. m. *Ad. f.*
HOODED CROW (*ca.* ⅛)

p. 407

Ad. m. *Juv.* *Ad. f.* Northern, *ad. m.* (*upper*)
LONG-TAILED TIT (⅓)

p. 406

Juv. f. *Juv. m.* *Ad. m.* *Ad. f.* *F., winter.*
BEARDED TIT (⅓)

PLATE
85

p. 409

Ad. f.   *Juv.*   *Ad. m.* (*upper*)
MARSH TIT (⅓)

p. 410

Ad. m. summer.   *Juv.*   *Ad. f. winter* (*lower*).   Northern, *ad. winter* (*upper*)
WILLOW TIT (⅓)

p. 412

Northern, *Ad. m.* (*upper*).   Scottish, *Juv.*   Scottish, *Ad. m.* (*upper*).
Central European, *Ad. m.* (*lower*).   Scottish, *Ad. f.* (*lower*).
CRESTED TIT (⅓)

PLATE
86

p. 414

Ad. m.   *Juv. f.*   *Ad. f.*
BLUE TIT (⅓)

p. 415

Ad. f.   *Juv. m.*   *Ad. m.*
GREAT TIT (⅓)

p. 413

Ad. m.   *Juv.*   *Ad. f.*
COAL TIT (⅓)

PLATE
87

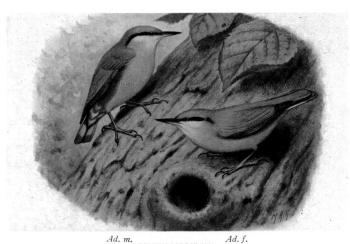

p. 417

Ad. m.   *Ad. f.*
NUTHATCH (⅓)

p. 419

Northern, *Ad. f.*   British, *Juv.   Ad. f.*   *Ad. m.*
TREECREEPER (⅓)

p. 418

Ad. summer.   *Juv.*   *Ad. winter*
WALLCREEPER (⅓)

PLATE
88

p. 349

Juv.   *Ad. m.*   *Ad. f.*
DIPPER (⅓)

p. 350

Ad. m. (upper) Juv. (lower) Ad. f.   *Ad. m.*   *Ad. f.*
WREN (⅓)   SHETLAND WREN   ST. KILDA WREN

p. 352

Continental *(upper) Ad. m.*   British *(upper) Ad. f.*
Hebridean *(lower) Ad. m.*   British *(lower) Ad. m. (middle) Juv.*
DUNNOCK (⅓)

PLATE
89

p. 357

1st winter m.   Ad. m. summer
1st winter m.   Ad. f.   1st winter f.   Ad. m. winter
RED-SPOTTED BLUETHROAT (⅓)

p. 357

Ad. m. summer   Juv.   Ad. m. winter   Ad. f. summer   1st winter m. (upper)
WHITE-SPOTTED BLUETHROAT (⅓)

p. 353

Ad. m.   Ad. f.   Juv.
ALPINE ACCENTOR (⅓)

PLATE
90

p. 354

Ad. f.   *Juv.*   *Ad. m.*
ROBIN (⅓)

p. 358

Ad. f.   *Ad. m. winter* *Juv.*   *Ad. m. summer*
BLACK REDSTART (⅓)

p. 360

1st winter m.   *Juv.*   *Ad. m. summer*   *Ad. f.*   *Ad. m. winter*
REDSTART (⅓)

PLATE
91

p. 355

Ad. f.   *Ad. m.*   *Juv.*
NIGHTINGALE (*lower*) (⅓)   THRUSH NIGHTINGALE (*upper*)

p. 363

Ad. f. summer   *Juv.*   *Ad. m. winter*   *Ad. m. summer*
STONECHAT (⅓)

p. 361

Ad. m summer   *Ad. f. summer*   *1st winter f.*   *Juv.*
WHINCHAT (⅓)

PLATE
92

p. 365

Ad. f. summer   Juv.   Ad. m. summer   1st summer male
WHEATEAR (⅓)

p. 365

Ad. m. winter   1st winter m.   Ad. f. winter   1st winter f.
WHEATEAR (⅓)

p. 366

Ad. m. (white-throated) winter.   Ad. f.   Ad. m. (white-throated) winter
Ad. m. (black-throated) summer.   Ad. m. (black-throated) summer
(Western) BLACK-EARED WHEATEAR (⅓) (Eastern)

PLATE
93

p. 368

Ad. m. summer.   *Juv.*   *Ad. f. summer*
RING OUZEL (⅓)

p. 369

Ad. f. summer.   *Ad. m. summer.*   *Juv. m.*
BLACKBIRD (⅓)

p. 373

Iceland, 1*st winter m.*   Common, *juv.*   Common, *ad. f.*
REDWING (⅓)

PLATE
94

p. 372

Ad. f.   *Juv.*   *Ad. m.*
SONG THRUSH (*ca.* ¼)

p. 375

Juv. m.   *Ad. f.*   *Ad. m.*
MISTLE THRUSH (⅓)

p. 371

Ad. f.   *Ad. m.*   *Juv.*
FIELDFARE (⅓)

PLATE
95

p. 367

Ad. m. winter. *Ad. f. winter.*
WHITE'S THRUSH (⅓)

p. 390

Juv. m. *Ad. m. (upper)* *Ad. f.*
WHITETHROAT (⅓)

p. 389

Ad. m. *Juv.* *Ad. f.*
LESSER WHITETHROAT (⅓)

PLATE
96

p. 387

1st winter f.   *Juv.*   *Ad. m.*   *Ad. f.* ·
DARTFORD WARBLER (½)

p. 392

Juv.   *Ad. m.*   *Ad. f.*
GARDEN WARBLER (⅓)

p. 393

Ad. m.   *1st winter m.*   *Ad. f.*
BLACKCAP (⅓)

PLATE
97

p. 388

Ad. m. summer   *1st winter m.*   *Ad. f. summer*
BARRED WARBLER (⅓)

p. 380

Ad. f.   *Juv. m.*   *Ad. m.*
SEDGE WARBLER (⅓)

p. 379

Ad. m.   *Ad. m.*   *Juv. m.*   *Ad. f.*
AQUATIC WARBLER (⅓)

Plate
98

p. 384

Ad. f.   *Ad. m.*   *Ad. m.*
GREAT REED WARBLER (⅓)

p. 382

Ad. f.   *Juv.*   *Ad. m.*
REED WARBLER (⅓)

p. 381

Ad. f.   *Juv.*   *Ad. m.*
MARSH WARBLER (⅓)

PLATE
99

p. 377

Ad. f.   *Juv. m.*   *Ad. m.*
GRASSHOPPER WARBLER (⅓)

p. 385

Ad. f.   *Juv.*   *Ad. m.*
ICTERINE WARBLER (⅓)

p. 394

Ad. f.   *Ad. m.* Yellow-browed (*upper*).   *Ad. m.* Pallas (*lower*).
YELLOW-BROWED WARBLER.   PALLAS'S LEAF WARBLER (⅓)

PLATE
100

p. 396

Ad. f. summer.   *Juv. f.*   *Ad. m. summer.*
CHIFFCHAFF (⅓)

p. 395

Ad. m.   *Ad. f.*
WOOD WARBLER (⅓)

p. 399

Ad. m. summer.   *Juv.*   *Ad. f. autumn.*
WILLOW WARBLER (⅓)

CHIFFCHAFF   WILLOW WARBLER

                  ICTARINE WARBLER

MELODIOUS WARBLER   GARDEN WARBLER

                  BARRED WARBLER

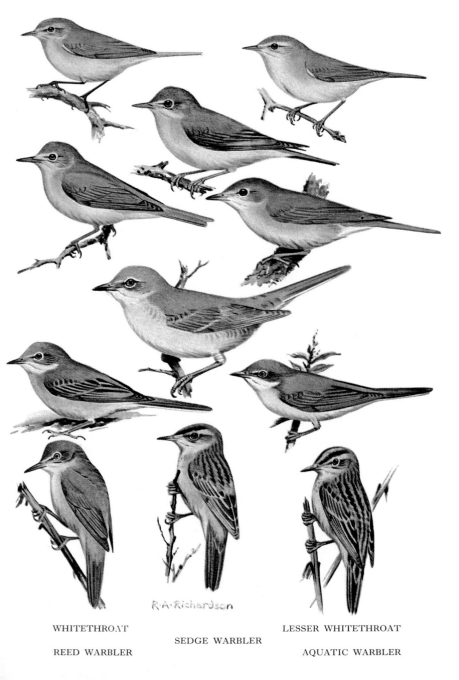

R·A·Richardson

WHITETHROAT   LESSER WHITETHROAT

               SEDGE WARBLER

REED WARBLER   AQUATIC WARBLER

PLATE
102

p. 404

Ad. f.   *Ad. m.*   *1st winter (upper).*   *Ad. f.*
RED-BREASTED FLYCATCHER (⅓) BROWN FLYCATCHER

p. 402

Ad. m.   *Juv.*   *Ad. f.*
FIRECREST (⅓)

p. 400

Ad. m.   *Ad. f.*   *Juv.*
GOLDCREST (⅓)

PLATE
103

p. 405

Juv. m.   M. winter.   Ad. f. (lower).   Ad. m. summer (upper).
PIED FLYCATCHER (⅓)

p. 346

Ad. f. summer.   Ad. m. summer.   Juv. f.
WHITE WAGTAIL (⅓)

p. 346

Juv.   Ad. f.   Ad. m.
PIED WAGTAIL (⅓)

PLATE
104

p. 403

Ad. m.   *Juv.*   *Ad. f.*
SPOTTED FLYCATCHER (⅓)

p. 344

Ad. m. winter.   *Ad. f. winter.*
GREY WAGTAIL (⅓)

p. 344

Ad. m. summer (upper).   *Ad. f. summer.*   *Juv. m.*
GREY WAGTAIL (⅓)

PLATE
105

p. 342

Ad. f.   *Juv.*   *Ad. m.*
BLUE-HEADED WAGTAIL (⅓)

p. 342

Ad. m.   *Ad. f.*
YELLOW WAGTAIL (⅓)

p. 335

Ad. m.   *Ad. f.*   *Juv.*
TAWNY PIPIT (⅓)

PLATE
106

p. 334

Ad. m. RICHARD'S PIPIT (⅓) *Ad. f.*

p. 341

Ad. m. winter. *Ad. m. summer.* *Ad. f. summer.* American, *Ad. m. winter.*
WATER PIPIT (⅓)

p. 341

Scandinavian, *ad. m. spring.* Rock Pipit, *ad. m. summer.*
Rock Pipit, *winter.* Hebridean, *spring.* *Juv.*
ROCK PIPIT (⅓)

PLATE
107

p. 337

Ad. m. (upper).   *Juv. m.*   *Ad. f.*
TREE PIPIT (⅓)

p. 339

Ad. f.   *Ad. m. (upper).*   *Juv. f.*
MEADOW PIPIT (⅓)

p. 340

F., winter.   *F., summer.*   *Juv.*   *M., summer (upper)*
RED-THROATED PIPIT (⅓)

PLATE
108

p. 347

Ad. f.   1*st winter m.* (⅓)   *Ad. m.*
WAXWING (⅓)

p. 426

Ad. f.   *Juv.*   *Ad. m.*
WOODCHAT SHRIKE (⅓)

p. 422

1*st winter m.* (*middle*).   *Ad. f.* (*upper and lower*).   *Juv.*   *Ad. m.*
RED-BACKED SHRIKE (½)

PLATE
109

p. 425

Ad. f. (upper). **1st** *winter m.*
GREAT GREY SHRIKE (⅓)   *Ad. m.*

p. 423

Ad. m. summer.   *Juv.*   *1st winter f. (upper).*
LESSER GREY SHRIKE (⅓)

p. 442

Ad. f. summer.   *Ad. m. summer.*   *Juv.*
ROSE-COLOURED STARLING (⅓)

Plate
110

p. 440

Ad. m. spring.   *Ad. m. summer.*   *Ad. f. spring.*   Shetland, *Juv.*
STARLING (⅓)

p. 440

Ad. m. winter.   *Ad. f. winter.*   *Juv.*
STARLING (⅓)

p. 444

Juv. (upper).   *Ad. f.*   *Ad. m.*
TREE SPARROW (⅓)

PLATE
111

p. 442

Ad. m. summer. *Juv. Ad. m. winter (upper).* *Ad. f.*
HOUSE SPARROW (⅓)

p. 466

Juv. *Ad. m. summer.* *Ad. f. summer.*
SNOW BUNTING (⅓)

p. 466

Ad. f. winter. *Ad. m. winter.* *1st winter m.*
SNOW BUNTING (⅓)

PLATE
112

p. 472

p. 472

Ad. f.   *Juv.*   *Ad. m.*
LITTLE BUNTING (⅓)

p. 465

Ad. m. spring.   *F. 1st winter.*   *M. 1st winter.*
LAPLAND BUNTING (⅓)

p. 473

Ad. f. summer.   *Juv.*   *Ad. m. summer.*
REED BUNTING (⅓)

PLATE
113

p. 470

Ad. f.   *Juv.*   *1st. winter f.*   *Ad. m.*
ORTOLAN BUNTING (⅓)

p. 471

F. winter.   *Ad. f.*   *Ad. m. winter.*   *Ad. m.*
RUSTIC BUNTING (⅓)

p. 474

F. winter.   *Ad. m. winter.*   *Ad. m. summer.*   *Ad. f. summer.*   *Juv.*
BLACK-HEADED BUNTING (⅓)

PLATE
114

p. 467

Ad. f.   *Juv. m.*   *Ad. m.*
YELLOWHAMMER (⅓)

p. 475

Ad. m.   *Juv. m.*   *Ad. f.*
CORN BUNTING (⅓)

p. 469

Ad. m.   *Juv. f.*   *Ad. f.*
CIRL BUNTING (⅓)

PLATE
115

p. 458

Ad. f.   TWO-BARRED CROSSBILL (⅓)   *Ad. m.*

p. 445

Ad. m. winter.   *Ad. f.*   *Ad. m. summer.*   *Juv.*
CHAFFINCH (⅓)

p. 446

Ad. m. summer.   *Ad. m. winter.*   *Ad. f. winter.*
BRAMBLING (⅓)

PLATE
116

p. 462

Ad. m.   *Ad. f.*   *Juv.*
BULLFINCH (⅓)

p. 458

Im. m.   *Im. m.*   *Im. m.*   *Ad. m.*
CROSSBILL (⅓)

p. 458

Ad. m.   *Juv. m.*   *Juv. f.*   *Ad. f.*
CROSSBILL (⅓)

PLATE
117

p. 461

Ad. m.   *Ad. f.*
SCARLET ROSEFINCH (⅓)

p. 462

Ad. m.   **Ad. f.**
PINE GROSBEAK (⅓)

p. 448

Ad. m. summer.   *Juv. f.*   *Ad. m. winter.*   *Ad. f.*
SERIN (⅓)

PLATE
118

p. 452

Ad. m. spring. Juv. m.   Ad. f.   Ad. m. summer.
LINNET (⅓)

p. 452

F. winter.   M. winter.   M. winter.
LINNET (⅓)

p. 454

Juv.   Ad. m. winter (upper).   Ad. f. summer (upper).
Ad. m. summer (lower).   Continental Twite, ad. m. winter (lower).
TWITE (⅓)

PLATE
119

p. 451

Ad. m.   *Juv.*   *Ad. f.*
SISKIN (⅓)

p. 457

Ad. m.   *1st winter m.*   *1st winter f.*
ARCTIC REDPOLL (⅖)

p. 455

Ad. m. winter.   *Ad. f. (upper).*   *1st winter m.*
REDPOLL (⅓)

PLATE
120

p. 449

Ad. m.   *Juv. m.*   *Ad. f.*
GREENFINCH (⅓)

p. 450

Ad. f.   *Juv.*   *Ad. m.*
GOLDFINCH (⅓)

p. 463

Juv. m.   *Ad. f.*   *Ad. m.*
HAWFINCH (⅓)

PLATE 121

1. BAR-TAILED GODWIT (*winter*). 2. BLACK-TAILED GODWIT (*winter*). 3. STONE CURLEW. 4. LAPWING.
5. WHIMBREL. 6. CURLEW. 7. AVOCET. 8. OYSTERCATCHER (*winter*).

PLATE 122

1. TEMMINCK'S STINT (*juv.*). 2. LITTLE STINT (*juv.*). 3. PURPLE SANDPIPER. 4. DUNLIN (*left, ad. summer, right, ad. winter*). 5. CURLEW SANDPIPER (*left, ad. winter, right, ad. summer*). 6. KNOT (*left, ad. summer, right, ad. winter*). 7. SANDERLING (*left, juv., right, ad. winter*). 8. GREEN SANDPIPER. 9. WOOD SANDPIPER. 10. COMMON SANDPIPER. 11. GREENSHANK. 12. SPOTTED REDSHANK (*left, ad. summer, right, ad. winter*). 13. REDSHANK (*ad. winter*).

PLATE 123

1. GREY PHALAROPE (*ad. winter*). 2. RED-NECKED PHALAROPE (*left, juv., right, ad. summer*). 3. JACK SNIPE. 4. COMMON SNIPE. 5. GREAT SNIPE. 6. WOODCOCK. 7. REEVE (*juv.*), RUFF (*ad. summer*). 8. DOTTEREL (*left, ad. winter, middle and right, ad. summer*). 9. TURNSTONE (*ad. summer*). 10. LITTLE RINGED PLOVER. 11. KENTISH PLOVER. 12. RINGED PLOVER. 13. GREY PLOVER (*left, ad. winter, middle, juv., right, ad. summer*). 14. GOLDEN PLOVER (*left and middle, ad. winter, right, ad. summer*).

J.C.Harrison.

Plate 124
Adult Males and Females of
1. Tufted Duck. 2. Teal. 3. Pochard. 4. Pintail. 5. Mallard. 6. Gadwall. 7. Shelduck
(*male*). 8. Shoveler. 9. Wigeon. 10. Garganey.

PLATE 125
ADULT MALES AND FEMALES OF
1. GOLDENEYE. 2. SCAUP. 3. LONG-TAILED DUCK. 4. COMMON EIDER. 5. VELVET SCOTER
6. COMMON SCOTER. 7. GOOSANDER. 8. SMEW. 9. RED-BREASTED MERGANSER.

PLATE 126

1. POMARINE SKUA (*left, ad. pale, middle, juv., right, ad. dark*). 2. ARCTIC SKUA (*left, ad. dark, middle, juv., right, ad. pale*). 3. GREAT SKUA. 4. LONG-TAILED SKUA (*upper, juv., lower, ad.*).

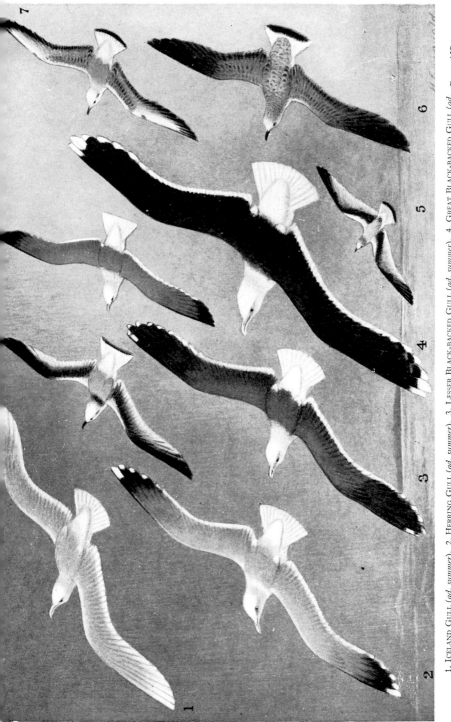

1. ICELAND GULL (ad. summer). 2. HERRING GULL (ad. summer). 3. LESSER BLACK-BACKED GULL (ad. summer). 4. GREAT BLACK-BACKED GULL (ad. summer). 5. LITTLE GULL (1st winter). 6. COMMON GULL (1st winter). 7. BLACK-HEADED GULL (1st winter). 8, 9. KITTIWAKE (ad. summer, 1st winter). PLATE 127

PLATE 128. Marsh terns in non-breeding plumages: top row, White-winged Black Tern (*Chlidonias leucopterus*); centre row, Black Tern (*Ch. niger*); bottom row, Whiskered Tern (*Ch. hybridus*). The three left-hand birds are juveniles, the rest adults in winter. Note the presence or absence of shoulder marks, the larger size and *Sterna*-like appearance of *hybrida*, and the white rump and dark "saddle" of the young *leucopterus*.

CUCKOO—*Cuculus canorus*

BIRD PLATE 70   EGG PLATE XIII

The upper-parts and breast are blue-grey, the rest of the under-parts whitish with dark bars; the tail is rather long. It is chiefly seen on the wing, when its *general appearance is superficially not unlike male Sparrowhawk, though the pointed wings and graduated tail with feathers marked and tipped with white* at once distinguish it. *Its note is distinctive*. The sexes are practically alike. Juvenile has upper-parts either grey-brown, little marked, or reddish-brown strongly barred; the under-parts in both types are buffish-white barred black, and there is a white patch on the nape. A rare colour phase of adult female is much like the rufous type of juvenile, but richer chestnut. Length about 13 ins.

Habitat. In the breeding-season it frequents a variety of country, from open woodland, thickets, and well-timbered cultivated districts to treeless sand-dunes, moors, and hill-country.

General Habits. On the ground it proceeds with a waddling gait or succession of awkward hops. It perches in trees, but also on bushes, walls, posts, rocks, etc., often alighting in rather clumsy fashion, steadying itself with wings and elevating tail. Flight is direct, hurried, with wings moving rapidly, and often with a long glide on extended wings before settling.

The song of male is the familiar "coocoo", with variants, uttered from any sort of perch or on the wing; sometimes at night. It is heard regularly in April, May and most of June, exceptionally in the first half of July. Female has an entirely different, water-bubbling chuckle, and there are other notes.

Food is chiefly insects. Centipedes, spiders, and worms are also recorded, and an egg from fosterer's nest is usually removed and eaten.

Nesting. It is parasitic on other species especially Meadow Pipit, Dunnock, Reed Warbler, Pied Wagtail, Robin, and Sedge Warbler, but over 50 species have been recorded. Each hen confines herself to a limited locality and shows a decided preference for some particular fosterer whose nests are found by watching the birds in the process of building. In many cases the Cuckoo's egg is laid on the same day on which the fosterer also lays, the Cuckoo removing one of the fosterer's eggs in her bill before laying her own directly into the nest. Up to 15–25 eggs are laid in a season commencing generally in the second half of May. They tend to resemble the fosterer's egg, ranging in ground-colour from bluish, greenish, reddish or grey to brownish, more or less speckled, spotted, or blotched with varying shades of darker brown and greys, small black spots frequently being present. Incubation is for about 12½ days; the young Cuckoo thus hatches out in some cases before the fosterer's eggs, and it ejects the eggs or newly hatched young one by one over the side of the nest. It flies when about 20–23 days old.

Status and Distribution. A summer-visitor, arriving from the end of March, or more usually in April, and continuing until late May. Adults leave in July and August, juveniles in August and September. It is generally distributed throughout the British Isles except in Orkney and Shetland where it breeds only irregularly. Abroad the race concerned, *Cuculus canorus canorus*, breeds from N. Scandinavia south to the Pyrenees and Balkan peninsula, and east into W. Asia. Other races occur in N.W. Africa, Spain and Portugal, and across most of Asia to Japan. Our birds winter in central and S. Africa.

YELLOW-BILLED CUCKOO—*Coccyzus americanus*

BIRD PLATE 70

Yellow-billed Cuckoo is a slim, dove-like bird with long tail, brown above and powdery white below. It is distinguished from the even rarer Black-billed Cuckoo (*Coccyzus erythropthalmus*) by *rufous on the flight-feathers*, which may often be seen in the field, *black tail feathers with large conspicuous white marks at tips*, and yellow of the lower mandible visible at close range. Length about 11 ins.

Habitat. In the breeding-season it frequents wood-borders, thickets, bushy roadsides, orchards, or cultivated grounds.

General Habits. A graceful and elegant, but secretive bird, slipping quietly and rather furtively through foliage and flying easily from tree to tree, moving in characteristic loping fashion. It keeps for the most part under protection of leaves, and frequently feeds on or near the ground.

It is mainly silent outside the nesting season.

Food is chiefly insects, and some fruit.

Status and Distribution. A rare vagrant, recorded only in autumn, and chiefly October, mainly from S.W. England and Wales between Hants and Cardigan. There are also records from several parts of Scotland and Ireland. The race concerned, *Coccyzus americanus americanus*, breeds in eastern N. America and winters in S. America. Other races occur in western N. America and S. America.

BARN OWL—*Tyto alba*

BIRD PLATE 71   EGG PLATE XVII (8)

Chiefly seen on the wing as a ghostly whitish form in the dusk, but also not rarely in daylight on winter afternoons or when it is feeding young; at such times its *pale appearance, with orange-buff upper-parts, pure white face and under-parts*, equally attract the eye, as it quarters the ground with buoyant, wavering flight and perhaps pounces down to seize a mouse or vole. The orange-buff upper-parts are finely mottled and spotted with grey and white; the grey is more pronounced in female. Sometimes there are a few fine spots on under-parts, especially in female. Length about 13½ ins.

Habitat. It is the most closely associated with man of the British-breeding owls, haunting the vicinity of farms, ruins and old buildings, and even occurs sometimes in towns, though also in localities with old timber not necessarily near human habitations, and sometimes remote cliffs and crags. It hunts chiefly over fields and open country.

General Habits. When perched the attitude is upright with long legs rather noticeable. It roosts during the day in ruins, church-towers, barns, dovecotes, clefts in cliffs, hollow trees, etc. Prey is taken chiefly from the ground, but it will also capture birds at roost, and it appears to have regular hunting beats; it also has regular "stations" at which prey is eaten or deposited.

The ordinary note is an eerie, long-drawn shriek, often uttered in flight. Both old and young make a hissing and loud snoring noise, and there are other calls.

Food is chiefly small rodents and not infrequently small birds; sometimes insects, frogs and fish.

Nests generally in ruins or unoccupied buildings, also in church-towers, hollow trees, and crevices in cliffs, both inland and on the coast, old nests of Jackdaws, etc. The white eggs, usually 4–7, but 3–11 recorded, are laid without nesting materials generally in April or early May, but it has occasionally been found breeding as early as February and as late as December. Incubation is by hen alone, for about 32–34 days. The young are fed by both parents and fly when about 64–86 days old.

Status and Distribution. A resident, generally distributed in the British Isles but not abundant. It breeds very rarely, if at all, in Caithness, N.W. Scotland, the Highlands, and is virtually unknown in Orkney, Shetland, and Outer Hebrides. The race concerned, *Tyto alba alba*, breeds also in W. Europe, Azores,

Canaries, N. Africa east to Egypt, and S.W. Asia. It is replaced from E. France north to S. Sweden and Poland, and south to Jugoslavia and Bulgaria, by the race *Tyto alba guttata* which has occurred here as a vagrant or irregular migrant mainly on the S.E. and E. coasts; this is normally a noticeably darker bird than ours, with upper-parts much more grey, and under-parts buff, more or less strongly spotted. Other races occur elsewhere in Africa, Asia, America and Australasia.

SCOPS OWL—*Otus scops*

BIRD PLATE 72

It proclaims its presence by a *persistent call*. It is much smaller than other owls with *ear-tufts*, while even when the latter are (as often) inconspicuous, the *delicately vermiculated pattern of greyish-brown plumage and much slimmer build* at once distinguish it from the plump, broad-headed Little Owl. The facial discs of Scops are rather longer than they are broad, giving the bird a questioning look in contrast to the flat-browed, frowning expression caused by the broad discs of Little Owl. Length about 7½ ins.

Habitat. It frequents open woods, parkland, gardens, etc., with a liking for avenues and roadside trees. It sometimes also haunts ruins, etc.

General Habits. It perches in an upright attitude, roosting by day on a branch of a tree, usually close up against the stem, where it is often very difficult to see even when not much concealed; or in bushes, creepers, etc. When aware of being observed it straightens itself up still more and assumes an attenuated appearance. Flight has the silent wavering action of the typical owls, and lacks the characteristic bounding undulations of Little Owl. It is mainly nocturnal, although sometimes seen abroad by day.

The best-known and characteristic note is the song, a low, short, musical, whistling "kiu" repeated with monotonous persistence for long stretches, with intervals of generally about 2 seconds (sometimes more) between each note; it is chiefly heard from dusk through the night, but occasionally by day.

Food is chiefly insects.

Status and Distribution. A rare vagrant occurring at long intervals mostly from April to June, but has been recorded in nearly every month. In England it has appeared mainly in the south and east from Hants to Yorks; it has been recorded several times in Ireland, in Scotland north to Shetland, also in Wales. The race *Otus scops scops* breeds in the Mediterranean region of Europe north to Switzerland and S. Czechoslovakia, also in N.W. Africa, Asia Minor and Syria. Other races occur in Cyprus and perhaps neighbouring islands, also S. Russia and W. Siberia. It winters in tropical Africa.

EAGLE OWL—*Bubo bubo*

BIRD PLATE 71

Its large size and long conspicuous ear-tufts distinguish it from all other owls on the British list. The upper-parts are mottled blackish and tawny, wings and tail barred; under-parts are buff with fine wavy bars, boldly streaked on the breast and more narrowly below. The facial disc is poorly marked, not developed above eye; it has a fierce expression. Orange eyes. Length about 25–28 ins., female larger than male.

Habitat. It frequents extensive forests or the vicinity of cliffs, crags, ravines, and rocky ground in both wooded or wild open country; locally even extensive reed-beds.

General Habits. It has an upright attitude. When perched on the bough of a tree it will draw itself up, with plumage tightly compressed, close to the trunk, much like Long-eared Owl; it has the usual noiseless flight of owls, slow and wavering, and generally low down, but in the evening sometimes rising high in the air. It hunts by preference in the dusk, but does not mind daylight.

Calls are extremely varied, but chiefly a feeble "oo-oo-*oo*", and a strident "kveck, kveck".

Food records include mammals from mice up to roe-deer in size, many species of birds from Capercaillie downwards, also reptiles, fish and large beetles.

Status and Distribution. A very rare vagrant, with records from Devon to Shetland, but most regarded as suspect and introduced birds have bred recently. The race concerned, *Bubo bubo bubo*, breeds in Europe from about the Arctic circle south to the Pyrenees, Sicily and Greece. Other races occur in Spain and Portugal, N. Africa, S.E. Russia and Asia.

SNOWY OWL—*Nyctea scandiaca*

BIRD PLATE 71

A very large white owl with plumage more or less barred brown.
The adult male is white or creamy, sometimes almost unmarked
even on the upper-parts; female is more strikingly barred and
spotted except on face, throat and to a variable extent on under-
parts. The eyes are yellow, not black as in Barn Owl. The flight
action is distinctive even at a great distance. It frequents exclusively open country, and is largely diurnal. Length about 21–24 ins.;
female considerably larger than male.

Habitat. In its wanderings in winter southward from the Arctic
it frequents open tracts, such as moors, coastal flats, marshes, etc.

General Habits. Flight is more suggestive of a diurnal bird of
prey, such as a buzzard, than a typical owl but it has a jerky,
swaying action with quick upstroke and slow downstroke of
the deep-beating wings; at times rapid and it will kill birds on the
wing, striking them down like a falcon. When quartering the
ground for mammals it often hovers for a few seconds. It usually
alights on the ground or a rock, sometimes a post or stump and
occasionally on trees. It often sits down, resting on breast, or
stands with body slanting forward at an angle of about 45°. Usually
rather shy and not readily approached.

It is usually a silent bird when not breeding. Shriek on the wing
resembles a loud "krow-ow", repeated three or four times; also a
wild, loud "rick, rick, rick".

SNOWY OWL

Note fingered primaries.

Food includes mammals to the size of hare, birds, insects and worms.

Status and Distribution. Bred in Shetland 1967 to 1975; otherwise a rare almost regular winter visitor, sometimes semi-resident, to Highlands and islands of Scotland. It has also often been recorded in Ireland, but only as a vagrant in England. Most occurrences fall between September and April, but there have been a few in summer. The bird breeds in N., sometimes central, Scandinavia, N. Russia, N. Asia, arctic N. America and Iceland. There are no subspecies.

LITTLE OWL—*Athene noctua*

BIRD PLATE 72   EGG PLATE XVII (10)

The small size and very compact, plump form, with flat head and short tail, and *greyish-brown plumage, spotted, barred, and mottled with whitish, are distinctive.* Flight is characteristic, usually low down, with a *bounding action recalling woodpeckers*, though the rounded wing and general appearance proclaim it an owl, but when hunting in dusk the flight is often much more direct. The under-parts are whitish with dark markings forming streaks. The outline of the facial discs is flattened above the eye, giving a frowning expression. It is frequently abroad by day. Length about 8½–9 ins.

Habitat. It frequents mostly more or less open, especially agricultural, country, where hedgerow or other old timber, pollard willows, orchards, or farm out-buildings provide breeding-sites, but also treeless sand-dunes, islands, and rocky localities, as well as wood-borders and vicinity of quarries, ruins, and even occupied buildings.

General Habits. It perches with erect attitude on branches, hedges, walls, posts, telegraph-wires, etc., as well as on rocks or ground. A characteristic action when suspicious or agitated is a comical bobbing, the bird bowing down and straightening itself up again in rapid alternation. It hunts chiefly at dusk and early morning. Holes in trees, the ground, etc., are sometimes used for dismembering larger prey, forming so-called "larders", and at times more may be accumulated than can be eaten.

The ordinary note is a monotonous, rather plaintive "kiew, kiew" with variations, and it has other less frequent calls.

Food is largely insects, also mice, rats and other mammals, Starlings, Sparrows and other small birds. Some reptiles, frogs, fish, molluscs, worms, etc., also recorded.

Nests often in holes of trees, but also in holes of walls or farm buildings, in rabbit-burrows, under wood-stacks, in quarries, and even sea-cliffs, and at times in old nests of Stock Dove, Jackdaw, etc. The white eggs, usually 3–5, but 2–8 recorded, are laid generally in the latter part of April and in May. Incubation is usually by hen only, for about 28–29 days. The young are fed by both parents and fly when about 35–40 days old. One brood normally, two occasionally.

Status and Distribution. A resident, introduced in the latter part of the 19th century and now widespread in England and Wales; in Scotland breeding (first in Berwick 1958) recorded sporadically north to Forth. There have been very few occurrences in Ireland. The race concerned, *Athene noctua vidalii*, breeds in W. Europe from Holland to Portugal. Other races occur elsewhere in Europe south of the Baltic, in N. Africa and across Asia to China.

TAWNY OWL—*Strix aluco*

BIRD PLATE 73   EGG PLATE XVII (9)

Tawny Owl is one of the most thoroughly nocturnal species. If disturbed during day-time or seen on the wing in dusk it appears as a *moderately large mottled brown bird with disproportionately large head, broad rounded wings*, and typical owl flight. At rest the *black eyes*, absence of ear tufts, and more portly form distinguish it from the smaller Long-eared Owl. Upper-parts are generally rufous-brown mottled and streaked dark brown, with whitish patches on the scapulars and wing-coverts; under-parts are buff, broadly streaked and faintly barred dark brown; wings and tail barred. A greyer phase is rare in Britain. The facial discs are greyish-brown, well-developed. Length about 15 ins.

Habitat. It inhabits woods, copses, well-timbered old gardens, parks or farm-land; and is sometimes frequent in quite thickly populated suburban localities. More rarely it haunts open country where old buildings, ruins, crags or isolated hollow trees afford shelter.

General Habits. It perches chiefly on branches of trees, and roosts in hollow trees or on a branch, close up against the trunk where foliage affords cover, or amongst ivy; more rarely in barns, ruins, rocks, etc. It seldom emerges before dusk, and usually hunts in or near woods or well-timbered places, but at times far from trees. Prey is taken largely from the ground. It is bold in defence of nest and will sometimes stoop at and strike the head of an intruder.

Most owls have a variety of calls, but one or more having the character of songs, consisting of either one note or a simple combination of notes. The mellow and musical "song" (the well-known, so-called "hoot") of the Tawny Owl consists typically of a prolonged, more or less distinctly di- or trisyllabic "hoo-hoo" or "hoo-hoo-hoo" followed by a long pause then a faint low "oo", a brief pause, and finally a long-drawn, quavering "hoooooooooo"; not ordinarily uttered before dusk. It is heard regularly from mid-January to June, less frequently from mid-December until the latter part of July, also in late September and October, and exceptionally during the rest of the year. The call-note most often heard is a sharp "kewick".

Food includes mammals (especially vole, mouse, rat, mole, shrew and rabbit), birds (principally Starlings and Sparrows), also fish, frogs, molluscs, worms and insects.

Nests in holes of trees, on squirrel's dreys, old nests of other birds, and occasionally in barns, on ledges of rocks, and at times on the ground. The white eggs, normally 2–4, sometimes 1–7, are laid generally, without the addition of nesting material, in March or early April. Incubation is by hen only, for about 28–30 days. The male provides much of the food for the young which fly when about 30–37 days old, but which remain dependent on their parents for a further 2½–3 months. Single-brooded.

Status and Distribution. A resident, generally distributed in Great Britain but uncommon in the west and rare in N. Sutherland. It is unknown in the Outer Hebrides except Stornoway and does not occur in Orkney, Shetland, Isle of Man or Ireland. The race *Strix aluco sylvatica* is apparently confined to Great Britain. Other races occur from central Scandinavia south to N.W. Africa and Asia Minor and east to W. Siberia and the Himalayas.

LONG-EARED OWL—*Asio otus*

BIRD PLATE 73   EGG PLATE XVII (6)

Owing to its nocturnal habits it is seldom seen by day, unless encountered by chance as it stands with much attenuated body, close to the trunk of a tree. *Its smaller size, prominent ear-tufts, and yellow iris* distinguish it from Tawny Owl. In flight it looks *greyer*, less tawny, than Short-eared Owl, and the wings appear less long, being broader and more rounded, but both wings and tail are longer than in Tawny Owl, though the ear-tufts are then laid flat and usually invisible. Upper-parts are mottled and vermiculated greyish-buff and dark brown; under-parts buff broadly streaked dark brown, with wavy transverse barrings visible at close quarters. Length about 13½ ins.

Habitat. It is essentially a tree-haunting species. It prefers conifer woods and plantations especially of spruce and pine (but quite small clumps and belts suffice), but it occurs regularly in non-coniferous woods and copses, also nests in thorn-thickets in old Magpie's nests. It hunts over open country as well as in woods, and in some districts breeds on open heaths, dunes, or marshes.

General Habits. It perches in trees, roosting amongst thick foliage of conifers or other evergreens, usually close to the trunk, but may also at times be flushed from the ground. On the wing it has the usual silent wavering action of owls. Usually seen singly, but in winter, as well as on migration, not rarely occurs in little parties in favourable localities.

The principal and most characteristic note is the song, a long-drawn, low "oo, oo, oo . . .", a cooing moan rather than a hoot, with notes spaced at regular intervals of about one every third second, heard mainly in early spring. The food-call of young in early June, a whining metallic "zeen" like a swinging rusty iron gate, very high pitched and far-carrying, is often first indication of presence of breeding birds.

Food consists of small mammals, birds, and insects.

Nests in old squirrels' dreys, old nests of Magpie, Crow, etc.; also, but less frequently, on the ground at foot of a tree in woods, or in heather in open country. The white eggs, usually 4–5, but sometimes 3 to 7 or 8, are laid generally in March or early April, sometimes earlier. Incubation is apparently by hen only, for about 27–28 days. The young leave the nest when about 23 days old. Normally single-brooded.

Status and Distribution. A resident, widely distributed in Great Britain in wooded localities but becoming scarcer and local in much of England and Wales. Breeds some years in Shetland, and is rare in the Outer Hebrides. In Ireland it is the commonest owl. It also occurs as a passage-migrant on the east coast of Great Britain and in the northern isles. The race concerned, *Asio otus otus*, breeds from arctic Scandinavia south to N.W. Africa and the Azores and east to Japan. Other races occur in the Canaries, Ethiopia and N. America.

SHORT-EARED OWL—*Asio flammeus*

BIRD PLATE 73   EGG PLATE XVII (5)

Its terrestrial and largely diurnal habits, long wings, and regular occurrence in open country distinguish Short-eared from other owls. The wings in flight look conspicuously long in proportion to the size of the bird, and suggest those of some diurnal bird of prey in combination with head and body of an owl. The ear-tufts are hardly discernible even at close range. Upper-parts are richly marbled with buffs and dark brown; wings and tail barred; in general effect is paler and more tawny than Long-eared Owl and more blotched than streaked. Under-parts are buff, broadly streaked dark brown without trace of transverse barrings. The facial disc is well defined, but darker round eyes. Length about 14½–15 ins.

Habitat. It inhabits open country: moors, fells, bogs, marshes, heaths, and sand-dunes. In winter it is also often flushed from root-fields, stubble, etc.

General Habits. It ordinarily settles on the ground, but will sometimes perch on trees; also on bushes, fences, stumps, etc. Normal carriage is less upright, with body more slanting, than in most owls. Flight is slow, noiseless, and when hunting is usually wavering and rolling, and low down, but at other times more direct

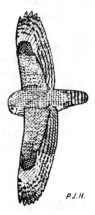

P.J.H.

SHORT-EARED OWL

In flight shows dark carpal patches on upper and underwing.

and sometimes at a great height. Frequent gliding and wheeling on rigid wings heightens the resemblance to a diurnal bird of prey. Although hunting chiefly at or towards dusk, it is often abroad in full daylight. It is slightly gregarious, but during vole "plagues" remarkable numbers may assemble in affected areas, and parties may be observed at migration times. The bulk of its prey is taken on the ground, but it will capture birds on the wing.

It is generally silent, but when nest is threatened it utters a hoarse, barking "kwowk" and raucous, nasal noises. Its song is a low-pitched, hollow "boo-boo-boo-boo . . .".

Food consists mainly of small mammals (principally field-voles), also small birds and some insects.

Nests on the ground among heather, in rank grass, sedge, or gorse. The dull white eggs, normally 4–8, sometimes 3 to 13 or 14, are laid generally in late April or the beginning of May, sometimes earlier, in a roughly-lined scrape. Incubation is by female alone for about 24–28 days. The young are fed by female on food provided by male; they leave the nest at about 12–17 days but are unable to fly till about 24–27 days old. Normally one brood, but two reared in vole years.

Status and Distribution. A resident, also a winter-visitor from about September to mid-May. In England and Wales it nests occasionally in many counties, while a few pairs now nest regularly in coastal areas of N. Kent, Essex, Suffolk, also Breckland, (almost annual Norfolk), and in several counties in central and N. Wales. Northwards from mid-Lancs and mid-Yorks and throughout Scotland it nests locally and sparingly in most counties, but not Lewis and Harris or Shetland although regularly in Orkney. In Ireland it has nested in Galway. As a winter-visitor it is fairly generally distributed, and both as breeder and migrant numbers fluctuate considerably, and are greatly augmented at times of vole-plague. The race concerned, *Asio flammeus flammeus*, breeds also in Iceland, and from arctic Europe and Asia south to France, Sicily, Macedonia, Afghanistan; also in parts of N. and S. America. Another race occurs in Hawaii.

TENGMALM'S OWL—*Aegolius funereus*

BIRD PLATE 72

It is only slightly larger than Little Owl, though the browns are rather warmer, more chocolate, and the light parts nearly pure white; but the *very large rounded head*, with better defined *facial discs not depressed over the eyes* as in Little Owl, give it a quite different appearance, more like a miniature Tawny Owl so far as shape is concerned, but the head is relatively even bigger. *Legs and toes are clothed in long white feathers to the tips of the latter*, while the toes of Little Owl are merely bristly, and the crown is closely sprinkled with white spots instead of streaked as in Little Owl. Under-parts tend to be less definitely streaked than in most Little Owls, and are more mottled. Juveniles are chocolate-brown both above and below with only a few white markings. Length about 10 ins.

Habitat. It chiefly haunts coniferous or predominantly coniferous woodland.

General Habits. In central Europe it is almost exclusively nocturnal, roosting by day well concealed in the thick crown of conifers and nearly impossible to see. Flight is not like Little Owl and is more like that of Long-eared Owl but with quicker wing-beats.

The song is a single soft liquid and rather musical note repeated 3–5 times, in quality somewhat recalling Hoopoe's. Other notes are rarely heard.

Food is chiefly small mammals, also a few birds and beetles.

Status and Distribution. A rare vagrant, appearing chiefly between October and February. It has occurred mainly in the N.E. and E. coastal counties of England, but once or twice south to Kent and west to Salop. There are also a few records for Scotland. The race concerned, *Aegolius funereus funereus*, breeds from N. Scandinavia south to mountain ranges from France to Bulgaria and parts of Russia. Other races occur in S. Russia, W. Siberia, temperate Asia and N. America.

NIGHTJAR—*Caprimulgus europaeus*

BIRD PLATE 74   EGG PLATE V (16A & 16B)

It is crepuscular in habits. When seen in the dusk, *the shape and flight* are sufficient to distinguish it from any other night-flying bird: it has *rather long wings and tail; the flight is easy, silent and wheeling* with sudden twists and zigzags in pursuit of insects, the wing-beats deliberate, varied by gliding and floating on extended wings. Its churring song often directs attention to the bird's presence. In daytime it is usually quiescent, resting, with eyes

NIGHTJAR
male

nearly closed, on the ground amongst scanty vegetation, or on a fallen log or low horizontal branch of a tree. The broad flat head, very small bill (but enormous gape) and large eyes are characteristic. The general colouring is remarkably protective on the ground, being grey-brown, pleasingly and delicately mottled, spotted, streaked and barred with dark brown and pale to rufous buff. *Male has white spots on the three outer primaries, and the outer tail-feathers are broadly tipped white*, conspicuous in flight; female and young lack these markings. Length about 10½ ins.

Habitat. In the breeding-season it inhabits woodland and wood-borders, commons, hillsides, moors, sand-dunes and other open wastes, with cover of bracken, heather, gorse, or bushes.

General Habits. It normally perches lengthways on branches, resting on the breast, also with body more slanting, on bush, stump, or (especially when "churring") on the tip of a young conifer, etc., or on outer twigs near the top of a larger tree. It sometimes hovers if taking food from the ground, as well as under other conditions. During the breeding-season the wings are clapped during flight in display, also apparently as a call. It migrates in flocks, but is not otherwise gregarious.

Common flight-call of male is "coo-*ic*". The song is a sustained, vibrant, churring trill, like an excessively rapid but slightly muffled tapping, continuing for occasionally as much as 5 minutes on end without variation except for a rhythmical rise and fall. It is heard regularly from the first half of May to the second half of July, and less frequently into the second half of August.

Food consists of insects taken chiefly on the wing.

Nests on bare ground often close to bits of dead wood. The eggs, normally 2, are laid generally in late May and early June in a scrape without nesting material. Incubation is by both sexes for about 17–18 days. The young are fed by both parents and fly when about 16–18 days old. Double-brooded.

Status and Distribution. A summer-visitor, arriving between the end of April and the end of May and leaving from mid-August to late September. Formerly it was generally distributed in suitable localities in Britain and Ireland; however, with widespread decreases extending over the past fifty years many previous haunts have been abandoned, and few or none remain in, for example, Essex, Cambridge, Oxford, and several Welsh counties; in Scotland it is now perhaps restricted to the Clyde/Solway area, and a vagrant in the north. Abroad the race concerned, *Caprimulgus europaeus europaeus*, breeds from Scandinavia south to France and apparently Asia Minor. Other races occur in N.W. Africa, S. Europe and parts of W. and central Asia. It winters in Africa south to the Cape.

SWIFT—*Apus apus*

BIRD PLATE 74   EGG PLATE XVII (13)

Swifts can only be confused with members of the swallow family, from which the very *long and narrow scythe-like wings*, short tail and, in the case of the present species, the *uniform sooty-brown plumage at once distinguish* them. The tail is moderately forked; the throat whitish. Juveniles have more white on the throat and a narrow white border to wing-feathers. Length about 6½ ins.

Habitat. An exclusively aerial species which may be seen at times over every sort of country from lowlands to the tops of our highest mountains, but local abundance in the breeding-season is mainly dependent on the proximity of suitable breeding-places; hence it occurs chiefly in well-populated areas with substantial buildings. However, even at mid-summer some tend to move south to avoid depressions when the number of air-borne insects is greatly reduced, and large numbers of Swifts may travel long distances, including over the sea, in such temporary weather movements.

General Habits. Flight is very rapid and highly characteristic, only that of the swallow family being at all like it; it wheels and dashes through the air with frequent changes of direction, and a succession of rapid wing-beats alternating with long glides on extended wings, never with wings partially closed like swallows. It is pre-eminently aerial and does not voluntarily settle on the ground, the short legs being only adapted for clinging to rocks, masonry, etc. At times it courses low over pastures or sheets of water, at others it hawks for food high overhead, and on fine summer evenings flocks sometimes mount in circles to a great elevation till lost to view.

Ordinary note is a long-drawn harsh screaming "sweer" or "sweeree", which may be heard throughout the bird's stay in this country. On passage however it is usually silent.

Food consists of insects taken on the wing.

Nests generally in colonies, in crevices under eaves of houses or in holes of thatch, and occasionally in natural fissures in cliff faces, old nests of House Martins, and nest-boxes. The white eggs, 2–3, occasionally 4, are laid at the end of May or early June in a nest composed of bits of straw or grass, seeds of trees, feathers, etc., picked up floating in the air and agglutinated with saliva to form a low cup. Incubation is by both sexes, for about 18–20 days, sometimes longer. The young are fed by both parents and fly usually when about 6 weeks old, but the period may vary from 35 to 56 days. Single-brooded.

Status and Distribution. A summer-visitor arriving in late April and in May, with passage continuing into June. The return movement, commencing in early July, is virtually over by the end of August although stragglers occur in September and sometimes October. The bird is generally distributed in the British Isles, but few breed in N.W. Scotland, and none in Outer Hebrides, Orkney or Shetland, although occurring there fairly regularly on passage. Abroad *Apus apus apus* breeds from arctic Europe and Siberia, south to the Mediterranean and N.W. Africa, and east to Transcaucasia; it winters in S. Africa. Another race occurs from Asia Minor to Manchuria.

ALPINE SWIFT—*Apus melba*

BIRD PLATE 74

It is larger than Swift and easily distinguished by the *paler brown upper-parts and white belly*, both of which are readily seen at a long distance as the bird turns in the air. It has a brown breast-band. Length about 8¼ ins.

Habitat. An exclusively aerial species, occurring in the breeding-season chiefly in mountains, but also about cliffs and high crags from sea-level, as well as buildings and old walls.

General Habits. In flight and general habits it much resembles Swift.

Birds on migration are silent.

Food consists of insects taken on the wing.

Status and Distribution. A vagrant, noted annually in recent years, which has occurred in various parts of England, but chiefly in the southern half between April and October. There are also several records from Ireland, Scotland and Wales. The race concerned, *Apus melba melba*, breeds in N. Morocco and Europe north to S. Germany. Other races occur elsewhere in Africa, and parts of Asia.

KINGFISHER—*Alcedo atthis*

BIRD PLATE 75   EGG PLATE XVII (17)

It is unique amongst our native birds in the brilliance of its coloration, while the *stumpy, short-tailed build and long dagger-shaped beak* are equally unlike any other British species. *The upper-parts are dazzling cobalt-blue* or emerald-green according to the incidence of the light; the under-parts, chiefly noticeable when the bird is stationary, are warm chestnut; the feet sealing-wax red. Its shape and flight, the latter astonishingly swift, with rapidly whirring wings, are equally characteristic, even if colours are not evident. The cheeks are chestnut, the throat and patch on sides of neck white. The sexes are similar. Juveniles resemble adults, merely a little duller. Length about 6½ ins.; bill about 1½–1¾ ins.

Habitat. It haunts fresh waters of all kinds, streams, canals, lakes, fen-drains; also, particularly in winter, tidal estuaries, gutters on salt-marshes, and rocky sea-shores.

General Habits. It perches on a branch or root overhanging water or on a post, rock, etc., watching for fish or aquatic insects and crustaceans, which are captured by a sudden plunge. It also hovers over water. Larger fish are beaten on a branch or other perch before swallowing. Though usually flying low over water, it will sometimes rise to a fair height over land or in courtship chases.

Usual note is a loud shrill "chee" or "chi-kee", two or three times repeated or in longer, more rapid sequence if excited. The song, which is infrequent, but heard mainly from mid-February to mid-April, more rarely from January to early June and again from late August to early October, consists of trilling whistles, sweet and varied, and sometimes a rich warble.

Food is mainly small fish; also insects, tadpoles, small molluscs and crustacea.

Nests generally in the steep banks of slow-flowing streams, but also at times in sand-pits or banks at a considerable distance from water. The glossy white eggs, normally 6–7, sometimes 4–10, are laid generally from late April or early May onwards in a circular chamber without nesting material at the end of a slightly rising tunnel of about 1½–3 feet in length, bored by both sexes. Incubation is by both sexes for about 19–21 days. The young are fed by both parents and fly when about 23–27 days old. Double-brooded: sometimes in the same hole.

Status and Distribution. A resident, widely but thinly distributed in England and Wales on slow-flowing streams, often moving to coasts in autumn and severe weather. A few pairs breed regularly in S.W. Scotland, and sporadically north to S. Argyll, Aberdeen, E. Ross. The bird is almost unknown in Orkney, Shetland and Outer Hebrides. In Ireland it is rather local but breeds in every county. Abroad this race, *Alcedo atthis ispida*, breeds from mid-Sweden south to Spain, N. Italy and Roumania. Other races occur in N.W. Africa, S.E. Europe, and over much of Asia.

BEE-EATER—*Merops apiaster*

Bird Plate 75

In flight the characteristic outline, with *pointed wings and central tail-feathers projecting considerably beyond the rest, a rather Swallow-like action and constantly used note* afford ready

BEE-EATER

means of identification, though the colours are inconspicuous except in favourable lights. When perched its *upright carriage, pointed tail and long bill* are distinctive. The main features of the colour-scheme are: upper-parts chestnut, shading to more golden on lower back, throat bright yellow, rest of under-parts greenish-blue. Fore-head is whitish; lores, ear-coverts and band below the throat are black; wings blue-green and brown with chestnut on coverts; tail greenish-brown. The sexes are similar; young resemble adults, but are rather duller, with central tail-feathers scarcely projecting. Length about 11 ins., bill about 1½ ins.

Habitat. In the breeding-season it frequents chiefly plains and the neighbourhood of rivers, where there are enough trees, telegraph-wires, etc., to afford perches.

General Habits. Direct flight is slightly undulating, usually with a succession of quick wing-beats alternating with momentary closure of the wings. When hawking for insects it has an easy and graceful wheeling action, in which more or less brief periods of rapid wing movement alternate regularly with intervals of sailing round on rigid wings. It is gregarious at all seasons.

Note, constantly employed at all seasons, is a cheerful if rather monotonous "cruuk, cruuk" of liquid, yet somewhat croaking, quality.

Food consists of insects taken on the wing.

Nests usually in colonies, both sexes burrowing a tunnel from 3 to 9 feet into perpendicular banks of streams, cuttings by road-sides, sandpits, etc., or in almost flat ground. The glossy white eggs, usually 4–7 and sometimes more, are laid generally from mid-May to early June in a circular chamber without nesting material. Incubation is by both sexes for about 20 days, and both parents feed the young, which fly when about 20–25 days old. Single-brooded.

Status and Distribution. A vagrant, which occurs annually and sometimes in small parties, chiefly in May and June, occasionally in April and in autumn. A pair attempted to nest near Edinburgh in 1920, and 3 pairs bred in a sand-pit in Sussex in 1955. In England it has been recorded in all the east and south coast counties, but more thinly elsewhere; there are several records for Scotland, Ireland and Wales. The bird breeds from N.W. Africa and S.W. Europe north to N. Italy and Czechoslovakia, and east to Kashmir. It winters in Africa south to the Cape, and in S. Arabia. There are no subspecies.

ROLLER—*Coracias garrulus*

Bird Plate 75

Its general appearance suggests a Jay or corvine bird, but the *mainly greenish-blue plumage and chestnut back* are distinctive even when settled; the appearance is then less striking, however, than in flight, when effect of the *brilliant turquoise blue of the wings*, largely hidden when at rest, contrasted with the chestnut mantle and black quills is most beautiful. The sexes are similar; the young rather duller. Length about 12 ins.

Habitat. In the breeding-season it generally frequents well-wooded country with old trees, deciduous or conifer.

General Habits. It not infrequently settles on the ground, where it hops heavily. Ordinary flight is easy and buoyant with uniform, fairly rapid wing-action, which has been compared to that of pigeon, though the outline is quite different, and more corvine; it occasionally glides a short distance. It perches in exposed situations such as a bough of a tree, an old building, telegraph-wire, or even a bush or eminence on the ground, watching for insects, somewhat like a shrike.

Usual cry is a loud, harsh "rack-kack, kacker", etc., with rapidly repeated variants.

Food is largely insects taken on the ground.

Status and Distribution. A vagrant, recorded chiefly in May–July and September–October on the east coast of England from

Suffolk to Northumberland, fairly often on the south coast and at rare intervals elsewhere in England and Wales. In Scotland a few have occurred in most parts except the N.W. mainland, and there are about a dozen Irish records. The race concerned, *Coracias garrulus garrulus*, breeds in N.W. Africa, S. Europe north to S. France, Germany and Baltic States, and east into W. Asia; it winters in tropical and S. Africa. Another race occurs from E. Palestine to India.

HOOPOE—*Upupa epops*

BIRD PLATE 76   EGG PLATE V (11)

When settled, *the long curved bill, striking crest and pinkish-brown plumage, with boldly barred wings and lower back*, are unmistakable. In flight the *rounded wings barred black and white, and desultory, butterfly-like wing action* are equally distinctive: the wings are apparently almost closed at each beat. The tail is black, white at base; the crest feathers tipped black. The sexes are similar; young rather duller, with much shorter bills. Length about 11–11½ ins.; bill 2–2½ ins.

Habitat. In the breeding-season it frequents chiefly places with scattered old trees; wood-borders (deciduous or mixed), especially with fields and pastures adjacent, parklands, willow-fringed streams and bushy places, orchards, and cultivation. Often occurs near buildings.

General Habits. It feeds mainly on the ground, especially on lawns and paths or, alternatively, on refuse-heaps. The crest is depressed when at rest, but erected when excited or alarmed and for a moment on settling. It perches in trees, as well as on buildings, walls, etc., and is fond of dust- and sand-baths.

P.J.H.

HOOPOE

Ordinary note in the breeding-season is a low, soft "hoop-hoop-hoop", with considerable carrying power.

Food is chiefly larvae of insects.

Nests frequently in holes in trees at varying heights; also in loose stone-walls, heaps of stones and crevices in buildings. The whitish-grey or yellowish-olive eggs, normally 5–8, but up to 12 recorded, are laid generally in May or June in a nest sometimes containing rags, straws, feathers, etc., but normally with no nesting material. Incubation is by hen alone, for about 18 days. The young are fed by both parents and fly when about 20–27 days old.

Status and Distribution. Mainly a passage-migrant. It is regular in small numbers end March to May, but less frequent in autumn, in south coast counties of England, where a pair or two nest some years. North of the Thames it nests rarely, but occurs frequently on the east coast to Norfolk. Otherwise in England, Wales and Scotland it is a vagrant which has appeared at all times of year but more often in autumn in the north. In Ireland it is an annual passage-migrant in spring and autumn on the south coast, but a vagrant elsewhere. Abroad *Upupa epops epops* breeds from Baltic States and S.W. Siberia south to N.W. Africa and N. India. Other races occur in Egypt, tropical and E. Africa, S. and E. Asia. European birds winter in tropical Africa.

WRYNECK—*Jynx torquilla*

Bird Plate 76   Egg Plate XVII (7)

A rather slim, elongated-looking, grey-brown bird, with upper-parts delicately mottled, streaked and vermiculated, much like those of Nightjar, and with under-parts more barred; it looks *in the field much more like a passerine bird than a relative of the woodpeckers*. There is little difference between adults and young. It is rather secretive and elusive, easily overlooked but for note. Length about 6½ ins.

Habitat. In the breeding-season it inhabits open parkland, heaths, hedgerows, etc., with old timber; sometimes orchards, gardens, or open deciduous woods.

General Habits. Though spending much time in upper branches, it also feeds largely on the ground, moving by short hops with elevated tail, and will perch on low bushes, etc., as well as in trees. It usually perches across boughs in passerine fashion; also clings to trunks like a woodpecker, often obliquely and without assistance from the tail. It does not bore for food like woodpeckers, but picks up insects from bark, leaves, or ground by exceedingly rapid movements of the long, worm-like tongue, and occasionally flutters in the air to seize an insect. Flight is rather slow and hesitant, undulating, often looking much like a big, long-tailed warbler or similar passerine.

Usual call is a deliberate, shrill "quee-quee-quee-quee-quee . . ." decidedly suggestive of the cries of the smaller falcons or Lesser Spotted Woodpecker, but more musical than the latter. It is given regularly from early April to mid-June, less frequently to mid-July, and exceptionally into the first half of August and again in early September.

Food is chiefly insects.

Nests in a hole in a tree (frequently in an orchard), nesting box, a hole in a bank, thatch or post, or in a Sand Martin's burrow, etc. The dull white eggs, often 7–10, but 5–14 recorded, are laid generally from late May onwards on the floor of the hole without the addition of nesting material. Incubation is by both sexes, but chiefly by hen, usually for about 12 days. The young are fed by both sexes and fly when about 19–21 days old. Not infrequently double-brooded.

Status and Distribution. A summer-visitor, now sporadic, and passage-migrant in small and variable numbers. Following years of decrease it was reduced by the 1960s to a few pairs in Kent and Surrey, but now perhaps extinct as a breeding bird in England. It formerly bred north to Cumberland and west to Wales and Devon. In Scotland, however, it has summered with increasing regularity in Highlands, bred in 1969, and perhaps most years since. In Ireland there are a few records of migrants usually in autumn. It normally arrives from late March to mid-May and leaves in August or September, occasionally later. Continental birds, usually in small numbers only, occur as passage-migrants in easterly weather, mainly in autumn in late August and early September on the east coast from the N. Scottish isles south to the channel, and to a lesser extent on the S. and W. coasts. The race concerned, *Jynx torquilla torquilla*, breeds from mid-Scandinavia south to France, Switzerland, Bulgaria and east into Asia. Other races occur in and around Italy, in Algeria and E. Asia. Our birds winter in tropical Africa.

GREEN WOODPECKER—*Picus viridis*

BIRD PLATE 77   EGG PLATE XVII (14)

Woodpeckers are rather short-tailed sturdily-built birds with strong pointed bills. The general habits of the British species are all much the same. They ascend tree-trunks in a succession of jerky hops with stiff tail-feathers pressed against the trunk; occasionally descending a foot or two backwards with similar jerky movements, but never head first, though they will also move along the underside of boughs. In their search for insects on tree-trunks and branches they frequently make a loud tapping, but this is much less rapid than, and quite distinct from, the "drumming" of the spotted species. *Flight* is very characteristic, consisting of *a succession of marked undulations with wings closed to the sides for an appreciable interval every 3 or 4 beats*. None are at all gregarious. The Green Woodpecker is the largest British species; *the green plumage*, darker above and paler below, and *crimson crown* are distinctive, as is the note. The rump is bright greenish-yellow; the region round the eye black; moustachial stripe is crimson, bordered black, in male, but black in female. Juvenile has light spots and markings above, the sides of head and under-parts streaked and barred blackish. Length about 12½ ins.

Habitat. It is found regularly in open deciduous woodland, but still more in well-timbered meadow- and parkland, heaths with scattered trees, orchards, and even large gardens; it occurs much less frequently in conifer woods.

General Habits. It feeds much more on the ground than the other species, especially where there are ants' nests, and it may be met with feeding in the open far from any trees; the tail is pressed on the ground while at rest, and the carriage is rather upright. It roosts singly in holes in trees and, if necessary, special roosting holes appear to be excavated.

Ordinary cry is a loud, clear, laughing note fairly rapidly repeated, "queu-queu-queu-queu-queu . . .". Drumming occurs only exceptionally.

Food is chiefly larvae of wood-boring insects, and ants. Some seeds and fruit are also eaten.

Nest-hole is bored by both sexes into the trunk of a tree, sometimes only about a yard from the ground, but usually considerably higher. The white eggs, usually 5–7, sometimes 4–9, are laid generally from the end of April onwards, without nesting material except a few chips at the bottom of the hole. Incubation is by both sexes normally for about 15–17 days. The young are fed by both parents and fly when about 18–21 days old, but up to 28 days recorded. Single-brooded.

Status and Distribution. A resident, fairly generally distributed in England and Wales and breeding in every county. In Scotland first bred in 1951 and has since spread north to Inverness, Moray basin and has been recorded in E. and W. Ross. Absent from the Isle of Man and Ireland. Abroad the race concerned, *Picus viridis pluvius*, appears to be the form breeding in France, Belgium and Holland. Other races occur over most of Europe and in S.W. Asia.

GREAT SPOTTED WOODPECKER—*Dendrocopos major*

BIRD PLATE 77   EGG PLATE XVII (15)

It is distinguished from Green Woodpecker by *boldly pied plumage* and smaller size, and from Lesser Spotted Woodpecker by its larger size, *black back, white shoulder patches, and crimson under tail-coverts*. The sides of the face are white, separated by a black mark from white throat and white patch on side of the neck. The crown is black; with a crimson patch on nape in male, absent in female. Juveniles of both sexes have the crown crimson. Wing-quills are barred black and white; the central tail-feathers are black, the outer ones largely white with black bars. Under-parts buffish-white. Its presence is often announced by the characteristic note, or a mechanical "drumming". The latter is a loud, hard,

GREAT SPOTTED WOODPECKER

vibrating sound, produced by both sexes by an extremely rapid rain of blows with the bill, generally on a dead branch. It may be heard exceptionally from September to February, regularly from the end of February to April, and less frequently till mid-May. Length about 9 ins.

Habitat. It principally inhabits woods and copses; it also frequents hedgerow and parkland timber (but much less than Green Woodpecker), and sometimes orchards and large gardens. In the north of England and in Scotland it appears to prefer coniferous woodland, but in central and S. England is more in deciduous woods.

General Habits. In general behaviour, flight, etc., it resembles Green Woodpecker, but settles on the ground much less frequently. Pine-cones worked by Great Spotted Woodpecker are often indistinguishable from those worked by Crossbill; they are usually wedged in a crevice of bark, which may be intentionally enlarged for the purpose. Special roosting-holes may be excavated at any time of year.

Main note is an abrupt, far-carrying "tchick, tchick".

Food is mainly larvae of wood-boring insects; spiders are freely taken, and sometimes nestling birds. Nuts, seeds and berries are also taken.

Nests rarely less than 10 or 12 ft. from ground, and usually considerably higher, in a hole bored by both sexes in the bole of a tree, with an elliptical entrance 2¾ ins. high by 2¹/₁₆ ins. broad. The rather glossy white eggs, normally 4–7, but 3–8 recorded, are laid generally in the second half of May in a neatly rounded chamber with no nesting material except a few chips. Incubation is mainly by hen for about 16 days. The young are fed by both sexes and fly when about 18–21 days old. Single-brooded.

Status and Distribution. A resident, widely distributed and breeding in all counties in England and Wales including Isle of Wight and Anglesey, while in Scotland range recovery has extended it north to Sutherland and perhaps Caithness, also to the Inner Hebrides. It does not breed in Ireland or Isle of Man. The race *Dendrocopos major anglicus* is confined to Great Britain. The race *Dendrocopos major major*, which breeds from N. Scandinavia south to N. Poland, is a winter-visitor, apparently fairly regular in small numbers, but periodically more abundant, on the east coast from Suffolk to Shetland and occasionally elsewhere in England and Scotland; it has also occurred a number of times in Ireland. It is indistinguishable in the field from our bird, but the whites are purer and the bill stouter. Other races occur elsewhere in Europe, N. Africa, Canaries, and across N. Asia to Japan.

LESSER SPOTTED WOODPECKER—*Dendrocopos minor*

BIRD PLATE 77   EGG PLATE XVII (16)

It is a tiny black and white woodpecker *scarcely larger than a sparrow*, with pattern differing from Great Spotted Woodpecker chiefly in the *whole wings and lower back being barred black and white*. There is no crimson on the under tail-coverts. Fore-head is brownish-white; the crown dull crimson in male, whitish in female, while juveniles have some red on the crown in both sexes. Upper back, nape, stripes over the eye and from base of bill to neck are black, the rest of the head and under-parts white. The tail is much like Great Spotted Woodpecker's. A rather elusive little bird, keeping largely to the upper branches of trees, and easily overlooked, but for its *call* and drumming. The latter is usually feebler than the drumming of Great Spotted Woodpecker, and is heard exceptionally from September to late February, regularly from the end of February to the second half of April, less frequently to the end of May and exceptionally in the first half of June. Length about 5¾ ins.

Habitat. It frequents open woods, copses, well-timbered parkland, gardens, avenues, orchards, etc.

General Habits. Flight is rather slow and hesitant with characteristic woodpecker action; habits resemble those of other woodpeckers, but it is very seldom seen on the ground, and in trees is inclined to flutter from branch to branch more than larger species and to examine smaller branches and even twigs in its search for food.

Usual note is a rather loud shrill "pee-pee-pee-pee-pee", without variation in tone, liable to be confused with Wryneck's cry, but lacking its musical resonance.

Food is chiefly larvae of wood-boring insects; also spiders. Berries are occasionally taken.

Nests only in decayed wood of a branch or stem at varying heights from a few feet to 60 or 70 ft. from the ground. The glossy white eggs, usually 4–6, occasionally 3 to 7 or 8, are laid generally in May in a hole bored by both sexes, with an elliptical entrance about 1¾ by 1½ ins.; there is no nest material except a few chips. Incubation is by both sexes for about 14 days. The young are fed by both parents and fly when about 21–28 days old. Single-brooded.

Status and Distribution. A resident, generally rather local in S. England (probably excluding Isle of Wight) and the Midlands, becoming extremely local in Yorks, very rare in Lancs, but it has nested in Cumberland. In Wales it is fairly distributed in scattered pairs, except in the extreme west. There are a few records for Scotland, doubtfully Ireland. The British race is *Dendrocopos minor comminutus*. Other races occur over most of continental Europe, in N.W. Africa and from Asia Minor to Japan.

WHITE-WINGED LARK
and in flight.

SNOW BUNTING
and in flight 1st winter and
adult male.

Note differences in distribution of white on spread wing.

WHITE-WINGED LARK—*Melanocorypha leucoptera*

BIRD PLATE 79

It is a large, heavy, short-tailed and stout-billed lark, lacking a crest; the *white wing patch* on secondaries is most noticeable but the diagnostic *white outer web of the leading primary* can be prominent under favourable conditions in flight and on ground. In male the chestnut tint on crown, lesser wing-coverts and tail, and white under wing-coverts are distinctive; the back is tawny-brown, with centres of the feathers darker, throat and breast tinged buff, and there are indistinct rufous-brown spots on the throat, gorget and flanks. The rest of the under-parts are white. Female has the crown streaked brown like back, and both sexes have white in the outer tail feathers. Confusion must be avoided with Snow Bunting, in the greyest mantled examples of which the pale chestnut head is striking. Legs brown. Length about 7 ins.

Habitat. It frequents mainly arid grass-steppes.

Food is chiefly insects.

Status and Distribution. A very rare vagrant which has only occurred in east England, in autumn or winter. It breeds in S.E. Russia and central Asia. There are no subspecies.

SHORT-TOED LARK—*Calandrella brachydactyla*

BIRD PLATE 79

A *small, rather pale, sandy-looking* lark with the *under-parts unmarked and nearly white*, except for a vaguely defined band of buffish across the breast. The tail is conspicuously darker than the rest in flight, looking blackish with a whitish border. Dark patches at the sides of upper breast are distinctive when visible, but this is a very uncertain character in the field, the mark being commonly quite concealed unless the bird stretches up its head. The upper-parts are streaked dark, not very conspicuous in adults, but juvenile appears fairly strongly speckled. Bill rather stout. A crest is faintly indicated, sometimes not perceptible. Length about 5½ ins.

Habitat. It haunts barren sandy wastes and dunes or steppe country with or without meagre scrub, dried salt-marshes and pastures, and fallow fields.

General Habits. Flight is undulating, and usually low. It does not perch in trees. Outside the breeding-season commonly in parties, which squat silently when approached and rise suddenly.

Ordinary flight-call is a short chirruping note, harder and less rippling than Skylark's and recalling House Martin's, typically "chi*chirrp*".

Food is chiefly small seeds, also insects.

Status and Distribution. A vagrant of annual occurrence, in spring and autumn, which has appeared more often on Fair Isle and Scilly than elsewhere. There are records from other N. and N.W. Scottish islands and most English south and east coast counties, and it has been almost annual in Ireland in recent years. Many resemble the race *Calandrella brachydactyla brachydactyla* which breeds in the Mediterranean area of Europe, and winters in Africa; especially on Fair Isle examples have also resembled *Calandrella brachydactyla longipennis* which is slightly paler and greyer and breeds in central Asia. Other races occur in Africa and W. Asia.

CRESTED LARK—*Galerida cristata*

BIRD PLATE 78

It is distinguished from Skylark by a *long crest*, conspicuous even when depressed, *very broad, rounded wings, short tail which is buff, not white, at the sides, and striking note*. A rather stouter bird than Skylark, with upper-parts more uniform looking. The underside of the wing, when visible, shows orange-buff. Length about 6¾ ins.

Habitat. It inhabits open country in plains and mountains, and is less addicted to grasslands and more constantly to arable or rather barren, sandy or rocky ground than Skylark. In some parts it is common about roads, railways, villages, and waste land on the fringes of towns.

CRESTED LARK   SKYLARK

Note Crested Lark's long, upstanding crest.

General Habits. Flight is rather undulating, resembling Woodlark. It will perch on bushes, low walls, buildings, or even telegraph-wires and, infrequently, on trees. Out of the breeding-season it is less prone to flock than Skylark. It is often very tame.

Usual note is a liquid, melodious, somewhat whistling "whee-wheeoo", with variants. Also a cat-like mewing note.

Food is more vegetable than animal, chiefly grain and seeds.

Status and Distribution. A rare vagrant which has appeared mainly in autumn, but also spring, usually in southern England, also Wales and Shetland. The race concerned, *Galerida cristata cristata*, breeds on the Continent from the English Channel to Hungary, north to N.W. Russia and south to Sicily. Other races occur elsewhere in S. and E. Europe, N. and central Africa and in S.W. Asia.

CRESTED LARK   SKYLARK

Note Skylark's more pointed wings, white in tail, and
white-tipped secondaries.

WOODLARK—*Lullula arborea*

BIRD PLATE 78   EGG PLATE V (13)

It is distinguished from Skylark by the *short tail* which is
specially noticeable in flight, the *richer, more strongly contrasted
pattern of the plumage, buffish-white eye-stripes meeting across
the nape*, and very different *note*. At close quarters it shows also
a finer bill, a dark brown and white mark at the edge of wing,
and pinkish-brown, not yellowish-brown, legs. Under-parts are
buffish-white with streaked breast. Tail is blackish without a white
border, but with whitish tips. The crest is well-developed, but
often inconspicuous in the field. In juveniles light tips and edgings
to the feathers of upper-parts give a more spotted appearance.
Length about 6 ins.

Habitat. It haunts a fair variety of country providing a combination of open greensward with sprinkling of scrub, bracken or
brambles, and *scattered trees*: scrubby hillsides, sandy heaths,
warrens, thinly timbered meadowland, derelict farmland with
ragwort, dock and other weeds, and borders of woods. Chiefly, but
not invariably, on light, dry soils.

General Habits. It feeds on the ground, moving quietly and
inconspicuously over turf, but perches freely on trees and bushes.
Flight is more undulating and jerky than Skylark. It is usually
found in family parties after breeding and at times in larger flocks,
but is less gregarious than Skylark. In winter somewhat nomadic, it
may roam well away from breeding haunts.

Call and anxiety note on ground or wing is a liquid melodious "titloo-eet". The song, though lacking the variety and vehemence of Skylark's, is sweeter, more musical and mellow, delivered as a sequence of short phrases in a song-flight when the male with fluttering action circles round over a wide area, at a more or less constant and often considerable elevation. It is also given from a tree or the ground and frequently at night. It is heard regularly from the beginning of March to mid-June, fairly frequently from late January to early August and again in the second half of September and most of October, exceptionally until the end of November.

Food is largely animal matter especially insects; also spiders. In autumn many seeds are taken.

Nests on or close to the ground in a rather deep depression, sheltered by bracken, grass or heath. The eggs, normally 3–4, very rarely 6, are laid generally at the end of March or early in April in a neat and substantial nest built by both sexes of bents, with finer grass, sometimes horsehair, etc., in the lining. Incubation is apparently by hen only, usually for 13–15 days. The young are fed by both sexes, and leave the nest before they can fly, at about 12 days old. Two broods as a rule, sometimes three.

Status and Distribution. A resident or partial migrant, locally distributed in small, fluctuating numbers. It breeds mainly in East Anglia and southern England especially Surrey and Hampshire. It has disappeared from a number of areas including Yorks, Lincoln, Essex and parts of Wales, and become scarce in other localities. Some breeding areas are vacated in winter. In Scotland it is a vagrant, mainly recorded from Fair Isle; a rare vagrant in Ireland, where it has bred. The race concerned, *Lullula arborea arborea*, breeds from S. Scandinavia south to France, Hungary and central Russia. Other races occur further south in Europe, in N.W. Africa and W. Asia.

SKYLARK—*Alauda arvensis*

BIRD PLATE 78   EGG PLATE V (12)

Typical larks are predominantly terrestrial, streaky brown birds, walking, not hopping, on the ground and differing from pipits in stouter build, less nimble gait, less slender bills, and the presence of a distinct crest. Owing to rarity of the other species,

Skylark is only likely to be confused with Woodlark, from which it differs in having a *longer tail and less pronounced, though somewhat variable, eye-stripe*. The crest is not so long as Woodlark's, but often more conspicuous. *White outer tail-feathers* and to a less extent the greyish-white edging of the hind margin of wing are noticeable in flight. Light edging to the feathers give a more spotted or "scaly" pattern to the plumage of juveniles. Length about 7 ins.

Habitat. It haunts open grasslands or cultivation, from plains, meadows, marshes, peat-bogs or sand-dunes at sea-level to mountain pastures or moors; it is absent from tree-fringed fields of small or moderate size, and narrow valleys.

General Habits. It crouches when uneasy. Flight over short distances is commonly rather fluttering and wavering, but when more prolonged is strong and slightly undulating, several wing-beats alternating with a sudden closure, but with a perceptibly slower, more "floppy" wing-action than other small birds of the open country. It hardly ever perches on trees; often takes dust baths on roads or light soil. It is gregarious outside the breeding-season, and sometimes occurs in large flocks.

Note is a liquid rippling "chirrup" and variants. The song, a loud shrill warbling, pleasantly modulated, is delivered with great spirit sometimes from the ground or low perch, but usually in song flight; the male mounts steeply with a vigorous fluttering action to a high elevation where it remains poised, and presently sinks gently downwards, completing the descent by an abrupt drop to the ground. It is heard regularly from late January to early July and again in October, and less regularly at other times of year except from early August to late September.

Food includes seeds in quantities. Animal matter consists mainly of worms and insects.

Nests always on the ground in a depression in grass or growing crops, occasionally on shingle or in sand. The eggs, normally 3–4, rarely 7, are laid generally from the latter half of April onwards in a nest built probably by the hen only, of bents and grasses, lined with finer grasses and sometimes a little hair. Incubation is by hen only, for about 11 days. The young are fed by both sexes, and leave the nest after about 9–10 days and can fly 10 days later. Two or three broods.

Status and Distribution. Present throughout the year, common and widespread as a breeding bird, but is largely absent in winter from high ground, especially in N. and W. Scotland. Many, if not most, home-bred birds leave in autumn, when passage-migrants and winter-visitors arrive from central and N. Europe.

Southward and westward movement occurs from late August to November (and similar hard-weather movements through the winter), and the return from mid-February to early May. Our birds belong to the race *Alauda arvensis arvensis* which breeds in the Faeroes and from N. Scandinavia south to S. France, Austria and central Russia. A few examples of the race *Alauda arvensis intermedia* from central Asia, with cleaner-looking upper-parts and whiter under-parts, have been found in Scotland and Ireland. Other races occur in S. Europe, the Mediterranean, N.W. Africa and across Asia.

SHORE LARK—*Eremophila alpestris*

BIRD PLATE 79

The pinkish-brown upper-parts with contrasted pattern of yellow face and throat, black lores and cheeks, and a broad black gorget are distinctive. Adult male has the black band across the front of crown prolonged into a pair of slender erectile "horns". *The under-parts are whitish*, almost unstreaked. The outer tail-feathers have whitish borders, inconspicuous. The beak is short. Females and young males have less black, and in both sexes the black is obscured after the autumn moult by yellowish edgings to feathers, rendering the head pattern less striking and the birds are more easily overlooked. Length about 6½ ins.

Habitat. In winter-quarters it frequents the sea-shore, saltings, and stubble-fields or waste ground near the sea.

General Habits. Keeps more in the open than Skylark; usual gait a rapid run. It will perch on rocks and buildings, but not trees. Flight is more bounding than Skylark. It usually occurs in small parties in winter, sometimes associating with Lapland or Snow Buntings, etc., and often feeding amongst seaweed along tide-marks; usually not shy.

Commonest note in winter is a shrill "tsee-tsi", rather Meadow Pipit-like, but louder; also "tsissup" rather like Pied Wagtail.

Food includes seeds and insects; also small molluscs and crustacea in winter.

Status and Distribution. A winter-visitor arriving early October to mid-November and returning from mid-March to late April. In England it is annual on the east coast from Yorks. to Kent, occasional on the south coast and is very rare inland. In

Scotland some are seen every autumn on E. coasts, a few often winter; one or two occasionally summer in the Highlands where it bred in 1977, perhaps also 1973. It is a vagrant in Ireland. The race concerned, *Eremophila alpestris flava*, breeds in arctic Europe, coming farther south in Scandinavia, also in N. Siberia. An example of the N. American race *Eremophila alpestris alpestris* has occurred in Outer Hebrides. Other races breed in N. Africa, S.E. Europe to Lebanon and across mid-Asia.

SAND MARTIN—*Riparia riparia*

BIRD PLATE 80   EGG PLATE XVII (12)

It is smaller than Swallow or House Martin and slenderer-looking than the latter. It is *uniform brown above and white below, with a brown band across the chest*. The tail is only slightly forked. Juveniles are less uniform, with warm buff or pale fringes on the feathers of the upper-parts. Length about 4¾ ins.

Habitat. It frequents open country, but is even more closely attached to the vicinity of water than Swallow and House Martin, and more restricted in its occurrence owing to the nature of its breeding-sites.

General Habits. Very gregarious at all times and as much at home in the air as other hirundines, but its flight has not the sweep and grace of Swallow, being more fluttering and erratic; it is less inclined to glide on outstretched wings. It feeds chiefly over water, but like Swallow will occasionally pick up insects from the ground while on the wing. It perches on telegraph-wires and low branches, projecting roots, or vegetation over water and at breeding-places. Breeding birds also cling freely to faces of pits and banks containing their nests. Outside the breeding-season it roosts socially, frequently in great numbers, in reed-beds, osiers and swamp vegetation.

Note is a rippling or chirruping twitter of characteristically hard quality. The song, inferior to that of other British hirundines, is a harsh twittering, little more than an elaboration of ordinary notes. It may be heard from the first half of April to early September, but is most frequent from late April to mid-June.

Food consists of insects taken on the wing.

Nests in colonies, in sand- and gravel-pits, railway cuttings, banks of rivers and sea-cliffs, making a horizontal burrow 2 or 3 ft.

long with a chamber at the end; exceptionally also in drainpipes in walls, holes in brickwork, in spoil-heaps, etc. The white eggs, usually 4–5, sometimes 3–7, are laid generally in late May or early June in a nest consisting of straws, feathers, etc., picked up in flight and carelessly arranged; both sexes work at boring the tunnel. Incubation is by both sexes for about 14 days. The young are fed by both parents and fly when about 19 days old. Double-brooded as a rule.

Status and Distribution. A summer-visitor arriving from mid-March to mid-April, and continuing until June. They move south again from the second half of July to September, with stragglers in November. It is widely distributed in the British Isles, but local, with numbers seriously decreased since the mid-1960s; scarce in much of Scotland, especially in the north, and does not breed in Outer Hebrides, Orkney or Shetland. The race concerned, *Riparia riparia riparia*, ranges over practically all the continent of Europe, N.W. Africa, W. Asia, N. Siberia and N. America. Other races occur in N.E. Africa, central and E. Asia.

SWALLOW—*Hirundo rustica*

Bird Plate 80 Egg Plate V (10a & 10b)

In form and behaviour swallows and martins are unlike any other British birds, excepts perhaps swifts. Their slender build, long wings and forked tails no less than great powers of flight and manner of hawking for insect prey are very characteristic. Swallow differs from martins in its *uniform blue-black upper-parts, elongated outer tail-feathers, and chestnut-red throat and fore-head*. The throat is bounded by a dark blue pectoral band. The under-parts are white to pinkish-buff; the tail-feathers have white subterminal marks. The sexes are alike, but female is rather duller, whiter below and with usually rather shorter "streamers" to tail. Juveniles are considerably duller, with the chestnut paler and "streamers" much shorter. Length (adults) about 7–7½ ins., according to length of streamers.

Habitat. It inhabits all sorts of open country, particularly near water. Its presence in the breeding-season is chiefly dependent on suitable breeding-sites, hence it occurs especially about cultivated country and habitations.

General Habits. It spends much time on the wing, but settles freely on buildings, telegraph-wires, etc., on cliffs and crags where available, and to a much less extent on bare boughs of trees or on bushes, perching in an upright attitude. Except when collecting nesting material it is seldom on the ground. Flight is light and easy; though more direct when migrating, the chief feature as a rule is its graceful irregularity with constant changes of direction, and at varying heights in the air. Insects are picked from the surface of water, and sometimes from vegetation, or even from the ground, as well as captured on the wing, and birds sip water as they skim the surface. Less gregarious in the breeding-season than martins, but at other times is usually in parties. The gatherings preparatory to autumn migration are familiar, and the birds roost gregariously, often in hundreds, in reed- and osier-beds, frequently over water.

Usual notes, used especially on the wing, "tswit, tswit tswit", are more twittering than House Martin's, and often run together into a regular twitter. The song is a simple but pleasing warbling twitter intermingled with a little short throaty trill, uttered chiefly on the wing. It is heard regularly from late April until the middle of July, less frequently earlier in April and until mid-September, and exceptionally into early October.

Food consists of insects taken on the wing.

Nests generally on rafters in sheds and outhouses, but in some districts many pairs breed inside chimney stacks. The eggs, usually 4–5, sometimes 3–8, are laid generally from mid-May till

SAND MARTIN (upper left)
    SWALLOW, adult and juvenile.
HOUSE MARTIN (lower left)

Note the short tail of young Swallow. Only House Martin
has a white rump.

August in a nest built by both sexes of mud with bits of straw
worked in to hold the material together: it is more saucer-shaped
than that of House Martin, open at the top and resting on a support
of some kind as a rule. Incubation is apparently mainly by hen
only, for about 14–15 days. The young are fed by both sexes and
usually fly when about 21 days old. Two broods normally, three
occasionally.

Status and Distribution. A summer-visitor, early arrivals
appearing in the second half of March, but the main body not until
April and with passage continuing through May, or into June. The
return movement lasts from July to October with stragglers in
November, and birds occasionally stay into the winter. It is
generally distributed in the British Isles but is scarce in N.W.
Scotland, Orkney, Shetland and Outer Hebrides; our birds winter
in S. Africa. The race concerned, *Hirundo rustica rustica*, extends
over most of Europe, N.W. Africa, the Mediterranean, and much
of Asia. Other races occur in Egypt, Palestine, E. Asia and
N. America.

HOUSE MARTIN—*Delichon urbica*

Bird Plate 80   Egg Plate XVII (11)

The tail is less deeply forked than Swallow's and the entire
under-parts are pure white, but the readiest distinction is *the white
rump* which contrasts strongly with blue-black back and black
wings. White-feathered legs are conspicuous when the bird is on
the ground or clinging to nest. Juveniles are browner. Length
about 5 ins.

Habitat. It inhabits open country, from remote rocky localities
to highly cultivated districts, but chiefly the latter; it occurs more
in towns and about dwelling-houses than Swallow.

General Habits. Like Swallow, it spends much of its time on
the wing, but settles freely on buildings, telegraph-wires, bare
boughs, etc. Flight, although similar in general character, is less
rapid and twisting than Swallow's, and it is inclined to fly higher.
It has much the same habits as Swallow but is more genuinely
sociable.

Usual note is more chirruping than Swallow's, a slightly hard
"chirrrp" or "chichirrrp". The song, much less frequently uttered
than that of Swallow or Sand Martin, is a very soft but sweet

twittering. It may be heard from the end of April to the second half of September.

Food consists of insects taken on the wing.

Nests usually on the outer walls of houses under eaves, often in considerable numbers. Exceptionally it also nests inside roofs or sheds; also on the face of cliffs. The white eggs, usually 4–5, sometimes 2–6, are laid from the latter part of May onwards in a nest shaped like a section of a cup with a narrow entrance between the top and the eaves, built by both sexes of mud and with pieces of bents to hold the material together. The lining is of feathers, bits of straw, etc. Incubation is by both sexes for about 14–15 days. The young are fed by both parents and fly when about 19–22 days old. Double-brooded: three not uncommonly.

Status and Distribution. A summer-visitor, arriving from the beginning of April but mainly in May, with passage extending well into June. The return movement lasts from late July to late October, with stragglers occasionally into December. It is generally distributed, but more local than Swallow, especially in Ireland. It is a scarce breeder in N.W. Scotland and Inner Hebrides, seldom in Orkney and Shetland, and exceptionally in the Outer Hebrides. Our birds winter in S. Africa. The race concerned, *Delichon urbica urbica*, breeds over most of Europe and parts of W. Asia. Other races occur in N.W. Africa, S. Spain, and parts of Asia east to Japan.

RICHARD'S PIPIT—*Anthus novaeseelandiae*

BIRD PLATE 106

A conspicuously large long-legged and upstanding pipit with a heavy bill and with dark brown upper-parts boldly marked, except on the nearly uniform rump. The breast is buff, moderately streaked, belly whiter. *The outer tail-feathers are pure white*, contrasting with blackish central feathers, noticeable when hovering before landing. In winter a broad whitish stripe over the eye and under the ear-coverts may give the head a very light appearance. In autumn it can be confused with young Tawny Pipit, which see. Length about 7 ins.

Habitat. In the breeding-season it frequents well-watered grassy steppe and damp meadow-land; in winter quarters chiefly rank grasslands, marshes and ricefields.

RICHARD'S PIPIT
immature.

Note the shaded patch on the side of head,
extending from bill to ear-coverts and em-
bracing eye.

General Habits. It usually moves with a swift run; carriage is erect. The flight is strong and undulating; wagtail-like. It often hovers at 10–20 feet for several seconds before landing. It perches on rocks or bushes, and exceptionally on trees. Is inclined to be shy and wary.

Usual note is an explosive, strident "schreep", recalling sparrow but with great carrying power.

Food is largely insects; also worms, grasshoppers and vegetable matter.

Status and Distribution. A vagrant of annual occurrence chiefly from September to November, few April–May, rarely winter, in various parts of England but mainly in coastal counties in the southern half of the country, also Wales and Fair Isle, but few records elsewhere in Scotland or in Ireland. The race *Anthus novaeseelandiae richardi* breeds in central Asia; other races occur in N.E. India and China.

TAWNY PIPIT—*Anthus campestris*

BIRD PLATE 105

A large, slim, *noticeably pale, sandy-coloured pipit with rather long legs*, varying from bright yellowish to more flesh-coloured. It has a distinct light eye-stripe and whitish or buffish outer tail

TAWNY PIPIT
immature

feathers. The markings of the upper-parts are inconspicuous in adults, the under-parts paler and unstreaked or nearly so. Young in autumn, having the breast distinctly streaked and the upper-parts often quite boldly marked, are readily confused with Richard's Pipit. Richard's, however, is normally darker and larger, with decidedly longer legs, a heavy dark mark on the side of the neck, and a rather different note; even in flight seems bulky and pot-bellied. Tawny is the most wagtail-like of the pipits. Length about 6½ ins.

Habitat. In the breeding-season it haunts sandy wastes, heaths, and dunes, arid pastures or cultivated land. In winter-quarters it is found largely on similar ground, but also in moist cultivation and on the banks of lagoons and waterways.

General Habits. On the ground walks or runs with great speed, frequently, and especially when suspicious, moving the tail up and down like a wagtail, a habit shared, however, with the smaller less wagtail-like pipits. Flight is in long undulations, wagtail-like. It perches chiefly on the ground or on rocks, walls, etc., sometimes on bushes or telegraph-wires.

Flight-note is a sparrow-like "chirrup". Other notes include: "tzic", "tzucc", "sweep" recalling Yellow Wagtail, etc.

Food is chiefly insects.

Nests in a depression of the ground well sheltered by a tussock, clod or bush. The eggs, usually 4–5, rarely 6, are closely spotted or mottled with brown, and violet shell-marks, on a whitish ground. They are laid generally in May or June in a nest built of grasses, roots, dead weeds, etc., lined with some hair. Incubation is for about 13–14 days. The young fly when about 14 days old. Possibly double-brooded.

Status and Distribution. A vagrant of annual occurrence on the south coast, and in E. Anglia, mainly in September or October and occasionally spring (May) and it may perhaps have bred. Elsewhere in England it is rarer and few have been found in Scotland. There have been several records in S. Ireland in recent years. The race concerned, *Anthus campestris campestris*, breeds in Europe from S. Scandinavia south to the Mediterranean and west across Asia to Mongolia; also in N.W. Africa. Another race occurs in part of central Asia.

TREE PIPIT—*Anthus trivialis*

BIRD PLATE 107   EGG PLATE II (1A, 1B, 1C, 1D, 1E & 1F)

The smaller pipits are all closely similar, recalling typical larks in plumage—brown above with darker markings, and light below with more or less streaked breast and flanks—but with slenderer bills, slimmer form and more active, graceful movements. The tail is often moved like a wagtail, but less conspicuously because it is shorter. The present species closely resembles Meadow Pipit, and shows similar *white outer tail-feathers* in flight, but is *rather more stockily built, a sleeker-looking bird*, a trifle larger and tending to carry itself more erect. *The breast is more suffused with yellow-buff* than most Meadow Pipits, but some Meadow Pipits in spring have the breast quite strongly buff, and colour alone is not always a secure guide. Streaks on the breast tend to be larger and fewer than in Meadow Pipit, the legs more distinctly flesh-coloured, less brownish, and in very favourable circumstances the short hind-claw can occasionally be made out, but the *call-note* is the most reliable character outside breeding-season. In the case of breeding birds the song of male precludes confusion. Length about 6 ins.

Habitat. In the breeding-season it haunts meadowland, commons and heaths (especially with pines), hillsides and bushy places, where there are *scattered trees*, and the borders or open parts of woods; also railway cuttings, etc., where telegraph-wires afford song-posts.

General Habits. Flight action is flitting and jerky, rising and falling in a somewhat erratic manner. Unlike Meadow Pipit, it settles habitually on tall trees, as well as lower perches, and usually flies into trees when disturbed, though, like others of this genus, it is essentially a ground bird. In general it is rather quieter and less active than Meadow Pipit.

Call, heard generally when the bird is flying for some distance, is a somewhat rasping, or hoarse "teez". The song, much superior to Meadow or Rock Pipit's, and with exceptional carrying power, leads up to a shrill, musical, Canary-like "seea-seea-seea . . ." with which the song finishes. A curtailed version is often given from a perch, but the full song is only delivered in a special flight from a tree when the male flutters steeply upwards, begins singing near the peak of the ascent and continues as it parachutes down, with wings inclined upwards and tail spread, to the same or an adjacent perch again. The bird never rises to anything like the height reached by larks. It is heard from mid-April to mid-July, less frequently to the end of July.

Food is chiefly insects; also spiders.

Nests in a depression of the ground. The eggs, usually 4–6, rarely 8, are extraordinarily variable; the three main types are reddish, brown, or grey in general appearance, but in each type the eggs may be uniformly speckled, with well-defined zone or cap, or with blotches and streaks. They are laid generally in the latter half of May and early June in a nest substantially built of dry grass and bents, with moss in the foundation, lined with finer grasses and a varying amount of hair. Incubation is by hen only, for about 13–14 days. The young are fed by both parents and fly when about 12–13 days old. Two broods in some cases.

Status and Distribution. A summer-visitor, fairly distributed and locally common in England and Wales, but it does not breed in W. Cornwall. In Scotland it is plentiful in most of the west and north, more thinly scattered in central lowlands, and scarce or absent near the east coast from Aberdeen southwards. A passage-migrant in Shetland and Orkney, but rarely recorded in Outer Hebrides although breeding on several of Inner Hebrides. It occurs regularly in S. Ireland in autumn, but less frequently in spring. The birds begin to arrive in early April and passage continues until early June. The return movement lasts from end of July to mid-October. The race concerned, *Anthus trivialis trivialis*, breeds in Europe from N. Scandinavia south to N. Spain and Greece and far into Asia. Other races occur in central Asia. Our birds winter in tropical Africa.

MEADOW PIPIT—*Anthus pratensis*

BIRD PLATE 107   EGG PLATE II (4A & 4B)

It closely resembles Tree Pipit. For characters and distinctions, see under that species. Length about 5¾ ins.

Habitat. It is exclusively a bird of open country. It breeds on rough grasslands, heaths, moors, sand-dunes, etc.; in winter high moorlands are largely deserted, and the birds resort to lowland pastures, marshes, sewage-farms, root-fields, sea-coast and the shores of inland waters.

General Habits. Its ordinary movements are like Tree Pipit, but it is a rather more lively, active bird. It perches less habitually in trees than Tree Pipit, but does so freely on migration and not rarely at other times where trees are available. Outside the breeding-season it frequently occurs in flocks, but birds maintain only rather loose contact, and, when disturbed, rise in ones and twos or little groups rather than in a body.

Usual note when flushed is a thin, feeble, squeaky "tsiip", sometimes uttered singly, but, when startled, often rapidly repeated. The song, delivered typically in a fluttering song-flight, is a tinkling sequence of feeble notes gathering speed as the bird rises from the ground, and succeeded by a succession of slightly more musical notes ending in a trill as the bird descends with a Tree Pipit-like glide. It is heard regularly from mid-March to early July, less frequently for a month earlier or later, and exceptionally into September.

Food is mainly insects; also earthworms, spiders, and occasionally seeds.

Nests in a depression of the ground, sometimes completely sheltered from above, in tussocks or in heather. The eggs, usually 4–5, sometimes 7, are variable; ordinary types are brown or grey, finely mottled or more boldly marbled; others are almost uniform ochreous or pale leaden-grey, with dark hair-streaks, and some unmarked on pale blue ground. They are laid generally from the latter part of April onwards in a nest built of dry grasses and bents, lined with finer material and some horsehair. Incubation is probably by hen alone for about 13–14 days. The young are fed by both parents and fly when about 13–14 days old. At least two broods are usually reared.

Status and Distribution. Present throughout the year, and abundant in open country, but the majority leave higher and more northern situations in autumn and many emigrate to S. Ireland, W. France, Spain and Portugal. Immigrants from N.W. Europe and Iceland pass through and many winter here. Movement occurs from August to late November and from late February to May. Abroad it breeds from Iceland and N. Europe to S. France, Sicily and S. Russia, also in Asia to W. Siberia. In winter it reaches N. Africa. There are no subspecies.

RED-THROATED PIPIT—*Anthus cervinus*

BIRD PLATE 107

In general the plumage resembles Tree Pipit; it is rather darker above, more boldly marked, and lacking the greenish tint of Meadow Pipit. In spring and summer the *pale rusty red of throat and breast* is distinctive, though varying in intensity. In autumn and winter this is lost or much reduced, and the *broadly streaked, instead of practically uniform, rump and upper tail-coverts* appear to be then the only infallible plumage character in the field, but the *note* is quite diagnostic. Length about 5¾ ins.

Habitat. In winter-quarters it is found chiefly on damp grass-lands, borders of rivers, lakes and marshes, and wet cultivation, more rarely on coastal dunes and edge of desert.

General Habits. Gait, carriage, and flight are like Tree Pipit. It perches freely on bushes, fences, telegraph-wires, buildings, etc., and on trees where available. On the whole it appears to prefer more bushy ground than Meadow Pipit.

Note, distinct from Tree Pipit's, when uttered loudly is a full, musical, rather abrupt "choop", both on wing and when flushed or while perched; also a note "skeez", closer to, but usually more drawn out than Tree Pipit's. Both these are used by migrants.

Food is principally insects.

Status and Distribution. A vagrant recorded almost annually. It occurs mainly in May or September–October, in England, more often on Fair Isle, and it has appeared on a few other islands in Scotland and S. Ireland. It breeds in the Arctic from N.E. Scandinavia to Siberia, and winters mainly in tropical Africa and Asia. There are no subspecies.

ROCK PIPIT/WATER PIPIT—*Anthus spinoletta*

BIRD PLATE 106   EGG PLATE II (5)

A number of races of this species occur in the British Isles, the subspecies from the mountains of central and southern Europe being sufficiently distinct from our native Rock Pipit to be known as Water Pipit. Its description is given in the final paragraph of this account. Rock Pipit is larger than the other British breeding pipits, with a relatively longer bill giving the head a more elongated appearance. The olive-shaded *plumage is darker, less strongly marked both above and below, the legs are dark brown and the outer tail-feathers smoky-grey*, not white. Young are more streaked than adults. Length about 6¼ ins.

Habitat. In the breeding-season in this country it is normally confined to rocky coasts and islands. On passage and in winter it is also found on mud-banks, estuaries, saltings and sandy shores: exceptionally, stray individuals occur inland by reservoirs or other waters.

General Habits. Flight and gait are as Tree Pipit, and it ordinarily perches on rocks or other eminences. In winter it often occurs in small parties, but seldom in regular flocks except on migration.

Note is "tsup", rather fuller, more metallic, and less squeaky than Meadow Pipit's. Song resembles Meadow Pipit's, but is louder, with notes fuller, rather more musical, and more metallic, with the terminal trill more pronounced. It is given in a Meadow Pipit-like song flight and is heard regularly from late March to early July, less frequently from mid-March and until early August, and sometimes in September, October and February.

Food consists of insects, animal and vegetable matter picked up on or close to shore or cliff-tops.

Nests in a hole or recess of some kind in a cliff, often sheltered by vegetation, less often in grassy banks, but nearly always close to the seashore, though sometimes at a considerable height, and on cliff tops. The eggs, normally 4–5, in some cases 2–6, are laid generally from the second half of April onwards. Incubation is by hen alone for about two weeks. The young are fed by both parents and fly when about 16 days old. Two broods.

Status and Distribution. Present throughout the year. It is generally distributed on rocky shores, and does not breed between Kent and S. Yorks., in Lancs or Dumfries. It occurs on many flat shores in autumn and winter and occasionally inland. The race is *Anthus spinoletta petrosus* which occupies the British Isles and breeds also in the Channel Isles, N.W. France and Norway. The race *Anthus spinoletta littoralis*, from the Baltic and White Seas, has been recorded occasionally; but in winter plumage, when it is most likely to be seen, it is indistinguishable from our native birds; in summer a vinous flush on throat and breast and lack or reduction of streaks on the breast are often distinctive. The Water Pipit, *Anthus spinoletta spinoletta*, which breeds in mountains from the Mediterranean to Switzerland and Germany, and east to Asia Minor, is a regular winter visitor in small numbers to lowland freshwater habitats. It has occurred in all months from September to April, occasionally August and rarely May; chiefly in S.E. England, but also through the Midlands and the south-west to Wales and Ireland, also in Shetland. In full summer plumage Water Pipit is characterized by a *pinkish flush on unstreaked breast, a broad whitish eye-stripe*, and greyish tint of the upper-parts. At all seasons it differs from the preceding races in having *pure white (instead of smoky) outer tail-feathers*, and in autumn and winter in *warmer brown upper-parts and whitish under-parts and eye-stripe*. At this season the breast is quite strongly streaked and the whole plumage more recalls Meadow Pipit, from which it differs in larger size, Rock Pipit-like form and carriage, dark legs, only faintly marked upper-parts, without olivaceous tint, and whiter breast. The American race *Anthus spinoletta rubescens* which is distinctive in having buff, not white or olivaceous under-parts, and white outer tail-feathers, has been recorded as a rare vagrant in Scotland and Ireland. Other races occur from central Asia to Japan.

YELLOW WAGTAIL/BLUE-HEADED WAGTAIL—*Motacilla flava*

BIRD PLATE 105   EGG PLATE II (6A & 6B)

Wagtails are slim, graceful, primarily terrestrial birds, with longer tails than pipits, not mainly brown-plumaged, spotted or streaked like the latter, but with yellows, greens, greys, white and black predominating, and with characteristic flight and carriage. The Yellow Wagtail and allied races have all yellow breasts, but differ from Grey Wagtail, which also has a yellow breast, in much shorter tail, greenish back, and less aquatic habits. Breeding male Yellow Wagtail has a *bright yellow head, with crown and ear-coverts more or less greenish*. The mantle is olive-green, wings and tail blackish-brown with two buffish wing-bars and white outer tail-feathers. Female, and both sexes in autumn, are duller, browner above, and paler yellow below, with a buffish eye-stripe. The same features are still more pronounced in young, which have throat surrounded by a kind of bib of dark markings. Length about 6½ ins. Besides Yellow Wagtail (*Motacilla flava flavissima*), another form of this species occurring regularly in the British Isles is Blue-headed Wagtail (*Motacilla flava flava*) of which the breeding male has bluish-grey, not greenish, crown and ear-coverts, a white, not yellow, eye-stripe and white chin, the white usually extending back beneath the ear-coverts. Breeding females are a good deal duller, but the same characters, in less pronounced form, are generally sufficient to distinguish them from Yellow Wagtails, and this is also true of males in autumn plumage; immatures, and often females in autumn, are indistinguishable. Blue-headed and Yellow Wagtails at times interbreed, which may in part account for the occasional appearance in S.E. England of breeding birds with almost lavender crowns with or without eye-stripe, a variety resembling *Motacilla flava beema* of W. Siberia. Other variants occur which do not match any particular race. Rare or very rare vagrants are the following races of this bird: Grey-headed Wagtail (*Motacilla flava thunbergi*) darker than Blue-headed Wagtail and male without eye-stripe, but with yellow throat; Ashy-headed Wagtail (*Motacilla flava cinereocapilla*), intermediate between Blue-headed and Grey-headed as regards upper-parts, the eye-stripe of male being little more than a spot behind and above the eye, and with the white of chin extending well on to the throat; Black-headed Wagtail (*Motacilla flava feldegg*) male typically has a very distinctive black head without eye-stripe and with yellow throat, but some resemble Grey-headed Wagtail, as do females.

Habitat. In the breeding-season it mainly frequents lowland pastures, marshes, and cultivated fields, commonly, but not necessarily, near water. Locally it breeds on heaths and moorland.

General Habits. Actions on the ground and in the air are similar in all wagtails. The gait is a brisk walk or swift run, with a backward and forward motion of the head and the *tail constantly moved up and down*; it frequently takes a little flutter into the air after a passing insect. Flight is strongly undulating, in long curves, with wings closed perceptibly longer than in the case of less pronouncedly undulating fliers, such as larks or finches. The present species perches freely on fences, bushes or trees, and delights to feed amongst cattle. It is gregarious outside the breeding-season.

Usual note is a rather prolonged, shrill, musical "tsweep". The song is a brief and simple warble interspersed with call-notes; it is delivered in flight or from a perch and may be heard fairly frequently in May, exceptionally in the latter part of April, in June and early July.

Food is mainly insects; also small molluscs.

Nests generally in a depression on the ground in thick herbage, sometimes also in fallows or crops. The eggs, usually 5–6, sometimes 4–7, are laid generally in May or early June in a nest built by the hen, with male accompanying her, and composed of bents and roots, thickly lined with a pad of cow- or horse-hair, and an occasional feather or two. Incubation is by both sexes for about 12–13 days. The young are fed by both parents and usually leave the nest when about 12–13 days old. Normally double-brooded in the south, and occasionally elsewhere.

Status and Distribution. Yellow Wagtail is a summer-visitor, arriving from late March to mid-May, and leaving between mid-August and the end of September, but has exceptionally been recorded in winter. It is distributed throughout England and Wales but breeds rarely in the west. A few pairs breed in Scotland, centred on the Clyde area, rarely north-east to Aberdeen. In Ireland it used to breed in the north and south-east but now seems sporadic. Abroad it extends from N.W. France to Norway. Blue-headed Wagtail, and/or variants with bluish heads, breed in small numbers in S.E. England (Kent/Sussex/Surrey/Middlesex), and have done so in several other counties; otherwise Blue-headed Wagtail is an occasional passage-migrant chiefly in the south and often on Fair Isle. It breeds in Europe from S. Scandinavia south to central France, and east through S. Russia into Asia. The Grey-headed Wagtail comes from N. Europe and W. Siberia, Ashy-headed Wagtail from the central Mediterranean area, and Black-headed Wagtail from S.E. Europe and Asia Minor. Other races occur in S.W. and E. Europe, Egypt, Asia and Alaska. The species winters in the tropics.

GREY WAGTAIL—*Motacilla cinerea*

BIRD PLATE 104   EGG PLATE II (7A & 7B)

The yellow of the under tail-coverts and often of the breast, the blue-grey upper-parts and very long tail are distinctive, the last two characters distinguishing it from all races of Yellow Wagtail.

The rump is greenish-yellow, the outer tail-feathers white. Male in spring has a whitish stripe above and below the eye and has a *black throat*. Female has a whitish throat, without or only obscurely marked with black. In autumn and winter both sexes have buffish-white throats and paler under-parts. Young birds have the throat and breast pale buff with some dark markings at the sides of throat and can be confused with young Pied Wagtails, which also have buffish breasts, but in Grey Wagtail the buff shades into *distinct yellow on the under tail-coverts*, and it has a longer tail. Length about 7 ins.

Habitat. In the breeding-season it is found principally on swift and rocky, but to some extent on shallow gravelly, streams, and sometimes lakes, in hilly and mountainous districts; it is also locally frequent in lowlands on less sluggish streams or where locks and lashers cause increased movement of water. In winter it is more general on lowland streams, ponds, watercress-beds and the like or on the coast, and, though chiefly confined to the neighbourhood of water, it occasionally visits farmyards and other places some distance away.

General Habits. It is commonly seen flitting along streams and perching on boulders or over-hanging trees. Its actions are like those of other wagtails. The movement of the tail is especially conspicuous owing to its length. Usually it occurs in pairs or singly.

Common note is rather higher pitched and more metallic than Pied Wagtail with syllables usually perceptibly shorter, "tzitzi". Song is infrequent, and may be heard from late March to early May; exceptionally through May and early June and from late September to mid-January.

Food is mainly insects.

Nests in a hole of cliff, rocky ledge or cavity in a wall, occasionally on a steep bank or among tree-roots, and generally quite close to running water. The eggs, normally 4–6, sometimes 3–7, are laid generally in the latter half of April or early May in a nest built by the hen, accompanied by male, and constructed of moss, small twigs, leaves, roots, and grasses, lined with hair, and an occasional feather. Incubation is by both sexes, for 11–13 days. The young are fed by both parents and fly when about 13 days old. Double-brooded in some districts.

Status and Distribution. Present throughout the year and widely spread, but breeds only sparingly in the east and centre from mid-Yorks to Kent. It is more common elsewhere in England, also in Wales, Ireland and most parts of Scotland, but is scarcer in N. Scotland and Orkney and is only a visitor (apart from one or two breeding records) to Shetland and Outer Hebrides. A southward movement from breeding places occurs in autumn. The race concerned, *Motacilla cinerea cinerea*, breeds from S. Scandinavia to N.W. Africa and east to central Asia. Other races occur in the African Atlantic islands and N.E. Asia.

PIED WAGTAIL/WHITE WAGTAIL—*Motacilla alba*

Bird Plate 103   Egg Plate II (8a & 8b)

Both races have a contrasted plumage pattern of black, white and grey. Pied Wagtail male has the crown and *whole upper-parts black*, the throat and upper breast black in summer, meeting the black of the upper-parts; the fore-head, sides of face and belly are white, the flanks sooty, wings and tail blackish with a double white wing-bar and white outer tail-feathers. In winter plumage the throat is white, bounded by a horseshoe-shaped black bib. Female has the back more grey, and less black on the crown and breast. Juvenile is brownish-grey above, with sides of the face dirty white, throat dull white, crescentic breast-band blackish, and the rest of breast and flanks grey-buff. In first autumn and winter the young of both sexes have the crown black and back mainly or completely grey; there are usually some black marks on the fore-head and the white parts are tinged yellowish. White Wagtail in the breeding-season has the *mantle and rump clear pale grey*, duller in female. In spring some first year female Pied Wagtails are almost as pale as Whites, but *in Pied the grey shades into black on the rump*. Also White Wagtail has the wings rather browner with wing-marks less distinct, and *flanks grey, not sooty*. In autumn grey-backed young Pieds may be very similar to male Whites, but *female and young male Whites differ from all post-juvenile plumages of Pied in having the whole top of the head grey*, without white fore-head or black on crown. Length about 7 ins.

Habitat. It occurs in a variety of more or less open country, but chiefly about farms, buildings and cultivation, preferably, but not necessarily, near ponds, streams or other water. Its presence at particular places in the breeding-season is mainly conditioned by the availability of suitable nesting-sites.

General Habits. It feeds much near water, but also much on open grassland and cultivation. From autumn to spring it roosts gregariously, often in hundreds, in widely varied situations, of which reed-beds and tangled aquatic vegetation are commonest; buildings such as glasshouses are sometimes used. Usual note is a shrill "tschizzik". The song, which is rather infrequent, is a simple but lively warbling twitter. It is heard mainly in March, April, July and from September to early November, exceptionally in most of January, February, May, June, late August and early September.

Food is chiefly insects.

Nests in holes of walls, sheds, banks, ivy, woodstacks, thatch, etc. Less commonly it re-lines the old nest of some other bird. The eggs, normally 5–6, occasionally 3–7, sometimes pure white, are laid generally from the latter part of April or May onwards in a nest built by hen alone of moss, dead leaves, twigs, roots, bents, etc., lined with hair, feathers or bits of wool. Incubation is chiefly by hen for about 13–14 days. The young are fed by both parents, and fly when about 14–16 days old.

Status and Distribution. The Pied Wagtail, *Motacilla alba yarrellii*, is present throughout the year, as a breeding bird generally distributed throughout the British Isles, but not in Shetland where it is an occasional visitor and has rarely bred, or interbred with White Wagtail, the usual race there. Many migrate southwards from mid-August to late October and return from the end of February to end of April. Some reach S. Spain. Abroad it has bred from N.W. France to S.W. Norway. The White Wagtail, *Motacilla alba alba*, is chiefly a coastal passage-migrant from mid-March to early June and from mid-August to early October. It is much more occasional inland and has occasionally bred (more often interbred with Pied). Abroad it breeds from Iceland and the Arctic Ocean to the Mediterranean and N. Asia, wintering south to tropical Africa. Other races occur in Africa and across Asia.

WAXWING—*Bombycilla garrulus*

Bird Plate 108

It is about the size of a Starling. *The prominent crest, general vinaceous brown colouring* and rather short, conspicuously *yellow-tipped tail* with white and yellow markings on the wings and a black throat, are unmistakable. The deep sienna-brown under tail-coverts also are noticeable from below. On the wing the yellow tips of the tail-feathers are striking at moderately close range, but at

WAXWING

Note Starling-like flight.

longer range the *grey lower back and rump* catch the eye first. Young birds are duller, with shorter crests, no black on throat, and buffish streaks on the under-parts. Length about 7 ins.

Habitat. In its winter incursions it appears largely in open places with scattered trees (often gardens), but with little preference for any definite type of ground, its haunts being principally determined by the presence of suitable berry-bearing trees or shrubs such as rowans, thorn, rose, cotoneaster, etc.

General Habits. It is principally arboreal, often perching on the tops of trees, but also low down and amongst branches. Its attitudes when feeding in trees recall Crossbill or tits, and it will catch insects in the air. In sustained flight, well up in the air, the action is Starling-like, strong and buoyant, in long sweeping undulations, with wings closed at intervals. It drinks freely. It is often very tame, and rather sluggish, sitting for a long time immobile. In Britain it appears chiefly in small parties or singly, but sometimes in considerable flocks.

Usual note is a high feeble trilling "sirrrrr".

Food in winter consists mainly of berries.

Status and Distribution. A winter-visitor, a few appearing in most years but periodically in considerable numbers (apparently when food supplies are scarce in N. Europe) and occasionally as late as April. It is most frequent on the east side, but has occurred in most counties, although more occasionally in west England and west Scotland, and still more rarely in Wales and north Scotland. In Ireland it has been recorded in most recent years chiefly in the east and north, but sometimes reaching the west. The race concerned, *Bombycilla garrulus garrulus*, breeds from N. Norway to N. Siberia. Another race occurs in N. America.

DIPPER—*Cinclus cinclus*

BIRD PLATE 88   EGG PLATE XVII (18)

The plump form and short tail, suggesting a gigantic Wren (but with the tail not, or only slightly, cocked), *the slaty brown plumage and white throat* of adult, and its aquatic habits are all distinctive, precluding confusion with any other bird. The head and nape are chocolate-brown, the rest darker, more slaty, with black margins to the feathers of the back giving a scaly pattern at close range, though looking uniform at a little distance. The white gorget is bordered below by a chestnut band merging into the blackish of flanks and belly. Juveniles are greyer above with dingy white under-parts mottled grey, while young birds in first autumn and winter have whitish tips to the coverts and secondaries. Length about 7 ins.

Habitat. It is found typically on swift streams and rivers and shallow margins of lakes and tarns in hilly or mountainous country, but in some districts is quite frequent on suitably shallow and stony streams in lowlands, especially where bridges or other masonry afford good nesting-sites. In mountainous regions the lower reaches of rivers are more frequented in winter and even the coast is visited.

General Habits. It remains usually in pairs or singly and territorial even in winter, occupying a definite reach of stream which it is reluctant to leave, doubling back beyond a certain point if pursued. It delights to perch on a stone or rock protruding from the water, bobbing and curtseying as if hinged on its legs, with an accompanying downward jerk of the tail and blinking of white eye-lid. It also perches on low branches near water. In pursuit of food it wades into water and deliberately submerges, settles on the surface and dives, or plunges straight in from the air or a stone. Under water it walks deliberately over the bottom; on the surface it can swim buoyantly. It is never ordinarily seen far from water. Flight is direct and rapid, usually low down following the course of a stream.

Ordinary note is a loud, tuneless "zit, zit, zit". The song is a very sweet rippling warble, somewhat Wren-like in general pattern, uttered equally freely by both sexes. It is heard regularly from the beginning of October to the beginning of July, less frequently in August and September.

Food is chiefly aquatic insects; also small molluscs, crustacea, worms, tadpoles, and small fishes.

Nests on faces of cliffs and rocks by rapidly flowing streams, also in holes of walls and bridges, among ivy or tree-roots and under waterfalls, but always over or close to water. The white eggs, usually 5, sometimes 3–7, are laid generally about the end of March or later, in a cup-shaped nest built by both sexes and constructed of moss, dry grasses, etc., with a lining of dead leaves, and a superstructure chiefly of moss with an overhanging roof partly concealing the entrance. Incubation is apparently by hen only, for about 16 days. The young are fed by both parents and fly when about 19–25 days old. Double-brooded as a rule, possibly three occasionally.

Status and Distribution. A resident, generally distributed in suitable localities in Ireland, Wales and Scotland north to Caithness (apparently no longer in Orkney or Isle of Man); also in W. and N. England, but it is a vagrant east of Derby, Warwick, Oxford, Hants. The race *Cinclus cinclus gularis* breeds only in England, Wales and most of Scotland, the race *Cinclus cinclus hibernicus* occupying Ireland, the Hebrides and parts of W. Scotland; the latter race is darker above and generally has less chestnut below but cannot certainly be separated in the field. A few examples have also occurred in England, Scotland and Ireland in winter and spring of the form *Cinclus cinclus cinclus* which breeds from N. Scandinavia and Russia south to E. Prussia, also apparently in parts of France, Spain and Portugal. It is distinguished from our bird by the virtual absence of the chestnut band on the under-parts. Other races occur elsewhere in Europe, in N.W. Africa and in Asia.

WREN—*Troglodytes troglodytes*

Bird Plate 88   Egg Plate III (17A & 17B)

The diminutive size and russet-brown colouring (paler, more buff, below) *and plump, stumpy build with short tail, usually cocked up*, are characteristic. The wings, tail and flanks are distinctly, and the back more obscurely, barred; it has a pale buffish eye-stripe. Juveniles resemble adults, but are more mottled below, and less barred. Length about 3¾ ins.

Habitat. It occupies a great variety of habitats, frequenting almost any sort of cultivated or uncultivated ground which provides some kind of low cover, from lowland hedgerows, gardens, thickets, woodland, or reed-beds, to an occasional bush or bramble patch on upland moors and rock faces, boulder-strewn tops of high mountains, and rocky coasts or marine islands.

General Habits. Bustling and active, it is constantly on the move, hunting for insects in cover or the open, and often disappears from view amongst tangled vegetation or as it examines every little crevice of tree trunks or rocks. It occasionally goes quite high in trees, but keeps for the most part low down and is often flushed from under overhanging banks and other hidden nooks and corners. It flies quite swiftly and straight, but generally for a short distance only, with rapid whirring wing-action. It is not generally gregarious, but numbers sometimes roost together in hard weather.

Commonest note is a hard, rattling, slightly tremulous "tic-tic-tic". The song, delivered with great vehemence and remarkably loud for the bird's size, is a rattling warble of clear shrill notes in quick time, which is given usually from some low perch, but not infrequently on the wing and occasionally at night. It is heard throughout the year, regularly in December and from the beginning of February to early August, less frequently at other times.

Food is mainly insects; also spiders and some seeds.

Nests in hedges, ivy, sides of stacks, thatch, out-buildings, old nests of other birds, etc. The eggs, usually 5–6, sometimes 3 to 7–11 or more, sometimes unmarked, are laid from the latter part of April onwards in a nest built by the cock, which makes several but does not line them, the lining being added by hen to that nest used for breeding. It is constructed of moss, dead grass, bracken, dead leaves, etc., neatly domed, with a rounded entrance at the side and freely lined with feathers. Incubation is by hen alone, usually for about 14–15 days. The young are fed by both parents and fly when about 16–17 days old. Normally two broods.

Status and Distribution. Resident and generally distributed but some coastal passage occurs between mid-September and mid-November and between March and May. Separate races occur on isolated island groups: on St. Kilda *Troglodytes troglodytes hirtensis*, which is larger, rather greyer-brown above and paler below than the common form; in Shetland *Troglodytes*

troglodytes zetlandicus, distinctly darker and looks bulkier; the Fair Isle bird, *Troglodytes troglodytes fridariensis*, is closer to the mainland form; in the Outer Hebrides, *Troglodytes troglodytes hebridensis* resembles the Shetland race but is not so dark below. The race nesting in most parts of the British Isles, *Troglodytes troglodytes troglodytes*, also breeds in Europe from about the Arctic Circle to N. Spain, Sicily and S. Russia; also in Asia Minor. Other races occur in Iceland, Faeroes, N.W. Africa, Spain, Mediterranean islands, from S. Russia across Asia and in N. America.

DUNNOCK (or HEDGE SPARROW)—*Prunella modularis*

BIRD PLATE 88   EGG PLATE III (16)

It lacks conspicuous features, but the moderately plump build, *slender bill and combination of brown and grey* serve to distinguish the species. The general colour of adults is warm brown, broadly streaked blackish, with the breast, throat and head grey, and the ear-coverts and crown browner, the latter with dark markings. It has a narrow buffish wing-bar. Juvenile is less rufous and more spotted, with a browner head. Length about 5¾ ins.

Habitat. It favours gardens, shrubberies, spinneys, hedgerows and bushy places rather than actual woodland. It also occurs to some extent amongst low scrub of open moorland and other comparatively barren land, and even rocky marine islets.

General Habits. Unobtrusive rather than secretive, its presence is often first proclaimed by the insistent call-note and, during the greater part of year, by song. It feeds much on the ground proceeding by leisurely short hops or a kind of creeping walk, with the body carried almost horizontal and legs much flexed, with belly near the ground. It usually perches low, chiefly in the cover of foliage and often flicks its wings in a characteristic manner. It is not really gregarious at any time.

Main call is a shrill, piping "tseep", somewhat prolonged as alarm-note. The song is a short high-pitched warbling strain, more subdued and more musical than Wren's. It is delivered usually from a hedgerow or bush, but sometimes from fair-sized trees, and is heard exceptionally during most of August and the first half of September, more regularly to mid-October and in the second half of July, and regularly for the rest of the year.

Food is almost entirely seeds in winter, but much animal matter in summer.

Nests in hedges and evergreens, also often in stick-heaps and in ivy, on banks and occasionally in old nests of other birds. The eggs, usually 4–5, occasionally 3–6, are laid generally from April onwards in a nest, built by hen only, with a foundation of twigs, much moss with bents, a few dead leaves, roots, etc., and lined neatly with moss and hair or wool: feathers are occasionally freely used. Incubation is by hen for about 12–13 days. The young are fed by both sexes and fly usually when about 12 days old. Two broods regularly, three occasionally.

Status and Distribution. Mainly a resident, generally distributed but scarce in Orkney, and it nested in 1965 in Shetland. There is some southward movement from late September to early November, with return from March to May. The breeding bird in most parts of the British Isles (also W. France) is *Prunella modularis occidentalis*, but it is replaced in the Hebrides and part of W. Scotland by a darker race, *Prunella modularis hebridium*. Also occurring as a regular but scarce passage-migrant is the race *Prunella modularis modularis* which breeds in most parts of Europe, except the south-east and south-west, also in W. Asia; it is usually paler below and brighter brown above than our bird, but is indistinguishable in the field. Other races occur in parts of Spain, Portugal, S. Russia and W. Asia.

ALPINE ACCENTOR—*Prunella collaris*

BIRD PLATE 89

In appearance it suggests a large, robust, brightly-coloured Hedge Sparrow with a *whitish bib spotted with black*, and with conspicuous *chestnut feathers with light borders on the sides. Light tips to the dark brown tail-feathers* are conspicuous in flight and whitish spots on the coverts form a double white wing-bar. Juveniles are duller with greyish, unspotted throats, and first winter plumage resembles adult, but many young birds have unspotted throats as late as September. Length about 7 ins.

Habitat. In winter it occurs chiefly amongst mountains, but also on rocky and scrubby ground in lowlands.

General Habits. Quiet and unobtrusive in habits, it is frequently first seen when flushed from amongst rocks when it flies low for a short distance with rather undulating action. Carriage is like Hedge Sparrow, and it occasionally jerks its tail and flutters its wings. It will occasionally perch on a low bush or plant stem.

Usual note when flushed is a characteristic rippling "tchirriri-*rip*", sometimes rather lark-like.

Food in autumn and winter consists chiefly of seeds and berries; insects in summer.

Status and Distribution. A rare vagrant which has occurred mainly from August to January, rarely in spring, chiefly appearing in the southern English counties, but there are records from Wales and Fair Isle. The race concerned, *Prunella collaris collaris*, breeds in the mountains of N.W. Africa, S.W. and mid-Europe. Other races occur in S.E. Europe and across Asia.

ROBIN—*Erithacus rubecula*

BIRD PLATE 90 EGG PLATE III (15A & 15B)

The familiar and distinctive plumage of adults, olive-brown above with *bright orange fore-head, throat and breast* bordered by pale grey, scarcely requires description, but the juvenile lacks the orange breast and has a noticeably spotted appearance. Length about 5½ ins.

Habitat. It is found alike about gardens, shrubberies, hedge-rows and the neighbourhood of habitations, and in woods and copses with considerable undergrowth far from cultivation.

General Habits. Its engaging manners and trustful disposition towards man render the Robin perhaps most generally known of British birds. Though essentially a bird of thick undergrowth and capable of exceedingly skulking and secretive behaviour during moult in late summer, when often only its irrepressible scolding note proclaims its presence, it ordinarily feeds freely in the open (though not as a rule far from cover), on lawns and about houses and cultivated ground. It frequently flicks the wings and tail; also bobs, especially when excited. Flight as a rule is low and for a short distance only. It perches in all sorts of situations, but usually low down except sometimes when singing. It is pugnacious toward its own kind and other birds, individuals of each sex occupying and defending separate territories from August to mid-winter.

Commonest note is the scolding "tic, tic", also much used at roosting time. Calls are a high-pitched thin "tswee" and a soft, thin "tsit". The song, melodious and varied though with a certain melancholy quality, consists of short liquid warbly phrases, some rather shrill. It is delivered usually from low down, often from

cover but sometimes well up in trees, occasionally on the wing,
ground and at night. It is heard throughout most of the year,
regularly from the end of July through to mid-June, and less
frequently to mid-July. The female also sings.

Food is mainly insects. Also spiders and centipedes; and
vegetable matter includes seeds of many kinds, fruit and berries.

Nests often in a hollow on bank side, occasionally in a stump or
hole, also amongst ivy, in thick growth of hedges and at times in
sheds or even in old tins, etc. The eggs, normally 4–6, sometimes
3–9, are laid generally from the end of March or early April
onwards in a nest, built by the hen only, with a foundation of dead
leaves and moss, neatly lined with hair and sometimes a feather or
two; it is generally rather bulky, but often cleverly concealed.
Incubation is by hen only, usually for 13–14 days. The young are
fed by both parents and fly when about 12–14 days old. Double-
brooded, sometimes three.

Status and Distribution. Present throughout the year, and
generally distributed, but local in the extreme north Scottish
mainland and in Orkney, and absent from Shetland. Our breeding
birds belong to the race *Erithacus rubecula melophilus*, which
is confined to the British Isles and Channel Islands (perhaps
also Portugal). Many are strictly sedentary, but especially in the
north considerable southward movements occur in autumn, and
some birds cross the channel. In addition, from September to
November passage-migrants and winter-visitors arrive from the
Continent, appearing mainly on the east side north to Shetland,
and returning from March to May. These birds, which belong to
the race *Erithacus rubecula rubecula*, are less domesticated,
wilder and often much more skulking than the British bird, and in
the hand are distinguished by their paler colouring; they breed
from N. Scandinavia south to mid-Spain, Sicily, Greece, and S.
Russia, also in the Azores, Madeira and W. Canaries. Other races
occur in the Mediterranean, S. Spain, N. Africa, E. Canaries and
W. Asia.

NIGHTINGALE—*Luscinia megarhynchos*

BIRD PLATE 91   EGG PLATE III (14A & 14B)

The unique *song* is the best guide to the bird's presence, but it is
recognized when seen by the *uniform russet-brown upper-parts
and more rufous upper tail-coverts and tail*, conspicuous in flight.

Under-parts are pale greyish-brown tending to whitish on the throat and abdomen. The sexes are similar. Juveniles have a spotted and mottled appearance much like young Robins, but with rufous tails. Length about 6½ ins.

Habitat. In the breeding-season it haunts open deciduous woods with thick under-growth, thickets and bushy places, and tangled hedgerows, tending to avoid hilly country.

General Habits. Form, carriage, and mannerisms somewhat suggest a large Robin, but the build, though sturdy, is better proportioned and more graceful, and movements though alert and sprightly, are more deliberate. It is more constantly skulking than Robin, generally keeping amongst cover of foliage not far from the ground. It is partial to moist places, and feeds much on the ground, largely amongst undergrowth. Its carriage is rather erect, legs fairly straight, and tail commonly cocked up. Flight is much as Robin, usually low and for a short distance only.

Calls are a soft "hweet", very like Chiffchaff and Willow Warbler, but often louder, and a hard "tacc, tacc" or softer "tucc, tucc". Alarm notes are croaking, or harsh and grating. The song, remarkable for its richness and variety and the extraordinary vigour of its delivery, consists of a succession of repetitive phrases, mostly in quick time and many *much* quicker than any other first-rate British songster. Most striking are the extremely rapid, loud "chooc-chooc-chooc-chooc-chooc . . ." and the fluty, much higher-pitched "pioo" repeated rather slowly in a magnificent crescendo. It sings chiefly from low cover or amongst the foliage of lower branches of trees, but sometimes fully exposed. It is heard regularly from mid-April to early June, less regularly for a fortnight longer and exceptionally into July.

Food is mainly worms and insects. Spiders, fruit and berries are also eaten.

Nests generally on or close to the ground, occasionally a few feet above it, among coarse grass, nettles, or trailing ivy. The eggs, usually 4–5, occasionally 3–6, are laid generally in May in a nest built by hen alone with a bulky foundation, mainly of oak or other dead leaves, and lined with dead grasses and sometimes hair or a few leaves. Incubation is by hen alone for about 13–14 days. The young are fed by both sexes and leave the nest when about 11–12 days old. Single-brooded.

Status and Distribution. A summer-visitor to S. parts of England, becoming scarce in some areas, but still fairly well distributed, not extending much north or west of a line from the Humber to Severn but breeds regularly north to Shrewsbury; also locally in Monmouth and irregularly in S. Yorks. It does not breed

in Cornwall. It has occurred on very few occasions in central and
N. Wales, N. England and Scotland, and very rarely in Ireland.
Abroad the race concerned, *Luscinia megarhynchos megarhynchos*
breeds from Denmark, W. Poland and S.W. Russia south to N.W.
Africa, Sicily, and Cyprus; and winters in tropical Africa. Other
races occur in S. Russia and W. Asia.

BLUETHROAT—*Luscinia svecica*

Bird Plate 89

In form it resembles a slim Robin. *The brilliant blue gorget of
male in spring, with chestnut border below*, is very striking, but the
bright reddish base to the dark brown tail is diagnostic at all ages,
conspicuous in flight and when tail is spread. A chestnut patch in
the middle of the gorget distinguishes male of the Red-spotted race
from male of the White-spotted race, which has a satiny white spot
on the gorget or occasionally no spot at all. Females and young of
the two races are not certainly distinguishable. Female has the
gorget whitish, defined by a dark breast-band and stripes at the
sides, with some dark spots and sometimes more or less blue round
the borders and with traces of chestnut. Autumn birds are readily
identified by the tail-pattern and *conspicuous white eye-stripe*, but
vary rather bewilderingly in throat-pattern. Adult male is then
more like female, but with a good deal more blue and chestnut,
though somewhat obscured by light edgings. Young males may be

Tail of Bluethroat

Note the (reddish) patches
on each side of the basal
half of the tail.

much like some females, while young females lack the dark throat-spots of adult and have normally no trace of blue. Juveniles are considerably darker than young Robins, with much more streaked, rather than spotted, pattern, and tails as adults. Length about 5½ ins.

Habitat. As a passage-migrant it frequents scrub, gardens, etc., with bushes, rank grass and rootfields in the neighbourhood of the coast, and even cliffs.

General Habits. It is very skulking, spending most of its time on the ground amongst rank vegetation or in the case of migrants, often amongst root-crops. When flushed it flies low, for a short distance only, with Robin-like action, and dives into cover again, but almost always flattening out at the last moment instead of diving vertically down like most other small migrants in similar circumstances. If undisturbed will emerge to feed in the open. The tail is cocked well up and frequently flirted in a lively way; it also spreads tail on alighting and bobs like a Robin.

Usual note is a chat-like "tacc, tacc" varied by a more plaintive "hweet".

Food consists of insects, also small snails, worms and seeds.

Status and Distribution. A regular autumn passage-migrant from the end of August to mid-October, less often observed in spring, occurring on Scottish islands, especially Fair Isle and Isle of May, and the E. coast of England, but apparently only occasionally on the S. coast. It has also occurred several times in Ireland. A nest was found in the Moray area in Scotland in June 1968. The Red-spotted Bluethroat, *Luscinia svecica svecica*, which is the race mainly concerned, breeds from Scandinavia across N. Russia to W. Siberia. Some examples have also occurred of the White-spotted Bluethroat, *Luscinia svecica cyanecula*, the males of which are distinguished as described above, and which breeds in middle Europe from central Spain, Switzerland and Jugoslavia north to Belgium, Denmark, the Baltic States and W. Russia. These races winter in W. Africa and S.W. Asia. Other races occur in W. France, S. Russia and in Asia.

BLACK REDSTART—*Phoenicurus ochruros*

BIRD PLATE 90   EGG PLATE XVII (4)

Has the typical Redstart tail, but its darker colouring and *absence of any trace of orange or buff on the under-parts* are distinctive at all ages. Adult male is darker grey above than

Redstart, with *the breast as well as the throat black, a whitish patch on the wing* in full plumage and usually no white on the fore-head. Females and young are darker than Redstarts, with *grey under-parts*, and the juveniles hardly differ. Male in autumn has the black obscured by greyish edgings. A good many young males breed in immature plumage, looking more like females, with little or no white in the wing. Length about 5½ ins.

Habitat. In the breeding-season it haunts the vicinity of buildings, ruins and old walls, open and waste ground near habitations, and showed a particular preference for bomb-damaged buildings in large towns; it also frequents rocky and boulder-strewn ground and marine or other cliffs. In winter it occurs in similar places, as well as downs with rocky outcrops, the sea-shore and waste places; in S. England it is particularly addicted to unsightly "dumps" and heaps of rubble or old buildings near the shore.

General Habits. Flight, carriage, tail movement and other mannerisms are like Redstart, but it is much more on the ground, perching chiefly on rocks or other eminences and on buildings, walls, etc.; when on trees or bushes it keeps to exposed perches. It is adept at hawking insects on the wing, often hovering while so engaged.

Call-note is "tsip", shorter and less plaintive than Redstart's. This note also frequently introduces the alarm or scold, "tucc-tucc". The complete song is a quick warble like that of the common species, but less rich and loud, interrupted towards the end by a remarkable sound exactly like a handful of small metal balls shaken together. It is heard regularly from late March to early July and again from late August to early October.

Food is mainly insects. Spiders and millipedes are also taken, and berries in late summer and winter.

Nests in a hole or ledge in buildings, in fissures or holes of rocks, or inside sheds, or rafters under eaves, etc. The white eggs, usually 4–6, are laid generally from early April onwards in a nest normally built by hen alone, loosely constructed of dry grasses, moss, fibre, etc., and lined with hair and feathers. Incubation is by hen alone for about 12–13 days. The young are fed by both sexes and leave the nest when about 16–18 days old. Two broods normal; occasionally three.

Status and Distribution. Present throughout the year in England, a few pairs nesting more or less regularly in the London area, also at coastal sites in Sussex, Kent and E. Anglia, and in the Midlands, after establishment in most of these localities following the bomb-damage of 1940–1941. A very few pairs, however, had bred in Middlesex and Sussex in the preceding 15–18 years. At its post-war peak breeding occurred temporarily as far afield as Yorkshire, Shropshire and S.W. England. Breeding quarters are mainly deserted in winter, movement occurring from August to late November and the return from March to May. It winters regularly in the S. and especially S.W. counties of England and fairly frequently in S. Wales. It is more widespread on passage, occurring fairly often as far north as Shetland, but is rare on the W. side and Scottish mainland. In Ireland it is fairly regular in autumn and occurs too in winter and spring, chiefly on the S. and E. coasts; rare elsewhere. The race concerned, *Phoenicurus ochruros gibraltariensis*, breeds from S. Scandinavia south to the Mediterranean countries and Morocco; and winters mainly in the Mediterranean area. Other races occur in W. and central Asia.

REDSTART—*Phoenicurus phoenicurus*

BIRD PLATE 90   EGG PLATE III (13)

Redstarts are distinguished at all ages from all other British birds by the *orange-chestnut tail, constantly moved with a quivering up-and-down motion* quite different from the flicks of other chats. Adult males of both species have a black face and throat, but common Redstart has *the breast and flanks orange* like the rump and tail, french-grey upper-parts, and *white forehead*, and cannot well be confused with Black Redstart. Females and young of the two species are more similar, but in the present species the upper-parts are lighter greyish-brown and the under-parts a delicate orange-buff instead of grey. Juvenile Redstarts have mottled plumage rather like young Robins (but with the characteristic tail), while juvenile Black Redstarts are very like adult females. Length about 5½ ins.

Habitat. In the breeding-season it inhabits old deciduous woods and parkland, commons with scattered trees, orchards, stream sides with pollard willows, open hilly country with loose stone walls, and to some extent ruins and rocky localities.

General Habits. An active and restless bird, constantly flitting about amongst branches or making little fluttering and hovering excursions into the air after insects. Flight, carriage and gait hardly differ from Robin and it has the same trick of bobbing, but is seldom long on the ground and much more arboreal. It perches freely on exposed branches of trees, often high up, as well as on bushes, fences and buildings, but also at times skulks in foliage.

Call-notes are a plaintive "hooweet", very like that of Willow Warbler, and a rather liquid "twick" or "tooick". The song is a very brief but melodious, rather Robin-like warble petering out in a characteristic little jangle of notes curiously mechanical in effect. It is heard regularly from early April to the second half of June, with less frequency into July and exceptionally in August.

Food is mainly insects. Spiders, small worms and berries are also taken occasionally.

Nests generally in a hole of a tree or stump in the south, also in walls and occasionally in old sheds or outhouses. Farther north a common site is in loose stone walls. The eggs, normally 6, sometimes 5 or up to 10, occasionally with fine speckles, are laid generally from mid-May onwards, in a nest built usually by hen alone of grasses, strips of bark, moss, roots, and lined with hair and feathers. Incubation is chiefly by hen for about 12–14 days. The young are fed by both sexes and fly usually when about 14–15 days old. Double-brooded frequently.

Status and Distribution. A summer-migrant, widely distributed in Great Britain, but local and fluctuating. It does not nest in Cornwall and parts of Devon and is rare in the extreme north of the Scottish mainland and in E. midlands. As a passage-migrant only, it is well known in Orkney and Shetland, but scarce in the Outer Hebrides. It does not breed in the Isle of Man, and very rarely in Ireland where a sprinkling appear annually on migration on the S. and E. coasts. Our birds arrive from early April to the second half of May, with passage continuing to mid-June; the return movement lasts from July to October. They belong to the race *Phoenicurus phoenicurus phoenicurus* which breeds from N. Norway and W. Siberia south to N.E. Spain, Sicily and W. Asia Minor, and east to central Asia; wintering in tropical Africa. Other races occur in the Iberian peninsula, N.W. Africa, and E. Asia Minor to Iran.

WHINCHAT—*Saxicola rubetra*

Bird Plate 91   Egg Plate III (11)

Stonechat and Whinchat are rather short-tailed birds perching especially on the tops of bushes or other plants and resembling one another in habits and behaviour. Male Whinchat, with streaked brown upper-parts, and dark lores and ear-coverts bounded by a *prominent white eye-stripe* above and white mark below, cannot be mistaken for the black-headed Stonechat, but females and young of the two species can be confused. The *eyestripe* of female Whinchat, however, though duller and buffer than in adult male, is distinct at all ages, while *white at the sides of the base of tail*, and the *under-parts a delicate warm buff* instead of dull reddish are further good characters. Its carriage is less upright and build slighter, less stocky, than Stonechat. The wings and terminal part of the tail are blackish; there is a broad white wing-mark in male, smaller in female and absent in juvenile. Male in autumn is duller, more like female. Length about 5 ins.

Habitat. In the breeding-season it inhabits a fair variety of open country, but generally rough grasslands of some sort with a few bushes, bracken, etc., ranging from lowland meadows, marshes, and commons to upland pastures and hillsides. In autumn root-fields, etc., are visited.

General Habits. Carriage is rather upright, and it bobs and flicks the tail and wings. It perches chiefly on the tops of bushes or sprays of ground plants in the open, flying low from one to another with rapidly moving wings and jerky flight; it also perches freely on trees and telegraph-wires, but not in the cover of foliage. It is rather crepuscular in habits, remaining active till dark. It sometimes occurs in family parties in autumn.

Chief note is a scolding "tic-tic", akin to, but not so hard as, Stonechat's note, combined with a liquid, musical "tu". The brief warbling song shows close affinities with other British chats, but is rather variable. It is heard regularly from the latter part of April to the end of June, and less frequently in the first half of July.

Food is mainly insects, also spiders and worms.

STONECHAT   WHINCHAT

Note Whinchat's eyestripe and more chequered back.

Nests usually on the ground in mowing grass, or at the foot of a low bush. The eggs, normally 5–6, rarely 4–7, are laid generally in the second half of May or early June in a nest built by hen only, of dry grass with moss in the foundation, lined with finer bents and hair. Incubation is by hen alone for about 13 days. The young are fed by both parents and leave the nest when about 13 days old. Double-brooded at times.

Status and Distribution. A summer-visitor, widely distributed and locally fairly numerous in Scotland and Wales and English uplands but has decreased in lowland areas throughout England and is now scarce or missing in many counties, especially south of a line from Wash to Severn. It is scarce in Outer Hebrides and does not breed now in Orkney or Shetland; irregular or absent from many Irish counties. It arrives in April and May, with passage lasting into June, and returns from mid-July to early October; on rare occasions individuals have wintered. Abroad the bird breeds from N. Scandinavia and W. Siberia south to N. Portugal, Sicily, and N. Iran, and winters in tropical Africa. There are no subspecies.

STONECHAT—*Saxicola torquata*

Bird Plate 91   Egg Plate III (12)

It perches like Whinchat on the tops of bushes, constantly spreading and flirting its tail and flicking wings, and is particularly attached to gorse. *The black head of male, with a white patch on the sides of the neck, white wing-patch*, and white rump more or less obscured by dark markings, are distinctive. Female and young have streaked brown upper-parts, without white on the neck or rump, and are more like Whinchats, but are duller looking, without eye-stripe or white at sides of the tail and with dull reddish, not buff, breasts. Male has back almost black in spring and under-parts chestnut; in autumn brown edgings to the black feathers make the pattern duller. Wings and tail are blackish. Length about 5 ins.

Habitat. Its habitat overlaps with Whinchat's, but the Stonechat has an even stronger liking for neglected ground and occurs less in cultivated country. In the breeding-season it frequents gorse-grown commons, wastes, especially near the sea, rough hillsides or upland moors with a few bushes, brambles, etc.

It occurs to a less extent about road-side hedgerows and neglected corners in cultivated country, and in autumn and winter is more frequent in such places, also visiting reed-beds, etc.

General Habits. These and behaviour are very like Whinchat, though build is plumper and carriage generally more erect. It perches less on trees, preferring top sprays of gorse or other bushes, and is active and restless. It tends to lead a rather nomadic existence in winter, commonly in pairs.

Usual notes are an insistent, hard "tsak, tsak" like two pebbles struck together, and a plaintive "hweet"; often the two in combination. The song is somewhat variable, sometimes much like Hedge Sparrow, and is delivered from a prominent perch or in a vertical dancing song-flight. It is heard sometimes in the first half of March, thereafter regularly until mid-June and less regularly again until mid-July.

Food is chiefly insects; also spiders and worms.

Nests often on the ground at the foot of a clump of gorse or thick bush, with sometimes a run leading up to it, but occasionally as much as 2 ft. above the ground. The eggs, normally 5–6, rarely 3–8, are laid from late March to June or July in a nest, built by hen only, of moss and grasses, sometimes bits of dead thistle, gorse or wool, neatly lined with bents, hair, and sometimes feathers. Incubation is nearly always by hen for about 14–15 days. The young are fed by both sexes and leave the nest when about 12–13 days old, flying a few days later. Two broods normally; probably three occasionally.

Status and Distribution. Present throughout the year. It has decreased considerably in England and Wales, and as a regular breeder is largely confined to south and west coastal counties, also Northumberland, East Anglia and inland in Surrey, Shropshire and Montgomery. It remains widely scattered in Ireland and Scotland north to Orkney; it has only occasionally bred in Shetland, first in 1961. Some adults are resident but in many districts, especially inland, it is only a summer-visitor, and in other areas a winter-visitor. It can be severely hit by hard weather in winter. Movement and emigration occur between August and November, the return from mid-February to May. British birds belong to the race *Saxicola torquata hibernans* which also breeds in N.W. France and Portugal. A few examples have been obtained in this country in autumn resembling *Saxicola torquata maura* from E. Russia and W. Siberia which is paler than our bird, particularly on the rump. Other races occur in middle and S. Europe, N.W. Africa, and across Asia to Japan.

WHEATEAR—*Oenanthe oenanthe*

BIRD PLATE 92   EGG PLATE III (10)

Wheatears are active, dapper looking, rather short-tailed, ground-living birds of open country, all with much the same habits and mode of behaviour. *The white rump and base of tail* separate the common Wheatear from all our other native birds of similar habits. Male in the breeding-season has french-grey upper-parts, a black mark on the sides of the face bordered by white above, blackish wings, and white under-parts faintly to strongly tinged with sandy-buff on the breast. The broad terminal band and central feathers of the tail are black. Female is brown above and buff below, with the blacks replaced by dark brown, the dark facial mark being often quite obscure; male in autumn is similar. Juveniles have a spotted appearance, but the tail and wings are like old female. Length about 5¾ ins.

Habitat. In the breeding-season it haunts bare hillsides and upland pastures, stony mountain-tops, sea-cliffs, warrens, and other barren, rocky, or waste places.

General Habits. It is active and restless, moving on the ground in a quick succession of long hops, frequently halting on some little eminence or flitting a short distance from one such perch to another, or making little fluttering dashes into the air after insects; it occasionally hovers. At rest the carriage is rather upright, but it is seldom long still, constantly bowing and bobbing and at the same time spreading the tail and moving it up and down. It also perches on stone walls, fences, and sometimes bushes, almost always flying low till close to the perch. It readily takes shelter in holes or under rocks, etc.

Note is a hard "chack, chack" or "weet-chack-chack". The song, superior to that of other British chats and delivered with great gusto, is a short, pleasantly modulated warble in which melodious rather lark-like notes are mingled with harsh, creaky and rattling sounds. It is delivered from some little eminence or in song-flight, and sometimes in ordinary flight; it is sometimes heard in late March, regularly from April to mid-June, sometimes to mid-July and exceptionally in mid-September.

Food is chiefly insects. Also small molluscs, centipedes, and spiders.

Nests in a hole in the ground or under stones, or in old walls, drain-pipes, old tins, etc. The eggs, normally 6, sometimes 3–8, occasionally showing dark spots, are laid generally in May or late April, in a nest built chiefly by hen with male usually helping, constructed of grasses and sometimes moss, lined with grass and hair, feathers or bits of wool. Incubation is chiefly by hen for about 14 days. The young are fed by both sexes and leave the nest when about 15 days old. Usually single-brooded.

Status and Distribution. A summer-visitor, but it appears in winter very occasionally. It is still widespread, though local, in much of northern and western Britain and Ireland, but in the southern half of England is now very scarce or no longer nests in a number of counties from Scillies to Lincs. It arrives from early March to late April, with passage continuing until early June; the return movement extends from late July until the second half of October, occasionally later. Our breeding birds belong to the race *Oenanthe oenanthe oenanthe* which ranges throughout Europe (except S. Spain) and N. Asia and winters in tropical Africa and S. Arabia. The race *Oenanthe oenanthe leucorhoa*, breeding in Greenland, N.E. Canada and Labrador, is a regular passage-migrant through Great Britain and Ireland; it tends to have a more upright stance, and to perch not merely on bushes, but even quite high up in trees; moreover in spring some males of this race have deeper buff under-parts, but a large proportion are quite unidentifiable in the field. Other races occur in S. Spain and N. Africa.

BLACK-EARED WHEATEAR—*Oenanthe hispanica*

BIRD PLATE 92

The bold contrasts of male plumage are greater in this species than in any other light-backed wheatear. *Males are dimorphic, with either a black mark through the eye, and throat whitish, or the whole throat black*. The general colour is *pale sandy-buff, often shading to nearly pure white on the crown*, and whiter below, but occasional individuals have the mantle practically pure white in summer. The colour of the upper parts at once distinguishes the Black-eared phase from the common Wheatear, which has also not so much white on the tail, though rump and tail pattern are otherwise similar. *Very black wings, specially emphasized by the black extending over scapulars*, form another difference. Female is much like common Wheatear, but has the scapulars, wings, and tail as male, though the blacks are browner, and general colour more sandy. In autumn stronger buff colouring and buff edgings to the wing-feathers and scapulars make pattern of the male a trifle less striking, and young males are duller than adults, which may have the buff of the upper-parts very bright; immatures are very easily confused with common Wheatear. Length about 5¾ ins.

Habitat. It frequents chiefly dry, stony and barren places, arid pastures or rough cultivation.

General Habits. In behaviour it is almost exactly like Wheatear, though perhaps rather more prone to perch.

Notes are of the usual Wheatear type, but include a distinctive, rasping "tshrrrek".

Food is apparently almost entirely insects.

Status and Distribution. A rare vagrant which has appeared in spring (March–June) and September–October. The records are widely scattered in England, Scotland and Ireland. They refer both to the race *Oenanthe hispanica hispanica*, which breeds in the Mediterranean region of Europe and Africa from Sicily westwards, and to the race *Oenanthe hispanica melanoleuca* which breeds from S. Italy eastwards to W. Iran. Eastern males usually become whiter in spring and summer than those of the western race and in the black-throated phase the black extends farther down the throat, while black-eared examples have more black on the forehead. The species winters in tropical Africa.

WHITE'S THRUSH—*Zoothera dauma*

BIRD PLATE 95

It is characterized by a *bold pattern of crescentic black markings over the upper- as well as the under-parts.* Movements and general appearance are suggestive of Mistle Thrush, but at close range the crescentic markings are distinctly visible. *A broad black band on the underside of the wing with a white band behind it* at once identifies the bird in flight. The ground-colour of upper-parts is yellowish, of under-parts white. The tail has central feathers brown, but the sides are darker, with whitish tips. Young Mistle Thrushes, which have a more particoloured appearance than adults, show remote resemblance to the much bolder and richer pattern of White's Thrush and have a white under-wing; moreover their rump and upper tail-coverts are only faintly marked, while in White's Thrush the crescentic pattern extends to the very base of the tail. The sexes are similar, and the young are much like adults. Length about 10½ ins.

Habitat. Dense forest with heavy undergrowth is its normal habitat.

General Habits. It is very shy, and extremely difficult to observe in the thick cover which it haunts. It feeds principally on the ground, but flies up into trees when disturbed, and is solitary in habits. Flight is very undulating, like that of Green Woodpecker. A very silent bird as a rule, but has a characteristic Bullfinch-like melodious piping call-note.

Food is largely insects.

Status and Distribution. A rare vagrant occurring almost always in winter. It has been recorded in a number of widely scattered English counties and a few times in Scotland and Ireland. The race concerned, *Zoothera dauma aureus*, breeds across Siberia and in Japan. Other races occur in S. Asia and Australasia.

RING OUZEL—*Turdus torquatus*

BIRD PLATE 93   EGG PLATE III (4A & 4B)

The sooty-black plumage with white crescent on the breast distinguishes adult male. The secondaries and coverts have greyish edges, so that, unlike Blackbird, the *closed wing appears paler than the rest* in all plumages. After the autumn moult it has also light edgings to the body feathers, especially of the under-parts. *Its loud chatter often serves for identification at long range.* Female is browner, with the light edgings more prominent, and has a *narrower brown-tinged gorget.* Juveniles lack the gorget entirely and are not unlike young Blackbirds, but are much less rufous, more greyish, brown, with under-parts more closely mottled with dark brown and whitish, and have whitish-buff, drop-shaped shaft marks on the coverts. Immature females in first autumn and winter may have the gorget barely distinguishable, but immature males are much like adults. Length about 9½ ins.

Habitat. In the breeding-season it haunts moorlands and rocky or scrubby hill- and mountain-sides. On migration it also occurs in lowlands, chiefly where there are tall berry-bearing hedgerows and bushes, but also sometimes in open country near the sea.

General Habits. Carriage and actions on the ground resemble Blackbird, and like that species, it elevates its tail on alighting, and is noisy at nightfall, but is much more a bird of the open, perching freely in exposed positions, and is much shyer and less approachable. It is bold and aggressive, however, in defence of nest. Flight is bolder than Blackbird's, generally rapid and direct. It is gregarious at migration seasons.

It has a clear piping call, a hard loud "tac-tac-tac", and a "chick-chick" note less shrill than Blackbird's; also on migration a more trilling note recalling the ordinary note of Dunlin. The usual form of song is a mere repetition of a loud, clear, single or double piping note, but at the beginning of the season it has also a fuller song. It is heard regularly from late March till the second half of June, less frequently to the first week in July.

Food in summer consists of worms, insects and small molluscs. In autumn berries and fruit are also taken.

Nests among heather-grown banks of water-courses, on broken moorland in rocky ravines and old buildings. The eggs, normally 4, occasionally 3 or 5–6, often resembling the more boldly marked types of Blackbird, are laid from mid-April onwards, in a nest built by both sexes of coarse grasses, with a few heather twigs and earth in the foundation, and lined with fine dry grasses. Incubation is by both sexes for about 14 days. The young are fed by both sexes and fly when about 14 days old. Usually double-brooded.

Status and Distribution. It is a summer-visitor and passage-migrant normally arriving from the first half of March to May and leaving from late August to early November, but it occasionally stays throughout the winter. In Scotland it is generally distributed on the mainland and nests on most of the Inner Hebrides; also rarely in Orkney and Shetland but not Outer Hebrides; apparently not Isle of Man; in Ireland it is thinly distributed in the wilder mountain districts of each province; it nests in most Welsh counties; in England it breeds regularly in hilly districts in Devon and Somerset, on the Welsh border and the Pennines northwards, also in N.E. Yorkshire. It has visited most English counties on migration and nested exceptionally in several entirely outside its normal range. Our bird belongs to the race *Turdus torquatus torquatus* which breeds in Scandinavia, occasionally Finland, and winters in the Mediterranean area. Other races occur in S. Europe and W. Asia.

BLACKBIRD—*Turdus merula*

BIRD PLATE 93   EGG PLATE III (5A, 5B & 5C)

The glossy black plumage of male with *orange bill* and eye-rim is unmistakable. Female is *umber-brown above, lighter and usually more rufous-brown below, with more or less distinct dark mottlings* and a paler, more whitish, throat. Juveniles are lighter and more rufous than females, with mottling of the under-parts more pronounced and rufous shaft-streaks on the upper-parts. Young males have blackish bill and browner plumage than adults. Partial albinism is not uncommon and males with a white patch on the breast have sometimes been mistaken for Ring Ouzels, but the latter have duller, less jet-black plumage than adult Blackbird, whitish borders to the coverts and secondaries, and a different note. Length about 10 ins.

Habitat. It inhabits gardens, shrubberies, hedgerows, and woods with undergrowth, as well as more open localities such as rough hillsides, bushy commons, etc., in both cultivated and uncultivated districts, and occasionally even treeless islands.

General Habits. On alighting the tail is raised with an easy and graceful motion and the wings often drooped. More skulking than other thrushes, it readily takes shelter in and underneath bushes, and when feeding in the open is seldom far from hedges or other cover. It usually flies low and for short distances only, when the action appears rather weak and wavering. Much of its food is regularly obtained by turning over dead leaves; fruit and berry-bearing trees and shrubs are an attraction in summer and autumn. Except on migration it is never really gregarious.

Common note when disturbed is a low "tchook, tchook, tchook"; when startled it flies off with a characteristic "alarm rattle". The flight note, used especially on migration is a grating "dzzeeb". A persistent "chick-chick-chick . . ." is much used when going to roost. The rich fluty song is loud and fluent but the notes are not clearly defined as in Song Thrush, being merged into a continuous short warble. A certain languid ease of delivery is characteristic, and it is lower pitched, also richer and mellower, but tends to tail off into a feeble ending of subdued, creaky, chuckling notes. It is heard exceptionally or as subsong from about mid-December to early February, by the end of which month full song is regular, lasting to early July, but ceases entirely early in August; there is a slight recrudescence from late August to late September.

Food includes fruit, berries and seeds, also worms, insects, spiders, molluscs, etc.

Nests usually a few feet up in hedges, bushes and ivy, locally on banks or buildings, even in sheds, on the ground, or at a considerable height in trees. The eggs, rarely more than 4–5, often 3, occasionally unmarked clear blue, are laid mainly in April and May (some March), in a nest normally built by the hen and not unlike that of Song Thrush but usually with more moss, solidified with mud and also lined with it, but with an inner layer of dry grasses. Incubation is usually by hen alone for about 13–14 days. The young are fed by both parents and generally fly when 13–14 days old. Two or three broods normally.

Status and Distribution. Mainly a resident, and generally distributed, but local in the Outer Hebrides and Shetland. It is however much more common in winter in the N. and W. Scottish islands, a considerable immigration of Continental birds to these and other parts of Great Britain and Ireland arriving from late September until the end of November, returning in late February, March and April. Our birds belong to the race *Turdus merula merula* which breeds from Scandinavia south to N. Portugal and east to central Russia. Other races occur in S. Spain, N. Africa, S.E. Europe, W. and S. Asia.

FIELDFARE—*Turdus pilaris*

Bird Plate 94

The slate-grey head, nape and rump, contrasted with chestnut back and the blackish tail are distinctive, as is the flight-note. In flight the white axillaries and under-wing are conspicuous, as in Mistle Thrush. The crown is streaked black, the superciliary stripe whitish, throat and breast golden-brown streaked black; the rest of the under-parts are white, flanks boldly marked black, and the wings blackish-brown. The sexes are similar. Juveniles after the autumn moult are much like old birds, but the greys are browner. Length about 10 ins.

Habitat. In winter it is chiefly found in open country, on rough pasture, root-fields, etc., but also in open woodland, where a sufficient food supply of berries is available. The Blackbird-like nest is built in a tree or bush.

General Habits. It is shy and wary in winter, and *strongly gregarious*, leading a nomadic existence often in flocks up to several hundred. These keep up a constant clamour as they pass to and fro, and feed chiefly in the open, scattered in loose formation over the fields, and flying up into trees if disturbed, where they sit as a rule all facing one way. In woodland it never skulks in undergrowth like Song Thrush or Blackbird, but perches always in the open on bushes or branches of trees. Carriage and behaviour on the ground resemble Mistle Thrush, and it has a rather similar leisurely flight.

The characteristic note, chiefly in flight, is a harsh "cha-cha-cha-chack".

Food in winter is varied, including slugs, worms, insects, spiders, many kinds of berries, and some seeds.

Status and Distribution. It is generally distributed throughout the British Isles as a winter-visitor and passage-migrant arriving between late September and mid-December and returning from late March to early May or later. Nesting, first in Orkney in 1967 and later Shetland, is now perhaps annual in the northern half of Scotland, and has occurred sporadically in England. It breeds from N. Norway south to Switzerland, recently in Denmark, and east to N. Siberia; also Greenland. It seldom migrates as far south as the Mediterranean in winter. There are no subspecies.

SONG THRUSH—*Turdus philomelos*

BIRD PLATE 94   EGG PLATE III (2A & 2B)

It differs from Mistle Thrush in smaller size, *warmer brown upper-parts, and warmer buff of the breast and flanks*, with *smaller, narrower spots*. In flight the axillaries and under-wing are golden-brown. Tail-feathers are uniform; buffish tips to the coverts form two faint wing-bars. Juveniles have buff streaks on the upper-parts. Length about 9 ins.

Habitat. It inhabits gardens, shrubberies and woods with undergrowth, thickets, and hedgerows, and shows a liking for the neighbourhood of habitations.

General Habits. The carriage is usually rather upright when standing still. Unlike Mistle Thrush and Fieldfare it resorts freely to cover, although foraging much in the open, where in intervals between short runs it stands, usually with head on one side, intent on detecting any movement. Flight is direct or only slightly undulating, the wing movement appearing faster than in Mistle Thrush. It is not really gregarious except on migration.

Usual note is a thin "sipp" or "tick" not unlike Redwing's, but not so penetrating or prolonged. The loud, clear, vigorous song is a succession of simple, but musical, phrases distinguished by their repetitive character, great variety and clear enunciation. It is delivered as a rule from well up in a tree, sometimes from a building, low bush, or the ground; also infrequently on the wing, and occasionally at night. It is heard exceptionally from mid-September to mid-October, more frequently to mid-November and regularly from then to early July, with a little song sometimes persisting in August.

Food consists largely of worms and molluscs, especially snails after breaking the shell on stones, etc. Insects, spiders, fruit and berries are also taken.

Nests in hedgerows, bushes, trees, among ivy, and occasionally on banks or in buildings. The eggs, usually 4–5, sometimes 3–6 or more, at times unmarked, are laid mainly in April and May (some March), in a well-built nest, constructed by hen alone of grasses, roots and at times moss, leaves and twigs, solidified with earth, and lined with a smooth coating of rotten wood or dung mixed with saliva. Incubation is by hen alone usually for about 13–14 days. The young are fed by both parents and fly usually when 13–14 days old.

Status and Distribution. Present throughout the year and generally distributed in the British Isles as a breeding bird except in Shetland where the nesting is now only occasional. The race mainly concerned is *Turdus philomelos clarkei* which also breeds in France, Belgium and Holland; however, the Outer Hebrides (excluding Stornoway) and Skye are occupied by the race *Turdus philomelos hebridensis* which is decidedly darker on the upper-parts and more thickly spotted below. The continental race *Turdus philomelos philomelos* which is rather greyer and paler than the British bird, but usually not distinguishable with certainty in the field, breeds from N. Scandinavia south to N. Spain and east to mid-Siberia; in Britain it is a passage-migrant and to some extent a winter-visitor, which has been identified in the northern isles, and on many parts of the E. and S.E. coasts, and on a few occasions elsewhere. Song Thrushes are common autumn-migrants on E. coast. In autumn, from late July onwards, many British birds move south, some wintering in Ireland and in Europe from Belgium to Spain. The return movement occurs from February to April.

REDWING—*Turdus iliacus*

BIRD PLATE 93   EGG PLATE III (3)

In size and coloration it much resembles Song Thrush except for the *broad buffish-white superciliary stripe and chestnut-red flanks* and axillaries, which at once distinguish it; the breast and flanks are streaked. Juveniles have much less chestnut on the flanks and are extremely like juvenile Song Thrush except for the prominent eye-stripe. Length about 8¼ ins.

Habitat. In Scotland it breeds in large gardens and deciduous woods, often with good cover near wet grassy areas. In winter it chiefly frequents open pastures and grasslands, sometimes stubble and rootfields or open woods.

General Habits. Gait, flight, and behaviour when feeding are like Song Thrush, but it is habitually gregarious in winter, feeding in loose flocks on the ground and resorting to trees when disturbed or preparing to roost; it often consorts with Fieldfares, but is less of a berry-eater than that bird or Mistle Thrush.

The call-note used especially in flight, and habitually by migrants passing over at night, is a soft, thin, far-carrying "seeih" or "seeip"; the corresponding note of Song Thrush is nearly always less prolonged and penetrating. Song is often a descending phrase of about five fluty "trui" notes, seldom heard outside breeding areas, but low chattering subsong is sometimes given by flocks in winter and early spring.

Food in winter includes worms, molluscs, insects and berries.

Nests in trees, bushes, or often on banks and broken ground. The eggs, 5–6 as a rule, are laid generally in May in a nest built of grasses, twigs and earth, lined with grasses and sometimes a few lichens or bits of moss on the outside. Incubation is apparently by both sexes for about 13 days. The young are fed by both parents and fly when about 12–14 days old. Double-brooded.

Status and Distribution. It is generally distributed as a winter-visitor and passage-migrant, arriving from mid-September onwards, and leaving by mid-April. Sometimes pairs remain in England during summer, but it has recently become a regular breeder in the northern half of Scotland, particularly Sutherland, Ross, Inverness, and is extending southwards. In Ireland bred Kerry 1951. Our visitors include both races, *Turdus iliacus iliacus* breeding from N. Scandinavia south to Germany and east into Siberia, and *Turdus iliacus coburni* from Iceland. The latter is rather the darker of the two, but generally speaking they cannot be separated in the field. The species winters south to the Mediterranean area.

MISTLE THRUSH—*Turdus viscivorus*

BIRD PLATE 94   EGG PLATE III (1A & 1B)

The larger size, greyer upper-parts, under-parts more boldly marked with bigger and broader spots, and quite *different note*, all serve to distinguish it from Song Thrush. The greyer appearance is noticeable on the wing, when its characteristic flight action and, at close range, whitish tips to the outer tail-feathers make it easy to recognize. From below, the white axillaries and under-wing provide a further distinction from other thrushes except Fieldfare, which, apart from conspicuous differences of the upper-parts, has a darker tail, less stout build and wing closure less prolonged. The sexes are similar. Juveniles have the head spotted whitish, and broad whitish marks on the coverts and mantle feathers, emphasized by dark brown borders towards the tips, producing a much more variegated effect than in adults. Length about 10½ ins.

Habitat. In the breeding-season it frequents woods and plantations (often conifers), gardens, orchards and well-timbered country; locally also in almost treeless regions. After the breeding-season, it occurs mainly on rough pasture, arable and moorland, with a predilection for wild, open, and often hilly country.

General Habits. Much time is spent on the ground, where the typical attitude is rather upright, bolder and more assertive-looking than Song Thrush, with head well up, tail down, and wings often slightly drooped. *The flight is distinctive, characterized by relatively prolonged closure of the wings* at fairly regular

MISTLE THRUSH   SONG THRUSH

Note Mistle Thrush's bolder spotting and more upright, strained stance; its spread tail (centre figure) shows whitish tips of outer feathers.

intervals, and is regularly at a greater height than usual for Song Thrush or Blackbird. In autumn it frequently occurs in loose family parties and small flocks. Like Fieldfare it does not resort to undergrowth and feeds much on hedgerow fruit. It is quarrelsome and intolerant of food-competitors and fearless in defence of its nest, though at other times wary and suspicious of man.

Usual note is a harsh churring chatter, becoming much louder and more rattling when excited. The song consists of short phrases of loud, challenging notes of Blackbird-like quality repeated again and again, and given usually from the upper branches of a tree. It is heard fairly frequently from mid-November until the end of the year and then regularly to early June; also exceptionally in late August and early September, and again in October.

Food is largely fruit and berries, but also includes molluscs, worms, insects and spiders.

Nests usually in a fork of a tree or sometimes out on a bough, often at a considerable height above the ground, also, near the coast, in recesses of rocks. The eggs, normally 4, occasionally 2–6, tawny-cream to greenish-blue in ground-colour, are laid generally in March or April in a nest built by hen only as a rule, constructed of bents, roots, moss, etc., with earth to solidify it, lined with dry grasses, and sometimes decorated with lichens, bits of wool, linen, feathers, etc. Incubation is almost always by hen only, for about 13–14 days. The young are fed by both parents and fly usually when 14–16 days old. Two broods frequently recorded, occasionally in the same nest.

Status and Distribution. Present throughout the year. It is generally distributed throughout the British Isles except in the higher mountains and treeless districts, but is only thinly distributed in N.W. Scotland, irregular in Orkney, and absent from Outer Hebrides and Shetland except as an occasional migrant. In southern counties adults are mainly sedentary, but northern birds move south in autumn and may reach Ireland or France; and continental immigrants arrive from mid-September to the end of November, returning mainly from mid-February to early April. Our birds belong to the race *Turdus viscivorus viscivorus* which breeds from N. Sweden south to the Mediterranean and east to Syria. Other races occur in N.W. Africa, and from E. Europe to central Asia.

CETTI'S WARBLER—*Cettia cetti*

Proclaims identity at almost all seasons by explosive song. Seldom allows a clear view, appearing a rather dark rufous bird with dull whitish eye-stripe, pale greyish under-parts, and graduated tail which is often cocked. Unlike Nightingale, tail is not more rufous than rest. Length about 5½ ins.

Habitat. Thickets and tangles near water or swampy places and reed-beds with rank undergrowth; sometimes by streams in woods; rarely in bushy places not near water.

General Habits. Very skulking, usually in thick cover, but occasionally exposing itself for a few seconds.

Song is a sudden, brief outburst (1–3 secs.) of loud, clear notes such as "che, che*wee*choo-*wee*choo-*wee*choo-wee", ceasing as abruptly as it begins.

Nests May onwards, in thick bushes and rank swamp growth. Probably more than one brood.

Status and Distribution. Partial resident. First occurred in England in 1961; has nested in Kent since 1972 and subsequently spread, as breeder or visitor, to many counties south of Wash/Bristol Channel. Also occurred in Wales, Scotland and Ireland. Abroad it has recently spread into west and central Europe from its traditional range in Mediterranean, Black Sea and Caspian countries.

GRASSHOPPER WARBLER—*Locustella naevia*

BIRD PLATE 99   EGG PLATE II (15A & 15B)

Being very secretive it would often escape notice but for the peculiar *song* which is the best character, but when seen it is recognized by *olive-brown, dark-streaked upper-parts*, pale whitish or buff under-parts, a few streaks on the breast, and *graduated tail*. It often appears yellower in the field than might be expected from skins or descriptions. There are faint markings on the rump, dark streaks on the under tail-coverts, and it has an obscure eye-stripe. Young are warmer brown than adults, though latter vary somewhat. Legs pink. Length about 5 ins.

Habitat. In the breeding season in a variety of both marshy and dry situations where rank grass and vegetation grow up amongst scattered bushes; e.g. bushy fens, osier-beds, neglected hedgerows, moors, furzy commons, and young fir plantations.

General Habits. It frequently sings well exposed, but takes cover at the least disturbance, slipping with astonishing facility through tangled undergrowth. On alighting it sometimes raises the tail over back, when the streaked under tail-coverts are conspicuous. It spends much time low down or on the ground amongst grass or thick cover, creeping along horizontal branches and looking peculiarly slim and tapering. It is reluctant to fly, except during territorial or sexual chases, and when driven usually flits only a few yards before diving into cover again.

Usual call is a sharp, rather hard "tchick". The song is a rapid and uniform high-pitched trill, sustained for sometimes as much as 2 minutes, of peculiarly mechanical effect, not unlike the sound of a line running off an angler's reel. The bird sings at all hours, including night, but chiefly in the early morning and late evening, fairly frequently from mid-April to the end of July and again in mid-September; sometimes early August.

Food consists of insects; also spiders and woodlice.

Nests on the ground or raised a foot or so above it, usually carefully hidden in a tussock, the bird entering and leaving by a run. The eggs, normally 6, sometimes 4–7, are laid generally in late May or early June in a nest built by both sexes of dead grasses and stalks with dead leaves in the foundation, lined with finer materials and a few hairs. Incubation is by both sexes for about 13–15 days. The young are fed by both sexes and fly when about 10–12 days old. Two broods regularly in the south, but less frequently in the north.

Status and Distribution. A summer-visitor, arriving between mid-April and late May and leaving during August and September. It is local, and variable in numbers, fairly evenly distributed in suitable localities in England and Ireland, but scarcer in Cornwall and in Wales. In Scotland it is local and thinly distributed north to Perth, perhaps regularly to Caithness. Our birds belong to the race *Locustella naevia naevia* which breeds abroad from N. Spain to the Baltic and east to the Caucasus. Other races occur in E. Russia and W. central Asia.

SAVI'S WARBLER—*Locustella luscinioides*

The bird has re-established itself as a British breeding species, having nested in Kent since 1960 or earlier, and later spread to Suffolk and perhaps elsewhere.

A soberly-coloured brown bird, darker than, say, a Reed Warbler, which it is not unlike (though with the form of a Grasshopper Warbler) with *strongly graduated tail* and lighter below, palest on throat, but not always white, as sometimes stated. Plumage lacks distinctive features but, at least in the breeding season, *the trilling song* precludes confusion with anything but Grasshopper Warbler and possibly River Warbler (*Locustella fluviatilis*). It is distinguished from the former by *unspotted plumage* and from the latter by absence of throat-streaks as well as different habits, while the trills are also distinguishable. Length about 5½ ins. (14 cms.).

AQUATIC WARBLER—*Acrocephalus paludicola*

BIRD PLATES 97 and 101

It resembles Sedge Warbler, but is distinguished by *buffer eye-stripes and a broad yellow-buff band down the centre of the crown.* (Some young Sedge Warblers in autumn show quite a distinct pale band, but never so pronounced or sharply defined as in Aquatic Warbler.) The streaking of the mantle is more prominent and *continues over the rump*, the ground-colour of upperparts in adults being paler, more greyish- less tawny-buff in summer, though decidedly more yellowish or bright sandy-buff in autumn and winter and in young birds; *the breast and flanks have distinct dark streaks in summer* and often to some extent in winter. (Sedge Warblers more rarely show a few streaks.) At least in summer it looks paler in flight than Sedge Warbler. Legs creamy flesh-coloured. Length about 5 ins.

Habitat. On passage it occurs in reed-beds and any kind of aquatic vegetation in which Sedge Warblers might be found, but at other times normally avoids reed-beds and tall or close growth of willows or bushes, preferring lower marsh vegetation.

General Habits. It will perch on reeds and tall sprays of marsh plants, but prefers to skulk in low vegetation and may be kicked up repeatedly from tussocks of sedge or rush in open marsh, flitting from one to another as disturbed.

Scolding "tucc" and churring notes are almost, if not quite, identical with Sedge Warbler's.

Food is chiefly insects.

Status and Distribution. A vagrant which occurs regularly on autumn passage in very small numbers. It occurs mainly in August and September, and most often on the south coast of England, and in Norfolk. Recorded Scotland mainly on Fair Isle and Isle of May, and a few times in Ireland. It breeds in central Europe from Germany to E. Russia, also Italy, and winters in Africa. There are no subspecies.

SEDGE WARBLER—*Acrocephalus schoenobaenus*

BIRD PLATES 97 and 101   EGG PLATE II (18A & 18B)

It is distinguished from Reed Warbler by the *prominent creamy eye-stripe and blackish streaking of crown and mantle*. The less uniform appearance is further emphasized by light edgings to the dark brown wing-feathers. *The unstreaked tawny rump*, contrasting with duller brown of mantle, is noticeable in flight. Differences from Aquatic Warbler are given under that species. The crown is strongly streaked blackish, and the mantle more faintly marked; the sides of face are brownish. Under-parts are creamy-white, shading to yellowish-buff at sides, strongest on the flanks. Coloration of the young is rather richer and yellower, with faint spots on the breast. Legs are pale dun-grey. Length about 5 ins.

Habitat. In the breeding-season it inhabits principally osier- and reed-beds with rank undergrowth, hedgerows bordering ditches, and tangled vegetation on marshy ground; more rarely in copses or bushy places away from water.

General Habits. It frequently descends to the ground amongst tangled vegetation, but seldom in the open. It creeps about with much facility amongst thick cover, clinging to and sidling up stems, but also perches quite freely on osiers, bushes, or tall plants. It usually flies low and for short distances only, with tail spread and depressed.

Notes are a scolding "tucc", often run together, and a grating "chirr". The song is a loud, hurried, vigorous medley, much less repetitive and more varied than Reed Warbler, with sweet and musical passages freely interspersed with harsh, strident, and chattering ones; strongly imitative. It is heard regularly from mid-April to mid-July, less frequently to the end of that month and exceptionally in August and early September; delivered from cover or from an exposed perch, also in song flight or sometimes during ordinary flight, and frequently at night.

Food is chiefly insects; also spiders, small worms and in autumn some berries.

Nests generally within a foot or two of the ground, but exceptionally 6 ft. or so above it, in rank waterside vegetation, but also in hedgerows and bushes at a distance from water. The eggs, normally 5–6, rarely 3–8, are laid generally in the latter part of May and early June in a rather bulky nest, but not so deep or cylindrical as Reed Warbler. It is built by the hen of stalks and grass, with moss and dead grasses as a foundation, and generally lined with hair, willow-down, grassheads and occasionally a few feathers. Incubation is chiefly by hen, usually for 13–14 days. The young are fed by both sexes and fly when about 13–14 days old, but if disturbed will leave the nest earlier. A second brood sometimes reared.

Status and Distribution. A summer-visitor, arriving from about mid-April with passage lasting into June, and returning mainly in August and September; it has occurred exceptionally in winter. It is generally distributed in England, Wales and Ireland; in Scotland it is local in the north-west but breeds Orkney (not Shetland) and quite widely in the Outer Hebrides. Abroad it breeds from N. Norway south to central France and east through the Balkans to N. Iran and Siberia; also in N. Africa. It winters in Africa. There are no subspecies.

MARSH WARBLER—*Acrocephalus palustris*

BIRD PLATE 98   EGG PLATE II (17A & 17B)

It very closely resembles Reed Warbler, the colour distinctions requiring a close view and much caution in the field, but the upper-parts are *colder, more earth- or olivaceous-brown, without a rufous tint*, while the under-parts, especially throat, usually appear whiter. The legs are pale flesh-coloured, as against the darker brown or greyish of Reed Warbler. Young birds are not separable from Reed Warblers in the field, and even in the hand cannot always be correctly identified. It is rather stouter in build than Reed Warbler, with carriage often more like a Garden Warbler than an *Acrocephalus*. Much the best distinction, however, is the striking *song*. Eggs and nest are also characteristic. Length about 5 ins.

Habitat. In the breeding-season it inhabits osier-beds, lowland copses or bushy places with vigorous undergrowth, ground overgrown with meadow-sweet, willow-herb, nettles or other tall plants, orchards, corn and other cultivated fields, and thick hedgerows on such ground. It is commonly found near water, but also on quite dry ground.

General Habits. Though sometimes secretive and hard to see, it is less creeping and skulking in habits than Reed Warbler, more ready to take wing, and in general more excitable and demonstrative. Especially when singing, it tends to perch higher and on more exposed sprays of tall plants, bushes, and even trees.

Chief alarm- or scolding-notes are a chirring, higher-pitched and less grating than Sedge Warbler's; sometimes developing into regular rattle or, again, more craking in effect, and a loud (sometimes very rapidly) repeated "tic" or "tchic" with variants. Full song, of striking beauty and vivacity, is a far richer and more diversified warbling than that of others of this genus, with typical *Acrocephalus* chirrings at times, but generally without the extreme harsh notes of Sedge Warbler, and mimetic to a remarkable extent. Of its own notes, certain high, clear, liquid, Canary-like shakes and trills and a very nasal, iterated "za-wee" are especially characteristic. It sings regularly in the latter part of May and June, less frequently during the first half of July, and exceptionally in August or September; uncommonly at night.

Food is chiefly marsh-haunting insects.

Nests up to 7 or 8 ft. in osier-beds, also low in tangled hedge bottoms, etc. The eggs, 3–5, rarely 6, are laid generally in June in a nest shallower and more like that of a *Sylvia* than of Reed Warbler, and fixed by "basket-handles" to supporting vegetation or bushes. It is built by both sexes of dry grasses, dead plants, etc., and lined with roots and a few hairs. Incubation is by both sexes for about 12–13 days. The young are fed by both sexes, and fly when about 10–14 days old. Single-brooded.

Status and Distribution. A summer-visitor arriving in late May or June. It is scarce and local and only known to breed regularly in Worcester, Gloucester, and perhaps Somerset and Dorset. It has nested in a number of other southern counties west to Devon and north to Cheshire, but not definitely in East Anglia. Vagrants are reported annually on north Scottish islands. Abroad it breeds from the Baltic south to S. France, N. Italy, Macedonia and N. Iran. It winters in Africa. There are no subspecies.

REED WARBLER—*Acrocephalus scirpaceus*

Bird Plates 98 and 101 Egg Plate II (16)

Acrocephali are soberly-coloured, slim, compact, round-tailed warblers, chiefly haunting marshy places and with characteristic churring notes in the song. Reed Warbler has *brown upper-parts inclining to rufous, especially on the rump*, and under-parts light buff, shading into white on the throat. It is distinguished from Sedge Warbler by *lack of dark markings or definite eye-stripe*, but, by plumage, only with difficulty from the rarer Marsh Warbler. Legs flesh-coloured or brown, usually tinged greyish or bluish. Length about 5 ins.

Habitat. In the breeding-season it frequents reed-beds, osier-beds, or sometimes other rank vegetation or bushes near water, exceptionally occurring in gardens or parks far from water.

General Habits. It is found commonly amongst reeds actually over water. It seldom leaves cover, clinging to stems and sidling up them with a quick jerky action and hopping or flitting from one to another with restless activity. It also perches, chiefly amongst foliage. It seldom flies for more than a short distance, low over reeds or across a bit of open water, usually with tail spread and slightly drooped in the manner characteristic of the genus. Though restriction of sites often imposes almost colonial breeding-habits and some numbers may occur together on migration, it is essentially non-gregarious.

Usual note is a low "churr". The song has a certain general similarity to Sedge Warbler's, but is more uniform and lower pitched, and is delivered in a rather slow and "conversational" manner. The basis of the song is a sequence of rather low chirping phrases, *each repeated two or three times*, frequently changing pitch without otherwise altering. It is mimetic to a limited extent; delivery is commonly from cover, occasionally on wing, and not infrequently at night. It is heard regularly from late April to mid-July, less frequently until the end of that month or into August, and exceptionally in the first half of September.

Food is mainly aquatic insects; spiders, slugs and molluscs are also recorded, and berries in autumn.

Nests generally in reeds or osiers, but occasionally in hedges or bushes; also in rank marsh vegetation, nettles, willow-herb, etc. The eggs, normally 4, occasionally 3–5, blotched to a varying degree, are laid generally in June in a cylindrical nest with a deep cup built chiefly by the hen on to and around reeds or branches, and constructed of grasses, reed-flowers, etc., lined variously with grasses and feathers, wool, hair, reed-tops, etc. Incubation is by both sexes in turn for 11 days as a rule. The young are fed by both sexes, and fly usually when 11–12 days old. Many are double-brooded in the south.

Status and Distribution. A summer-visitor, fairly distributed throughout S. and mid-England north to S. Yorks and Cheshire and west to Scilly Isles. It also breeds very locally in S.E. and N. Wales and in a few localities in Lancs., Westmorland, Cumberland and Northumberland. It occurs annually in Scotland, mainly on E. side north to Shetland where it has bred; also a few Ireland where it breeds sporadically. It arrives in the second half of April and in May, and leaves during August and September. Our bird belongs to the race *Acrocephalus scirpaceus scirpaceus* which breeds abroad from the Baltic south to N.W. Africa, east to the Balkans and perhaps Asia Minor. It winters in tropical Africa. Another race occurs in S. Asia.

GREAT REED WARBLER—*Acrocephalus arundinaceus*
Bird Plate 98

In form and colouring it closely resembles Reed Warbler, but is *much larger*, has a *prominent whitish eye-stripe* and a characteristic *song*. When only the head is visible the noticeably long straight bill, appearing of almost uniform depth for nearly its whole length, is sometimes a useful character. Length about 7½ ins.

Habitat. In the breeding-season it frequents reed-beds, preferably where there is a certain amount of open water and commonly with some bushes or trees. On passage it also occurs along ditches, in gardens, etc.

General Habits. Its habits and actions are similar to Reed Warbler, although it is definitely heavier in its movements. Though also keeping much in the cover of reeds, and on some days very skulking, it appears genuinely a rather less secretive and bolder bird as from its size it is necessarily more conspicuous; it is more prone to perch on bushes or trees, or even telegraph wires, and attracts notice as it flies a short distance with spread tail, rapidly moving wings and rather jerky action, noticeably heavier than that of smaller *Acrocephali*, low over reed tops or across a strip of open water.

Notes are a harsh "tack" or "chack" and a deep churring croak. The song, though variable, has commonly the same general character as Reed Warbler's, but is much louder, more guttural and croaking with frog-like noises, interspersed with shriller, more piping, components.

Food is largely insects, also spiders. Berries are recorded in autumn.

Status and Distribution. A vagrant which has occurred rarely in Scotland and Ireland, but appears most years in S.E. England, rather more often in spring than autumn and occasionally individuals have remained for a period during summer. The race *Acrocephalus arundinaceus arundinaceus* breeds from S. Sweden and the Baltic States south to the Mediterranean and N.W. Africa and east to Syria, wintering in tropical and S. Africa. Other races occur elsewhere in Asia and in Egypt.

ICTERINE WARBLER—*Hippolais icterina*

BIRD PLATES 99 and 101

It resembles a large, stockily built *Phylloscopus* with *yellow under-parts, bluish-grey legs*, and a wider bill. It has olive upper-parts, wing and tail browner, with lemon-yellow under-parts and eye-stripe. The under-parts are paler in autumn and winter, when the upper-parts are browner, and very pale in young birds; sometimes all trace of yellow is lacking, the under-parts being pale buff or greyish-brown. The *long pointed wings* are noticeable in flight, if view is good. In fresh plumage there is a *pale patch on the closed wing* above the dark primaries, caused by the pale edges of the secondaries and appearing yellow in adults in spring and off-white in immatures in autumn. The very similar Melodious Warbler (see Plate 101) generally lacks this pale patch, has shorter, more rounded wings and rather browner legs. Length about 5½ ins.

Habitat. In the breeding-season it frequents gardens with fruit, lilac or other trees and bushes, copses with rich under-growth, hedgerow trees, and scrub growth of elder, osiers, etc., often in damp situations.

General Habits. Icterine is an active and lively bird, though heavier in movements than the *Phylloscopi*. It spends much of its time amongst the foliage of trees, especially rather isolated ones, where it is often very hard to see, and seems to like the vicinity of houses or cottages; seldom on the ground. Flight recalls Spotted Flycatcher. Carriage is rather upright when perched. The crown feathers are erected when excited or curious, giving the bird often a characteristic big-headed appearance.

Chief notes are a liquid, melodious "dideroid", "diderid" and variants, and a hard, *Sylvia*-like "teck, teck". Song is variable, distinctly acrocephaline in character, and at best much like Marsh

ICTERINE WARBLER

Note pale panel on closed
wing, (very rarely does
this occur in Melodious
Warbler).

Warbler, loud, vehement and varied, with rich musical notes, but
usually much interspersed with extraordinary shrieking, chattering, chuckling, churring and other discordant and grating noises,
which often form the bulk of the utterance, while less striking and
varied forms, deficient in both the more musical and more exaggerated harsh notes, are not uncommon; most notes and phrases are
repeated several times and are often markedly imitative.

Food is chiefly insects. Ripe fruit and berries are also eaten.

Nests in the fork of a bough, often of lilac, syringa or osier, from
4 to 8 ft. above the ground as a rule. The eggs, normally 4–5, of
dull rose or very pale pinkish-violet, sparingly spotted and
streaked with black, are laid generally at the end of May or early
June in a nest neatly built by both sexes of vegetable down, grasses,
wool, etc., interwoven with bark-fibre or roots, decorated outside
with birch-bark or bits of paper, and lined with grasses, roots and
hair, sometimes feathers. Incubation is by both sexes for about 13
days. The young are fed by both sexes and fly when about 13–14
days old. Apparently single-brooded.

Status and Distribution. A passage-migrant in very small
numbers which has bred in Wiltshire: it occurs sometimes in
spring, but is seen mainly in September on the east coast from
Kent to Shetland and on the English south coast; it is also regular
in S. Ireland. Abroad it breeds from the Arctic circle in Norway
south to E. France and Italy and east to N. Iran and Siberia. It
winters in S. tropical Africa. There are no subspecies.

DARTFORD WARBLER—*Sylvia undata*

Bird Plate 96   Egg Plate III (9)

Though very skulking, its small size, *dark coloration, and long tail* are distinctive, even when the bird is only seen in brief flight from one bit of cover to another. Male has dark brown upper-parts, shading into slate-grey on the head, and under-parts a *dull vinous colour*, while female and young are paler and browner, both above and below. The throat shows small white spots in autumn. The tail is graduated, with a narrow white border. Eye and orbital rim are reddish-orange. Length about 5 ins.

Habitat. It frequents heaths with rank growth of heather and usually some admixture of gorse, and gorse-grown commons or downs.

General Habits. As a rule it is extremely secretive, slipping through thick cover with utmost facility and easily eluding observation, especially in dull weather. In fine bright weather it is more inclined to show itself, emerging into view for a brief space now and again, and when the young are hatched it becomes much more demonstrative. The tail is usually carried cocked up and is frequently flicked. If flushed it usually flies a short distance only, close to the ground, with weak undulating action, the long tail bobbing up and down in characteristic top-heavy fashion, and dives straight into fresh cover. Where common it will join up into parties in autumn and wander about the heaths, the males in song.

Notes are rather like Whitethroat's, but have a distinctive quality and are readily recognized when once known. They consist of a somewhat grating, rather metallic "tchirr" and a hard, incisive "tucc", becoming a very rapidly uttered "tututututucc" when excited. The song is a short, rather Whitethroat-like warble, but of more metallic quality and as a rule distinctly more musical, sometimes not unlike Stonechat.

Food is chiefly insects; also spiders.

Nests chiefly in long heather or gorse; in heather generally low down, but in gorse at varying heights. The eggs, normally 3–4, occasionally 5, dirty white or pale greenish in ground-colour, are laid generally towards the end of April in a compact nest built chiefly by hen, but male makes flimsy "cock's nests". It is constructed of bits of ling, grasses, a little thistledown, wool, bits of paper, moss, etc., and lined with fine grass, roots, and sometimes a feather or two, down or hair, and studded externally with cocoons of spiders. Incubation is chiefly by hen for about 12 days. The young are fed by both sexes and fly when about 13 days old. Regularly double-brooded and evidence of a third occasionally. **Status and Distribution.** A very local resident, fluctuating in numbers and much reduced by severe winters. It breeds regularly in Dorset and Hampshire, and usually Surrey, and in years of high population may extend from Sussex to Cornwall. It formerly bred in several other southern counties. A rare vagrant in the southern half of England outside breeding areas and it has occurred in Scotland and Ireland. The race *Sylvia undata dartfordiensis* is confined to England. Other races occur in the Channel Islands, S.W. Europe and N.W. Africa.

BARRED WARBLER—*Sylvia nisoria*

BIRD PLATES 97 and 101

It is a large, robust, rather long-tailed warbler. Adults are ashy-grey above, with greyish-white *under-parts barred dark grey*; the wing-coverts and quills have more or less distinct light borders and tips, and there is white in the outer tail-feathers. Females are browner and less distinctly barred than males, while *young in autumn show little or no barring* except on under tail-coverts and have under-parts more buff, looking something like large, grey long-tailed Garden Warblers, but with a *heavy bill*, unusually pale tips to the flight feathers and a steep forehead like Whitethroat. *The staring yellow eye is a striking feature of adult*, but immature birds have the iris dark greyish-brown. Legs and feet are stout, looking disproportionately large in the field. Length about 6 ins.

Habitat. In the breeding-season it frequents bushy places and thickets, especially of thorns.

General Habits. It is shy, restless and skulking, moving with much facility through thick cover, and seldom settles on the ground. Flight is often rather heavy, and sometimes shrike-like in passage from tree to tree. It raises the crown feathers and jerks tail when excited.

It has, like others of the genus, a "tacking" and a churring note.

Food is largely insects; in autumn berries and worms are also eaten.

Status and Distribution. Immature birds occur regularly in small numbers on autumn passage in the northern isles, and on the east coast of Britain, mainly in September; more rarely in the south. In addition, it has been recorded in Wales and inland in England; in Ireland perhaps annually, mainly on Great Saltee. Abroad it breeds from Denmark and the Baltic south to N. Italy and Iran and east to Mongolia. It winters in Arabia and N.E. Africa. There are no subspecies.

LESSER WHITETHROAT—*Sylvia curruca*

Bird Plates 95 and 101   Egg Plate III (8)

It is rather smaller and more compact-looking than Whitethroat, greyer above and whiter below, *without rufous edgings to the secondaries* and with *ear-coverts distinctly darker than the rest of the cap*. The outer tail-feathers are white, *tail looking shorter than Whitethroat's*. Young in autumn hardly differ from adults, but are rather browner. Length about 5¼ ins.

Habitat. In the breeding-season it occurs largely in similar places to Whitethroat, but also in tall thick hedgerows, gardens, shrubberies, and places with closer and taller bush growth and more trees than the latter species likes. It is rarely found in sparse hedgerows like Whitethroat.

General Habits. It is more skulking than Whitethroat, though particularly noisy and demonstrative when with fledged young, and it frequents the foliage of trees more, though also freely occurring in low cover. Otherwise its habits, flight, carriage, etc., are like Whitethroat.

Chief note is a persistent, hard, Blackcap-like "tacc, tacc", much heard in late summer when young are about, and a hoarse "charrr", like Whitethroat, less often used. The song is loud rattling repetition of one note, a rapid "chikka-chikka-chikka-chikka-chikk", often, but not always, preceded by a soft low, varied and musical warbling audible only at close quarters. It is delivered usually from thick hedgerows or bushes, often while moving about, and is heard regularly from late April to the end of June, fairly frequently in the first half of July and exceptionally in late July, late August and the first half of September.

Food is chiefly insects, and occasionally spiders and small worms. In summer and autumn fruit and berries of many kinds are also taken.

Nests in thick hedges and bushes, generally between 2 and 5 ft.

from the ground. The eggs, 4–6, occasionally 3–7, are laid generally from mid-May onwards, in a nest smaller than a Whitethroat's and lacking its thick base. It is built by the cock but finished and lined by the hen; constructed of dry stalks and roots and a dead leaf or two, decorated with spiders' cocoons, and lined sometimes with roots only and sometimes freely with horsehair. Incubation is mostly by hen for about 10–11 days. The young are fed by both parents and fly when about 11 days old.

Status and Distribution. A summer-visitor from April–May until July–September with passage continuing in October. It is generally distributed in England, but local in the north and only breeds occasionally in Cornwall and in most Welsh coastal counties. In Scotland it is a scarce breeder south of the Forth, at times north to Aberdeen; on passage is rare on the mainland but regular on Fair Isle and Isle of May and perhaps elsewhere. It is probably of annual occurrence in Ireland. Our breeding birds belong to the race *Sylvia curruca curruca* which breeds in Europe from central Scandinavia and N.W. Russia south to the Pyrenees and Balkan Peninsula; also in W. Asia. It winters in N.E. Africa. Several examples of the race *Sylvia curruca blythi* from E. Russia and Siberia have also occurred in September and October on Scottish islands, especially Fair Isle, but they are indistinguishable from our birds in the field. Other races occur elsewhere in Asia.

WHITETHROAT—*Sylvia communis*

Bird Plates 95 and 101   Egg Plate III (7a & 7b)

The grey cap descending below the eye and contrasted with *white throat* at once identify male in the breeding-season, but the *reddish-brown edgings to secondaries and wing-coverts* are distinctive at all ages, giving a warm rufous appearance to the closed wing, contrasting with the duller brown of the mantle. This feature, with slimmer build, longer tail, and *white outer tailfeathers* readily distinguish the brown-capped female, young, and male in autumn from the stouter, more compact-looking Garden Warbler. Distinctions from the Lesser Whitethroat are given under that species. Breast and flanks are buff, with a distinct pink flush in adult male. A slight raising of the crown feathers commonly gives a characteristic peaked appearance to the head. Length about 5½ ins.

Habitat. In the breeding-season it occurs largely in more open localities than Blackcap or Garden Warbler: untrimmed hedge-rows and field borders, rough ground with tangled vegetation or bushes, commons, osier-beds and glades in open woodland or outskirts of woods; gardens and cultivated fields are visited chiefly in late summer and autumn.

General Habits. Though skulking at times, it is less secretive than most warblers. It frequents principally hedgerows and low vegetation and is sprightly and active, moving with much facility amongst tangled growth. On the wing, except in song-flight, it is chiefly seen in short, flitting, rather jerky flights from bush to bush or along a hedgerow, low down and ending with a dive into cover.

Notes are a scolding, hoarse "charr", varying a good deal in quality, a sharp "tacc, tacc" and a more "conversational" "wheet, wheet, whit-whit-whit-whit". The song is a short, rapidly uttered warble, brisk and lively, of rather poor quality. It is delivered usually from low cover or an exposed spray of hedge, etc., or a wire or in dancing song-flight; it is heard regularly from mid-April to mid-July, fairly frequently to the end of July, and exceptionally in August and the first three weeks of September.

Food is mainly insects. Currants, raspberries, and peas are occasionally eaten, also wild berries in autumn.

Nests in low bushes, brambles, etc., and occasionally in corn, heath, long grass, etc., usually close to the ground, but also at times at some height above it. The eggs, usually 4–5, exceptionally 3–7, are very variable, with ground-colour generally greenish or stone, and markings ranging from big blotches to fine stippling. They are laid from early May onwards but mostly in the second half of the month, in a nest built by both sexes, and sometimes founded on a cock's nest built before the arrival of the female. It is usually substantial, with a deep cup, made of dead grasses, roots, etc., and well lined with hair, generally black, and decorated by the hen with bits of down or wool. Incubation is by both sexes for about 11–13 days. The young are fed by both parents and fly when about 10–12 days old. Usually double-brooded.

Status and Distribution. A summer-visitor, generally distributed in England, Wales, Ireland and S. and central Scotland. In N. Scotland it is thinly distributed and local; sporadic in the Outer Hebrides, Orkney and Shetland. Most birds arrive between mid-April and mid-May but movement extends from the end of March to early June, and in autumn from mid-July to mid-October. Our birds belong to the race *Sylvia communis communis* which also breeds in N.W. Africa and in Europe from the Mediterranean north almost to the Arctic Circle. It winters in Africa. Other races occur in Asia.

GARDEN WARBLER—*Sylvia borin*

BIRD PLATES 96 and 101   EGG PLATE II (19A & 19B)

It is a medium-sized, rather plump and compactly-built warbler, characterized by a complete lack of any prominent features, yet the *soft and pleasing shade of the pale buff below, combined with darker hair-brown upper-parts* produces a (rather pale) general effect not quite like any other British species. Adults and young are similar. Autumn birds are quite variable and can be confused with Barred, Marsh and other rare warblers. It is very secretive and would often escape notice but for its song. Length about 5½ ins.

Habitat. In the breeding-season it inhabits open deciduous or mixed woodland with an abundant undergrowth of bushes and briars, and bushy places, often with scattered trees, but also (unlike Blackcap) where no trees are present; less often osierbeds and untrimmed hedges. Occasionally it is found in conifer woods with deciduous secondary growth.

General Habits. Active, but quiet in movements, it spends most of its time amongst the cover of foliage. Other habits, flight, etc., are like Blackcap. The young remain with female for some weeks after fledging.

Ordinary notes are a hard "tacc, tacc", like Blackcap's, and a low grating "churr". The song is a sweet, even-flowing warble, more uniform, more subdued and more sustained than ordinary song of Blackcap, though the more subdued warblings of the latter may be difficult or hardly possible to distinguish. It is usually delivered from cover, often while moving about, and is heard regularly from the end of April to mid-July, occasionally later in that month or in August.

Food in spring and early summer is chiefly insects; also spiders and occasionally worms: later fruit and berries are also taken.

Nests in shrubs, brambles and sometimes in trees or rank vegetation. The eggs, normally 4–5, rarely 3–6, whitish to yellowish or greenish in ground-colour with considerable range of variation in markings, are on average rather larger and more glossy than Blackcap's, but not distinguishable with certainty. They are laid generally in late May or early June in a nest built by both sexes of grass stalks and bents, thicker and more substantial than used by Blackcap, sometimes a little moss or a dead leaf; and lined with finer grasses, rootlets, and hair. The male also makes "cock's nests". Incubation is mainly by female, for about 12 days. The young are fed by both sexes and fly usually when 9–10 days old. Generally single-brooded, but exceptionally a second.

Status and Distribution. A summer-visitor, arriving from mid-April to the end of May, with passage continuing to mid-June, and returning from mid-July to the beginning of October. It is generally distributed in England and Wales, but rather local, and scarce or absent in W. Cornwall, S.W. Lancs and the Fens. In Scotland it is fairly common in the Lowlands and scarcer to Inverness and E. Ross. It is regular on passage in Shetland. In Ireland it is very local, unknown in most districts, but nests up Shannon valley and north to Lough Erne. Abroad it breeds from N. Norway south to the Mediterranean, and east to Transcaucasia and W. Siberia. It winters in central and S. Africa. There are no subspecies.

BLACKCAP—*Sylvia atricapilla*

Bird Plate 96   Egg Plate III (6A & 6B)

The sharply-defined *glossy black cap*, extending to the level of the eye, at once distinguishes male, while the *reddish-brown cap of female*, though less conspicuous, is equally distinctive. Upperparts are greyish-brown, the sides of head, neck and under-parts being ashy-grey in male, more brown in female. Young males in autumn often have some admixture of brown in the black cap. Length about 5½ ins.

Habitat. In the breeding-season it frequents open woodland and copses with thick undergrowth, other overgrown and bushy places, and gardens or shrubberies, where trees are present. There is no clear-cut difference from Garden Warbler in its choice of habitat, but it is more partial to evergreens.

General Habits. It is active and lively, often keeping in the cover of trees and bushes, but perhaps less retiring than Garden Warbler. It seldom settles on the ground. Under ordinary conditions, like other small warblers, it is disinclined to fly far and usually seen merely in short, rather jerky flights from one bit of cover to another.

Usual notes are a hard, scolding "tacc, tacc" like two pebbles struck together, and a "churr". The commonest phase of song consists of clear, rich warbling notes, with much more definite form and phrasing than the relatively uniform and even warbling of Garden Warbler, but usually in shorter phrases, and fairly stereotyped in general pattern. It sings principally from cover, and is heard regularly from early April to the end of June, less frequently in the first half of July and exceptionally as late as mid-September.

Food consists of insects, fruit, and berries.

Nests usually higher than Garden Warbler in bushes, hedge-rows, among honeysuckle or briars, etc. The eggs, normally 5, occasionally 3–6, are laid generally during the second half of May in a slight nest built chiefly by hen, of bents, roots and grasses, and lined with finer materials, and sometimes horsehair. Incubation is by both sexes usually for 10–11 days. The young are fed by both sexes, and fly when about 10–13 days old. Often double-brooded in the south.

Status and Distribution. It now winters regularly in small numbers in Ireland, S.W. and S. and probably N.E. England and often Scotland; otherwise it is a summer visitor, arriving mainly in April and May, sometimes late March, and leaving from mid-August to mid-October, with stragglers into November. It is somewhat local, but fairly well distributed in England, and most parts of Wales except the N.W., where it is rare. In Scotland it breeds sparsely north to Dunkeld and the Spey valley, and has attempted to do so in Orkney and Shetland, where it is a regular autumn migrant. Breeding in Ireland is very local, rather erratic, and mainly in the east. The race concerned, *Sylvia atricapilla atricapilla*, breeds abroad from N. Norway south to N.W. Africa and east to Iran and W. Siberia. It winters in S. Europe and N. Africa. Another race occurs in Madeira and the Canaries.

YELLOW-BROWED WARBLER—*Phylloscopus inornatus*

BIRD PLATE 99

Its small size, light green above and whitish below, as well as the prominent pale yellowish superciliary stripe and double wing-bar are all noticeable characters and make it quite easy to distinguish. Some individuals show a faint light stripe down the centre of crown, and the rump tends to be paler and greener than the back. Length about 4 ins.

Habitat. In its winter-quarters it frequents all kinds of wooded or partly wooded country, and is found in scrub and brushwood as well as higher timber.

General Habits. Its carriage and behaviour are typically phylloscopine and it has a Willow Warbler-like habit of flicking the wings and tail. It frequently feeds with flycatcher-like actions. Note, variously rendered "sweet", "weesp", etc., resembles Willow Warbler's in general character, but is sharper and much shriller.

Food is largely small insects.

Status and Distribution. A passage-migrant, probably regular in very small numbers along the east coasts of Great Britain and especially in Fair Isle from mid-September to late October. It also occurs fairly regularly in the Scillies and S.W. Ireland. It is rare in spring. The race concerned, *Phylloscopus inornatus inornatus*, breeds in N. Siberia from the Urals eastwards and normally winters in S.E. Asia. Other races occur in central and S.E. Asia.

WOOD WARBLER—*Phylloscopus sibilatrix*

Bird Plate 100   Egg Plate II (12A & 12B)

It is distinguished from other British *Phylloscopi* by *rather larger size*, relatively longer wings and shorter tail, and *brighter, "cleaner", more contrasted colouring, which is yellowish-green above, with a broad yellow superciliary stripe, sulphur-yellow throat and breast, and the rest of the under-parts pure white.* Yellowish edging to the browner wing-feathers is often conspicuous. Colouring is dullest in autumn and in young birds. Length about 5 ins.

Habitat. In the breeding-season it inhabits chiefly well-grown woods and wooded parkland, especially beech and oak, but extending to stunted growths at the upper limit of woodland in hilly districts. Ground vegetation is relatively unimportant, but it generally occurs only where secondary growth (coppice wood, etc.) is sparse or absent.

General Habits. It often droops loosely-folded wings so that the tips show in silhouette apart from the body. It does not flick the tail like Chiffchaff and Willow Warbler. Its habits resemble those of other leaf-warblers, but it is more thoroughly arboreal, even outside the breeding-season. It frequently makes little aerial sallies after insects, or hovers to pick them from the under-sides of leaves.

Usual call and alarm-note is a plaintive, piping "puu". The song is heard regularly from the 2nd half of April to early July and less frequently to the end of July. It has two phases: (1) typically a repetition of a single note, increasing in speed and passing into a shivering trill, "stip-stip-stititititipp sweeeee", delivered while perched or moving about in the canopy; (2) a plaintive liquid "puu" repeated about 7–14 times, either delivered separately or introduced at brief intervals in the sequence of ordinary songs; it is less regular than the latter, but quite frequent.

Food is mainly insects; berries are occasionally taken in autumn.

Nests in undergrowth of bracken and brambles, making use of a natural hollow in the ground. The eggs, normally 6–7, occasionally 4–8, are laid generally in the second half of May or early June in a domed nest with a side entrance, built by hen only, of dead bracken, dead leaves and grass, neatly lined with fine bents, and occasionally a few hairs, but no feathers. Incubation is by hen only, for about 13 days. The young are fed by both sexes and fly when about 11–12 days old. Only one brood as a rule; rarely a second.

Status and Distribution. A summer-visitor, most arriving in the latter part of April and first half of May, but some a week or two earlier, and leaving in late July or August, with stragglers into September. It is widely distributed but often local in England and Wales in well-wooded districts, but rare in places especially in the east. In Scotland it is fairly common in the W., north to Sutherland, but sporadic in most eastern counties; few regular on passage in Orkney, Shetland and the Outer Hebrides. It is extremely scarce in Ireland where it has been found nesting on rare occasions. Abroad it breeds from S. Scandinavia south to central France and Serbia and east to the Caucasus. It winters in central Africa. There are no subspecies.

CHIFFCHAFF—*Phylloscopus collybita*

BIRD PLATES 100 and 101   EGG PLATE II (13)

Phylloscopi are small, slim and graceful, active warblers, spending much of their time amongst foliage, mostly with more or less greenish or yellowish in the plumage; they are much alike and most readily distinguished by habits and notes. The *song* of the Chiffchaff is unmistakable. In appearance it closely resembles Willow Warbler, but *generally has darker, sometimes blackish legs*; it is

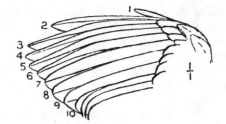

CHIFFCHAFF
Note short 2nd primary and emarginated
6th primary.

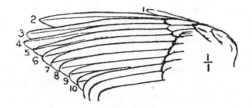

WILLOW WARBLER
Note longer 2nd primary than in Chiffchaff,
and 6th primary not emarginated.

also a trifle smaller, and *dingier in colouring*, dirtier brown above
and more buff, less yellowish, below. Plumage is brownest above
and under-parts least buff (more whitish) about midsummer, and
the yellowish tint is strongest in autumn, when, however, Willow
Warbler is also correspondingly yellower; but plumage distinctions require much caution, nor as a rule is the shorter, more
rounded wing a character of much value in the field. In the hand
the two species may be separated by the wing characters, as shown
in the text figure. Length about $4\frac{1}{4}$ ins.

Habitat. In the breeding-season it haunts woods and shrubberies with rich undergrowth, well-timbered old hedgerows
and bushy places; it is more strictly dependent on trees than
Willow Warbler, but seldom found in unmixed conifer woodland.
In Scotland the presence of rhododendrons is often important. In
winter-quarters it keeps preferably to bushy places, gardens, and
the like, often, but not necessarily, with some trees, and much in
low vegetation, reed-beds, etc.

General Habits. Flight is somewhat jerky and flitting, often at
a fair height from tree to tree. In the breeding-season it feeds
mainly in the foliage of trees, hopping or flitting from twig to twig
with restless activity, gently flicking the wings and tail at frequent

intervals, darting out to catch a fly in the air or fluttering for a few seconds to pick an insect from a leaf; but on arrival and in autumn and winter it feeds much in lower growth. Earliest arrivals are often in bushes near water. Usual call and alarm-note is a soft, plaintive "hweet", like that of Willow Warbler but more monosyllabic. The song is a measured repetition of two notes "chiff-chaff", one rather higher-pitched than the other, in very irregular sequence. It is heard regularly from late March to mid-July, and less frequently until early October but nearly always with a gap during the first 2 or 3 weeks in August; exceptionally in November, January and February.

Food is chiefly insects.

Nests generally at some little height from the ground, in clumps of brambles and rank herbage in woods, or low bushes; also among thick branches of yews, hollies, etc. The eggs, usually 6, occasionally 4–7, are laid generally in May, sometimes in April, in a roughly spherical nest with a rather wide and shallow side entrance; it is built by the hen, more loosely than Willow Warbler's, and usually with dead leaves as foundation, and constructed of moss, stalks, etc., with a thick lining of feathers. Incubation is by hen alone for about 13 days. The young are fed mainly by the hen and normally fly when 14 days old. Two broods are not unusual in the south.

Status and Distribution. Mainly a summer-visitor, sometimes arriving early in March, but most from the latter part of the month to the end of April, with passage continuing into the second half of May. The return movement lasts from August to mid-October. A few birds winter in S. England, S. Wales and Ireland, and exceptionally in Scotland. In summer it is well distributed in Ireland and Wales, also in England except East Anglia and the N.E. where it is rather local. In Scotland it breeds in the W. and more locally in E., north to perhaps Perth, becoming sporadic in rest of mainland and Inner Hebrides, and song is frequently reported from Outer Hebrides; otherwise it is a scarce but regular passage-migrant. Our birds belong to the race *Phylloscopus collybita collybita* which breeds in central Europe south of the Baltic, east to the Balkans and south to S. France. Passage-migrants probably regularly include birds of the race *Phylloscopus collybita abietinus* which breeds from arctic Scandinavia south-east to N. Iran, but is seldom identified in this country; it is generally greyer above and whiter below than our bird, but is often indistinguishable from it, while on the other hand adults may have white under-parts and so overlap in appearance the race *Phylloscopus collybita tristis* from Siberia, which has also occurred a few times, including winter, in England, Scotland and Ireland; regular on Fair Isle. The call note of *Phylloscopus collybita abietinus* is sometimes, but not always, shriller and louder than our birds, while that of *Phylloscopus collybita tristis* is a good deal more plaintive and perhaps nearest to a single note sometimes uttered by Coal Tit. Other races occur in Spain, Portugal, the Canaries and in parts of Asia. Our birds winter in the Mediterranean region and N. Africa.

WILLOW WARBLER—*Phylloscopus trochilus*

BIRD PLATES 100 and 101   EGG PLATE II (14A & 14B)

When in *song* no other distinction is needed. Its appearance is extremely like Chiffchaff, but it tends to have *lighter brown, not blackish, legs*, is slightly larger and *"cleaner" in colouring*, more greenish above and more yellowish below, and as summer advances the upper-parts become browner and the under-parts whiter. The yellow tint is strongest in autumn and is decidedly stronger on the under-parts of young than adults. See also under Chiffchaff. Length about 4¼ ins.

Habitat. In the breeding-season its habitat is less restricted than Chiffchaff's, extending from open woodland or bushy ground to almost any places with tussocky grass and ground vegetation plus a few trees.

General Habits. These and flight, etc., are much as Chiffchaff, but it is perhaps slightly less active and restless, and more varied in its haunts, frequenting hedgerows and low growth more extensively, and is usually much more numerous.

Call and alarm-note is a plaintive "hooeet", very like Chiffchaff's but more definitely disyllabic. Song, simple but pleasing, is a continuous, liquid, rippling phrase of closely similar notes, usually faint and low at first, but gaining loudness and emphasis, and then sinking away again to a fainter but more distinctly phrased ending. It is heard regularly from early April to early July, with revival towards the end of the month and in early August, and exceptionally until late September.

Food is chiefly insects, also spiders and occasionally small worms. In autumn some berries are taken.

Nests normally on the ground among grass in hedge-bottoms, open glades in woods, etc., and occasionally in a low bush. The eggs, usually 6–7, sometimes 3–9, some finely freckled, others blotched, are laid generally in May, sometimes late April in a domed nest with a neat entrance at the side, built by the hen alone, of green moss, inter-woven stalks, grasses, sometimes bracken, and lined freely with feathers almost invariably. Incubation is by hen alone normally for about 13 days. The young are fed by both sexes and as a rule fly when 13–14 days old. Many apparently are single-brooded, but some second broods occur. **Status and Distribution.** A summer-visitor in the British Isles, abundant and widely distributed, but local in N. Caithness, the Outer Hebrides and Orkney, and very rarely breeds in Shetland where it appears on passage. It has very occasionally been recorded in winter in England and Wales. Spring movement may extend from mid-March to early June. The main body of summer-visitors arrives in April, and departs from mid-July to September, with passage migration lasting into early October and stragglers a week or two later. The majority of English breeding birds belong to the race *Phylloscopus trochilus trochilus* which extends in Europe from central France and central Italy north to S. Sweden and east to Romania, and winters in tropical and S. Africa; in Scotland most appear to resemble the race *Phylloscopus trochilus acredula*, breeding over most of Scandinavia and across N. Europe to Siberia. The latter race typically is less greenish above and whiter below.

GOLDCREST—*Regulus regulus*

Bird Plate 102   Egg Plate II (11)

The diminutive size, dull greenish upper-parts and flanks and *orange-yellow crest*, bordered black, are characteristic, but the plump, compact form, shorter tail and slenderer bill than tits are readily recognizable even if the colours are not distinguished. The under-parts are dingy whitish, shading to dull greenish on the sides. The crest is orange in the centre in male, lemon-yellow in female, and absent in juvenile. The wings have two white bars and a dark band. Differences from Firecrest are given under that species. Length about 3½ ins.

Habitat. In the breeding-season it inhabits fir and other conifer woods, mixed woods and gardens containing conifers, and to a much less extent non-coniferous woodland, thickets, etc. After the breeding-season and in winter it frequents deciduous trees more freely, though still keeping principally in conifers; also sometimes in thickets and hedgerows.

General Habits. Flight is tit-like, with rapidly moving wings. It is indifferent to observation, but active and restless, and has a flicking movement of the wings similar to that of tits and leaf-warblers. In trees it generally keeps well up, flitting from twig to twig examining the foliage, or hangs suspended in tit-like fashion, but its actions are less acrobatic and more warbler-like than those of tits, its frequent associates. It is gregarious outside the breeding-season, in family parties or consorting with flocks of tits and Treecreepers.

Call is a very thin, shrill "zeec-zeec-zeec". The song, also extremely thin and high-pitched, is a repetition of a single almost disyllabic note followed by a little terminal flourish. It is heard regularly from March to early July, less regularly in the second half of February and to the end of July, and again from mid-August to mid-November.

Food is chiefly spiders and insects.

Nest is normally suspended under thick foliage towards the end of a branch of some conifer, but sometimes built against tree-trunks in ivy, in furze, or among boughs of evergreens and whitethorns. The eggs, usually 7–10, occasionally 11–13, varying from white to ochreous in ground-colour, are laid generally from the end of April onwards in a nest built usually by both sexes of green moss woven together with spiders' webs and freely lined with feathers. Incubation is by hen only, for about 14–16 days. The young are fed by both sexes and fly when up to 23 days old. Double-brooded.

Status and Distribution. Present throughout the year, and generally distributed almost everywhere, but only thinly in the Outer Hebrides and breeding is sporadic in Orkney and Shetland. There is considerable southward movement in autumn from August to November, with return in March and April. Our birds belong to the race *Regulus regulus regulus*, which also breeds from N. Scandinavia south to the Pyrenees, Sicily, Macedonia and Syria. Continental birds are common passage-migrants on the east coast in varying numbers and are also regular in the north, arriving from mid-September to the end of November, returning in March and April. Other races occur in the Azores, Canaries, Asia and N. America.

FIRECREST—*Regulus ignicapillus*

BIRD PLATE 102

It has a general resemblance to Goldcrest, but is readily distinguished by the *conspicuous white superciliary band and black stripe through eye, with some more white below it*. The whole plumage is much brighter and cleaner-looking than Goldcrest, *the upper-parts being brighter green and under-parts whiter*; there is a noticeable bronzy tint on the sides of the neck. The orange-red centre of crown in both sexes (richest in male) is more extensive, with less yellow at the sides, than in male Goldcrest, but the facial markings are a much more effective means of identification, and are usually indicated to some extent even in young, where the crest is lacking. Length about 3½ ins.

Habitat. Often associated with Norway spruce, pine, tall holly, but is much less restricted to conifers than Goldcrest and outside the breeding-season occurs largely in deciduous woods, gardens, etc., with a partiality for ilexes; sometimes amongst scrub or dead bracken.

General Habits. It occurs more often than Goldcrest in bushes and relatively low cover; its actions and habits are otherwise much the same, and, like it, often consorts with tits, etc., in winter.

Note is "zit, zit, zit" perceptibly lower in pitch, less thin and feeble, than Goldcrest's and often given singly. The repetition of a similar note is the basis of the song, which is rather stronger than Goldcrest's; the notes increase in volume during the course of the song-phrase, which normally ends in a flourish.

Food consists of small insects; also spiders.

Status and Distribution. Small numbers breed widely, but very locally, mainly in S. and E. England; it has also nested in Wales; first found in 1961. Otherwise the bird is a scarce but regular passage-migrant and winter-visitor along the English coast from the Scillies to Norfolk, occurring sometimes in September but mainly October, until March–April. It is found more rarely in a number of inland and northern counties up to the border, and about annually in Scotland; more frequently in Ireland especially in S.W. The race concerned, *Regulus ignicapillus ignicapillus*, breeds from Denmark and Poland south to N.W. Africa and Asia Minor. Other races occur on some Mediterranean islands and Madeira.

SPOTTED FLYCATCHER—*Muscicapa striata*

BIRD PLATE 104 EGG PLATE II (9A & 9B)

The mouse-grey plumage, whitish below, with dark streaks on the head and breast, lacks striking features, but the bird is at once identified by its *pose and behaviour*. It sits in a rather upright attitude with head somewhat sunk between the shoulders, on a bare branch or other exposed perch, making frequent sallies after insects, and returns often to the same perch. The sexes are similar; the young have a paler ground-colour and dark borders to feathers of the upper-parts, giving a more "scaly" or spotted appearance. Length about 5½ ins.

Habitat. In the breeding-season it inhabits open woodland, gardens and parkland.

General Habits. When feeding, flight is fluttering and erratic, often with rapid swerves and twists as it pursues an insect, but when prolonged, flight is rapid and somewhat undulating like many other small birds. In trees it usually perches on the lower branches, seldom near the top, but is seldom seen on the ground. It shows little tendency to gregariousness but forms small parties in autumn.

Call-note is a thin "tzee", much like Robin's, but shriller and more scratchy. Alarm is "tzeec-tzucc". Migrants give a sharp "tchick".

Food is almost entirely insects.

Nests against a wall or tree-trunk, or resting on a beam or branch, and sometimes in a hole or the old nest of another bird. The eggs, normally 4–5, rarely 6, occasionally unmarked pale blue, are laid generally in the second half of May or early June in a nest constructed by both sexes, slightly built of moss, wool and hair, compacted with cobwebs. Incubation is by both sexes for about 12–14 days. The young are fed by both parents and usually fly when 12–13 days old. Normally one brood, but two not infrequently reared.

Status and Distribution. A summer-visitor and passage-migrant arriving from mid-April to early June, but mainly in the second half of May; the return movement lasts from late July to October. It is generally distributed, but is local in N. Scotland, and is irregular in Orkney and the Outer Hebrides; it is only a passage-migrant in Shetland. Abroad the same race, *Muscicapa striata striata*, breeds from N. Norway and the White Sea south to Romania, Czechoslovakia and across W. Europe to N.W. Africa. Other races occur in some Mediterranean islands, the Balkans and W. Asia. It winters in tropical and S. Africa.

RED-BREASTED FLYCATCHER—*Ficedula parva*

Bird Plate 102

A small, rotund flycatcher, ashy-brown above and buffish-white below, with broad *white patches at either side of the basal half of the tail*; the patches are conspicuous in flight and when settled they are prominently displayed by a *frequent upward flick of the tail*, which is often cocked over the back like Wren. *Male has an orange-red throat at all seasons*, but females and young males lack this. Juveniles have the spotted, "scaly" pattern of other young flycatchers, but tail as adult; young in autumn differ from adult females in having buff spots on the wings. Length about 4½ ins.

Habitat. In winter-quarters it occurs almost anywhere where good-sized trees are to be found, in forest, in open cultivation or in the neighbourhood of towns and villages, but also in reed-beds and low vegetation.

General Habits. Shy and secretive, it keeps mainly amongst the foliage of tall trees, though sometimes "flycatching" from fences, securing insects in a typical flycatcher fashion, but it is active and restless and sometimes compared to a *Phylloscopus* in habits. It seldom makes more than a momentary excursion to the ground to catch an insect. Not gregarious.

It has a characteristic chattering or rattling note reminiscent of Wren, though less loud; also an abrupt "chick".

Food consists of insects, chiefly taken on the wing. It is said to take berries in autumn.

Status and Distribution. A scarce passage-migrant on east coast between Shetland and Norfolk in autumn, also S.W. areas.

Red-breasted Flycatcher

The white patches at base of the tail show when tail is flirted.

Most are recorded in September and October, rarely in spring. It has also occurred in several other English, Scottish and Irish counties. The race concerned, *Ficedula parva parva*, breeds from Denmark eastwards through central Europe to Iran and winters in W. India. Other races occur elsewhere in central Asia.

PIED FLYCATCHER—*Ficedula hypoleuca*

BIRD PLATE 103   EGG PLATE II (10)

It is plumper than Spotted Flycatcher. The pied plumage of male in the breeding-season, *black above and white below*, with white fore-head and broad *white wing-bar*, is distinctive and conspicuous. Female is unobtrusively coloured, not unlike a hen Chaffinch, olive-brown above and whitish below, and in a bad light or unfavourable position can be confused with Spotted Flycatcher, but the buffish white wing-bar (narrower, however, than male's) and sides of tail at once distinguish it. In autumn the sexes are similar, both old and young males resembling females, but the former have usually some white on the forehead. Juveniles have a similar "scaly" pattern to juvenile Spotted Flycatcher, but show white in wings and tail much as adults. Length about 5 ins.

Habitat. In the breeding-season it haunts old woodland, particularly oak and birch in hilly country, well-timbered parks, gardens, etc., as a rule near a stream or other water. It is also locally common about villages and roadside trees.

General Habits. Unlike Spotted Flycatcher, it seldom, if ever, returns to the same twig after darting out to catch an insect; at times it clings, tit-like, to a tree-trunk for an instant and often feeds on the ground. It frequently moves the tail up and down and flicks wings, especially on settling. As soon as the young are fledged, they and the old birds may virtually disappear from the breeding haunts, often keeping high up in thick trees, and quite silent.

Notes are a sharp, Chaffinch-like "whit" and a short repeated "tic", sometimes combined. Alarm-note is usually "p'hweet". The simple but pleasing song has a preliminary hesitant repetition of the same note, and a rapid, more trilling conclusion. It may be heard from late April to the end of May, and less frequently throughout June.

Food is chiefly insects. Worms are taken occasionally.

Nests in holes of trees, walls or buildings, and nest-boxes, sometimes close to the ground. The eggs, normally 5–9, but sometimes 3–10, are seldom laid before the second half of May, in a nest loosely built by female of leaves, strips of honeysuckle bark, moss, bents, and roots, lined with hair, and sometimes bits of wool or feathers. Incubation is by hen alone for about 12–13 days. The young are fed by both parents and fly when 13 or more days old. Single-brooded.

Status and Distribution. A summer-visitor and passage-migrant, arriving from mid-April to early June, and returning from August to October. It breeds regularly in considerable numbers in the Forest of Dean (Glos) and over much of Wales except the south-west. It is also well distributed from Yorkshire to S. Scotland. In England between these two main areas there are a series of isolated breeding spots down the Pennines, in the West Midlands, and Welsh Border counties; it also breeds in small numbers in Devon and Somerset, and has done so exceptionally in many other counties. In Scotland scattered breeding extends north to Perth and occasionally Spey, W. Ross. There are recent records of nesting in N.E. and S.E. Ireland. As a passage-migrant it occurs in considerable numbers in spring and especially autumn along the east coast from Shetland to Kent, in smaller numbers on the south coast, and less frequently inland; a few regularly in S. Ireland. The race concerned, *Ficedula hypoleuca hypoleuca*, breeds in Europe from the Arctic Ocean south to S. France and S. Russia; also in W. Siberia. It winters in tropical Africa. Other races occur in S.W. and S.E. Europe, W. Asia and N.W. Africa.

BEARDED TIT—*Panurus biarmicus*

Bird Plate 84   Egg Plate V (9)

It is found only in reed-beds. *The predominantly tawny-brown colouring and, in male, the striking head pattern* at once distinguish it from Long-tailed Tit, the only other bird which might be confused with it. *Head of male is lavender-grey with a broad, tapering moustachial stripe of glossy black.* There is some white at the sides of the tail; the closed wing appears banded lengthwise with whitish (outer border), rufous-brown, blackish, and pale buff on inner border; the under tail-coverts are black, and the bill rich yellow. Female is duller, without moustache or black under tail-coverts, and has the whole upper-parts brown, usually with some dark streaks on the mantle; under-parts paler. Young resemble female, but with the middle of back and sides of tail blackish and sometimes with dark streaks on the head. On the wing it appears mainly brown, not unlike a small rufous-looking

Sparrow with an inordinately long, graduated tail. Length about
6½ ins.; tail about 3 ins.

Habitat. It inhabits extensive reed-beds.

General Habits. Flight is rather laboured, slightly undulating,
with rapid whirring wing-action, usually just over tops of the
reeds, accompanied by a peculiar rhythmical movement of the tail.
It moves up and down reeds with a jerky action and assumes a
variety of acrobatic postures, or creeps amongst the vegetation at
their base. It is extremely confiding at the nest, and is gregarious
outside the breeding-season.

Calls are a distinctive ringing, vibrant "ping, ping" and a less
distinctive "ticc".

Food includes insects but in winter is seeds of reed chiefly.

Nests generally among sedge, reeds or other aquatic vegetation
in swampy ground, not far from the edge of bed, and low down.
The eggs, normally 5–7, but sometimes up to 12, are laid generally
from mid-April onwards in a characteristic nest built by both sexes
of dead leaves of reed or sometimes sedges, warmly lined with
flowering tops of reeds and often a feather or two. Incubation is by
both sexes for about 12–13 days. The young are fed by both
parents and fly when about 9–12 days old. Two broods regularly;
three at times, possibly more.

Status and Distribution. For many years restricted as a
resident to Norfolk and Suffolk and several times almost exterminated by severe winters; but autumn eruptions from East Anglia
(and even Netherlands) in the 1960s and early 1970s scattered
birds as far as Scotland for the first time, and in Ireland a small
breeding group was formed in Wicklow. In England breeding
spread very locally and in some cases temporarily, south to Kent,
west to Devon, north to Humber and Lancs. It was previously
only a rare vagrant to S. and central England. Our birds belong to
the race *Panurus biarmicus biarmicus* which breeds over much of
Europe south and west from the Baltic. An allied race occurs in
Hungary and other parts of S.E. Europe, and in W. Asia.

LONG-TAILED TIT—*Aegithalos caudatus*

BIRD PLATE 84   EGG PLATE V (8A & 8B)

The small size, *very long narrow tail* and *combination of pink,
blackish and dull white* in the plumage are distinctive. The head is
dingy white with a broad blackish band from lores over the eye to

mantle, the upper-parts blackish mixed with pink, the rump and scapulars mainly pink, the under-parts are dull white shading to pinkish on belly and flanks, the wings and tail blackish with whitish edgings to secondaries and conspicuous white in the outer tail-feathers. Young are duller, lacking pink, with sides of the face dark and with shorter tails. Length about 5½ ins.; tail about 3 ins.

Habitat. In the breeding-season it haunts principally hedge-rows, thickets and bushy places or outskirts of woods, less in regular woodland and only where it is open and well provided with bushes and undergrowth; more rarely in gardens, etc. Outside the breeding-season it is more general in woods, though also regular in hedgerows, etc., as above.

General Habits. Flight is rather laboured, with rapidly moving wings, and irregularly undulating when prolonged, the long tail giving a characteristic appearance. It feeds in trees, also much in lower undergrowth and hedgerows, but rarely settles on the ground. Its restless activity and acrobatic actions resemble those of other tits, but the flicking movement of wings and tail is exaggerated owing to the length of the latter. It associates freely with other tits, but also often occurs in unmixed family or larger parties. It visits gardens less than other tits, and bird-tables only exceptionally.

Distinctive note is a low, rather abrupt "tupp" with a slightly tremulous quality difficult to describe, but highly characteristic. Also a colourless, thin "zee-zee-zee", like other tits, but more penetrating and persistently repeated.

Food is chiefly insects, occasionally centipedes, seeds, fragments of buds, and frequently spiders.

Nests usually in thorn bushes, furze or brambles, but also in trees at 30–70 feet. The eggs, normally 8–12, sometimes more or as few as 5, at times almost unmarked, are laid generally in mid- or late April in a large, upright and ovoid-shaped nest with entrance hole near the top; it is built by both sexes, chiefly of moss woven together with cobwebs and a little hair, and externally covered with lichens, lined with a great profusion of feathers of various kinds. Incubation is chiefly if not entirely by hen, for about 14–18 days. The young are fed by both sexes and fly when about 15–16 days old. Normally single-brooded.

Status and Distribution. A resident, generally distributed in most parts of the British Isles, but rare in some very barren districts including Isle of Man, and almost unknown in the Outer Hebrides, Orkney and Shetland. The race *Aegithalos caudatus rosaceus* is confined to the British Isles. A few birds have occurred in eastern counties with white heads, whiter under-parts and secondaries, resembling the race *Aegithalos caudatus caudatus* which breeds from arctic Scandinavia south to E. Prussia and Romania. Other races occur elsewhere in mid- and S. Europe and across Asia.

MARSH TIT—*Parus palustris*

BIRD PLATE 85   EGG PLATE V (6)

It is about the size of a Coal Tit, from which it is distinguished by the *absence of a white patch on nape, the brown, not olive-grey, shade of upper-parts* and the absence of wing-bars. It is very similar to the Willow Tit, under which species the distinctions are given. *The crown is glossy black in adult*, but in young it is dull sooty like Willow Tit. The cheeks are white; wings and tail brown, as mantle; chin black; and under-parts dull whitish, with flanks more buff. Length about 4½ ins.

Habitat. It haunts woods, chiefly deciduous and especially open oak-wood, copses, hedgerows, orchards, and more rarely gardens, both in damp and dry situations, with no special preference for the former, notwithstanding its name.

General Habits. Flight and habits are much like other small tits, but it tends to feed less in the canopy and more in lower growth than other species, except Willow Tit.

Notes are varied in detail. The typical call (with no counterpart in Willow Tit), is a distinctive double "pitchuu", with variants; it also utters a thin "tsee-tsee-tsee . . ." and a harsh nasal "tchaa-tchaa-tchaa-tchaa . . ." commonly prefaced by the "pitchuu" note. The song, a simple repetition of notes with a peculiar liquid

MARSH TIT   WILLOW TIT

Note Willow Tit's pale wing patch.

bubbling quality, is regular from mid-January to mid-April, less regular for a month earlier and later, and heard exceptionally from mid-May to the beginning of August and again from October to December.

Food is chiefly insects; also seeds, beechmast and berries.

Nests usually in natural holes of willows, alders, etc., sometimes slightly enlarging or altering the opening, and rarely making its own hole; it occasionally breeds in nesting-boxes and holes in stone-walls. The eggs, normally 7–8, occasionally 5–10, occasionally unmarked, are laid generally at the end of April or early in May on a thick pad of felted hair, rabbit's fur or down, with a foundation of moss. Incubation is apparently by hen for 13 days. The young are fed by both sexes and fly when about 16–17 days old. Possibly at times double-brooded.

Status and Distribution. A resident, widespread in England and Wales, but somewhat local and especially so in W. Cornwall, Cumberland and N.W. Wales. In Scotland it breeds not uncommonly in some parts of Berwick, in Roxburgh since 1966, also perhaps E. Lothian and Selkirk. It does not occur in Ireland. The race concerned, *Parus palustris dresseri*, is confined to Great Britain. Other races occur in Europe, except in the south-west and south-east, also in N. Asia east to Japan.

WILLOW TIT—*Parus montanus*

BIRD PLATE 85   EGG PLATE V (7)

It very closely resembles Marsh Tit, the safest distinction being the *difference in notes*, while the negative character, that Willow Tit has nothing like the well-known "pitchuu" note of Marsh Tit, should not be overlooked. On the whole the best plumage distinction is a broad *light patch on the secondaries in the closed wing*, often very marked, though considerably obscured by abrasion in summer, while some Marsh Tits show indications of such a mark. *The dull sooty, instead of glossy, black crown* is a valid character under favourable conditions, but requires care. A bird showing strong gloss is a Marsh Tit, but in poor lighting the gloss may not be very obvious, while in strong lights a faint gloss may be discernible even on Willow Tit. Even when the degree of gloss is in doubt, however, the looser texture of the feathers tends to give a less sleek, "well-groomed" appearance to Willow Tit's crown.

Subsidiary characters are: the flanks are more strongly buff than in Marsh Tit, whitish of cheeks tend to extend further over the sides of the neck, and the dark cap further back over shoulders, and the dark chin patch tends to be more extensive, with less sharply defined borders. Young of both Marsh and Willow Tit have dull sooty heads. Length about 4½ ins.

Habitat. Its habitat is not sharply defined from that of Marsh Tit, both species often occurring together, but Willow Tit usually shows a distinct preference in the breeding-season for more or less marshy spots or the vicinity of water; thus it occurs especially in damp woods and copses, alder-holts, etc., where there are plenty of soft, rotten stumps. Also, particularly in winter, it is more regular than Marsh Tit about hedgerows, thickets, and bushy places, and even heaths, away from woods.

General Habits. In these it closely resembles Marsh Tit, but is rather less active and less noisy.

Main notes are: a rather thin, sibilant "eez-eez-eez", a contact or feeding note which is probably the commonest utterance; an extremely high-pitched, thin "zi-zi-zi-zi", or rather less shrill "zit-zit-zit-zit"; a prolonged, emphatic "zi-zurr-zurr-zurr", deeper, more nasal and harshly slurred than any note of Marsh Tit. This note is absolutely diagnostic and it may be heard at any time of year, although bird is often silent for long periods. Song is erratic, and full song comparatively infrequent, differing from all other tit utterances in including "series of sweet warbling notes of striking richness"; it may be heard from mid-January to mid-May and from late July to mid-September, also exceptionally at other times but not in the first half of July or most of November.

Food seems very similar to that of Marsh Tit.

Nests in a hole excavated by the birds themselves in very soft rotten wood, usually in birches, willows or alders, generally in marshy ground. The eggs, normally 8–9, sometimes 5–13, are laid generally in late April or early May on a thin pad of rabbit-down mixed with wood-fibre, and moss only found very exceptionally, but often a few feathers. Incubation is by hen alone for about 13–14 days. The young are fed by both sexes and fly when about 17–19 days old. Apparently one brood.

Status and Distribution. A resident, widespread in England and Wales but local and generally occurring in smaller numbers than Marsh Tit. In Scotland, where the Marsh Tit is not found except in the S.E., the Willow Tit is local and thinly distributed, breeding only in the S.W. as far north as the Clyde valley; elsewhere as a vagrant it has occurred north to Sutherland. It is unknown in Ireland. The race *Parus montanus kleinschmidti* is confined to Great Britain. One example of the race *Parus monta-nus borealis* has occurred in Glos., others possibly in Herts and Fair Isle; this race breeds from S. Scandinavia and E. Prussia to N.W. Russia and can be separated in the field from our birds by its larger size, very white cheeks and generally greyer appearance with prominent greyish-white edgings to the secondaries. Other races occur elsewhere in Europe except in the south, also in Asia and N. America.

CRESTED TIT—*Parus cristatus*

BIRD PLATE 85   EGG PLATE V (5)

The pointed crest, dull whitish with black centres, and the characteristic trilling note at once separate it from other tits. The sides of the head and neck are dingy white, bounded by a black gorget prolonged as a narrow black collar; a blackish mark through the eye curves round behind the ear-coverts, upper-parts are hair-brown, wings and tail darker; the under-parts whitish, buffer on the flanks. Length about 4½ ins.

Habitat. It inhabits pine forests, but is not averse to a considerable local admixture of birch, alder, etc.

General Habits. Its actions and habits resemble those of Coal Tit.

Characteristic note is a lively, rather low, purring trill, impossible to reproduce vocally.

Food consists of insects and larvae; also pine seed and berries.

Nests in holes or crevices excavated in old and decayed pine stumps, also in alders and birches and sometimes in fencing posts, iron and wooden. The eggs, usually 5–6, rarely 8, are laid generally in late April or early May in a nest built almost entirely by the hen, of dead moss, and lined with hair of deer and hare, sometimes feathers or wool. Incubation is by hen alone for about 13–15 days. The young are fed by both sexes, and normally fly when 17–18 days old. Nearly always single-brooded.

Status and Distribution. The British race, *Parus cristatus scoticus*, is confined to Scotland, resident principally in the Spey valley, but extending into Nairn, Moray, Banff and Ross. Examples of the Continental races *Parus cristatus cristatus* (breeding from Scandinavia south-east to the Balkans and Russia) and *Parus cristatus mitratus* (breeding from the English Channel to Romania) have occurred as rare vagrants in England. Both these races are less dark brown than our bird, but they cannot be separated in the field. Other races occur elsewhere in Europe.

COAL TIT—*Parus ater*

BIRD PLATE 86   EGG PLATE V (4)

It differs from other black-capped and white-cheeked tits in having a *large white patch on the nape*. The head pattern otherwise is as Great Tit, though the bird is much smaller and duller, with *buff, not yellow, under-parts* and no black band down the centre. It differs further from Marsh and Willow Tits, which are approximately the same size, in the olive-grey shade of the upper-parts, *double white wing-bar* and distinctly shorter tail. Length about 4¼ ins.

Habitat. It frequents woods, copses and gardens, and has a marked, though not exclusive, preference for conifers; also sometimes orchards, etc. Outside the breeding-season it occasionally visits hedgerows, etc.

General Habits. Flight and habits are like those of other small tits, but it feeds more than other species on trunks where it moves with Treecreeper-like action, though also feeding freely on branches. More gregarious than Marsh Tit, it often occurs in considerable parties where common.

Notes are nearly all sweeter and clearer in tone than those of any other British tit. Commonest is a piping, often rather plaintive "tsuu", etc. It has also a thin "tsee-tsee-tsee . . ." common to most tits, which is often not unlike Goldcrest. Song is a repetition of a double note, comparable in form to Great Tit's, but much sweeter and more piping in tone; "*tee*chu-*tee*chu-*tee*chu . . .". It is usually delivered from a high perch in a conifer or other tree, and is heard during much the same periods as Great Tit's song.

Food is mainly insects; also spiders. Seeds are also sometimes eaten, and like other tits it will feed on meat and fat.

Nests in a hole either in or close to the ground in an old stump, or tree, often in a bank; also recorded in foundations of large nests in trees. The eggs, normally 7–11, occasionally 5–14, at times pure white, are laid generally in late April or early May in a nest built by both sexes of moss with a thick layer of felted hair or down; feathers are used. Incubation is chiefly or entirely by the hen for perhaps 17–18 days. The young are fed by both parents, and fly when about 16 days old. Normally single-brooded.

Status and Distribution. A resident, generally distributed throughout the British Isles, more especially in wooded parts, but it is little known in the Outer Hebrides (bred Stornoway 1969 and formerly recorded as breeding there) and has never been recorded in Orkney and Shetland. The race *Parus ater britannicus* occurs in Great Britain and N.E. Ireland. However, many birds in W. Scotland and W. Wales resemble the typical Irish bird, *Parus ater hibernicus*, which differs typically in the yellowish tint of cheeks and nape patch, most pronounced in winter; moreover, birds resembling the British form may be found almost anywhere in Ireland. In addition to these resident races, Continental birds of the race *Parus ater ater*, which breeds from the Arctic south to France and the Balkans, are recorded occasionally on the east coast, and have reached Ireland. Other races occur elsewhere in Europe, N.W. Africa and parts of Asia.

BLUE TIT—*Parus caeruleus*

Bird Plate 86   Egg Plate V (3)

It is the only short-tailed British tit, other than the unmistakable Crested Tit, which lacks a black crown, and is the only one with *bright blue* in its plumage. *The crown is cobalt-blue*, bordered white; the *whole side of the face is white*, with dark border extending from chin to meet a dark line passing through the eye, and a white patch on the nape. Mantle is yellowish-green, underparts sulphur-yellow with a dark mark down the belly, tail and wings blue with a white wing-bar. Young are duller, with greenish crowns and the white on the head replaced by yellow. Length about 4½ ins.

Habitat. It inhabits woods and copses, chiefly deciduous, and parks, gardens, orchards, hedgerows, and thickets. In winter it is more widely dispersed; it visits reed beds and reedy ditches more than other tits.

General Habits. Flight and general habits resemble Great Tit, and it sometimes moves on tree-trunks with a creeper-like action. It is especially confiding about houses; it is the chief culprit in periodical outbursts of milk-bottle opening and paper-tearing.

It has a considerable variety of call-notes, the chief being "tsee-tsee-tsee, tsit" (mostly in early spring), with minor variants, and a thin "tsee-tsee-tsee" also given singly. The song is a rapid, liquid trill introduced by two or three single notes, "tsee-tsee-tsu-tsuhuhuhuhuhu". Its seasonal occurrence is similar to Great Tit's song.

Food of an animal kind is mainly insects, with some spiders and millipedes. Fruit, grain, seeds and buds are also eaten.

Nests in holes of trees and walls, occasionally inside open nests of other species or in the foundations of nests of large birds. Where natural sites fail, holes of any kind may be used. The eggs, 7–14, sometimes only 5–6, sometimes unmarked, are laid generally in late April or early May in a nest built by both sexes, having a foundation of moss mixed with grass, and lining of hair or wool with feathers. Incubation is by hen only, for about 13–14 days. The young are fed by both sexes, and fly usually when about 19 days old. One brood normally.

Status and Distribution. An abundant resident, generally distributed throughout the British Isles, but local although spreading in N.W. Scotland, and only occurring rarely in Orkney and Shetland; the Outer Hebrides were colonized about 1962 and Scilly Isles in late 1940s. Our breeding birds belong to the race *Parus caeruleus obscurus* which also occurs in Alderney (Channel Islands). *Parus caeruleus caeruleus*, the Continental race breeding from the Arctic Circle in Norway south to central Spain, the Balkans and Asia Minor, appears in this country as an irregular autumn-migrant, mainly on the east coast; it is a little paler than our bird, but not distinguishable in the field. Other races occur in S.W. Europe, N. Africa, Mediterranean islands and W. Asia.

GREAT TIT—*Parus major*

Bird Plate 86   Egg Plate V (2A & 2B)

Tits are small, plump, thick-necked, stumpy-billed birds of gregarious tendencies, often with black on the crown. Great Tit is the largest species, with *crown and nape a glossy blue-black*, which extends behind the *white cheeks* to join the black of throat, and a *broad black band down the centre of sulphur-yellow underparts*. Mantle is yellowish-green, the rump, tail and wing-coverts blue-grey, with white outer tail-feathers and a white wing-bar. Young birds are duller and paler, with a dark brown cap and yellowish cheeks, all colours looking washed out. Length about 5½ ins.

Habitat. It haunts woods and copses, chiefly deciduous or mixed, and gardens, orchards, hedgerows, and thickets.

General Habits. All members of the present genus are much the same in action and behaviour. When on the ground they hop, while flight most commonly takes the form of short more or less direct passages from tree to tree or along a hedgerow, though longer (and then distinctly undulating) flights at fair height across open spaces are not infrequent. Though tolerably swift, flight appears rather weak and laboured, especially in the smaller species, with rapid wing action. They feed mainly in trees though also frequently foraging amongst dead leaves, etc., on the ground, and are active and sprightly in their movements, the small ones particularly, clinging to or hanging from twigs in a variety of acrobatic postures, and gently flicking wings and tail as they move about. Hard seeds, etc., are held down with foot while hacked open. From autumn to spring they tend to gather in parties, often of several species, which roam woods and hedgerows. Great Tit is on the whole less gregarious than the rest, although flocks predominantly or even exclusively of this species are frequent in woods in autumn and winter.

Its repertoire of calls is the most varied of all tits, prolific in combinations and complicated by a tendency to imitate. Notes are generally fuller and louder than other tits, and most have a distinctive metallic quality. Common calls are a ringing, Chaffinch-like "tink, tink, tink"; a quick, short note, rising at the end, repeated several times, "tui, tui, tui"; a thin "tsee-tsee-tsee" and similar notes, and a scolding churr. The chief form of song is a strongly metallic "*tee*chu-*tee*chu-*tee*chu" which is heard regularly from January to mid-June, less frequently until mid-October, but with a month's break in July–August, and only exceptionally after mid-October.

Food includes insects, spiders, small molluscs, earthworms; also fruit, peas, seeds and buds. Young birds are occasionally killed.

Nests usually in a hole of a tree or wall, occasionally in the foundations of nests of larger birds. Nest-boxes, flower-pots, and almost any kind of hole may be used in default of natural sites. In a few cases open nests have been found in thick hedges. The eggs, normally 5–11, but more recorded, some unmarked, are laid generally in late April or early May in a nest built by both sexes of moss, with a few bents, and lined with a thick layer of felted hair or down. Incubation is apparently by hen only, usually for 13–14 days. The young are fed by both parents, and fly generally when 18–20 days old. One brood normally.

Status and Distribution. A resident, generally distributed throughout the British Isles from the Scillies to the north coast of the Scottish mainland; it first bred in the Outer Hebrides in 1962, and is only an occasional visitor to Orkney and Shetland. The race to which our birds belong, *Parus major newtoni*, is confined to the British Isles. Continental birds of the race *Parus major major*, breeding from the Arctic Ocean to the Mediterranean, are irregular autumn- and winter-visitors here, mainly to the E. coast from Shetland to Kent; they are indistinguishable in the field but have the bill shorter and decidedly more slender than our bird. Other races occur in N.W. Africa, S.W. Europe, Mediterranean islands and across Asia to Japan.

NUTHATCH—*Sitta europaea*

BIRD PLATE 87   EGG PLATE III (18)

The plump form, short tail, woodpecker-like, pointed bill, and coloration are alike distinctive. The upper-parts are blue-grey, under-parts buff, with more chestnut on the flanks; there is a black stripe through the eye; cheeks and throat are white; lateral tail-feathers black at base, with some white in the outer ones. Young are duller, without chestnut flanks. Length about 5½ ins.

Habitat. It inhabits woods, parks, or large gardens with old deciduous trees, rarely occurring in unmixed conifers.

General Habits. *It moves on tree trunks with short jerky leaps, upwards, sideways or downwards with equal facility* and does not use tail in climbing like Creeper; it occasionally settles on walls or buildings, and in shrubs or bushes. It sometimes feeds on the ground, moving by hops. Flight is undulating when prolonged, but the bird chiefly confines itself to short direct flights between neighbouring trees. Hazel-nuts, acorns, beechmast and yew seeds are wedged in crevices of bark and hacked open with the bill, each blow delivered with the force of the whole body hinging on the legs. Its presence is often proclaimed by loud, woodpecker-like tapping during these operations. It commonly occurs in pairs, and is not gregarious, but may associate with foraging parties of tits.

Chief calls are a loud metallic "chwit-chwit", and variants; a shrill repeated "tsit"; a loud, clear, piping repeated "twee"; and a very rapid trill.

Food is largely hazel-nuts in autumn: also beechmast, acorns, seeds and insects.

Nests usually in a hole in the stem or large branch of a tree at varying heights, occasionally in holes of walls or banks or in old Magpies' nests. Nesting boxes are also often occupied. The entrance to the hole is reduced in size with hard mud, and crevices are filled up. The eggs, normally 6–11, occasionally 4–13, at times unmarked, are laid generally in late April or May in a nest built as a rule by both sexes and lined with flakes of bark, or dried leaves of oak and beech. Incubation is by hen alone, normally for 14–15 days. The young are fed by both sexes and fly when about 23–25 days old. One brood usually.

Status and Distribution. A resident, widely distributed in England north to a line from the Wash to Mersey and in Wales where it has now spread to the west; much more local in northern England and relatively recently colonised Northumberland and Westmorland. It has occurred a few times in Scotland north to Fair Isle, but not in Ireland. The race *Sitta europaea affinis* is confined to Great Britain. Other races occur from S. Scandinavia south to N.W. Africa and east to Japan.

WALLCREEPER—*Tichodroma muraria*

BIRD PLATE 87

The grey upper-parts, crimson wing-coverts, and distinctive pattern and action on the wing preclude confusion with any other species. The bill is long, slender, and curved. Throat and breast are black in summer, whitish in winter. Young are much as winter adults but with nearly straight bills. In flight the *rounded wings, white spots on the blackish primaries and corners of the tail*, as well as the red coverts, are distinctive, as is the *desultory, flitting, butterfly-like action*, much resembling that of Hoopoe. Length about 6½ ins.; bill about 1 in.

Habitat. In winter it haunts buildings and ruins as well as rocks.

General Habits. It spends much of its time climbing about rock-faces, or masonry, or amongst boulders, with little jerky hops, not using the tail as support like Treecreeper, probing crevices for insects, and constantly half opening and closing its wings with a flicking action, displaying the red. It only exceptionally settles on trees.

The note, seldom heard, is described as a thin, but clear and pleasing, piping.

Food is almost entirely insects.

Status and Distribution. A very rare vagrant, in autumn, winter and spring, which has occurred north to Lancs, but mainly in S.E. England. It breeds in the mountains of central and S. Europe, and across Asia to Mongolia. There are no subspecies.

TREECREEPER—*Certhia familiaris*

BIRD PLATE 87   EGG PLATE V (1A & 1B)

Creepers are the *only small British passerines with relatively long decurved bills*. The chief characteristic of the soberly coloured Treecreeper is its constant hunt for insects, in which it ascends trunks or limbs of trees in a succession of little jerks, then flies down to another tree and again ascends. The upper-parts are brown, streaked pale buff, rump more rufous, the eye stripe whitish, under-parts silvery-white, and wings barred buffish. Young birds have a more rufous-yellow tinge and more spotted appearance than adults. Length about 5 ins.

Habitat. It haunts well-grown woodland, and well-timbered parks or old gardens; in Britain more often in deciduous than conifer woods. At times it visits hedgerows and other trees in the open.

General Habits. It climbs with feet wide apart, aided by the stiff, pointed feathers of the graduated tail, which are pressed against the bark like a woodpecker. It often climbs along the under-side of boughs, and very rarely descends trunks head downwards like Nuthatch. It feeds at times while clinging tit-like to small outer foliage and occasionally on the ground. Flight is slightly undulating, tit-like, seldom for more than a short distance. Not gregarious, but outside the breeding-season it associates habitually with roving parties of tits or Goldcrests. Wherever Wellingtonias are available roosting hollows are excavated in the bark.

Notes are a shrill "tsuu", often rapidly repeated, and a softer "tsit". Song is thin and high-pitched, with a characteristic trisyllabic ending. It is usually delivered while climbing and is heard regularly from mid-February to mid-May, irregularly at other times but not from late July to late August and only exceptionally from mid-November to the end of the year.

Food is almost entirely animal; chiefly insects.

Nests usually behind loose bark on trunks of trees, in cracks in stem, or behind ivy roots where separated from the stem; also occasionally in crevices of buildings. The eggs, normally 6, occasionally 3–8, are laid generally from late April to June in a nest built probably by both sexes. It has a foundation of birch twigs, moss, roots, grass, etc., and is lined with feathers, bark and bits of wool, with a few twigs in the outer rim. Incubation is chiefly by hen, for about 17–20 days. The young are fed by both sexes, and fly usually when 14–15 days old. Sometimes double-brooded.

Status and Distribution. A resident, generally distributed in suitable localities, but very rarely seen in Orkney and Shetland, or in the Outer Hebrides until it became a breeding resident in Stornoway in 1962. The race concerned, *Certhia familiaris britannica*, is confined to the British Isles, but the race *Certhia familiaris familiaris*, breeding in Scandinavia, the Baltic and E. Europe, is an occasional visitor to northern isles and E. coast. Other races occur elsewhere in Europe, also in Asia and America.

GOLDEN ORIOLE—*Oriolus oriolus*

Bird Plate 81   Egg Plate V (14)

Male is *brilliant yellow with black wings and tail*, with some yellow at sides of the latter. Female and young are yellowish-green, with wings and tail darker and under-parts lighter; occasionally female is almost as bright clear yellow as male. Male is unmistakable when seen, but is exceedingly secretive, often only detected by a *musical whistle* while remaining invisible in the canopy, or affording merely a fleeting view as it flies to another tree. Length about 9½ ins.

Habitat. In the breeding-season it frequents deciduous or mixed, and less commonly coniferous, woodland, well-timbered old gardens, parks and river banks, chiefly in lowlands. Most typical haunts are districts with scattered woods and copses, especially oak, birch and alder.

General Habits. A strictly arboreal bird rarely descending to the ground. Flight, except over short distances, is in long undulations, somewhat suggesting a short-tailed Mistle Thrush, swift, but rather heavy and with a curious unstable action. The sweeping upward curve by which the bird usually reaches the centre of a tree from below is characteristic. It bathes freely. Mostly seen in pairs or singly.

The most distinctive note is that of male, a loud, clear, and very musical flute-like, whistle, "weela-weeo", with minor variants. Others include harsh screeching notes.

Food is largely insects in spring, but much fruit in autumn.

Nests in an angle of two horizontal boughs. The eggs, usually 3–4, occasionally 6, are laid generally in late May or early June in a nest built almost entirely by hen. It is slung like a hammock, but attached firmly to boughs on both sides, built of grass-stalks, sedges, strips of bark, wool, etc., and lined with flowery grass-heads and frequently containing bits of paper woven into it. Incubation is by both sexes for about 14–15 days. The young are fed by both parents and fly when about 14–15 days old. Possibly double-brooded.

Status and Distribution. Mainly a spring passage-migrant in late April and May, appearing annually in very small numbers in S.E. and S.W. England; scattered elsewhere, including Scotland and Ireland. In addition it is a rare summer-visitor, breeding regularly at least in E. Anglia and sporadically in other eastern and southern counties, rarely elsewhere including Fife. The race concerned, *Oriolus oriolus oriolus*, breeds in Europe from S. Sweden and E. Finland south to the Mediterranean, excluding Greece, also in W. Asia, and winters mainly in tropical and S. Africa. Another race occurs in India.

GOLDEN ORIOLE
male

RED-BACKED SHRIKE—*Lanius collurio*

BIRD PLATE 108   EGG PLATE I (1A, 1B, 1C & 1D)

Shrikes are medium-sized, trimly-built passerines of predatory habits and fierce aspect, with hooked, hawk-like bills, rather long, graduated tails, and a habit of sitting on an exposed point of vantage in more or less open country. Red-backed Shrike is the only one regularly visiting Britain in summer, and is distinguished by *blue-grey crown, nape and rump, and chestnut back of male*. The tail is black with white at the sides, especially towards base. *Female is duller, russet-brown above and buffish below*, without black facial markings, and usually with *crescentic dark markings* indicated on the upper-parts and more pronounced below; but the bird is variable, and some show an approach to male colouring. The young resemble typical female, but with the "scaly" pattern of crescentic dark markings much more pronounced. Length about 6¾ ins.

Habitat. In the breeding-season it frequents old hedgerows, thickets, rather open places with some bushes, old overgrown quarries and the like.

General Habits. The pointed wings and long tail are noticeable in flight, which, when prolonged, is markedly undulating as a rule. Flight from bush to bush or other lookout is usually low down, with an abrupt upward sweep to the new perch. Posted on the top of bush, tree, or telegraph-wire, it turns its head in all directions, watching for a passing insect or other prey, which is seized in sudden dashes either in the air or on ground; but it also hunts, hawk-like, along hedgerows, etc., and sometimes hovers while searching for or about to seize prey. As with other shrikes, the tail is frequently expanded and moved up and down or swung from side to side. At times very inconspicuous, crouching "frozen" on perch. Prey is frequently impaled on a thorn; sometimes particular bushes or parts of a hedge are used repeatedly, forming so-called "larders", where surplus food is placed and often left uneaten, but this habit is inconstant. It is never really gregarious, though several pairs sometimes breed close together, and numbers may be present in the same area on passage.

Commonest note is a harsh "chack, chack" of irritation or alarm, but it has numerous others. The song is a subdued jerky warbling which incorporates varied imitations of notes and songs of other birds; it is heard infrequently in England from the beginning of May to mid-July.

Food includes insects, birds and their young, small mammals, frogs, worms, etc.

Nests in thick clumps of brambles, etc., orchards or straggling hedgerows, usually 3 to 6 ft. from the ground. The eggs, usually 4–5, rarely 7, vary in ground-colour from brownish to pale greenish, or unmarked white. They are laid generally towards the end of May or early June in a rather large nest built almost entirely by the male, of green moss, bents, stalks, etc., neatly lined with fine roots and hair, with a little wool or down at times. Incubation is normally by hen only, for 14–16 days. The young are fed by both sexes and fly when 14–15 days old as a rule. Single-brooded.

Status and Distribution. A fast disappearing summer-visitor and passage-migrant arriving between late April and the beginning of June, and leaving from August to October. It is barely surviving in eastern England. Surprisingly, a few pairs bred in N. and N.E. Scotland in 1977–1979, but not earlier. Its range formerly extended from southern England west to Pembroke and north to Cumberland. Small numbers occur on passage on the south and east coasts north to Shetland; elsewhere it is rare. Almost annual in Ireland. Abroad the race concerned, *Lanius collurio collurio*, breeds from central Scandinavia south to N. Spain, Sicily and Greece, also in W. Asia; it winters in tropical and S. Africa. Other races occur across Asia.

LESSER GREY SHRIKE—*Lanius minor*

Bird Plate 109

The general colour and plumage pattern resemble Great Grey Shrike, but it has a *shorter tail and more upright stance*, and size is approximately like Red-backed. Adults have the under-parts tinged vinous, *black marks on the sides of face united across the fore-head as a broad black frontal band* (which is less developed, however, in the female), and *lacking the Great Grey Shrike's whitish eye-stripe*; the *scapulars are mainly grey like the rest of the back*. The rump is grey, where Great Grey may show a fair amount of white. Young have buffish-grey, not pure grey, upper-parts and the black does not meet across forehead; they may be distinguished by upright stance, stubby beak, and have proportionately shorter tails and longer wings than Great Grey, the wings extending well down tail at rest, whereas in the larger bird they appear to meet at the base of the tail. In flight it presents a strongly parti-coloured appearance with a *broad white patch on the*

LESSER GREY SHRIKE
immature

It has better defined black
ear-coverts than young
Woodchat, and paler, more
sandy-grey, plumage.

black wings, the white being confined to the primaries. Length
about 8 ins.

Habitat. In the breeding-season it frequents mainly grasslands
or the outskirts of cultivation with scattered trees or bushes,
gardens, groves, borders of woods, and roadside trees; principally
in lowlands. On passage and in winter-quarters it is found in scrub
and thorn-bush country.

General Habits. These are much like Red-backed Shrike and
flight similar, but it is perhaps more prone to gliding with extended
wings.

All shrikes have a harsh chattering cry and a considerable range
of other more or less hard grating or strident notes, as well as often
more piping or whistling ones. Usual note of Lesser Grey Shrike is
a harsh "sheck, sheck".

Food is apparently chiefly insects; millipedes and fruit also
recorded.

Status and Distribution. A vagrant of almost annual appearance which has occurred more often in spring than autumn. It has
been recorded from Shetland to the Scillies, also Wales and rarely
Ireland, but most from S.E. England. In Europe it breeds from
the Baltic States west to central France and south to the Balkans;
also in W. Asia. It winters in tropical and S. Africa. There are no
subspecies.

GREAT GREY SHRIKE—*Lanius excubitor*

BIRD PLATE 109

The large size combined with *grey upper-parts and black and white pattern of the wings and tail* distinguish it from all other shrikes. Differences from Lesser Grey Shrike are given under that species. The upper-parts are pale grey, *scapulars white or whitish*, showing as a conspicuous white band above the black of the closed wing; there is a broad black mark from lores to ear-coverts (but not across the fore-head); adults usually (but young birds seldom) show a white eye-stripe above the black eye-mask; the under-parts are whitish, sometimes with a faint pink tinge; the flaunting, almost unwieldy, tail is black with white sides, disproportionately longer and more graduated than in Lesser Grey Shrike. The bird counter-balances its considerable tail-length with a *forward-leaning*, sometimes thrush-like posture. Wings are black with a white bar narrower and longer than in Lesser Grey, usually extended to the secondaries, giving the effect of a double bar on the closed wing; the secondaries are tipped to a varying extent with white. Female is duller, commonly with faint crescentic marks on the under-parts. Young are brownish-grey above and more marked on under-parts. Length about 9½ ins.

Habitat. Outside the breeding-season it is found chiefly in open country, frequenting old hedgerows and places with scattered trees or bushes.

LESSER GREY SHRIKE
adult

GREAT GREY SHRIKE
adult

In flight: Great Grey (northern and southern races)
and Lesser Grey Shrikes.

General Habits. It perches sentinel-like on the top of a tree or bush or on telegraph-wires, from which it swoops down on prey or makes sallies at passing hawks or other birds. It is very aggressive. Like other shrikes it constantly moves its tail up and down while perched. Flight is markedly undulating when prolonged; on shorter flights from perch to perch it usually drops almost to the ground, flies low for some distance, and then sweeps upwards with extended wings to a fresh lookout. Habitually hovers. Prey may be jammed in the fork of a branch or spiked on a thorn, and "larders" are sometimes formed in winter as well as in summer.

Alarm-note is a harsh "sheck, sheck" which may become a Magpie-like chatter. Call-note "truu".

Food is largely small birds; also insects, small mammals and reptiles.

Status and Distribution. A scarce autumn- and winter-visitor along the east side of Great Britain, arriving from the second week in October onwards. It is much more irregular in spring and only occasional in summer. Elsewhere it is very irregular, especially in the west, and is rare in Ireland but occurs particularly in Ulster and Leinster. The race concerned, *Lanius excubitor excubitor*, breeds in Europe northwards into the Arctic from central France, N. Jugoslavia and W. Romania, also in W. Siberia. In addition, examples have occurred twice on Fair Isle of the race *Lanius excubitor pallidirostris* from Caspian Sea area, distinguished by its much paler colouring, more extensive white wing patches and pale bill. Other races occur in S. Europe, and parts of Asia, Africa and America.

WOODCHAT SHRIKE—*Lanius senator*

BIRD PLATE 108

At rest the *chestnut crown and nape and strikingly pied plumage* with gleaming white breast are distinctive. In flight the conspicuous white scapulars and *white rump*, contrasted with the black mantle, at once separate it from Lesser Grey Shrike, whose wing-pattern, with broad white bar, is much the same. The rufous cap is bordered by a broad black frontal band meeting the black of the shoulders; the tail is black with less white at the sides than in Grey Shrikes. Female is rather duller. Young may show a narrow whitish wing-bar but are otherwise much like young Red-backed

Shrike, although generally paler (especially on rump), greyer and less rufous, and at close range show a more pronounced "scaly" pattern of crescentic dark markings both above and below; the scapulars are paler than the rest, often strikingly enough for this character alone to suffice for identification. Length about 6¾ ins.

Habitat. In the breeding-season it inhabits almost any ground with scattered trees and scrub; sometimes also in fairly thick woodland.

General Habits. These and flight, etc., are much like Red-backed Shrike. Though perching freely on the tops of trees, bushes, posts and wires, it sits more habitually in trees, amongst foliage and branches, than other shrikes.

It has harsh chattering notes "kiwick, kiwick" and various others.

Food includes small birds and insects, also worms.

Status and Distribution. Annual passage vagrant, mainly coastal, in S. and E. England as far north as Norfolk, and in S. Irish sea area (Scillies, Lundy, Skokholm, Great Saltee); rare to Shetland. All occurrences have been between spring, mainly May and June, and autumn. The race *Lanius senator senator* breeds from Belgium, Poland, Hungary and S. Russia south to the Mediterranean, also in N.W. Africa; and winters in tropical W. Africa. Other races occur in the Mediterranean and from Palestine to Iran.

WOODCHAT SHRIKE adult and immature.
RED-BACKED SHRIKE immature (bottom).

Note small white patch at base of
primaries of young Woodchat.

JAY—*Garrulus glandarius*

BIRD PLATE 81   EGG PLATE IV (7)

The *vinaceous body colour*, white and black erectile crown-feathers and *bright blue, barred black, of wing-coverts* are distinctive at close range, but it is restless and wary and difficult to view well when settled; usually first seen flying away, when pure *white rump*, contrasted with black tail, and harsh note identify it. The wings have a broad white patch. Length about 13½ ins.

Habitat. It frequents woods and coverts, preferring more open types with tall secondary growth, also some urban parks and open spaces. At times, especially outside the breeding-season, it visits hedgerows, gardens and orchards, but rarely far from trees. Except for suburban birds, oaks are almost essential for winter food.

General Habits. It is the most arboreal of the crow family. It moves by rather heavy hops both in branches and on ground, frequently jerking its tail. Flight in the open appears weak and laboured, with rather quick, jerky, flapping action of rounded wings, but on the wing in coverts it shows much dexterity. Outside the breeding-season it commonly occurs in pairs or small parties, but at times in larger flocks.

Usual note is a loud, very harsh "skaaak, skaaak", audible for a long distance, with subsidiary variations. It also has a prolonged mewing note, and other less frequent cries.

Food is largely vegetable, chiefly fruits in the widest sense, especially acorns. Animal food includes young birds, eggs, mice, slugs, worms, insects and spiders.

Nests generally in undergrowth and not as a rule high; the outcrop from the trunk of a big tree is also a favourite site. The eggs, usually 5–6, occasionally 3–7, have ground-colour sage-green or olive-buff. They are laid generally in May in a nest built of sticks and twigs and a little earth, with a thick internal layer of fine black roots. Incubation is mainly if not entirely by female, for about 16 days. Young are fed by both parents and fly when about 20 days old. Single-brooded.

Status and Distribution. Present throughout the year. In England and Wales it is generally distributed and locally abundant, penetrating central London. In Scotland it is rather local, breeding in the Solway, Clyde to N. Argyll, Tay, and a few parts of the Tweed and Forth areas; recent expansion has taken it north-east to Aberdeen. It is unknown elsewhere except as a rare migrant. Irish birds, which now breed in all counties except

Kerry, Sligo, Leitrim, Derry and Donegal, belong to the race *Garrulus glandarius hibernicus* which is rather darker than, but not safely distinguishable in the field from, the race *Garrulus glandarius rufitergum* which occupies the rest of the British Isles and also occurs in adjacent parts of the continent. British birds do not migrate although irregular movements have occasionally been reported. Also occasionally in autumn and winter Jays of the race *Garrulus glandarius glandarius* are found in S.E. England. This race, which can only be detected in the hand, is greyer and paler than our own, and breeds in Europe from the Pyrenees to the Balkans and north almost to the Arctic Circle. Other races occur in the Iberian peninsula, N.W. Africa, the Mediterranean area and parts of Asia.

MAGPIE—*Pica pica*
BIRD PLATE 82   EGG PLATE IV (6)

The pied plumage and long wedge-shaped tail are distinctive. Its unmistakable cry often reveals its presence when concealed in thick cover, but it is constantly seen in the open, usually in pairs or small parties, and sometimes in larger numbers, but very rarely more than about 30–40. Young resemble adults, but are less glossy. Total length about 18 ins.; tail 8–10 ins.

Habitat. It frequents chiefly grasslands with thick hedges and some trees, thickets, and outskirts of woods, and to a lesser extent comparatively open country.

General Habits. It feeds largely on the ground, moving at a walk, varied by brisk sidling hops when excited; the tail is usually somewhat elevated. Flight is direct, rather slow, with fairly rapid wing-beats, parties travelling usually in single file. It will hoard surplus food, as well as coloured or glistening objects which attract it.

Usual note is a harsh, chattering "chatchatchatchatchack".

Food consists mainly of insects; also small mammals, carrion, young birds, eggs, slugs, snails, worms, ticks, etc. Vegetable matter includes cereals, fruits, nuts, berries and potatoes.

Nests usually in tall trees, sometimes in thorny bushes. The eggs, usually 5–8, rarely 10, vary in ground-colour from greenish-blue to yellowish-green. They are laid generally in April, in a nest built by both sexes, constructed of sticks with a lining of earth and over it a layer of fine roots. A dome of sticks, usually thorny, covers the nest, but is occasionally absent. Incubation is by female alone, normally for 17–18 days. The young are fed by both parents and leave the nest when about 22–27 days old. Single-brooded.

Status and Distribution. A resident, generally distributed and locally numerous in England and Wales and spreading into suburban areas. In Scotland it is rather local on the mainland, being plentiful in some places and rare or absent in others; very scarce in the N., N.W. and S.E. In Inner Hebrides, it has bred on Skye, is unknown in Outer Hebrides and Shetland and a very rare vagrant in Orkney. In Ireland it is numerous and breeds even in cities where there are trees, but is scarcer in the extreme west. Our birds belong to the race *Pica pica pica* which breeds through much of Europe from arctic Norway to Italy and the Balkans, and in Asia Minor. Other races occur in Spain, Portugal, France, Belgium (?), N. Sweden, Finland, central Russia; also in W. and central Asia, N.W. Africa and N. America.

NUTCRACKER—*Nucifraga caryocatactes*

Bird Plate 82

When settled, the *dark brown, white-flecked plumage* distinguishes it from all other *Corvidae*. In flight it appears a broad-winged bird with *rather short tail and noticeably long, pointed bill*; there is a *broad white border to the tail, and white under-tail coverts* are conspicuous. Length about 12½ ins.

Habitat. Outside the breeding-season it may visit coniferous and deciduous woods, hazel coppice, etc.

General Habits. It feeds much on the ground, hopping in rather a heavy fashion. Its flight and other actions in general recall Jay, but it is less shy, keeping less to cover, flying freely over tops of trees and delighting to perch on topmost shoots of fir trees.

A noisy bird whose usual call is a fairly high-pitched "kraak", harsh, but less strident than Jay's and audible for a long distance.

Food is mainly seeds of conifers, but also nuts, berries, grain, insects and flesh.

Status and Distribution. A vagrant which has usually occurred from October to December, chiefly in S. and E. England, a few times in Wales and Scotland. However, a remarkable invasion in

1968, involving hundreds of birds, began in August. Most have been of the race *Nucifraga caryocatactes macrorhynchus* which breeds in Siberia and N.E. Russia and which in some years is common in winter over most of Europe west to the Pyrenees. But one or two Nutcrackers found in England have been attributed to the more sedentary race *Nucifraga caryocatactes caryocatactes* which breeds in Europe from France to the Balkans and north to the Arctic. This latter race is the thicker-billed of the two, but they are not certainly separable in the field. Other races occur in central and E. Asia.

CHOUGH—*Pyrrhocorax pyrrhocorax*

BIRD PLATE 81   EGG PLATE IV (5)

It is only likely to be confused with Jackdaw from which it is distinguished by the absence of grey in purple-black plumage, more slender form, *long curved red bill and red legs*. Young have an orange bill. Length about 15 ins.; bill 1¾–2 ins.

Habitat. It haunts maritime cliffs or crags close to coast and, increasingly at the present time, hilly districts inland. It feeds on pastures and rough ground close to breeding haunts.

General Habits. Flight is stronger, and more buoyant, than Jackdaw's, with primaries widely separated, and their tips often curving upwards. Progress ordinarily is by a succession of leisurely flaps and glides but at times is steeply undulating. It also performs aerobatics about cliffs and frequently soars. On the ground it

P. J. H.

CHOUGH

The wings are broad and deep-fingered.

walks, runs and hops. It has a habit of flirting up tail and tip of wings when it calls. Pairs appear to keep together throughout the year, and it is sociable in all but nesting-habits.

Ordinary note is "kyaa", rather closely resembling Jackdaw's but clearer, more musical, rather higher-pitched and more prolonged.

Food consists chiefly of insects. Crustacea, molluscs, spiders as well as lizards are also recorded.

Nests largely in crevices of sea-cliffs or holes in roof of sea-caves, but sometimes in quarries, inland cliffs, or occasionally ruinous buildings. The eggs, 3 or 4–6, 2–7 also recorded, are whitish, creamy or very pale greenish in ground-colour and are laid generally from late April onwards in a bulky nest built of sticks, heather-stalks, or furze-stems, dead plants, etc., and thickly lined with wool, hair, etc. Incubation is entirely by hen for about 17–18 days. Young are fed by both sexes and leave the nest at about 38 days. Single-brooded.

Status and Distribution. A resident which has greatly decreased, but in recent years numbers on whole appear to be stationary. It breeds now in Wales in some sea-cliffs and in a few places close to the sea and fairly numerously in several localities inland; in the Isle of Man; and some of the Inner Hebrides especially Islay and Jura. In Ireland it breeds on many sea-cliffs, mainly in west and south, and inland in Kerry, but it is absent from the east coast. Our birds belong to the race *Pyrrhocorax pyrrhocorax pyrrhocorax* which also breeds in N.W. France. Other races occur in the Alps, Pyrenees, Iberian peninsula, Mediterranean, N.W. Africa and in Asia.

JACKDAW—*Corvus monedula*

BIRD PLATE 82   EGG PLATE IV (8A & 8B)

The grey nape and ear-coverts of adult are distinctive. Young are browner, but at all ages the Jackdaw's smaller size, dapper appearance and a certain pert alertness in actions distinguish it from Rook or Crow. It is distinguished from these species on the wing by more compact form, especially of the head, due to shorter bill, and by its notes. Length about 13 ins.

Habitat. It frequents especially parks and wooded districts with plenty of old timber, the vicinity of towers and old buildings, and coastal or inland cliffs, foraging mainly on grassland.

General Habits. Movements on the ground are less sedate than Rook or Crow; it walks with a quick jaunty action. Flight is faster, with quicker wing-beats and rather pigeon-like action, and it often performs aerial evolutions. Very sociable in habits, and commonly seen in flocks of several dozens or even hundreds, often associating with Rooks or Starlings in fields, being like them mainly a ground feeder. It shares with others of its family a propensity for hiding food, as well as inedible objects.
Usual note is a short, fairly high-pitched "tchack", also "kyow".

Food is largely animal matter consisting mainly of insects, also young birds, eggs, mice, frogs, snails, slugs, worms, etc. Vegetable matter includes cereals, potatoes, fruit and berries.

Nests usually in a hole, whether of tree, building, rock, or rabbit-burrow, many breeding close together, but it sometimes builds a large open nest of sticks with deep cup, occasionally roofed, in trees. Also breeds in the foundations of old Rooks' nests. The eggs, usually 4–6, at times 2 to 7 or 8, sometimes have bold black blotches and shell-marks; others are unmarked. They are laid from the second half of April onwards in a nest, built by both sexes, which varies according to site, enormous quantities of sticks being used in some cases, but absent from small holes, which are merely lined with wool, hair, fur, grass, etc. Incubation is apparently by hen alone, for about 17–18 days. The young are fed by both parents and fly when about 30–35 days old. Single-brooded.

Status and Distribution. Present throughout the year, and common except in N.W. Scotland where it is scarce, Outer Hebrides where it only breeds in Stornoway, and Shetland where a few pairs have bred since 1943. It is abundant in Orkney. It does not breed in the isles of west Ireland, with few exceptions. Some appear to emigrate in winter, while numbers of continental birds arrive from mid-October to early November and leave from mid-February to April. British breeding birds belong to the race *Corvus monedula spermologus* which breeds in N.W. Africa, W. and S. Europe east to Romania and north to Denmark. A few examples of the race *Corvus monedula monedula* from Scandinavia, sometimes recognizable by its paler grey "collar", becoming whitish at the base of the neck, have occurred in spring in Shetland, Sutherland, Yorks and Suffolk.

ROOK
juvenile

CARRION CROW

Note Rook's looser feathering on thighs.

ROOK—*Corvus frugilegus*

BIRD PLATE 83   EGG PLATE IV (4A & 4B)

Adult is distinguished by *bare greyish-white face*, noticeable at rest or in flight, causing bill to look longer and head more peaked than Crow's. Young, until face becomes bare, resemble Carrion Crow, but bill is more slender and the culmen usually less curved. At all ages the baggy appearance of thighs, due to loose flank feathers, distinguishes it from Crow on the ground. Length about 18 ins.

Habitat. Prefers agricultural country with at least enough trees for nesting, frequenting both pasture and arable land, but commonest on heavy soils. Moorland, heath, marshes and unreclaimed land are less frequented, and heavily wooded country is usually avoided. It is often associated with smaller human settlements, farms, villages and open towns, but disappears from very large built-up areas. In England the main concentration of rookeries is below 400 ft.

General Habits. Essentially gregarious, it is usually, though not invariably, in parties or flocks up to several hundreds strong, and feeds mainly on ground in the open. Gait is a sedate walk, with occasional hop. Sustained flight is direct and deliberate, with regular wing-beats rather faster than Crow's; it also glides or soars at times. Flocks fly in loose straggling formation. In autumn and winter it roosts in woods, usually at the site of a rookery, often in very large numbers and commonly with Jackdaws. Hides food for later consumption.

The usual note is familiar "caw", or better "kaah", and variants, less raucous than Carrion Crow's ordinary note, but it has a varied vocabulary. Juveniles appear to be silent.

Food. Vegetable matter predominates, and includes cereals, potatoes and other roots, fruits, seeds and berries. Animal food includes insects, worms, molluscs, millipedes, spiders, carrion, small mammals, young birds and eggs.

Nests in colonies usually in large trees, but occasionally in bushes and small trees, and quite exceptionally on buildings such as church-spires or chimneys. The eggs, usually 3–5, rarely 7, vary in ground-colour, like Crow's, from light bluish-green to greyish-green but are never so blue, and rarely show so much of ground-colour. Laying generally begins in the latter half of March and early April in nest built by both sexes preferably in the upper and slenderer branches of a tree. It is constructed of sticks solidified with earth, and often on an old nest of previous year, and is lined with grasses, dead leaves, roots, etc. Incubation is by hen alone, fed by male, for about 16–18 days. The young are fed by both parents and fly after 29–30 days. Single-brooded. Normally first breed when two years old.

Status and Distribution. Present throughout the year, and generally distributed as a breeding species, where trees exist, throughout the British Isles including Hebrides and Orkney, and since 1952 in Shetland. Winter-visitors from northern-central Europe and Scandinavia arrive in great numbers on the east coast of Great Britain in October and November and depart from mid-February to April. The race concerned, *Corvus frugilegus frugilegus*, breeds from mid-France, N. Italy and S. Russia north to southern Scandinavia and Finland, and winters south to the Iberian peninsula and Mediterranean. Other races occur in W. temperate and E. Asia.

HOODED CROW—*Corvus corone cornix*

Bird Plate 84   Egg Plate IV (2a & 2b)

Hooded and Carrion Crows are now regarded as races of the same species, generally quite separate both in breeding range and appearance but in zones of geographical overlap a variety of hybrid forms appear. Hooded Crow's typical *grey mantle and under-parts* prevent confusion with Carrion Crow or Rook. Young are browner than adults. Length about 18½ ins.

Habitat. It frequents the same type of country as Carrion Crow. Winter migrants favour open country, especially near the coast.

RAVEN   CARRION CROW

Note Raven's long, diamond-shaped tail, long neck
and heavy bill.

General Habits. In these it resembles Carrion Crow but
winter-visitors in Britain are more frequently gregarious. In the
Outer Hebrides it usually roosts amongst long heather on islands in
lochs, in huge roosts of many hundreds.

Its notes are similar to Carrion Crow.

Food is very varied, including carrion of all kinds, small
mammals, birds, enormous quantities of eggs, also molluscs,
frogs, insects, earthworms and some vegetable matter.

Nests preferably in a tree, but often in a low bush on the side of a
steep bank, or on a ledge of sea-cliff; occasionally among heather
on low islets in lochs. The eggs, usually 4–6, rarely 7, much
resemble Carrion Crow's, the ground-colour varying from light
blue to deep green, sometimes unmarked. They are laid generally
in late March or April in a nest built by both sexes, strongly
constructed of sticks, heather-twigs, seaweed-stems, moss, and
earth, lined with wool, hair and sometimes feathers. Incubation is
by hen for about 19 days. The young are fed by both parents, but
chiefly by hen, and fly when about 4–5 weeks old. Single-brooded.

Status and Distribution. It is resident in Ireland, breeding in
every county, and in the Isle of Man and in Scotland, where it is
abundant in the north and north-west and most islands. It overlaps
the breeding-range of Carrion Crow, and often interbreeds with it,
the main area of hybridization extending in a broad band from
Wigtown north to Caithness. It very occasionally breeds in S.E.
Scotland, where it is chiefly known as a winter-visitor in rather
small numbers. In England it has bred occasionally, mostly in the
eastern counties and seldom inland; but it is a regular autumn- and

winter-visitor in small numbers on east coast, irregular on south coast, and in the Trent valley and E. Midlands. It is occasional further inland and in western counties, and very scarce in Wales. Winter-visitors from the Baltic countries and Scandinavia arrive on the east coast from the second week of October to third week November and depart from early March to the third week of April. The race concerned, *Corvus corone cornix*, breeds in the Faeroes, in N. and E. Europe south to the Caucasus, Sicily and Italy, and west to the river Elbe (Germany), south-west of which its place is taken by Carrion Crow. A zone of overlap and inter-breeding occurs at the boundary. Other races of Hooded Crow occur in Corsica, Sardinia, the Balkans, Egypt, S.W. Asia and W. Siberia.

CARRION CROW—*Corvus corone corone*

BIRD PLATE 83   EGG PLATE IV (3A & 3B)

It differs from Hoodie in its uniformly black plumage and from adult Rook in *fully feathered base of bill*. It is easily confused with immature Rook, but usually distinguishable by its *stouter bill*, though some individuals differ little in this respect. Plumage also has a rather greener gloss and is more compact than Rook's, which tends to hang loosely, especially over the thighs. Readily distinguished from Rook by voice. Length about 18½ ins.

Habitat. It frequents cultivated and uncultivated districts, choosing open to well or moderately well timbered, rather than closely wooded, country. Seen chiefly on arable and grasslands, on heaths, hill country, and both rocky and low-lying coasts; often on sea-shore and the borders of lakes and estuaries. It frequents parks in towns when not disturbed.

General Habits. Like others of this genus, it feeds mainly on the ground in the open, with movements as Raven. Flight is straight, rather slow, with regular wing-beats, which are a little slower and more deliberate than those of Rook; rarely as high as Raven and it does not ordinarily soar. Comparatively solitary and commonly seen in pairs; sometimes in small flocks, but, unlike Rook, rarely more than two or three dozen at most, except at roosts. It smashes molluscs, crabs, walnuts, and other hard-shelled articles of food by dropping them from a height.

Usual note is a deep, hoarse, croaking "kraah", subject to considerable variation and modulation; also "konk, konk", and others.

Food is very varied, including carrion, small mammals, small or wounded birds, eggs, frogs and toads, fish, molluscs, insects, worms and vegetable matter, chiefly grain, fruits and seeds.

Nests chiefly in stout forks of trees, but in hills often in small bushes on hillsides: also on ledges of cliffs. The eggs, usually 4–5, rarely 1–7, are like Hooded Crow's but perhaps averaging a little paler and not so green. They are laid generally from early April onwards in a nest built by both sexes, which closely resembles Hooded Crow's, constructed of sticks and twigs, earth, moss, etc., thickly lined with hair and wool. Incubation is by female alone, for about 18–21 days. Young are fed by both parents, and fly when about 4–5 weeks old. Single-brooded.

Status and Distribution. It is resident and common, widespread in England and Wales; also in Scotland on the east side as far north as E. Sutherland and on the west side to Clyde area, extending into N. Argyll. It is scarce in Skye and Orkney. An occasional visitor to Shetland, Fair Isle, Inner and Outer Hebrides and becoming more frequent in north of Scotland. It frequently interbreeds with Hooded Crow where their ranges overlap, and this zone continues to shift northwards. Small numbers occur annually in Ireland, and it has bred there. It is not a numerous winter-immigrant but some continental birds may reach Scotland and E. England between early September and November, returning between mid-February and mid-April. The race concerned, *Corvus corone corone*, breeds in western Europe from S. Spain to Germany west of the Elbe, east to N. Italy. Another black race occurs in Asia; the distribution of the conspecific grey races is given under Hooded Crow.

RAVEN—*Corvus corax*

Bird Plate 83   Egg Plate IV (1a & 1b)

It is distinguished from Carrion Crow by its large size, *much stouter bill and unmistakable note*. It has also a *more graduated tail* and somewhat more pointed, narrower wings than Crow, and gives the impression of having a longer neck. Pointed throat-feathers may be noticeable at close quarters. Length about 25 ins.

Habitat. It haunts mainly mountainous and wild hilly districts, with or without trees, and coastal or other cliffs; also occurring in wooded lowlands in some districts. Indifferent to altitude, it ranges from sea-level to mountain-tops.

RAVEN

General Habits. It is often seen on the ground, where gait is a walk, with an occasional clumsy hop if hurried. It perches much on crags, also on trees where available. Flight is direct with powerful, regular wing-beats, generally rather slower than Crow, and often at a great height. It glides and *soars freely* and, mainly during the breeding-season, performs aerobatics. Pairs associate throughout the year, and where sufficiently numerous may congregate in flocks for foraging purposes and roosting.

Usual flight-note is a repeated, deep "pruk, pruk", and it has various other notes, especially in the breeding-season.

Food is very varied, including carrion of all kinds, occasionally lambs or helpless sheep, small mammals up to the size of rabbit, and birds, eggs, reptiles, molluscs, insects and some vegetable matter including corn.

Nests in cliffs and rocks, and to a minor but increasing extent in trees. The eggs, usually 4–6, sometimes 3–7, light blue to greenish in ground-colour, and rarely unmarked, are laid generally in February and the first half of March, in a nest built by both sexes, solidly constructed of sticks, heather-stalks, rarely seaweed, mixed with earth, warmly lined with moss, leaves, grass-tufts, and internally with hair and wool. Incubation is apparently by hen alone, for 20–21 days. The young are fed by both parents, and fly after 5–6 weeks.

Status and Distribution. A resident, breeding in considerable numbers on the coast of S.W. England from Isle of Wight to

Cornwall and up the Bristol Channel to Somerset, extending into Gloucester, and in fair numbers inland, especially Devon and Somerset; in Wales it is comparatively common, and most suitable crag nesting-sites, as well as many tree-sites, are occupied, and it extends over the border into Hereford and Shropshire; has bred Worcs. In the Cumbrian hills it is numerous, rather scarce in the Pennines, and comparatively numerous in Isle of Man. It is a rare visitor to the midlands and eastern counties, and last bred on the Sussex coast in 1945. In Scotland it breeds fairly commonly in the west, and in higher districts and on islands, particularly Hebrides and Shetland; it is rare or absent in east coast counties from Moray Firth to the border, and in the central lowlands, and declining in the south. In Ireland it breeds on the wilder sea-cliffs and some mountains, especially in west. It is more widely distributed in Scotland from late autumn to spring when immigrants are regularly present. The race concerned, *Corvus corax corax*, breeds in Europe from the Arctic to Portugal and the Caucasus, and in Asia from W. Siberia to Afghanistan. Other races occur in the Faeroes, Iceland, N. America, Mediterranean, Sahara, S.W., central and E. Asia.

STARLING—*Sturnus vulgaris*

BIRD PLATE 110   EGG PLATE I (11)

Plump form, short tail and moderately long, pointed bill (combined, in flight, with short pointed wings) give a distinctive outline both in the air and when settled. The *iridescent plumage* of adults has a spangled appearance in winter, more marked in female than male and most in first-year birds. *Juveniles are nearly uniform mouse-brown* with whitish throat. Length about 8½ ins.

Habitat. Catholic in choice of haunts, it frequents town and country, cultivated and uncultivated ground, even treeless islands and shore-line. As a rule it scarcely ascends above the limit of cultivation, though sometimes ranging up on to high moors and pastures in autumn and winter. In the breeding-season many frequent woods and built-up areas for nesting, but these are otherwise avoided, except for roosting or when caterpillars in woodland trees attract flocks in early summer.

General Habits. On the ground its bustling activity and quick jerky walk are characteristic; it also runs and, less frequently, hops. Flight is swift and direct, with rapidly moving wings (closed momentarily occasionally), varied by glides with wings extended, but when hawking for high-flying insects it adopts a distinct wheeling and gliding action recalling Swallows. Usually feeds in close flocks on the ground in open fields, etc., constantly probing surface with its bill. It roosts gregariously, often in immense numbers in reed- and osier-beds, dense coverts and, especially in London, on large buildings; also in caves and cliffs on Scottish islands. Some birds travel 12–20 miles or more to the assembly and flocks usually perform spectacular massed evolutions in the air before finally "rocketing" down into the roost. Roosts may be occupied to some extent even in the breeding-season.

The usual note is a grating "tcheerr". The song, normally given from an elevated position, is a lively rambling melody of throaty warbling, chirruping notes, musical whistles and pervaded by a peculiar creaky quality. It may be heard throughout the year, regularly from mid-August to mid-May but only exceptionally in late June and most of July. Flocks at roost keep up a continuous twittering chorus.

Food taken in the breeding-season is principally animal and includes insects, earthworms, spiders, centipedes, woodlice, snails, slugs, and crustacea. Vegetable matter includes fruit, cereals, potatoes and roots, acorns, seeds and berries.

Nests generally in loose colonies, but also at times singly, in holes, most frequently in tree or building, but also among rocks and occasionally in the foundations of larger birds' nests, in holes in ground, etc.; exceptionally in thick evergreens. The eggs, 5–7, sometimes 4–9, are laid generally about mid-April onwards, exceptionally in autumn or winter, in an untidy nest built by male before mating and subsequently lined by female, constructed of straw, lined with feathers and sometimes containing leaves, wool, or moss. Incubation is by both sexes for about 12–13 days. The young are fed by both sexes and fly after about 20–22 days. Most pairs are single-brooded, but some breed twice.

Status and Distribution. Present throughout the year and generally distributed. A few British birds may emigrate in winter, when the population is vastly increased by visitors from N.E. and N. Europe which arrive mainly from end of September to mid-November, returning from mid-February to the end of April. Winter weather movements also occur. The Starlings of Shetland and Outer Hebrides, *Sturnus vulgaris zetlandicus*, cannot be separated in the field when adult, but juveniles are recognizably darker. Otherwise British breeding birds and immigrants belong to the race *Sturnus vulgaris vulgaris* which breeds from north-ernmost Scandinavia south to S. France and east into Russia, wintering largely in the Mediterranean. As an introduced bird it has spread over much of N. America. Other races occur in the Faeroes, Azores, S.E. Europe and Asia.

ROSE-COLOURED STARLING—*Sturnus roseus*

BIRD PLATE 109

The adult's *rose-pink body with black head, tail and wings and conspicuous crest* are unmistakable. Young birds are duller and juvenile is like the uncommon pale sandy type of young Starling, with darker wings and *yellow* base to *bill*. Length about 8½ ins.

Habitat. Outside the breeding-season it occurs in every type of open country, though cultivation and grassy lands are chiefly preferred.

General Habits. General form and actions are very like Starling, and it is indistinguishable on the wing when distance or light prevents colours being seen. Movement on the ground is similar, but more sprightly. A sociable bird, flocks foraging freely with Starlings and especially among cattle. It hawks flies like Starling.

Voice is Starling-like, but more scratchy and higher-pitched.

Food includes insects, worms, fruit and seeds.

Status and Distribution. A vagrant, which has been recorded from many parts of England, chiefly on the east side but often in Devon and Cornwall. It has also often occurred in Scotland, including the northern isles, less often in Ireland and seldom in Wales. It has occurred in every month, but most between June and August. It breeds in S.E. Europe west to Hungary, and in W. Asia, wintering in India, but wanders north and west of its normal range at irregular intervals. There are no subspecies.

HOUSE SPARROW—*Passer domesticus*

BIRD PLATE 111   EGG PLATE I (3A & 3B)

The bird's appearance is universally familiar and only Tree Sparrow can reasonably be confused with it. Male has warm brown upper-parts streaked black, *dark grey crown* (*brown at the sides*), *black throat, greyish-white cheeks* and under-parts; a fairly distinct, but short, white wing-bar and *grey rump* are noticeable on its taking wing. Female and young are duller brown, lacking grey on the crown and rump and without a distinct wing-bar. The bill is rather stout. Length about 5¾ ins.

Habitat. It is closely confined to cultivated land and the vicinity of human habitations, from large towns to isolated farmsteads or crofts.

General Habits. It is bold and impudent, yet wary and suspicious, with a perky and bustling demeanour. Mainly a ground-feeder where it hops with a frequent flicking movement of the tail, but it constantly perches on trees, buildings, etc. The rapidly moving wings convey the effect of some exertion in flight, which is more variable in character than finches, from typically undulatory to practically straight. Usually remains faithful to mate and nest-site for life. It is gregarious at all times, and consorts in autumn and winter with finches in fields. It roosts socially, often closely packed, in groups of trees, thatch, ivy, etc., or under eaves of buildings.

It is very noisy, especially in spring and summer, the main call being a loud, penetrating and somewhat variable "chee-ip".

Food in agricultural districts is chiefly corn; in towns, insects and street refuse; in fruit-growing districts, insects; but worms, seeds, buds, etc., are also eaten.

Nests in almost any kind of hole or niche about houses, or in creeper, also not uncommonly at considerable heights among branches of trees, among foundations of Rooks' nests and in holes of cliffs. The eggs, normally 3–5, occasionally 6–7, are variable in colouring, one egg in the set being generally much lighter than the rest. Although they have been found in almost every month they are laid generally between May and August, in a characteristically untidy nest built by both sexes of straw, and domed, with a side entrance when in the open, but merely a lining when inside a small hole; it is warmly lined with feathers and sometimes a little hair, wool, etc. Incubation is chiefly by hen for about 12–14 days. Both sexes feed the young which fly when about 15 days old. Three broods are frequent.

Status and Distribution. A resident, widely distributed throughout the British Isles; it is local in many parts of Ireland, but found on some western isles. British birds appear to be mainly sedentary, but there seems to be some dispersal in autumn, probably of young birds. The race *Passer domesticus domesticus* breeds in Europe generally but is absent from the extreme north, and is replaced by other races in Italy, Corsica, Balearic Islands, as is also the case in N. Africa and temperate Asia. It has spread across Siberia; it has also been introduced and spread over much of N. and S. America and Australasia.

TREE SPARROW—*Passer montanus*

BIRD PLATE 110　EGG PLATE I (2A & 2B)

The sexes are alike, differing from male House Sparrow in rather smaller size, trimmer build, *black patch on ear-coverts and a chocolate, not grey, crown*. The double white wing-bar is another less obvious distinction. Young resemble adults. *The flight-note is distinctive*. Length about 5½ ins.

Habitat. It is less attached to habitations and cultivation than House Sparrow. It haunts pollard willows and old hedgerow trees, orchards, secluded gardens, old quarries, and, less often, the vicinity of farm or other buildings; locally common in the suburbs of some large towns. Occasionally it is found on rocky coasts and islands and even exposed uplands. In winter it visits stubblefields, stackyards, and farm bartons.

General Habits. It is more shy and retiring than House Sparrow. Flight and movements are similar, but more agile. From October to April or May flocks habitually join with House Sparrows, Chaffinches, Greenfinches, etc.; they also sometimes form unmixed parties.

Notes have a general resemblance to House Sparrow's, but are more musical and higher-pitched. More distinctive is the flight-note, a rather hoarse, hard "teck, teck".

Food includes seeds of weeds and corn as well as insects and spiders.

Nests in holes in ivy-covered trees, pollarded willows, thatch, holes in buildings, cliffs, and old nests of Rooks, etc. The eggs, normally 4–6, rarely 9, are much smaller than House Sparrow's, darker and rather browner. They are laid sometimes at the end of April, but often later, in a nest built by both sexes, very similar to a House Sparrow's, though smaller. Incubation is by both sexes for about 12–14 days. The young are fed by both parents and fly when about 12–14 days old. Two broods normal, sometimes three.

Status and Distribution. A widely spread resident but local, especially on the west side of Great Britain, largely absent from Devon, Cornwall, parts of W. Wales, and the Scottish mainland (except its eastern fringe) north of the Tay. Colonies have at times been established on many of the islands off N. and W. Scotland. In Ireland it breeds locally in most coastal counties. British birds flock and wander to a certain extent in winter, while some immigrants arrive in October and November and return from March to May. The race concerned, *Passer montanus montanus*, breeds in Europe from the Mediterranean to N. Scandinavia and east to Siberia. Other races occur in Asia.

CHAFFINCH—*Fringilla coelebs*

Bird Plate 115   Egg Plate I (9A, 9B & 9C)

In flight both sexes, but especially male, show a *broad white shoulder patch* with less prominent whitish wing-bar behind it and *conspicuous white on outer tail feathers*; the rump is yellowish-green. When settled the plumage is distinctive: male with slate-blue crown and nape, chestnut mantle, sides of head and underparts deep pinkish-brown, wings and tail blackish with white marks as above; female rather pale yellowish-brown, lighter below. The head is slightly peaked in male, less so in female. Juveniles are as female, but less green on the rump; young males soon begin to show a more chestnut back. Length about 6 ins.

Habitat. It frequents gardens, hedgerows, and bushy commons, copses and deciduous and coniferous woods, resorting outside the breeding-season to stubble and root-fields, stackyards and the like, and often to roads, to feed.

General Habits. It has a typical undulating finch flight and usually settles well up in trees, though also on lower perches. It is gregarious outside the breeding-season and forms flocks not infrequently of one sex only, often consorting with Bramblings, Greenfinches, Sparrows, and Yellowhammers.

The usual call is rather metallic "chwink, chwink". The flight note, especially in autumn, is a low "tsup, tsup", and in spring the characteristic note of the male is a clear, loud "wheet". The song is short, loud, vigorous and rattling, but not unmusical, rendered "chip chip chip tell tell tell cherry-erry-erry tissi cheweeo"; the terminal flourish may be omitted and other minor and local variants occur. It is heard mainly from January or February to July, with some revival in September–October.

Food of a vegetable nature predominates, with seeds of many kinds, seedlings, some corn, and fruit. Animal matter includes insects, spiders and earthworms.

R.A.R.

CHAFFINCH   BRAMBLING
Note Brambling's white rump.

Nests in bushes and small trees, as a rule. The eggs, usually 4–5, but up to 8 recorded, have normally greenish-blue to brownish stone ground-colour, exceptionally clear blue or olive. They are laid generally in late April or May in a nest well and compactly built of grasses, wool, roots, moss, etc., decorated externally with lichens fastened together by spiders' webs, sometimes with fragments of birch-bark or paper, neatly lined with hair and sometimes a feather or two. Incubation is almost always by hen only, for about 11–13 days. The young are fed by both sexes and fly when about 13–14 days old. Normally single-brooded.

Status and Distribution. Present throughout the year. Abundant and widely distributed throughout Great Britain and Ireland, including Orkney and parts of Outer Hebrides. It has bred in Shetland. Our residents, comprising the race *Fringilla coelebs gengleri*, flock in winter and move about the country, but there is no evidence that they emigrate abroad. Large flocks, however, of the continental race *Fringilla coelebs coelebs* (slightly paler and pinker on cheeks and underparts than our breeding birds) arrive here from mid-September to mid-November as passage-migrants or winter-visitors, extending to the west coast of Ireland, and leave again from mid-March to May. The bird breeds in Europe generally, from the Mediterranean to northernmost Scandinavia. Other races occur in the Atlantic Islands, N.W. Africa and W. Asia.

BRAMBLING—*Fringilla montifringilla*

BIRD PLATE 115

It is the same shape as Chaffinch, but with *white rump* conspicuous in flight, while the *orange-buff shoulder patch of male and breast of both sexes*, and *brown or blackish heads* immediately distinguish them amongst Chaffinches on the ground. Breeding male has head and mantle glossy black, but in winter these are mottled brown. Female and young are dull brown above. Wings are much as Chaffinch, but the anterior white band is less extensive, especially in hen. The tail is more distinctly forked, slightly shorter, and shows less white. *Call-notes* are diagnostic. Length about 5¾ ins.

Habitat. In the breeding-season it haunts birch and mixed woods and the outskirts or open parts of conifer forest; in winter especially beech-woods and plantations, also stubble and root-fields, stackyards, etc., but it often resorts to conifers in spring before leaving winter-quarters.

General Habits. Flight and movements are as Chaffinch. In winter it is gregarious, feeding, often with Chaffinches, on beech-mast under trees or with mixed flocks of finches in fields, flying up into trees when disturbed.

Flight-note is "chucc-chucc-chucc . . ." slightly hoarse and lower-pitched than flight-call of Chaffinch and uttered in more rapid succession. Call-note is a hoarse, rather metallic "tsweek". In spring sometimes a prolonged "dweee".

Food. In winter it feeds on seeds of knot-grass and other weeds, beechmast, wheat, berries, etc.

Nests in birch and conifers, usually from 5 to 10 ft. from the ground, but sometimes considerably higher. The eggs, usually 6–7, but 4–9 recorded, often darker and greener than normal Chaffinch's eggs, are laid generally in the second half of May or June in a nest larger and less finished than Chaffinch's, with stouter walls of grasses, bents, etc., generally decorated with bits of birch-bark and lichens, lined with hair, feathers, and sometimes down. Incubation is by female alone. The young are fed by both sexes. Probably single-brooded.

Status and Distribution. Mainly a winter-visitor in varying numbers, arriving from the end of September to mid-November and leaving in March, April and early May, in some years not reaching the extreme S.W. and W. of England and Wales. In Ireland it is scarce in the west. In Scotland also, numbers are greatly influenced by weather conditions, and it is most regular and abundant in the S.E.; in S.W. and N.E. more irregular, although sometimes occurring in large numbers, but it is much scarcer in the north-west and Outer Hebrides; regular on passage in Orkney and Shetland. Very few summer, occasionally in England, but mainly N. Scotland where a pair or two have bred since 1979. It breeds from N. Scandinavia east into Siberia and south possibly to N. Italy and Jugoslavia but not regularly south of the Baltic; it winters south to the Mediterranean. There are no subspecies.

SERIN—*Serinus serinus*

BIRD PLATE 117

A small finch with a *small, stumpy bill*, short forked tail, two rather indistinct yellowish wing-bars, and colouring like mule Canary, with *lemon-yellow rump* showing in flight in both sexes. Male looks a streaky, greenish-brown bird, with *bright yellow on head and breast*. Female is duller, more streaked and less yellow; confusion is only likely with hen Siskin, which, apart from different habits, has a longer, finer bill and yellow at sides of the tail. Young are still duller, browner and more streaked than female and without the yellow rump. Length about 4½ ins.

Habitat. It frequents gardens, vineyards, avenues, copses, etc., with a strong liking for cultivation and is common in towns on the Continent and round villages. It is generally scarcer in uncultivated country.

General Habits. It feeds a good deal on the ground, but usually not far from trees. Flight is undulating, with similar light, dancing action to Goldfinch or Redpoll. It is commonly found in small flocks, and is markedly sociable at all seasons, groups often nesting in close proximity.

Flight-note is "tirrilillit", with many variants. It has a peculiar little jangling song distinctly reminiscent of Corn Bunting's, though much softer, less discordant, and with somewhat sibilant tone, delivered from a tree, commonly at a fair height (about 30 ft. upwards), or telegraph wire, or in bat-like nuptial flight.

Food includes seeds of various weeds and garden plants; also of alder and birch.

Status and Distribution. Formerly a vagrant; its appearances had become annual by the mid 1960s and it first bred in S. England in 1967; intermittently since. Most occurrences have been between October and May, the bulk of them in counties bordering the Channel, a few on the east side north to Durham, also Scotland, Wales and Ireland. It breeds in N.W. Africa, Asia Minor, and Europe north to the Baltic. There are no subspecies.

GREENFINCH—*Carduelis chloris*

Bird Plate 120   Egg Plate I (17A & 17B)

The stout bill, olive-green plumage with brighter yellow-green rump, *and bright yellow patches on the primaries and at sides of the tail* are diagnostic. Female is duller than male, having upperparts faintly streaked at very close range and with less yellow. Juvenile is browner, fairly strongly streaked above and below and with a brown rump, but wings and tail are as adult. In flight at all ages the plump form and rather short, distinctly cleft tail are characteristic *and the yellow wing and tail patches* conspicuous. Length about 5¾ ins.

Habitat. It frequents localities well supplied with trees and bushes, but not closed woodlands; chiefly gardens, shrubberies, plantations, and borders of woods. Outside the breeding-season it visits arable land, stackyards, etc.

General Habits. It perches principally in trees, though also low down. Flight has a slightly undulating character which is common in varying degrees to most finches, few rapid wing beats alternating with momentary closure, with a brief glide on extended wings only when about to pitch. It is distinctly sociable, and from autumn to spring flocks with other finches and buntings to forage for seeds and waste grain.

Usual note, chiefly on the wing, is a rapid twitter "chichichichichit". The spring and summer call of male is a persistent, drawn-out, nasal "tsweee". Song, based mainly on calls, is delivered while perched, usually at top of a tree, or in bat-like song-flight with slowly flapping wings. It is heard regularly from mid-March till the latter part of July, and occasionally from mid-January, during August and in October or early November.

Food is mainly seeds, berries, and buds of fruit trees, occasionally a few beetles and other animal matter. The young are fed partly on insects.

Nests in hedgerows, evergreens and bushes, numbers sometimes breeding close to one another. The eggs, usually 4–6, rarely 3–7, are normally rather sparingly spotted and streaked but some with zone of spots, others thickly spotted or white with no markings. They are laid generally in early May or late April in a nest built of twigs and moss, mixed with a few bents, bits of wool, etc., and usually lined with roots and hair but sometimes feathers are freely used. Incubation is by hen alone for about 13 days. The young are fed by both sexes and fly when about 13–16 days old. Two broods, three occasionally.

Status and Distribution. Present throughout the year and common in most parts, but only a passage- and winter-migrant to Shetland and most Outer Hebrides, though it breeds in Stornoway. British birds are largely sedentary though there is a tendency with some to an autumn southward movement. Passage-migrants and winter-visitors arrive on the E. coast from October to mid-November and depart mid-March to the end of April. The race concerned, *Carduelis chloris chloris*, breeds in Europe from central France and the Balkans north almost to the Arctic Circle. Other races occur in the Azores, N.W. Africa, Iberian Peninsula, S. France and parts of Asia east to Japan.

GOLDFINCH—*Carduelis carduelis*

Bird Plate 120   Egg Plate I (15)

The black wings and tail with broad band of brilliant yellow on the former and white terminal spots on quills of both are distinctive at all ages, as is additionally the *red, white, and black pattern of head* in adults, and the *note*. Sexes are similar. Juvenile is streaked, lacking the red, white, and black on head, but wings and tail are as adult. Length about 4¾ ins.

Habitat. In the breeding-season it frequents chiefly gardens, orchards, and open cultivated land with a sprinkle of trees, and less regularly, open woodland, resorting largely to open ground to feed. In autumn and winter it occurs principally on such ground, especially rough, neglected pastures, roadsides, and waste land, with thistles and other weeds.

General Habits. It feeds much near the ground on thistles and other composites, flitting from plant to plant, fluttering butterfly-like about the seed-heads or hanging on them like a tit, but less on the ground itself. In trees it perches principally on the uppermost or outer twigs rather than amongst foliage. Flight has the usual finch undulations, but with noticeably light, flitting and "dancing" action. It visits alders, birches, etc., but less constantly than Siskins or Redpolls. It is usually gregarious.

Ordinary note is a constantly uttered "tswitt-witt-witt . . ." with a peculiar liquid, trickling quality difficult to convey in words, but unmistakable. The song is a pleasing liquid twittering elaboration of the call-note, with variations and modulations. It is regular from mid-March to mid-July and is occasionally heard from the end of January and until early December, but with a break from late August to late September.

Food consists of seeds and insects, but chiefly the former.

Nests especially in chestnuts and fruit trees, often far out on spreading boughs; occasionally also in hedges and evergreens. The eggs, usually 5–6, 3–7 also on record, are laid generally from early May onwards in a nest neatly built by the hen of roots, bents, moss, and lichens, interwoven with wool, lined with vegetable-down and wool. Incubation is by hen alone, for about 12–13 days. The young are fed by both parents and fly when about 13–14 days old. Normally two broods; three at times.

Status and Distribution. A resident, local but fairly generally distributed, but scarce or absent from many parts of Scotland, and only a scarce vagrant in extreme north, the Hebrides, Shetland and Orkney. In autumn and winter local migration of flocks occurs especially on the south coast and a number emigrate. The race concerned, *Carduelis carduelis britannica*, is confined to the British Isles and Channel Islands. Other races occur throughout Europe except in the north, in N.W. Africa and parts of W. Asia.

SISKIN—*Carduelis spinus*

Bird Plate 119   Egg Plate I (16)

Predominantly yellow-green plumage with black crown and chin and yellow rump distinguish male. Wing-bar and sides of tail are greenish-yellow. Female is duller and greyer with little yellow, and *no black on the head*, and with under-parts more striped. Young are similar, but the striping is still stronger. When colours are not distinguishable, it may be separated from Redpoll by its stouter bill and shorter tail (distinctly cleft in both). Length about 4¾ ins.

Habitat. In the breeding-season it haunts coniferous or sometimes mixed woods, especially spruce. In autumn and winter it chiefly frequents birches and alders, in copses, along streams, etc., increasingly visiting suburban gardens in early spring.

General Habits. Although sometimes descending to the ground, it generally keeps in trees, where its restless activity and varied postures recall tits. In the breeding-season it keeps much to tops of firs. It is quick and light on the wing, with typical finch action. To the greater part of Britain it is known only as a winter-visitor, when it is essentially gregarious, usually consorting with Redpolls to feed in alders and birches and in spring in larches; at times amongst thistles. It is also seen in small parties in the breeding-season.

Main call is a shrill clear "tsuu" or "tsyzing" freely used on the wing. Flying flocks also give a very hard twitter. Song is a sweet, lively to tolerably varied twittering terminating in a prolonged creaking note; it is uttered from a tree or during special song-flight and mainly heard from mid-February to the end of April.

Food is mainly seeds of trees; in gardens, pea-nuts and suet.

Nests in conifers, often at a great height from the ground, frequently far out near end of branch. The eggs, 3–5, also 2–6 recorded, are laid generally in early April (Ireland), or early May (Scotland), in a nest built by hen only, of small dead twigs with lichens attached; moss, bents, wool, etc., lined with roots, feathers, down and hair. Incubation is by hen only, for about 11–12 days. The young are fed by both parents and fly when about 15 days old. Two broods.

Status and Distribution. It is a resident in Ireland, breeding locally throughout the country. In Scotland its range has expanded with afforestation and it breeds in almost every mainland county, but as yet remains scarce in most parts south of the Tay/Clyde and in Caithness and Inner Hebrides. In England small numbers nest in Cumberland, Pennines, Breckland, New Forest, Devon and elsewhere, and N. 'Wales. Otherwise it is a winter-visitor to England and Wales, widely distributed but local, arriving from late September to early November and leaving in April and early May. The bird breeds in Europe from the Arctic Circle south locally to the Pyrenees and Bulgaria, also in Asia east to Japan. The Mediterranean area is occupied in winter. There are no subspecies.

LINNET—*Carduelis cannabina*

BIRD PLATE 118   EGG PLATE I (13A & 13B)

It is larger than Twite and Redpoll. Male is distinguished by the *chestnut of mantle*, greyish head, white edgings of tail-feathers and wing-quills more pronounced than in Twite, and more strikingly in summer by *crimson crown and breast*, without the black chin of Redpoll. Female does not acquire crimson, and the other features are less strongly marked, the mantle duller, less chestnut, and more striated. Young is much like female, but striping is more pronounced. Tail is cleft. Bill is greyish in the breeding-season, more horn-coloured at other times, and in young birds. Length about 5¼ ins.

Habitat. In the breeding-season it frequents especially gorse-grown commons and rough ground with a sprinkling of bushes or scrub, or young plantations; to a less extent gardens, and bushy places amongst cultivation. In winter it almost completely vacates its summer haunts, occurring locally, but often abundantly, in cultivated country, on stubble, fallow fields and waste ground; also frequently on shore, etc.

General Habits. It prefers low to lofty perches, settling more on bushes or fences than on tall trees. Flight is rapid and undulating like other finches, often with a more wavering and dancing action, as birds flit over feeding grounds. It is gregarious from autumn to spring, but more exclusive than some finches, though often mixed with Chaffinches, Goldfinches, Greenfinches, buntings, etc. Flocks, sometimes hundreds strong, roam the country in search of seeds, gathered mainly on the ground.

Flight-note is a rapid twittering "chichichichit", slightly metallic, but less so than Twite and much less than Redpoll. Song is a pleasant, musical and tolerably varied twittering without set form, usually delivered from an exposed spray of bush or tree. It is heard from late March to mid-July, less frequently from January to end of October.

Food consists mainly of seeds of weeds and some insects.

Nests chiefly low down in gorse, bramble, and thorn-bushes, but also commonly in hedgerows, etc., and locally in marram-grass on sandy coasts, sometimes showing a tendency to breed socially. The eggs, 4–6, occasionally 7, sometimes without markings, are laid from mid-April onwards, in a nest built by hen alone of stalks, bents, moss, and sometimes twigs, lined with hair, wool, and sometimes down or feathers. Incubation is chiefly by hen for about 10–12 days. The young are fed by both parents and fly usually when 11–12 days old. Two or even three broods.

Status and Distribution. Present throughout the year, widely distributed in the British Isles as a breeding bird, but local in the Highlands and Inner Hebrides, and is a vagrant in the Outer Hebrides. It breeds Orkney but not Shetland. A proportion of our birds move south in September and October, some reaching S.W. France and N. Spain, and return from mid-March to mid-April; a large number of continental birds winter in Britain. The race concerned, *Carduelis cannabina cannabina*, breeds in Europe generally, north almost to the Arctic Circle, but it is replaced by other races in the Atlantic islands, the Mediterranean, Crimea, also W. Asia.

TWITE—*Carduelis flavirostris*

BIRD PLATE 118   EGG PLATE II (2)

It is most likely to be confused with female or juvenile Linnet (cock Linnet is at once differentiated by chestnut back and, in breeding-season, red on crown and breast), but is darker, more tawny, and the *warm, almost orange-buff, shade of lores and throat* is often noticeable, while male (only) has *rose-pink rump. In winter the yellow bill* at once separates it from Linnet (but not from Redpoll) but in the breeding-season this is greyish. It has a white wing-mark as Linnet, but not so distinct and is a slightly smaller bird with a relatively longer tail. *Note also is quite distinct.* Length about 5¼ ins.

Habitat. Exclusively a bird of open country. In the breeding-season it frequents chiefly the fringes of heather moors, rough pastures and bracken-grown slopes, mainly in hilly districts, but also occurs locally in lowland mosses and on rough, often rocky, ground near sea. Although some localities such as the Pennine moors are frequented all the year, in winter it largely deserts higher land, resorting especially to shore and salt-marshes; more rarely rough pastures, stubble-fields, stackyards, waste ground, etc., generally preferring the vicinity of the coast.

General Habits. It feeds much on the ground, but perches on bushes and railings, etc., and even on tall trees. Flight and movements are Linnet-like. It is gregarious outside the breeding-season and often occurs in considerable flocks.

The call and alarm-note, "chweek" or "tsooeek", is distinctly more nasal and twanging than Linnet's, while twitter, though similar, is perceptibly harder, more metallic, though less so than Redpoll's. Song is Linnet-like in general type and is heard occasionally from early March to mid-August, regularly from mid-April to late July.

Food is mainly seeds of weeds; also insects.

Nests almost in colonies, frequently close to or actually on the ground; in the west and south often in long heather; in north in loose stone-walls or gorse. The eggs, usually 5–6, sometimes 4–7, are bluer and with more decided markings than Linnet. They are laid generally in late May and early June in a nest built entirely by hen of grasses, stalks, etc., with a few twigs and some moss, lined with hair and wool and sometimes a few feathers. Incubation is by hen only, usually for 12–13 days. The young are fed by both parents and fly when about 15 days old. Two broods not infrequently.

Status and Distribution. Present throughout the year. In Ireland it breeds mainly on west and north coasts, also some mountains. In Scotland also it is fairly generally distributed especially on W. coast and Hebrides, Orkney and Shetland, but probably no longer breeds in the south and has become scarce or absent in many parts of the central Highlands. In England it breeds very locally on moorlands in Cumberland (scarce), W. Yorks, Lancs, N. Derby, N. Staffs and E. Cheshire but not farther south. It bred in N. Wales in 1967. In winter it is regular on the E. coast and in Kent and Sussex, uncertain in Dorset and Hants, scarce in Devon, Cornwall and Wales. These winter movements involve both our own birds, of the race *Carduelis flavirostris pipilans* which is confined to the British Isles, and some visitors from Scandinavia of the race *Carduelis flavirostris flavirostris*. The latter, slightly paler than British birds but indistinguishable in the field, arrive on the E. coast in October and November, returning in March and April. Other races occur in Asia south to Asia Minor.

REDPOLL—*Carduelis flammea*

BIRD PLATE 119   EGG PLATE I (14)

It is recognized, when adult, by *crimson fore-head and black chin*, and it has a *distinctive flight-note*. The upper-parts and flanks are streaked; the breast and rump of male in summer are strongly tinted pink. Juvenile has only an ill-defined, grey-black chin patch, but is still distinguishable by its general shape, differing from Twite and Linnet by rotund form and shorter tail, and from young Siskin by longer tail and no trace of yellow. Length about 4¾ ins.

Habitat. In the breeding-season its favourite haunts are birch copses, but it is also found in alder-holts, osier-beds, conifer plantations, gardens, etc., often near water. In autumn and winter it haunts chiefly birches and alders, but also hedgerows and open places with rank vegetation.

General Habits. Flight has the usual finch undulations, but is noticeably light and free as compared with most and is often high up. From autumn to spring it roams the country in closely-packed flocks, feeding upon seeds of birches and alders and (less often) of herbaceous plants, especially thistles, etc. In its acrobatic postures and continual twittering it resembles Siskin, with which it frequently associates. In the breeding-season it is less in evidence and would be easily overlooked, but for curious and characteristic song-flight.

Flight-note is a twittering "chuch-uch-uch-uch", more metallic than Linnet's or even Twite's. Song is merely a brief rippling trill delivered most characteristically in a looping, circling song-flight with slow, hesitant wing-beats, but also freely from a perch or in ordinary flight.

Food is chiefly seeds, but also minute insects and larvae.

Nests are often isolated although it tends to breed sociably. Sites are varied, including high hedges or isolated bushes, outskirts of plantations and young conifers, but also at considerable heights in forest-trees, in osier-beds, alder swamps, and exceptionally in tall heather. The eggs, usually 4–5, and rarely 3–7, sometimes unmarked, are laid generally in May or early June in a nest built by hen and recognizable by the foundation of twigs and the roughly-finished external appearance due to ends of coarse bents and stalks; it is lined with white down, sometimes hair and feathers. Incubation is apparently by hen alone for 10–11 days or more. The young are fed by both parents for about 11–14 days. Sometimes double-brooded.

Status and Distribution. Present throughout the year. In Ireland it is generally distributed even in the bare west; also in most wooded districts in Scotland but is uncommon in the north-west. It breeds sparingly in the Inner Hebrides, and is said to have nested in Orkney, but is rare at any time in Shetland. In England and Wales it breeds in most counties, but is local, increasingly so towards the south and west until in W. Devon and Cornwall it is rare or absent even in winter, when it becomes more generally distributed elsewhere. Some of our birds appear to emigrate in winter. They belong to the race *Carduelis flammea disruptis* (Lesser Redpoll) which also breeds in the Alps, and winters south to the Mediterranean. Other races occur in the north, of which *Carduelis flammea flammea* (Mealy Redpoll) breeding in N. Europe, Siberia and Canada, is an irregular autumn- or winter-visitor along the whole east coast of Britain especially in the north, from mid-October to May, but only occasionally elsewhere. Typical examples, but not all individuals, of this slightly larger race (length up to about 5 ins.) may be separated from our own bird by their paler coloration, having a greyer, less warm brown appearance and the wing-bar whiter, less buff. As an autumn passage migrant birds of the race *Carduelis flammea rostrata*, breeding mainly in Greenland, also occur fairly regularly in northern and western Scottish isles and occasionally in Ireland, very rarely England. Generally speaking, the two last named cannot be reliably separated in the field, but in favourable circumstances affording direct comparison, the Greenland bird shows its larger size and darker coloration (which is nearer to that of our breeding birds), also bulging bill and upright posture.

ARCTIC REDPOLL—*Carduelis hornemanni*

BIRD PLATE 119

The white unstreaked rump and white under-parts distinguish it from Redpoll, but some Mealy Redpolls in worn plumage in late winter look almost as pale. Its upper-parts are also paler, the broad white edgings of the wing-coverts and white inner webs of the secondaries forming a light patch on the closed wing. Length about 5 ins.

Habitat. Outside the breeding-season it occurs chiefly in alders birches, or larches, much as Redpoll.

General Habits. These do not appear to differ in any way from those of Redpoll.

The voice is also similar.

Food consists of seeds and small insects.

Status and Distribution. Examples of both races of this species have occurred as very rare vagrants in autumn or winter mainly on the east coast from Shetland to Yarmouth, especially Fair Isle and Yorkshire; probably Ireland. These races are probably not separable in the field, although *Carduelis hornemanni exilipes* which breeds in Lapland, North Russia, and the northernmost portions of the continents of Asia and America, is slightly smaller and has the white area not so pure as *Carduelis hornemanni hornemanni* which breeds only in N.W. Greenland and normally winters in N.E. Canada.

TWO-BARRED CROSSBILL—*Loxia leucoptera*

BIRD PLATE 115

The double white wing-bar is distinctive at all ages. At a glance it can be mistaken for a Chaffinch. The brilliant pink rump of the adult male is very noticeable. Length about 5¾ ins.

Habitat. It haunts coniferous, especially larch, forests.

General Habits. Its habits are as Crossbill, but it feeds especially on larch cones.

The note, "wheet", is distinct from Crossbill, being louder and more musical.

Food is chiefly seeds from cones of various conifers.

Status and Distribution. A vagrant which has only rarely occurred in recent years, formerly recorded a good many times from various parts of England, but mostly on the east side; in some years a number together. There are several records from Scotland, few Ireland and one Wales. The race concerned, *Loxia leucoptera bifasciata*, breeds in N. Russia. Siberian birds are probably of the same race, but another occurs in N. America.

CROSSBILL—*Loxia curvirostra*

BIRD PLATE 116   EGG PLATE I (10)

Owing to its tameness it is usually possible to examine the bird at close quarters when its *crossed mandibles*, varying plumages and parrot-like postures are easily recognizable, while on the wing the *unmistakable note* and short deeply forked tail identify it. Adult male is brick-red, of very varying intensity, young male more or less orange, female yellowish-green, and juvenile is greenish-grey, much more strongly streaked than female, especially below, and with rump inclined to yellowish. In both sexes the wings and tail are dark at all ages. There is an obscure pale wing-bar, and the absence of a double white bar distinguishes it from Two-barred Crossbill at all ages. Length about 6½ ins.

Habitat. It is seldom seen outside coniferous woods and plantations, chiefly Scots pine, larch and spruce, but often with some deciduous admixture.

General Habits. Apart from regular visits to pools or streams to drink, it seldom descends to the ground, where it hops clumsily.

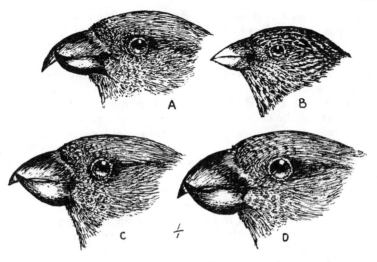

Crossbill (*Loxia curvirostra*). A. Adult. B. Nestling.
C. Scottish Crossbill (*Loxia scotica*). D. Parrot Crossbill (*Loxia pytyopsittacus*).

Flight is rapid and undulating, usually above the level of tree-tops. When feeding, birds flutter from perch to perch, sidle along branches, or clamber parrot-fashion about them, occasionally aided by bill, and hang in acrobatic postures to attack cones. These are usually wrenched off and held in foot while seeds are extracted. "Crossbilled" cones on the ground afford useful evidence of the presence of birds but many are not always distinguishable from the work of woodpeckers. At times it will hang from thistle heads like Goldfinch to extract seeds, or pick aphides off leaves. It is gregarious in habits, and parties of apparently non-breeding birds often associate throughout the nesting season.

The main note given in trees, and constantly on the wing, is a loud incisive "chup, chup" uttered with peculiar, almost "explosive", emphasis, which is distinctive. Song is somewhat variable, often rather Greenfinch-like, and always intermingled with the call. It is heard frequently from mid-January to early August, and exceptionally from mid-September to mid-November.

Food is normally the seeds of conifer cones, but also apple-pips, hawthorn and other berries, and seeds and some insects.

Nests in Scots pines preferably on the outskirts of clumps or belts of these trees or in openings. The eggs, usually 4, rarely 2–5, sometimes unmarked, are laid generally in March and April but sometimes as early as January or as late as July. The nest, built by hen alone, has a characteristic, strong foundation of pine twigs, with superstructure of grasses, wool, etc., and is lined with grass, rabbit's fur, hair, feathers, etc.; it is somewhat flattened in shape. Incubation is by hen only, for about 12–13 days. The young are fed by both sexes and fly after 17–25 days. Probably two broods sometimes.

Status and Distribution. Present throughout the year. In most parts of the country its occurrence is limited to passage or rather temporary immigration of continental birds which arrive from mid-June to August, irregularly in most districts especially in the west but perhaps regular in some, but as a result it now breeds regularly, and seems resident, in Norfolk and Suffolk since 1910, and more recently Hampshire. Elsewhere in England nesting has followed periodic irruptions, every three to ten years, when the bird has arrived in great numbers and frequently stayed over the following spring. Thus during the past 100 years there have been breeding records in most English and several Welsh counties; in some parts, as in Surrey, Sussex and Bucks, the birds have at times persisted several years before disappearing. In Ireland also it is not indigenous but following irruptions became resident in Tipperary and elsewhere; reliable evidence of continued nesting is now lacking. In Scotland, including the northern isles, immigration is as evident as elsewhere in the United Kingdom, and breeding has sometimes occurred in the south, but in the Highlands the position is obscured by the presence throughout the year of the identically plumaged but heavier-billed Scottish Crossbill. Our Crossbills belong to the race *Loxia curvirostra curvirostra* which breeds in Europe generally and N. Asia. Other races occur in the Mediterranean area, Caucasus, central Asia and N. America.

SCOTTISH CROSSBILL—*Loxia scotica*

Taxonomic opinions have changed a number of times regarding the relationships of the crossbills occurring in Britain. Currently, Scottish Crossbill (*Loxia scotica*), Crossbill (*Loxia curvirostra*) and Parrot Crossbill (*Loxia pytyopsittacus*) are considered to be three separate species. All are identical in plumage, details of which will be found in the account of the Crossbill on pp. 458–459. While Parrot Crossbill is slightly larger than Crossbill, its bill is disproportionately heavier, strikingly stout and arched on both mandibles, giving a distinctive appearance as shown in the sketch on p. 459. The Scottish Crossbill is intermediate in size, and its bill is only slightly less heavy than that of Parrot Crossbill; satisfactory separation in the field would generally be unlikely but fortunately Scottish Crossbill is thought to be strictly resident and confined to Scotland, whereas Parrot Crossbill is only known to have occurred once on the Scottish mainland.

Habits are largely similar, but Scottish Crossbill (like Parrot Crossbill) seems more essentially associated with pines than is Crossbill which is regarded as better adapted to feeding on spruce cones. There are also said to be differences in voice, that of Parrot Crossbill being the deepest.

The Scottish Crossbill breeds mainly in the Highlands between Perth and S. E. Sutherland.

SCARLET ROSEFINCH—*Carpodacus erythrinus*

BIRD PLATE 117

The carmine head, breast and rump of adult male, with browner wings and tail and *stout bill* are unmistakable. Female and young male are somewhat like Corn Buntings in general coloration, but much slimmer; *the double whitish wing-bar* and streaked throat and breast are distinctive in conjunction with the conical bill and a characteristic "dumpy" stance with head sunk between shoulders. The head is domed and the large dark eye noticeable. Length about 5¾ ins.

Habitat. In winter-quarters it frequents open country and cultivation.

General Habits. It has a typical undulating finch flight. In winter it feeds very largely on the ground amongst undergrowth and crops, flying up into trees when disturbed.

Call-note is a soft "twee-eek".

Food is entirely vegetable-matter, seeds and buds.

Status and Distribution. An annual but rare autumn-visitor mainly in September, occurring especially in Shetland, also Orkney, Isle of May and elsewhere on east and south coasts of Britain; a few in Wales and Ireland. Increasingly from the 1960s it has also appeared in spring (May/mid-June), singing males have been seen in several areas, and a nest found in the Highlands in 1982. The race concerned, *Carpodacus erythrinus erythrinus*, breeds from Finland south-east through E. Germany to the Volga and into Asia. Other races occur in other parts of Asia and the Caucasus. It winters normally in Asia.

PINE GROSBEAK—*Pinicola enucleator*

BIRD PLATE 117

It somewhat suggests a *gigantic, long-tailed Crossbill* but is as big as Starling and has a *symmetrical stout bill and double white wing-bar*. Male is rose pink with darker wings and tail, and grey belly. Female has the pink replaced by bronzy colour. Immature birds are much as female. Length about 8 ins.

Habitat. In winter it occurs chiefly in conifer and mixed woods.

General Habits. In branches it hops and clambers like a Crossbill, but it feeds a good deal on the ground, hopping about and occasionally walking a few paces. Flight is strongly undulating. The bird is often exceedingly confiding. It flocks in winter, when it is especially attracted by rowans, extracting kernels from the berries.

Call-note is a fluty whistle "tee-tee-teu".

Food is chiefly berries, catkins of birch, seeds and buds of willow.

Status and Distribution. A very rare vagrant, which during the present century has occurred in Northumberland and Kent in May, and Isle of May in November. The race concerned, *Pinicola enucleator enucleator*, breeds in N. Europe and N. Siberia, extending to countries south of the Baltic in winter. Other races occur in Kamchatka and N. America.

BULLFINCH—*Pyrrhula pyrrhula*

BIRD PLATE 116   EGG PLATE I (12A & 12B)

At rest, *the stout bill, grey back, black cap*, wings and tail, and *under-parts rose-red in male* or pinkish-grey in female are unmistakable, but it is secretive in habits, and most often seen flitting along a hedgerow or crossing from one bit of cover to another, when the *pure white rump* identifies it. Juveniles are browner than female, without black cap. Length about 5¾ ins.

Habitat. It haunts woods, shrubberies, and copses with undergrowth of thorns, etc., thickets, and old hedgerows, requiring plenty of dense and tall cover. Gardens and orchards are visited especially in spring.

General Habits. Not often seen on the ground. Flight is undulating. It is seldom far from cover where it perches chiefly in bushes, etc., seldom high up, but it visits gardens to feed on fruit buds. It is generally found in pairs throughout year, or in family parties in summer and autumn; occasionally in early spring in considerable flocks.

Call-note is a low, piping "deu" or "deu-deu", with considerable carrying power which often first reveals its presence. There is no proper song, but between late February and the end of August both sexes at times give a low, broken, piping warble of poor and creaky quality.

Food comprises seeds, berries, etc.; in spring chiefly buds of fruit trees and shrubs. The young are fed on caterpillars.

Nests usually about four to seven feet from ground in thick hedges, clumps of evergreens, and in plantations. The eggs, usually 4–5, occasionally 7, are laid generally in May in a nest sometimes extremely slightly, at others very stoutly, constructed of fine twigs and some moss or lichens, lined with a thick layer of interlacing fine roots nearly always black. Incubation is chiefly by hen, for about 12–14 days. Both sexes feed the young which fly when 12–16 days old. At least two broods.

Status and Distribution. Resident, and generally distributed, but rather local in Scotland including Inner Hebrides; is absent from Outer Hebrides, Orkney, Shetland, also Isle of Man. Our breeding birds are relatively sedentary and belong to the race *Pyrrhula pyrrhula nesa* which is confined to the British Isles. In addition the race *Pyrrhula pyrrhula pyrrhula*, which breeds from N. Scandinavia to the Balkans and which in the field even at a little distance is distinctly larger and brighter looking than our bird, visits this country as an irregular autumn- and winter-immigrant. It has been recorded as far south as Sussex but occurs mainly in the north-east and especially in Shetland. Other races are found in W. Europe, Azores, Caucasus and Asia.

HAWFINCH—*Coccothraustes coccothraustes*

BIRD PLATE 120   EGG PLATE II (3A & 3B)

The enormous bill, stout, "bull-necked" appearance and short tail are distinctive both at rest and in flight. When flying from ground or low down, the *ruddy brown mantle, broad white border to tail and broad whitish patch on wing-coverts* catch the eye, and if close enough, the narrower white marks on wing quills; but it often flies high, the whitish wing patches looking transparent from below. Usually shy and secretive, it would more often be overlooked but for *its note* or the presence of shredded pea-pods or split fruit-stones where it has fed, but is sometimes noisy in early spring. Rump, head and under-parts are paler than the mantle, with greyish nape and black throat. Juvenile has yellow throat and the under-parts spotted and barred. Length about 6½ ins.

Habitat. In the breeding-season it haunts well-grown deciduous or mixed woods, old wooded gardens, orchards, and bushy places with scattered trees. In winter it is sometimes found in more open country.

General Habits. Likes to perch on topmost twigs of tall trees and feeds by preference in upper branches, but also often on the ground where it hops rather heavily with erect carriage. Flight is quick with rapid wing-beats and is moderately undulating except over short distances. Outside the breeding-season it often associates in flocks.

Usual note is an abrupt, clicking "tzik" or "tzik-tzik", uttered in flight or from a perch. Song is infrequent and halting but occurs mainly from mid-March to the end of May.

Food is mainly kernels and seeds of many kinds; also green peas and beechmast. Young are fed on insects.

Nests on horizontal branches of fruit-trees, occasionally in forest-trees or thorn-bushes at varying heights. The eggs, usually 4–6, but 2–7 recorded, vary in ground-colour from light bluish to warm buff. They are laid generally in May in a slight and shallow nest built of roots, lichens, bents, etc., with a layer of small twigs as foundation, and lined with fine roots, hair or fibre. Incubation is by hen only, for about 9½ days. The young are fed by both parents and fly when about 10–11 days old. There is evidence of a second brood occasionally.

Status and Distribution. A resident, local but generally distributed in England except in the extreme west, being rare in Devon and unknown in Cornwall as a breeding bird. In Wales also it is rare or unknown in the west except in Carmarthen where it breeds sparingly. In Scotland it breeds locally in small numbers in most of the counties south of the Forth/Clyde valley and north to Perth, and has bred in Fife and probably Aberdeen; elsewhere a straggler as far north as Shetland. To Ireland it is a rare vagrant mainly in autumn. There is sometimes a little movement in Great Britain in winter and spring, although no regular migration occurs. The race concerned, *Coccothraustes coccothraustes coccothraustes*, breeds over most of Europe from S. Norway southwards, but other races occur in S. Spain, N.W. Africa, S.E. Russia, and Asia.

LAPLAND BUNTING—*Calcarius lapponicus*

BIRD PLATE 112

The black face and throat, separated from black crown and chestnut nape by a V-shaped white band, are distinctive of male, though much obscured by brown in autumn. The upper-parts are brown, streaked black; under-parts whitish, streaked black on the flanks. Females in the breeding-season have a head pattern like male, but much dulled and with throat whitish. Autumn females and young have the distinctive chestnut nape undetectable and look much like rather large, stout female Reed Buntings, but have pale centre to crown, black "corners" to ear-coverts, shorter tail, and a *different note*. Whitish edges to the median coverts are a further distinction. Length about 6 ins.

Habitat. In winter-quarters it is chiefly found on stubble or rough ground near the coast, but also on hilly ground inland.

General Habits. The ordinary gait is a quick run, but it can also hop. It usually occurs in treeless country in company with Skylarks or mixed flocks of finches and buntings, but will perch in trees where available. Flight is undulating, more so than Snow Bunting.

The chief notes of migrants in autumn are a hard rattle "ticki-tick", and a full melodious descending whistle, "teu", harder than the corresponding note of the Snow Bunting.

Food in this country is chiefly seeds of grasses and other plants.

Status and Distribution. An autumn passage-migrant arriving from the end of August to end of October, regular on the northern and western isles, and E. and S.E. coasts, also at times in considerable numbers in N.W. Ireland. A few normally winter in some places on the east coasts of England and Scotland, but it is very rare

LAPLAND BUNTING
immature
Note whitish V pattern on
back like "braces".

RUSTIC BUNTING
female

in spring except on Fair Isle where it is regular; exceptional in summer, but bred in the Highlands in 1977–1980 (about a dozen pairs in 1979). It has occurred in other parts of England, in Wales and the Isle of Man as a vagrant. The race concerned, *Calcarius lapponicus lapponicus*, breeds from arctic America and Greenland across N. Europe to Siberia; our birds probably come more from Greenland than Scandinavia, this being one of the few passerines regularly to make a crossing of the N. Atlantic. Other races occur in E. Asia and Alaska. The winter range of European birds is obscure.

SNOW BUNTING—*Plectrophenax nivalis*

BIRD PLATE 111   EGG PLATE I (4A & 4B)

A rather stockily-built bunting recognized in autumn and winter by the *white under-parts of both sexes and large amount of white in the wings and tail of males*, the females and young having much less. Birds passing overhead look mainly white. In adult male at all seasons almost the whole wing is white, apart from black primaries and bastard wing, and is very striking in flight. Breeding males have the *back and central tail-feathers black and the rest pure white*, while hen has the head and back greyish-brown flecked with black. After the autumn moult, when the bird is most familiar in the British Isles, male has *white much obscured by rusty brown* on the head and chest, and the *back is warm brown mottled black*, while females or young, except for less white on wings and tail, are much the same, but a paler, duller brown; some greyer birds occur. Legs black. Length about 6½ ins. See also drawing p. 322.

Habitat. In the breeding-season it is confined in the British Isles to bare, stony mountain-tops, not usually below 3,500 ft. In winter quarters it haunts principally the sea-shore or rough land near the coast; to a less extent open hilly country and upland moors inland, and sometimes even stackyards, etc.

General Habits. It spends most of its time on the ground, seldom perching on trees. Flight is swift and undulating. Flocks often fly rather high, and after an abrupt descent skim a few yards before settling. When uneasy it flicks the tail and slightly flicks up the wings. It is gregarious outside the breeding-season, assemblages varying from small parties to flocks of several hundreds, not as a rule associating much with other species.

Flight-note a musical, rather rippling twitter, "tirrirrir*rip*". Also a loud, musical "seeoo" and a Brambling-like "swayeek" from flocks. The song is short, but musical, bold and loud for the bird's size. It is given from a rock or other low perch and on the wing.

Food in summer is largely insects, as well as seeds, grasses and buds; in autumn and winter mainly seeds.

Nests among screes on mountain-sides or among loose boulders in crevices of rocks, placing the nest well out of sight among stones. The eggs, normally 4–6, occasionally 7–8, vary in ground-colour from yellowish-white to bluish or greenish. They are laid generally at the end of May and the beginning of June in a nest built by hen, chiefly of dead grasses, stalks, moss, lichens, lined with finer grasses, hair, wool and feathers. Incubation is apparently by hen only, for about 12–14 days. The young are fed by both sexes and fly when about 10–12 days old. Sometimes double-brooded.

Status and Distribution. Probably throughout the year in Scotland where a few are found breeding in most years on mountains in the northern half of the mainland: it is mainly a winter-visitor, not only to the islands and coasts, but also inland and on the hills. Elsewhere in the British Isles it is a winter-visitor chiefly to the coasts, but often inland on hills, though only occasionally on the plains, arriving in varying numbers between early September and late November, and returning from mid-March to mid-May. There are also records for every summer month on the N. and W. coasts of Ireland. Abroad this race, *Plectrophenax nivalis nivalis*, breeds in Scandinavia, arctic Europe, Asia and America. The Icelandic race *Plectrophenax nivalis insulae* has also occurred in the British Isles. Other races occur in Siberia and the Bering Sea.

YELLOWHAMMER—*Emberiza citrinella*

BIRD PLATE 114   EGG PLATE I (7A, 7B & 7C)

Like most buntings, it differs from typical finches in having a slighter build and longer tail. *Yellow head and under-parts* and chestnut upper-parts, streaked black except on the rump, distinguish male. The head has dull greenish-brown markings, reduced or almost lost in summer, but the extent and intensity of yellow varies considerably; there is an obscure streaky cinnamon band across the chest; *white on outer tail-feathers* (inner web) is conspicuous in flight. Female is dull, with much less yellow and the dark markings much more pronounced on the head; it scarcely differs from female Cirl Bunting, except in having a *chestnut rump*. Juveniles and young females are still darker, only faintly

YELLOW-BREASTED BUNTING, 1st winter.
YELLOWHAMMER, 1st winter.

Note wing-bars, crown-stripe and eye-stripe of
Yellow-breasted Bunting.

yellow below and with hardly any on the head. Length about 6½ ins.

Habitat. In the breeding-season it frequents mainly grasslands or arable with hedgerows, bushy banks or similar cover, but not too much timbered; also bushy commons, heaths, etc. After the breeding-season and in winter it is also commonly found in stubble and root-fields, stackyards, etc.

General Habits. Like its allies, it feeds almost exclusively on the ground, but perches freely on bushes and trees. Slightly flicks its tail from time to time. Flight action is somewhat variable, from almost straight to irregularly undulating, with periodical momentary wing closure as in finches. It is gregarious from autumn to spring, often associating with other finches or buntings.

Notes are "tink", "twink" or "tweek" with a rather ringing quality, resembling the opening notes of song; a single "twick" or "tillip" is used in flight. Song is a single phrase consisting of a tinkling repetition of the same high-pitched note followed by a more prolonged one, roughly suggested by the traditional "Little bit of bread and no cheese". It is heard regularly from late February to mid-August, at times some weeks earlier or later, and occasionally in October or early November.

Food is chiefly vegetable: corn, seeds, wild fruits, leaves, grass, etc. Insects constitute most of the animal matter, also spiders, slugs, millipedes and earthworms.

Nests mainly in hedge bottoms, or at the foot of bushes, generally on or near the ground and frequently partly hidden by grass. The eggs, usually 3–4, sometimes 2–6, normally have few bold markings and much finer lines than Cirl and Corn Buntings. They are laid generally from late April or May onwards in a nest built of stalks, bents, and a little moss, lined with horsehair and fine bents. Incubation is chiefly by hen for about 12–14 days. The young are fed by both sexes and fly when about 12–13 days old. Two or three broods.

Status and Distribution. Present throughout year, generally distributed in British Isles, but in Outer Hebrides a scarce migrant (has bred), and in Shetland a scarce migrant and winter-visitor. Our breeding birds flock in winter, but there is little evidence that they emigrate. Immigrants from the north or east appear on the E. coasts of Great Britain from the end of September to third week of November and return from late March to mid-May. The race breeding in S.E. England, *Emberiza citrinella citrinella*, breeds also from northern Scandinavia south to N. Spain and Hungary. N. and W. England, also Scotland and Ireland, is occupied by the slightly darker and richer coloured *Emberiza citrinella caliginosa*. Another race occurs in E. Europe and W. Asia.

CIRL BUNTING—*Emberiza cirlus*

Bird Plate 114   Egg Plate I (6a & 6b)

Male is distinguished from Yellowhammer by *black throat and mark through eye, dark crown and greyish-green band across the chest*. The sides of the breast are rich chestnut behind the greenish band, and the rest of the under-parts are yellow; otherwise it is much as Yellowhammer, including white in outer tail-feathers, but *the rump is olive-brown*, not chestnut. Female and young are only reliably distinguished from Yellowhammers by *voice* and brown rump, as above, though Yellowhammer is in fact a rather longer-looking, less compact bird. Length about 6¼ ins.

Habitat. It is found chiefly in pasture-lands well provided with hedgerow timber, especially elms, often near the sea, on bushy slopes on sheltered aspects of chiefly limestone or chalk hills or downs, sites of felled woodland, and sometimes well-timbered cultivated land, parks, etc. In winter it frequents mainly open fields.

General Habits. It is more addicted than Yellowhammer to tall trees, especially elms, often in roadside hedgerows. Flight is more dipping and volatile than Yellowhammer. From autumn to spring it occurs in open country in small parties, often with Yellow-hammers and other species, or where common in flocks.

It has only one call, a rather thin "zit" or "sip", sometimes run together in flight to produce a characteristic sibilant "sissi-sissi-sip". The song, a rattling repetition of the same metallic note, not unlike Lesser Whitethroat's rattle, is heard regularly from late February to early September, and occasionally during the rest of the year.

Food is chiefly corn and seeds of weeds and grasses; also insects.

Nests mainly in bushes generally above the ground, but also on it. The eggs, normally 3–4, occasionally 2–5, are better marked than Yellowhammer's. They are laid generally from mid-May onwards in a nest built usually by hen only, of bents, roots, much moss, and sometimes with leaves in the foundation; lined with fine grasses and horsehair. Incubation is normally by hen only, for 12–14 days. The young are fed chiefly by hen, and fly when about 11–13 days old. Two broods at least, sometimes three.

Status and Distribution. Present throughout the year, but following long-term decrease few pairs now remain, almost re-stricted to coastal areas in S.W. England, especially Devon. It is a rare vagrant in Scotland and Ireland. There is no evidence of overseas migration although the bird wanders in winter. The race concerned, *Emberiza cirlus cirlus*, breeds from the Mediterranean north to N. France and Bulgaria, also in Asia Minor. Another race occurs in Corsica.

ORTOLAN BUNTING—*Emberiza hortulana*

Bird Plate 113

Greyish-olive head, rufous under-parts and yellow throat and "spectacle" round eye are distinctive of adults, but females and autumn males are duller and may lack the spectacle. The upper-parts are brown streaked black, and there is an olive moustachial stripe at the sides of throat. *Bill and legs pinkish.* Autumn females and young are still browner and may be confused with young Yellowhammers or Cirl Buntings, but show *golden-buff rumps*, more prominent patterning in blackish and whitish on the upper-parts, pale bill and legs, and often traces of adult colouring on head and under-parts. Outer tail-feathers are white whereas Yellow-hammer does not have white on the *outer* webs. *Flight-note is distinctive.* Length 6¼ ins.

Habitat. Outside the breeding-season it largely frequents cultivation, particularly cornfields in autumn.

General Habits. It is a rather quiet, secretive bird, but at times wild and shy, perching high and flying far when only slightly disturbed. Flight and movements resemble other buntings.

Notes include a soft liquid "tlip" and a loud "cheup".

Food is largely seeds; also insects and snails recorded.

Status and Distribution. A vagrant or drift migrant of annual occurrence in small numbers in spring or autumn on the east coast and particularly Fair Isle. It also occurs on the south coast and islands in the S. Irish Sea area (Scillies, Lundy, Skokholm, Great Saltee) and S.W. Ireland, but otherwise is rare in west of England and Ireland as it is anywhere inland. The species breeds from northern Scandinavia south to the Mediterranean and eastwards in Asia to W. Mongolia; it winters chiefly in Africa. There are no subspecies.

RUSTIC BUNTING—*Emberiza rustica*

BIRD PLATE 113

The bright rusty breast-band of large spots as well as similar spots on the flanks show up distinctly on the *silky white underparts* and make it readily distinguishable from other buntings. Male has black crown and sides of head (mottled brown in winter) with a broad white eye-stripe and white throat, the upper-parts are chestnut streaked black, and there is *white in the outer tailfeathers*. Female is duller, with the black of the head replaced by dark brown. Length about 5¾ ins.

Habitat. In the breeding-season it frequents damp places often with considerable undergrowth; in winter it is found in woods as well as open country and cultivation.

General Habits. A restless bird, commonly flying close to the ground and playing about among roots of trees, usually near a swamp.

Call is a sharp "tic, tic" comparable to Robin's.

Food is chiefly seeds.

Status and Distribution. A vagrant which has occurred almost annually in spring and autumn on the east side of Great Britain from Shetland to Sussex, but mainly in the N. Scottish islands and especially Fair Isle; also recorded Scillies and S.W. Ireland. It breeds eastwards from N. Scandinavia to N.E. Siberia, European birds normally migrating S.E. There are no subspecies.

LITTLE BUNTING—*Emberiza pusilla*

BIRD PLATE 112

It is a dull-looking little bird, distinctly smaller and shorter-billed than Reed Bunting or Meadow Pipit, but *rufous sides of the face* should always be looked for, although not always apparent. Male has the crown rufous, like the sides of the face, with a black band at side. The rest of the upper-parts are duller chestnut, streaked black, and can show two widely-spaced creamy-white stripes running parallel down the back; the outer tail-feathers are white. Female is duller, with a light eye-stripe. Under some conditions the bird can look distinctly dark-headed. In addition to its smaller or slimmer appearance, it is readily distinguished from Rustic Bunting by its duller, more greyish-white under-parts, with fine black streaks. Legs pale brown. Length about 5¼ ins.

Habitat. On passage in this country it is chiefly found in rather open coastal areas, arable lowland, or among vegetables and similar low cover.

General Habits. It is usually rather shy outside the breeding-season. It feeds much on the ground, creeping about in a low crouching, hunch-back attitude, but will also stand on a raised perch and flick and fan tail like a Reed Bunting. On migration and in winter it frequently associates with other birds such as buntings and pipits.

Note of migrants is a high quiet Robin-like "tick".

Food consists of seeds; also insects in summer.

Status and Distribution. A passage-migrant, rare and irregular in spring, but occurs annually in very small numbers in autumn mainly in September and October and most regularly on Fair Isle: there are a number of records from the Isle of May (Forth) and fewer elsewhere in Scotland. In England it is recorded

LITTLE BUNTING

less regularly, occurring mainly on the east side south to Sussex, occasionally inland. There are a few Irish and Welsh records. The species breeds from Finland to Siberia and winters in central and E. Asia. There are no subspecies.

REED BUNTING—*Emberiza schoeniclus*

BIRD PLATE 112   EGG PLATE I (5A & 5B)

The black head and throat and white collar of male are conspicuous characters, whilst brown head, buff eye-stripe and throat, with well-defined moustachial streak, and *white outer tailfeathers* identify female and young. Legs dark brown. Length about 6 ins.

Habitat. In the breeding-season it frequents bushy fens and reed-beds, rank vegetation fringing waters of all sorts, withy-beds and rushy pastures; locally even regularly on wooded islets in lakes with little or no marshy ground, reeds or sedge. Recently it has also been found breeding in many areas in dry habitats, sometimes far from water. In winter it also occurs on cultivated fields and open ground, including upland grass moors, well away from water.

General Habits. It clings to reed stems or perches on bushes, water-side vegetation or willows, seldom high up, frequently flicking its wings and tail and spreading and closing the latter. Flight is jerky rather than undulating. In winter the breeding haunts are largely, but not completely, deserted, and many join with Yellowhammers and finches in the open fields. The first flocks of returning migrants in early spring, often associated with Pied Wagtails and Meadow Pipits, usually consist of males only.

Calls are a shrill "tseep", and a ringing, metallic "ching". Song is a tinkling "tweek, tweek, tweek, tititick", with variants. It is heard regularly from the latter part of March to mid-July, less frequently for about a month earlier and later.

Food is chiefly seeds of marsh plants, grasses and grain, also small molluscs and crustacea, and in spring and summer insects are taken.

Nests generally in marshy ground, in tussocks, osier stumps, etc., on or near the ground but sometimes higher in bushes. The eggs, 4–5 normally, occasionally 6, rarely bluish without markings, are laid generally in May or late April, in a nest built by hen, chiefly of bents and a little moss, lined with finer grasses, horsehair, and sometimes reed-flowers. Incubation is by both sexes for about 13–14 days. The young are fed by both sexes and fly when about 10–13 days old. Two, occasionally three, broods.

Status and Distribution. Present throughout the year, and generally distributed throughout the country, but scarce in Shetland where a pair or two have bred since 1949. Most of our birds move south in autumn and some emigrate, while numbers arrive from the Continent in September and October, returning from late March to mid-May. The race concerned, *Emberiza schoeniclus schoeniclus*, breeds across central Europe, north to the Baltic and east to Siberia. Other races occur in N. and S. Europe and parts of Asia. European birds reach N. Africa in winter.

BLACK-HEADED BUNTING—*Emberiza melanocephala*

BIRD PLATE 113

The large size, uniform yellow or yellowish under-parts and no white in the tail are distinctive. The male with striking coloration marking it out from any other European passerine and more suggestive of a tropical weaver-bird than anything else, has the crown and sides of head black, and rich chestnut upper-parts; in autumn the head is browner and the colours are obscured. Female is brown above with dark streaks, and pale yellowish below, becoming *brighter yellow on the under tail-coverts*. Juvenile has pale buffish *unstreaked* under-parts. Length about 6½ ins.

Habitat. Outside the breeding-season it affects cultivation and scrub.

General Habits. In winter quarters it feeds on the ground amongst cultivation and flies up into trees when disturbed.

Call is a sharp "zitt" of typical bunting character.

Food is mainly seeds, insects being freely taken in summer.

Status and Distribution. A rare vagrant which has occurred in May or June and in autumn, with a scatter from Shetland to Scillies and S. Ireland, but it is often difficult to eliminate the possibility of escaped cage-birds. It breeds in S.E. Europe and W. Asia from Jugoslavia and S. Italy to Afghanistan. There are no subspecies.

CORN BUNTING—*Miliaria calandra*

The dull brown, streaked plumage lacks outstanding features, but its size (between Sparrow and Thrush), *robust form with rather heavy head and bill, and absence of white outer tail-feathers* distinguish it from any other similarly coloured bird. Moreover in summer the persistent song at once identifies male, while the peculiar flight-note distinguishes flocks flying by, which might be taken for hen Sparrows. Length about 7 ins.

Habitat. In the breeding-season it haunts arable and grasslands with hedgerows or bushes, gorsy commons or downlands, rough pastures and scrubby wastes, especially near coast though also in elevated stonewall country in Midlands; ordinarily it avoids areas much dominated by trees. In winter it frequents chiefly cultivated land, stackyards, etc.

General Habits. Flight is much as Sparrow, in undulations when prolonged. Feeds much on the ground, but perches freely on bushes, telegraph-wires, etc., not much on trees. On leaving a song perch male often flies with legs dangling. Gregarious from autumn to spring, in unmixed parties, or in company with other buntings and finches.

Characteristic flight-note of flocks, from the end of July onwards, is a repeated, abrupt "quit", or when run together, "quit-it-it". Song is short and hard, consisting of a sequence of similar ticking notes, gaining speed and leading up to a singular discordant finish aptly likened to jangling of a bunch of small keys. It may be heard throughout the year except from mid-August to mid-October, and is regular from mid-February to mid-August.

Food is mainly vegetable matter, wild fruits, seeds, leaves, occasionally buds, ivy-berries, and corn. Animal matter is largely insects, also spiders, millipedes, snails, slugs and earthworms.

Nests generally among rank grass, especially with clumps of thistle, knapweed, etc., in brambles and even hedgerows, less frequently in corn and other crops. When in bushes it may be as much as five feet from the ground. Many males are polygamous. The eggs, usually 3–5, but 1–7 recorded, have ground-colour ranging from greyish-white to light brown, sometimes unmarked. They are laid generally in late May or June in a nest somewhat loosely built by hen alone of bents and grasses, lined with finer grasses and roots with a few hairs. Incubation is by hen alone for about 12–13 days. The young are fed by hen, normally unaided by cock, and fly when they are about 9–12 days old. Double-brooded in some districts, but not in others.

Status and Distribution. Present throughout the year, widely but locally distributed, declining; absent from large areas in E. Anglia, S.W. England, almost all Wales; also most of Scotland except near E. coast, parts of S.W. and Hebrides, and Orkney; in Ireland it is very local, confined to some coastal districts. Abroad the bird breeds in Europe from S. Norway to the Mediterranean; also in N. Africa and W. Asia. There are no subspecies.

INDEX

INDEX

The first figure in bold type after an English name is the text page number; the figure or figures in clear type indicate the plate number or numbers, and the roman numeral indicates the egg plate number. Against scientific names, only the text page number is given.